Surveillance and Spies in the Civil War

Ohio University Press Series on
Law, Society, and Politics in the Midwest

STEPHEN E. TOWNE

Surveillance and Spies in the Civil War

EXPOSING CONFEDERATE CONSPIRACIES
IN AMERICA'S HEARTLAND

Ohio University Press – Athens

973.786
Tow

Ohio University Press, Athens, Ohio 45701
ohioswallow.com
© 2015 by Ohio University Press
All rights reserved

Printed in the United States of America
Ohio University Press books are printed on acid-free paper ⊗ ™

25 24 23 22 21 20 19 18 17 16 15   5 4 3 2 1

Library of Congress Cataloging-in-Publication Data
Towne, Stephen E., 1961–
 Surveillance and spies in the Civil War : exposing Confederate conspiracies in
America's heartland / Stephen E. Towne.
     pages cm. — (Ohio University Press series on law, society, and politics in the
midwest)
 Includes bibliographical references and index.
 ISBN 978-0-8214-2131-4 (hc : alk. paper) — ISBN 978-0-8214-2103-1 (pb : alk.
paper) — ISBN 978-0-8214-4493-1 (pdf)
 1. United States—History—Civil War, 1861–1865—Secret service. 2. Spies—
United States—History—19th century. 3. Spies—Confederate States of America.
I. Title.
 E608.T69 2014
 973.7'86—dc23

2014038526

CONTENTS

ILLUSTRATIONS

Plates

Map

ACKNOWLEDGMENTS

Research for this book began in 1992, when I was working at the Indiana State Archives. One day, a visitor arrived who wished to see records documenting Henry B. Carrington's tenure in Indiana during the American Civil War. In those days, I had not long been out of graduate school studies in English history, and Carrington's name was unfamiliar to me (a fault since remedied). I scrambled to find relatively low-hanging archival fruit to occupy the visitor. In the meantime, I raced upstairs to the Indiana State Library (in those days the archives were housed in the State Library Building, as was the Indiana Historical Society) to do some quick research on Carrington and what he might have been doing in Indiana. The patron left, no doubt unsatisfied with the service I provided. But what I had quickly found in the secondary historical literature intrigued me. Wild things had happened in Indiana during the Civil War, and I wanted to learn more about them. In the days, weeks, and months to come, I began to read the standard works on Indiana's experience during the rebellion and soon became fascinated by what I found. I was especially taken by the widespread suppression of the newspaper press throughout the state, and, on my lunch hours over the next several years, began to read the surviving Civil War–era newspapers kept in the State Library's collection. I also read many of the manuscript collections in the State Library and Indiana Historical Society and started to get a sense of the extraordinary events that occurred in Indiana during the rebellion.

Realizing that most of the Civil War records in the Indiana State Archives languished in a jumbled mess, long neglected and in disarray, I devoted much of my time to organizing the records of Governor Oliver P. Morton and his administration. I uncovered and recovered Civil War–era records that had been lost for generations or perhaps had never been examined by either archivist or researcher. Almost every day brought new discoveries. I read the records carefully in the process, and what I saw often conflicted with the existing historiography of Indiana in the period. Driven both by the archivist's duty to bring new records to light as well as the historian's duty to interpret the past using all the available evidence, I took on the responsibility to advertise this long-hidden and nearly inaccessible wealth of Civil War records by demonstrating through new scholarship what the records said. I began to publish my research findings.

My research in Indiana records led me to broaden my documentary horizons. Was Indiana's experience similar to that in neighboring states? Research trips to archives and manuscript repositories throughout the Midwest followed. I also began almost annual visits to the National Archives, in Washington, DC, and to Chicago. There, I found long-ignored records that fit hand in glove with the sorts of records I found in the Indiana State Archives. About ten years ago, I determined that I needed to pour my findings into a book-length study of U.S. Army intelligence operations in the Old Northwest (as the Midwest was called in the mid-nineteenth century).

My research forays to archives and repositories from coast to coast have made me greatly indebted to archivists, manuscripts curators, and librarians throughout the United States, too many to thank individually here. Their collective generosity and patience is greatly appreciated. I foremost acknowledge my heartfelt thanks to the friendly staffs of the Indiana State Archives and the Indiana State Library, who have long suffered my frequent visits and incessant requests. Many thanks are due to the archivists of the National Archives in Washington, DC, especially to DeAnne Blanton, who first assisted me in finding my way through its massive holdings. Special thanks are due also to Martin Tuohy and Scott Forsyth both formerly of the National Archives and Records Administration's regional holdings at Chicago.

I have received generous financial support for my research. The Office for Professional Development at Indiana University–Purdue University Indianapolis gave me funds to conduct important research in New England repositories. The National Endowment for the Humanities awarded me a Summer Stipend, which afforded me two glorious months of intensive research in the National Archives and the Library of Congress. The IUPUI University Library allowed several short research leaves affording trips to archives and time to write. And the Charles E. Young Research Library Department of Special Collections at UCLA granted me one of their James and Sylvia Thayer Short-Term Research Fellowships to read their extraordinary collection of papers of General William S. Rosecrans. Finally, my colleagues at IUPUI kindly approved my application for a yearlong sabbatical in 2009–10. During that time, I conducted more research in Washington, Chicago, and elsewhere and wrote most of the first draft of this book. This study would not exist without the extended time away from professional duties for research and writing that the sabbatical allowed.

Many thanks are due the historians who have read and commented on versions of this research in the form of conference papers, manuscripts, and book chapters. The congenial crew of scholars who form the Civil War Study Group have heard me spout off endlessly on spies and detectives. They are much to be thanked. I especially thank Professors June Klees and A. James Fuller for kindly reviewing draft chapters and correcting numerous problems. Of course, all errors in this volume are my own.

Last, but most important, I wish to thank my family for suffering through years of almost monomaniacal dinnertime drones about researching and writing this book. I owe them more than I can express.

The Secret History of the Civil War in the North

IN 2013, when this book was taking its final form, daily reports of the activities of a young computer technician named Edward Snowden flashed across newspaper headlines and television news worldwide. As an erstwhile low-level private contractor working for the supersecret United States electronic surveillance agency, the National Security Agency (NSA), Snowden had smuggled untold millions of secret reports and data off NSA servers and began to feed it in well-timed droplets to major news organizations. The leaks revealed the breathtaking scope of sophisticated American electronic espionage on international targets. Largely in reaction to the post–September 11, 2001, terrorist attacks on the United States, the American government had seemingly abandoned all restraint to ensure that the country would not again be attacked by foreign terrorists. But the information that Snowden gave to reporters also showed that the NSA intercepted communications of leaders of major governments closely allied to the United States. Moreover, it became clear that the NSA also collected information on the billions of electronic communications made daily by American citizens within the United States, in apparent contravention of U.S. laws. Indeed, the comprehensiveness of the electronic eavesdropping was perhaps the most startling aspect of the stories.

According to news reports, the NSA acted like a massive computer vacuum cleaner to sweep up and analyze massive quantities of personal communications sent through commercial networks; moreover, beyond collecting the "metadata" of personal electronic messages, the agency worked diligently to de-encrypt the messages themselves. The news leaks from Snowden had the effect of shaking American diplomacy around the world as well as severely affecting the popularity of the incumbent U.S. president. American citizens, wedded to their electronic communication devices, did not appreciate the fact that their communications had been so closely monitored. At the time of this writing, several civil suits filed by individuals and groups challenging the legality of the NSA's actions were working through the federal courts. Americans became acutely sensitive to the problem of government intrusion into private communications.

But this is not the first time in American history that such government surveillance efforts have occurred. During the American Civil War, the U.S. Army kept a widespread surveillance over many persons in the loyal North. Army commanders suspected (with good reason, as will be shown) that large numbers of civilians in Northern states acted to impede the government's steps to suppress the Southern rebellion. Government officials examined private telegraphic and postal correspondence to learn the thoughts and plans of citizens. Commanders hired detectives and sent officers and enlisted soldiers to watch and report on persons deemed to be threats to the survival of the national Union. They followed prominent political leaders and other persons who were suspected of aiding the rebels-in-arms. Agents infiltrated secret groups to collect information about their plans for resisting the government and fomenting insurrection.

One example of surveillance on a prominent figure shows the scope of the activity. During much of the war, army detectives maintained a careful watch on antiwar leader and former Ohio congressman Clement L. Vallandigham. Major General Ambrose E. Burnside sent officers in disguise to report on the Democratic leader's speeches. Troops later arrested him, tried him by military commission, and sent him into exile on the evidence of the officers employed as detectives. Commanders closely observed the Ohioan in Canada and worked to detect the secret communication network that connected him to his stateside followers and friends. Discovering the channels of communication, army generals received permission from postal officials to open and read Vallandigham's mail. Thereby, commanders learned that he issued orders to his followers in the United States. The information helped officers prepare for potential unrest.

This is the story of the rise of army intelligence in the lower Old Northwest states (Ohio, Indiana, and Illinois) and Michigan during the rebellion. Army espionage operations arose in the multistate region for a purpose: after civilian law enforcement efforts failed to detect and counteract growing criminal conspiracy, including resistance to government war measures, the army stepped in to fill the void. Widespread desertion and resistance to federal conscription on the home front prompted concerned commanders to act against the growing threat to the integrity of the army and stability in the region. They gathered information about disaffection in the ranks that prompted desertion and traced the source to an organized effort to sow soldier dissatisfaction. Later, officers identified armed and organized groups behind plots to resist the draft and, even more alarming, to attack the army's prisoner-of-war camps that housed thousands of captured Confederate soldiers. Army spies collected evidence that Northern opponents of the war effort communicated with Confederate authorities to foment insurrection in a desperate bid to weaken the Union cause and divert government forces from Southern fronts. Armed with copious evidence of conspiratorial activities, gathered by a cohort of spies and informers, commanders arrested and brought to trial in military courts leaders of organized subversive groups.

Historians of the American Civil War have long understood the importance of military-intelligence operations during the rebellion. Edwin Fishel and William B. Feis have produced fine studies of tactical intelligence operations conducted by U.S. Army commanders *in the field,* showing how generals and their staffs worked to learn the strength, location, and intentions of their battlefield opponents. Their works portray how skilled officers attached to army headquarters directed large staffs of spies and detectives who worked to cross rebel lines and carry away useful information that would aid military movements.[1] Historians have fueled the popular imagination about spies and traitors, focusing on women's espionage exploits, telling and retelling tales of plucky Rose Greenhow, Pauline Cushman, Elizabeth Van Lew, or Belle Boyd.[2] Indeed, popular histories of espionage activities in American history have given undue emphasis to such "amateur" efforts, while usually neglecting the more productive, if less thrilling, endeavors of professionals, who were often in the military.[3]

Historians have mostly focused on intelligence activities on the battlefield and in areas of the South under occupation, thus neglecting U.S. Army operations targeting the Northern home front. This study of military intelligence in the Old Northwest remedies that neglect to show the widespread reach of the army's espionage efforts during the war. Officers worked diligently to "ferret out" the sources of disaffection and threats to political stability in the North. Using large numbers of soldiers—both officers and enlisted men—and paid civilians as their detectives, they investigated manifestations of what they perceived as disloyalty that threatened the army's ability to maintain its strength to fight and suppress the Confederate rebellion. Officers also employed information proffered by thousands of informers—women and men who reported what they saw or heard to military authorities. Historian Joan M. Jensen's sweeping history of military surveillance of Americans posits that during the Civil War the U.S. Army did very little of the sort. This book challenges that analysis, demonstrating that the army did not hesitate to employ its full gamut of resources to watch citizens, even frequently intercepting and opening private postal communications to read their contents and learn the plans of suspected persons.[4]

Moreover, military-intelligence operations occurred in the North wherever U.S. Army personnel were located. During the massive mobilization of national manpower and economic resources prompted by the rebellion, the army maintained posts throughout Ohio, Michigan, Indiana, and Illinois to superintend a variety of important activities. Posts sprang up at Cincinnati, Cleveland, Columbus, Dayton, and Mansfield in Ohio; Dearborn and Detroit in Michigan; Evansville, Indianapolis, and New Albany in Indiana; and Cairo, Chicago, Mattoon, and Springfield in Illinois, not to mention dozens more temporary recruiting and rendezvous camps for volunteer troops. Added to that were prisoner-of-war camps located at Johnson's Island and Columbus in Ohio; at Indianapolis; and at Chicago, Rock Island, and Alton in Illinois. On top of that, the passage of the Enrollment Act, in March 1863, created a bureaucratic apparatus to administer the draft—the Provost Marshal General's Bureau—spread over the entire landscape. Located in every county, draft officers reported to officials in the War Department in Washington, DC, the administrative home of the army. Each one of these draft officers was charged with finding and capturing deserters and draft dodgers, as well as arresting spies. To attain these goals, local officers hired myriad detectives to scour the local landscape. Thus, in its ubiquity, the army was well positioned to gather information on disaffection and disloyalty on the home front that threatened its ability to fight the rebellion successfully.

Despite the army's ubiquity, army intelligence operations in the Old Northwest arose in an unsystematic, decentralized, and ad hoc manner, without direction from Washington. Operations arose when it became clear that state and federal civilian law enforcement authorities were incapable of investigating the growing evidence of conspiracy in the Old Northwest. In a short period, local commanders collected significant evidence of conspiracy in Ohio, Indiana, Illinois, and neighboring states. Sometimes cooperating with civil officials, they formulated plans to counteract the plots. In late 1864, on the eve of state and national elections, officers and state governors agreed on a plan to arrest the leaders of the secret organizations and try them in military courts for conspiracy, employing the army's spies and informers as prosecution witnesses. The War Department, and, tacitly, President Abraham Lincoln, gave their assent to the plan, which produced the treason trials at a critical moment, before Northern voters went to the polls.

This study of army intelligence operations in the Northwest aims to answer two related historical questions: Did secret Democratic conspiratorial organizations exist and pose a threat to order in the North? Or, did Republican politicians and politically minded officers conspire to fabricate the existence of such Democratic conspiracies in an effort to smear their partisan foes? To the first question, the answer is yes; to the second question, no. This work concludes unequivocally that during the Civil War secret political organizations with ties to elements of the Democratic Party arose that conspired to obstruct the federal government's war effort. As the war wore on, the conspirators became increasingly ambitious in their aims, evolving from mutual-protection groups to groups aiding deserters and draft dodgers to plotting the release of Confederate prisoners of war en masse and raising insurrection in the North. Army intelligence officers amassed significant evidence of the existence of conspiracy, seized records of the secret groups, opened the private correspondence of participants, obtained numerous confessions of members, collected reliable information from informants, and inserted spies into the organizations to learn their secrets and plans.

Throughout the war, army commanders and politicians, working together to uncover the conspiracies, voiced genuine concern about the threats posed by the secret plots. They found the copious evidence their spies and informers supplied convincing. Officers believed that the conspiracies were widespread and threatened civil war in the North. They scrambled to counteract the threats. The fact that the army's spies infiltrated the secret groups with seeming ease and supplied significant information to commanders has been a stumbling block for historians, leading them to conclude erroneously that the threat was minimal and easily managed. For example, in his history of wartime Indiana politics, historian Kenneth M. Stampp scoffed at the idea that the secret organizations posed a genuine threat to stability in the North and that authorities feared for the future: "Knowing every move the Order made," he wrote, "[Governor] Morton and [General] Carrington had no reason to fear it as a menace to domestic peace. Instead, the Governor held the society 'as a plaything in his hands,' allowed it to grow, and 'even coerce[d] it into his service.'"[5] What Stampp and other historians misunderstood was that while local commanders had knowledge of conspirator's plans, they had few troops at hand with which to confront organizations that, their information accurately told them, boasted tens of thousands in each state in the region. In the summer of 1864, amid imminent threat of insurrection, generals could call on only a few scattered companies of troops. Ohio, Indiana, Illinois, and Michigan were stripped bare of troops, all available units having been sent to the front. Authorities possessed insufficient military power to arrest the leadership of the secret order, let alone confront the broader membership. Hence, they voiced grave fears. Some historians have suggested that Republicans and army officers were delusional in their belief that the conspiracies were large and threatening.[6] The weight of evidence mustered in this book points to the opposite conclusion: officers and officials who investigated the conspiracies were clear eyed and level headed in their assessments of the threat. The threats were real.

By concluding that widespread conspiracies existed in the Northwest during the Civil War and were not fabrications of army officers and associated politicians for partisan political purposes, this study challenges the works of historian Frank L. Klement, who schooled generations of historians to believe that the Midwestern landscape harbored no widespread secret organizations that aimed to subvert the Union war effort. His studies of the copperheads sought to rehabilitate what he saw as a maligned segment of the population who were patriotic in their own way. He argued that only a tiny handful of "dreamers" among them, with little political consequence or influence, talked loudly of aiding the Confederate rebels against the Lincoln administration. Instead, the real conspirators were the "politically-minded" officers who, with malevolent Republican politicians, concocted stories of monstrous conspiracies to frighten voters into opposing the Democrats and supporting Republican candidates.[7] Klement's works have been enormously influential in training historians to dismiss evidence of secret societies and their conspiracies in the Northwest and other regions. Consequently, historians have portrayed a North that, while divided by ideology and class, faced no dangerous internal fissures that threatened violent upheaval.[8]

This book directly challenges Klement's narrative and points in another direction to show that, based on the reliable evidence gathered by detectives and spies, upheaval and violence were close to the surface throughout the region as ideologically driven secret political groups threatened large-scale unrest.

Moreover, the current study points to numerous significant errors of fact and misreading of records that undermine the Klement thesis.[9]

In the course of the Civil War, officers in the U.S. Army stepped in to investigate conditions in the Northwestern states when law enforcement officials failed to address the growing signs of criminal conspiracy. From the start of armed rebellion, evidence emerged of sympathy and assistance offered by Northerners to the Southern rebels. But state governments lacked investigative capacity, while U.S. marshals and attorneys were hamstrung by a minuscule federal law enforcement bureaucracy more intent on saving money than pursuing criminals. At the time, federal law made it difficult for marshals and attorneys to hire detectives, and their cries for help to investigate criminality directed to leaders in Washington were in vain. By 1862 increasing unrest and opposition to the Union cause became manifest in the region, opposition that threatened the army's ability to recruit volunteers and stop desertion. Starting in southern Illinois, local commanders began to investigate signs of secret organizations that existed in their areas. Soon, other commanders also began their own investigations. In late 1862 an officer in Indianapolis obtained confessions that soldiers in camps around the city had joined secret groups, which he tied to the rising contagion of desertion then plaguing the army. That officer, Colonel Henry B. Carrington, promptly compared notes with Indiana governor Oliver P. Morton, who from early in the rebellion had tried to get a handle on evidence of criminal conspiracy by secret political organizations that opposed the war effort. For most of the rest of the war, Carrington and Morton worked together to investigate secret conspiracy in Indiana and the Northwest.

In early 1863 military efforts to investigate and contain unrest on the Northwestern home front spread to Ohio, where commanders in Cincinnati noted that secret groups opposed to the war were supplying themselves with arms to resist the government. Most important, war opponents vowed to help army deserters avoid capture and resist the newly passed Enrollment Act, which established a national conscription system. With the approval of Major General Horatio G. Wright of the Department of the Ohio, the multistate command encompassing states of the Northwest and much of Kentucky, officers established detective bureaus of hired civilian detectives and soldiers detailed from their units who fanned out into communities throughout the region to track arms sales, hunt down deserters, and investigate secret organizations. Soon, district commanders in the department established their own detective staffs. As well, the Provost Marshal General's Bureau created under the Enrollment Act created another layer of investigative capacity when it hired hundreds of "special agents" to track down and arrest deserters and draft dodgers. Working together, the detectives from the military commands and the Provost Marshal General's Bureau began to amass large amounts of evidence pointing to the existence of secret political organizations that aimed to subvert the Union war effort. Detectives maintained surveillance on many important antiwar Democratic politicians, including exiled Clement L. Vallandigham, who had taken up residence in Windsor, Canada West, just across the river from Detroit. Officers investigated ties between Vallandigham and other Democrats and the secret groups and rebel agents in Canada. They discovered that the secret organizations called themselves different names, but went under the umbrella name of the Knights of the Golden Circle (KGC).[10] Later, army detectives learned that the organization's name changed to the Order of American Knights (OAK), and still later, in 1864, to the Sons of Liberty.

In late 1863, military-intelligence efforts in the Northwest scored their first victories by breaking up plots to attack prisoner-of-war camps in Ohio to release Confederate soldiers. This effort led to arrests of prominent persons and indictments in a federal civil court in Cincinnati. Further successes came in 1864 when spies infiltrated leadership of the secret groups and learned their plans, which included fomenting insurrection. Learning the full scope of the threat, military commanders and political leaders pressed Washington, including President Lincoln, for troop reinforcements and other help. But the president was preoccupied with the war in the South, and national leaders were dismissive of the possibility of massive unrest. The administration was unwilling to divert troops from combat to chase down civilians. Rebuffed, the generals and governors in the region resolved to act on their own initiative to combat the threat of uprisings. They made plans to arrest some of the leading conspirators and try them in military courts, having seen that the civil trials in Cincinnati had ground to a halt. In August 1864 two plots to instigate uprisings in Indianapolis and Chicago collapsed and large quantities of guns and ammunition were seized in Indiana, all thanks to intelligence efforts and the fortuitous arrival of troops in Indianapolis and the rumor of reinforcements in Chicago that intimidated conspirators. Washington leaders, including Lincoln, fearing the possibility of Democratic election victories, finally agreed to the military plan to arrest and try leading conspirators, including ordering widespread surveillance over persons suspected by the Lincoln administration. Afterward, army commanders in Indianapolis arrested some of them and put them on trial for conspiracy by a military commission. The tribunal convicted them based primarily on evidence supplied by the army's spies and informants. As the war wound down, in 1865, commanders in the region dismissed their detectives and broke up their investigative units in the general demobilization.

While this study mostly focuses on military-intelligence activities in the lower Midwestern states of Ohio, Indiana, and Illinois, significant attention is also directed toward neighboring states. The Department of the Ohio and the Northern Department, the army's geographical commands that encompassed the Old Northwestern states for much of the war, also included Michigan, where officers stationed at Detroit ran detectives into Canada to watch rebel agents, escaped prisoners of war, deserters, draft dodgers, as well as exiled Congressman Vallandigham and his friends. These officers worked closely with departmental commanders to learn the plans of Confederate soldiers and their collaborators in the Northwestern states who targeted insurrection in Ohio, Indiana, and Illinois. Similarly, the efforts of military commanders in Louisville and Lexington, Kentucky come under study. In 1864, seeing the threat of sabotage and unrest, the commander of the District of Kentucky, Major General Stephen G. Burbridge, pressed the generals and governors north of the Ohio River to take dramatic steps to counter the secret organizations. His aggressive efforts to lobby his Northwestern comrades were key in the decision to arrest the leaders of the multistate conspiracy. Likewise, the investigations of Major General William S. Rosecrans and his aide, Colonel John P. Sanderson, both of the Department of the Missouri, followed evidence of conspiracy into the Northwest. Seeing a large-scale threat to the integrity of the United States, Rosecrans shared his findings with his comrades in the affected states and worked closely with them to combat the danger. All told, army detectives from the Northwest ranged far and wide, from Canada and New York down the Mississippi River into the occupied South, to investigate leads or tail suspects. Thus, to study the experience of the principle three states in question, this book ranges well beyond the geographic confines of their borders.

This book demonstrates that the national emergency created by the Confederate rebellion prompted widespread government efforts to spy on citizens of the North during the Civil War. The U.S. Army took steps to watch persons who actively opposed the war effort in the lower Midwestern states of Ohio, Indiana, and Illinois, as well as in neighboring Northern states. Commanders hired civilian detectives and detailed officers and enlisted men to sniff out evidence of misdeeds, which included arms smuggling, harboring deserters and draft dodgers, organized resistance to the draft, as well as collaboration with Confederate secret agents to foment insurrection. With cooperation from private telegraph companies and government postal officials, officers intercepted private correspondence to learn specifics of secret conspiracies that existed in the North. The actions of these commanders and the detectives and informers who supplied them with information have largely been forgotten. But they served as precedents for the widespread government surveillance of private communications that newspaper reporters have revealed is a pervasive feature of early-twenty-first-century life.

ONE

"Secret Secessionism in Our Midst"

The Failure of Civilian Investigations in the Old Northwest, 1861–62

THE NEWS of the Confederate attack on Fort Sumter, in Charleston harbor in South Carolina, produced an explosion of indignation in the Old Northwest. In cities, towns, and countryside, men, women, and children gathered to hear the latest reports. One small-town Indiana observer's description of the scene was representative of the larger region: on hearing the first reports of the attack, people gathered in the streets before daylight; "old gray haired men" were "wrought up" with emotion; "mechanics quit their shops and with men from the country, spent the day on the street. There was no business." In impromptu rallies, farmers and tradesmen voiced their outrage and vowed to defend their country, the national Union, against secessionist violence. Rallies became recruiting drives as thousands responded to President Lincoln's call for seventy-five thousand volunteers to serve for three months to put down rebellion.[1]

While the response to the call to arms in the North was massive, it was not universal. Many Northerners responded to the call to suppress rebellion and treason with countercalls to redouble efforts for reconciliation and compromise. These calls did not derive from pacifist, nonviolent ideologies (though several religious groups present in Ohio, Indiana, and Illinois held such views),[2] but from views regarding the roles of the federal government and the individual states. Many Americans, including many Northern Democrats, held strict *states' rights* or *state sovereignty* views of the constitutional relationship between the federal government and the states. These two views, quite distinct themselves, stood in opposition to nationalist views of the United States and how government should function held by many Republicans, reflecting their Whig Party antecedents. In simple terms, states' rights ideology espoused a "dual-federalism" relationship between states and the federal government in which the Constitution delegated separate responsibilities to states and the nation; the national government had certain powers and responsibilities, while the states held others. Federal and state governments held equally sovereign powers in this conception of the Constitution. Stephen Douglas championed this states' rights view of dual authority in his career through the secession crisis. State sovereignty, on the other hand, evolved from the notion that when the former colonies rejected allegiance to Great Britain in the War of Independence, they became separate states, independent and sovereign entities. According to this view, the Articles of Confederation and the Constitution, created by the several states, served as contracts for common understanding and action among the states but did not create a unified nation. States retained sovereign powers in all matters, and the federal government served merely as the agent for the individual states. John C. Calhoun, the late South Carolina nullifier, political philosopher, and defender of the benefits of slavery, had been the leader of state sovereignty thought. Many of the Southern rebellion's political leaders adhered to state sovereignty views. These two views, similar enough to allow respective adherents to cooperate in politics, were distinct enough to split the Democratic Party in 1860 and allow Lincoln, the nationalist, leading a Republican Party limited to the North with no Southern support, to prevail in the presidential race with less than 40 percent of the popular vote.[3] The more moderate states' rights notion of dual sovereignty held by Douglas and his Northern Democrat followers allowed them to unite with Republicans in a nationalist endeavor to subdue rebellion and preserve the national Union.

Some Northerners, though, held strict states' rights and state sovereignty views, holding to the supremacy of the state over the federal government. During the secession crisis of 1860–61, for example, the editors of a Democratic newspaper in northern Indiana wrote that "we favor the right of secession."[4] When war came, these Northerners rejected a coercive war on the South to force the rebel states back into the federal union. They held that the Southern states had the right to secede from the Union if they wished to preserve slavery as the cornerstone of their social and economic systems. Such views on federalism and the relationship between the federal government and the states animated many people's political views, and in the course of the Civil War these views would be enunciated by Northern opponents of the Union war effort.

In the electric atmosphere of the moment, Northern calls for compromise, moderation, and peace based on states' rights or state sovereignty ideologies prompted violent responses from advocates of war and retribution. Northern speakers and newspaper editors who voiced such sentiments suffered violent attacks, intimidation, and threats of violence. Likewise, in communities where pro-South sentiments and views of the constitutional propriety of Southern secession prevailed, Unionists felt the wrath of the majority and suffered violent attacks and intimidation. Crowd violence erupted frequently in towns and villages in the Old Northwest states, and residents feared it throughout the war.[5] Consequently, many Northerners kept their eyes and ears open to the words and actions of their neighbors. Many reported to state and federal authorities in Illinois, Indiana, and Ohio that they had heard expressions of sympathy for the rebel cause. They told of neighbors who declared that the South was in the right and that states had the right under the Constitution to secede. Reports of rallies in favor of Southern rights, of recruiting for the army of the Confederate States of America, sabotage of the war effort, organizing in opposition to the government, and other instances of "treason" arrived in government offices throughout the region. The officials who received the reports took them seriously.

Illinois

In the days and weeks after the attack on Fort Sumter, reports about sentiments in the state of Illinois streamed into newly elected Governor Richard Yates's Springfield office. A former Whig-now-Republican politician, friend of Lincoln, and ardent abolitionist who served in the state legislature and the U.S. House of Representatives, he was a seasoned public servant with strong knowledge of his state. His political contacts and constituents supplied him with reports that problems existed in the state. Secessionist sentiments were strong in parts of the state, they warned. "Egypt," the southernmost tip of the state, which jutted deep into Dixie, posed a special challenge. During the secession crisis, many there asserted that the South possessed the right to leave the Union. When war came, some threatened to sabotage the Illinois Central Railroad line should federal troops be sent south over it. Others reported that men had banded together to cross the Ohio River to Kentucky to join Confederate forces.[6] Elsewhere, correspondents wrote that men who flew the U.S. flag were threatened with mob violence. Pro-Union men and women voiced uneasiness in their communities. People wrote the governor to ask for arms to be supplied to local "Home Guard" militia companies to afford protection from "rampant secessionists."[7] A Wabash County resident in eastern Illinois warned that men there had formed a company led by secessionists who declared they would not drill under Yates or Lincoln. An "undercurrent [was] at work," he noted.[8] Constituents wrote that they had inklings of conspiracy in Illinois. One correspondent noted, "I feel almost certain that there are sworn secret political societies here which are in league with the Southern traitors."[9] Another reported to the governor that Unionists in Perry County believed that a "deep laid plot against the Government" existed "right here among us."[10] Still another correspondent relayed information that Tennessee Confederates maintained communications with rebel sympathizers in and around Cairo and plotted an attack on the Union base. Such information was echoed by influential figures such as David Davis, Lincoln's campaign manager in the recent election.[11] State leaders believed the reports. Prominent Illinois Republican and attorney Orville Hickman Browning, in Springfield in the days after the attack on Fort Sumter, recorded in his diary that government leaders in the state capital believed that a "scheme had been set on foot" by "traitors" in southern Illinois who conspired with rebels in Missouri and Tennessee to seize Cairo and take the southernmost part of Illinois out of the Union. "To prevent the execution of so diabolical a plot it was deemed advisable to anticipate them in the occupation of Cairo."[12]

The defeat of federal forces at Bull Run, in Virginia in July, bolstered antiwar, pro-South sentiment in the North and prompted many displays of antigovernment strength in communities. More reports of secret undercurrents arrived on Springfield desks. A correspondent wrote the governor that Union men received many threats in Washington County and that "secret organizations have been formed, & secret meetings are weekly being held by them, which we learn is the case in most of the counties south of us." A "demonstration" was feared in his home community if and when recruits left for the front.[13] A Marion County writer stated that the Southern sympathizers were organizing and had their headquarters in Jefferson County. "I am creditably informed that they are organizing lodges of the famous organization, known as the Knights of the Golden Circle." The organization spread across Jefferson, Hamilton, Wayne, and Marion Counties.[14] Others reported that secessionists were holding private meetings, to the alarm of the Union people.[15]

Unionists managed to get informants into the secret organizations forming in their communities. A writer in Perry County reported on a secret group in that and adjoining counties; "in Jefferson county they number about 1300 in franklin about 900, in Washington co they are said to be strong[,] in Jackson county they are also said to be strong." The leader of the group had recruited a local young man "of high standing" into it who was actually a Unionist. The young man reported that they drilled regularly with the intent to resist any draft or the payment of taxes to support the war.[16] Elsewhere, a man wrote that his sister was married to a member of a pro-secession company in Hancock County, in western Illinois, who were "working secretly." My sister "is my informant," he wrote, and she planned to leave her husband "in consequence of his course and threatment [*sic*] of her."[17]

Correspondents around the state served as the governor's eyes and ears and provided information on the activities and sentiments of their neighbors. Undoubtedly, some of the information was the product of great anxiety and fear. One correspondent in Carbondale wrote that "strong bands of the Golden Circle [are] increasing rappidly [*sic*]," that local informal Union militia were not adequate for defense, and he urged the dispatch of a regiment of troops to keep them at bay.[18] But their fears were often justified, for in locales where antiwar sentiment was predominant, Union men and women experienced assault and other forms of violence. Correspondents understood that the extraordinary information they shared may not appear credible and used phrases such as "entirely reliable," "reliably informed," "a reliable man," "creditably informed," and "settled opinion," to support the accuracy of their statements.[19]

Governor Yates received these written reports, as well as many more verbal reports, of affairs in his state. He credited the reports. In August he wrote an indignant letter to a Democratic politician in Clay County who had complained to him regarding the arming of Republicans in the county:

> I will not disguise the fact that having received reliable information
> that bands of disloyal men have made unlawful combinations and
> formed secret organizations with the avowed purpose of subvert-
> ing the Government of the United States; I have taken measures to
> furnish good reliable men with arms and ammunition with which
> to protect the friends of the Union against the unprovoked assaults
> which have been made upon them on account of their loyalty to the
> best government the world ever saw.
>   This infamous rebellion must be put down, the supremacy of
> law must be maintained and to this end the most vigorous measures

must be used against traitors abroad and at home and abroad [*sic*], those in our midst being by far the most formidable.[20]

Yates worked with military commanders in and near Illinois to request assistance and arms from them for the defense of the state and to quell internal disturbances. Writing to Major General John C. Frémont, commanding at Saint Louis, the governor inquired if troops could be posted at Chester, Illinois, on the Mississippi River, halfway between Saint Louis and Cairo, to guard against invasion. The troops would also be handy to suppress insurrection in his state. "I regret to inform you," he wrote, "that my correspondence with southern Illinois indicates much larger secession numbers than we anticipated—the least encouragement would make them a formidable force."[21]

In October military commanders at Cairo and other points on the rivers investigated smuggling activities between federal- and Confederate-controlled areas. Brigadier General Ulysses S. Grant, commanding the District of Southeast Missouri with headquarters at Cairo, received reports from sources that indiscriminate sales of contraband goods occurred back and forth across the Mississippi River. Arms were among the items passed freely, "without regard to politics." Grant also learned that military companies raised in Illinois intended to march south to join the Confederates. Naval commanders patrolling the Ohio River near Shawneetown, Illinois, also reported efforts to intercept recruits leaving Illinois to join rebel forces.[22] A number of arrests occurred. In early November, Grant and Brigadier General John A. McClernand informed Yates that arrests of civilians near Shawneetown had provoked excitement there and that citizens of the town had come to Cairo to plead the loyalty of the town's people. The generals in turn professed their innocence in ordering the arrests and referred the people to the governor. Grant and McClernand wrote that they "had heard of the existence of a secret political order known as the 'Knights of the Golden Circle' in some portions of Illinois." They added that it should be "repressed." The governor drafted a reply to the officers that he was "well advised of the movements of the 'Knights of the Golden Circle.'"[23]

In 1861, Governor Yates collected information from correspondents in his state reporting serious disaffection and the existence of organized combinations intent on subverting the Lincoln administration's war effort. The governor relied on constituents and political allies to feed him information. Evidence suggests that some Unionists managed to infiltrate the secret organizations then forming. His information, however, remained vague and nebulous. His counterpart to the east, in Indiana, shared the same problem.

Indiana

Indiana voters elected Oliver P. Morton to be lieutenant governor in 1860, but he served in that position only one day before Republicans in the General Assembly selected Governor Henry S. Lane to serve in the U.S. Senate. Elevated to the governor's office when war came, Morton turned his indefatigable energies to mobilizing the state for war. Like Yates, the young new governor received numerous reports of expressions of sympathy for the rebels. Informants warned of county officials suspected of being secession sympathizers and that some men should not be trusted to command Indiana Legion (state militia) units after being heard to "halloo" for Jefferson Davis, the president of the Confederate States.[24] Others requested state arms be sent to them to counteract a military company that was being formed for the "avowed purpose . . . to resist the laws of the state."[25] Correspondents along the Ohio River reported that Union people received threats from secessionist sympathizers both in Kentucky and in Indiana; "we look for trouble here as soon as the troops is moved from here," wrote a Warrick County man. "It is unsafe for a Union man to express his sentiments on the streets."[26] A Washington County writer reported that "considerable opposition" from "those who are not favorable to the prosecution of the war" was interfering with recruiting. Another man from Harrison County complained, "We cannot disguise the fact . . . that we have living secessionists here among us" who tried to stop men from joining the legion.[27] Morton's informants were an admixture of local political officials and private citizens.

As in Illinois, the federal disaster at the battle of Bull Run in Virginia in July played havoc in Indiana, prompting a bold outpouring of pro-South sentiment around the state. A Republican newspaper editor wrote to Lazarus Noble, adjutant general of Indiana, "It is a fact, well authenticated" that Democrats in Blackford County, in northern Indiana, "exulted over the defeat of the Union forces at Manassas [Bull Run], and some of them hurrah for Jeff. Davis."[28] Reports from Boone County, northwest of Indianapolis, of U.S. flags being torn from their flagpoles reached the governor. A correspondent wrote that "a body of secessionists went in open daylight with axes and other instruments to the terror of the loyal citizens and cut down a Pole bearing the Stars and Stripes and trailed them in the dust and completely distroued [sic] them."[29] The secessionists were running "rampant" after the defeat, and the loyal people were unarmed, frightened, and needed protection, wrote one correspondent.[30] Requests for arms to equip local legion companies became more urgent as the weeks passed. Indiana Legion companies became lightning rods for antiwar harassment and threats, serving as symbols of support for the Lincoln administration's war policies. Membership in the legion became dangerous without arms. A Greene County man warned, "we are in the midst of secessionists and the strong probability is that we will soon need arms to protect the laws, ourselves, and good citizens."[31] In those circumstances, wrote one legion officer, either arm them or they will disband. "My men ar [sic] tired of handling cornstocks[stalks]."[32]

At this time, reports sent to the governor's office mentioned that expressions of antiwar sentiment were making way for organized opposition. The colonel of the 10th Indiana Volunteer Infantry Regiment reported, "Disloyalty and insurrection have got to such a pitch in some places in my county [Boone] that as many as three companies are being drilled with an avowed and declared purpose of assisting the brethren rebellion [sic] if necessary."[33] A Lawrence County man wrote that armed secessionists were threatening loyal people and pro-secession speeches were made in Paoli, the county seat of Orange County, just a few miles away. We anticipate "truble," he wrote.[34] Another report noted that "a responsible man" from Fountain County told of the organization of the Knights of the Golden Circle. They had become "quite numerous" in Jackson Township, where they boldly "denounce the government and all who uphold it openly."[35]

Late in August, Governor Morton received a curious telegram message from Michigan City, a town on the shores of Lake Michigan in far-northern Indiana. "We have a traitor spy here evidence positive," read the message, "What shall we do with him Answer immediately."[36] Local authorities had arrested a man who with his wife had been residing at Michigan City for several weeks past. His name was John C. Brain. He posed as an "artist" (photographer) and was photographing local scenes. According to a newspaper account, Brain was "mistrusted and his movements watched closely." Two local men entrapped him by saying that they sympathized with the Southern rebels. He revealed to them that his purpose was to recruit troops for the Confederacy; that he was "commissioned to organize the K.G.C.'s." He revealed the operations of this "secret conclave" to the men: that it exists all over the South to aid the rebellion, and it operated in the North as well. He showed them unreadable "hyerogliphics" purporting to be encoded messages allowing free passage throughout the South and told them how arms were smuggled to the South "under direction of the Lodge [the KGC]." "He showed the letters he had received from the South, recommending him and his mission to the disloyal men of the North." The two men informed an army officer encamped at La Porte, who duly arrested Brain and held him under guard. Commanders later turned him over to county authorities for a judicial hearing. At the hearing several soldiers from the 9th Indiana Volunteer Infantry Regiment testified that they had seen him at Philippi, in western Virginia, where the regiment had campaigned in June. The newspaper report noted that papers found with Brain indicated that he had recently traveled extensively in the South, came from Nashville, Tennessee, and had a brother in the rebel service. The judge set bond for $6,000 and held Brain for trial.[37] Federal authorities soon took over, however, and removed him to Fort Lafayette, in New York harbor, and Fort Warren, in Boston harbor, military prisons where the army held many political prisoners.[38]

Other Indiana citizens supplied information about perceived disloyalty. Governor Morton received protests from Fulton County residents about a local physician, Dr. Charles L. White, a Virginia native, who was an applicant for an appointment as surgeon in one of the volunteer regiments then being raised. White was "utterly unworthy" of any appointment in the "loyal army," wrote the local postmaster, who had opened one of White's letters. Eight hundred men in the county were willing to "fight for the rights of the South," he quoted. Stand firm and "kill every damned Republican that dare to set foot on the Sacred Soil of Virginia."[39]

Morton's informants had not been idle, and neither was the governor. In addition to raising Indiana troops, he played an important role in supporting Kentucky's Union supporters during the commonwealth's "neutrality"; he had an active intelligence-gathering operation in the Blue Grass State. He reported to Washington that his "secret scouts" in Kentucky kept him apprised of affairs and were supplying him with intelligence on the plans of its secessionists.[40] Alerted by his many informants around Indiana, Morton also acted on the reports of disaffection at home. During efforts to rush federal troops to Kentucky in late August, Governor Morton telegraphed the War Department that he had "detected a plan to burn the bridges on the [rail]roads" in Indiana leading to Louisville, "to prevent the movement of troops." He detailed troops to guard the railroads and warned national authorities "not to suffer affairs to drift on until it is too late."[41] That month Morton spoke at a Union rally near Rockville, in the western part of Indiana. After dissecting and condemning the arguments made for ending the war effort and compromising with the Confederate rebels, he thundered out a public warning to those who sympathized with rebellion: "Vigilant men watched them, and the moment they put a foot one inch beyond the line of strict legal action, they should feel the consequences."[42]

In late November an anonymous informer supplied Morton with details of a secret organization spread over western Indiana and eastern Illinois. Indiana attorney general John P. Usher, of Terre Haute, shared the detailed report with U.S. Senator Henry S. Lane. The document described an organization then in existence in Terre Haute called the "M.P.s, or Mutual Protection," which was in communication with rebels in the South. Its stated intent was opposition to the Lincoln administration and to federal taxes to pay for the war. Members, who included incumbent congressman Daniel W. Voorhees and former congressman John G. Davis, swore "not to take up arms against the Southern Confederacy and only in self defense or the order." According to the "memorandum," their plans also contemplated sabotage of railroad tracks carrying troop trains and the murder of army officers.[43] A month later the *Indianapolis Daily Journal*, the organ of the state Republican Party, published an exposé of the "M.P.s." clearly based on the informer's report, often quoting word for word from the original but omitting names. The newspaper's editor added that the information came from a source inside the secret group, and that detectives watched its meetings. The *Indianapolis Daily State Sentinel*, the state organ of the Democrats, claimed it to be a lie and challenged the *Journal* to print names or else be known as a "wholesale slanderer and villifier." A newspaper feud ensued, spreading to other papers, which added details. But the Republican organs did not meet the challenge to print names and dropped the matter, fearing lawsuits for libel. Similar newspaper "exposés" and feuds erupted in neighboring states over the existence of secret organizations and the KGC specifically. Vociferous Democratic counterattacks and Republican admissions of being duped by fraudsters demonstrated the difficulty of making newspaper accusations stick.[44]

Despite the denials and counterclaims, in 1862, Morton and his allies continued to pursue evidence of antiwar machinations. In one instance, Morton ordered an investigation prompted by a letter written by a Confederate prisoner of war at Camp Morton to a Terre Haute Democrat suggesting a "secret understanding" between them.[45] At another time, during a Union rally of Republicans and War Democrats, he read aloud a report about a secret political society in Brown County, prompting more newspaper jousting.[46] He penned a letter to Secretary of War Edwin M. Stanton sharing his grave apprehensions. "The fact is well established," he wrote, "that there is a secret political organization in Indiana" to oppose the war. It operated throughout the state and its members were "bound by oaths and their meetings are guarded by armed men." He continued, "These facts have been coming to me for some weeks past from all parts of the State, substantiated by evidence which leaves no doubt in my mind of their truth." He concluded by asking for guns with which to arm the Indiana Legion against the threat.[47]

Evidence points to Governor Morton receiving information of disloyalty and organized opposition to the war from a wide range of informal correspondents. Some informants passed on hearsay evidence, while others stated their information was from reliable eyewitnesses. One informant opened private U.S. mail to reveal its contents. Another was an insider of a secret group in western Indiana. Some reports were clear, others were indistinct and uncertain. Records show Morton's active efforts to gather information arose from his uneasiness about internal threats. Similar action occurred in Indiana's neighbor to the east.

Ohio

As in Illinois and Indiana, many expressions of antiwar sentiment arose in Ohio in the early weeks and months of the war. Accounts of threats to tear down U.S. flags as well as attempts to torch a barracks for newly raised troops circulated around the state.[48] Citizens recounted in letters to state authorities stories of rebel sympathizers' threats to burn down towns.[49] Republican governor William Dennison, Jr., elected to office in 1859 to fill a two-year term, fielded the reports as he scrambled to organize Ohio's enormous war effort. The rebel victory at Bull Run in July dealt a devastating blow to Ohio Unionists' hopes for a speedy end to the war. Information filtered into the governor's office that the federal defeat gave encouragement to the "Breckinridge traitors," informants wrote.[50] A man from Jackson County, in southern Ohio, reported that the sympathizers there had hoisted a secession flag in celebration. Please send us arms to protect ourselves, he wrote.[51] Another wrote that sympathy for the Southern secessionists had strengthened in Pike County, and the sympathizers had resorted to "insulting" Union men.[52] Several reports came in from around the state that "Demo-sessionists" worked to retard recruiting efforts. Southern sympathizers were working to defeat the organization of a regiment of volunteer troops, wrote one Highland County man. A Morgan County man wrote that his community was a "secessionist hole," and that a former state legislator was circulating through the county spreading false information and discouraging potential recruits. Men passed for Union supporters but actually spoke treason, he complained. A Muskingum County man said opponents of the federal government called the war effort "unholy" in their effort to prevent men from enlisting. Another reported that Delaware County men claimed the war against the South was unconstitutional.[53] As the weeks passed, both reports of efforts to discourage recruiting and slow progress in raising troops arrived in the mail at the statehouse; the authors of these reports ascribed the problems to "traitors" and their calls for compromise to end the war.[54]

Reports received in the governor's office took a darker turn. In the late summer and early fall of 1861, Ohio observers reported to state authorities that war opponents were forming military companies in their communities. A Findlay man warned that a military organization forming in northwestern Ohio had applied for arms under the militia law. The men who composed the company were opponents of the government and cheered for Jefferson Davis in the presence of Union men.[55] Opponents of the war raised a company in Gallia County, in southeastern Ohio, wrote another informant. Only Democrats were members of it, and they said they would kill all the "damned abolitionists."[56] A man from Holmes County, in the hills of northeastern Ohio, wrote to warn of a company made up solely of antiwar, pro-secession Democrats. One of the leaders of the company had rejoiced when "abolitionists" in the federal army "bit the dust" in Virginia. The informant believed that the company intended to serve as bodyguards for the Democratic newspaper editor in Millersburg, who was a bold and outspoken opponent of the Lincoln administration.[57] Other reports alerted authorities to developments in Delaware County, immediately north of Columbus. Men there were organizing a military company, all the members of which were pro-slavery sympathizers with the Southern rebellion. The company drilled at night. Its leader was an avowed secessionist who believed that any state had the right to secede from the Union, and who said that if he had to fight it would be for the South.[58]

William Coggeshall, a private secretary for Governor Dennison and ardent supporter of the war, noted in his diary the latest insider information to circulate in the governor's office. In late July he recorded that facts showed that opponents of war had formed a "party" for peace; this party discouraged enlistments in the army and otherwise gave aid and comfort to the rebels. Days later he recounted a private conversation between the governor and a political ally on affairs in Ohio and Kentucky. The ally voiced concerns about the rise of secessionism in Kentucky and that Ohio farmers resented the embargo on goods and commodities placed on Kentucky, shutting off commerce. The governor said he did not fear a rebellion of the farmers, but secret societies forming in Ohio had to be watched carefully.[59] Another Ohio insider voiced concerns about secret movements in the state. Samuel Galloway, a leading Republican, shared his apprehensions privately with another party man. "Our people are becoming entirely sensitive as to this secret secessionism in our midst," he wrote. Perhaps alluding to the ongoing federal investigation in northern Ohio (see below), he hinted, "I would not be surprised if the air should bristle with weapons" and news of the "arrest [of] internal enemies before October."[60]

In Ohio, as in Illinois and Indiana, the reports that filtered into the governor's office spoke to a growing threat in the state. Informants told of secret movements among antiwar groups. Added together, these remarkably similar reports of illicit activities by war opponents in the three states were numerous and appeared reliable to their recipients. But neither Yates nor Morton nor Dennison possessed the means to verify the reports. None possessed a police detective force nor had a state fund to pay for detectives or other investigators. They could not take steps to reign in the groups. Instead, they relied on trusted partisan friends to report on political conditions around their states, and they called on federal law enforcement authorities for assistance. But, like the state governors, those federal officers also lacked the means to investigate growing political conspiracy.

Federal Law Enforcement Investigations of Criminal Conspiracy under the Lincoln Administration

The crisis of civil war proved to be a daunting challenge to the small cadre of federal officers who enforced federal law throughout the Union. Confronted with strong evidence of serious crime and conspiracy by persons who sought to aid the Southern rebellion, federal law enforcement officials in the Old Northwestern states appealed to their superiors in Washington for guidance, support, and tools to arrest criminal acts. But the three top officials responsible for upholding federal law—President Lincoln; his attorney general, Edward Bates; and Secretary of the Interior Caleb B. Smith, who managed the Judiciary Fund—were preoccupied with the war effort, the legal challenges posed by rebellion, and controlling the high costs of waging war. They failed to support their local law enforcement officers when those officers called for assistance. Undeterred, some officers instituted investigations in their jurisdictions that detected evidence of conspiracy to aid the Confederate rebellion and undermine the federal war effort. Generally, however, federal law enforcement languished, held back by an unresponsive and misguided leadership.

United States attorneys and marshals enforced federal law throughout the country. U.S. marshals sought out and arrested persons wanted on warrants for trial in federal courts. They also served subpoenas on witnesses, disposed of seized and condemned property, housed prisoners awaiting trial, and provided for the needs of judges—from cleaning courtrooms and supplying court stationery to buying spittoons.[61] U.S. attorneys prosecuted criminal cases in federal district and circuit courts according to federal law and defended the United States in civil suits. As officers of the courts, marshals and attorneys served as the eyes and ears of the U.S. government throughout the country and operated with minimal supervision from Washington. At the outset of the Civil War, the attorney general of the United States commanded no central law enforcement bureaucracy. By law, the Office of the Attorney General boasted a staff of one assistant, four clerks, and one messenger.[62] (Today's Department of Justice came into existence only in 1870, after the end of the war, when the attorney general officially became a member of the president's cabinet. Up to that time the attorney general attended cabinet meetings as the president's counsel.) In the course of the war, the attorney general provided legal advice to executive and law enforcement officers throughout the Union, as well as represented the executive branch before the U.S. Supreme Court.[63]

Overall, the onset of civil war presented enormous challenges to the law enforcement system of the United States. Most of the federal judiciary and officers located in the Southern states resigned their posts in allegiance to the new Confederacy. The federal law enforcement network in effect ceased to exist in roughly half of the United States. But that was the least of the worries of the new attorney general, Edward Bates of Missouri. Simple as his administrative functions were, the Civil War raised myriad questions that puzzled legal minds both in and out of government. Questions arose surrounding the status of belligerents in a civil war, the confiscation of property of rebels, prisoners of war, the laws of neutrality, international law and naval blockades, presidential pardons, the admission of new states such as West Virginia, as well as soldiers' bounties, military arrests of civilians, guerrilla warfare, and treason. Bates often researched and prepared important opinions and briefs singlehandedly.[64]

Along with Bates, U.S. marshals and attorneys ran up against daunting problems in their local jurisdictions in the course of enforcing federal law. Many vexing questions arose concerning ways to deal with evidence of collaboration with the Southern rebels. Federal law enforcement officers communicated with the attorney general for direction and legal advice. But Washington authorities provided little or no help to those on the front lines of civil war; indeed, Washington leaders' narrow readings of existing law effectively crippled federal officers' efforts to investigate and stop secret pro-rebel collaboration in the North. The Lincoln administration's neglect of these efforts to combat collaboration had significant repercussions for Northern politics during the war.

In the first days of the war, newly minted federal marshals and attorneys, with their commissions fresh in hand, wrote to Washington for instructions. The U.S. attorney in New York City reported that he had knowledge of persons shipping war munitions to the South and reported on local efforts to recruit men for the rebel army. He also noted efforts to fit out ships as privateer vessels to wage private war on the United States. The attorney at Chicago reported that arms and ammunition destined for the South were expected to arrive imminently and requested instruction on how at act. The district attorney for Iowa telegraphed from Dubuque, "I have directed Marshal to prevent all shipments to [seceded states] am I right? Shall I pursue same course in regard to shipments of Powder lead and produce to States the Governors of which have refused compliance with Presidents requisition."[65] Some officials acted on their own initiative. Two weeks after Fort Sumter fell and four days after taking office the new marshal for the Northern District of Ohio at Cleveland, Earl Bill, reported that he had conferred with the U.S. attorney and the federal district judge about the best means to intercept shipments of contraband goods to the South. Together the three officials developed a plan of action. He instructed his deputies to seize all goods shipped to people "known to be connected with the pretended Govt of the Rebel States" as prima facie evidence of their contraband status. Shipments to private persons suspected to be linked to the rebels were to be stopped and investigated. All arms and munitions not directed to the U.S. government or a state officer of an "adhering State" were to be seized.[66] In May the marshal at Cincinnati seized revolvers hidden in a barrel of dried apples being sent south. The owner contested their confiscation in federal district court, however, and Judge Humphrey Leavitt agreed with him.[67]

Once troops from the North arrived at a beleaguered Washington in May, national leadership calmed down and returned to supervising officials around the country. In a cooperative effort with the War Department to investigate Northern collusion with the Southern rebels, Bates authorized a widespread effort to collect private telegraph messages sent between the North and South in the months leading up to the start of war. Marshals went to telegraph offices in several northeastern states, as well as Delaware and Maryland, and seized thousands of copies of telegraph messages "with purposes hostile to this Government." Marshals seized over a quarter of a million telegrams from the telegraph offices in New York City alone. Newspapers reported that the marshals delivered them to a War Department panel composed of "highly respectable men" who sifted through the piles of messages in secrecy.[68] A similar sweep occurred in Louisville in September.[69]

Federal officers acted diligently to investigate and intercept contraband trade with the South. It soon became evident, however, that the task was too large for them. The U.S. marshal for Connecticut, David H. Carr, wrote to

Washington for help. His state was a leading producer of firearms and munitions. New Haven, he wrote, was full of manufacturers of firearms, percussion caps, powder flasks, and other munitions that were transported to various points by sea and land. Carr asked that a small sum from secret service funds be sent to him to keep watch on arms dealers. "Aside from the high consideration of public safety," he added, "I think it would be a paying investment." Bates, who had no secret-service funds or any similar discretionary funds available, consulted Secretary of State William H. Seward, who did. Carr received the $200 he asked for and hired extra eyes to help watch.[70]

George A. Coffey, the U.S. attorney in Philadelphia, wrote to Bates "There are beyond doubt *some* traitors in our midst, and *some* sources from which the rebels are supplied with material aid for treason." He said he was eager to discover the offenders and punish them. "But to do this effectually," he wrote, "we should have a *special* detective force." He applied for funds to that end and asked that Bates support his application. "If we could be thus aided & furnished I am sure that we can detect treason & most effectively stop the manufacture of arms, munitions & stores for the rebels. The officers of the law do tolerably well as it is," he added, "but with aid, we can systematize our operations, and procure evidence to arrest, try, convict, and punish."[71] The new U.S. marshal for the Southern District of Illinois, David L. Phillips, wrote for money. "It is highly important that many persons charged with the crime of treason should be arrested and indicted, all of which cannot be done without some money." Men were being recruited for the Confederate army in Illinois, he added, and others were hindering efforts to recruit for the U.S. Army.[72] Phillips worked closely with Governor Richard Yates to detect what he perceived to be traitorous activities. In September he wrote, "I am watching the Bond Co. secessionists. [I] hope to catch the ringleaders." He also kept an eye on Democratic politicians who he believed were "bent on mischief," and nudged the governor to follow up efforts to break up the emerging secret combinations.[73] He later wrote to voice suspicions that recruiters from Missouri ostensibly recruiting for the volunteer service were actually recruiting for the rebel army. "Men have been here and across the state to the Wabash [River], whose conduct has been most suspicious." He also warned Yates that the Knights of the Golden Circle "will make much trouble. They are all about here."[74]

In late summer and fall of 1861, several officers communicated with the attorney general their concerns about nefarious activities in their districts. W. H. L. Gurley, the U.S. attorney in Iowa, wrote to Bates, enclosing two letters he had obtained from an informant. One of the letters was written in cipher, the other only partly in code. Gurley suggested, "If these men are engaged in an enterprise of the character indicated in the letters, they are undoubtedly connected with others in higher walks of life whose discovery might be of great importance to the Government. You will notice that the last letter is from Washington City July 25th 1861."[75] The marshal in Iowa wrote from Des Moines to ask for advice about seditious articles in local newspapers.[76] The U.S. marshal for the Northern District of New York wrote from Lockport asking for instructions on how to handle treason and treasonous speech. His deputies had arrested people and seized packages of New York City newspapers.[77] The governor of New York, Republican Edwin D. Morgan, also wrote to Bates and enclosed copies of letters received from his constituents. The letters included reports of groups holding secret meetings and arming themselves to oppose the government. The letters were merely a sample of what he received every day from all over his state, he wrote, and he asked the attorney general to "suggest some practical course for them to take with regard to meetings, newspapers, and individuals clearly in sympathy with the rebels."[78]

Bates, a conservative ex-Whig, viewed it as improper as attorney general to offer direction to the marshals and district attorneys who wrote for advice. His replies consistently reminded them to "act on your own responsibility under the law" and not to ask him for advice in the difficult cases before them. He did not possess the authority to provide policy leadership, he replied. He and his assistants told them to use their "good discretion" to decide how to proceed and choose which cases to investigate and prosecute. He refused to give advice about the recently enacted Confiscation Act, writing, "This is the proper business of the Courts" and that district attorneys were to act "upon their own convictions" in each case.[79] Unofficially, he offered fatherly advice to some of the attorneys who faced vexing legal challenges. To the district attorney in his home town of Saint Louis, Asa S. Jones, Bates noted that the Lincoln administration put "great importance" on intercepting shipments of war materiel from the North to the Southern insurgents and they expected that Jones would be vigilant. Prosecuting such cases would produce an "excellent moral effect," but care must be taken to avoid an adverse reaction: "Better let twenty of the guilty go free of public accusation,—than to be defeated in a single case." Also, he suggested that pursuing conspiracy cases rather than treason cases would "help the cause by rubbing off the varnish from romantic treason, and showing the criminals in the homely garb of vulgar felony." To the Philadelphia attorney's questions about habeas corpus cases, he responded that he could not help him, merely adding that the Constitution required the president to put down insurrection in an undefined manner and that the armed forces should be the means of suppressing rebellion. "Draw your own inferences," he concluded.[80] Beyond such bromides Bates was careful not to venture.

Federal law enforcement officers continued to ask for money to hire detectives to uncover illegality. Flamen Ball, Jr., the U.S. attorney for the Southern District of Ohio at Cincinnati, wrote for funds. Several arrests for treason had been made in his district, "some of whom I believe to be guilty," he wrote, "but the proof is generally confined to the testimony of the officers making the arrests or that & the papers found upon the persons of the accused." These sources often furnished grounds for suspicion "without furnishing the necessary legal evidence for the conviction of the parties." He continued, "I often am embarrassed for the want of means to employ special agents to go to distant points & find out and procure testimony on behalf of the Government." Without money to employ such agents, "it is useless to attempt to hold even guilty parties." In reply, Bates's assistant lamented that the attorney general had no coffers "to be used for the purposes of procuring evidence in the cases you mention." He regretted that it was so, as he received many requests to investigate similar cases. "But Congress having failed to provide [investigatory funds,] you will be compelled to rely on the ordinary agencies used in detecting and convicting offenders."[81]

Having told their law enforcement officers there was no money to support investigations, Washington authorities perversely pushed officers to increase investigatory efforts. Bates wrote to his marshals and attorneys to chase down law breakers and uncover criminal acts and conspiracy. Information from the Treasury Department of shipments of tin from New York City to Kentucky prompted Bates's office to inform marshals in Ohio and Indiana to "give your attention to this matter" and prevent the transportation. The attorney in Kentucky received instructions to "counteract" an "evil" uncovered by New York City police detectives. After the marshal at Cleveland reported to the attorney general about illegal communications between Northerners and the Southern rebels, Bates replied, "I can give you no specific instructions as to the manner of proceeding" and blandly suggested that "a well-concerted espionage might produce much good."[82] Such instructions must have been akin to rubbing salt in the wounds of these hard-pressed law enforcement officers.

The Withers Letter Investigation
and the Knights of the Golden Circle in Northern Ohio

The most important federal law enforcement investigation of conspiracy in 1861 occurred in northern Ohio. Marshal Earl Bill, a former state senator and publisher of a Republican newspaper in Sandusky, had energetically undertaken the responsibilities of his new office. In late June he obtained a curious letter that had passed from the Crestline postmaster to a Richland County Republican. The letter, dated June 15, 1861, was by one W. T. Withers to a John Thompson, both of whom appeared to be traveling slowly across northern Ohio canvassing and collecting names of Southern sympathizers in the area. "Here we have many true friends of the South ready to help us if a safe plan can be found," Withers wrote. After naming several, he added, "I have selected a place to put the arms. . . . It will take immense work to go all over the Northern States to carry out the plan. It will make the damned Abolitionists feel that there is a South to be feared. . . . I am going into Wyandotte [sic] and Seneca counties. . . . We must not forget to go to the K.G.C. at Cynthiana in July, by that time we can tell what is to be done." The letter included several cipherlike markings, and above Withers's name was the closing: "Yours, D.K.2.B.9."[83]

Bill went to Crawford County to investigate the matter personally and identified the people named in the letter. Returning to Cleveland, he ordered his deputies to be alert for conspirators against the federal government.[84] He also communicated his findings to his superiors at Washington and promptly hired a "secret agent," longtime Mansfield resident Mansfield H. Gilkison, to keep watch primarily in Crawford County and collect "facts and information."[85] In a long and highly detailed report to Washington, Bill explained that the only way for Gilkison to obtain good information was "by assuming the role of opposition to the War and to the Government, and thus acquiring the confidence of the persons suspected of complicity with the rebellion." He reported, "Mr. G. is very competent to the work assigned him." Gilkison confirmed that "a man named Withers was, at or about the date of said letter and for a period subsequent thereto, perambulating that section" in the guise of a peddler selling dry goods from a wagon.[86] Bill reported that "secret lodges or associations" sprouted up about the time of Withers' visit, which were active and met at regular times and places. The groups posed as "mutual protection" societies but were "in reality the 'Knights of the Golden Circle' of the South, modified revised and shaped to suit the climate." He had the names of local leaders and other details. The groups hid caches of arms. He believed they were hostile to the federal government, though "whether, however, it is so far actually treasonable as to subject its members to the penalties of the act of Congress on that subject is not yet so clear." Following advice from the U.S. attorney, he deferred making arrests or searching for the arms. He solicited instructions from Washington and offered to share more information if the

"Government still deems the subject matter of sufficient importance to prosecute the investigation further."[87]

The local federal officers kept Washington informed of the progress of the investigation. The district attorney at Cleveland, Robert F. Paine, wrote to Bates in early September to urge prompt arrests "for treason & conspiracy against the Government." The KGC was known to exist in ten counties in the district and had multiple hidden caches of arms. "I have not before disturbed them [the caches] for the reason that I desired further evidence of their Guilt," he explained. "This I hope I have secured." Paine urged haste to arrest twenty "Officers of the Order" to stand trial for conspiracy.[88] But Bates balked at Paine's idea of hiring a prominent War Democrat as cocounsel for the prosecution and dithered in making his decision. Precious days were lost in negotiations between Cleveland and Washington.[89]

Finally, Bates agreed to the hiring of the War Democrat, but further delays ensued. The first arrest by deputy marshals occurred on October 5, three days before the state elections for governor and legislators. Further arrests followed, which election-day newspapers in the state reported. Republican and War Democrat newspapers trumpeted the arrest in headlines that read: "Alarming Treason in Ohio!" and "Important Arrest! A 'Castle' of the Knights of the G. C. Assaulted by the U.S. Marshal: The Records Seized: A 'Commander' Taken." Newspapers quoted sworn affidavits of Marion County men filed as complaints prompting the arrest, saying that an arrested man initiated them into the secret organization and swore them to oaths to protect fellow "constitutional Democrats" and oppose the Lincoln administration.[90] If the district attorney and the marshal, as well as Washington leaders, had wanted to time the arrests to achieve maximum electoral effect (which is entirely likely), they had missed the boat with the back-and-forth dithering in September that forced weeks of delays.[91] The impact of the arrests arrived during pretrial judicial hearings that only occurred one full week *after* the election and which were reported in minute detail by the Cleveland dailies.

Pretrial examinations before U.S. Commissioner Bushnell White in Cleveland stretched over five days. Testimony revealed widespread secret activities in several Ohio counties during the summer and early autumn. Some of the witnesses testified that they had been asked to join the Knights of the Golden Circle. They had been told that the purpose of the organization was to protect Democrats from "abolitionist" mobs then making threats against Democrats who voiced opposition to the war, as well as to prevent volunteering and drafting. One witness stated he was told that the secret order had three hundred members in Marion County and that there were nine hundred in

Columbus and Franklin County. Defense lawyers acknowledged the existence of an organization in the county but were at pains to show that it had no connection to "the organization known as the Golden Circle." They called their own witnesses who testified that it was merely a group made up of Democrats to deter mob attacks on fellow Democrats. They also denied knowledge of any arms hidden in the area.[92]

Commissioner White summarized the presentation of the evidence and the arguments made in the hearings. He concluded it made no difference if the secret organization was the KGC or another group. He said the evidence showed that the KGC did exist in the area but that evidence also suggested that there were two connected organizations coexistent there. He concluded that conspiring to drive Lincoln out of office was conspiracy to overthrow the government under the new Conspiracies Act and held the defendants to trial.[93] In the following days the federal sweep widened and in early November federal marshals arrested seven more on charges of conspiracy.[94] The trials before Federal District Judge Hiram V. Willson approached with much anticipation. On the first day of the trial, however, after Willson gave a stern charge to empaneled grand jurors on the law of conspiracy and treason, the prosecution case collapsed. U.S. Attorney Paine rose in court to announce that no prosecutions of the defendants held for conspiracy would proceed. An important prosecution witness had backed out under threats from neighbors and fled to safety in the army. Another witness suddenly and inexplicably died shortly after the hearings. The *Plain Dealer*, Cleveland's War Democrat paper, asked, "Is there any significance in his dying at this time?" The *Crawford County Forum*, an antiwar Democratic newspaper in neighboring Bucyrus that ridiculed the hearings, countered that he had died from "fear and remorse" for committing perjury.[95]

The prosecution's case collapsed when the witnesses felt the full force of the threat from neighbors in their home communities. They broke under the pressure. The fruits of Earl Bill's months-long investigation and infiltration of the KGC in Ohio came to naught when witnesses feared the repercussions of testifying in open court. Bill's "secret agent," Mansfield Gilkison, was not heard in court, nor did other insiders who had supplied information to him step forward.[96] Democrats afterward pronounced the arrests and attempted prosecutions a "humbug" and a "deliberately planned piece of villainy" based on forged documents, perjury, and false accusations by political enemies.[97]

The investigation by federal law enforcement officials at Cleveland was the most aggressive and far-reaching effort to prosecute conspiracy among secret groups in the North in the early months of the Civil War. They had uncovered secret movements to recruit opponents of the federal war effort to support the rebel cause through information gathering and the use of a hired "secret agent" to investigate and infiltrate the secret organization. As shown by their reports to their Washington superiors, Bill and Paine sincerely believed that they had uncovered a dangerous secret conspiracy against the federal government. Their failure to prosecute the conspirators presaged the difficulties that federal law enforcement officials would have in the course of the war. Conspirators succeeded in effectively intimidating potential witnesses into silence. Furthermore, given the slippery nature of conspiracy and the secret organization in question, officials could not make their accusations stick. More important, the episode illustrated the weakness of the federal officials' legal tools to bring conspirators to justice. In the summer of 1863, Paine and a federal grand jury at Cleveland would return to the issue of the existence of secret societies composed of "unprincipled men and villainous traitors," reporting that authorities had "reliable information" based on testimony of witnesses and entertained "no doubt" as to their intentions. But they pursued no cases against anyone.[98] Law enforcement authorities proved unprepared to handle conspiracy on the scale encountered in the North during the Civil War. As shown below, a significant reason for that weakness derived from parsimonious distribution of federal funds.

Strangled Investigations: Holding the Purse Strings of the Judiciary Fund

Attorney General Bates was in a difficult position in the early months of the war. Barraged by federal law enforcement officers with requests for funds to deal with the additional demands the war placed on them, especially for cash with which to hire detectives to investigate criminal activities, he had no material support to offer to them and was powerless. His office had no money at its disposal to send to federal officers around the country to assist them in the investigation, arrest, and prosecution of conspiracy. In fact, federal funds to maintain the courts and officers of the courts were by law under the control of another government department. Congress created the Judiciary Fund in 1852 and placed its administration in the hands of the secretary of the interior. The law specified what expenses the fund would cover and tasked the secretary with the responsibility of doling out money to federal law enforcement officials and officers of the federal courts. An 1853 law set a schedule for the fees that marshals and other officers could be paid for services rendered. In the first two years of the war, President Lincoln's appointee Caleb Blood Smith had control of the Judiciary Fund. A brief excursion into its administration will shed light on an obscure corner of federal-government bureaucracy and will illuminate an important reason for the failure of civil law enforcement authorities to take on the investigation and trial of Northern conspiracy during the war.

Boston-born Indiana politician and attorney Caleb Smith played a pivotal role in securing Lincoln's nomination at the 1860 Republican National Convention at Chicago by securing the votes of the whole Indiana delegation to him. He later led the vote-getting effort in Indiana, which went for the Illinoisan and his electors. As a reward, Lincoln nominated him to head Interior.[99] As chief of one of the largest civilian agencies in Washington, encompassing several large bureaus, Smith administered vast expanses of western territories and maintained friendly relations with native Indians. Administration of the Judiciary Fund was only one of many important functions he undertook. However, it clearly occupied a significant portion of his time.[100] In his first weeks in office, Smith faced vexing questions about paying off expenses of outgoing Buchanan administration law enforcement officers. Those expenses involved activities not covered by the fee schedule and were, in his view, salaries—something that marshals could not receive. He fought hard against establishing a precedent for paying salaries.[101] "Admit the right of a Marshal to incur such an expense and at once a rule is established which would open a wide door to abuses," Smith advised. Marshals and their deputies had an "undoubted right to certain fees or, in lieu thereof, certain travelling expenses." But the government would not pay them salaries. "The law imposes the duty upon the Marshal. If in grave cases, such as the present one, he incurs . . . expenses exceeding his lawful compensation there is no remedy."[102]

Secretary Smith answered requests for funds from U.S. marshals and attorneys for other purposes; his answers reflected his rigid interpretation of the law. For example, he denied the U.S. attorney in New York City an advance for work to suppress the slave trade. In another case, he turned down a request from the U.S. attorney in Philadelphia for funds to detect counterfeiters of U.S. coin and traitors by stating that no law authorized it.[103] Though he routinely refused extraordinary applications for funds, however, the secretary held out a ray of hope. He advised officers that if they would provide a detailed written statement about how funds were to be spent he might be persuaded to part with some of the Judiciary Fund. It is this method of extracting detailed information about the way funds would be expended that explains the detailed report by U.S. Marshal Earl Bill to Smith about conspiracy in northern Ohio.[104]

However, having received specific requests from law officers for Judiciary Fund money, Smith was sometimes loath to advance it. David L. Phillips, the marshal for southern Illinois at Springfield, repeatedly wrote to the attorney general requesting assistance to break up the trafficking of arms and supplies to the rebels from his district, whereupon Bates forwarded the requests to the secretary. Smith turned them down based on his narrow interpretation of the law. "While I agree with you in the importance of the Government taking prompt steps to effect this object, I do not think an advance can be properly made from the Judiciary Fund for the purpose," he wrote. The expenses could not be considered judicial expenses, he added. "There are no legal proceedings pending against any parties, and no process of court which he is commanded to execute." To Smith's eye expenditures for investigation and detection of crime did not fit the criteria of the fund because they were not directly related to court-ordered proceedings such as carrying out arrest warrants or subpoenas. "I beg leave to suggest that the matter might be a fit subject for the action of the War Department," he concluded.[105]

Indeed, Smith soon began to forward requests for funds from law enforcement officers to the War Department for their information and action, reasoning that the matter related to the suppression of the rebellion and not to court-ordered actions.[106] But an order from Lincoln of November 1 put an end to this bureaucratic battling. It required that arrests called for by the Departments of War or State and executed by U.S. marshals be paid from the Judiciary Fund. The order must have come as a blow to Smith. Nevertheless, he responded with a time-tested bureaucratic tactic: increase the paperwork burden and perhaps others might reconsider. A few days later he informed Secretaries Cameron and Seward that U.S. marshals ordered to make arrests under orders from their departments must submit their expenses first to those departments' auditors for verification, who would then forward them to the Department of the Interior for payment under the fund.[107] Still, he was not happy about Lincoln's order. To the first auditor in the Department of the Treasury he complained that these bills would be unprecedented and "many of the expenses incurred will be of a character so extraordinary as to demand the exercise of unusual liberality."[108]

In 1862, Smith continued to respond with parsimony to requests for Judiciary Fund money to cover war-related investigations. He wrote to the Iowa district attorney to deny payment for expenses incurred at the request of a military officer that, while important, were not for judicial service and "not embraced in any provision of the law authorizing payment for services."[109] He refused a request from Secretary of the Treasury Salmon P. Chase for funds to detect and arrest counterfeiters of treasury notes. Smith wrote that he would be happy to aid this important work, but he had grave doubts that the Judiciary Fund could be used to "defray the expenses of detectives engaged in endeavoring to discover persons who are violating the law." Furthermore, Congress had appropriated $5,000 in 1860 specifically for the "detection and bringing to trial of persons engaged in counterfeiting the coin of the U.S." By making a special appropriation for this purpose, he argued, Congress "indicated, very clearly, their opinion that the general judiciary appropriation could not be so applied." To reinforce his view, Smith applied to Attorney General Bates for an opinion on the matter: did the law give him the authority to make payments to detect treasury note counterfeiters, he asked? In April, Bates produced his opinion, concluding that Smith had no power to supply money from the Judiciary Fund to marshals for detection of treasury note counterfeiters.[110] Armed with Bates's opinion, Smith replied triumphantly to a request for payment from the first comptroller of the treasury based on Lincoln's order of November 1, 1861:

> Attorney General Bates has recently decided that the judiciary fund cannot be legally applied to pay detectives of persons engaged in counterfeiting Treasury notes. I concur in the opinion and have declined to make requisition upon the [fund] for that purpose. If the fund cannot be legally used to employ detectives for that purpose, *it certainly cannot be used to employ detectives of persons guilty of political offenses.*[111]

Due to Smith's stubborn penny-pinching, marshals and district attorneys gave up seeking dollars from the Judiciary Fund to investigate criminal activities and conspiracy in their jurisdictions. Other civilian government officials likewise gave up efforts to use the fund for investigations. Moreover, in an effort to rein in the burgeoning federal-government budget, Congress even considered reducing the rates of compensation paid to officers of the court under the 1853 fee schedule.[112] Clearly, Congress was not in the mood to spend more money for law enforcement investigations while a war raged. Smith's efforts to protect the Judiciary Fund from raids on it by other departments for uses other than those laid out in the 1852 law had the effect of killing efforts by civilian departments to employ detectives to investigate political crimes. U.S. marshals and district attorneys had repeatedly asked for means with which to make investigations. But Attorney General Bates offered merely moral support while placing increasing demands on them, and Secretary Smith turned down their requests for funds by his narrow reading of the law. Efforts by other federal executive departments to use his money to investigate law breaking of various sorts were also stymied by his limited interpretation of the law. Smith's actions in handling the Judiciary Fund played a critical role in creating the conditions for the slow, weak, and ineffectual response of the Lincoln administration's civilian law enforcement officials to the exigencies they faced during the war. Congress passed laws broadening the definition of acts against the government deemed illegal and treasonous, but it failed at the same time to give the executive branch the means to pursue the law breakers. Smith's reading of the law hampered effective civilian investigations of large, sophisticated, and complicated criminal conspiracies.

Frustrated by Smith's intransigence, federal officials developed other means. Secretary Chase and the Department of the Treasury opted to rely on a makeshift unit of detectives operating out of the War Department in Washington led by Lafayette C. Baker to detect and arrest counterfeiters of coin and notes.[113] In 1862, Congress made specific appropriations for investigations of counterfeiters of treasury notes and, in the next year, established a detective operation in Chase's department under the supervision of the solicitor of the treasury; this operation became the Secret Service in 1865.[114]

These makeshifts, however, did little to assist U.S. attorneys and marshals in the Northwest, who continued to try to investigate criminal collaboration with the southern rebels. They sometimes received assistance from political leaders in their jurisdictions. In Indiana, Governor Morton turned to the federal grand jury. In July 1862 he wrote to a Republican confidante in Terre Haute, "Where is the man who came over with you last winter and exposed that secret society in your town? Can't you get him to go before the grand jury this week, in the Federal Court[.] Send his name to [U.S. Attorney] John Hanna that he may be subpoenaed."[115] Empaneled in May, the grand jurors at Indianapolis heard weeks of testimony from over two hundred witnesses about secret movements in the state. They indicted several persons for collaboration with rebel guerrillas during the raid on Newburgh. In early August, before it adjourned, the jurors prepared a presentment, or report, for the court on its investigations of a "secret and oath-bound organization," the KGC. They reported that it went by several names, was found all over the state, and, if drafted, its members vowed not to harm fellow members arrayed against them in battle. Made public, the report created a sensation in the Northwest.[116]

Law enforcement officers also took their cue from a War Department order issued August 8, 1862 by Secretary of War Edwin M. Stanton designed to enforce a recent law, the Militia Act, passed by Congress. Enacted to create a draft in states that failed to meet their quotas of troops, the order authorized civilian officials to arrest and imprison all persons "who may be engaged, by act, speech, or writing, in discouraging volunteer enlistments, or in any way giving aid and comfort to the enemy, or in any other disloyal practice against the United States." In addition, the order suspended the privilege of the writ of habeas corpus—the constitutionally guaranteed right of prisoners to know the charges against them—for "all persons arrested for disloyal practices."[117] The order produced a wave of arrests throughout the North. Accordingly, the U.S. marshal at Cincinnati obtained affidavits from three Champaign County men attesting to having been recruited to join the KGC and efforts to discourage enlistments in the U.S. Army. He arrested a young man named Bethuel Rubart and forwarded him to Washington for trial by military commission. The prisoner languished there for months while Ohio friends attempted to free him.[118] In another case, the marshal in Iowa aggressively pursued the KGC in 1862 and 1863 with assistance from military authorities. He employed "an experienced detective" (how he paid the detective, if he did at all, is not known) to procure information on secret organizations that supplied arms to Missouri guerrillas and plotted to resist the draft.[119]

State and federal law enforcement officers received numerous reports of criminal conspiracy in the Northwest to aid the rebels. As evidence of the existence of secret political organizations to oppose the war mounted, alarmed officials attempted to investigate. But their efforts were ineffectual and failed to stop secret movements. A significant reason for their failure was their inability to obtain federal funds to hire investigators. Failing federal civilian help, desperate state officials would turn to the U.S. Army for assistance. For their part, army commanders would develop a widespread espionage apparatus to deal with threats to the welfare of military organizations arising from growing antiwar sentiment, rampant desertion, and resistance to the draft in the North. The army would fill the void left by a civilian law enforcement bureaucracy rendered incapable of pursuing major criminal conspiracy.

Investigating Desertion and Disloyalty

Henry B. Carrington and the Knights of the
Golden Circle in Indiana, 1862–63

IN THE summer of 1862, rising opposition in the North to the war prompted Washington, DC, leaders to issue an order clamping down on acts and speech deemed to be discouraging or disloyal. The August 8 order from the War Department gave civilian law enforcement officers broad authority to make arrests and imprison citizens. In the following days, weeks, and months, officials made numerous arrests. But owing to penny-pinching by Secretary of the Interior Caleb Smith, armed with a legal opinion from Attorney General Bates, federal marshals and attorneys could not dip into federal funds to investigate reported instances of disloyalty or discouragement of volunteer enlistments. They could not employ detectives to uncover worrisome movements. In their stead, the U.S. Army stepped in. Growing antiwar sentiment in the North disturbed commanders as much as it did civilian authorities. Discouragement about the war and the ability of the federal government to suppress the rebellion was manifested in slowed recruitment. Especially problematic were reports of organized groups that encouraged desertion. As a consequence, individual officers responded by employing their soldiers as detectives to uncover individuals and groups who fomented unrest in the ranks. The most important commander to investigate conspiracy was Colonel (later Brigadier

General) Henry B. Carrington, who zealously chased down movements that threatened the army's integrity in Indiana. A close look at how he became involved in investigations and surveillance reveals the ad hoc, contingent start to the army's involvement in espionage in the Old Northwest.

Army Espionage in "Egypt"

The first-known military investigations of unrest in the Old Northwest occurred deep in southern Illinois. During the spring and early summer of 1862, reports of unrest among opponents of the war continued to arrive in Governor Yates's Springfield office. While western armies made significant progress in subduing rebellion and occupying large portions of the Confederate South, the eastern Army of the Potomac's Peninsula campaign in Virginia collapsed in retreat. That setback emboldened antiwar adherents, who called for peace talks with the rebels. Citizens reported they saw ominous portents of violence around them. A Jefferson County woman's letter to Governor Yates serves as an example of the tensions felt in the state. She wrote that the Knights of the Golden Circle were organized into armed companies in her county and were prepared to fight. She implored the governor to send a spy to infiltrate them, learn what they were doing, and make them "quit talking treason."[1] Similar reports of trouble in the state, coupled with increasing threat of guerrilla raids from Kentucky, reached government authorities.[2] In Carbondale four purported members of the KGC, "avowed secessionists," were arrested for giving aid to the rebels.[3] Writing from Cairo, U.S. Marshal David L. Phillips informed Yates that Democrats were "intensely agitated" and "almost desperate" throughout the region; they were "ready for anything." Union supporters in Jackson and Williamson Counties were threatened with being driven from their homes. Referring to antiwar Democrats, he suggested, "We must watch them constantly, or we shall have trouble." He noted that the military commander of the District of Cairo, Brigadier General William K. Strong, was fully in agreement with him on the need for troops in the region to quell unrest. Phillips stated that Strong "thinks most energetic measures will be necessary to keep these disturbed elements still."[4]

As part of his energetic measures, General Strong, a War Democrat from New York, employed his provost marshal, Major Joseph W. Merrill, to investigate disloyalty in the district. Merrill, a Massachusetts-born resident of northwestern Illinois, commissioned in the 27th Illinois Volunteer Infantry Regiment, played an active role in policing Cairo and the surrounding region.[5] For two months Merrill investigated the signs of the existence of a secret organization in counties of southern Illinois, employing several "agents" to infiltrate the meetings of the organization. Merrill himself reputedly "visited several [KGC] lodges in person" in the course of the summer's investigation.[6] He collected affidavits from his agents, eyewitnesses, and others that attested to prominent southern Illinois Democratic politicians taking leading roles in the activities of the KGC. On August 14, Merrill, acting on instructions from General Strong, led squads of troops and conducted a sweep of several towns to arrest prominent Democratic politicians implicated in the secret organization. Among the men arrested was William "Josh" Allen, member of Congress for the 13th congressional district of Illinois. Merrill held the prisoners in Cairo for two weeks, after which Marshal Phillips conveyed them to Washington, where they were held in the Old Capitol, turned into a prison to hold political prisoners. Federal authorities held them there into November, until after the Illinois elections were over.[7] Merrill based his arrests on affidavits of witnesses who claimed to attend meetings of KGC lodges guarded by armed sentinels. Witnesses claimed to see local prominent Democrats speak to the groups and swore that Allen and a former congressman, Samuel S. Marshall, were KGC leaders. While in prison and afterward, the arrested men challenged the veracity of Merrill's affidavits. Influential Union leaders such as former congressman, then brigadier general, John A. Logan intervened with President Lincoln on behalf of his brother-in-law to state that he could not have attended a certain secret meeting. Lincoln freed the prisoner. Other prisoners claimed the affidavits were lies.[8] Though his accusations collapsed, Merrill's investigations set the stage for subsequent military espionage efforts in the Northwest. The most important military investigations emerged in neighboring Indiana.

Carrington's Arrival in Indiana

The rise of Henry Beebee Carrington to become the U.S. Army's most important intelligence officer to investigate conspiracy in the North during the Civil War occurred completely by chance. His arrival in Indiana resulted from the army's need to post an efficient military bureaucrat to organize mobilization efforts in the state. While there he investigated problems in recruiting and desertion, which he accurately ascribed to conspiracies to subvert the army and the war effort. Despite his desire to fight in the field, Carrington's newfound effectiveness as an intelligence officer kept him in Indiana for most of the war, where he collected important evidence of secret organizations.

In the summer of 1862, Governor Morton of Indiana had a problem. That spring, after a series of western federal victories—among them the battles at

Mill Springs, Forts Henry and Donelson, Pea Ridge, the capture of New Orleans, the occupation of Nashville, Island Number 10 in the Mississippi River, and the tactical draw at Shiloh that turned into a victory when rebel forces retreated from the battlefield—Secretary of War Edwin M. Stanton quite suddenly and without warning halted volunteer recruitment efforts for the U.S. Army. The rebels would soon end their resistance, he reasoned, reflecting Northern public opinion that the war effort would soon crush the Southern rebellion. More troops were unnecessary and would only add greater debts to the already strained federal treasury.[9] Morton disagreed and tried without success to persuade Stanton to reinstitute recruiting efforts quickly.[10] Only after the collapse of the months-long Peninsula campaign of the Army of the Potomac under Major General George McClellan in early July did the pressing need for more troops become clear to Washington leaders. On July 2, Lincoln issued a call for three hundred thousand volunteer troops. Still, that was not enough, and on August 4 the president made an additional call for three hundred thousand troops, to be raised by conscription, the drafted men to serve for nine months. Morton and other Northern governors, whose responsibility it was to raise volunteer troops in their states, restarted their recruiting efforts with a vengeance. Indiana's quota under the two calls was 42,500 new soldiers. The new recruits could not be raised too quickly. Federal commanders everywhere needed more troops, and Confederate armies appeared to be rallying on the offensive in several theaters to push back federal forces. Most notably, Confederate cavalry commander John Hunt Morgan's raids in Kentucky and Tennessee showed vividly that federal communication and supply lines in those states were stretched dangerously thin and underprotected. The progress won by Union forces in the winter and spring might disappear without more troops to bolster the effort.

Morton's immediate problem existed in the form of Colonel John S. Simonson, a veteran of the War of 1812. The ranking U.S. Army officer in Indiana in the summer of 1862, responsible for organizing new volunteers, equipping, paying, and sending them to the front, he had returned from retirement to active service. Old and tired, he lacked organizational talent and could not meet the demands that the emergency placed on him. Needing an officer who could handle the pressure of organizing thousands of new recruits quickly, Morton telegraphed Stanton in early August to find a replacement.[11] Relief came days later in the form of Colonel Henry B. Carrington, then serving at Columbus, Ohio, as commander of the 18th U.S. Infantry Regiment. On August 15 the War Department sent orders to Carrington to report at Indianapolis for duty to replace Simonson as chief mustering and disbursing officer (Simonson retained command of the post of Indianapolis). He arrived shortly thereafter and quickly set to work. The change for the better in the management of military affairs at Indianapolis was immediately visible. Both major partisan newspapers in the city reported that Carrington entered into his new work with energy and zeal.[12] The new appointment was fortuitous, as reports of Confederate general Edmund Kirby Smith's advance into Kentucky and the parallel movement of Confederate general Braxton Bragg's advance northward from Chattanooga shortly thereafter reached federal commanders, suggesting a grave threat. Carrington efficiently organized the new Indiana volunteer regiments and sent them into the field. Dozens of new Indiana volunteer regiments reinforced federal armies in Tennessee and Kentucky. The governor, pleased with the assignment that the War Department had made, wired Stanton: "Thanks for sending Col Carrington[.] A better appointment could not have been made."[13]

Carrington had long served as an organizer in Ohio, in both civilian and military capacities. Born in 1824 in Wallingford, Connecticut, he exhibited the desire from an early age to be a military man and wished to enter the U.S. Military Academy at West Point, New York, to begin an army career. However, poor respiratory health, perhaps a form of tuberculosis, plagued him from an early age, destroying his dreams of West Point. Diminutive and frail, Carrington suffered from this disease during his surprisingly long lifetime (he died in 1912). Denied a West Point education, Carrington settled for Yale College and graduated in 1845. After teaching school in New York, he returned to Yale to study law and taught at a women's school in New Haven on the side.[14] In 1848 he left for Ohio to work in a cousin's law office in Columbus while he studied for admission to the Ohio bar. After admission he began a corporate and railroad law practice, later partnering with prominent attorney and Whig political leader William Dennison. In 1851 he married Margaret Sullivant, daughter of a leading Columbus family, and in the following years fathered a number of children, several of whom died young. Among his activities, he formed a temperance organization in Ohio and spoke at meetings throughout the state. A devout Christian evangelical, driven both by nervous energy and by Christian zeal, Carrington was a workaholic.[15]

Though he never ran for public office, Carrington took part in Whig politics in Ohio, becoming one of the leading antislavery Whigs in the state. Carrington proudly proclaimed his abolitionist beliefs and represented fugitive slaves who escaped from the South.[16] During the excitement over Stephen A. Douglas's Kansas-Nebraska Bill, in 1854, Carrington played a role in the fusion of the various antislavery elements in Ohio that formed the Republican

Party.[17] He also became an acolyte and friend of Ohio's leading antislavery champion, Salmon P. Chase, who selected the military-minded Carrington first to be the state's judge advocate general and later appointed him adjutant general to reform the state's militia. Though the latter was only a part-time position (he continued to practice law), Carrington worked hard to try to bring order to the state militia system. He assembled militia companies from around the state and commanded them in mass exercises and drill. When William Dennison succeeded Chase in the governor's office, he retained his law partner, Carrington, as adjutant general.

With the outbreak of armed hostilities, in April 1861, Ohio's state militia was in better condition than that found in neighboring states. Still, the demands of mobilization laid bare the impoverished condition of militia organization throughout the country, including Ohio's. Buckeyes rallied to the Union in numbers that overwhelmed state government's ability to manage them.[18] Carrington, as adjutant general, received much blame from both friends and foes for the chaotic mess that descended on Columbus in the early days and weeks of the war.[19] Nonetheless, Carrington worked diligently and succeeded quickly in organizing Ohio volunteer regiments to send to the relief of Washington in the first days of the war. He also organized the Ohio expeditionary force of nine infantry regiments sent into western Virginia under Ohio general George McClellan and Colonel William Rosecrans to quell secessionism and secure that largely pro-Union region for the Union.[20] In the face of the newspaper criticism heaped on him, Carrington was quoted to say, "The letter writers must write; let them write."[21]

Despite the criticism of his service as adjutant general of Ohio, Carrington's efforts were welcomed in Washington and he received an unsolicited offer of the colonelcy of one of the new regular-army regiments created by Congress in the summer of 1861.[22] He took command of the newly created 18th U.S. Infantry Regiment, the headquarters of which were established at a newly built military camp, Camp Thomas, three miles north of Columbus. With his characteristic energy, he launched into building a new regular-army regiment from scratch. Carrington ran a strict operation and expected high standards of his officers and men that reflected his Calvinist moral outlook. One junior officer testified publicly to the temperance vow he took to abstain from alcohol: "I am indebted to the powerful influence of your example set me in sobriety."[23] Carrington stripped noncommissioned officers of their rank for drunkenness and ran recruiting advertisements in newspapers that only "temperate men need apply."[24] Another soldier testified to the colonel's kind treatment when in midwinter a battalion shipped out for the front: "When on guard after landing at Cincinnati, at 10 o'clock at night, I told him that I was suffering for want of a pair of gloves, and thereupon without a moment's hesitation the Colonel took off his own gloves and gave them to me. So I think there can be no fear of a man of that character mistreating a young man in his own ranks."[25] The portrait of Carrington as a kind, paternal figure to the soldiers also emerges from a description written by an Indiana soldier at the draft rendezvous camp commanded by Carrington in 1865:

> General Carrington is a little dried up fellow [who] wears a moustache, beard, and long flowing hair, [is] uneasy in his manner, has keen black eyes, handles a cigar in exquisite style, speaks kindly to men and officers, and is *always* at work. He was "out calling" among the boys this evening—drinking coffee and passing jokes. The last I saw of him he was knee deep in mud, instructing and helping the boys pitch their tents. The General drives a peg equal to any old circus hand.[26]

The 18th Infantry quickly outpaced the other newly created regular-army regiments in recruiting, and Carrington sent the first twelve companies to Kentucky in December; a mixed brigade of his regiment and volunteer regiments was promised him when the regiment filled its complement, established at over twenty-five hundred men. The federal law creating the new regular-army regiments stipulated, however, that the field officers of each regiment were responsible for recruiting the regiments to full strength, and Carrington was obliged to remain in Ohio recruiting.[27] He was still at work recruiting the regiment when ordered by the War Department to Indianapolis to superintend mustering of the Indiana volunteer regiments. He left for Indiana on August 18 and took up his new duties immediately.[28]

Carrington entered into his Indianapolis work with characteristic energy. News from Kentucky was uppermost on the minds of the people, and reports of the debacle at Richmond, Kentucky, of August 30 shook the state. Several newly organized Indiana volunteer infantry regiments that had been rushed to the front had been mauled before they surrendered to Kirby Smith's advancing Confederate army. Rebel troops threatened Cincinnati and Louisville. Carrington rapidly processed new Indiana volunteers, mustered them into regiments, and sent them to Louisville or Cincinnati. In the last stretch Bragg turned aside near Bardstown, allowing Major General Don Carlos Buell's army to reach Louisville. Refreshed with reinforcements and supplies, Buell set out at the beginning of October to find and bring Bragg's army to battle. As a summer drought stretched into fall, the two armies stumbled onto each other while thirsty troops from both armies searched for water. The battle at the town of Perryville, on October 8, resulted in Bragg's invading army retreating into Tennessee.[29]

With Kentucky preserved for the Union, Carrington continued in his work of mustering and disbursing troops. Though nominally subordinate to post commander Simonson, Carrington exercised real authority in Indianapolis, a fact that the older man probably welcomed.[30] Carrington wasted no time. He quelled camp mutinies. He designed and supervised the building of new camps in the city, the better to accommodate recruits. In appreciation, troops named one of the new camps in his honor, Camp Carrington. The newspapers reported that he was quite sick, apparently suffering from typhoid fever. The city's main Republican organ solicitously suggested that he had "worked too hard for his health since he had been in this state. No man could exhibit more energy and efficiency in the numerous and important duties of his post than he."[31] The newspaper later remarked that Carrington appeared to fight illness by "constant labor."[32] The city's Democratic newspaper also suggested that he worked too hard, claiming that he had ordered a bayonet charge on civilians who had interfered in the arrest of a deserter. "The most charitable construction that can be put upon this act of Col. Carrington is, that he is crazy—too much labor or honor has made him mad."[33]

In tandem with his zealous evangelicalism, Carrington's military ambitions drove him to work hard. He dreamed of commanding a division of troops— soldiers he had himself drilled to perfection—in the field. He looked around and saw men of (he thought) lesser abilities and achievement obtain high rank and field appointments. "I feel annoyed at seeing men who received their first military schooling under me, made Major Generals," he confided. Though he claimed "no desire to push into the race for office or untimely promotion," he lamented that the epaulets on his shoulders were "not starred."[34] "I am sincerely anxious for promotion, in due time in the *regular service,* by brevet, for *services* rendered . . . & *finally, fully* as Brig Genl." Nor did he turn up his nose to an eventual "*Maj Genlship.*"[35] Circumstances would keep him off the field of glory.

Confronting Dissent and Resistance

As Carrington took increasing control of military affairs in the city and state, he was drawn into state politics. In early October, days before state elections, he published a notice in the newspapers that, though distasteful, "anonymous communications" charging disloyalty and interference with recruiting and the draft would be pursued "in proportion to the influence of the guilty."[36] Following the War Department's orders of August 8, he furnished five hundred troops to quell a draft riot at Hartford City, Blackford County, in northern Indiana. Troops lingered in the county for several days until after election day and guarded polling places in order to catch rioters if they tried to vote.[37] Elsewhere, acting on affidavits supplied by the U.S. marshal, he sent troops to arrest Democratic politicians in several places around the state who spoke at political meetings against the war and the Lincoln administration. In one instance, he wired Washington for instructions as to how to proceed in a case where a former state senator, Harris Reynolds, "made a treasonable speech" and "called upon the people to resist the draft by blood and to meet . . . to act together." Noted Carrington, "This is become too frequent and needs example in this region."[38]

In September the Army of the Potomac under Major General George McClellan had managed to turn back Confederate general Robert E. Lee's invasion of Maryland at Antietam Creek. Though not a resounding Union victory, President Lincoln used the occasion to proclaim that slaves in the rebel states not under federal occupation would be free men and women on and after January 1, 1863. The Emancipation Proclamation had a stunning effect on politics in the North. Conservative Democrats, disgusted by the proclamation, which they viewed as proof of the radical intentions of Lincoln's Republican Party, redoubled their efforts to kick the "abolitionists" out of office. Coming just weeks before October elections in many states, including Indiana, the timing of the proclamation proved a hindrance to "Union Party" hopes as many War Democrats recoiled from their previous alliance with the Republicans.[39] Moreover, although federal forces repulsed the Confederate invasion of Kentucky, the invasion scare rippled through Old Northwest communities north of the Ohio River and brought home the fears of civil war. Finally, while Indiana furnished its state quota of volunteers, the draft still went forward in townships that failed to meet their quotas.[40] Intense opposition to the draft exacerbated hostility to the war effort to suppress the rebellion. War weariness on top of growing animosity to war measures began to appear in many communities, and renewed calls for a negotiated peace settlement with the rebels emerged.

Mounting objections to the war measures of the Lincoln administration contributed to Democratic victories in the October elections. Lincoln's suppression of Democratic speech and newspapers, the arrests of critics, the confiscation of rebel property (including slaves), the promised emancipation of African American slaves, war taxes and tariffs, economic disruption, the institution of a draft, and many thousands of dead and wounded soldiers turned many voters against the Republicans. Democratic candidates achieved significant victories in Indiana, winning most of the congressional races and securing majorities in both chambers of the Indiana General Assembly. Ohio races also went to the Democrats (with the notable exception of Clement L. Vallandigham's district around Dayton, which had been gerrymandered to favor a Republican challenger). Illinois, which held its elections in November, followed suit. Indiana's Republicans were stunned. They assigned much fault to the ineptitude of some of the Union's commanding generals, most notably McClellan, Buell, and Henry Halleck, known to be Democrats, for their slow and ineffectual leadership. They also noted that tens of thousands of Indiana soldiers had been prohibited the franchise while serving in the field, and they believed (with justification) that these soldiers would have voted with the Republicans.[41] Republicans also detected an ominous undertone in their opponents' rhetoric. Governor Morton's private secretary (and brother-in-law), William R. Holloway, reported to his Washington counterpart, John G. Nicolay, Lincoln's secretary, that Democrats from Indiana and Kentucky advocated forming "'a great Central Government,' cut off from New England and the Cotton States." Men who once had been counted as "sound union men" now advocated the plan put forward by leading Indiana Democrat Thomas A. Hendricks at his January 8, 1862, party speech. They would form a "north and southwestern Government."[42]

Days later, Morton wrote to Lincoln to outline what he believed the victorious Democrats were thinking and planning. "The fate of the Northwest is trembling in the balance," he began. The Democrats in the Old Northwest "assume that the rebellion will not be crushed" and that the Confederacy must before long be recognized. For the last year Democrats had been thinking of a "Northwestern Confederacy" preparatory to joining with the Southern Confederacy. "It was the staple of every democratic speech" during the campaign that the Northwest's interests were with the Southern states, he wrote, that they are connected by the Mississippi River, and that the Northwest could not be separated from them. His "deliberate judgment" was that if the Union war effort failed, Ohio, Indiana, and Illinois could be stopped from secession and joining the Confederate states only "by a bloody and desolating civil war." The only way to avoid this catastrophe was an all-out military campaign to secure the Mississippi River and rebel states west of the river.[43]

Beyond the dangers apprehended by Morton and others, political turmoil on the home front had significant repercussions for the soldiers in the field and in camp. Both soldiers in the army and soldiers' parents attempted to use the privilege of the writ of habeas corpus to gain release from service. They appealed to Democratic judges in various courts to issue the writ. Parents frequently claimed that their child was under age and enlisted without requisite permission. Officers went to great lengths to prove consent or to prove that the enlisted soldier claimed to be eighteen years old; commanders saw many judges' actions as politically motivated gestures to hinder the war effort.[44] Carrington and his subordinate officers received subpoenas from Indiana courts to release soldiers, including from the Indiana Supreme Court. Chief Justice Samuel E. Perkins, a Democrat, entertained petitions to his court to issue the writ. In October, Carrington appealed to him to assist in curtailing abuses relative to the writ.[45] Perkins replied that he would not discourage enlistments in the army.[46] In the weeks to come, however, clashes between the court and the army continued. On December 31, Perkins issued a writ of habeas corpus for a deserter under arrest and sent an arrest order for a captain holding the deserter, "declaring that the streets should flow with blood but the party should be produced." Under Carrington's instructions the captain declined to surrender the deserter. Carrington met with the chief justice to protest his move, "especially, as the Court had agreed in similar cases, to abide by the decision of the Secretary of War." Nonetheless, as a precaution he placed both the officer and the deserter under a protective guard of troops. The following day Perkins called on Carrington and "apologized for his language." Carrington showed the jurist the enlistment papers of the deserter, and, satisfied, Perkins withdrew the attachment to arrest the captain. Carrington concluded that "firmness is vital at this juncture in the northern states, and our only salvation" to preserve federal authority.[47]

Meanwhile, desertion from the U.S. Army increased dramatically through the winter of 1862–63 and reached crisis proportions. Military authorities in Indiana reported the arrests of four hundred deserters per week in December 1862, but many more deserters escaped army dragnets.[48] In February 1863, General-in-Chief Henry W. Halleck reported to Stanton that of total army strength of 790,000 troops, fully 282,000 soldiers were absent from their commands. The figure constituted 36 percent of total army strength, the largest proportion coming from desertions from armies in the field.[49] Growing dissatisfaction with the war effort was manifest in the army. Many soldiers complained about Lincoln's recent Emancipation Proclamation. The war was no longer fought to preserve the Union, some thought; it was now to free the slaves. Other soldiers wanted a respite from campaigning. Soldiers melted away from their regiments, slipped away from camps and garrisons, and walked or rode the rails home.

Desertion in the Army of the Cumberland, then concentrated around Murfreesboro and Nashville, Tennessee, vexed its commander, Major General William S. Rosecrans. During the cold winter, while the army recovered from the three-day battle of Stones River, thousands of his troops disappeared from their units and sneaked homeward to Illinois, Indiana, and Ohio. In February, Rosecrans took steps to stem the exodus, appointing one of his generals, Brigadier General Milo S. Hascall, to superintend the roundup of tens of thousands of deserters in the three-state region and send them back to the army.[50] Rosecrans solicited the cooperation of Major General Horatio G. Wright, commander of the Department of the Ohio, in the roundup effort. He pointed to the sources of the desertion problem: "Treasonable documents are circulating through the mails, sent by traitors at home causing discontent and intended to procure desertions."[51] Wright promised full cooperation in efforts to stop desertion and round up deserters.[52]

Uncovering Conspiracy in the Ranks

In December 1862 reports reached Carrington that soldiers in units stationed in the camps around Indianapolis had become involved in secret organizations in their home communities. Some soldiers knew the signs, handshakes, and passwords of the organizations and reported their knowledge to camp commanders. Carrington questioned them and took sworn affidavits. One such affidavit came from a trooper in the 3rd Indiana Cavalry Regiment who recounted that while visiting at home in Shelby County he attended a Democratic meeting. Men told him they were a society "to perfect the organization of the Democratic party, and that whatever was done or said was to be kept secret." He received instructions in making and recognizing signs, grips (handshakes), and passwords. "I asked if the obligations would interfere with my duties as a soldier and was answered that they would not." Men made speeches, stating that the war was to abolish slavery and that they were opposed to it. A "sentinel" guarded the door where they met. Back in camp in Indianapolis, he said, another Shelby County trooper, John O. Brown, "gave me a sign or signs similar [to what he had learned] and passed his hand over his face to attract my attention." The trooper gave the name of the order as "the Band of Brothers" and explained that it had twelve thousand members in Indiana and included army officers and "some of our Northern Generals." The purpose of the order was to "perfect the Democratic Party and produce peace," the soldier said, and told him a Rush County man named Conway was one of the state leaders of the order. Other soldiers also "belonged to the order," he swore.[53]

A quick investigation ensued. On December 22, Carrington telegraphed Secretary Stanton that he was mailing an important letter to be shown the president and cabinet concerning the existence in Indiana of a secret order to incite desertion, resist arrest of deserters, stop enlistments, and prevent continued conscription: "in short, a distinct avowal to stop this war." Soldiers were involved, but civilians were the "originators" of the order. How, he asked, was the army to reach these civilians? The existence of the secret order "affords a clue to the alarming desertions now so prevalent in this State."[54]

Carrington's mailed letter provided more details of his investigation. The secret organization was sometimes called the Holy Brotherhood, but also Knights of the Golden Circle. Members urged soldiers to desert with their arms and horses (if cavalry), but if they could not escape with their weapons, arms would be provided to them by the organization. Its objects were also to stop the "abolition war" and "thwart the Government in the efforts to suppress this rebellion." Carrington quoted affidavits that stated the organization aimed to "maintain the Constitution as it is, the Union, as it was."[55] It was operated by citizens, possessed signs, oaths, and passwords, and met in private. They employed "party elements" that "sympathized with the southern element" to defeat the government. He noted that his sources for this information came from affidavits taken of soldiers "who have been detected in the use of the signs" of the secret order. The soldiers had been arrested and interrogated, and though they served in different companies in different regiments, their statements were "nearly uniform" and agreed as to signs and oaths. He added that the soldiers had been assured that their signs would protect them if captured. They were also assured that "prominent federal officers" were connected with the order, a notion that Carrington dismissed as "absurd." Still, "the effect is no less prejudicial over the minds of the soldier." "Volunteering is practically suspended," he wrote; a draft undertaken in Indiana under the current conditions would be met by violence. Carrington again raised the question of how to deal with the civilians who were at the root of the "plot." "To convict before a jury is uncertain and causes delay," but if the problem was not stopped it would only grow worse. Quoting from an affidavit that the order wanted the army to "waste away" on account of desertion, the issue at hand, he ventured, was the preservation of the army as a viable war-fighting instrument. He concluded that he was assisting Governor Morton with these investigations of growing problems in the army.[56]

Carrington shared his information with the governor. Morton seized on the new evidence as confirmation of the serious danger confronting them. He tied Carrington's investigations to his own, drawing a link to the Northwestern

Confederacy movement, about which he had warned Washington. Shortly after Carrington reported to the War Department on his investigation, the governor wrote to Stanton to press the point in stark language: the "treasonable, political secret organization, having for its object the withdrawal of the Northwestern States from the Union, which exists in every part of this State, has obtained a foot hold in the Military camps of this city." Important arrests had been made and investigation was ongoing. Morton added that Carrington had worked diligently in procuring these facts. But the colonel had received orders to take command of his regiment in the field. "I think it of the utmost importance that Col Carrington should remain here until this business is disposed of," he wrote.[57] Carrington "is the man for the emergency, and there are great signs of trouble here, such as I cannot telegraph."[58] The War Department promptly wired to the governor to suspend the order sending Carrington to his regiment.[59] Morton acted to retain Carrington in Indiana without consulting with the colonel, who had already closed up his accounts preparatory to leaving for Tennessee. Carrington wished to join his regiment and fight at the front, but Morton overrode that wish. This was the first of a series of contingencies and mishaps that prevented him from attaining his dream of soldiering in the field.[60]

At this time, in early 1863, the Democrats who controlled both chambers of the Indiana General Assembly sought to clip Morton's wings and gain complete control over state government. Efforts to strip Morton's control over military appointments to the volunteer units and the Indiana Legion prompted Republican legislators to "bolt" the capitol and the state, evade return, and deny Democrats the required quorum. Tensions rose, and commanders called out army units to surround the statehouse; an artillery battery exercised its guns and fired blank rounds to intimidate the Democrats inside.[61] Amid the tension, fearing that Democrats planned to seize control of the state arsenal, Morton administratively transferred all the state's arms and ammunition to Carrington.[62]

Detained in Indiana, Carrington proceeded to bring trooper John O. Brown to trial by court-martial. Military authorities charged him on three counts: exciting mutiny, failing to provide information of an intended mutiny among the soldiers, and advising soldiers to desert. Brown pled guilty to the first charge but not guilty to the other two. The witnesses in the military trial were all fellow soldiers in various companies and regiments stationed at Camp Carrington. One, Urias W. Stober from the 5th Indiana Cavalry Regiment, appears to have been used by commanders as a spy, employing his acquaintance with their secret signs and passwords to work his way inside the secret organizations.[63] He testified Brown told him he had initiated fifteen men of his company and one from another into the order called Star in the East. He also stated that Democratic attorneys in Indianapolis and Shelby County would help to get soldiers out of the service. Other soldiers testified that Brown initiated them into a society, variously called the Butternut Society or Star in the East, with grips and signs, and that they were all armed to protect each other and soldiers who deserted from the army. Brown offered no defense but only asked for mercy from the court. Showing no mercy, the court found him guilty on all three counts and sentenced him to be shot to death.[64]

During the trial Carrington wrote to President Lincoln, repeating the points he had made to Stanton about the existence of secret societies in Indiana and adding that "further examination confirms my judgment." The objects of the societies were to oppose the prosecution of the war and "compel peace." He echoed Morton's belief that, failing to stop the war, the societies aimed to "break up the Union and consolidate the South and North-west." The societies made plain their objects, and "quite a number of newspapers avow similar purpose and policy, under a thin veil of subterfuge. Public meetings are full of it. Toleration gives them boldness." He cited various phenomena in the army as evidence: desertion was rampant; habeas corpus appeals were frequent; courts accepted false oaths that soldiers were underage. "Our army is wasting rapidly," Carrington wrote. Besides the effect on the army, state authorities were constantly on the alert, and he kept an armed guard around the state arsenal "to prevent its seizure." Everywhere were signs of rebellion in the state, he added, and "to rule, or ruin, seems the motto; and the loyal people are beginning to apprehend serious trouble." Carrington suggested that "firm measures, decided, but quiet," were needed. But he voiced pessimism in his outlook. Governor Morton thought that they were then passing through the worst stage, but Carrington disagreed. It was, he believed, perhaps the work of God to test the people and "bring this people to a higher stand point of political principle. . . . We shall bear the strain and triumph; but not until we are purified by our very trials."[65]

In addition to examinations of soldiers, authorities collected affidavits of civilians providing evidence of potential dangers. A Union man from Brown County, in southern Indiana, swore out a statement that the KGC, which boasted six hundred men in the county and 125,000 in the state, frequently threatened the Union men in the community. They also intended to march on Indianapolis, he claimed, to seize the state arsenal and to take Morton prisoner with assistance from members in the city. Men claimed to be in communication with Southern rebels, who voiced willingness to compromise with a Democratic-controlled federal government. The affidavit also stated that money and clothing were furnished to deserters and that "letters have been written to [soldiers] requesting them to desert, and come home, and the Knights will protect them from arrest."[66]

Carrington wrote to General Wright at Department of the Ohio headquarters, in Cincinnati, to alert him to his findings. He reported on the court-martial and noted that secret societies "extreme in their views and treasonable in their aims" existed extensively in Indiana. He suggested that army officers who assisted soldiers to desert should be dismissed from the service.[67] Wright promptly wrote back to assure Carrington, "you shall not lack the full support of my authority in your endeavors to correct the evils and break up the illegal combinations to which you refer."[68] Carrington also wrote to the War Department for instructions and to offer suggestions for action. "Citizens are continually inducing soldiers to desert," he wrote. "Shall such offenders be dealt with by the U.S. Marshall, for treason, or by me?" He added, "A statute is greatly needed to meet such needs."[69]

The Morgan County Incident

At the end of January 1863 a violent incident in Morgan County, Indiana, one of many that occurred at this time, helped shape the government's response to manifestations of assistance to deserters and resistance to the government. A party of three cavalry troopers sent from Indianapolis into Morgan and Johnson Counties, the latter about fifteen miles south of the city, succeeded in capturing deserters. However, they met with resistance from a band of mounted men who fired on the troopers in the woods. None of the soldiers was wounded, but they fled to Indianapolis, leaving the deserters behind to escape. The next day Carrington sent a larger force of cavalry—twenty-six troopers in total—into the area. The force rearrested the deserters and continued on their way when they were fired on by a mounted band, which quickly rode off. About a quarter of a mile later the mounted band reappeared and again fired on the cavalry force. This time the cavalry lieutenant in command gave the order to his force to charge after the armed men. The cavalry captured several members of the band and brought them back to Indianapolis. There Carrington turned them over to the U.S. marshal for trial before the U.S. District Court.[70] He apprised General Wright of the occurrence and asked that he be given "ample powers in this state" to handle such incidents.[71] Writing to the War Department, he noted that the condition of Indiana "borders upon open resistance to Federal Authority" and asked for specific instructions to deal with attempts to rescue deserters and that his authority be extended over the whole state.[72]

The federal grand jury, then assembled in Indianapolis, promptly brought indictments against the Morgan County men for conspiracy under the July 31, 1861, law, and their trial took place two weeks later in U.S. district court, before newly appointed federal judge Caleb B. Smith. The trial attracted great interest and merited detailed reports in the Indianapolis newspapers. Witnesses testified that they had heard about secret meetings in the neighborhood; others admitted to belonging to a secret organization "for mutual protection against unlawful arrests."[73] Testimony brought out that the meetings focused on the question of whether members were obliged to defend deserters from arrest.[74] Carrington, who testified early in the trial regarding his orders to the cavalry sent to round up deserters, voiced his satisfaction at the convictions handed down at the trial. He wired Lincoln and confidently stated, "We shall be able to expose the secret treasonable associations fully."[75] However, to Judge Advocate General Joseph Holt he complained that the light fines handed the convicts by Judge Smith "will not save further trouble." He predicted that he would have over one hundred indicted by the grand jury for treason and inciting soldiers to desert, adding, "I have obtained the signs etc of the treasonable societies and hope to break up the order."[76]

Carrington had requested orders from Washington regarding the way to deal with civilians implicated in efforts to subvert the army. But federal leadership remained mute. Lacking instructions, he instead devised a strategy to indict, prosecute, and convict suspects in federal court under federal law. In the following weeks and months, Carrington and state and federal officials pursued his strategy and brought several hundred Indiana citizens under indictment for war-related violations of federal laws. At the end of the trial for the Morgan County incident, with the sentences of the convicts announced, Carrington issued a proclamation denouncing treasonous secret societies. Such groups were "public enemies" and would be dealt with harshly—soldiers by martial law, civilians by civil law. Secret societies aided the escape of deserters, he noted. "I know the oaths, I know the leaders," he warned. "Patiently and calmly I have watched these movements." He lamented that he knew men of "seeming respectability" who visited the secret lodges. He called on soldiers to "avoid the snare" of the organizations, as it "strikes at your honor, which is dearer than life." He called on civilians to rise above false oaths and obligations and stand by the Union.[77]

At this time, a federal grand jury also returned to the investigation of secret organizations in Indiana. Someone leaked two presentments made by the grand jury to the *Indianapolis Daily Journal* for publication. Both reports pertained to witnesses called before the grand jury who refused to testify about aspects of the KGC organization, in which they acknowledged membership. One concerned Jesse McHenry, an Indianapolis attorney, who testified that he was member of an organization called Mutual Protectionists, with two to three hundred members who met regularly in Indianapolis. Similarly, a George Hughes of Johnson County testified that he was a member of the KGC organization and had initiated other persons into membership. The organization had from forty to sixty members in his township. Both men provided information about oaths, grips, and signs, but refused to provide more details for fear of incriminating themselves.[78]

While Carrington battled the rise of secret societies in the army and their efforts to encourage desertion, Governor Morton attempted to raise a sense of urgency in Washington about the political conditions in Indiana and the Old Northwest. In a long letter to Secretary Stanton marked "strictly confidential," he laid out his understanding in stark and blunt language. "The Democratic scheme may be briefly stated thus: End the War by any means whatever at the earliest moment." They would let the Confederates leave the Union and recognize them as an independent country. "They will then propose to the Rebels a re-union and a re-construction upon the condition of leaving out the New England States." This "North Western Confederacy" scheme, he added, had broad support among Democratic leaders and party masses, abetted by "Secret Societies" like the "Knights of the Golden Circle" who were organized "in every county and township" in Indiana. To remedy the problem, he again recommended a vigorous military campaign focused on securing the Mississippi River to open commercial traffic. Morton sent the letter to Washington in the hands of Indiana War Democrat Robert Dale Owen, a friend of Stanton, who knew the "situation of affairs here."[79] Owen traveled to Washington, met with Stanton, and reported back to the governor in a letter. Stanton "thinks very highly of *Col Carrington,* and says he shall remain where he is, to aid you," he noted, adding that the secretary "fully believes in the plot to reconstruct leaving New England out." However, he "feels sure it cannot succeed." Significantly, Owen added his impression: "In my judgment [Stanton] does not fully appreciate the imminence of the danger."[80]

The Army Fights Homegrown Conspiracy

While Carrington fought organized efforts to encourage desertion and Morton worked to disclose the Northwestern Confederacy scheme, soldiers in the field took a significant part to stop the rot they perceived in the ranks. Troops at the front saw evidence of Northern civilians' efforts to weaken the army in the form of a massive letter-writing campaign directed at the soldiers. Officers and enlisted men alike voiced their alarm at the wholesale efforts of Northern civilians to induce soldiers in the field to desert and hide at home, sheltered from arrest by friends and family who promised to feed, pay, cloth, and defend them from arrest. The phenomenon was widespread in the Northwestern states and affected scores of regiments from the region.

Many soldiers, angered by the flood of discouraging letters from home written to induce them to desert, passed them on to their officers. In turn, officers complained to their governors and other officials. The letters, officers stated, started with political diatribes against the Lincoln administration, cataloging the many errors and sins committed by the administration in the handling of the war effort. The colonel of the 54th Illinois Volunteer Infantry Regiment stationed in Memphis, Tennessee, wrote that he had spent the day reading letters written to his soldiers from hometown civilians who advised them to desert and come home. The civilians offered protection from arrest, and some claimed membership in the Knights of the Golden Circle. The officer promised, "I will get up a bunch of those letters & send you so that you may see for yourself."[81] Another soldier from the 54th Illinois wrote that "letters are received almost daily, from pretended friends, extolling the K.G.C. [and] asserting that there is no harm in the order" and advising the boys to desert the "abolition army . . . at all hazards."[82] An Illinois captain wrote to Governor Yates that many deserters from Illinois regiments stationed in Tennessee had been induced to desert by letters written by KGC members who swore to protect them.[83] Another Illinois soldier wrote to his state legislator to complain of the efforts to sow discontent in his regiment. "We have evidence of the loyalty of the Illinois copperheads," he wrote, "by the efforts they are putting forth to induce the soldiers in the field to desert." People back home sent money "to *buy* them off, and pay their expenses home, promising them protection, and assistance to resist any effort made to induce them to return to duty."[84] An officer at Louisville reported that Indiana citizens who traveled south to visit the army ostensibly to support Indiana troops in the field had actually "attempted to produce dissatisfaction among the troops and to encourage desertions."[85] An Indiana colonel wrote that several men had recently deserted from his regiment and ascribed that to the receipt of letters from home. "Letters [were] almost daily coming to my regiment" from the southern Indiana counties where the regiment was recruited "denouncing the war and advising the men to desert," he wrote. "These letters are not infrequently written by fathers to their sons." He added that "it is clear that the KGCs are industriously at work to demoralize the army."[86] A lieutenant in the 100th Indiana Volunteer Infantry Regiment reported that he had seen a letter from a mother-in-law to one of his soldiers "advising him if he could get out no other way to shoot himself." She suggested that he shoot himself in the foot. The soldier later suffered a gunshot wound in the foot, "the wound in the foot was just what the Letter advised him to do and made in precisely the manner indicated."[87]

Colonel Thomas W. Bennett, commander of the 69th Indiana Volunteer Infantry Regiment fighting in Louisiana, complained, "You can form no idea of the mischief they are working in the army. The most stupendous efforts are being made to demoralize, and destroy the Indiana regiments." "Disloyal" newspapers were being circulated among the soldiery for free; printed speeches of Democratic politicians like Clement Vallandigham and Indiana's Chief Justice Perkins were "sown broad cast." Finally, a "pre concerted system of lying treasonable letter writing is carried on" and arrived in "every mail from the North." Bennett claimed that the "treason at home" had induced six soldiers to desert, "and others were contemplating it." To combat the problem Bennett reported that he made a speech to his regiment about the evils of the "proposition" offered to the soldiers by their friends at home. He told them if he heard one more word of abuse of the government or another threat to desert, "I should begin to shave heads and drum out. Since then not a word has been uttered out of the way." However, he warned that if home sentiments continued as they had, "we had as well lay down our arms now, and submit to our disgrace at once."[88]

Having received letters from home telling them to desert and come home, many soldiers reacted in anger. While officers forwarded some of the letters sent to their soldiers to state or local officials as evidence of the attempts to induce desertion, indignant soldiers sent letters they had received to the editors of their hometown newspapers and asked that the letters be published.[89] Many such letters appeared in the columns of Republican newspapers in Northwestern states, naming those who wrote the letters and adding bitter statements about the treason and sympathy with the rebels evinced in them. The published letters appeared in newspapers at the same time that regiments and brigades from Northwestern states sent carefully prepared petitions and resolutions to their state legislatures threatening retribution on those who opposed the war effort, called for an armistice, or advocated other action soldiers perceived to be disloyal.[90] C. H. Clark of the 39th Indiana Volunteer Infantry Regiment passed on letters to the *Portland Jay Torch-Light* and summed up a widely held attitude in the army. "We are tired of receiving such letters as some of our Company are getting almost daily from men in Jay Co., purporting to be our friends," he added. He warned the letter writers that if they persisted the soldiers had their names and would seek vengeance on their return home. "The Negro question is played out," he wrote. "The boys here are for the Government."[91] The soldiers' forceful response to the letter-writing campaign had a powerful impact. One Illinois observer writing to Governor Yates noted that the Democrats in the state were being held in abeyance only by the moral force of the soldiers' reaction to the threat to the army and the Union: "In other words," he wrote, "*a voice has been heard* from our brave men in the field—that and nothing but that, has calmed the rising storm."[92]

Government authorities seized the opportunity to single out and punish one letter writer for inducing a soldier to desert. A letter from Benjamin Jemison, formerly postmaster under the Democratic Buchanan administration in Centreville, Indiana (Governor Morton's hometown), to a soldier who subsequently deserted from the 14th Indiana Light Artillery Battery, appeared in the *Indianapolis Daily Journal.* Morton's secretary, William Holloway, sent Jemison's letter to the U.S. attorney in Indiana, John Hanna, and asked him to arrest and charge Jemison. The federal grand jury indicted Jemison for encouraging desertions and a deputy U.S. marshal subsequently arrested him. The arrest and a similar one in Illinois served as exemplary warnings to other letter writers to cease the practice or else face punishment.[93]

Military authorities dealt more harshly with an Indiana deserter. Private Robert Gay of the 60th Indiana Volunteer Infantry Regiment deserted his unit and fled to rebel lines. Rebel authorities paroled him and he made his way northward en route for Indiana. Military police arrested him, and the army tried him by court-martial for desertion, found him guilty, and sentenced him to death. Carrington and other military authorities wished to use Gay as an example to other soldiers of the consequences of desertion and interceded with Washington authorities to confirm the death sentence. "My sympathies are sufficiently warm," wrote Carrington, "but I feel that we need this exhibition of the power [of] the government, and the danger of the crime of desertion, at this crisis."[94] Lincoln confirmed the sentence, and in a carefully staged formal, solemn, and fearsome ceremony, superintended by Carrington, thousands of troops lined up in formation and witnessed the firing-squad execution of Gay.[95]

Military authorities in the region also took stringent measures to deal summarily with civil authorities who interfered with the arrest of deserters. In March military authorities from Indiana sent troops into eastern Illinois to arrest deserters. There they rounded up several deserters. However, the mother of one of the deserters obtained a warrant from a local justice of the peace to arrest the soldiers making the arrest, and the Clark County, Illinois, sheriff executed the warrant, arresting them and sending them before the judge of the Clark circuit court, Judge Charles H. Constable. Constable bound the soldiers over for trial on the charge of kidnapping. Word arrived in Indianapolis of the arrest of the soldiers, and Carrington immediately notified General Wright and the War Department of the incident. Wright ordered Carrington to send a strong military force to arrest the judge and "liberate" the soldiers. Carrington commanded the expedition himself, and with a force of over two hundred troops descended on Marshall, Illinois, quietly surrounded the courthouse, entered the courtroom, politely interrupted the proceedings in the case of the soldiers, arrested Judge Constable, and rescued the soldiers. While a crowd of hundreds of armed men surrounded the military force, Carrington returned to Indiana with his prisoner. There, after long deliberations by military, political, and judicial leaders, it was concluded to turn Constable over to the federal district court at Springfield, where Judge Samuel Treat held a brief hearing and dismissed the prisoner. Commanders intended Constable's arrest to signal the army's determination to suffer no opposition in the restoration of deserters to their army commands, as well as to fight illegal measures undertaken by secret organizations to weaken the army.[96] They responded with strong force to a similar incident in Indiana. A squad of soldiers sent from Indianapolis to near Raleigh, in Rush County, southeast of the city, arrested deserters in the neighborhood. A group of armed horsemen estimated to number two hundred confronted the troops and rescued the deserters. When news of the incident reached Indianapolis that night, Carrington immediately dispatched one hundred infantry to the town on a special train, disembarked at the nearest railroad station, marched six miles to the town, surrounded it, and before daylight arrested the deserters and the "ringleaders" of the mounted band at daylight. He turned the prisoners over to the federal court for trial. Reporting to Cincinnati headquarters, Carrington suggested that "prompt, cool but energetic action now alone will prevent insurrections. I am exercising authority wherever in Indiana the Government is resisted."[97]

Henry Carrington's arrival in Indiana came in response to the dire need for effective administration of the recruiting service in the state. While in Indiana, his attention turned to threats to military effectiveness and the army's ability to recruit new troops and retain its veterans. He combated efforts to discourage enlistments, disrupt the draft, and encourage desertion from the army in camp and in the field. Evidence shows Carrington began investigations into secret organizations in Indiana in December 1862 in response to threats to the integrity of the army and its ability to remain a strong fighting force. He and other military authorities took steps to halt desertion and efforts to induce desertion and to shield deserters from arrest. Governor Morton's fears of a Northwestern Confederacy conspiracy among Democratic politicians, which long predated the arrival of Carrington and the beginning of the officer's investigations, constituted a parallel political investigation to Carrington's, though both the military commander and the governor saw them as linked elements of a larger movement to undermine the war effort. Carrington's success in exposing efforts to encourage desertion came from evidence generated by affidavits and statements made by soldiers and civilians knowledgeable of the secret organizations involved. His efforts to expose the movement were aided by angry soldiers in the field who received letters encouraging desertion. They showed clearly the existence of secret organizations working to undermine the army. To date, Carrington and military officers under his command in Indiana had undertaken minimal espionage and detective work in their investigations to halt desertion's wasting effects on the army. Such espionage work only later characterized Carrington's and other officers' efforts to uncover Northern conspiracies during the war. Soon, following Carrington's example, commanders in other cities and states in the Old Northwest would establish intelligence operations in efforts to counteract problems that arose in their commands.

THREE

"They Are Doing Us an Immense Amount of Good"

The Rise of Army Intelligence Operations in the Old Northwest in 1863

DETECTIVES PROWLED the Cincinnati docks and frequented city saloons in search of deserters. Others sifted through warehouses looking for contraband goods. Still others loitered in city hotels eying travelers who sojourned there. Army commanders sent spies to trail persons suspected of carrying "rebel mails" through the lines back and forth to the Confederacy. Detectives embarked on packet boats or on trains, watching the movements and communications of their targets and reporting to headquarters. Others combed the hinterlands in search of contraband arms and arms smuggling throughout the Old Northwest. Crisscrossing the increasingly embattled region, army detectives observed and reported on developments that greatly worried their military commanders. With a multiplicity of army headquarters, each with its own spy operations, Cincinnati emerged as the intelligence center for a multistate military command that soon spawned several local detective bureaus.

The Queen City as Army Headquarters

Citizens and visitors to Cincinnati alike affectionately dubbed that Ohio River metropolis the Queen City. By the years of the Civil War, the city boasted a population of over 160,000 residents employed in industry and commerce. Situated on the northern bank of the Ohio River, the city was the influential center of a transportation network connecting river steamboats plying the Ohio and the Mississippi, as well as all the tributary rivers flowing into the Ohio. It also served as a railroad hub for a number of lines running both east and west, connecting eastern cities and states to the West, as well as northward into the heartlands of Ohio and Indiana. Along with Ohio goods, much of Kentucky's and Indiana's farm production flowed into Cincinnati, where trains and boats distributed it far and wide.[1]

During the Civil War, Cincinnati served also as a military hub. Enormous quantities of military supplies flowed into the city from manufacturing centers throughout the Northern states by rail, canal boat, or river steamboats. Much war production churned out of the city's factories as well. Miles Greenwood's great iron works forged artillery pieces and caissons to equip batteries. Factories constructed wagons. A clothing manufacturing center both before and during the war, thousands of men and women—many of the latter soldiers' wives and widows—labored in U.S. Army–owned and –operated factories sewing together uniform tunics, shirts, hats, coats, and trousers.[2] Commissary stores (foodstuffs) collected in great warehouses and on wharf boats awaiting shipment to the front. Farmers from Ohio and Indiana drove herds of hogs and cattle to the city to be slaughtered, packed in barrels, and loaded on shallow-draft riverboats that could run up the Tennessee, Cumberland, and Green Rivers to supply federal armies in Kentucky, Tennessee, and northern Mississippi and Alabama. The army's Quartermaster Department also let contracts to buy thousands of horses and mules to equip cavalry regiments and artillery batteries and to pull the wagons carrying the army's supplies. Collected from a radius of hundreds of miles, wranglers herded animals onto steamboats to be shipped south. The city's wharf handled scores of vessels daily loaded with troops, livestock, and supplies. Cincinnati's several daily newspapers (including German-language titles) had a wide circulation and a national reach, carried on the rails east and west in the North and on the riverboats far into the occupied South to supply the soldiers' ravenous demand for news. During the war thousands of travelers passed through the city by train or boat daily, staying in fine hotels and taking in theater, opera, and other entertainments; they gambled, drank, and caroused in its many saloons and brothels. It was both a wide-open and a cultured city.

As Cincinnati commanded the economy of a wide area, it was a natural to be an army command center. Major General Horatio G. Wright, commander of the Department of the Ohio, established his headquarters at Cincinnati in late 1862 and remained there into the following year. Commanding much of Kentucky and West Virginia as well as Ohio, Indiana, Michigan, and Illinois, the geographical reach of the department was enormous. With the increasing difficulty in handling opposition to the war effort and the Lincoln administration in those Northern states, direct command of the department became problematic at a time when Washington authorities hoped to advance into eastern Tennessee and relieve the sufferings of its pro-Union people. The army had posts scattered throughout the various Northern states reporting to Wright, and while regulations governed how post commanders divided jurisdictions in the geographical spaces between the posts, he agreed with his subordinates that a better command structure was needed. He already had district commanders under his command in Kentucky and West Virginia. Applying army command structures uniformly across his department, in March and April 1863 he appointed some of his post commanders to state district commands. Wright named Brigadier General Jacob Ammen, who had been commanding the Camp Douglas prisoner-of-war camp outside Chicago, as commander of the District of Illinois, with headquarters at Springfield. He appointed Colonel Henry B. Carrington to command the District of Indiana with headquarters at Indianapolis, and placed Brigadier General John S. Mason in command of the District of Ohio with headquarters at Cincinnati. After a couple of weeks, Brigadier General Jacob D. Cox, commanding military forces at Columbus, Ohio, switched places with Mason and assumed command of the District of Ohio. These commanders reported directly to Wright at Cincinnati.

Serious difficulties arose in all of Wright's Northern state district commands, not the least of which was widespread opposition to the war effort in the form of encouraging desertion and harboring deserters. In one instance, in Noble County in southeastern Ohio, hundreds of armed men rallied to prevent the arrest of deserters by troops and a deputy U.S. marshal. As happened in similar instances in Indiana and Illinois, letter writers from the community enticed soldiers to leave the army. One Noble County man wrote to a soldier in the 78th Ohio Volunteer Infantry Regiment decrying the illegal measures taken by "King Abraham" Lincoln's administration and the perversion of the war to save the Union into a war to abolish slavery. The prospect for revolution was great, the man wrote. "Things begin to look glowing indeed. Threats are thrown out by western editors to kick New England out, and the South & West to form a new Confederacy." The writer advised the soldier to "come home if you can possibly get home."[3] Troops marched into the community and arrested several persons who had resisted the capture of deserters and brought them to Cincinnati for trial before the U.S. federal court.[4]

Officers at Department of the Ohio headquarters perceived two related phenomena at work in the Northwestern states: rampant desertion from the army and the efforts by civilians to harbor and protect deserters, and the fact that those same civilians were *arming* themselves in opposition to the government. Most worrisome were the recent reports of large assemblies of armed civilians rallying to protect deserters from arrest or who intimidated small squads sent to capture them. The reports came from throughout the department's Northern states. Carrington, the best informed of Wright's district commanders, reported that secret societies meeting in Indianapolis were distributing arms and ammunition to their members.[5] The recent passage by Congress of the Enrollment Act, which instituted a federal draft to be administered by the War Department and replaced the state-administered draft under the Militia Act of 1862, further enraged opponents of the war. Reports flowed into department headquarters that armed citizens vowed resistance to the imposition of a draft.[6] Closer to home, officers took note of the traffic in arms and ammunition going on in the city. Wright wired Washington with his concerns: "Arms and munitions of war are being sold daily in this city and perhaps others in the Dept, without regard to loyalty of purchasers, or use for which they are intended. There appears to be no authority here for prohibiting such sales. The matter should be regulated in some way at once. Can it be done[?]"[7] In reply, the War Department authorized him to seize all government-owned arms in the possession of Cincinnati's mayor, as well as all government arms not then in service.[8] Not satisfied, on March 14 Wright issued an order prohibiting the sale and shipment of arms and ammunition in Cincinnati.

Carrington also perceived troubles arising from arms sales in Indiana. Before the order issued by Wright was promulgated, an informant in Richmond tipped Carrington off to the arrival of a shipment of arms intended for "disloyalists." Troops dispatched to the town seized revolvers bought by a local dealer from Cincinnati wholesalers and removed the arms to Indianapolis.[9] On March 17, Wright issued a new order, General Orders 22, extending the ban on sales of arms and ammunition to the entire Department of the Ohio. He immediately wired the order to Carrington in Indianapolis, who promulgated his own version of it for Indiana.[10] Carrington arrested several people in Indianapolis for trying to buy revolvers "for neighbors who sent to the city for them." He seized the guns and later resold them to the shops where they had been purchased.[11]

At this time, in response to the related problems of desertion and arms flowing into the hands of opponents of the government, Wright quietly took steps little noted by contemporaries then or by historians later, but which influenced events in the Northwestern states during the rest of the war. On March 19, 1863, Wright authorized the creation of a detective force to report to the post commander at Cincinnati, Lieutenant Colonel Seth Eastman of the 115th Ohio Volunteer Infantry Regiment. His action came about in response to the Cincinnati post adjutant, Captain Andrew C. Kemper, seconded from the 52nd Ohio Volunteer Infantry Regiment, who complained of the swarms of deserters in and around the city. The post's provost guard patrols could not capture them all. What was needed, Kemper suggested, was to hire "spies or detectives" to work to find the deserters in their lairs. Patrols would then be dispatched to make the arrests. He thought that a force of six detectives would be sufficient, hired at a salary of seventy-five to one hundred dollars per month each.[12] Wright promptly embraced the suggestion, and departmental headquarters authorized hiring a "corps of Spies & detectives not to exceed six in number." Post command immediately hired three detectives and added to the force as needs and funds occasioned; at one point in June 1863, departmental headquarters approved hiring detectives in excess of the authorized number as need warranted.[13] Headquarters called on the post's detective force frequently to gather information in the city and throughout the multistate region regarding the extent of opposition to the government. Soon, separate post, district, department, and Provost Marshal General's Bureau headquarters in the city each would have its own detective force to provide intelligence. Not to be outdone, subordinate commanders throughout the department would mimic the detective corps in Cincinnati and establish their own forces to furnish information on disaffected groups and individuals. All reported to Cincinnati headquarters. In this manner, the Queen City became a spy center.

Military Intelligence in the U.S. Army

All army commands *in the field* employed networks of spies to provide intelligence on rebel movements, strength, and operations on the battlefield or in contested regions. Typically called scouts or guides by army commanders (as *spy* was generally thought to be a pejorative epithet), men and women operated under provost marshal commands to venture into rebel-controlled areas at the risk of their lives to supply commanders with information.[14] Officers also collected information from escaped or liberated African American men and women who informed on rebel troop movements. Aside from battlefield operations, several army detective operations that operated outside and behind the lines existed at the time. Such operations served as models for Eastman and Kemper's request. Department of the Ohio forces were in constant contact with the Department of the Cumberland's headquarters in Tennessee immediately to the south. There, department commander Major General William S. Rosecrans, with headquarters at Murfreesboro, established a large and far-reaching provost marshal operation under Captain William Wiles to police the department and provide tactical intelligence for commanders. He augmented it by the creation of a separate "Army Police" department under the command of "Colonel" William Truesdail. A civilian businessman from Erie, Pennsylvania, and later Saint Louis who never obtained a military commission, Truesdail had a wide-ranging charge from Rosecrans to hunt down and break up fraud and corruption in the department, encompassing Tennessee and parts of Kentucky, but also to detect rebel espionage, smuggling operations, and the so-called rebel mails—the smuggling of communications between persons North and South, often communicating contraband military information about troop movements or strength. With headquarters at Nashville, Truesdail's numerous operatives—estimated by one historian at over two hundred men and women—tracked down deserters, rebel spies and couriers, smugglers, corrupt contractors, and thieves of army property. They also inspected packages and mail sent by both private express companies and the U.S. post. His spies also went behind rebel lines to provide intelligence for Rosecrans's military operations, even infiltrating Confederate general Braxton Bragg's headquarters. Truesdail was in frequent contact with commanders in Cincinnati and other Northwestern posts, and his operations were well known to officers in the Department of the Ohio.[15]

An example of a provost marshal office operating an extensive military detective program existed at the post of Cairo, Illinois. Though north of the Ohio River in the state of Illinois, since the early months of the war the post of Cairo had belonged to army departments such as the Department of the Mississippi or the Department of the Tennessee, frontline commands in regular contact with rebel forces or that occupied large areas of rebel states. Military authorities at Cairo operated like other posts in its department found closer to the front by supporting provost marshal operations with fines or taxes imposed on local populations. Money raised from licenses to operate saloons, hotels, and other public amenities, as well as fines charged for illegal sales of liquor, went to pay the salaries and expenses of a number of spies who operated out of Cairo. Post records show Cairo's provost marshal covered travel expenses and costs of buying civilian clothes for soldier-spies to disguise themselves.[16]

Another model might have been Allan Pinkerton's operation for General George McClellan's Army of the Potomac in the East in 1861 and 1862.

Pinkerton, a Scottish immigrant, established a private detective agency in the early 1850s in Chicago and worked for railroads, express companies, and other corporate clients. General McClellan, former Illinois Central Railroad executive, now commander of the Army of the Potomac, employed him and his detectives to provide intelligence on Confederate forces in Virginia. The War Department poured many thousands of Secret Service Fund dollars into his operations, sucking up the vast majority of secret-service expenditures during the war.[17] The results, however, were mixed at best. Pinkerton's faulty estimates of rebel forces greatly exaggerated their real strength. Unfortunately, McClellan placed great weight on the faulty intelligence and proceeded slowly and cautiously against rebel forces, always believing that he confronted massive Confederate armies in northern Virginia. Pinkerton, loyal to the general, also spied on the Lincoln administration for McClellan. He resigned from most secret-service work for the government after McClellan was removed from command. His failures notwithstanding, Pinkerton in later years boasted of his wartime work and built a false reputation as a detective genius.[18]

Another possible model existed in the War Department's in-house detective operation run by Lafayette C. Baker. Secretary Stanton and other department officials often employed Baker's corps of detectives in odd jobs, from policing the District of Columbia in arresting drunken soldiers and breaking up army contract frauds, to sending spies behind rebel lines or investigating rebel operations in Canada and Northern states. Baker was most effective in assisting treasury officials in breaking up treasury note counterfeiting operations; evidence suggests he played at most a marginal role in the army's efforts to detect secret organizations in the Old Northwest during the rebellion.[19]

Closer to Cincinnati and more effective than Pinkerton's or Baker's outfits were two detectives hired by the Commissary General's Department to detect fraud and waste within that department, responsible for feeding the armies. Often operating out of Cincinnati, John Newbury and John B. Pollard began their "special detective" careers for the federal government in Saint Louis in August and September 1861, respectively. Often working together as a team, they roamed widely through the Northwest, especially in the Department of the Ohio, but also in western Virginia, Kentucky, Iowa, and Missouri. They visited depots, warehouses, wharf boats, camps, and any other place where army officers kept commissary stores. They rooted out fraud, theft, waste, and neglected and lost stores. They also kept an unofficial eye open for fraud in the Quartermaster Department, frequently sharing information on corruption and waste in that realm. The pair met with resounding success, uncovering "glaring acts of fraud and peculation."[20] They estimated that the corruption they uncovered and subsistence stores recovered were worth millions of dollars in savings to the federal government. Paid seventy-five dollars per month each, they appealed to the War Department to have their pay increased, as their extensive travel exhausted their meager salaries; even detectives had families to feed.[21] However, their unglamorous work rooting out fraud and waste in the army bureaucracy attracted little attention, and War Department bureaucrats regularly questioned Commissary Department officers about the need for commissary detectives. Commissariat officials invariably reported that the work done by Newbury and Pollard was of great benefit to the service and should be expanded.[22]

Pollard and Newbury also undertook detective work in political matters, perhaps moonlighting to supplement their salaries. For example, Pollard and Newbury reported to Department of the Ohio headquarters that they investigated an armed organization in Highland County, Ohio, that was prepared to resist the arrest of deserters and the federal draft.[23] Later, Henry Carrington reported that Pollard had been "of great service" to him in his own investigations.[24] The two detectives investigated political shootings in Brown County, Indiana, and while in Indianapolis, Pollard captured a rebel spy.[25] Later, while working in western Kentucky, a provost marshal hired him to arrest deserters.[26] Shortly after the creation of the Cincinnati post's detective force, Department of the Ohio headquarters staff suggested that Pollard and Newbury might work in tandem with the force to save money.[27]

Most important, another inspiration for establishing a detective force in the Cincinnati post was the city's own police force. As American cities grew and became densely populated, complex, unwieldy, and unruly, the 1850s witnessed the transition from night watches and simple patrols of city streets to more extensive operations and saw the establishment of police forces in large American cities modeled on the London metropolitan police; with the creation of urban police agencies came additional efforts to detect crime and criminal conspiracy.[28] At the time of the Civil War, the regular Cincinnati police force had no detectives on its roster. Instead, the police hired independent detectives to hunt down criminals and fugitives. The private detective agency's chief was James L. Ruffin, who had for several years served on the city police force. Born in Ohio in 1814, he led efforts to bring order to the rough-and-tumble riverfront. His detectives-for-hire also chased down counterfeiters and arrested them in several states. The printing and distribution of false bank notes constituted perhaps the largest and most far-reaching criminal conspiracies in mid-century America, and police detectives worked hard to stop them. Attempts to halt widespread counterfeiting operations served as the impetus for the rise of detective police forces across the country. When Republicans won Cincinnati's municipal elections in April 1863, the new Republican mayor and council restored Ruffin to the police force and appointed him the new chief of police. His private detective agency continued under the name Cincinnati Independent Detective Police, and Ruffin employed them to work with the city police to investigate crime and hunt down criminals.[29]

Cincinnati post commanders hired Ruffin and two of his Cincinnati private detectives to be their first army detectives, with the city police chief serving as the head of the army force. Several more private detectives served on the post payroll in the course of the war.[30] There is no indication that Ruffin or his detectives relinquished their city and private employment while also employed by the army. Military commanders and city officials no doubt found the synergies derived from police detective work and the army's needs compatible. Indeed, like the police detective forces of Philadelphia and New York, which supplied detective skills and services to military commanders, the Cincinnati detectives had experience working for army commanders. In 1861, Ruffin and other Cincinnati detectives had worked for then brigadier general William S. Rosecrans in western Virginia in "secret service," supplying information on rebel operations in that region.[31]

Investigating Arms Sales

Days before the creation of the Cincinnati post detective corps, post commanders called on private detective Ruffin to employ his special skills. General Wright ordered Eastman to put a strict watch on the city's largest gun dealer to stop any violation of the army's sales ban. "Information received today indicates that this firm is largely engaged in the business of selling arms to persons who will use them for disloyal purposes," he explained. The firm had salesmen scouring the region hunting up orders for arms. Eastman was to avoid creating any suspicion that the salesmen were being watched, he ordered.[32] Kittredge and Co., the firm in question, "are selling arms to persons who will use them for disloyal purposes," Captain Kemper explained.[33] Ruffin and his private detectives went to work immediately. Meanwhile, military commanders placed a guard around Kittredge and Co.'s premises. Days later, acting on information from Mattoon, Illinois, that an agent for the firm was trying to sell guns in that disaffected area, Kemper sent a detective there to investigate with orders to "exercise great care" to avoid suspicion. In the meantime, having found evidence of violations of Wright's order, Cincinnati post commanders revoked the permits to sell arms and ammunition of thirteen city businesses. Still, Kemper ordered Ruffin to handle Kittredge and Co. with special care. The detective in Illinois reported that he could not establish as fact that the dealer sold arms to a local firm for resale to disloyal persons. Not surprisingly, he reported, "no one could be found to swear that they were disloyal or would connive at disloyalty." He did note that many people in Coles County and adjoining counties in Illinois were in open "mutiny" against the government, "avowing their sympathy with the south, [and] organizing drilling and arming themselves" to resist the government. Kemper passed the information on to departmental headquarters.[34]

On a related note at this time, Colonel Carrington developed a major report "at the request of Governor Morton" for President Lincoln and the War Department on the growing threat of "domestic treason" in Indiana and neighboring states in the North. The arming of the government's opponents was a central theme of the report. In the days before finalizing and sending the report, he visited Cincinnati to confer with Wright, so it is likely that he shared the information found in the report with the general and obtained approval to forward it to Washington.[35] Carrington reiterated his findings that a movement existed to undermine and break up the U.S. Army by securing desertions, resisting future drafts, and interfering with volunteer enlistments. The aim of the persons behind the movement, identified as the Knights of the Golden Circle, was to "stop this war." The new evidence he cited was the organization's push to arm its membership. "In February and March alone," he wrote, "nearly 30,000 arms, revolvers, etc. have entered Indiana." The number, he stated, was based on sales invoices he had examined, and "undoubtedly thousands more have been brought from the East of which I have no knowledge." Just the day before, when the ban on arms sales took effect in Indianapolis, "nearly 1,000 revolvers were contracted for and the trade could not supply the demand." In addition to firearms, he reported, gunpowder sales exceeded peacetime sales levels. Boxes containing arms were smuggled to local dealers by being marked as containing hardware items. With these arms, the organization aimed to stop what it considered to be the despotism of the Lincoln administration and to overthrow it by force if required. Carrington stated that its leaders claimed to be in communication with rebels in the South and planned cooperation with rebel raiders such as John Hunt Morgan. His sources, he reported, came from two general groups: "good and true citizens who report" to him, as well as the "statements of deserters" whom he had captured and interrogated. An informant in the Indianapolis lodge indicated that eighty-five of Indiana's ninety-two counties had organized lodges of the KGC. He believed the organization was strongest in rural communities. "The ostensible leaders here are not the leaders of the Democratic party," he observed. Indeed, in private meetings state Democratic Party leaders had voiced alarm to him at the rising tide of desperation and discontent in the party's ranks. The organization had grown faster than party leaders intended, he said, and had become uncontrollable.[36] Carrington assured Washington that he would meet the challenge with energy, firmness, and discretion. He aimed to promote a "popular reaction" against the movement that would restore calm.[37] But if there was a widespread uprising coupled with a rebel raid on Kentucky, as Wright, Rosecrans, and other commanders anticipated, "there would be great danger" requiring reinforcements from the East. He requested "discretionary power" in the state to handle the threat.[38]

The army's efforts to intercept arms shipments into the Northwest encountered difficulties. While General Wright designed his departmentwide order to keep arms out of the hands of persons perceived to be disloyal, it created havoc for people of all political persuasions. Dealers who abided by the order complained that it failed to prevent arms wholesalers located outside the region from shipping guns into the department. A manufacturer of gunpowder in Xenia, Ohio, suggested that if there was to be a ban, it had better be expanded to the whole northern United States.[39] Still others appeared to have been ignorant of the order's existence.[40] Gradually, in the days and weeks that followed, it became clear that the order was having no effect in the department. Dealers disregarded the order and sold to anyone who would buy. The quartermaster at Chicago reported that Chicago dealers sold large quantities of pistols to citizens in downstate Illinois and other states in defiance of the order.[41] A Sandusky, Ohio, man reported that local "secessionists" easily avoided the ban and bought from a dealer in nearby Tiffin who ignored the order, or else bought from sources out of state. Even the Cincinnati dealers began to defy the ban and resumed arms sales.[42] Kittredge and Co. announced its wish to apply for permission to sell arms again, stating in its defense that wholesalers in Saint Louis and New York, outside the department, and even Chicago, inside it, sold in the region and stole all their business.[43] Army commanders in Ohio pointed the finger of blame at each other for lax enforcement of the ban, citing reports that no one enforced it in Hamilton, Xenia, Dayton, and Hillsborough, while in Marion guns came from Philadelphia.[44] Arms seizures, though few, prompted complaints. The proprietor of one of Cincinnati's opera houses wrote to protest the seizure of his muskets used in stage productions, stating that the weapons were more dangerous to anyone who might try to fire one than anyone targeted.[45]

Evidence suggests that large quantities of arms and ammunition poured into the Northwestern states at this time. Only in rare cases were military authorities able to intercept the shipments. The quartermaster stationed at Mattoon, Illinois, pointed to carloads of gunpowder unloading at railroad stations there and in nearby towns, much of it consigned to persons considered to be "disloyal." He noted that while the order allowed sales in small quantities for "sporting purposes," he thought seven thousand percussion caps for one of the consignments excessive for one individual's personal sporting purposes. Suspicious, he opened the package purportedly containing the caps and instead found revolvers. General Ammen, to whom headquarters forwarded the query, ordered that the consignments for persons considered disloyal be seized.[46] Until the end of the war, the traffic in large quantities of arms into the hands of "disloyal" citizens remained a chief concern of military authorities in the Northwest.

Burnside Takes Command

Amid the increasing tensions, a change in command occurred that would have fateful consequences for the region. When the Senate voted not to confirm Wright's promotion to major general of volunteers, the general indignantly requested that he be relieved of his Cincinnati command.[47] The War Department and Lincoln responded by sending the battle-hardened Major General Ambrose E. Burnside. Born in Union County, Indiana, in 1824 and a West Point graduate, Burnside had succeeded in independent operations in coastal North Carolina and had commanded a corps in the Army of the Potomac under McClellan. In the fall of 1862, when Lincoln removed McClellan from command, he called on Burnside to take command and attack Robert E. Lee's rebel Army of Northern Virginia. Reluctant to assume command of the eastern army, he nonetheless pushed ahead in an effort to outflank Lee and bring him to battle near Fredericksburg. Delays in the federal advance and obtaining pontoons to cross the Rappahannock River allowed Lee's army to entrench safely near the town. Burnside pressed ahead, but on December 13 brave frontal assaults on Lee's well-protected forces at Fredericksburg produced horrible casualties in the federal army and failed to dislodge the rebels. A month later, in January 1863, the Union commander planned a swift maneuver to attempt to flank Lee and smash his numerically inferior force. But drenching rains for four days snarled the movement, dubbed the Mud March, and allowed Lee to prepare and wait. Burnside halted the advance, but the morass of mud hindered the retreat as badly as it did the forward movement. The army's top commanders fell to infighting and recriminations, making Burnside's position as commander of the Army of the Potomac untenable.

Lincoln promptly removed him from the command.[48] He believed the general was a good officer, however, and two months later, in March, appointed him to the command of the Department of the Ohio when that important position opened up. Transferring Burnside's 9th Corps to the department with him, Lincoln intended for the new commander promptly to organize an advance into eastern Tennessee to relieve Unionists there. His orders were to gather troops in the department and prepare for a campaign. Burnside was also to supply troops to Generals Rosecrans and Grant to assist them in their advances against rebel forces in the West.

Burnside arrived in Cincinnati on March 24 and conferred with Wright as to conditions in the department.[49] Political matters took priority, as increasing evidence of dissent, opposition to the war effort, and open, armed hostility to the government would hinder his ability to push into Tennessee. The need to suppress outbreaks in the Northwest tied up troops throughout the department. While Brigadier General Hascall's efforts continued apace to round up deserters in the states of Illinois, Indiana, and Ohio, assisted by Lincoln's presidential proclamation for deserters to return to their units, the problem continued to plague the army and weaken units everywhere.[50] Shortly after Burnside's arrival, Carrington (days before confirmed by the Senate as brigadier general of volunteers) wired to his new commander with his latest intelligence. Governor Morton had information of arms shipments from New York to Indiana intended "for disloyal purposes." He added that he would order railroad agents to report all arms shipments into the state and to "seize subject to proof as fact all cases of arms not invoiced to some competent officer."[51] Reports of ninety to one hundred thousand arms being shipped to Ohio and Indiana were surely a "great exaggeration," but "it may be well to notify authorities in Ohio[.] I will take care of Indiana."[52] Accordingly, Burnside continued Wright's ban on arms sales and shipments throughout the department.

Reports from around the department arrived at Burnside's headquarters that were worrisome. In Illinois in February, weeks after the Emancipation Proclamation took effect, Governor Yates had written to Washington noting that the political condition of the state was akin to a gunpowder magazine: the smallest spark, even the arrest of a deserter, could "precipitate revolution" unless the government should back down and allow the deserter to be released. He noted instances in which deserters had been rescued by "mobs." In addition, some Illinois volunteer regiments refused to return to service and seemed bent on mutiny. For the protection of the state against revolution he asked that four veteran regiments be sent to Illinois under the guise of recruiting, but actually to enforce the authority of the government. He concluded,

"I should not trouble you thus did I not believe it *absolutely essential.*"[53] Yates sent the letter by Illinois brigadier general John M. Palmer, a War Democrat and friend of Lincoln's, who delivered it to the president and awaited his questions. Palmer recorded in his memoirs,

> Mr. Lincoln, in response to the letter of the governor, handed him by me, answered with one of his jokes which cannot be repeated, and said: "Who can we trust if we can't trust Illinois!" and referred me to the secretary of war. . . . I called on . . . Mr. Stanton . . . and after I told him my business was from Governor Yates, and that he asked authority to raise four regiments of cavalry for service in Illinois, he said: "You are to command these troops, are you not?" and when I replied, "No, I am not, and would refuse the command of troops raised for service in my own state and amongst my own people. . . ." He then said: 'That shows the d—d nonsense of the whole thing; if you thought your own family and friends were in danger, you would be willing to command troops raised to protect them."[54]

In March, a report considered "reliable" by state officials indicated that in one community "copperheads 300 strong are fully armed except powder, & bent on mischief."[55] Yates also forwarded to Cincinnati headquarters a report that a large quantity of gunpowder and some arms were in the hands of Jefferson County citizens intent on resisting the draft.[56] General Ammen had information that speakers at public meetings in southern Illinois advised their listeners to organize and drill in order to resist the draft enrollment.[57] In early April, Yates wired Burnside that "reliable intelligence" left no doubt that a "formidable insurrection" was being planned in Illinois and "will break out with[in] a very few days in southern half of this state." The governor lamented that there were hardly any troops available in the state to suppress it.[58] Burnside credited the report and wired the commander of the Department of the Missouri at Saint Louis, quoting Yates and adding that it "coincides with information I received from Belleville, Xenia [Ohio] and other places."[59] Both commanders received reports of arms being smuggled from Illinois into Missouri to supply the guerrillas running rampant in that state; both credited reports of groups "secretly organizing" in the towns along the Mississippi River.[60]

Back in Ohio, in response to reports that organizations were forming to resist the draft, departmental headquarters sought legal advice about how best to suppress them. Commanders called on the federal attorney in Cincinnati, Flamen Ball, for assistance. Ball's advice was unsatisfactory. He opined that Congress had passed no law authorizing civil authorities to suppress disloyal organizations. Section 25 of the recently passed Enrollment Act provided that any person who resisted the draft or aided others in resistance to the draft could be indicted. However, he wrote, "in as much as no draft or enrollment has yet been attempted by the Government, there has been no opportunity given to such evil disposed persons to resist the action of the Government."[61] Civil and military authorities would have to wait until acts of resistance were attempted before acting to suppress them.

Such a passive attitude failed to please Burnside. Under pressure from the War Department to act on his orders to advance into eastern Tennessee, the commanding general wanted to suppress disloyalty quickly and decisively in his geographical command. On April 13 he announced General Orders 38, declaring that military authority would be employed in the department to regulate speech or publication deemed to be disloyal. "It must be distinctly understood," he stated in the order, "that treason expressed or implied will not be tolerated." The order reflected the attitude held by many in the army who pointed the finger at partisan speech—Democratic speech—as the source of the desertion problem and prolongation of the war. Days before, Brigadier General Jacob D. Cox spoke at Warren, Ohio, and accused Democratic news-papers of causing desertion. "It will not be thought strange," he said, "that the army should feel that these enemies at home are more dangerous than those they meet in the field."[62] A few days later, Burnside spoke at a Union rally in Hamilton, Ohio, and explained his intervention into civilian and political affairs. He was a military man, not a civilian ruler, he said. "I am probably invested with a little more power than the majority of you in suppressing anything like treason, and acts that tend to create dissention."[63] Republicans cheered Burnside's order and his aggressive posture toward opponents of the Lincoln administration. General Carrington wrote to Burnside to thank him for the order, stating that it would assist matters in unsettled Indiana. "The results will be the thorough vindication of the Government and the protec-tion of all good citizens."[64]

Designed to intimidate the war's opponents, Burnside's General Orders 38 failed to quell resistance to the government in the department. On April 15 a crowd of armed men surrounded two men who had arrested deserters at Anna, Union County, Illinois, at the southernmost tip of the state. Frightened, the two men released the deserters to the crowd and fled. The crowd pursued them and shot one dead; the other escaped. Local civil authorities took no steps to arrest the perpetrators. Military authorities scrambled to respond. General Ammen, at Springfield, was too far away and had few effective troops to call on. He wired the commander at Cairo, Brigadier General Napoleon Bonaparte

Buford, for assistance. Buford sent one hundred troops to Anna and made dozens of arrests of men suspected of participation in the incident. To avoid the possibility of habeas corpus requests for the prisoners, Buford sent them to Columbus, Kentucky, to the headquarters of his immediate superior.[65] Another shooting nearby prompted Buford to send more troops to make more arrests. He requested a regiment be sent to occupy the area.[66] Burnside, who learned of the incident only through the newspapers, telegraphed orders to arrest the perpetrators and send them to Cincinnati for trial by military commission. He ordered a strong force be sent to make the arrests, armed with orders "to shoot down any person who may resist their authority."[67]

Also at this time, Burnside learned that a Marion County, Illinois, Democratic leader, Dr. William White, had organized a "brigade of Copperheads" to act in cooperation with the Missouri Confederate guerrilla leader, General Jeff. Thompson. A local man, J. B. Allen, swore out an affidavit that White told him that he planned to lead four thousand men who were "in favor of the South and southern rights." According to Allen, White awaited a carload of gunpowder, caps, and rifles at a southern Illinois railroad station scheduled to arrive between the fifteenth and twenty-fifth of April.[68] General Alexander S. Asboth, commander at Columbus, Kentucky, to whom Buford reported, sent Allen to Cincinnati to speak with Burnside.[69] Asboth also sent a report of a captain of the 2nd Illinois Cavalry Regiment who had been ordered to investigate conditions in southern Illinois. The report confirmed the existence of the KGC throughout southwest Illinois, from Quincy, on the Mississippi River, through Springfield to Cave-in-Rock, on the Ohio River. There they had a secret crossing where members of the organization smuggled contraband supplies to the rebels, along with men for the Confederate army.[70] Local military and Illinois Central Railroad officials expected arms for White's men to arrive in boxes marked "dry goods" at a station on the line.[71] Burnside ordered Ammen to intercept the arms and arrest White and send him to Cincinnati.[72] In response to these reports, commanders put Cairo under martial law as a precaution and issued orders not to recognize civil process in efforts to release deserters and prisoners.[73]

On April 18 two separate violent incidents in Indiana also signified great danger to military authorities. In Danville, Hendricks County, immediately west of Indianapolis, tensions that had been simmering for months boiled over in a shootout at a Democratic Party rally. Armed horsemen wearing butternut emblems on their lapels rode into town to attend the rally and got into a fight with local Unionists. A general gun battle ensued in which several participants were shot and wounded. Legion militia units in nearby towns arrived too late to capture the armed horsemen, who escaped. Carrington sent a mixed force of cavalry and infantry to the town to prevent further fighting. The troops arrested seven "ringleaders" of the mounted force and handed them over for trial in the federal court. Three of the prisoners made sworn affidavits before the U.S. commissioner that they were members of the KGC. They admitted to taking oaths, learning signs, and being advised to arm themselves.[74]

On the same day as the Danville shootout, a Union rally took place in Brown County, a rural county about forty miles south of Indianapolis. During the rally a verbal altercation between a cavalry trooper in the county to arrest deserters and a former Democratic state representative resulted in a gunfight. The legislator, Lewis Prosser, shot the soldier dead. In instant retaliation, another soldier present, Captain A. D. Cunning, drew his revolver and shot Prosser in the leg. Bystanders carried Prosser to his house, where, according to various accounts, an armed force estimated from three hundred to three thousand strong gathered to protect him from arrest. Democratic newspaper accounts called them a posse comitatus, while Republican versions called them the KGC.[75] A witness to the shootings reported privately to state officials that another Democratic legislator, James Hester, drilled the assembled force of "some 500 KGCs" in the manual of arms.[76] After lingering for several weeks Prosser died of his wound.

Carrington reported to Cincinnati headquarters about the two incidents and canceled a planned trip to the river city. Instead, he requested that Burnside quietly travel to Indianapolis to confer with him and Governor Morton. He suggested that Generals Ammen and Cox, district commanders of Illinois and Ohio respectively, also come "to consult as to concerted action respecting secret societies of which I have the full evidence. Two attacks upon men made yesterday with fatal results."[77] He later wired to Burnside that "the extent and plans of treasonable societies are not realized facts are stranger than my statements even men dare not speak legality for fear of fire and murder in some counties. I know what I say I shall prudently but firmly take large responsibility if necessary I regret you could not come here."[78]

Carrington's panicky-sounding message alarmed Burnside, not so much in the content of the message, which was consistent with other reports of organized resistance, as its strange syntax and tone. No doubt he was reminded of the warnings that the general-in-chief at the War Department had voiced about Carrington. Henry W. Halleck personally disliked Carrington, a regular-army colonel and now brigadier general of volunteers who was not a West Point man and had never seen action in the field.[79] He insinuated to Burnside on his taking command of the department that Stanton wanted him to investigate Carrington "as it is feared that the officer . . . may by imprudence cause difficulties."[80] On his arrival in Cincinnati, Burnside had conferred with Wright about Carrington, who had assured him that the Indianapolis officer was sound. Burnside wired to Halleck, "Wright says there is no trouble at Indianapolis, and I shall assume responsibility of not going there till I receive an answer to this."[81] Not to be outdone, shortly thereafter Halleck wrote an "unofficial" letter offering "hints" to Burnside on a variety of subjects, one of which was Carrington. Stanton, he falsely insisted, believed that Carrington was "entirely unfitted for such a command. From my conversations with Governors [David] Tod [Ohio] and Morton, I think the Secretary is right."[82] On receipt of this letter Burnside telegraphed Stanton to absolve himself of blame, that Wright had appointed Carrington to the Indiana command before he had arrived. "I will investigate as to his fitness and relieve him at once if he is found deficient or I will relieve him at once if you wish."[83] A confused Stanton, unaware of Halleck's machinations and who had assured Morton's emissary that Carrington was doing good work in Indiana, replied that he had no desire to remove the general or "interfere with his command unless you [find] it necessary."[84]

As Halleck had deviously hoped, Burnside's suspicions were raised and he lost confidence in the Indianapolis commander. After he received Carrington's erratic-sounding message, he wired in reply, "There is no cause for alarm." He counseled that "haste and indiscretion in the exercise of military force often creates trouble," and patronizingly advised him to consult with Governor Morton, "who is thoroughly posted in the state affairs."[85] Carrington replied that Burnside could "rely upon my prudence[.] I entertain no alarm but wish to anticipate sharp issues."[86] Nonetheless, the next day Burnside relieved Carrington of the Indiana command, ordered him to report to headquarters, and replaced him with General Hascall, then in Indianapolis superintending the arrest of deserters in the Northwest.[87]

The news of Carrington's removal from command came like a thunderbolt to Morton. The governor had become increasingly dependent on the hardworking officer. Most important, Morton relied on him to collect useful information regarding the secret organizations then flourishing in Indiana. In the past month, since assuming command of the district, Carrington's troops, acting on tips, had intercepted guns and gunpowder shipments to nearby communities and dealers.[88] The general had also worked to raise awareness of the moral evils of secret political societies by preaching about their illegal acts: carrying concealed weapons in violation of state law, resisting the arrest of deserters, and defiance of federal laws generally.[89] He attempted to induce a popular reaction in the state against the groups. In a published order he announced that he would employ troops to protect civilians who were threatened by their neighbors for having Unionist views if civil authorities would not act.[90] Using the information he had gathered from interrogations of captured deserters and insider informants, he planted articles in Republican newspapers that exposed the oaths and obligations sworn in the societies, showing their members to be collaborators with the Southern rebels against the Lincoln administration.[91] Most significantly, forces under his orders had arrested and forwarded to the federal court scores of prisoners for trial on various charges related to subversion of the war effort. A number of convictions had already occurred, and a new federal grand jury had been impaneled and charged to investigate what Judge Caleb B. Smith considered the proved existence of secret political societies intent on resisting federal laws.[92] In short, in Morton's view the removal of Carrington would undo the progress made to counteract the rising tide of opposition to the war effort.

Morton pressed Burnside to retain Carrington in Indiana. He invited the general to Indianapolis, where community leaders leaned on him to keep Carrington in place. Morton shared with him a letter sent from Democratic legislator James Hester of Brown County showing the tense situation existing there. Hester had written that the danger of a "general uprising" from Democrats banded together in secret political organizations in self-defense against lawless military tribunals and injustice was "imminent."[93] Burnside remained unmoved. In the following days, however, Morton persuaded him not to launch a military expedition into Brown County. Instead, the governor sent a bipartisan commission to investigate the facts of the Prosser shooting case, take sworn testimony, and assuage bruised feelings in the neighborhood.[94] He also persuaded him to allow Carrington to return to Indianapolis to wrap up his office business. Significant partisan street battles in Greensburg, Fort Wayne, and Centreville at this time further highlighted the political tension in Indiana. Carrington managed to linger in Indianapolis for several weeks, unofficially helping the governor. Morton at this time told confidantes that he could not travel to Washington on business as he felt uneasy leaving the state in the hands of Hascall, testimony to the faith he put in Carrington's intelligence efforts. "Carrington has been removed, and a new man appointed who knows but little about the state," he lamented.[95]

Burnside's plan initially was to send Carrington to serve in the field. But Carrington's health, always bad, collapsed completely at this juncture, and physicians diagnosed that he had diphtheria. Burnside eventually sent him to Cleveland to command a rendezvous camp, organize troops, and recruit his health. While in Ohio, Carrington wrote his political mentor, Salmon P. Chase, that Burnside told him that the "radical defect" leading to his removal from command "was my use of the grand Jury and civil Courts, and that the military commission should have been used only."[96] Carrington, ever desirous of work and purpose, languished in Ohio for several weeks, sick and inactive. His intelligence efforts temporarily ceased.

While turmoil in the Indiana command mounted, the detective corps working out of Cincinnati continued its work. Civilian detectives hired by the post command ranged over the Ohio landscape and beyond to investigate reports of disloyal activities. Responding to reports that the KGCs in the Dayton area were collecting arms and ammunition in preparation to resist the government, post adjutant Kemper sent detectives. There they found that locals possessed plenty of arms and were prepared to resist the draft; "it's the common talk to resist the draft," they reported. Local plotters met secretly in a local schoolhouse to initiate new members.[97] Another detective working in Greene County posed as a rebel soldier from Kentucky wanting to buy $1,000 worth of gunpowder for his command. He reported that a local powder manufacturer "dident [sic] care how he got his money" and was willing to sell to both rebels and local butternuts who planned to resist the draft.[98] Post commanders also employed soldiers as detectives to gather information on disloyal activities. Prompted by letters sent to soldiers, officers detailed a sergeant of the 115th Ohio to go to Stark County, in northeastern Ohio, to investigate. The soldier reported that he was suspected of being a spy as soon as he arrived, and that "affairs quieted down."[99] Kemper also sent a sergeant of the 50th Ohio Volunteer Infantry Regiment to Louisville, Kentucky, to work his way into rebel-sympathizing circles to investigate tailors and clothing manufacturers who were selling to the rebels. Working in cooperation with local military authorities, the soldier also attempted to infiltrate KGC "lodges" by posing as a rebel smuggler and mail carrier. Failing that, he worked on intercepting rebel mails.[100]

Military authorities at Cincinnati requested and received authority from postal authorities to intercept and open U.S. mails. Captain Kemper, acting under orders from Burnside, intercepted correspondence of known "rebel mail" couriers operating between the city and areas of the South under occupation.[101] Postal authorities at Washington grudgingly granted permission. They found examination of private mails distasteful and ungentlemanly and sent instructions to the commanders to minimize the intrusions. In compliance, for example, Brigadier General Jeremiah T. Boyle at Louisville ordered an officer to "make examination yourself or order a sensible and prudent officer to do [it] in the presence of the post master. The examination should not be indiscriminate but of such letters as are suspicious. Do not allow mails to be removed from the custody of the post master."[102] Despite their unease, postal officials regularly cooperated with military commanders and turned over to them letters that raised suspicions. In the days after the military arrest of Clement Vallandigham and the riot at Dayton, that town's postmaster turned over to departmental headquarters letters directed to the former congressman and others.[103] The interception and opening of mail by military authority was a widespread practice.

The Proliferation of Intelligence Operations

In the spring of 1863, with Cincinnati headquarters actively employing civilians and soldiers as detectives, other commands in the Department of the Ohio began to develop their own detective operations. Such intelligence operations derived from officers' frontline experiences employing scouts, guides, and informers to gather tactical intelligence about Confederate forces. Veteran commanders translated their battlefield and occupation experiences to their duties on the Northern home front. The transfer of battlefield intelligence-gathering tactics to sorting out domestic dissent and perceived disloyal activities in the North marked an important turning point in authorities' efforts to combat Northern subversion.

On April 24, Major William Reany received orders from Department of the Ohio headquarters to report to District of Ohio headquarters for special duty.[104] Arriving at district headquarters, General Cox named him superintendent of the "Special Police and detective force" for the district.[105] A former Cincinnati police detective who had obtained a commission in the 7th Ohio Cavalry Regiment, military authorities called on Reany to employ his detective talents. He had served on the Cincinnati police force for a number of years and had been lauded in the press as an "accomplished detective police officer," most notably for breaking up counterfeiting rings in western states.[106] In 1861 he had served with James L. Ruffin under Rosecrans in western Virginia providing military intelligence. In his new capacity, Reany and the force under his command, made up of soldiers detailed from their units, ranged all over Ohio to investigate "disloyal sentiments," violations of General Orders 38, arms shipments from Cincinnati dealers, rebel spy operations, the escape of rebel prisoners from prison camps in the state, as well as to arrest deserters.[107] The arrest of Clement L. Vallandigham and the resultant riots, arson, arrests, and imposition of martial law on Dayton heightened tensions throughout Ohio and increased the challenges to quelling disorder. In July,

Cox named Reany provost marshal for the district.[108] Reany performed his duties as a chief of military detectives effectively, as evinced by a letter sent by his commander to Governor Tod, who had offered to share a detective working for him in uncovering secret political organizations in the state. Cox thanked the governor for the kind offer, but replied,

> Maj. Reany my Prov. Marshal who has charge of my detectives has examined him and we find that we have already more information than [the governor's detective] is able to furnish on the subject, and have reliable detectives working the same clues for further information. Under these circumstances I do not know that I have use for him, especially as our present mode is a more economical one than his would be likely to be.[109]

Another Ohio army commander sought to strengthen his military detective operation at this time. Brigadier General John S. Mason commanded at Columbus, where he had responsibility for Camp Chase, a large prisoner-of-war camp. He also maintained a watchful eye on political affairs in the state capital and surrounding region and maintained surveillance of leading antiwar Democrats.[110] Mason had investigated the sale of civilian clothing to soldiers to help them to desert, using troops under his command.[111] However, he was not satisfied with their service, complaining that it was "impossible to get any evidence through soldiers."[112] He requested authority from Cox to hire three civilian detectives, a move he believed would "advance the interests of the service." A staff officer at district headquarters denied the request, stating that both district and departmental headquarters detailed soldiers as detectives. The officer suggested that Mason contact the head of the newly established Provost Marshal General's Bureau—created by the Enrollment Act passed in March—for assistance. The new bureau had authority to employ civilian detectives; the officer suggested "you had better communicate with Col Parrott," the new acting assistant provost marshal general for Ohio, "for the purpose of making if possible some arrangement by which you can use the detectives employed by him."[113] The going salary for civilian detectives was seventy-five to one hundred dollars per month, roughly equivalent to commissioned officers' pay. Enlisted men in the army were paid thirteen dollars per month; higher noncommissioned ranks received slightly higher pay. With travel and other expenses added on to civilian wages, using soldiers seemed like a cost-effective method. Pressed further by Mason, Cox explained that Burnside was unwilling to hire civilian detectives, owing to the "liability to run into excessive expenditure." He would consider temporary use of civilian detectives only "in special cases which are first reported to these headquarters." Referring to the new Provost Marshal General's Bureau in the War Department, Cox noted that the duties of the new bureau "will be similar, & in many respects coincident" with ours, and he urged cooperation with it to employ civilian detectives in joint investigations. In detailing soldiers to detective duties, he advised,

> By a little care in selecting men, detectives can be found among the officers & enlisted men at posts, who will be quite as efficient as any. I am employing several so selected, and regard them [as] equal to any in the state in efficiency & skill. The Quartermaster department can be ordered to furnish the necessary clothes for disguise in cases when the wearing of uniform would defeat the purpose of investigation.[114]

Also at this time, the commander of the Department of the Missouri established a military command at Keokuk, Iowa, and installed a local figure, Captain J. M. Hiatt, as "Provost Marshal General of the Iowa and Missouri Border." Hiatt kept busy dealing with "copperhead judges," arresting deserters, feeding and sheltering "contrabands," and combating guerrillas and illegal trade along the Mississippi River. He also gathered information on secret organizations. In March he forwarded to departmental headquarters at Saint Louis news that he was "in possession of the signs, passwords etc of the Secret, Copperhead organization, of the country." He requested that he have the services of a "good detective or two" to obtain more information on the organization. He promptly warned Iowa governor Samuel Kirkwood of an assassination plot.[115] His reports evidently made their way up to the War Department, as in early May Hiatt visited Burnside's headquarters bearing a letter of introduction from Secretary Stanton. Stanton commended Hiatt's services "in detecting and arresting Guerrilla movements and contraband trade," among "other matters greatly beneficial to the United States," and noted that Keokuk was located at a central juncture for three military departments. The secretary also noted reports that guerrillas organizing in Hancock County, Illinois, planned raids in Missouri.[116] In a rare move, the War Department issued Hiatt $1,000 in secret-service funds.[117] Burnside issued orders giving Hiatt authority over portions of Illinois adjoining his border district.[118] Soon he was back in Keokuk and irritating federal officers in Illinois and Iowa by ranging throughout their districts arresting deserters and other persons.[119]

General Ammen at Springfield, Illinois, also requested authority from departmental headquarters to hire civilian detectives while battling outbreaks in several counties in the far south of the state. He investigated illicit arms and ammunition distribution in eastern Illinois and received numerous reports of the organization of armed groups opposed to the government. He also fielded requests from both citizens and officers in neighboring military commands in Kentucky and Missouri to stop the smuggling of contraband goods between North and South, a trade undertaken in part by the armed groups.[120] Numerous reports arrived on his desk that described disloyal activities requiring his assistance. Governor Yates also shared information and requested his help to detect the operations of the secret organizations they believed were in league with the Southern rebels. However, departmental headquarters, always with an eye toward economy, refused Ammen's request for authority to hire civilian detectives.[121]

Further evidence that Burnside preferred to employ soldiers as detectives is found in the fact that, through Captain Kemper, he sent two officers, Captains Harrington R. Hill and John A. Means of the 115th Ohio, in civilian disguises to watch Clement Vallandigham and record his speech at Mount Vernon, Ohio. Based on their reports, troops quietly took a special train to Dayton and in the dark of night broke down the former congressman's door and arrested him for violating General Orders 38. Burnside quickly brought him before a military commission in Cincinnati and tried him. Hill and Means, the soldier detectives, were the chief witnesses at the trial.[122]

While conscious of costs, Burnside took intelligence activities seriously and devoted considerable attention to gathering information on domestic activities. Burnside appointed Brigadier General Nathaniel C. McLean to be his departmental provost marshal general, and the two worked diligently to stamp out dissent and disloyalty in the department. Arrests for alleged violations of General Orders 38 occurred throughout the department, and McLean organized military commission trials to punish violators. Troop details from all over the Northwestern states filled Cincinnati's military prisons with hundreds of prisoners awaiting trial on a variety of charges, including desertion, participation in the Dayton riots, spying, carrying rebel mails, and violations of General Orders 38. Daniel Read Larned, one of Burnside's young aides-de-camp, assisted the general on intelligence matters and accompanied the general on visits to Kemper Barracks, a military prison. He wrote about his work in his diary, noting that the general personally interrogated prisoners of "all classes, conditions, and sexes." Some prisoners "wilted in about two seconds; others were so humble and craven that it was pitiable to see them cower before him."[123] Larned asked his sister to send him his civilian clothes, as he was in need of them daily, adding cryptically that "there are many instances when I am called on duty that requires citizens clothes." Burnside felt himself plagued by violently pro-rebel women in his department, especially Kentucky women, many of whom participated in the smuggling of rebel mail and contraband goods. He asked the War Department for permission to deport them to the South.[124] "The General says he can send me to see them because he knows I will not insult them, even if I do get mad," wrote Larned.[125]

Larned also sat in on meetings with spies. Writing in his diary, Larned described the "most interesting hour I have spent in a long time" in discussion with "detectives from Rosecrans['s] army, from our own Department and from New York." He was fascinated by "how they manage" and marveled at the "secrets they can reveal." He reflected on the ungentlemanly nature of espionage work:

> Their life is a strange one, and one they would abhor in ordinary times but they feel (and perhaps not unjustly) that the times demand any sacrifice of principle for the furtherance of our cause. They are doing us an immense amount of good, in giving us information of what is going on in our midst and forewarning us of suspected persons, so that when they "*call* to shake hands with the General" he knows how to receive them.[126]

Larned's journal entry provides a revealing glimpse into intelligence operations at departmental headquarters in Cincinnati. The "detectives from Rosecrans['s] army" were probably agents in the employ of "Colonel" Truesdail of the Department of the Cumberland Army Police. In late April, Truesdail reported to Rosecrans that his spies had discovered the "existence of a League, for the overthrow of the Union—which is of Southern Origin and growth and which is now spreading over the north." It was a "most dangerous enemy" and required "close attention." He had, he reported, sent some of his detectives "north to discover as much as possible in regard to it."[127] Two weeks later, Truesdail wrote to Cincinnati post headquarters to report that he had sent a "Capt Palmer" to Louisville to "obtain some important facts pertaining to political secret associations," and to "mingle under disguise" with people in communication with rebels. Palmer was under orders to report "any important discoveries" to Burnside, and he was to go to Saint Louis on similar duty.[128]

Larned's mention of one or more detectives from New York was a reference to an army operation undertaken by Cincinnati post and Ohio district detectives to uncover a scheme by Ohio businessmen trading with the Confederate government for contraband cotton via the Mexican port of Matamoros. Implicated in the scheme was Democratic congressman S. S. Cox of Cincinnati, who had written letters of introduction for constituents to Spanish officials at Havana, Cuba. Military officials in New York assisted in the investigation.[129]

Adjutant Kemper corresponded with a lieutenant of the 115th Ohio Regiment who had been sent to New York City and communicated with a detective who investigated the cotton-trading scheme.[130]

In the spring and summer of 1863, the intelligence operations in the Department of the Ohio were large, multifaceted, and involved numerous commands within the department. They were also expensive. Though records of expenditures for the department are not extant, we have hints as to their size and scope. In early June 1863, Burnside relieved General Hascall of command of the District of Indiana and replaced him with Brigadier General Orlando Bolivar Willcox. As Willcox was from Michigan, Burnside added that state to his district. One of Willcox's first acts after being installed at Indianapolis was to ask for secret-service funds for his new command. No records indicate that either Carrington or Hascall, his predecessors, had received secret-service funds. On arrival in Indianapolis, Willcox asked for $5,000 worth of the funds. A princely sum, Burnside nonetheless wired back that he would send the amount as soon as possible. When the funds failed to arrive promptly, Willcox dunned his commander for the money: "Please hurry forward five thousand dollars secret service fund. agent[s] all awaiting." After continued reminders, the funds arrived in Indianapolis later in the month.[131] Willcox appointed a fellow Michigander, Major George Collins Lyon of the 17th Michigan Volunteer Infantry Regiment, to be his provost marshal for the district and oversee his intelligence program. Lyon had served under Willcox in a similar post in Kentucky and had worked to intercept couriers traveling between Confederate forces and occupied Kentucky and the North. In Indiana, Lyon investigated secret organizations and arms sales to people deemed disloyal to the government. In June, Willcox reported to Burnside that the KGC were "quite extensive and determined" in Indiana.[132] Military arrests and interrogations of persons involved in violent resistance to draft enrollments yielded useful information. Willcox informed his superior that "some prisoners acknowledge that they belong to secret society to resist draft."[133] He badgered Burnside for a new military proclamation restricting the sale of firearms and ammunition. "I have information that the members of secret orders are extensively supplying themselves," he telegraphed.[134] In early July troops arrested arms dealers in Lafayette after investigations growing out of the arrest, trial, and confession of a deserter from Carroll County who had shot dead a man who had tried to arrest him. The investigation implicated the dealers in arming disloyal persons in the area.[135] Lyon undertook other arrests around the state for suspicion of disloyal activities, compiling a list of persons to be arrested.[136] Willcox and Lyon also spent their secret-service funds at Detroit spying on rebel refugees, escaped prisoners-of-war, and secret agents congregated across the Detroit River in Windsor, Canada West.

Events in the summer highlighted suspicious activities in the department and alerted commanders to the importance of intelligence efforts. In June a company of rebel cavalry under the command of Captain Thomas Henry Hines secretly crossed the Ohio River into Indiana and rode northward, the purpose and destination of their mission unclear to both contemporaries and historians. After local legion troops discovered them to be Confederates, Hines and his force raced for the river to escape into Kentucky, with legion forces in close pursuit. Federal troops battled the rebels on a river island, killing and wounding several rebels, while others drowned in attempting to cross. Hines swam across and escaped to safety. General Burnside commented to the War Department that Hines and his cavalry were "conducted by the sympathizers of southern Indiana," adding that "Kentucky is today a more loyal state than either Ohio Indiana or Illinois." In recent weeks rebel spies, recruiters, and mail couriers had become rampant in the Northern states, he wrote, and he asked for authority to impose a "stringent policy" on the Northern states in his command.[137] Weeks later, Morgan's command of twenty-five hundred veteran rebel cavalry captured two steamboats and ferried themselves across the Ohio into Indiana. Legion forces failed to stop their crossing and were brushed aside in a pitched battle at Corydon. Morgan's force rode north and east, burning, pillaging, and stealing horses, food, and trinkets from local peoples. Indiana Legion harassed the rebels throughout their sojourn in Indiana, and federal cavalry doggedly pursued them eastward into Ohio. Many Indiana citizens expressed indignation at the raid, and the large turnout of legion members and volunteers to resist Morgan attested to their anger. But immediately after the raid federal officers who had pursued the raiders reported that Morgan had received willing assistance from some Indiana people en route. Captain J. S. Hobart, who spied on a lodge of the KGC near Indianapolis for Governor Morton, rode in the vanguard of the federal pursuit and claimed that he communicated with local people using KGC signals along the way. His commander, Colonel L. S. Shuler, also reported that Indiana residents assisted the rebels during the raid.[138] In the summer of 1863 commanders in Indianapolis continued to observe with concern the secret meetings of opponents of the government and noted their "extraordinary efforts" to arm themselves to fight the government.[139]

In the spring of 1863 detective operations arose in various commands within the Department of the Ohio in response to the dangerous challenge to government control of the Northwestern states represented by the secret organizations that aided desertion and were arming to fight the federal draft. While commanders employed experienced police detectives like James Ruffin and William Reany to investigate political conspiracy, many of the spies employed by military commanders came from the army units stationed in the department. It is difficult, at the remove of a century and a half and with gaping holes in the surviving documentation, to assess how effective these soldier-detectives were in their employment. However, the evidence is clear that military commanders in the Department of the Ohio were well informed of the secret political organizations that existed in the Old Northwest.

FOUR

An Odious System of Espionage

The Intelligence Network Created by the Enrollment Act, 1863

AN ARMY detective, acting under orders, ventured into the gentle hills of eastern Illinois in the "guise of a Drafted Man and Democrat fleeing from the authorities and seeking concealment and protection." Pretending to be fearful of revealing his fugitive status, he unburdened himself to a small-town hotelkeeper who passed him to other sympathetic persons in the town. They assured him that they would shelter him safely from authorities; indeed, they promised to supply him with firearms with which to resist the "damned Abolitionists." His aiders introduced him to Confederate escapees from Northern prison camps who also found shelter in the neighborhood and vowed to fight with them to shield deserters and draft dodgers. Together with organized and armed bands who stood "ready at a moment's notice," they would "bushwhack" and ambush troops who ventured into the area. The detective slipped away and reported his findings to military commanders.[1]

In addition to military-intelligence operations run by post, district, and department commanders, the Enrollment Act, created to establish a national system of conscription, also created an intelligence-gathering apparatus throughout the North. "Special agents" hired to chase down deserters and draft dodgers provided significant information on organized efforts to obstruct enrollments and the draft, and aid and shelter deserters and draft dodgers throughout the Old Northwest. Together, the two bureaucracies developed an overlapping system to collect information on local resistance efforts and organized movements that threatened to subvert the war effort. As a consequence, both draft administrators and military commanders became well informed of threats and disposed of their often meager military forces accordingly.

The Provost Marshal General's Bureau and Intelligence Gathering

On March 3, 1863, Congress passed an Enrollment Act to provide for a national system of conscription for the U.S. Army. The measure replaced the Militia Act of 1862, which had given the responsibility of administering the draft to the states. While the earlier measure succeeded in raising troops for the army in the fall of 1862, several states struggled to raise their quotas. Therefore, Congress devised a more efficient and comprehensive method to correct deficiencies.[2] Authored by Senator Henry Wilson of Massachusetts, the law provided for a new bureau under the War Department to be under the charge of a provost marshal general. All able-bodied white men between the ages of eighteen and forty-five years (with certain exceptions) were to be enrolled and liable for military service; each state's enrollment and draft apparatus was to be administered by a military officer appointed by the War Department who would be called the acting assistant provost marshal general for that state; provost marshals would be appointed for each congressional district who would report to the state officer; boards of enrollment in each district would oversee the enrollments and medical examination of each man eligible to be drafted. Congress authorized the president to set quotas for each state and district whenever necessary to make a draft. Congress also crafted a system for drafted men to provide substitutes to serve in their place. Drafted men could also pay a commutation fee of $300 to avoid service.

The law gave provost marshals the duty to arrest all deserters wherever they might be found. They were to "detect, seize, and confine spies of the enemy" and turn them over to military authorities. The law specified that any person who assaulted or obstructed an officer, or counseled resistance to the draft in any form, would be subject to "summary arrest" by the provost marshal and delivered to civil authorities for trial. It also criminalized enticement of desertion and harboring of deserters, establishing fines and imprisonment as punishment.[3]

Wilson's original bill enjoined provost marshals to "inquire into . . . all treasonable practices" and to report them to the provost marshal general in the War Department. While the language breezed through the Republican-controlled

Senate with relative ease, Democratic minority representatives in the House voiced grave concerns about it. Charles J. Biddle of Pennsylvania referred the House to the tyrannical War Department orders of August 8, 1862, which authorized arrests for speech deemed to discourage enlistments and reminded his colleagues of Lincoln's September 24, 1862, proclamation suspending the privilege of the writ of habeas corpus, a violation, he said, of the Constitution. As contemplated in the bill, the envisioned apparatus would "cover the whole country with a network of military authority" and would light the "flame of social revolution" among the people of the country provoked into disobedience by it. Most of the debate focused on the vagueness of the term *treasonable practices*. What were they? Why not simply say treason, as defined in the Constitution? Who would decide what treasonable practices were, the provosts? Speeches by Daniel W. Voorhees of Indiana and Clement L. Vallandigham, eloquent antiwar Democrats, raised dark questions about the bill's language and reminded members of the many illegal misdeeds of the Lincoln administration in suppressing speech and arresting political rivals. Only one representative, Robert Mallory, a Union ticket man from Kentucky, brought attention to the other part of the phrase, *inquire into*. He noted that the powers to be given to provost marshals under the bill would make them "a band of informers" who would "invade the privacy of families." The bill would institute an "odious and oppressive . . . system of espionage" like that established in France under Napoleon I and his Bourbon successor. Sensing the growing resistance, Republican sponsors offered to amend the offensive language—"inquire into and report to the provost marshal general . . . treasonable practices"—and replace it with the instruction "detect, seize, and confine spies of the enemy." This text passed out of the House and became law.[4]

Secretary Stanton appointed Colonel James B. Fry to be provost marshal general to head the new bureau. A regular-army officer and West Point graduate, he had served as chief of staff under Major General Don Carlos Buell in the Army of the Ohio and was an efficient administrator. Stanton also selected acting assistant provost marshals general for the various states, choosing regular-army Lieutenant Colonel James Oakes of the 4th U.S. Cavalry Regiment for Illinois, Colonel Conrad Baker of the 1st Indiana Cavalry Regiment for Indiana, and Colonel Edwin A. Parrott of the 1st Ohio Volunteer Infantry Regiment for Ohio. The officers made their headquarters in the state capitals of their commands. District provost marshals appointed by Washington set up their offices in the principal cities and towns of their respective congressional districts. In April the War Department issued regulations based on the new law governing the newly established Provost Marshal General's Bureau.[5]

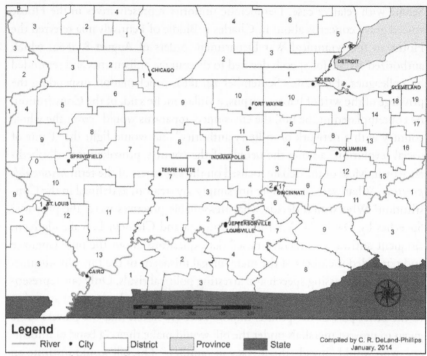

Congressional Districts of the Lower Midwestern States of the Thirty-Eighth Congress, March 4, 1863–March 3, 1865. *Map by C. R. DeLand-Phillips*

Each state provost marshal was to "communicate freely" and share information with governors and other state officials. District provost marshals were to appoint two deputy provost marshals, hire clerical staff, and appoint a board of enrollment to examine the drafted men. Quickly grasping that large western states had expansive districts in some cases stretching hundreds of miles north to south, east to west, encompassing sometimes ten or twelve large counties, in June the War Department revised the regulations and granted a deputy provost marshal to each county.[6]

War Department regulations also established a large force of "special officers or agents for detecting and arresting deserters and spies." Regulations allowed up to four such special agents for each congressional district, "to be employed when necessary." Most district provost marshals maintained the full complement of agents during the war. One district provost marshal, working the 9th Congressional District of western Illinois, requested and received War Department approval for an additional fifteen agents in the summer and autumn of 1863 to round up the multitude of deserters hiding in the area's forests and swamps. For a few months, he had nineteen agents on his books busily scouring the district, but he dismissed the fifteen agents in December and reverted to his regular four.[7]

Agents' pay was set at forty to sixty-five dollars per month. Records indicate that most agents received pay at the higher end of the range. Regulations initially established a five-dollar reward for the arrest of each deserter. The War Department soon raised that amount to ten dollars.[8] Administrators then established a thirty-dollar reward for the arrest of deserters, making civilians eligible to receive it. However, Washington received complaints that rewards had been paid to agents for arrests of persons who proved not to be deserters. Colonel Oakes at Springfield, Illinois, lectured one of his district officers that "men may be found sordid enough to resort to disreputable means to obtain the coveted bounty."[9] In November authorities directed that the thirty-dollar reward for agents was revoked unless the agents relinquished their monthly pay.[10] Agents would either get monthly pay and reimbursement for expenses (but not meals) or work strictly on commission.[11] Months later the district provost marshal at Peoria, Illinois, reflected on the change and pleaded on behalf of his agents. Depriving agents of the reward had "materially decreased" the number of deserters arrested and proved a hardship for the agents in a time of high prices. "The salaries paid to agents are scarcely sufficient for themselves and family to live on." Significantly, the marshal pointed out that agents often bought information on the whereabouts of deserters, "but as they have not the means to pay with, the information of course is not forthcoming, and the deserter goes at large." He concluded that "even *copperheads*, for a trifle, have betrayed the whereabouts of deserters and thus secured their arrest. . . . Money is everything in this business as in most others."[12] The bureau's man in Michigan concurred: "In practice I have no doubt but that information leading to the arrest of a deserter is paid for by the special agent making the arrest."[13]

The agent's work was dangerous, and they typically worked alone to arrest deserters. A district provost marshal in Iowa enjoined one of his men to go armed in his work. When encountering violence during an arrest, the agent should call on citizens for help. But if the resistance was organized, he should call troops for assistance.[14] The provost marshal in Chicago wrote to Springfield headquarters that his agents were "entirely unarmed" and requested revolvers be supplied to his agents and deputies. "My detective agents are making arrests of deserters every day, the deserters presume they are armed, should it transpire that they are not, the consequences might be serious."[15] Agents received orders to be diligent and unflinching in their duties. Another district provost marshal in Iowa ordered an agent to recapture a deserter who escaped, reminding him that he could pursue him into any county of any state in the Union to catch him. He was to "persevere, let him have no abiding place in your heart, *hunt him* as you would a *wild beast*, and *take him dead or alive.* Always remember a deserter is a felon at common law and if one flees *you may shoot them dead*, if they should *otherwise escape*."[16] Apprehending deserters and draft dodgers was a deadly business. In one of many violent incidents, in October 1864, south of Grinnell, Iowa, an armed band of draft dodgers ambushed a deputy provost marshal and an agent on a road and shot them dead.[17] During the war, thirty-eight bureau officials were killed and sixty were wounded doing their duties.[18]

Many agents and county deputy provost marshals devised different methods to find and arrest deserters. One district provost marshal described the work of one of his agents: "While in my employ his duties were those of a Spy and Detective, ascertaining the haunts of deserters and apprehending them."[19] Some agents and deputies concealed their identities as government officers. They were ordered to find out where deserters were hiding and report back to headquarters. Troops would then be sent to apprehend the deserters. Others acted openly and boldly, hiding neither their identities nor their objectives when collaring deserters themselves. District marshals often left the methods of finding deserters to their agents. Good information was the key to success. An Iowa district provost marshal advised a county deputy, "It is to be your special duty to keep perfectly posted on [deserters' whereabouts] in your county. . . . In these duties you must keep well informed. To do this, you must travel over the county frequently."[20] The bureau's deserter branch in Washington collected and distributed information on the whereabouts of deserters to district offices around the country. Agents then received orders to find them. Many agents frequented saloons and public gathering places, picked up loose talk over beer or whisky, or overheard conversations. Others operated in disguise. One deputy in northwestern Illinois wrote, "I start today to play a high game of disguises etc., to capture a desperate character."[21] A district provost marshal described the work of his agents as ungentlemanly, distasteful, and low. "These detectives do most of their business by deception," he sniffed. "The class of men who are engaged in the business of arresting soldiers are not as scrupulous in their manners as some other classes."[22] Many agents faced hindrances from local government officials who were often in sympathy with the deserters. Captured deserters sometimes filed habeas corpus petitions in sympathetic local courts to obtain release, against which the bureau developed elaborate procedures.[23] In one instance local authorities arrested an agent in Fulton County, Illinois, for entering a house to arrest a deserter without a search warrant. The local authorities also insisted that "agents must have attached to their appointments the seal of the United States."[24] Still, amid the friction and conflict in their communities, some provost marshals voiced high praise for the work of the agents. Captain Benjamin F. Westlake in western Illinois described his agents as "men of prudence & energy and devoid of fear."[25]

These special officers, variously called agents, secret agents, detectives, or spies in the records of the bureau, constituted a new "system of espionage" that worked in tandem with the intelligence operations of the military posts and districts in the Northwestern states. In addition to their primary work of chasing down and arresting deserters, as well as arresting rebel spies, agents undertook jobs that others would not do. Agents and county deputies sometimes took over the work of canvassing communities to enroll names for the draft when acts of violence and intimidation drove off the regular enrolling officers. At other times they assisted civil and military government authorities in investigations and intelligence work. In one instance, a downstate Illinois agent arrested a band of counterfeiters and handed them over to federal authorities.[26] Another time, the military commander at Chicago borrowed an agent to investigate a report of gunpowder being smuggled in barrels marked as containing rice. The agent inquired, found the gunpowder, and seized it.[27] In return, military commanders frequently provided troops to provost marshals to assist agents in the arrest of deserters, especially in situations where the deserters were numerous, organized, armed, and poised to resist arrest.

Additionally, the bureau employed other detectives who ranged over the states and investigated various matters. For example, Colonel Oakes at Springfield employed detectives not listed in district employee rosters as special agents. These men were assigned to state headquarters and engaged in investigations of political matters. One such detective was Lieutenant Thomas G. Barnes, a disabled soldier then attached to the Invalid Corps, organized under the Provost Marshal General's Bureau. Oakes described Barnes as a "secret agent" and employed him as a roving detective, checking and double-checking the reports of resistance and dissent received at headquarters. Barnes served as an intermediary with Union League leaders in Illinois who fed Oakes, General Ammen, and Governor Yates with information on the machinations of antigovernment groups. He also accompanied troops dispatched to hot spots around the state.[28]

In scouring their counties and districts to ascertain the whereabouts of deserters, special agents and other detectives provided valuable intelligence about the secret groups that hid, sheltered, fed, and sometimes armed the deserters. One district provost marshal reported that resistance to enrollment took place in Fulton County, Illinois, by persons well supplied with firearms and ammunition. However, he wrote, "I am closely watching these fellows through a Spy in their midst." Another "Secret Spy" in his employ in Brown County, Illinois, provided information on "an organized band" who had "pledged to Resist the Draft and also the further arrest of Deserters."[29] These groups were more than just the immediate family and friends of deserters. Agents found evidence that the secret organizations, which in early 1863 had endeavored to weaken the army by inducing desertion, later actively sheltered and subsisted deserters and draft dodgers. After the passage of the Enrollment Act, armed groups planned organized resistance to the enrollment and the collection of conscripted men. Detectives in the Provost Marshal General's Bureau "inquired into" the various plots to subvert the U.S. government that arose in the Old Northwest as part of a national espionage network.

Illinois

The top Provost Marshal General's Bureau officer in Illinois, the scene of significant draft resistance, was a capable regular-army officer. Lieutenant Colonel James Oakes was a West Point graduate (class of 1846) and Mexican War veteran with long experience in the cavalry. Assigned to command the bureau in Illinois, he took up his post in late May 1863 and worked to become familiar with state conditions. In early June, Colonel Fry at bureau headquarters in Washington sent him a clipping from the *Chicago Tribune* of the previous month. The article, written by "Zeta," a nom de plume of Joseph K. C. Forrest, the sometimes-Springfield man for the *Tribune* who had been the center of controversy during the previous year's state constitutional convention, quoted at length from letters sent to the governor regarding conditions around the state, and concluded that the KGC was the moving force behind the arming of the "copperheads." Fry asked for Oakes's assessment of the article's accuracy.[30] In reply, Oakes produced a long report on conditions in Illinois. His study of records and discussions with knowledgeable people convinced him that a "wide-spread disposition" existed in the state to "oppose and intimidate" federal and state government authorities. In some places the opposition was organized. He cited and quoted reports from the state Union League secretary, whom he believed reliable, who had furnished letters from fellow Union League members about conditions in their communities. In one case, a local Union League chapter had planted a spy in an armed group in Clark County that drilled under the instruction of rebel soldiers.[31] The spy reported that he had heard that the Democrats in the Illinois General Assembly planned to pass a secession ordinance and that they would attempt to seize the state arsenal during the upcoming Democratic state convention in Springfield. Oakes remarked that he did not know if this statement was true, but he verified that the groups had "large quantities of arms & ammunition" at their disposal. He also shared information on the KGC that General Ammen had furnished him. He concluded that "I cannot doubt" that what the *Tribune* stated was true: that "affiliated societies" existed mostly in southern and eastern Illinois "actuated by a common *sentiment* of hostility to the Government, the War, the Enrollment & draft, the arrest of deserters, and to the collection of the Federal Tax." However, Oakes dismissed the danger of an imminent "outbreak, or of *concerted armed* resistance to the State & Federal authorities." Careful steps to avoid irritating the people would maintain the peace. For example, an "ostentatious military demonstration" during the upcoming Democratic state convention would be imprudent. The true policy should be to "let the people see & feel that the government trusts them." Victory in the field would make opposition cease. But if Union forces met with defeats, "the danger of insurrection and civil war in Illinois would be extreme." He thought it best to keep military forces at Saint Louis, Cairo, and Indianapolis on alert in case of uprising at Springfield.[32]

Other military officers in Illinois shared Oakes's understanding of conditions. General Buford, commanding at Cairo, stated that Illinois might experience civil war should the armies in the field meet with defeat. He estimated that one quarter of the population of southern Illinois was disloyal. Intelligence gathered by his officers told him that opponents were smuggling large quantities of arms and gunpowder into the region, "which can only be intended for the rebels, or for use against the Government at home."[33] He shared information with Ammen that he had evidence of a planned uprising in southern Illinois. To counter it, he suggested a joint cavalry raid to capture arms, ammunition, and deserters.[34]

At this time, in early June, the Illinois General Assembly, which had adjourned in February, reconvened in Springfield. Fearing that Democratic legislators would pick up where they had left off and resume efforts to trim the governor's powers, Governor Yates seized on a mistake proffered him by his partisan opponents. Democratic leaders of the state's house of representatives and senate blundered in appointing two different dates on which the legislative session would adjourn. According to the state constitution, in cases of disagreement the governor had the power to appoint the date. Yates thought now was as good a time as any and on June 10 sent a message to the assembly ending the session immediately. Democrats were dumbstruck, claimed the move was unconstitutional and illegal, and at first refused to accept it.

Democratic legislators lingered in the capital for a few days but realized that they had failed and went home grumbling.[35]

Yates's bold move, which enraged Democrats around the state, raised tensions even higher. Ammen made preparations for a "disloyal demonstration" during the state Democratic convention in Springfield planned for June 17.[36] Along with keeping troops at Springfield in their camps under strict orders but available to be called out on five minutes' notice, he hid 150 soldiers "in close confinement" within the state arsenal, to repel any attempt on it.[37]

Amid the uproar over the abruptly closed session, Yates received word that men with whom the governor was "well acquainted" planned to kill him on the eve of the convention. Plotters planned to seize Springfield "while the sitizens [*sic*] are in confusion and uproar."[38] Another informant wrote that Fulton County Democrats had been overheard to say that they were going armed to the convention, hiding revolvers and shotguns in the straw of their wagons.[39] The mayor of Mattoon reported that multiple sources informed him that copperheads planned to provoke a conflict with military forces during the convention, thereby initiating the "movement."[40] Amid these reports, the governor wrote to Secretary Stanton to refuse to raise any troops to serve anywhere but Illinois. Since Burnside's recent effort to suppress the *Chicago Times*—the leading antiwar Democratic newspaper in the state and perhaps the Northwest—Democrats were rampant and "excitement [was] intense."[41] Some of his sources believed, he said, that the Democratic convention was to "inaugurate direct opposition to the Government if not revolution in our midst. Under these circumstances, I do not feel at liberty to promise you troops from Illinois—should the convention prove harmless then Illinois will do her *full share*."[42]

Though speakers tore into Yates for dismissing the legislature and vehemently criticized the war effort of President Lincoln, the convention passed over without a serious clash between troops and attenders and no uprising occurred. But in the following days and weeks events in Illinois were violent and dangerous. Reports of groups of armed mounted men confronting enrollment officers reached bureau headquarters. On July 2 an armed band estimated at from forty to sixty men stopped an enrolling officer and warned him to stop the enrollment in Shelby County. When on the following day the band went to the town of Oconee to seize him and his records, the officer eluded them and hid his papers in another town. Ammen dispatched one hundred troops on a special train to restore order and guard enrolling officers in the county while they completed their rounds.[43] "Secret agent" Lieutenant Barnes accompanied the troops to Oconee and reported to Oakes afterward, concluding, "there is probably no *positive evidence* that these men gathered for any unlawful purposes—and yet there is no *doubt* that their intention was to destroy the enrolling papers."[44]

Reports arrived at Springfield from eastern Illinois indicating the resolve of opponents of the draft to resist it by violence. Edgar County Unionists reported, "We are boldly and openly told that the law of congress cannot and shall not be carried out."[45] From nearby Coles County a man reported that armed men drilled all around the area. Five hundred men drilled near the town of Windsor, hundreds more did the same at Sullivan. War opponents planned a mass drill demonstration at Mattoon. They also rescued deserters from soldiers. Loyal people wanted troops sent to the area "to let us know that we had a government."[46] A captain in the Invalid Corps stationed at Mattoon reported that armed groups massed in the various counties of the region. He estimated them to be two thousand strong each in Coles, Edgar, Clark, and Shelby Counties, and one thousand each in Douglas, Cumberland, Jasper, and Moultrie Counties. They sported regimental and company organization and planned an advertised mass meeting in Mattoon. "They claim," he wrote, "that they are organized to resist the draft." In turn, loyal people in the vicinity gathered arms in town and "secreet [*sic*] them they intend to be here and ready to defend the flag as well as they can."[47] Amid scattered violence in surrounding counties, the meeting in Mattoon of three thousand men—an estimated six hundred of them armed—came off peacefully. Men marched and cheered for Democratic heroes like Vallandigham and New York governor Horatio Seymour, as well as for rebel leaders Jefferson Davis and John Hunt Morgan. An eyewitness reported that a "slight provocation would have ignited and exploded this pent up magazine of highly combustible material."[48]

Events in the 11th Congressional District in southeastern Illinois were likewise dramatic. In July, Oakes received reports that groups seized enrollment records from officers in Fayette, Crawford, and Clark Counties, where armed groups openly paraded and bid defiance to authorities. One evening the commissioner of the enrollment board for the district, with headquarters at Olney, in Richland County, learned that a group of three hundred armed men, mounted and in wagons, were seven miles north of the town, believed to be intent on seizing the draft enrollment records at headquarters. By "preconcerted plan" another force estimated at two hundred was south of town. On receipt of the news, townspeople armed and organized themselves to resist attack. In the meantime, the commissioner gathered up district draft records and escaped on a train to Springfield, where he handed them to Colonel Oakes. A delegation of townspeople went out to the group north of town and brought them to the county courthouse in town for a meeting, after which the armed groups dispersed, averting a battle.[49]

The district provost marshal of the 13th District, Captain Isaac N. Phillips, needed assistance from General Buford to make the enrollment of Williamson County and arrest deserters banded together. Buford considered Williamson "the most disloyal county in the state" and scraped together forces to help Phillips.[50] Ammen sent cavalry to assist him.[51] Affairs quickly got out of hand. In the course of enrolling the county, Phillips seized the Democratic newspaper in Marion, declared martial law, and refused Democratic congressman William "Josh" Allen a pass to leave town without swearing an oath of allegiance. Afterward, Oakes dressed Phillips down for grossly overstepping his authority. Allen's arrest during the previous year had stirred up a hornet's nest, and Oakes did not wish to repeat it. "I do not at all doubt the excellence of your aims & purposes," wrote Oakes, "but the declaration of martial law was nevertheless a very grave error."[52]

Elsewhere in the state, efforts to arrest deserters prompted violent clashes with armed groups. Numerous incidents occurred throughout the state. In July a group of 150 armed and mounted men stopped the Franklin County deputy provost marshal and freed a captured deserter.[53] The deputy marshal in Fulton County reported that deserters had banded together with enrollment resisters and drilled in three places in the county.[54] Unionist farmers had their wheat and hay burned and fruit trees cut down, while arsonists torched a Schuyler County farmer's barn, killing his horses. Men also fired into the house of the county deputy one night while the family slept.[55] In August, at Vandalia, in the 11th District, citizens resisted the arrest of deserters and fired on troops, wounding two. Troops arrested four of the citizens. The next day an armed force estimated at five to seven hundred men gathered and threatened to seize Unionists and hold them hostage for the return of the arrested citizens. The district provost marshal refused to yield to their demands and sent for infantry and cavalry. The crowd dispersed before troops arrived.[56]

In August at Danville, Vermilion County, on the eastern border of the state, tensions between Unionists and antiwar Democrats that had been simmering for weeks over recent local incidents boiled over. A large gunfight and brawl broke out in the town's central square. Along with revolvers, fighters wielded an assortment of knives, slingshots, rocks, and clubs. Several participants died, and more were wounded. One hundred troops dispatched from Lafayette, Indiana, and fifty sent from Springfield arrived after the fight. The senior officer brought citizens together and persuaded participants in the brawl to turn themselves over to law enforcement authorities to answer civil charges.[57]

General Ammen fielded reports of violence and draft enrollment resistance from all over the state. He responded as best he could by dispatching his few troops to all corners of the state to protect enrollment officers and assist provost marshals and agents to arrest deserters. He wrote to Cincinnati headquarters for reinforcements several times in July, stating that troops were needed at Chicago, Springfield, Mattoon, and Carbondale to assist enrollment and deserter-arresting operations, as well as to suppress feared outbreaks in those regions.[58] But Burnside was under War Department orders to forward as many troops as he could to reinforce Rosecrans and Grant; he also was preparing his own offensive into eastern Tennessee. As a consequence, Illinois, Indiana, and Ohio were strapped for troops.

The need for troops at the front did not stop Governor Yates from making urgent requests to Washington for troops to fend off revolutionary plots, enforce the draft, arrest deserters, and restore order generally. He also wished to raise troops to serve in Illinois "to defend the State against invasion, to suppress insurrection, and to aid the Federal authorities in enforcing the laws."[59] To support his requests, Yates cited a statement from Ammen noting that numerous organizations existed in Illinois and drilled under the pretext of self protection. However, he believed that they actually intended to resist the draft. "From the best information," he wrote, "I do not believe the draft can be made peaceably, with less than five good regiments in addition to the small number of troops now in the state."[60] Stanton disappointed Yates by turning down his requests. He deemed it inexpedient to weaken field armies to send troops to Illinois. He acknowledged the difficulties the governor faced and claimed to be not "insensible to the demonstrations made by the enemies of the Government," but military victories in the South would render the demonstrations "harmless." As a consolation, the secretary offered to supply the state militia with arms.[61] However, he soon reneged on that offer.[62] Events showed Stanton's prediction to be wrong. Union victories at Vicksburg and Gettysburg in early July had little immediate effect on the disaffected in Illinois, who continued to actively resist government measures.

The precarious state of affairs in Illinois continued into autumn. In November district provost marshal Captain William M. Fry reported to headquarters that one of his special agents had information that fifty deserters and over two hundred citizens had banded together, resisted arrests, and threatened to fight to the death in Scott County, near Manchester, just thirty miles from Springfield.[63] Authorities sent troops to the area to capture them. Fry soon received information that the "bushwhackers" were "strongly posted on a hill in heavy timbered country" twelve miles east of Manchester. Troops prepared a dawn attack, but learned that the insurgents had discovered their plans and dispersed in all directions. Dividing their troops into three groups, commanders scoured the region but found few men of arms-bearing age. "Whole neighborhoods had gone visiting—so said the women & children." Further efforts to round up the band led to a sharp gun battle in which one civilian man was killed and a soldier wounded. In all, troops took twenty-two deserters and thirteen civilians as prisoners. In his report, based on interrogations of prisoners and information from other sources, the expedition commander drew several conclusions: first, that a large organization existed through central and southern Illinois; that deserters and Confederate recruiting officers drilled it thoroughly, and that the organization possessed a variety of firearms. He stated that the "outbreak" in the area was "premature," but that the armed group expected to receive twenty thousand Enfield rifled muskets within a month, after which they planned an uprising. They sported company-, regiment-, and brigade-level organization, with corresponding officers. "Their leader lives in Chicago," he wrote, with subordinate generals elsewhere around the state. He added a personal opinion that while the organization ostensibly aimed to resist the draft and protect deserters, he had "good reason to believe that the real object is to bring upon the Southern & Central portions of this state, the same system of guerrilla warfare lately prevailing in Mo, Ky & Tenn." Its "head leaders are in the confidence & pay of Jeff Davis."[64] Bureau officers also obtained an affidavit that a rebel soldier served as drillmaster to the "copperheads" of Greene County and initiated deserters and locals into the KGC organization.[65] Information held by commanders at Springfield led them to believe that prominent antiwar Democratic attorney Richard T. Merrick of Chicago, son of a former U.S. senator from Maryland, was the state leader of the organization, and while the prisoners taken in the Manchester expedition were merely small fry, they believed the operation succeeded to "expose some important points of the organization" at the root of the problem.[66]

Throughout the hot summer and into autumn, military authorities in Illinois believed that they had amassed compelling information on the secret organization behind resistance to the draft enrollments. Oakes, Ammen, and Buford all had agents gathering information on affairs in the state. Buford stated that he had "daily evidence" of a plan to resist the administration's war policy in southern Illinois. He believed it large enough to require a "small army" to quell it.[67] Buford's immediate commander, General Alexander Asboth, sent an officer into southern Illinois to investigate secret organizations there. At the end of July he reported that many members of the Democratic

Party in the area were also members of the KGC. It had a regular military structure, and many of its leaders and officers were rebel soldiers who had been released by Buford on taking an oath of allegiance. He pointed to KGC companies in Massac and Pulaski Counties, Illinois, as well as a company on the Kentucky side of the Ohio River, naming the leaders of all three. Along with plotting resistance to the draft, they helped smuggle arms into southern Illinois and contraband goods into the South. He concluded that rank-and-file KGC members hoped that "the North West will unite with the South, or form a seperate [sic] Confederacy."[68]

Illinois army commanders shared these and other reports developed by their secret agents and spies among themselves. They took the threats of revolution from secret organizations seriously and planned accordingly. However, the army's weakness in the state limited its ability to strike at the groups beyond responding to local manifestations of resistance. Intelligence operations in Illinois allowed commanders to stretch their resources and move meager forces from flashpoint to flashpoint in response to local threats.

Indiana

Though Indiana's experience with enrollment resistance was not as severe as Illinois's, incidents of murder and violence required cool leadership from the officer who commanded the draft apparatus. Conrad Baker was that officer. A Pennsylvania-born Evansville attorney and Republican, he commanded the 1st Indiana Cavalry Regiment in action against rebel guerrillas throughout the Ozarks of Missouri and Arkansas. In late April 1863, the War Department assigned Baker to be acting assistant provost marshal general for Indiana. He devoted himself to preparing the new bureaucracy to administer the draft enrollment in the state. As an Indiana resident, he had the advantage of knowing the state and its people. As a prominent Republican, he was trusted by Indiana governor Morton. These attributes aided him in his administration of the draft. In April and May, Baker witnessed the power struggle between Morton and General Burnside over the best methods to employ to combat dissent and the rising threat of resistance to the government. In his subsequent administration of the bureau in Indiana, he collaborated closely with the governor to fashion a policy to control resistance and combat secret organizations.

Baker's tenure in Indiana in command of the bureau began inauspiciously. He inherited a state rife with murderous partisan tension, with Democrats and Republicans both wallowing in the belief that they were victims of illegal actions by the other and that violence was necessary to avenge perceived wrongs. Republicans employed the power of the army to punish their foes. Democrats responded by organizing secretly both to defend themselves and to wrest power from the Republicans. Violence was commonplace in all corners of the state. Clashes resulted from attempts to arrest deserters. In early June one of Baker's first orders was to borrow a company of fifty troops from Brigadier General Hascall to arrest deserters in Sullivan County. Arriving in the county, the soldiers found themselves surrounded by a band of two hundred armed and mounted men. The troops retreated and returned to Indianapolis, having failed in their mission.[69] Baker reported to Colonel Fry in Washington that Sullivan County "contains more disloyal citizens than any other" in the state and was controlled by Democrats who held the upper hand.[70]

Attacks on draft enrollment officers occurred in several counties in the state. Commanders in Indianapolis dispatched troops to Fulton, Johnson, and Montgomery Counties to assist the enrollment. Responding to enrollment resistance by a large band of armed men in Boone County, troops surrounded the village of Whitestown and arrested inhabitants to find the perpetrators.[71] Troops marched into Putnam County in response to a coordinated series of nighttime attacks on enrolling officers by masked horsemen who fired into the house of one of the officers, seriously wounding a boy. Troops arrested several men. In Rush County, men lying in wait in a wheat field next to a road shot dead the deputy provost marshal and wounded an enrolling officer who later died of his wounds. Another enrolling officer accompanying them suffered a nervous breakdown and was committed to the Indiana Hospital for the Insane.[72] Authorities dispatched a large military force to scour the area and arrest the perpetrators, who were believed to be deserters. Several days later men ambushed an enrolling officer along a road in Sullivan County and shot him dead. Baker requested federal judge Caleb B. Smith to reconvene the grand jury to indict people arrested for obstructing enrollments.[73]

The new military commander of the District of Indiana and Michigan, Brigadier General Orlando B. Willcox, wished to wield the iron hand of military authority to bring order to the state. "Sooner or later," he wrote to Burnside, "before the enrollment is completed, armed forces must be employed to crush the opposition."[74] But Baker sided with Governor Morton in pushing a conciliatory policy to avoid collisions between the army and citizens, thereby denying a pretext or provocation for reprisals and uprising. The two were "exceedingly anxious that everything which prudence can dictate shall be done to avoid a conflict, always being careful however not to compromise the authority of the Government."[75] They agreed that the government did not possess sufficient troops in the state to suppress an uprising, and that Union authorities should avoid any provocative actions. Instrumental in implementing Morton's and Baker's conciliatory policy was Brigadier General John Lutz Mansfield of the Indiana Legion, the state's militia force. In the spring and summer of 1863, Morton sent Mansfield to hotspots around the state to investigate difficulties and bring Democrats and Republicans together to air their grievances and reconcile differences. A German-born, university-educated former professor and state legislator, Mansfield possessed the singular gift of conciliating angered and aggrieved peoples. In May, Morton sent him to Switzerland County, on the Ohio River, to investigate the break-in of a local armory and the theft of legion muskets. Mansfield assembled the people and calmed them with a speech calling for unity and forbearance.[76] In early June a large brawl occurred in Williamsport, in Warren County, when a company of twenty-five soldiers of the 33rd Indiana Volunteer Infantry Regiment, visiting on furlough, smashed up a hotel saloon. The situation quickly blew up into an armed confrontation when hundreds of armed Democrats quickly surrounded the town and threatened attack. Morton sent Mansfield to Williamsport, where the general heard everyone's complaints, assembled townspeople of all parties in the courthouse, and gave a "conciliatory" address, assuring them that the governor would protect all persons equally under the law and promising civil trials for civilians and military punishment for soldiers. The assembled crowd gave him three "hearty" cheers after his speech.[77] In the following days and weeks, Mansfield followed troops sent to several counties where draft enrollment resistance occurred and spoke to assembled crowds "representing the views of the Governor."[78]

However much Morton attempted to conciliate a revolutionary-minded Democratic population, tempers continued to flare and threatened to spark unrest. Baker received reports from his district and deputy provost marshals, agents, and informers that detailed the activities of individuals and groups who aimed to subvert government authority. A Knox County man reported that local butternuts were armed and that a secret organization met weekly.[79] Washington County people had rescued a deserter captured by a bureau agent.[80] The deputy provost marshal reported that some Daviess County people declared that they would resist the draft and that they carried concealed weapons. He feared that local legion arms were in danger of being seized unless removed to safety. People cheered for Jeff Davis and Vallandigham, he added, and pickets guarding a KGC meeting place stopped a boy walking down a road who had stumbled on them.[81] Captain Blythe Hynes, the district provost marshal in the 1st Congressional District, in the southwestern corner of the state, had information about groups of deserters who resisted arrest and were aided by citizens.[82] He complained of the difficulties in arresting deserters in the area and reported that nineteen out of twenty men in most counties "act as 'guards'" who "telegraph" the approach of authorities.[83] Hynes also ordered an agent to arrest men who had been in the Confederate service, belonged to the KGC, and corresponded with people in rebel-controlled regions.[84] One informer reported that local KGC members across the Wabash River in Illinois harbored deserters and threatened a local uprising if authorities attempted to arrest them.[85] The provost marshal for the 2nd District reported that men in several counties in his district were purchasing Henry rifles—a new repeater—from New Albany and Louisville dealers.[86] Problems in Johnson County prompted fears of attacks by both Democrats and Republicans. After an incident in which Republican men and boys assaulted a man for wearing a butternut pin, the pin wearer obtained an order from a sympathetic justice of the peace and attempted to serve it on the aggressors. The Republicans resisted, leading to threats from the Democrats to form a posse to accompany the process server. The district provost marshal noted the irony that "it affords dangerous precedent for the friends of the government to resist process."[87]

Officers in northern Indiana districts also reported organized resistance. Northeastern Indiana contained several counties with strongly Democratic populations where resistance was widespread. Thieves stole boxes of government muskets shipped to a northern Indiana Legion company from the Huntington railroad depot; authorities feared the guns were in the hands of the local secret organization that regularly drilled and paraded, armed, on horseback through the town. Captain Calvin Cowgill of the 11th District ordered his Huntington County deputy to investigate the theft and arrest anyone he found with a government musket "unless you know he is 'allright' and can satisfactorily account for his possession" of it.[88] Days later, Cowgill learned that large quantities of gunpowder were being shipped to Huntington. His source was the toll collector on the canal at Toledo, Ohio, "who does not want it known that he gives the information." The "quantities shipped for sometime past have been so large and so frequent compared with the shipments to other points that [the collector's] suspicions have been aroused."[89] He reported that up to three hundred Huntington County men had been drilling regularly for weeks and warned that they planned to apply for arms under the state legion law. The leaders of the groups were "simpathizers [sic] with the rebels" who said they would not be drafted. Reliable men were watching them.[90] Serious difficulties in neighboring Wells County also resulted after two brothers assaulted an enrolling officer. Six men sent to arrest them discovered that thirty armed men guarded the house where they were hiding. Later, "several hundred men and boys congregated" in the area armed with rifles, shotguns, and revolvers and bid defiance to the law. Union men's property had been burned, and residents had been threatened and forced to leave the neighborhood. An enrolling officer found a note posted on a schoolhouse door, signed "KGC," telling him to leave the area.[91] Many residents were afraid to give information or file affidavits for fear of reprisals.[92] Cowgill wrote, "I know that there is an extensive organization in the counties of Wells—Huntington—Grant—Blackford and a portion of Madison to resist the draft. They are making loud threats and annoying Union men by burning their grain-barns, etc. They are all armed and the most reckless and desperate ones amongst them go in squads of 15 to 20."[93]

On receiving such reports, Baker investigated and worked to correct problems. He advised federal authorities that companies nominally organized under the state's legion (militia) law were actually units of the KGC attempting to secure legion arms.[94] On receipt of "reliable information" pointing to further violence against enrollment officers in Rush County, he ordered his officers to stop their work. "It will not do to have another officer killed in Rush Co."[95] Baker also studied interrogation reports and affidavits of the numerous persons arrested by troops dispatched to put down enrollment resistance. After hundreds of troops descended on Monroe County to arrest people who obstructed the enrollment officer in Indian Creek Township, he reported that "some of the parties arrested will I am convinced divulge the entire plot so far as they know it and I think valuable information will be elicited." He especially sought information on the leaders of organized obstruction and resistance: that "class of men . . . who practice law and politics and who seem to endeavor to be always near or upon the penitentiary line without crossing it."[96] Baker shared intelligence received from Cincinnati headquarters with his officers concerning gunpowder shipments to Wayne County dealers and ordered them to investigate.[97] In turn, they furnished him an affidavit from a Delaware County man who had been sworn into the local cell of the KGC, the oaths of which bound him to mutual protection, resisting the draft, and protecting deserters.[98]

In mid-July 1863 a bureau officer in Indiana cooperated with military commanders in an important intelligence operation. Captain James B. Merriwether, the provost marshal of the 2nd Congressional District of Indiana, headquartered at New Albany, an Ohio River town opposite Louisville, communicated startling information to military authorities across the river. George W. L. Bickley, the notorious founder of the Knights of the Golden Circle, was in New Albany, "direct from Richmond," Virginia. Bickley, the shadowy physician who had founded the KGC in the 1850s, had built up the membership of the secret society in Southern states before the war and had planned filibustering expeditions in Mexico and several Central American countries. He had generally been out of the public eye since the beginning of the war. His appearance in New Albany, Indiana, therefore, was alarming and raised questions among military officers well aware of the KGC and its activities in Indiana and neighboring states. A suspicious Merriwether asked for instructions from Brigadier General Jeremiah T. Boyle, the commander at Louisville. "Shall I arrest him?" he telegraphed.[99] Boyle immediately alerted Burnside at headquarters in Cincinnati. Burnside already had been warned of Bickley's movements by Major General Rosecrans of the Department of the Cumberland. A week previous, Rosecrans's provost marshal general, Captain William Wiles, had written to Burnside on Rosecrans's orders to apprise him of the movements of Bickley "and lady who represent themselves as direct from Richmond." Rosecrans had given the Southern travelers a travel pass to Cincinnati, but had his detectives follow their movements. Wiles wisely ordered the military conductor of the train from Nashville to Louisville "to watch him when he stops at Louisville and that he take route without delay to Cincinnati."[100] The captain also warned Burnside, "We fear they are not right."[101] Merriwether arrested Bickley and his female companion and handed them over to Boyle for safekeeping.[102] Military authorities searched the couple's luggage and their persons and found a significant amount of KGC papers and paraphernalia, including codes, as well as a rebel surgeon's commission.[103] Officers initially planned to try him by military commission at Cincinnati as a spy, but Secretary of War Stanton ordered the prisoner sent to the Ohio State Penitentiary at Columbus, the highly secure prison where prominent military prisoners received special attention.[104] Later, in 1864, the War Department ordered Bickley sent under guard to Fort Lafayette, in New York harbor, and later to Fort Warren, in Boston harbor, where he languished for the rest of the war without charge or effort to initiate a trial of any sort.

Baker and his officers collected significant information on organized resistance to the draft and the arrest of deserters in Indiana during the first months of the bureau's administration of the draft. But beyond responding to individual and local manifestations of resistance, Baker and his colleagues took no significant steps to rein in the problem. Like in Illinois, Morton and the military commanders did not have sufficient power to bring to bear on the conspirators in the state. Instead, authorities worked to conciliate the disaffected population in an effort to avoid revolutionary upheaval.

Ohio

As elsewhere, draft resistance in Ohio presented serious challenges to state and federal authorities. Officers appointed to administer the conscription system worked hard to combat violence, using the resources afforded them by the Enrollment Act. Edwin A. Parrott was an experienced soldier, man of business, and politician when Stanton appointed him to be acting assistant provost marshal general for Ohio. A Dayton native and graduate of Ohio Wesleyan College, he studied at the Harvard Law School and practiced as an attorney before going into the family linseed oil business. An antislavery Republican in the state's house of representatives at the beginning of the war, Governor Dennison immediately sent him to the relief of Washington, DC, in command of the first two thousand Ohio volunteers.[105] Appointed colonel of the 1st Ohio Volunteer Infantry Regiment, he commanded a brigade in the Army of the Ohio and the Army of the Cumberland and saw action in the field.

Like other newly appointed state provost marshals, Parrott quickly organized his administrative resources and prepared for the draft enrollment. Resistance to the draft and the arrest of deserters were prominent concerns from the outset. Governor David Tod received reports from around the state of plots to resist the enrollment. The former president of Kenyon College, in Knox County, wrote, "Almost all the male population are armed & united to protect the deserters & resist conscription."[106] A Pike County man warned the governor that a secret, oath-bound, armed organization existed in his county to resist the laws.[107] A Licking County man wrote that men openly avowed their plans to resist the enrollment and had made "fortifications & secret retreats," though since the Noble County incident of March (see chapter 3), "they have been more secret in their plans."[108]

Parrott's district officers also reported evidence of planned resistance around the state. His man in the 5th District, at Lima, in northwestern Ohio, reported that he had information of the "existance [*sic*] of four or five seperate [*sic*] and extensive organizations" in the counties of his district; these organizations expressed their intent to resist the enrollment of the draft. He wanted to have a military force on hand to prevent disturbances.[109] Others reported similar concerns in their districts. Captain B. F. Cory in the 11th District, in the southernmost part of the state, reported the existence of the KGC there and suggested that detectives be sent to "obtain particulars" about it.[110] Captain William Shunk at Mansfield in north-central Ohio reported resistance to the enrollment in Morrow County and that a "new formidable combination" was at work, the leader of which publicly justified the conduct of those who shot at an enrolling officer. Shunk asked whether he should arrest him.[111]

Anticipating their concerns, Parrott wrote to Washington to inquire about the use of detectives and his authority to make arrests for disloyal actions and speech.[112] Colonel Fry reminded him that the Enrollment Act did not provide authority to make arrests for disloyalty except under the section of the law pertaining to the apprehension of spies. He approved of Parrott's intention to forward information of disloyalty to Department of the Ohio headquarters for action.[113] Parrott instructed his district provost marshals to hire their quota of special agents and keep watch on secret groups around the state.[114] His district men reported that their "spies" were discovering the whereabouts of deserters and their deputies were arresting them.[115] He wrote to Captain James L. Drake of the 14th District, in northeastern Ohio, to have an agent watch the organization that Drake had reported was operating in his district. The agent "must work himself into [the] company and explore it. Have affidavits made of overt acts and send to this office."[116] He also instructed his officers to examine intercepted U.S. mails.[117]

Parrott soon reported to headquarters in Washington that resistance to the enrollment had occurred in several Ohio counties, much of it around Mansfield. Armed men had assaulted an enrolling officer in Holmes County on June 5. A deputy provost marshal aided by four citizens arrested the assaulters, but a group of seventy armed men surrounded and "violently rescued" them.[118] As well, an officer in Crawford County had been mobbed and incidents had occurred in Knox County. To remedy problems in that region, commanders stationed 150 troops at Mansfield to be dispatched promptly to quell violence and unrest.[119]

Holmes County soon became the focal point of concern.[120] Drake reported that several hundred men in Holmes County were busy fortifying themselves in "a speck of opposition," clearly intent on resisting the enrollment. He requested that Parrott send two companies of troops to lead them in an assault "over their works [fortifications]."[121] The "insurgents" numbered between six and nine hundred armed men and were not entrenched, but planned to "bushwhack." Relishing the thought of a bloody encounter, he thought that a force of about five hundred troops "would teach them a salutary lesson." He also revealed that he had a spy in the insurgent camp who supplied him with information.[122] Parrott notified military commanders in Mansfield, Columbus, and Cincinnati, who sent a cobbled-together force of infantry and artillery totaling roughly four hundred troops under the command of Colonel William Wallace of the 15th Ohio Volunteer Infantry Regiment. Wallace carried with him a proclamation to the "assemblage in arms" from Governor Tod. His orders were to give the proclamation to the insurgents with a warning to disperse at once and neither interfere with the enrollment nor hinder arrests. "Should you be compelled to use force to carry out your instructions, act promptly and with energy."[123] Arriving by train a day's march from the scene of anticipated action, Wallace's men advanced on the fortified positions in a three-columned pincer movement. His troops skirmished with armed men and charged with a yell, bayonets fixed. The insurgents scattered in flight. The troops arrested several of the resisters and captured the small artillery piece they wielded. A parlay occurred in which Wallace and Drake spoke to local Democratic leaders, including Democratic former U.S. representative Daniel P. Leadbetter, who agreed to try to persuade the armed men to give up both the deserters who had been rescued and the rescuers. After a day of unsuccessful negotiations with the men in arms, Leadbetter informed officers that "they could not reach the rescuers . . . and that we [the troops] would have to take them." Wallace left a company of troops with Drake with which to round up deserters and the rescuers and departed with his main force.[124] The situation died down. Parrott followed up the military expedition with requests to district officers to determine if a Mansfield arms dealer had supplied firearms to the insurgents.[125]

While the Holmes County rebellion collapsed quickly in the face of overwhelming military force, resistance continued throughout the district and state. Detectives sent into Ohio communities reported that hostility to the government continued. They were alert to the existence of secret organizations. One "secret detective," a soldier in "citizen's suit" ordered to Jackson County, in southern Ohio, reported that while resistance to the draft was threatened generally, and enrollment officers had been threatened with violence, he could detect neither any secret organization in the county nor any military preparations to resist the government. However, the same day the soldier-detective sent a follow-up report. He had new information that local businessmen had smuggled arms into the area in clothing boxes and had ordered four hundred small arms (pistols or revolvers) from Cincinnati dealers, so many that dealers had difficulty in quickly filling the order. The opponents of the government were meeting secretly and buying gunpowder, he added.[126]

Slowly and after great effort, in the face of resistance all around the state, officers completed the enrollments and bureau officials prepared to make the draft. At this time the state was thrown into panic by the invasion of John Hunt Morgan's force of Confederate cavalry. Having exited Indiana in haste on July 13, Morgan's cavalry division dashed across Ohio, skirting Cincinnati and skirmishing its way eastward and then northward parallel to the Ohio River, pursued by federal cavalry and shadowed by gunboats. Heavy rains in West Virginia raised the river, permitting gunboats to steam far upstream. Exhausted and depleted, with only a fraction of his original force of nearly twenty-five hundred cavalry troopers remaining, Morgan surrendered to Union forces on July 26 in northeastern Ohio, near the Pennsylvania border.[127] While most Ohio people turned out against the invaders, military and civilian authorities arrested a number of Ohio residents and indicted them in federal court for acting as willing guides for Morgan's forces.[128]

Amid the panic created by Morgan's raid, bureau officials prepared for the draft. Parrott was concerned about continued resistance. He sent orders to his district provost marshals to "set your detective[s] at work to ascertain if there is any purpose to create disturbance at time of draft." He enjoined them to "quietly take measures" in coordination with military commanders to meet any contingency. They were also to hide their draft records away from their offices as a precaution against attacks.[129] He informed Drake, in the 14th District, that he had information of a "conspiracy afoot" in the district to prevent the draft and asked for information.[130] Drake replied that three days before he had received information that "hellish mischief" was planned. But he did not credit any of it. "I have not forgotten," he wrote, "that I was a disbeliever in the reports that came to me from day to day that there was to be trouble in Holmes Co.—it came, it saw, it fizzled." Still, though an unbeliever in conspiracy plots, he quietly made preparations "to check any ordinary attempt at mischief."[131] Other officers reported undercurrents in their jurisdictions. The Darke County deputy reported that a document circulated through the community binding signers to stand by each other in resistance to the draft. His information came "through the revelations made by a young copperhead to a young female acquaintance in [Greenville] yesterday, but although well pumped he would not give any names."[132] Captain Daniel S. Brown in northwestern Ohio submitted that he had "positive information from several sources" that a large organization "of quite a number of persons" existed in two townships in Auglaize County intent on resisting the draft. Opponents of the draft had recently met to denounce the draft and pledge resistance collectively.[133]

Apart from his district agents, Parrott possessed his own sources whose reports confirmed the information received from around the state. He reported to Fry that "a regular organization exists" in several districts in Ohio and would act to prevent the draft "if it deems itself sufficiently strong." "I am constantly apprised of its movements through a detective," he wrote. "When sufficient evidence is accumulated I purpose to arrest the leaders, some of whom hold high political places." In the districts of southwestern Ohio, "slight evidences of designed mischief" existed, "but matters there are not sufficiently developed to show to what extent we ought to be apprehensive." He ordered his district marshals "to get all the information possible by means of their detectives of a purpose to oppose the draft." He also contacted Governor Tod to arm militia companies in Toledo and Cleveland to prevent outbreak where Irish immigrants were victims of misrepresentations about the draft. Elsewhere, he concluded, "I have no reason to apprehend trouble in any other parts of the State."[134]

Parrott supplied information furnished by his sources to his district marshals. In one case, he sent a letter he had received from a Delaware County resident about the existence of a secret organization intent on resisting the draft; he also alerted state military headquarters to the problem and asked that a detective be sent there to investigate.[135] In another instance, he shared information that an organization with one thousand armed members intent on resisting the draft existed in Knox County. He ordered the district marshal to "report the result of your investigation" and to "seize all government arms" in private hands he could find.[136] As the day of the draft approached, Parrott wrote to military headquarters that he had evidence of an organization in Butler County, north of Cincinnati, that planned to resist the draft. He requested that commanders shift troops from Dayton to the county in advance of the draft.[137] Reports continued to arrive from district and county officers that "something extraordinary is in [sic] foot." One deputy reported that the "butternuts" were arming themselves and firing themselves up with speeches about self-defense, civil liberties, and threats to the sanctity of the home. Troops would be needed to accompany marshals in serving draft notices, he wrote.[138]

The draft occurred without significant resistance, thanks to careful preparations. As during the enrollment, commanders positioned troops at central points in disaffected areas to be ready to put down violent resistance should it occur.[139] Armed groups of Union supporters also assisted in some areas to capture drafted men who refused to report, as well as to intimidate resisters.[140] Intelligence operations provided the information that both bureau and military commanders required to anticipate resistance and forestall widespread unrest.

Amid the tensions derived from strenuous opposition to the draft in Ohio, extraordinary political developments played out in Ohio. Following his military-commission trial in Cincinnati, military commanders carried dissident Clement Vallandigham through the front lines in Tennessee under a flag of truce and handed him over to Confederate troops. Conveyed eastward through rebel-held territory to the Atlantic Coast, the erstwhile congressman boarded a fast blockade runner at Wilmington, North Carolina, that could outsail U.S. Navy patrol ships. He traveled to Bermuda and thence to Halifax, Nova Scotia, in Canada East, a colonial possession of Great Britain. After a slow westward procession, received enthusiastically by many pro-South Britons and Canadians along his route, he took up residence in a hotel at Niagara, near the falls. Leading antiwar Democrats like Daniel W. Voorhees of Indiana and Richard T. Merrick of Illinois paid him calls. Ohio Democrat George E. Pugh, former U.S. senator and Vallandigham's defense counsel in his military trial and habeas corpus hearing, also visited him.[141] On the strength of his notoriety for being arrested and tried by military authorities and exiled as a victim of Lincoln's dictatorial tyranny, Ohio Democrats nominated Vallandigham to be their gubernatorial candidate in the fall election. Pugh received the nomination for lieutenant governor, and, in Vallandigham's absence, conducted the campaign.

In August, while Vallandigham was at Niagara Falls, the district provost marshal for the 5th District, Captain Brown, reported to Parrott that one of his "secret agents" had overheard Pugh in "public conversation" outside a hotel in Van Wert County. Franklin Collins of Wapakoneta, whom Brown employed to investigate the existence of the secret organization in the district,[142] on the morning of August 8 overheard Pugh say that "he (GE Pugh) had counseled and was now counseling CL Vallandigham to return to Ohio to visit his family and friends[,] address his constituency and that he (Pugh) would guarantee to him (Vallandigham) the uprising and armed protection of the people of Ohio in so doing." Brown assured his superior of the accuracy of the report: "you can rely upon the above statement as being perfectly correct."[143] Parrott sent the information immediately to General Cox at military district headquarters. Cox in turn promptly forwarded it to department headquarters.[144]

Events in the coming days and weeks would show that U.S. Army authorities were gravely concerned that Vallandigham would descend on Ohio to defy the government and inaugurate a general uprising. Thereafter, the army employed its growing espionage capacity to keep close watch on the exile to prevent such a revolution. In the summer and early autumn of 1863, large organized bodies of armed men had confronted enrollment officers and draft officials throughout the Old Northwest. Violence had occurred in numerous places as large armed bands challenged government officials carrying out their duties, killing some and wounding others. The extensive intelligence resources of the Provost Marshal General's Bureau in the Northwestern states afforded by the Enrollment Act joined those of military commanders to watch and listen for signs of domestic danger. Together they found plenty of evidence of organized opposition. The "network of military authority" and espionage that congressional Democrats had feared had come to fruition.

FIVE

Watching "Mr. Jones"

Army Surveillance of Clement L. Vallandigham, the Ohio Gubernatorial
Election of 1863, and Plots to Release Confederate POWs in the Fall of 1863

IN THE late summer and autumn of 1863, the intelligence operations of both the military commands and the Provost Marshal General's Bureau in the states of the Old Northwest matured sufficiently to provide important information of plans to attack prisoner-of-war camps in the region. Officers used the information to arrest plotters, reinforce garrisons, and brace for uprisings and invasion. Spies and informants also provided information on the rise of the successor organization to the Knights of the Golden Circle, the Order of American Knights. Commanders quietly shared information among themselves in efforts to prepare for insurrection.

Detectives in Detroit

"C L Vallandigham is at Windsor opposite this place," Lieutenant Colonel Joseph R. Smith, military commander at the post of Detroit, Michigan, wired on August 27, 1863. "The impression is he will cross into Michigan[.] If so shall he be arrest[ed] and where sent[?]"[1]

Vallandigham had left Niagara days before and taken a train to the small town of Windsor, Canada West, separated from Detroit only by the Detroit

River. Had Smith read the Democratic newspaper in that city he would have had warning of the notorious Ohioan's arrival. More than a week before his arrival the *Detroit Free Press* reported that Vallandigham was planning a trip to Quebec and then would go to Windsor, "where he will probably remain some time."[2] The exile arrived at the Windsor train station, accompanied by his wife and son, at seven o'clock in the evening of August 24 and took rooms at Hirons House, a hotel in the town. The *Free Press* reported the event in its edition of the following day and the next day observed that he received numerous visitors and delegations and warned the assembled crowd that when Americans are denied access to the ballot, the "right of revolution begins—not the right only, but the sacred duty. Give us a free ballot and we want no more!"[3]

Smith, a graduate of West Point (class of 1823) and longtime regular-army officer, veteran of the Seminole Wars and badly wounded in the Mexican War, was caught unaware of the Ohio politician's arrival opposite Detroit, which was a post in the Department of the Ohio. He was preoccupied with superintending the organization of new Michigan volunteer units. Departmental staff officers at Cincinnati were not so dilatory and promptly relayed Major General Ambrose E. Burnside's order that if Vallandigham crossed into Michigan he was to be arrested and immediately sent under a strong guard to Fort Warren, in Boston harbor.[4] Brigadier General Orlando B. Willcox, commander of the District of Indiana and Michigan, hence Smith's superior officer, wired that Vallandigham "must not be allowed to cross into Michigan." Should he attempt it, Smith was to warn him that he would be arrested and sent by steamboat to the prisoner-of-war camp near Sandusky, Ohio, Johnson's Island. Willcox asked if the sole naval presence on the Great Lakes, the U.S. steamer *Michigan,* was nearby. If so, he was to ask its commander for cooperation.[5] Smith replied that Detroit was quiet. "I will telegraph should anything occur of a riotous character."[6]

Indeed, military commanders at Detroit feared riot and uprising. Evidence of disquiet in and around Detroit worried army officer-observers. In previous weeks district and deputy provost marshals in the area reported that government opponents had voiced plans to resist the draft and local leaders had gone to New York City to buy arms for a secret "League" that existed in the area. Officers instructed their detectives to watch for the arrival of boxes of weapons, seize them, and arrest the persons asking at the railroad depots for them.[7] Officers were especially worried because Detroit, then a city of forty thousand inhabitants, was patrolled by only one company of men, a total of eighty troops. More troops were needed to guard against riot and violence, "which it is believed are in contemplation by certain disaffected citizens of the city."[8] The specter of the New York City draft riots of July, when hundreds were killed and wounded in wild street fighting, lingered in officers' minds.[9] The acting assistant provost marshal general for Michigan, Lieutenant Colonel Bennett H. Hill, an experienced regular-army officer, noted that the single company of provost guards, a handful of partially disabled men of the Invalid Corps, and some recruits were all he had to call on to quell violence. In addition, a federal arsenal at Dearborn holding over fifty thousand stands of military arms had only a small guard to protect it. There was no doubt in his mind of the existence of a "bitter opposition" to the government in Detroit and other parts of Michigan. During the New York riots he believed that should the riots not be quelled summarily, "the attempt to execute a draft here will lead to similar violence unless supported by strong military force."[10] Indeed, troops had already prevented a "demonstration" on the Dearborn Arsenal, but now those troops, the Michigan Sharpshooters Regiment, had been sent away to guard prisoners at Camp Douglas, in Chicago, and Detroit and the Dearborn Arsenal were exposed to the mercies of the "strong disloyal element."[11] In addition, the presence of over a thousand escaped rebel prisoners of war and refugees congregated at Windsor, along with hundreds of deserters and draft dodgers, who swelled the village's population to twice its usual size, loomed as an additional threat to the safety of the frontier city.

In response to Detroit's and the arsenal's exposed conditions, along with the arrival of Vallandigham at Windsor, Indianapolis headquarters sent the 116th Indiana Volunteer Infantry Regiment, a newly organized six-months regiment, to guard Detroit and Dearborn. There they quickly inaugurated an inauspicious record of theft, violence, and disorder that led to their prompt removal in disgrace.[12] Smith reported to Willcox that the Ohioan was still at Windsor and he was "taking every precaution" to arrest him should he try to cross, with troops ordered to act at a moment's notice. Smith also consulted with state officials and Michigan's Republican U.S. senator Zachariah Chandler, and requested that the sharpshooter regiment be recalled to guard the city.[13] He wired to the commander of the USS *Michigan*, then calling at Erie, Pennsylvania, to request that the ship steam to Detroit immediately in the interests of "important public business."[14] He also kept his ears open for rumors and reports circulating about Vallandigham's plans. Rebel "sympathizers have said Vallandigham would go in a few days to Ohio," he telegraphed, "shall relax no vigilance."[15]

In the place of a strong military presence to guard the border and protect the city, Smith employed detectives to learn the plans of the rebels and their sympathizers congregated in Canada. Commanders at Detroit immediately dispatched men to watch Vallandigham while he sojourned across the river. One spy, John Macafee, hired by the district provost marshal for Detroit, immediately began to watch Vallandigham and his movements. With easy access to Hirons House, he reported on the persons with whom the Ohio man met at the hotel and around the town. He filed a report of his surveillance during the first month of the exile's residence in Windsor, identifying Vallandigham as "Mr. Jones." Macafee's report showed that Vallandigham spent much of his time with Confederate military officers and "Secesh sympathizers" whom military authorities distrusted. The spy also reported conversations with one of Vallandigham's visitors who commented that he would "certainly" attempt to return to his home state before the October election, and that any attempt to arrest him "will ensure his Election."[16]

As the days passed and Vallandigham made no attempt to cross into the United States, military authorities began to systematically watch and investigate the rebel refugees, escaped soldiers, and others with whom he associated. To do so, commanders established a Military Police and U.S. Detective unit at Detroit. General Willcox appointed a young civilian clerk in the mustering and disbursing office, George S. Goodale, to serve part-time as the chief of the unit. When not working for the government, Goodale spent his free time serving as the theater critic for the *Detroit Advertiser and Tribune,* the city's Republican newspaper.[17] He assisted commanders to coordinate surveillance efforts of several detectives hired or borrowed from other army posts to watch the rebels in Windsor. Payroll records indicate that Detroit military commanders paid half a dozen men for detective work at this time.[18] Goodale corresponded with commanders at Louisville, Kentucky, to inquire after some of the rebels with whom Vallandigham mixed. Sometimes these rebels crossed the river to Detroit, and authorities wanted to catch them. A Louisville officer replied that "Cols Rodman, Steele, Smalley and Capt Richardson are confederate officers who have escaped to Canada, and should be arrested and treated as prisoners of war."[19] In addition, Smith contacted other command posts to gather information about the rebels across the way. He wrote to the provost marshal at Cincinnati about Smalley, formerly of Covington, Kentucky, who had requested an appointment to speak with him.[20] He alerted the district provost marshal at Cleveland to watch for John Hull, one of the men who met frequently with Vallandigham, who was believed to have gone to that city to buy arms and make arrangements for the Ohioan's return. "A steamer is said to be chartered," he wrote. "Have the movements of Hull watched. Call on Senator Chandler who is now in Cleveland who will point [out] Hull. Inform me immediately. Expenses will be paid by me."[21] In addition, Goodale wrote directly to Secretary Stanton to request authority to intercept and open U.S. mail directed to "desperate characters" in Windsor whose threats to set the city aflame worried officials. He added that he had "two or three detectives here for a month or two watching Vallandigham."[22]

One of the important detectives then at work at Detroit and Windsor was D. C. Gile, who was on loan from Louisville post headquarters via Major G. Collins Lyon, the provost marshal of the District of Indiana and Michigan. Gile, whose alias was Gilmore (who Macafee reported was also staying at Hirons House), watched Vallandigham closely at Windsor. He also reported to Louisville about rebels who sometimes crossed the river and made themselves vulnerable to arrest.[23] Gile was effective and productive, prompting Smith to try to supplant Goodale, who was only working as a part-time spy master. Gile, he wrote, "can give his whole time to the Military Police."[24]

In early September, Smith's detectives circulating in Windsor and elsewhere reported that they heard inklings of a plan for Vallandigham to return to Ohio. Smith telegraphed Willcox to report that "we think" that on September 12, Vallandigham would attempt to cross from Windsor with a chartered steamer and arms procured for the purpose. He did not know if they planned to cross to Michigan or head straight for Ohio. "Leading sympathizers have been heard to say that the 'dance will open on the 15th,'" he added. "We shall be watchful as possible, at this point."[25] Willcox forwarded Smith's message to Cincinnati, adding his own guess: "Dayton is the point I suppose at which he would aim."[26] Indeed, George E. Pugh's visit to Windsor prompted an anxious Willcox to travel to Detroit to be on hand should Vallandigham attempt a crossing. He wired Cox at Cincinnati to "look out for their turning up somewhere in Ohio."[27] In turn, Cox instructed General Mason at Columbus to confer with Governor Tod and Colonel Parrott, and asked that Parrott's district provost marshals along the Lake Erie coastline be "carefully instructed to be very watchful and forward any information they may get." He added that "the rumor is not very likely to have foundation," but if Vallandigham should try to return he would be arrested and trundled off to Fort Warren.[28] Pugh's departure from Windsor (accompanied by his wife, along with Vallandigham's wife and son) for Ohio on the fourteenth and Vallandigham's own travels eastward in Canada on the same day were closely watched. Smith reported, "Mr Vallandigham has gone from Windsor by Great Western Railroad to some point which I shall probably learn before long and will report."[29] The candidate made no attempt to cross.

Smith soon reported that the rebels in Windsor and other cities and towns in Canada "design to capture the USS Michigan near" Detroit. He added, however, that the warship's commander knew of the plan, was prepared for it, and hoped they would make the attempt. He also reported that "treasonable organizations are forming in Ohio" and that "Vallandigham has mentioned Toledo and Cleveland," Lake Erie port cities, as places "where he would be favorably received."[30] As the Ohio election neared, Smith asked General Cox for orders. "In case Vallandigham should be elected tomorrow, what instructions am I to receive with regard to his return to Ohio?" he telegraphed. "Rumor states, that steamers are to be sent from Ohio to conduct him to some port in that state." He suggested that the commander of the *Michigan* be requested to cruise in Lake Erie and pay visits to the Ohio ports of Cleveland, Sandusky, and Toledo.[31] However, Vallandigham's crushing defeat in the gubernatorial election by railroad executive and War-Democrat-turned-Republican John Brough the following day obviated the concern. Ohio's voters rejected the exile in overwhelming numbers. Ohio soldiers in the field, whose ballots were collected and sent home to be counted, added thousands more to the Union coalition candidate's totals. Brough bested Vallandigham by one hundred thousand ballots.[32] The Democrat's political threat dissolved overnight. Nonetheless, intent on keeping him in exile, in the coming weeks and months military authorities at Detroit continued to keep a close watch on Vallandigham while he resided at Windsor and conferred with rebels. Detectives hired by the army circulated in the saloons and lounges where rebels congregated and listened carefully to hear their hushed conversations. Detroit and Windsor would continue to be a center for intelligence operations for the remainder of the war.

Meanwhile, before the October election in Ohio, military authorities in their efforts to prevent an uprising in the state continued to watch vigilantly for Vallandigham's return. Cox reported to Burnside, who had departed on his long-delayed expedition to liberate eastern Tennessee, that all was quiet in Ohio. "The disloyal men have seemed desirous of a collision," he wrote, "but no considerable disturbance has occurred." He shared Willcox's information that Vallandigham would attempt a return. "His friends threaten an uprising to meet him, but I doubt their nerve."[33] He received reports from the officer commanding the small force retained at Dayton following the riots in May that Vallandigham's supporters among the city's political leadership, who were believed to be secret-society members, continued to make threatening noises. He advised the commander to be cautious and make no aggressive move that the civil authorities could use as a pretext. "I have seriously thought of withdrawing [the force] from Dayton entirely, but this is so strongly opposed by the Union people there," that it would remain there.[34] Forbearance was the rule. Commanders ignored the wearing of KGC badges as mere provocations.[35] Cox denied a request for troops to be sent to Lebanon to quell unrest at a local political rally, as "the appearance of soldiers would give the enemies of the government occasion for an outcry which we do not wish to incur on account of any small danger." He advised that "loyal men should scrupulously avoid interference or provocation."[36] The heated partisan atmosphere in Ohio could easily erupt into violence. Alluding to Burnside's heavyhanded and counterproductive tactics of the spring, he confided to his counterpart in West Virginia that "the political strife which has grown out of the attempt to apply severe measures to quasi-rebels here, has warned us that no economy of force will be gained in Ohio by summary interference with citizens by military power, since the cry of invasion of personal liberty etc. raised by demagogues aids the rebels more than we hurt them by our arrest of their friends."[37]

As senior commander in Ohio in Burnside's absence, Cox employed his intelligence resources to collect information on movements in the state that could threaten unrest. His detectives kept a watchful eye on leaders of the opposition who were secretly active in subversive efforts. Detectives of the Provost Marshal General's Bureau in Ohio reported that arms were coming into the state. One district provost marshal reported that three dozen pistols had been shipped from arms manufacturers in Connecticut consigned to persons in Trenton, Butler County, Ohio, who were not gun dealers. Local citizens feared that the guns were for "improper" purposes. Could the marshal seize the firearms? Bureau headquarters at Columbus replied that the Enrollment Act did not give him authority to seize the weapons, but he was to "watch them closely" and report if he believed they would be used illegally.[38] In addition, shortly before the election the district provost marshal at Richmond, Indiana, intercepted thirty heavily armed men riding trains headed east for Ohio. They carried revolvers, bowie knives, large quantities of ammunition, along with bullet molds and lead. He reported that the men acknowledged during interrogation that they intended to "interfere" in the Ohio election.[39]

Major William Reany, military provost marshal of the District of Ohio, kept his detective corps busy watching affairs. His force, made up mostly of soldiers from his own 7th Ohio Cavalry Regiment seconded to his command (including his sons William and Lafayette, privates in the regiment), prowled around the state gathering information. Headquarters forwarded him reports from Detroit of plans by Vallandigham and others to leave Canada and enter Ohio before the election.

The Camp Chase Plot

Two days before the election, two of Reany's soldier-detectives met with General Mason at Columbus to warn him of a plot to attack Camp Chase, the prisoner-of-war camp four miles west of the capital, holding over two thousand rebel soldiers.[40] The detectives, Privates Lewis A. Slade and Thomas Finn, both of Company A of the 7th Ohio Cavalry, detailed to Reany's office for special duty, reported that conspirators planned an attempt to release the prisoners in the camp that night. The arsenal at the camp was to be seized and arms distributed to newly freed Confederate soldiers. The rebels were then to proceed to the Ohio State Penitentiary, on the edge of the city, and release rebel General John Hunt Morgan and several dozen officers of his command. All were then to march south through the state and cross the Ohio River and make for Maysville, Kentucky, about sixty miles southeast of Cincinnati. The plot, they reported, was hatched by Ohio conspirators who were members of a secret organization active in the state. The detectives had infiltrated the organization. According to a report penned afterward by General Mason, one of the two detectives who shared this starling news "had been innitiated [sic] into the secret organization in Cincinnati and Covington." The leaders of the conspiracy sent one of the initiates to Columbus with letters to persons in the capital. "At the time the report was made by one of the detectives here," Mason wrote, "the other was having an interview with the parties."[41] Mason made immediate preparations at Camp Chase on the eve of the election, sending orders to its commander, Lieutenant Colonel Edwin L. Webber of the 88th Ohio Volunteer Infantry Regiment, to arm his men and "do it quietly." He further ordered that "the men will sleep with their accoutrements on and their arms by their sides."[42]

The conspirators then either got cold feet or encountered snags in their plans. "The premeditated attack was postponed from night to night," reported Mason. In the meantime, one of the detectives, Private Slade, met frequently with the conspirators, who "supplied him with money, chloroform and a fine pistol to be used by him" in the attack on the prison. Election day came, which turned out badly for Vallandigham. A week passed from the original date of the planned attempt, when Sunday night, October 18, was set for a new try. The conspirators agreed to meet at the editorial offices of the *Crisis,* the antiwar Democratic newspaper of Samuel Medary, at eleven o'clock that night. "I had parties watching the office," wrote Mason, "and also proper arrangements made for arresting the parties at the camp." However, only one of the conspirators and the detective appeared at the appointed time at the newspaper, "where they were received by Mr. Sam Medary." When the others failed to show up at the office, "the attack was again postponed."[43]

Authorities, hoping to catch the conspirators in the act, waited two weeks before making arrests. By then the election results obviated any attempt by Vallandigham to return to Ohio in triumph and dare the government to try to arrest him. Authorities may also have remembered the experience of the U.S. marshal in Cleveland two years previous when arrests made in advance of the general elections prompted accusations that they were motivated by partisan politics. Such would not be the case in this instance. Working in coordination with military commanders, the U.S. marshal at Cincinnati, A. C. Sands, made the arrests in Cincinnati and Columbus. At ten o'clock in the evening of Saturday, October 31, a special train rolled out of Cincinnati station with deputy marshals on board. Arriving in Columbus early the next morning, marshals arrested Charles W. H. Cathcart, the Democratic state school commissioner elected in 1862,[44] and J. D. Cresap, a businessman, formerly sutler for the 18th U.S. Infantry Regiment at Columbus (Henry B. Carrington's regiment), and two Confederate prisoners of war granted parole, Captain Thomas Watson and a Dr. Lazelle. The prisoners secured, the marshals carried them back to Cincinnati. As soon as the engine left for Columbus, other deputies fanned out in Cincinnati and arrested several persons: Samuel D. Thomas, a merchant tailor, and his wife, Mary A. Thomas, and Catherine Parmenter, a laundry woman who worked in one of the military prisons in the city, McLean Barracks, and who had access to prisoners. Military authorities undertook the arrests of James P. Patton of Covington, Kentucky, brother of a Confederate officer who had escaped from prison two weeks before, and Ruth McDonald, also known as Ruth Fleming, of Newport, Kentucky, in whose house several meetings to plan the operation occurred, and who also carried secret rebel mails through the lines.[45]

The Cincinnati newspapers were full of details of the arrests and the plot to release the Confederate prisoners, details evidently supplied by the detectives themselves. Major Reany swore out an affidavit that Samuel Thomas had conspired with others to assist in the escape of Patton's rebel officer brother and another Confederate soldier, and that he had conspired to release the rebel soldiers at Camp Chase and the state penitentiary. The plan at Camp Chase was for the guard on the perimeter of the camp to be "overpowered" with laudanum and chloroform, while the prisoners inside, notified and prepared in advance, were to make a rush on the wooden stockade walls when signaled. Axes were to be thrown over the walls to the prisoners to be used to chop their way out. Prisoners were to seize the arms of the guards both within and without the camp and, led by Cathcart, march on the state arsenal and seize the large supply of arms and ammunition stored there. That accomplished, the armed men were to attack the state penitentiary to free John Hunt Morgan and his officers. In the course of the attacks, telegraph lines and railroad tracks were to be cut and destroyed.[46]

According to newspaper accounts, Slade had introduced himself to the conspirators as a Confederate spy. Cathcart, who supplied him the "splendid pistol" to use in the attacks, had told him that he had been assured by rebel authorities that he would receive a Confederate army commission when he arrived at Richmond, Virginia. Slade also received money from Patton and laudanum from Parmenter with which to drug the guards. A meeting also occurred at her house on October 24 involving the Thomases and two detectives posing as rebels (including Slade), during which suspicions arose that a third detective named Gordon was a federal spy. They resolved to kill him and ordered Slade to do it. Slade and the other detective told Gordon to hide himself and reported back to the group that they had murdered the spy and buried his body.[47]

The *Cincinnati Daily Enquirer*, the chief Democratic newspaper in the city and state, also supplied copious information on the arrests, citing Major Reany for some of the details in its reports. However, the newspaper lost no time in throwing water on the existence of a plot and ridiculing the reports printed in Republican sheets. Democratic newspapers expressed much mirth in the fact that Parmenter cleaned laundry for her living, and editorials appeared mocking the pending preliminary hearings in federal court with titles such as "The Washerwoman at Large."[48] Even the pro-Union *Cincinnati Daily Times* mirthfully ridiculed the possibility of conspiracy.[49]

Federal authorities brought the prisoners before a U.S. commissioner for preliminary hearings to set bail. In the meantime, a week after the arrests U.S. Attorney Flamen Ball traveled to Washington to consult with national leaders.[50] On his return he promptly brought the cases before a grand jury, which returned indictments against the prisoners for treason and conspiracy to release the rebel prisoners. He suggested that instead of the preliminary hearings the prisoners should instead be arraigned formally and have bail set afterward. Ball charged Cathcart on four counts: one of treason and two for conspiring with the others to release Confederate prisoners of war at Camp Chase and the state penitentiary; he tacked on a fourth count of conspiracy to attack and seize the USS *Michigan*.[51] The attorneys representing the different prisoners, including George E. Pugh, raised a number of objections. William M. Corry, a prominent Democratic attorney and avid state sovereignty adherent representing Cathcart, filed a demurrer listing seven issues that required, he argued, that the indictments be thrown out, the most novel being "that treason or conspiracy against the United States after the refusal of some of the States to continue the constitutional compact is no longer possible." Judge Humphrey Leavitt dismissed it.[52] The court released the prisoners on bail and set trial for the next term of the court in the following year. The cases dragged on for months, however, as legal wrangling continued in the courts. Much of the difficulty was the prosecution's constitutional requirement to prove an overt act of treason. Flamen Ball wrote to Attorney General Edward Bates to voice his concerns about his ability to prove treason, conceding, "it is doubtful in my mind whether the overt acts can be fully made out. Some of the defendants are influential citizens & one of them, Medary, was formerly Gov. of Nebraska or Minnesota, I forget which."[53] The prosecutor's difficulty lay in the fact that authorities had wanted to arrest the conspirators in the act, but the plotters dithered. Eventually, he dropped the treason charges to focus on the conspiracy charges. Authorities made additional arrests. On May 20, 1864, after a new grand jury handed down indictments, the U.S. marshal arrested Samuel Medary for complicity in the conspiracy. Medary died shortly thereafter, before a trial could be had. Affairs dragged on and on, years passed, with summonses and subpoenas of the detectives as witnesses, filings, and more being called for. Finally, civil war ceased before the cases had been tried, and, eventually, in 1866 federal authorities dropped their prosecutions.[54]

In the end, the legal case may not have been a strong one. Soon after the arrests Republican newspapers suggested that "there is reason to believe that an exaggerated estimate of the verity and importance of the 'conspiracy' may have been entertained, and this will become quite apparent when the testimony is taken and subjected to analysis."[55] Even General Mason, whose Camp Chase was the target for the attack, belittled the threat. He opined, "We did not at any time consider the combination formidable, as we supposed they had not had time to complete their organization."[56] Nonetheless, military commanders had spies on the inside of the conspiracy. The spies kept commanders well informed about the plotters and their plans. It is important to note that Samuel Thomas, one of the conspirators, was a friend of the important Confederate agent Captain Thomas Henry Hines. In November 1864, after the collapse of the Hines-led plot to release rebel prisoners-of-war at Camp Douglas at Chicago, Hines escaped from Chicago, made his way to Cincinnati, and hid in a specially constructed hiding place in Thomas's house while troops searched it and surroundings. Samuel and Mary Thomas served as witnesses at Hines's secret marriage to Nancy S. Sproule in Covington on

November 10, 1864.[57] Many years later, John Breckinridge Castleman, a Confederate officer who also was active in Confederate secret service working with collaborators in the North, revealed the existence of the secret hiding space in Thomas's house in his memoir and described Thomas as an "intense Southerner" and a "perfectly reliable man."[58]

One sentence in the sensational report of one of the Cincinnati newspapers, and reprinted by several other Ohio newspapers and papers in other states, was especially noteworthy: "Since writing the above, we are informed by Mr. Slade that Cathcart stated, in the course of a conversation with him, that Dick Merrick, of Illinois assured him there were thousands of men in Illinois and Indiana already organized, and only waiting for the signal from Ohio to rise in arms against the Administration."[59] Private Slade, the soldier-detective, had offhandedly informed the newspaper reporter about coordination between conspirators in three states, and named a Chicago attorney, Richard T. Merrick, as a leader in it, the same Merrick who Illinois military commanders believed was a leader of the secret organization behind many of the problems besetting that state. The statement suggests that Cathcart was in communication and acting in coordination with Merrick and others in the Northwestern states to "rise in arms" at an appointed time.

The Order of American Knights

In November 1863, amid the excitement of the arrests in Cincinnati and Columbus, Ohio, copies of an extraordinary document circulated among the district provost marshals in Indiana. Colonel Conrad Baker, acting assistant provost marshal general for Indiana, sent copies of an affidavit of a detective to several of his district officers. The detective reported having joined a secret organization in Illinois called the OAK, with membership in that state and Indiana. The organization was active in raising money and procuring arms with the intent to capture Indianapolis and release the prisoners of war held at Camp Morton. The text of the document follows:

> Hd Qrs Prov. Mar. General
> Department of Ohio
> Cincinnati O

Nov 2nd 1863

Dr R S. Griffith deposes and says he has good reason to believe and does believe that on or about the 27th of September 1863 and at the town of Paris Edgar County Illinois and in the County of Viago [Vigo] County Indiana, there are many citizens who have a secret organization called "OAK" and I joined the so called O.A.K. in the month of October, they gave me a few grips signs and passwords, all which I found to be in resistance to the General Government, and further I know that on the 22 of September they had delegates sent from every district in Illinois & Indiana to a convention which was held in Chicago Illinois for the purpose of procuring money and munitions of war, and further as soon as they can arm themselves they are to elect their Brig Genl. who is to command their force. He is to capture Indianapolis, take all the arms and release the rebel prisoners and further I have heard many hurrah for Jeff—Davis and say they would fight for him and that they wanted the South to have their independence. There is one Johnson and Powderhorn who are commanding Companies in Edgar and Cole[s] counties Illinois. I have heard Johnson say that he was a rebel Captain from the Rebel Army, he is drilling large bodies of men and said that he would resist any force that the Government may send to take him or his men. I believe the said parties are traitors to this Government

R. S. Jeffries

Sworn to and Subscribed before me
this 2nd day of November 1863
Oscar Miner [Minor]
Capt and A.A.G.

An official copy
Conrad Baker [signature]
A.A.P.M.G[60]

This document merits careful scrutiny. First, the name of the deponent changes from the first line to the last. Originally, the name is "Dr. R S. Griffith," but later the document is signed by "R.S. Jeffries." The detective's name was actually Robert L. Jeffries (handwritten *L*'s and *S*'s look very much alike in nineteenth-century documents and readers frequently mistook one for the other). Jeffries was a Missouri-born physician, listed in the 1860 census as a twenty-two-year-old resident of Franklin County, Missouri, son of a wealthy attorney and landowner. In the spring of 1863, Jeffries was in Cincinnati, Ohio, and on April 21 found himself under arrest and held in the Kemper Barracks military prison on suspicion of being a rebel surgeon en route to the South with a trunk full of medical supplies. Army interrogators learned that he had lived in Missouri up to 1862, when he left the state on account of his bad health. A property owner in Mississippi, he avowed his opposition to the war but had refused a commission in the Confederate army as a rebel surgeon and had instead gone North with his family, who were then living in nearby Newtown, Ohio. Commanders arrested him when he jestingly (he claimed) asked a lady friend to tell a known rebel-sympathizing woman being sent south by military authorities to send his greetings to his friends in the South.[61] Jeffries protested his innocence, but military authorities held him in Kemper Barracks for several weeks. Finally, after Jeffries noted that his health was failing from lack of exercise in the prison, the acting judge advocate for the Department of the Ohio ordered his release from prison on taking an oath of allegiance to the United States and giving his parole not to leave Cincinnati.[62]

At some point after his release from arrest, military authorities in the Department of the Ohio recruited Jeffries to be a spy. Unfortunately, provost marshal general records of the department do not survive in the National Archives. Therefore, we cannot say when or for how long the office employed him. Jeffries later appeared on the payroll of the detective corps of the Cincinnati post command, beginning in November 1864.[63] While working on that force he infiltrated the Confederate network operating there and in northern Kentucky. But Confederate agents working for Captain Thomas Henry Hines, one of the Confederate government's leading secret agents, discovered his identity as an army spy. Hines's men seized him and executed him in the woods near Flat Rock, Kentucky, in January 1865.[64]

The document provides a useful clue that a detective employed by departmental headquarters in Cincinnati worked in Illinois and Indiana to infiltrate secret organizations in those states. It is probable that the name "Dr. R. L. Griffith" was his alias. The OAK, or Order of American Knights, was the successor organization of the Knights of the Golden Circle, a secret society that, after Carrington's efforts and exposés in Northern newspapers, along with George Bickley's arrest in July, appears to have become disorganized.[65] Jeffries's affidavit is one of the first mentions of the OAK name in army records, but references occurred elsewhere. A detective named David Turnbull working for Captain James Woodruff, the provost marshal for the 4th District of Illinois, reported in November on the organization in his area: "The order is known now by the name of American Knights. They had Vallandigham moved to Cannada [sic]. One of the highest of them from this county was in the Confederacy lately, and one of them from St Louis was here lately and pledged to the friends here ten thousand men when the time came for rising."[66] In December the commanding general at Saint Louis received an anonymous letter from Illinois of the existence of "the Golden Circle with a new name. The

Knights of America or Marion." A local cell of the group had been formed at Rock Hill, Illinois, within the last six weeks, the informer wrote. Its leader was named Hill and resided in Saint Louis, where they met regularly in secret. The order possessed signs, passwords, and symbols, and the informer had a copy of its printed pamphlet. She or he noted that the secret order plotted a "general uprising" in the West in order to "cripple the Federal Authority so that Peace will be obliged to be made & the south Acknowledged."[67] Also, according to a Republican newspaper in Richmond, Indiana, where the district provost marshal intercepted and arrested the heavily armed men traveling to Ohio before the Ohio gubernatorial election, authorities found a document on the train that had been left by one of the arrested men. A Richmond policeman who assisted the provost marshal in the arrests saw the man try to hide it under the train car's seat. A Richmond newspaper printed the text of the seized letter:

> Dear B———: I met you at Mendota last Friday, and we rode together to Galesburg. You remember the whole topic of our conversation. I now send you some of the friends. This will be handed you by Mr. A.B. L———, who will report to you fifteen good reliable Democrats from about here, who came on to be used to the best advantage. They are all tried men, upon whom you can rely on [in] an emergency. I send them to Dayton, to be distributed as is thought best. Mr. L——— will have the general supervision of the crowd. I have also given Mr. L. the name of W.H.G., Esq., of D———. You are acquainted with L———, give him an introduction to Mr. G. He has also a letter from the ——— to Merrick. Another lot from here have gone to Defiance county [Ohio].
> Hurrah for Vallandigham and the good cause.
> We have provided all the boys with money to pay their traveling expenses.
> Sincerely and truly yours. L——— will tell you who.
> The Company here is all O.A.K.
> *****[68]

Mendota and Galesburg are towns in northern Illinois. Especially note the references to "O.A.K." and "Merrick," the new organization and Richard T. Merrick of Chicago, respectively. This newspaper transcription predates the Jeffries affidavit by two weeks, before any newspaper accounts of the plan to attack Camp Chase appeared, and must be considered genuine.

The plan to attack Camp Morton, the prisoner-of-war camp in Indianapolis, mentioned in Jeffries's affidavit, shows similarities to the Camp Chase plot. The organization's efforts to procure arms are consistent with the intelligence that army commanders collected throughout the Northwest in 1863. Significantly, Jeffries also mentions the presence of Confederate soldiers acting as drillmasters for local companies of the secret organization. Records of Illinois military commanders reveal their awareness that rebel soldiers worked with groups in several communities in the state. Officers made unsuccessful efforts to try to capture them. Powderhorn was the nom de guerre of one of the rebel drillmasters active in eastern Illinois counties at the time.[69]

Colonel Conrad Baker sent official copies of Jeffries's affidavit to his district officers on November 9, a week after the spy swore out the statement. Accompanying it were copies of another document, a letter from a John H. S. Jones of Walnut Grove, Illinois (in McDonough County, in the western part of the state) to one Levi Croniger in Cincinnati, dated October 10, 1863. The letter was a rambling account ordering preparations in Cincinnati by various named persons. The letter noted that "the 15th [of November] is the time set all over the United States," and mentioned laying "every brick level with the ground in Cincinnati" and gathering a "big haul on 3rd Street say half a million. Fiar [Fire] all when a high wind is a blowing. Set fifty a fiar at once through the City."[70]

Baker received the Jones letter from Major William Reany, military provost marshal for the District of Ohio. Reany sent copies of the Jones letter to military commands in the Northwest, as well as to the headquarters of the Department of the Missouri at Saint Louis. In his cover letter to Saint Louis, Reany wrote, "Enclosed I send you a copy of a letter captured in Covington, Ky—we have detectives on the track trying to sift the matter. please inform me wheather [sic] you have any information in regard to Jones the writer of the letter or any of the parties, or if your detectives can find out."[71] Reany's detectives probably seized the document during the arrest of the Camp Chase conspirators. In his own cover letter, Baker wrote to his officers that the enclosed letters had been forwarded to him from Governor Morton. He advised them to alert local police forces and cooperate with legion commanders in their districts, but to keep their own counsel. He ordered them to report any occurrence in their district and to be prepared for anything.[72]

Surviving records show that local officers took their orders to heart and made earnest preparations. Captain Isaac Kinley at Richmond, Indiana, contacted legion company commanders in his district to be watchful for an OAK rising on November 15. He enjoined them to keep the matter secret but to notify legion, railroad, and police officials to be vigilant.[73] The top legion commander in Randolph County, Indiana, reported back that he had duly notified his legion officers, whose "movements created quite an excitement which is now abating."

He also reported that "the Knights" had posted pickets in places around the county on Monday night of the previous week and that he was "just getting into the secret of the Knights of the Golden Circle" in his county.[74]

The November 15 uprising did not happen. However, records show that military commanders took precautions and treated the evidence of a planned uprising seriously. They employed intelligence generated by their detectives to counteract the secret organization that planned the uprising. The episode reveals a significant degree of information sharing between military commanders in the region, as well as with Governor Morton. The provost marshal general of the Department of the Ohio at Cincinnati and the provost marshal for the District of Ohio forwarded information they had gathered to Morton for his use, and Morton shared it with Baker. He in turn alerted his district officers, who alerted local officials. Throughout this process no word of these precautionary steps emerged in the partisan newspaper press. Officials effectively enforced their orders to keep the matter quiet and out of the newspapers.

The Johnson's Island Expedition

Almost at the same time, intelligence operations warned of another planned attack on a prisoner-of-war camp in Ohio. Johnson's Island, a small island in a Lake Erie bay near Sandusky, had been selected by the War Department in 1861 to be a military prison camp. After construction was completed in the following year, authorities forwarded Confederate commissioned officers to the new prison, separating them from their enlisted men. The new prison, filled with over two thousand of the cream of Southern society, soon attracted the attention of Confederate authorities who devised plans to liberate their imprisoned officers.[75]

Detectives in the hire of military commanders at Detroit, ever watchful of the rebels located in Canada, got wind of Confederate plans about November 3. Their information was vague: "that an expedition was being organized, in some part of Canada, or in the Welland Canal," to release the prisoners at Johnson's Island. Lieutenant Colonel Smith immediately sent "special detectives" to Windsor to mingle with rebels and "disaffected persons" assembled there. After a few days their reports convinced Smith that trouble was brewing. He informed and consulted with Lieutenant Colonel Hill and local leaders.[76] George Goodale wrote of "desperate & dangerous persons" at Windsor, including secessionists, rebel refugees, and others, who were in "constant communication by mail" with the South and "who are plotting, I learn, from information, numerous schemes of arson, plunder, & even armed expeditions, to release prisoners of war at Johnson's Island."[77] Satisfied that the detective's reports were correct, Smith telegraphed Cox at Cincinnati to warn him that "we have every reason to believe that within a few days there will be an attack made upon Johnson's Island to release the prisoners." He added that "a steamer has been purchased at Montreal which will be in Lake Erie within a week manned by Morgan's men and other rebels."[78] Cox promptly telegraphed the commander at Johnson's Island, Lieutenant Colonel William S. Pierson, to share Smith's warning and to order him to communicate with Smith and keep headquarters posted.[79] Pierson, who commanded a garrison of about four hundred troops, requested that headquarters send him Major Reany "for a few days" to do some work in the matter.[80] Reany could not be spared at the moment, wired Cox in reply, but assured him the Montreal matter was being "looked after."[81] Cox had already telegraphed the consul general at Montreal, fellow Ohio Republican politician Joshua R. Giddings, to investigate and verify, if possible, the report of the steamer being fitted out there.[82] In the meantime, Smith sent another telegram reporting, "I am positively informed that within 48 hours 2 armed steamers will attack Johnson's Island. . . . We are powerless here," he added. "What can I do?"[83] Cox shared the report with Colonel Hoffman at Washington and wired General Mason that the "positive tone" of Smith's message prompted him to order troops from Columbus to Johnson's Island to reinforce the imperiled garrison.[84] He also informed Pierson that he did not "really credit" the report, but had ordered Mason to send reinforcements, including an extra artillery battery from Camp Dennison, near Cincinnati. He also agreed to send detective Reany to investigate.[85]

Hill, the acting assistant provost marshal general in Michigan, also lent a hand in investigations. He wrote to Giddings at Montreal to share intelligence received at Detroit. He usually viewed the rumors that emanated from Canada of movements and plans of the refugees and escaped rebel prisoners as "perfectly idle and have attached no importance to them." However, reliable sources said a rebel agent had just arrived at Windsor with certificates of specie from Judah Benjamin, the Confederate secretary of state, worth over $100,000 and more was on the way. The funds were for the purchase of a steamer to be built or bought at Montreal. Hill provided other tidbits of information gleaned from Detroit headquarters' spies in Canada relating to the presence of high-ranking Confederate officials and rebel naval officers who had recently been seen in Toronto. He concluded "that a project of some magnitude is on foot I have no doubt, to happen in a few days."[86] He also sent much the same information to Washington, adding, "Since writing above I am informed that nearly all the rebel refugees have left for Montreal, and the information points more positively to Johnson's Island."[87]

Following orders, Pierson and Smith communicated directly to inform each other of the latest developments. Smith and others were reassured that the USS *Michigan* was anchored a short distance away from the prison camp, guarding the entrance to the bay. He learned from his detectives in Windsor that many of the rebels there "had disappeared" from the town and had gone to man the vessels in preparation for the assault. He ordered them "to accompany some of the men" to learn their movements.[88] In the meantime, he telegraphed that "two detectives are sent to Port Stanley," on the Canadian north shore of Lake Erie, about eighty miles east of Windsor, "where the expedition is said to be organizing, as I learn today." He added, "I hear nothing from the Welland Canal. Rebels have all left Windsor. If there is a move at all," he surmised, "it will be soon."[89] He attempted to gather information from other sources, wiring the district provost marshal at Buffalo to ask him to send a "prudent detective" to inquire whether an ironclad steamer had passed through the Welland Canal connecting the east end of Lake Erie with Lake Ontario.[90] He dispatched a steamer from Detroit fitted with two mounted guns to cruise along the Canadian side of Lake Erie to look into Rondeau and Port Stanley, and scrounged around for large-caliber artillery pieces and ammunition with which to defend the Michigan city.[91] He reported to Cox that detectives found nothing at Port Stanley and that the steamer cruise discovered nothing suspicious. Nonetheless, he had sent another detective to traverse the length of the Canadian shore to the Welland Canal "with orders not to come back without finding where they are assembling."[92]

At this time, British government authorities in Canada independently got wind of the Confederate covert operation to attack Johnson's Island from Canadian soil.[93] Assessing that a violent attack on the United States from Canada would adversely affect already tense diplomatic relations between the United States and Great Britain, Canada's governor general, Lord Monck, the leader of the British government in the provinces, contacted the British minister at Washington, Lord Lyons, to notify the Lincoln administration of the impending raid on the prison camp and the plan to seize the USS *Michigan*.[94] Secretary Stanton immediately telegraphed the governors of the states bordering on the Great Lakes as well as mayors of cities along the shores most likely to be attacked by the Confederate raiders.[95] Telegraph services and newspapers published the warning, and the news became widely known throughout the United States and Canada. Learning that their plot was exposed in the newspapers, the Confederate naval officers in command of the expedition to attack Johnson's Island abandoned the effort.[96]

The news from Canadian authorities via Washington merely confirmed the information Smith's detectives had uncovered. Commanders viewed the news reports in that light and redoubled their efforts to reinforce Johnson's Island's defenses. Cox requested Governor Tod to send up to three thousand state militia troops to Sandusky and the island and went there in person under orders from Washington to superintend defense efforts.[97] But Smith soon reported that his detectives, who had followed and watched the Windsor rebels, told him that "the rebels are returning to Windsor who have been absent. They say there [sic] plans are frustrated. Only for the present. Our own precautions and those of the Canadian government oblige them to postpone their movement."[98] Cox, at Sandusky, forwarded the information to departmental headquarters and added, "I regard this as ending the immediate danger, but will keep the force here till [the detectives' report] is confirmed."[99] A couple of days later Smith wired to report that his detectives confirmed the news of the return of the rebels to Windsor and that all was quiet. He added, "I am told that Vallandigham was opposed to the movement. The information [is] not perfectly reliable."[100]

Military-intelligence operations in Detroit had detected plots to attack Johnson's Island and seize the *Michigan* and had alerted military commanders to prepare to meet the emergency. Commanders quietly reinforced the prison camp and took steps to provide a powerful defense against a seaborne attack on the island. However, it was the Canadian government's notification of the United States government, Stanton's prompt notification of civil authorities around the Great Lakes, and publication of the news that both the Canadian and U.S. governments knew of the impending attack that prompted the abandonment of the rebel scheme. The two routes of detection highlight the different ways in which intelligence was employed. The military commanders in Michigan and Ohio used the information their detectives picked up to prepare to meet the attack with a powerful defensive force capable of inflicting severe damage on the raiders and quite possibly defeating and capturing them. But an attack from Canada, either successful or unsuccessful, might have provoked calls for retaliation against Great Britain from an irate Northern public. By forestalling the attack, Stanton saved the British government the embarrassment of having allowed Confederate naval and military officers to attack the United States and avoided an international incident.

In the end, the episode prompted General Burnside, campaigning faraway at Knoxville, Tennessee, but still in command of the Department of the Ohio, to loosen his purse strings and supply secret-service funds to Smith at Detroit ($3,000) and Cox at Cincinnati ($2,000), replenishing already exhausted coffers.[101] Detectives under Smith's direction continued their surveillance of Vallandigham and the rebels at Windsor. As winter approached, commanders at Detroit continued to worry about the large number of rebels across the river, the rumblings they heard from them about attacks on the city and the Dearborn Arsenal, and reports that a new attempt on Johnson's Island would be made when Lake Erie's surface froze solid.[102] Washington officials were now alert to the exposed situation of the prison camp. War Department bureaucrats began to query commanders about the rumors and reports that they heard.[103] Owing to the poor anchorage near Johnson's Island, the USS *Michigan* could not winter in Sandusky Bay near the prison camp and its commander was forced to sail to Erie, Pennsylvania, for the coming months before navigation ended on the lake.[104] In its place, the War Department sent an idle division of troops from the Army of the Potomac under the command of Brigadier General Henry D. Terry to Sandusky to guard Johnson's Island during the frozen winter. Stanton also dispatched Corps of Engineers officers to survey the Lake Erie coast preparatory to constructing fortifications to guard against future rebel raids from Canada.[105]

Nonetheless, the prison camp continued to be exposed to future attack. Good intelligence would be needed to stop further attempts to free rebel prisoners of war. Commanders and political leaders alike began to grasp that information on the actions and intentions of the disaffected in the Old Northwest was vital to maintaining the Northern war effort. In the late summer and fall of 1863, military intelligence kept a sharp watch on Vallandigham and the host of rebels over the northern frontier. Major Reany's corps of soldier-detectives infiltrated and broke up a plot to release Confederate prisoners at Camp Chase. Spies working for Department of the Ohio headquarters and Provost Marshal General's Bureau commanders detected the rise of the successor organization to the KGC in Illinois and Indiana called the Order of American Knights. Finally, army detectives got wind of plots to cross the Great Lakes and attack Johnson's Island and other points on the northern frontier. The detective operations run by both military commanders and the Provost Marshal General's Bureau in the Old Northwestern states had supplied much useful information and would be relied on to continue to do so.

Governor Richard Yates of Illinois. *Library of Congress*

Governor Oliver P. Morton of Indiana. *Library of Congress*

Caleb Blood Smith, Secretary of the Interior. *Library of Congress*

Colonel Henry B. Carrington. *Library of Congress*

Major General Ambrose E. Burnside. *Library of Congress*

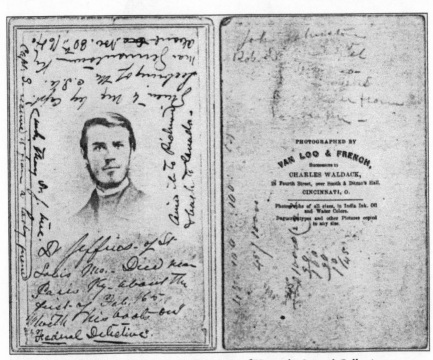

Robert L. Jeffries, U.S. Army spy. *University of Kentucky Special Collections, Thomas Henry Hines Papers*

Major General Samuel P. Heintzelman. *Library of Congress*

Major General William S. Rosecrans. *Library of Congress*

Sargent Parker Coffin, U.S. Army spy. *Miami County (Indiana) Historical Museum*

Lieutenant Colonel Bennett H. Hill. *Library of Congress*

Colonel Benjamin J. Sweet. *Library of Congress*

June 1864.

Felix G. Stidger

Felix Grundy Stidger, U.S. Army spy. *Filson Historical Society*

"It Is Impossible to Doubt This"

Army Intelligence in the Northern Department in Early 1864

WHEN WAR Department leaders shuffled Major General Samuel P. Heintzelman off to Columbus, Ohio, at the beginning of 1864, to lead a new army department, their aim was to rid themselves of another disappointing officer who yearned for a major field command. Given the new Northern Department, formed from the discontinued Department of the Ohio, Heintzelman's chief task was to guard the prison camps scattered around the Old Northwest. War Department functionaries gave him vague instructions and sent him away. Left mainly to his own devices, without staff officers and subordinates familiar with the situation, the general soon learned that guarding prison camps in a restive region was not a simple task. Post commanders in the department informed him of the threat of rebellion and attack from organized groups both within the region and from across the Canadian border. Grasping the extent and intent of the secret groups, he recognized the regional instability that imperiled his ability to protect the prison camps and keep down insurrection. Heintzelman came to rely on the efforts of Brigadier General Henry B. Carrington as his chief intelligence officer in keeping a lid on conspiracy and uprising.

Heintzelman's Arrival in Ohio

Loitering in Washington, awaiting word of a new army command, Samuel Peter Heintzelman recorded in his journal that the adjutant general of the U.S. Army, Lorenzo Thomas, told him that he was going to be posted to Columbus, Ohio, to assume command of a new army department. "I don't know what for," he wrote, "but I am disappointed. I expected certainly to go to Texas." Days later the major general recounted chatting with the wife of U.S. Senator John Sherman of Ohio, who had heard via the grapevine that he was being posted to Ohio. "I told her I had hoped it would be to Texas, to more active duties. I cannot see what I can have to do in Ohio," he grumbled.[1]

Heintzelman was a seasoned career officer. Born in Pennsylvania in 1805, a graduate of West Point in 1826, he had spent his long military career assigned to the army's frontier outposts from northern Michigan Territory to Florida, from Massachusetts to California. He had fought in the Mexican War and had served in a variety of tasks from recruiting, managing quartermaster supplies, and guarding the U.S.-Mexican border, to fighting Indians in Texas, Arizona, and California. At the beginning of the Civil War, the War Department ordered him to repair to Washington and appointed him to the command of the 17th U.S. Infantry Regiment, one of the new regular-army units created by Congress. He also accepted a brigadier general of volunteers appointment and command of a division near Washington. Fighting at Bull Run in July 1861, he suffered a serious wound in his right arm while attempting to rally panicky federal troops under his command. He never regained full use of the limb.[2] After he recovered, the War Department put him in command of an army corps in the Army of the Potomac, which he commanded through the Peninsula campaign and Second Bull Run. Placed in command of the Department of Washington, he guarded the national capital from rebel raids and policed the city with a full army corps under his orders until relieved, in the fall of 1863. Bitter at his removal from command and bored, languishing in Washington and hopeful of the command of the Army of the Potomac, he received a summons from Secretary Stanton to meet in his War Department office shortly after the new year. Stanton told him that soon he would receive a new command, but did not specify what it was. Heintzelman also hoped for Texas, where he had enjoyed his desert service and where he anticipated there would be plenty of fighting.[3] Rumors that he would be assigned to Texas swirled in the newspapers. The posting to Columbus came as a severe letdown. But the professional soldier accepted his orders. Shortly afterward, he met with General-in-Chief Henry Halleck, who provided unwelcome details.

"My principal duty is to take care of rebel prisoners," Heintzelman groused.[4] The next day he returned to the War Department to meet with Stanton, Halleck, and others about securing the services of trusted staff officers and to learn more about his tasks. Halleck provided still more details, showing that the War Department was alert to the threat from rebel operatives across the Canadian frontier. "The important thing now is to send an officer to Detroit, to learn what the secessionists are assembling there for—or rather to Windsor opposite," wrote Heintzelman.[5] The following day, before leaving for Columbus, he sent a trusted staff officer to Detroit with orders to meet with Lieutenant Colonel Joseph R. Smith, post commander, to learn about the movements of rebels and secession sympathizers at Windsor and other points in Canada. His orders noted that the rebels planned a "demonstration" on Johnson's Island.[6]

Heintzelman rode the rails to Ohio, arrived at Columbus on January 20, and assumed command of the new Northern Department, encompassing Ohio, Michigan, Indiana, and Illinois but now shorn of its Kentucky regions (except Newport and Covington, across the Ohio River from Cincinnati). The Department of the Ohio, formerly commanded by Major General Burnside, had been discontinued when that general turned over his army to John G. Foster at Knoxville, Tennessee, and went home to Rhode Island in December.[7] A new District of Kentucky was created with departmental powers, and Brigadier General Jacob Ammen left Springfield, Illinois and assumed command of it. Brigadier General Jacob D. Cox had gone south to command part of Burnside's army, leaving no district command in Ohio. Likewise, Brigadier General Willcox was commanding troops in eastern Tennessee, and his District of Indiana and Michigan was divided, and command duties devolved on the superannuated Colonel Simonson at Indianapolis and Smith at Detroit. Significantly, with the departure of the district generals went their staffs, including their provost marshals with extensive intelligence experience and knowledge of local political conditions. Most importantly, Burnside's Provost Marshal General's office in Department of the Ohio headquarters was dismantled, its intelligence capabilities broken up, and Brigadier General Nathan C. McLean sent away. No continuity of command structure remained. Moreover, the briefing Heintzelman received from the War Department had been cursory, providing poor guidance and almost no information to the new commander. Within days, friends (including President Lincoln) of an Illinois general lobbied him to appoint that officer as district commander in Illinois. "I don't yet know what I can do but think I will have to make sub-districts of the States," he confided to his journal.[8] He asked the War Department to approve the appointment of Brigadier General William W. Orme, Lincoln's friend, to command at Springfield, but he lacked information to make informed decisions for the other states.[9] Heintzelman still was not clear on his responsibilities in the new command. The department contained five major prisoner-of-war camps: Johnson's Island and Camp Chase in Ohio, Camp Morton in Indiana, and Camp Douglas and Rock Island in Illinois (Alton, Illinois, also contained a prisoner-of-war camp, but it was under the command of the Department of the Missouri). In the following weeks he attempted to learn the geographical boundaries of the department and what troops were available to him to use.[10] Beyond the camp garrisons and new recruits, there were scarcely any veteran troops stationed in the whole department, certainly none that could be employed in any campaign against rebels. From commanding a full army corps, Heintzelman now had only a few scattered companies of Veteran Reserve Corps (VRC) troops at his disposal. Furthermore, he wondered why he had been ordered to establish his headquarters at Columbus. A small city of twenty thousand, Columbus was overshadowed by Cincinnati as the economic and transportation center of Ohio and the region. Furthermore, Cincinnati offered more amenities—like opera, concerts, and theater—that Heintzelman appreciated. "The longer I stay the more disgusted I am at the situation of affairs. I wish my HdQrs were at Cincinnati," he complained.[11] He was "out of position here," and "Columbus [is] entirely out of the way," he wrote to Washington.[12] Attempts to persuade the War Department to move his headquarters closer to the front fell on deaf ears.

The only advantage that Columbus held over Cincinnati was its proximity to the rebel prisoner-of-war camps in Ohio. Camp Chase was there, of course, but Columbus was also one hundred miles closer to Johnson's Island. It was also closer to Detroit and the Canadian frontier. Heintzelman's staff officer, Major Granville E. Johnson, returned from Detroit after conferring with Smith and brought "no alarming news" of the Windsor plotters.[13] However, Johnson's written report laid out details of what Smith and his detectives knew of rebel movements across the Detroit River. The "Secessionists" in Canada numbered "two thousand men of the most desperate character" and had "nearly matured" a "second plan" to liberate the rebel officers at Johnson's Island in the absence of the USS *Michigan*. The plan was to cross on the thick winter ice of Lake Erie, attack the prison, release and arm the prisoners, and march south "to attempt to join [John Hunt] Morgan." However, the plan was frustrated by the "timely arrival of the Brigade commanded by Brig. Genl Terry." The warmer weather of the last week also had broken the ice on the lake, rendering such a plan impossible, he added. The rebels planned to attack and burn Detroit sometime in the near future. Johnson admitted that he "could gain no particulars of this design," but he had effected "arrangements" to be "fully and promptly informed of every particulars [*sic*]." The Confederates had sent men and money to Canada to raid on the northern frontier, he reported, and added that "one Dr. Blackburn at Toronto or Montreal is the Agent of the rebels."[14] He offered his opinion that good intelligence would protect the northern frontier: the "good faith" of the governor general of Canada, Lord Monck, along with the "various sources of information at our command, together with a strict vigilance on our part," would frustrate the rebels "in this or any design they may have."[15] A similar report of rebel plans to cross over the ice to raid Johnson's Island came from the acting assistant provost marshal general at Columbus, Colonel Edwin Parrott.[16] Other camps in the department reported difficulties, too. Camp Chase commanders wrote that their prison stewards and "detectives employed inside the prison" had uncovered plans between prisoners and rebel sympathizers outside the camp to overpower the guard and break out. Arms had been found in the possession of prisoners.[17] Heintzelman learned from Orme that a small plot to release prisoners at Camp Douglas had been discovered and dealt with.[18]

Aside from prison problems, reports arrived of planned resistance to the draft and unrest in various regions of the department. Union men in Sullivan County, Indiana, reported intimidation and threats of violence from deserters who ran rampant in the area.[19] A district provost marshal in southern Ohio reported that there were "unmistakable signs" that the "copperheads" planned to resist the draft and were holding secret meetings to that end. He suggested that a soldier posing as a deserter could infiltrate the organization and discover their plans.[20] In his first days at Columbus, Heintzelman came to realize the difficulties and complexities of the region he oversaw. He would need troops and constant vigilance to suppress unrest in the department. Heintzelman soon received welcome assistance in this task from a source previously unknown to him.

Carrington's Return

Soon after the departmental commander's arrival in Columbus, a forgotten but important figure introduced himself to his new superior officer. Brigadier General Henry B. Carrington, stationed at Indianapolis, wrote to Heintzelman, "I am engaged in organizing and drilling the Indiana troops, under the Governors [*sic*] directions, as per Special Order of the Secretary of War, and shall take pleasure at all times in furnishing all information in my power." He informed him he had formerly been in command of the District of Indiana, "was relieved by Genl Burnside—ordered to Ohio—thence returned here." He added that "Genl Ammen having been relieved in Illinois, and Genl Cox in Ohio, I supposed the District system had ceased to operate, until advised by Col. Simonson that his orders comprehended the District."[21]

Carrington's odyssey from the moment he was relieved of command of the District of Indiana, in April 1863, had brought him back to Indiana. Since then, he had been an outcast in the army. Governor Morton had tried to retain him in Indiana, but Burnside was adamant in his determination to send him to the field. His health collapsed with a serious case of diphtheria, and he languished in Ohio. Depressed by his inactivity, he rejoiced when orders arrived to drill recruits at Cleveland. But the arrangement soon collapsed. Governor Tod, jealous of his authority in Ohio, resisted Burnside's order to assign Carrington to the command. Governor Morton rescued him from limbo by persuading the War Department to order him to Indiana to serve on his personal staff to organize the Indiana Legion (state militia), as well as to superintend the organization of Indiana volunteer troops. Beneath the cover story, Morton wanted Carrington to return to his important work of investigating the secret organizations that still plagued the state and region.[22] Indiana newspapers first reported the news of Carrington's imminent return on July 7, 1863.[23]

Carrington arrived in Indianapolis on July 10, in the midst of the invasion of Confederate general John Hunt Morgan's division of cavalry raiders. He immediately set to work to organize the estimated forty thousand volunteers that turned the capital into "one vast camp."[24] Carrington dove into the work with his typical diligence and over the next three days worked almost nonstop completing the necessary paperwork organizing volunteer units. New regiments sprouted from his pen armed and equipped and departed to points in southern Indiana to intercept the rebel invaders. On July 13, Carrington received orders from General Willcox to take command of a brigade of newly formed regiments and ride a freight train from Indianapolis to Hamilton, Ohio, to attempt to cut off Morgan before he escaped far into Ohio. Carrington arrived at the train station, the troops having already boarded freight cars. Word arrived that another train was on the line blocking the dispatch of the troop train. All were impatient with the delay, especially the troops packed in cars that reeked of hogs. What happened next has been disputed by historians ever since. According to his own account written in later years, while awaiting the clearance of the tracks Carrington and other officers went to a house near the station "where refreshments were served freely." By his own admission, Carrington, visibly "worn out" by his almost incessant labors in organizing new regiments, on top of his continued frail health, agreed to the suggestion to relinquish command of the brigade and retired to his hotel, "where blood-spitting, long contended against, claimed the mastery."[25] However, other officers and soldiers on the train later wrote that Carrington collapsed on the train platform at the station "in a state of maudlin intoxication" and had to be carried away. Finding a replacement added to the delay, and the troop train departed Indianapolis and arrived in Ohio too late to cut off Morgan's force. Critics blamed Carrington for the delay and failure to catch the rebels. While drunkenness was widespread among officers in the army, and accusations of drunkenness commonplace when attacking rivals, everything we know about teetotaler Carrington negates the accusation leveled at him by contemporaries and historians that he was intoxicated.[26]

Morton had confidence in him and after the raid sent Carrington to southern Indiana to reorganize the legion and adjudicate claims regarding the thousands of horses that Morgan and the pursuing federal cavalry either stole or "borrowed." He also investigated evidence of collaboration between the rebel cavalry and local Indiana citizens. In the following months, he crisscrossed the state to organize, review, and drill the legion. He also spoke to assembled Legion troops, as well as to crowds of citizens. In speeches that lasted up to two hours, he adjured audiences to forebear the use of partisan epithets such as *copperhead* or *butternut* as only leading to hard feelings, political strife, and violence. It was the right of all citizens to criticize the administration, he said, and told soldiers to uphold the law rather than break it. He told listeners that they "must not attempt to interfere with the freedom of the press." After one such speech a Democratic newspaper observed that "this part of the address was most distasteful to the abolitionists on hand."[27] Such conciliatory utterances garnered praise from the Democratic press. A Democratic editor in Vincennes said his speech was "calm and free of slang and abuse. His denunciation of the applying the slang phrases of copperheads and butternuts to Democrats was well-timed and proper."[28] Even the *Indianapolis Daily State Sentinel,* the organ of the state Democratic Party, called him an "exceedingly felicitous" speaker.[29] Governor Morton gave Carrington greater authority over military matters in the state, giving him command over the organization camps for new regiments. The general worked diligently to superintend the camps in and around Indianapolis. While his health continued to be precarious, he kept active organizing legion artillery batteries to guard the Ohio River border. As his duties multiplied, he needed staff assistance. On Heintzelman's arrival at Columbus, Carrington wrote to him to apprise the new commander of his duties and accomplishments, and to request help. He had one volunteer officer who served as an aide, he wrote, but the aide's regiment was being called away. "I am daily at four camps, and in my state of health I need Lieut Flowers['s] services," he wrote.[30] Shortly thereafter Carrington visited Columbus and called on Heintzelman. We can conjecture that it was a courtesy call. The commander simply recorded in his pocket diary, "Gen. Carrington called."[31] The Indiana general was soon to acquaint the departmental commander with his true function as spymaster.

At eleven o'clock at night on March 2, after Heintzelman had gone to bed, a staff officer woke him with a telegram just arrived from the War Department. General Halleck had ordered him "to proceed forthwith to Paris Edgar Co Ill and suppress a rebellion—or rather insurrection." The first westbound train did not leave until two o'clock in the morning, so he had time to scan the newspapers. "There is not a word in the newspapers and I don't believe it amounts to anything," he recorded in his journal.[32]

Troubles had been simmering in eastern Illinois for months, and in the previous weeks several incidents occurred provoked by the presence of veterans home on furlough. Soldiers had assaulted Judge Charles Constable on the streets of Mattoon, in neighboring Coles County, and committed other abuses.[33] Incidents built up, and on January 31 an armed group of citizens estimated to number 150 men gathered outside Paris and advanced on the town. Officers on furlough in the town thought it best to assemble and arm soldiers, twenty-five in number, to take defensive positions at the courthouse and other places. The armed and mounted men drew near. The officers reported that they "dared us to fight and then fell back a bit; we sent out some men who were fired on and returned fire." "Powderhorn," the elusive rebel soldier who drilled and led the local armed organizations, was reported wounded in the exchange. An armed standoff ensued for several days, and reinforcements of troops arrived from Indianapolis and Terre Haute under the command of Richard W. Thompson. Soldiers arrested several people in the town, including the editor of the Democratic newspaper, and remained on alert for several days as reports filtered in of large bodies of armed men massing in the surrounding area.[34] The officers further reported that Amos Green, a Democratic leader and attorney in the town, admitted to ordering the armed band

> to come to Paris to protect some property against which no demonstration had been made by soldiers or any one else. He admitted this to the undersigned and two days afterward promised to send out and disperse the mob. He did send out one O'Hair former Sheriff of the Co and on the 4th inst. [February] we learned the mob had

dispersed. Amos Green clearly proved his control of the armed force by convening & dispersing them at pleasure and we consider him responsible for the attack & disturbance on the 31st ult.[35]

One month later, Governor Yates telegraphed Washington with an alarmed report of widespread insurrection in Edgar County after another incident arose between armed civilians and soldiers.[36] Newspaper reports circulated of one soldier and one civilian each shot dead in an ambush attack on soldiers.[37] General Halleck wired Colonel Oakes to depart immediately for Paris with two companies of troops, to act under the orders of Heintzelman.[38] Heintzelman rode westward and arrived at Indianapolis, where while awaiting another train he met with Morton and Carrington at the statehouse to learn the latest information. Heintzelman, whom an Indianapolis newspaper reporter described as gray-haired but as lively as a forty-year-old,[39] recorded that the two men "assured me it did not amount to anything." Orders were orders, however, and he pressed on to Terre Haute, where Thompson, the district provost marshal, briefed him with the latest news. He "knew all about the affair and gave us a full account and substantially correct, and also that all was perfectly quiet," the general recorded. Proceeding to Paris, he found no troops had arrived yet. Unable to contact Governor Yates, he learned that Oakes was en route. VRC troops arrived from Chicago. Finally a telegram came from Yates: he had requested two companies of troops be sent to Paris, "and that citizens had told him there were 2,000 copperheads in arms." Oakes finally arrived, without troops, and told the general that the "Gov. would not give him any information as to what he wished done, only to consult with citizens and be governed by circumstances," he wrote in his journal. "Col. Oakes showed me a copy of the Gov's telegram to the Secy of War. It was two battles and 2000 men in arms." Heintzelman gathered the facts: "It was only a collision between some copperheads 15 or 20 and some returned veterans." One copperhead would probably die of his wounds and two soldiers were wounded. "I decided to return by the next train," he wrote, and ordered Oakes and some of the troops to return to their posts. While in the Illinois town he impressed local Republican leaders, who were "well-pleased" with him and his tough talk.[40] The general passed through Indiana and arrived back in Ohio on March 7.[41] On his arrival at headquarters, he reported to Halleck with details of the incident, adding, "I took advantage of a delay of a couple of hours at Indianapolis to see Gov. Morton and learned that there was no serious outbreak. . . . I procured a statement of the different affairs and of the condition of the disloyal and enclose them." He also referred to "Powderhorn," also known as Johnson, who was believed to be a rebel who had escaped from Camp Douglas. If he could be found he would be arrested. "The arrest of a few of the most troublesome in the vicinity of Paris would aid in quieting this ill feeling," he advised, and he suggested that troops should be ordered to remain there to quell unrest.[42]

Heintzelman's Intelligence Chief

The Paris incident was a false alarm, but the general's trip to Illinois taught him one important lesson. Meeting with Morton and Carrington at Indianapolis, he had been thoroughly briefed on the supposed outbreak. More significantly, he learned of their intelligence operations and was impressed by their knowledge.

If Heintzelman needed prodding to place departmental intelligence matters in Carrington's hands, it came from the War Department. Days before, Colonel Conrad Baker, the acting assistant provost marshal general at Indianapolis, had written to Washington to warn that "evidence is daily accumulating" that "disloyal" citizens in Illinois and Indiana intended to "revolt against the Government as soon as their plans are perfected, and a favorable opportunity offers." He had "strong reasons for believing" that efforts to smuggle arms from Canada via Chicago, Fort Wayne, and other places were in progress and that leaders of "secret oathbound societies, the organization of which is fast being perfected all over the state," planned to whip their members into "open resistance to the Government." He suggested that "with proper skill and energy their treasonable scheme could be exposed and some of their leaders brought to merited punishment." Baker had in mind to use two men who were members of the organization as spies, "who connected themselves with it for the purpose of serving the Government, and both of whom I believe to be thoroughly loyal and reliable." They were John Jackson, who recently had enlisted as a soldier in the 101st Indiana Volunteer Infantry Regiment, and Dr. Henry S. Zumro, of Huntington County, Indiana, whom Baker described as "a man of good social position, a physician by profession quite intelligent and possessed of considerable property." He noted that Zumro "has already spent some money and much time in making himself acquainted with the plans of these men for the purpose of ultimately using the information for the benefit of the Government." He suggested that the physician could be hired at one hundred dollars per month "in the ordinary way through the Provost Marshal of the District," a salary "as would justify the risk of loss of life and property, he would incur in the event of his relations to the Government being discovered." Jackson, the new recruit, should be detailed for "similar duty" in Indiana; "the fact of this detail should not be made known to any person or officer in the State except himself and the officer to whom he might be directed to report." He further suggested that Jackson should "perform the part of a deserter, and return to his disloyal associates by whom he would be sure to be treated with new marks of confidence." Baker believed these two spies could also recruit other "reliable men" who would be "initiated into the order" to secure "complete exposure and the punishment of the most guilty." He added, "I am satisfied that the assassination of the Governor is one of the objects contemplated by some of the men connected with this treasonable organization, the design being to transfer the executive power of the State to disloyal hands by vesting it in an officer who is known to sympathize with treason." He suggested that Heintzelman be entrusted with the operation, and if an officer in Indiana should supervise them, that "Brig. Genl Carrington now on duty with Gov. Morton is well fitted for the duty." Baker knew that Carrington was actively investigating the secret organizations. He opined that the "disloyal portion" in Indiana was "less demonstrative" at the moment than it had been in the summer of 1863, "but it is also better organized and more determined and therefore more dangerous."[43] General Fry, at Washington, forwarded Baker's letter to Stanton, noting that "Colonel Baker is reliable in all his statements. I think the subject is worthy of attention." Fry added that his friends in Illinois also believed that "designs are entertained" similar to what Baker described.[44] Stanton's staff promptly forwarded Baker's report to Heintzelman and authorized the employment of Jackson and Zumro, and that he "give this matter early and diligent attention." Stanton also authorized "the employment of any other means, necessary and proper to carry out" the effort.[45] Heintzelman in turn forwarded the War Department's order to Carrington and began to use Carrington as his head of intelligence.[46] He ordered him to report frequently regarding his actions and findings "as to those secret movements. Your success will depend on the secrecy with which you act."[47] Carrington now had two spies paid for by War Department funds, a luxury he had not previously enjoyed. He quickly put the two spies to use. He replied to Heintzelman that he had "already commenced some investigations and will keep you advised fully of all developments." He reminded him that "in 1863, I was able to secure the whole work [of the KGC] and bring convictions by U.S. Courts in nearly 150 cases." Given the wider scope of his new brief, he added, "I think it may be well for me, quietly, to slip over to Springfield and have a conference with Gov Yates."[48]

Within days of his return from Illinois, Heintzelman began to channel information received at headquarters to Carrington. When the War Department forwarded reports of expected disturbances in Illinois and Indiana to him, he informed Oakes that, while he wished him to continue his investigations, "I have placed the immediate supervision of the matter in the hands of Brig Gen. Carrington."[49]

The records that Oakes turned over to Carrington included reports of David Turnbull, the deputy provost marshal for Warren County in western Illinois. Turnbull had learned in November that the new name of the organization was the American Knights. His source at that time was "one of the good Democrats" in the county, a county constable, who revealed to him the activities of the organization, including "the stuffing of the ballot boxes in several of the towns in this county" in 1862. It also had concealed weapons caches, and members were arming themselves on a large scale. Funds for the purchase of arms in Canada primarily came from the rebels in the South, with whom they were in regular communication; "the remainder is now called on in shape of a Tax on the party, so much from each county in the State." He reported that the organization numbered seventy-five thousand "enrolled men."[50] Turnbull continued to provide information on the machinations of the secret organization to the provost marshal. The Knights sported a thorough military organization, he noted, with a brigade for each congressional district and a regiment for each county. A Col. "Barry" of St. Louis [probably Dr. James Barret, one of the leaders of the OAK in Saint Louis] told the county organization that they had "friends" in army headquarters at Saint Louis and that the governor of Kentucky "had sold out" to them and "has promised to bring the authorities of that state in conflict with the U.S. authorities." The county organization procured rifles and ammunition through an Iowa gunsmith. He further reported that "P.C. Wright" (Phineas C. Wright) was the name of the "man from the South that organized the band of Knights to assist the South in Ill Iowa, Mis. [Missouri] & Indiana & Ohio." Wright had purchased all or part of the *New York Daily News* and was using the newspaper "for the benefit of the rebels." He was "the agent of the South in this whole matter and through his press these secrets are circulated." Secret plans were in process for the Southern rebels to make three raids in the early spring: one each in Ohio, Indiana, and Illinois. Longstreet was to raid across the Ohio River in the spring, "which may afford an opportunity for a rise." Lee was to move on Washington, and the Knights planned to "strike simultaneously" at prison camps. They boasted twenty thousand members in Chicago alone, and many in Canada would act in concert. They maintained a large cache of arms near Detroit with which to equip members, and Turnbull suggested that detectives should go to Canada to "ferret out" its whereabouts. He added that the "Supreme Council" of the order met in New York City on February 22, and that Robert Holloway was the Warren County delegate to the meeting, where representatives from New York, Missouri, Ohio, Indiana, Illinois, and Iowa met, each of whom promised many men to act in concert. Clement Vallandigham had met with representatives in Canada, who "agreed that at an appointed time he is to return home & if arrested the Knights was to rise immediately"; Vallandigham had "supervision" of arms in Canada for their use. The council "appropriated" $50,000 for him at the meeting. Turnbull's informant also told him that George B. McClellan, the former commander of the Army of the Potomac, also met with the council.[51]

Besides Turnbull, Carrington had many informants. In February, before he became Heintzelman's de facto intelligence chief, he obtained a report of a soldier from the 17th Indiana Volunteer Infantry Regiment named Henry Henley from Martin County about William A. Bowles, identified as a leader in the secret organization. Henley said that he had friends watching the "butternut conspiracy." The organization's leaders professed to have "free communication" with the Confederate army and said that "Jeff Davis" gave them directions. They planned to attack and capture Indianapolis, Springfield, Illinois, and Saint Louis; they claimed to have eighty thousand men poised to attack the Indiana capital. Henley's friends also watched "Dr. Bowles," the owner of the nearby French Lick Springs resort, in Orange County, Indiana. Bowles was "violently opposed to the war & the administration, & very active in all the secret organizations of 1863," Henley reported. "Previous to the break out of the rebellion [Bowles] brought his wife's slaves to the Springs where he resides and kept them there for several weeks & to avoid seizure ran them off in the night." Henley warned that Bowles "makes friends wherever he goes among the masses. He is smart and wields an extensive influence among the masses, especially the lower classes."[52]

As was Carrington's custom, he collected affidavits from his informants. In early March a Wayne County man, Thomas Elliott, a regular source, swore to a statement that recently he had been initiated into the "Knights of the Mighty Host," in neighboring Randolph County. He had attended only two meetings of the order and had not yet memorized the oath; "but [I] have heard [fellow spy] John Jackson's oath, and to the best of my recollection it is about the same," Elliott stated. Over 250 members were present at the meeting, held at a farmhouse north of Winchester. "A man from New York* [Carrington added in the margin, "*P.C. Wright of New York News"] made them a speech and talked to them about the manner of procuring arms. That if he could not get them in New York he could get them from Canada. I heard his name but have forgotten it." He believed that there were many arms hidden near Muncie, in nearby Delaware County. On the night of the meeting a collection was taken up with which to purchase arms netted $4,000. The order planned to seize the state arsenal at Indianapolis during the spring and assassinate Governor Morton if possible.[53]

John Jackson, the soldier detailed to Carrington, also furnished a statement in early March. He swore that he had joined the organization formerly known as the Knights of the Mighty Host, but was now known simply as the Knights, in August 1863 in his home community in Rock Creek Township, Wells County. He had attended a number of its secret meetings, which were usually held in barns or empty schoolhouses, with guards posted outside and passwords for admittance. The "object of the order is to defeat the present Administration, and to do all they can to keep men from going into the Army," he stated. They aimed to "cripple" the administration's ability to defeat the rebel states, and were prepared to resist "any arrest whatever of any person of the order who may have violated any military law or order." The "Johnson boys," the brothers who assaulted an enrollment officer and around whom hundreds of armed men rallied during the previous summer, "are to be sustained." Efforts were made to arm all the members, and those who did not have or could not afford to buy arms would be assisted by a "tax" on the membership. Jackson believed that ninety-three thousand men were enrolled in the order, with six thousand muskets and sixty thousand revolvers spread among them. "There is considerable talk about making arrangements to receive a large number of arms, through Vallandigham from Canada, who had beyond doubt furnished a good many arms to Ohio and Indiana." The arms would be shipped to Chicago, Cleveland, and other Great Lakes ports. He provided a long and detailed list of the "leading men in our lodge," including "H.S. Zimro" [Zumro, against whose name Carrington wrote, "U.S. Detective"]. He believed another member was involved in the theft of the legion arms at the Huntington railroad station in the summer of 1863. "The principal man in Huntington is L.P. Milligan [next to whose name Carrington noted, "Maj. Genl of order"]."[54]

Dr. Henry Zumro actively investigated the secret organization in his community around Markle, a town in Huntington County near Jackson's Rock Creek Township in Wells County. A forty-year-old Pennsylvania-born physician, Zumro supported his wife and several children on a thriving medical practice in the neighborhood. On March 19 he informed Governor Morton that a fellow Wells County physician who was endeavoring to obtain a military appointment as a regimental surgeon was an "active member of the

Knights" and speaking publicly against the Lincoln administration. Zumro warned that his medical colleague should not be given an appointment. "Mr. Jackson is sick with measles and will be at Indianapolis as soon as he is able to come," he stated. "The impression among the Knights here is that I was sent for by the provost of Indianapolis to appear and make restoration for treasonable language and other charges alleged against me," Zumro wrote, referring to a summons from Baker. "It has a very good effect," he continued, and suggested, in his poorly spelled letter,

> They appere to be more free in speaking to me upon their disigns. I think one among the best arangements to establish their confidence in me more strongly is to have me arested. From all that I can lern they are making big calculasions for the coming election. some say we will conquer or ~~perish~~ die at the stake. Eny time that I can be of eny service let me know. Here I am prying in to maters as fast as I can.

Zumro added a postscript that he would like to "here from Col. Schooler [Shuler] and also Col Baker."[55] Though a novice in spy work, Zumro had suggested that Baker, Carrington, and Morton enact a classic espionage maneuver to establish an agent's bona fides. The officers agreed and, days later, arranged for the arrest of the country physician. Carrington soon penned a letter to Baker to add to the charade, concluding that Zumro should be discharged without trial.[56] Armed with this phony document, Zumro would work to infiltrate the secret organization in his community.[57]

Watching Windsor

In the meantime, news arrived at Columbus from Detroit regarding developments across the river at Windsor. Lieutenant Colonel Smith reported to Major Johnson and sent documents about "conversations held with parties belonging (at present) in Windsor" and others. The rebels there placed "great faith" in John Hunt Morgan and expected him to raid in southern Illinois, Indiana, and Ohio "ere long." They were making preparations to join him, including "providing arms" to accomplices. "I am further assured that there is an extensive plot organizing in nearly or quite all the North Western States, to oppose the Government," he continued, "and as far as possible to assist the rebels." As part of the preparations, Smith noted that "emissaries have been here in consultation with Mr Vallandigham and other leading rebels in Canada." As well, a merchant offered to sell them "any number of revolvers which he said he was having shipped from the east as Medicines, and to go to Iowa."

Smith reported that he had detectives "on the lookout" for the firearms, but had not found them. He surmised that at the outset of the planned uprising the leaders would demand the restoration of Vallandigham, "and in case of refusal, they will try force." Many leading Democrats visited the Ohio exile and other "disloyal men" in Windsor. Headquarters digested Smith's report and forwarded it to Baker and Carrington for their information.[58]

A week later Smith provided additional details. The Windsor rebels' new plan was, when the ice on Lake Erie cleared, to seize a steamer and accompany two schooners then moored at Rondeau, on the Canadian north shore, to raid U.S. cities that lacked defenses. His detectives reported that one of the schooners was armed with two cannon and had a hold full of arms. He suggested that, as soon as the ice cleared, the USS *Michigan* cruise in the western end of the lake and that the government request British authorities to search the schooner's hold without alerting the conspirators.[59] Headquarters asked Smith who his source was.[60] Smith replied that one of his informants about affairs in Windsor was "not a recognized detective of mine; although he gives me a great deal of information." Rather than a mercenary detective, the informant was a "physician; and a gentleman; one, whom I believe, to be truly loyal, and perfectly reliable." He had just called on Smith "clandestinely" about "a very large organization, in the Northern, and N. Western States," well armed and intent on rising and initiating "a general time of rioting and incendiarism." The date for the rising was not fixed, he informed Smith, but was perhaps days or weeks away. A raid across the Ohio River by Confederate cavalry raiders John Hunt Morgan or Nathan Bedford Forrest might be the signal. But "if such an event does not occur, it is believed, that the Democratic Convention, at Chicago, will be the time decided upon." Smith added, "My informant is confident that Vallandigham is concerned in the proposed movement." Smith also provided additional information on two "rebel emissaries" from Missouri, one called Talbot of the Confederate artillery, "said to be a good officer," and the other called "Col Sneider," an influential man among the rebels, then in Canada. He also relayed information about Enfield rifles and tons of gunpowder that in the previous year had been shipped secretly up the Maumee River near Toledo. However, "either the failure to elect Vallandigham, or the failure to attack Johnson's Island" prompted the plotters to return the arms to Canada. He hoped that his detectives would learn of their whereabouts. "I believe it myself," he added. "I inform you of as much as I can communicate on paper," he wrote. "I have plans for ascertaining their contemplated movements, which I trust may be successful. At all events, I shall keep watch over their movements, as my Emissaries on the other Side, will."[61]

Heintzelman shared Smith's information with Halleck at the War Department, including the report of a schooner being fitted out north of Detroit on Lake Huron, but dismissed the threat. Sufficient force existed to prevent the vessel passing near Detroit into Lake Erie, he thought; nonetheless, the USS *Michigan* should be sent north when the ice melted.[62] He added that he had spoken with Governor Brough on security matters. Both men boarded in the same Columbus hotel and often conversed in the dining room. Brough, who had his own sources, had confided on several occasions about his misgivings about affairs in Ohio. He shared information about a possible raid by West Virginia rebels on Gallipolis, Ohio, where the army had important quartermaster depots. The general alerted the commander of federal forces in West Virginia and wrote to Washington about the exposed nature of that area. Still, Heintzelman was skeptical, concluding "the information is very indefinite and exaggerated."[63] Days later, the governor warned him of another imminent breakout attempt by the rebel prisoners held at the Ohio State Penitentiary, many of them officers from Morgan's cavalry force. Brough canceled a Cleveland appearance to remain in Columbus and monitor the situation.[64] Shortly afterward, as a precaution, the War Department ordered Heintzelman to send George W. L. Bickley, the founder of the KGC organization and imprisoned at the state penitentiary since his arrest in Indiana the previous summer, under guard to the highly secure military prison at Fort Lafayette, in New York harbor.[65] One day, the general had a "long talk" with Brough, during which the governor told him of General Grant's plans for the Army of the Potomac in the coming campaign season. Hearing of army strategy imparted to a politician by Washington officials but not confided to him annoyed the general. The "Governor told me this as he said I ought to know it," he recorded. "The War Dept don't think so."[66] Still, their dining room discussions were significant, and Heintzelman advised the War Department, "Should we meet with any serious reverses, or not some decided successes soon, I am satisfied that we will have much trouble with the disloyal in the states of this Dept and probably also in Kentucky."[67] As a precautionary measure, he requested the acting assistant provost marshal generals in the department to report to him on the likelihood of resistance to the coming draft. Colonel Baker of Indiana reported that as the state had met its volunteer quotas he could not "judge of the probabilities of resistance." He suggested, however, that there should be at least four more infantry companies at Indianapolis and that the new cavalry regiments then being organized could be armed and used to counteract difficulties.[68]

More Troubles in Illinois

Amid the worries about insurrection in the region, on March 28, in eastern Illinois, the simmering animosity between armed bands of war opponents and furloughed soldiers again boiled over into bloodshed. The day saw the opening of the Coles County circuit court session, and many people flocked to Charleston to attend court. As well, many came to town to enjoy a Democratic rally and hear speeches by their anti-Lincoln-administration congressman, John R. Eden. Soldiers of the 54th Illinois Volunteer Infantry Regiment, at home on leave, milled around the town and courthouse square. It was their last day of furlough and they gathered to prepare to depart. Despite the festive atmosphere, tensions were high. Soldiers of the regiment had participated in the violent incidents at Paris and elsewhere, had assaulted citizens, and left a trail of blood and bad feelings in their dealings with local Democrats. Many Democratic men came to town armed, with revolvers hidden in their clothing or in the straw in the back of their wagons. An exchange of insults between a soldier and a Democrat in the courthouse square quickly became a brawl, and both drew guns and fired. Nearby Democrats promptly uncovered their guns and fired a broadside at soldiers, most of whom were unarmed. Soldiers scrambled to find weapons of any sort—grabbing firearms, rocks, sticks, and other implements where they could—and rallied against the well-armed Democrats. The melee lasted only about a minute, but seven men—six soldiers and one Democrat—already lay dead in the streets. Two more—a Democrat and a Republican bystander—died shortly afterward when soldiers shot at a captured Democrat who tried to break and run, also killing the bystander. Twelve others were wounded.[69]

The colonel of the 54th Illinois rushed to the telegraph office and wired Mattoon for reinforcements, where the rest of the regiment was gathering and where other troops were to be found. In turn, Mattoon officers immediately telegraphed to Oakes at Springfield. Oakes notified Heintzelman, who notified the War Department. Oakes dispatched additional troops to Charleston and went there himself. In the meantime, many of the Democrats involved in the fighting fled town and met up with others in the countryside. There they gathered and prepared to renew the fight. Oakes arrived on March 30 with more troops from Springfield and arrested thirty persons thought to be involved in the fighting. He telegraphed Heintzelman that he believed reports of massing "insurgents" nearby and thought that they would soon attack the troops in both Mattoon and Charleston. Oakes also asked officers at Indianapolis to send five hundred troops.[70] As soon as he received the request, Carrington quickly diverted the 47th Indiana Volunteer Infantry Regiment, which was preparing to depart for the front after its veteran furlough ended. He ordered the regiment to stop at Mattoon to ascertain the situation and lend support if needed. He also sent along twenty thousand rounds of ammunition.[71]

That same day, Carrington received telegrams from Major General Stephen G. Burbridge, the new commander of the District of Kentucky. Rebel cavalry raider General Nathan Bedford Forrest and two thousand troopers had attacked and taken Paducah, Kentucky, on the Ohio River. Burbridge asked what troops he had available for river border defense. Carrington replied that he could put five thousand well-armed legion troops at Evansville; unfortunately, the new Indiana volunteer cavalry regiments then in the process of organizing had few horses and arms.[72] He telegraphed legion commanders along the river to have their arms inspected and be ready for action on the border.[73] To Governor Morton, away in New York City, he wired that he had notified the legion to prepare for action, adding that he "anticipat[ed] this movement [of Forrest] a week ago."[74] Though no overt link between Forrest and persons north of the Ohio River developed, Carrington continued to monitor the whereabouts of Forrest's troops.[75]

Carrington thought the Charleston riot and the Forrest attack at Paducah were not coincidental. The reports and affidavits he had collected spoke of rebel raids and concurrent uprisings in states north of the Ohio River. In sending the troops to Illinois he violated army protocols, as he was not the military commander at Indianapolis at the time. He explained, "I have satisfactory evidence that there is concert of action, as well as opinion, between some of the rebel leaders and the disaffected at home, and in such an emergency as this I have deemed the delay of *non-action,* more offensive to military propriety than to meet it by the best method possible."[76]

A short time afterward, when the armed bands near Charleston had melted away, most of the troops had dispersed, and many of the witnesses and prisoners had been questioned, Colonel Oakes prepared a long and detailed report to Heintzelman on the affair, accompanied by hundreds of pages of affidavits and other documentation. The attack was "preconcerted & premeditated," he concluded. Indeed, "it is impossible to doubt this. The whole conduct of the insurgents proves this. The documents forwarded herewith demonstrate it." The opening of the court and the Democratic rally to hear Congressman Eden had been pretexts used by the leaders in a "deliberate plot to murder the soldiers." He credited the quick reactions of the colonel of the 54th Illinois and other military commanders in promptly reinforcing him for "thwarting" the beginning of a "dangerous & extensive insurrection in that part of the State." He had "direct & positive proof" that some of the participants in the Charleston fight "were members of a treasonable secret society, known as the 'Golden Circle,' or more lately by some other name." The riot and murder was "planned & executed through that organization," he added, and he had no doubt that "by its agency a wide-spread conspiracy is being formed against the Govt which is only waiting a fitting opportunity for development." He advised against trying the prisoners in state or federal civil courts. "They would inevitably be either set at liberty without punishment, or dealt with so leniently as to encourage, rather than dissuade from, future acts of violence & treason." Instead, the prisoners should be tried by courts-martial or military commissions, conviction in which "could not fail to be of salutary & lasting effect."[77]

Also at this time, Carrington prepared the first of his major reports to Heintzelman outlining his extensive knowledge of the secret organization in Indiana, based on his investigations and interviews. He termed it a "partial report of progress in examination of disloyal societies in Indiana" and began with a brief review of the KGC in 1863, when the organization aimed to protect deserters, resist the draft, and furnish a "general opposition to the progress of the war." The organization also worked to import arms and distribute them to the members. Authorities seized many arms, "but many thousands [of weapons] were distributed for disloyal purposes" despite the army's best efforts. "A thorough system of espionage gave me possession of their entire machinery," he proudly wrote, which resulted in over one hundred and fifty convictions in federal courts. This, he claimed, demoralized the organization and it disbanded. He ascribed the failure of a rising during the Morgan Raid to his previous exposures. "They had been thoroughly exposed during the summer," he added, "so that Morgan, upon his invasion, was not only disappointed of substantial support, but found the masses of the people overwhelmingly his enemies." At present, he continued, based on statements of the "witnesses examined," the organization possessed two basic aims:

1st To prevent a four years succession of the war party

2nd To force a recognition of a Southern Confederacy bound to the North by an offensive and defensive league, in respect to foreign powers, while yielding to the Confederacy as a Slaveocracy, all rights to be secured by an efficient fugitive slave law, and kindred enactments. To this end they propose such th[o]rough armed organization, as will give them command of the North West, believing that this will control the politics of New England and other Eastern States.

The organization had divided the state into districts and begun to enroll members who were "positive opponents to the war." It aimed to prevent Lincoln's reelection by fraud at the ballot box or force. Carrington cited his insider informants regarding the organization's strength in Indiana. John Jackson said that the lodge in Huntington County circulated the number of members at ninety-three thousand. Wesley Tranter, a soldier in the 17th Indiana Volunteer Infantry Regiment from Martin County, reported that nearly one hundred thousand was the number mentioned in his lodge, while Thomas Elliott in Wayne County said that ninety-five thousand was the number given in his lodge. All three reported that Illinois had more members than Indiana and that arms were coming to Indiana from Canada and the East. "This accords with the opinion of Col Smith U.S.A. at Detroit, copy of whose letter was furnished me by General Heintzelman," he wrote. He reported on the "mock arrest" of Zumro, noting that he released him to secure the new ritual "which has been prepared to counteract previous exposures." He cited his spies on other matters, noting that Elliott had sworn that the organization's taxation scheme raised significant amounts of money with which to arm members. All his spies reported that members of their lodges spoke of the necessity of replacing Governor Morton with Indiana secretary of state James Athon, whom he characterized as a "bitter and unscrupulous opponent of the war." Leading Democrats provided him with information on the growth and extent of the organization in Indiana. Significantly, he quoted Joseph E. McDonald, a former Congressmen who shortly would win the party's nomination to challenge Morton in the fall gubernatorial contest and "opposed to the 'K.G.C.s' in 1863," as saying, "'These things cannot last. . . . if the people are forced into secret organizations to protect themselves, it will not be six months before the whole North West will be in a blaze of Civil War—they may force such men as me even, into it. I know the temper and feeling of the people—it will embrace one half of the North West, and a force the government cannot put down.'" Carrington suggested that the strength of the movement had grown beyond the point that the "conservatives of the party" could control it. He believed that the division in Democratic ranks between the radical revolutionaries and establishment old guard could be exploited. Still, he warned that the revolutionaries were "sufficiently desperate after power to require attention." Amid the clash of armies at the front and a passive willingness coming from Washington to trust in the "intelligence of the people," he noted the "natural tendency to lightly treat these domestic organizations." Against such complacency Carrington earnestly warned.[78]

The Arrest of Phineas C. Wright

At this time, the watch on the Detroit River continued by military authorities and detectives. Smith reported to Columbus headquarters that the U.S. attorney in Detroit, Alfred Russell, had called on him. A leading "War Democrat" of the city reported the presence of one P. C. Wright, "formerly from New York State, lately from New Orleans." He was a "bitter denouncer" of the government, reported the War Democrat. Wright had resided in a hotel in Detroit for the past month, "with no visible occupation, and no pecuniary interest . . . to keep him here." Furthermore, he visited Windsor and Port Huron and met frequently with "Peace Democrats" in Detroit. Wright had revealed to Russell's informant

> that within a very few weeks, there will be a rebellion against the Administration, in this city and other places, and in other States; and great blood shed, murders, incendiarism; the entire North next will rise, and by force of arms, compel the Government to withdraw the troops from the South. That there is an extensive organization, stretching from Canada, through Missouri and Kentucky, armed, whose plans will be matured in a few weeks, for forcibly overthrowing the Administration, and thus organize mob law, in this city and other places.[79]

Smith promptly put a detective on Wright's trail and continued his efforts to watch the Windsor rebels. He alerted Michigan's two Republican U.S. senators, Jacob M. Howard and Zachariah Chandler, who pressed Secretary Stanton for protection for Detroit. The secretary complied by authorizing the hire of a tug to patrol the Detroit River.[80] Russell also confided his information to Lieutenant Colonel Bennett H. Hill, the acting assistant provost marshal general for Michigan, who also relayed details to Heintzelman. The armed organization, he reported, had its headquarters in Chicago and planned on a rising to occur within two weeks to coincide with the appearance of Vallandigham on United States soil. The rising was to be large enough to "paralyse our armies in the field for a time, and to affect very materially the next political elections." Hill suggested that, as his own spies would be easily spotted, detectives from Columbus be sent to Windsor to watch Vallandigham, "persons who from their appearance and manners could pass for Southern refugees," and who could "readily obtain the confidence of Vallandigham's friends."[81]

Other Washington authorities received warnings of signs of revolution in the Northwest. A prominent New Yorker informed Secretary of State William

Seward that while in Toronto men there spoke to him of a "deep laid plan . . . to sever Illinois & Indiana from the Union—that the recent troubles in Illinois have their origin in this plan. They boast that the States have been sounded & are ripe—& that through those States the South will [secure?] peace on their own terms." Seward forwarded a copy of the letter to Heintzelman.[82]

Numerous reports of the imminent danger of revolutionary outbreak in the Old Northwest reached Washington in early April, so many that a sometimes negligent and preoccupied Lincoln administration was forced to act. President Lincoln ordered military authorities to arrest Phineas C. Wright. Secretary Stanton's War Department sent orders to General Heintzelman to make the arrest:

> Information has reached this Department that "there is one, P.C. Wright, formerly a New Orleans lawyer and owner of a plantation confiscated with the slaves, who has been staying at the Russell House, at Detroit, in correspondence with leading rebels now in Canada, and who, as Col. Smith, U.S.A., military commander there, has good reason to believe, upon information derived from good War Democrats, who do not like to have their names given, and who advise his arrest, is connected directly with a treasonable plot through the Northwest, to rise, as they did in Coles County, Illinois. Leading Peace Democrats are closeted with him."
>
> The President directs that you take measures to have P.C. Wright arrested and sent to Fort Lafayette, to await further orders, and that you report your action to this Department.[83]

Heintzelman received the order on April 23 and forwarded the order to Smith to carry out.[84] Smith's men tracked down Wright in Grand Rapids, Michigan, and arrested him on April 26. Smith reported that the officers found papers on him, including a "roll of manuscript, apparently a lecture, frequently delivered," along with other items, all of which Smith sent to headquarters. A staff officer and guard conveyed Wright eastward by steamboat and train to Fort Lafayette, in New York harbor, for safekeeping.[85] The Lincoln administration held him in military prison without charges until well after the rebellion ended.[86]

Heintzelman and his staff had known that P. C. Wright was the leader of the OAK when orders came from Lincoln to arrest him. Wright's name had been associated with the movement in Illinois earlier in the year, in reports forwarded from Oakes and written by the detective working for him, David Turnbull of Warren County, Illinois. On April 4, Turnbull called on the general at Columbus headquarters and presented letters from Springfield officials "about copperhead organizations." In his journal Heintzelman reflected to himself, "There is no doubt there are regular organizations and prepared to give trouble, if there is a raid, or we meet with reverses. I gave [Turnbull] a letter to Gen. Carrington to have him use his information. It is well enough to keep advised."[87]

In April, Heintzelman was greatly preoccupied with "copperhead demonstrations" in his department, remarking that Smith at Detroit was "always in trouble about something."[88] In his hotel dining room he met Governor Brough, who mentioned "going to Indianapolis about these copperhead demonstrations." Brough traveled to Indianapolis to meet with Morton and returned to persuade the general to join him on another trip later that week to meet Morton and other governors.[89] Heintzelman agreed and traveled to the Indiana capital with Brough and his wife. On April 15, at ten o'clock in the morning he met with Governors Morton, Yates, and Brough, along with General Carrington, in a room in the statehouse. Also present was a detective. A "long conversation" ensued in which the detective gave "a full account of the secret society and their books with the two lower degrees." The governors heard that the organization was spread through Canada, Indiana, Illinois, with some lodges in Ohio, Iowa, and Missouri. Heintzelman recorded in his journal the tenor of the discussion: "if we meet with any reverses they will act. If Forrest had captured Paducah and crossed the Ohio, the other day there would have been trouble." The meeting adjourned for luncheon, during which the governors' wives joined them. Having dined, the ladies retired and the gentlemen resumed their earnest discussions. They agreed that the governors would go to Washington to air their concerns with federal officials. Besides ventilating on their common problem of "copperhead demonstrations," the governors wished to press on Lincoln and the War Department the idea of tendering a force of three-months troops to relieve veteran troops of tasks such as guarding railroads and bridges in the occupied South, freeing them to fight at the front.[90]

As spring advanced and April rolled into May, military commanders in the Northern Department had compared notes they had collected from their detectives on the secret organizations in their midst. Heintzelman acted on his orders to protect the prisoner-of-war camps under his purview, but he also responded to the need from the Provost Marshal General's Bureau to suppress draft resistance. At the root of many of their problems were the secret organizations. Heintzelman's recognition that Carrington had special knowledge on the subject was a significant step forward in the army's ability to combat them. Carrington's diligent efforts to detect their machinations bore fruit, as reports obtained from his sources and spies in Indiana and Illinois enabled commanders to anticipate problems. Continued army surveillance of Vallandigham and the persons with whom he associated in Windsor helped keep the lid on the problem. Finally, the arrest of P. C. Wright, a leader of the OAK, the successor of the KGC, brought about by a tip from an anonymous and prominent War Democrat, was a major success and may have forestalled a planned uprising in the region that spring. Soon, cooperation from energetic military commanders at Saint Louis would bolster intelligence gathering and present a fuller picture of the threat.

SEVEN

"What I Say about Secret Dangers Is Well Considered and Based on Fact"

How Rosecrans's Detectives Infiltrated the Secret Organizations in Early 1864

MAJOR GENERAL William Starke Rosecrans was an experienced and adept user of intelligence resources. On his arrival at Saint Louis to command the sprawling Department of the Missouri, he quickly revamped army intelligence operations to make them more responsive to his needs. One of his key moves was to appoint as his chief intelligence officer Colonel John P. Sanderson. Together, Rosecrans and Sanderson rapidly built a wide-ranging detective force that provided important information on secret undercurrents both in his department and in the Northwestern states that neighbored it. Their detectives ranged from New York City to Canada to the cities and states of the Ohio and Mississippi River valleys to western Missouri. Significantly, Rosecrans shared the information his detectives obtained with military and political leaders in Illinois, Indiana, and Ohio. Together, they coordinated a unified response and began to formulate a plan to combat the growing threat of insurrection in the North.

Rosecrans Arrives at Saint Louis

In January 1864, Major General Rosecrans received orders to take command of the Department of the Missouri, headquartered in Saint Louis. One of the U.S. Army's most effective and brilliant generals in the Civil War, the victor of several important battles and campaigns to conquer the Southern rebellion, Rosecrans had been ordered by the War Department to take command of a guerrilla-ravaged sinkhole of a department wracked by internecine political hatreds among even the federal government's supporters. The vicious infighting between Conservatives and Radicals among the Missouri Unionists and Republicans had destroyed the effectiveness of his predecessors, Generals Samuel R. Curtis and John M. Schofield. The two generals had been caught in the crossfire between the two warring political factions. Missouri politics plagued President Lincoln and the War Department during the war, and the placement of a capable military officer in Saint Louis was an important step in pacifying a vast western region. Rosecrans's appointment was recognition of his known talent, reputation, and leadership.

But the Missouri command was a significant step down for the general and was seen by him, Washington leadership, and others as punishment for his one major defeat: the debacle at Chickamauga Creek, in northern Georgia. In October 1863, weeks after the battle, Lincoln removed him from command of the Army of the Cumberland. Rosecrans knew that the Saint Louis posting was no plum appointment. He knew that Secretary Stanton strongly disliked him and had probably sent him there hoping to torment him. That was fine with Rosecrans, who hated Stanton passionately in return. The general enjoyed a challenge, was dedicated to crushing the rebellion, and entered into his latest command intent on fixing the "Missouri imbroglio" and helping preserve the national Union.[1]

Rosecrans was born in 1819 in Delaware County, Ohio, and graduated from the U.S. Military Academy in 1842 fifth in his class. The high class rank won him a coveted assignment to the Army Corps of Engineers, and he served in various posts and fortifications. As a consequence, he missed the fighting in the war with Mexico. Finding promotion in the regular army glacially slow, and with a wife and several children to support on meager army pay, he resigned his commission and returned to Cincinnati, Ohio, to enter the coal and oil-refining businesses. An oil-lamp explosion burned his face badly, leaving scars and requiring over a year to recover. Possessing an active mind, during these years Rosecrans patented several new inventions.[2]

With the attack on Fort Sumter, Rosecrans soon obtained the command of the 23rd Ohio Volunteer Infantry Regiment. With his regular-army experience, he was a valuable commodity. As a prominent Ohio Democrat who supported the war effort to suppress rebellion, and Catholic besides, he soon obtained a brigadier general appointment in the regular army and commanded part of

George McClellan's force in western Virginia. It was Rosecrans's forces that won the small but significant battle of Rich Mountain, in July 1861. Rosecrans assumed command of the Department of the Ohio when McClellan departed to take command of the Army of the Potomac. He secured western Virginia for the Union, which later became a separate state.[3] During the campaign, Rosecrans employed Cincinnati police detectives effectively in the region.

Transferred to the great Union army in Tennessee and northern Mississippi under the command of Major General Henry W. Halleck, Rosecrans commanded troops in the drive on Corinth, Mississippi, in the spring of 1862. When Halleck broke up his massive force and spread it abroad to occupy captured territory, Rosecrans took command of the Army of the Mississippi, under the command of Major General Ulysses S. Grant. He commanded his force in two major Union victories in northern Mississippi, the battles of Iuka and Corinth in September and October, respectively, defeating the stronger forces of rebel generals Sterling Price and Earl Van Dorn, with little help from Grant's other troops.[4] He quarreled seriously with Grant, who had ordered a vigorous pursuit of the defeated rebels only to reverse himself and halt the chase. Rosecrans, possessor of a sharp temper and tongue, complained bitterly. In a fit of pique, Grant insulted Rosecrans by hardly acknowledging his victories. The two generals, both rising stars in the U.S. Army, fought a clash of egos.[5] Subsequently, as Grant rose in prominence in the army and in the eyes of the War Department, he worked out his anger at Rosecrans in various and subtle ways.

The War Department rewarded Rosecrans for the victories at Iuka and Corinth by promoting him in the regular army and giving him command of the Army of the Ohio, which was soon renamed the Army of the Cumberland, one of the three main commands in the U.S. Army at the time (the Army of the Potomac and Grant's Army of the Tennessee, near Vicksburg, being the other major commands). Advancing southeast from Nashville, Rosecrans commanded the army in a fierce three-day battle (December 31, 1862–January 2, 1863) fought along the banks of Stones River near Murfreesboro, Tennessee, against rebel forces under Braxton Bragg. The two armies bludgeoned each other to a tactical draw, but Bragg withdrew from the field, allowing Rosecrans and his army to claim a major victory.[6] Rosecrans spent the winter and spring months rebuilding his army, especially strengthening his cavalry force, in preparation for offensive action. He also crafted an enormous and highly effective intelligence apparatus to gather information on Bragg's forces as well as to disrupt rebel mails, subversion, and other pro-rebel activities in the regions his forces occupied. During this time he raised the ire of Halleck,

Stanton, and Lincoln for not moving south as fast as they wanted. He also angered Grant by not weakening his own forces to reinforce Grant's army near Vicksburg. Finally, that summer Rosecrans launched a brilliant maneuver that forced Bragg's army to evacuate Tennessee and retreat into northern Georgia. He relied on excellent intelligence from his spies and his improved cavalry force to great effect in the campaign. Rosecrans pursued the rebel force. However, in September, Bragg received reinforcements in the shape of General James Longstreet's strong corps from Lee's Army of Northern Virginia and counterattacked. The two armies clashed near Chickamauga Creek. Reacting to a (mistaken) report that a division in his line was out of position, Rosecrans sent orders to another division commander to shift his force. Longstreet's newly arrived troops poured into the breach in the federal line's right flank, crushing it and forcing a pell-mell retreat to Chattanooga. Rosecrans was caught up in the headlong flight of the troops of the right flank and could not rally them. Only the stubborn resistance of Major General George H. Thomas's left flank prevented an absolute rout, allowing the crushed right to escape northward.[7]

Rosecrans and his army rallied at Chattanooga and prepared to resist attack from rebel forces that besieged the city. But his reputation was in tatters. An assistant secretary of war, Charles A. Dana, who had lived with Rosecrans's headquarters staff during the advance into Georgia, sent dispatches to Stanton filled with damning accounts of Rosecrans's behavior, suggesting that the commander was unhinged. It was a deliberate campaign of character assassination. Notified of the defeat to federal troops, the War Department and Lincoln rallied reinforcements from all points and determined to sack the general. In October, Grant, who had months before forced the capitulation of the Mississippi River fortress at Vicksburg and had received command of all troops west of the Appalachians, arrived and relieved Rosecrans of command, replacing him with Thomas. With the reinforcements in hand, Grant attacked Bragg's forces on Lookout Mountain and Missionary Ridge and drove him south into Georgia.[8]

Rosecrans, ordered to Cincinnati to await word of a future assignment, itched for a new command. Rumors coming from Washington suggested that the Missouri post would be available. Knowing that the Saint Louis command would primarily require refereeing the warring political factions in the state as well as fighting guerrillas, he nonetheless yearned for the job. Finally, after much waiting, orders arrived to proceed to Saint Louis to take command of the Department of the Missouri. Rosecrans gathered up his trusted staff officers and left for Missouri at the end of January 1864.

Rosecrans Recruits John P. Sanderson

Shortly after arriving at Saint Louis and surveying the lay of the land, Rosecrans sent for another trusted staff officer. While still in Cincinnati, when the rumors of the Missouri command began to float around, he had spoken quietly with Colonel John Philip Sanderson, commander of the 13th U.S. Infantry Regiment, then stationed at Newport Barracks, across the Ohio River. Sanderson had impressed the commanding general as a man of sense, efficiency, and ability while serving on another general's staff. Rosecrans soon added him to his own staff, where he served in the battle as a dispatch rider, carrying the commanding general's orders to others. In his official report of the battle Rosecrans commended him for his bravery.[9] Sanderson, who wrote a journal in installments that he sent to his wife almost daily, recorded that Rosecrans had assured him that "he would apply to the War Dept to have me assigned to his Department for the purpose of giving me some important position."[10] Rosecrans returned to Cincinnati from Saint Louis and spoke briefly to Sanderson. The general, wrote Sanderson to his wife, had "looked round; he had seen enough to satisfy him that the Provost Marshal General was second only in importance to the Comd Genl there; that it must be a man after his own heart & according to his own mind; and that he had resolved to have me for the place, no matter who was urged, & meant not to ask Halleck or Stanton for me, but apply direct to the President. Thus matters now stand, all of which yet remains, of course, *strictly confidential.*"[11]

Sanderson's services were in demand at this time both in the army and out of it. Earlier in the fall, prominent Unionists of Louisville, Kentucky, approached him with the offer of taking over the editor's chair of the *Louisville Journal*, the leading newspaper of that city and one of the most important in the West, then edited by George D. Prentice. The Unionists meant to buy the *Journal*, or, failing that, to start a new daily newspaper in the city. They raised funds for the purpose and wanted Sanderson to be managing editor.[12] Also, Pennsylvania politicians had gone to Washington to lobby for Sanderson to be appointed the acting assistant provost marshal general to run the draft apparatus in the state. Secretary Stanton had agreed and was poised to send him to Harrisburg.[13]

Sanderson was a man of talents, recognized as such by his contemporaries, and praised for his organizational abilities. Born in 1818 in Dauphin County, Pennsylvania, he studied and practiced law and entered Whig Party politics in the 1840s, serving in both houses of the Pennsylvania legislature. A businessman, he turned to journalism and edited the *Philadelphia Daily News*, a major newspaper, from 1848 to 1856. He rose to become one of the top managers and then right-hand man for Simon Cameron, one of Pennsylvania's preeminent political leaders. He became involved in the Know-Nothings, a secret anti-immigrant and anti-Catholic movement, and enraged Pennsylvania Republicans in 1856 when he broke up an effort to fuse state Know-Nothings with the Republicans, thereby handing election victory to the Democratic Party. He eventually became an active Republican. Lincoln appointed him chief clerk of the War Department at Cameron's behest.[14] He later was appointed lieutenant colonel of the 15th U.S. Infantry Regiment. As was the lot of many regular-army officers, Sanderson filled important administrative posts besides working to fill his regiment to full strength, bringing valuable experience to the business of managing an army.[15]

On arrival in Saint Louis, Rosecrans and his staff immediately grasped that lowering the level of animosity between the two major Unionist factions would be key to solving the department's military and other ancillary problems. Replacing subordinate generals identified with one or other of the factions with officers from outside the state was essential, as was bringing in troops from other states instead of relying on Missouri militia forces.[16] As an experienced user of intelligence resources, Rosecrans immediately employed the detective corps at his disposal more aggressively than had his predecessors, who had used detectives in comparatively mundane and ordinary tasks. The records of the army post of Saint Louis show that within days of his arrival, and before Sanderson's arrival, staff detectives ranged farther afield and undertook a wider range of tasks than had been previously attempted, including searching and seizing private property, traveling to distant towns within and without the department, undertaking investigations, and making more arrests. Commanders fired many underperforming detectives.[17] Additionally, one of Rosecrans's staff officers wrote privately that "the feeling that is got up between two parties Radicals & con——s is very intense, and considering the grounds very unnecessary."[18] Days after arriving in the state, the general wrote to President Lincoln to ask for Sanderson's services: "The interests of the Service here [as] well as the national cause makes it expedient that an able officer not identified with local parties should be Provost Marshal of the Department."[19] Lincoln agreed to his request.[20]

Sanderson arrived at Saint Louis on March 3 and immediately reported to Rosecrans, who briefed him on his new job. Sanderson was impressed by the size of the staff he was to command, with two colonels to serve as his chief assistants, and an army of clerks and other assistants to handle the myriad matters that his office oversaw. His headquarters were near Rosecrans's in central

Saint Louis and occupied a "large three st[o]ry double brick building, and is filled with my officers and clerks from top to bottom, every room being occupied for office purposes."[21] The Provost Marshal General's Office in the department had grown over the years in response to the enormous guerrilla problem in the state. The army had divided the state into a number of districts and subdistricts, each with military commanders to oversee efforts to suppress guerrilla activity. Each district and subdistrict employed detectives to watch rebel activities, especially keeping an eye open for guerrillas. The brutality of the pro-rebel guerrillas and Unionist reprisals, and the almost equal severity of the army's efforts at counterinsurgency in Missouri, was perhaps unparalleled in United States experience, and the headquarters bureaucracy had grown commensurate with the challenge.[22] Sanderson voiced awe at the responsibilities placed in his hands. His new duties "are even more extensive than I had any idea of. The Provost Marshal is in truth, a power, and had devolving upon him an enormous amount of duty, responsibility, & patronage. He is second only in importance, as well as public estimation, to the Commanding General." He added that the different political factions received his appointment well; "each congratulates itself, in not having" someone "who is identified with the others, and all say that they are satisfied with me, because they know I belong to neither, and expect me to be impartial and independent, as I shall certainly strive to be."[23] His new duties were "arduous, and require all the mind, energy, skill, tact, & talent, I can command." But he found them "to my taste" and he believed he was "adapted and qualified" for them. He congratulated himself that his good relations with Rosecrans allowed for the smooth operation of his office: "we understand each other fully," he concluded, "and get along with each other most harmoniously and agreeably."[24] Sanderson and Rosecrans quickly established a system by which the colonel reported to the commanding general at a regular hour each day, usually late in the evening (which was the middle of Rosecrans's day, as he typically rose late in the morning and worked eighteen hours days, often until dawn), to review the day and plan ahead.[25] Sanderson briefed the general on all matters that arose in the provost marshal general's office, and records show that Rosecrans was aware of, directed, and sanctioned all the colonel's efforts.

Sanderson entered into the duties of his new post with enthusiasm and vigor. He was soon consumed by the myriad tasks. Among them was maintaining the military prisons in the city and Alton, Illinois, where thousands of rebel prisoners of war, guerrillas, and political prisoners were held. He undertook many interrogations of prisoners, as well as listened to numerous appeals for release or clemency. During his first week on the job he dodged an assassination attempt by a "lady smuggler of rebel mails" held in prison awaiting court-martial. Indeed, he penned to his wife, the woman was but "one of the intensely secesh females" in Saint Louis who undertook espionage work for the Confederate cause. The provost marshal's staff and corps of detectives kept close watch on many pro-Confederate women in the city and around the state.[26] The scale, scope, and incessant demands of his work soon ended Sanderson's daily journal letter. Before March was out gaps of several days began to appear, and the colonel apologized for the lapses. The last surviving entry he wrote to his wife began with the apology: "I find myself from necessity obliged to neglect my record. I hope soon to have more leisure, and shall then again resume my regularity. At present it is simply impossible."[27]

Also, within a week of starting in his new job, he encountered the problem of the existence of secret pro-rebel organizations in the state:

> Among other characters before me to day was a Rebel officer, who holds a high position in the organization of the Knights of the Golden Circle, and from whom I obtained much information, which I shall use to some purpose hereafter. Of course, this is a secret not to be repeated, known only to him & myself, & which, if made known, would probably loose [sic] him his head. But, all rebels, I believe, are precious scoundrels, and, acting on the motto that it takes a thief to catch a thief, I hope to make good use of his information & services.[28]

The following day, Sanderson wrote to his wife:

> I have had all sort of people to deal with during the day [among whom was] a Rebel Lt Colonel in the Rebel Army, now Paroled Prisoner professedly, but really in my employ as a spy upon Rebels & their sympathizers within the Department, and ferreting out the leading spirits and all the operations of the Knights of the Golden Circle. Another who is now imprisoned for Bushwhacking, giving me a very full, whether truthful or not remains to be ascertained, account of the doing of some grand rascals, who profess to be Union men; another holding the rank of Major in the Rebel Army, but in fact a spy, just from Richmond [Virginia].[29]

The rebel officer was one G. Byron Jones, alias "James C. Johnson," who told Sanderson of his activities as a Confederate army recruiting agent and organizer in northern Missouri. Military authorities arrested Jones in Nebraska and delivered him to Saint Joseph, Missouri, where he revealed the nature of his work.

Sanderson interrogated him in Saint Louis. Jones revealed that in the spring of 1863 the Missouri militia units in the northern part of the state, derisively called the Paw Paws, were riddled with disloyal officers who were active in the KGC.[30]

Also during that first week, the commanding general of the District of Cairo, Illinois, Brigadier General Hugh T. Reid, forwarded to Rosecrans "some papers in relation to an organization which is said supersedes the Knights of the Golden Circle, and whose Members are sworn to use their efforts to get up a Rebellion in the North West." The papers were carried to Saint Louis by a "Dr. Edward Everett, probably an assumed name," and who is "probably a great rascal, and not very communicative." Everett, reported Reid, "was probably frightened into making the Revelation" by "one of our Detectives," to whom he had divulged information. Consequently, Everett "concluded to make a clean breast of it. He promises to Report to you and I will give him a letter to you, and you may be able to gain further information from him."[31] Records from the provost marshal's office at Cairo confirm Reid's statement: on March 3 he authorized payment of fifty-five dollars to a Dr. M. C. Baker for "expenses detecting secret disloyal organization to St Louis by order." On March 8, Reid authorized five dollars for "Dr Everett expenses going to Saint Louis with documents for Genl Rosecrans."[32]

Reid enclosed two reports by his provost marshal at Cairo, Captain Isaac M. Talmadge, who succeeded Major Joseph Merrill in the post. Talmadge continued Merrill's work of spying on secret organizations active in extreme southern Illinois. His reports, dated February 8 and March 8, detailed the existence of the Order of American Knights (OAK). In the first report he outlined that its "design is armed resistence [sic] to the Federal Government in the North," and that "Lodges or 'Temples' as they are called are in existence in the States of New York, Indiana, Illinois Missouri and Ohio." The organization, with an officer in each state called a General Commander, administered five degrees to members. Talmadge described passwords, handshakes, and signals that the members used to communicate secretly. "Beyond the 2nd Degree I have no information," he wrote. He added,

> It is stated that a meeting of the "General Commanders" was held in the City of New York on the 22n of Feby. to organize an outbreak on the 10th of March (on the occasion of the Draft); but through the want of courage, or we may charitably hope lingering sparks of patriotism, in some of the number, it was indefinitely postponed until consultation could be held with Valandigham [sic] the Grand Commander.

In the second report, Talmadge added that a captain named Singleton in the Missouri State Militia was thought to be a member of one of two "Temples" at Kirkwood, Missouri. (Sanderson endorsed the document: "Capt Singleton is the man who recently shot a man at St Joseph, & refused to be arrested by the civil authorities. Would it not be well to follow up his case? JPS.") The two OAK temples at Kirkwood ran a "regular line of smugglers and mail carriers" to Sterling Price's rebel army, he wrote, and a run was planned for the following Saturday night carrying arms and a rebel mail.[33]

The existence of secret organizations in Missouri had been noted by previous military commanders. Many reports in 1862 and 1863 filtered into Saint Louis headquarters that the KGC was actively working there to assist the rebels. In the spring and summer of 1863 a district provost marshal at Saint Joseph collected numerous sworn statements of members who admitted to membership in the KGC, which also went by the names Lone Star," the "Copperhead Organization," or "Democratic Society."[34] However, aside from arresting and questioning local leaders and members of the secret organization, little evidence exists to suggest that military authorities in Missouri did much with the information.

Before Sanderson arrived at Saint Louis, Rosecrans had received warnings from Missouri citizens of the existence of a secret organization in the state. Three Callaway County men wrote in February that "something unusual was on foot" among the rebels and their sympathizers in northern Missouri. The men had "no doubt but secret organizations are formed in every vicinity," and that a "general uprising . . . will be attempted between this & the middle of March." Among other things overheard, the "disaffected" counseled their friends to divest themselves of "'greenbacks,' saying that paper money will not be worth ten cents on the dollar a month hence." More dangerous was the fact, they said, that the members of the secret organization "are all arming themselves with *guns & Revolvers* (principally, the latter) & laying in large supplies of *ammunition*." Moreover, "*they get those things let them cost what they may*—even though they have to pay fifty per cent. over the ordinary price." They advised the general that they were not "idle alarmists," and suggested that "experienced detectives" be dispatched to northern Missouri to investigate the facts.[35]

Sanderson soon had the provost marshal's office machine humming efficiently, but someone thrust a monkey wrench into the gears. Newspaper reports from Washington arrived that rumors swirled around the Capitol accusing Sanderson of cowardice on the battlefield of Chickamauga, throwing Senate confirmation of his promotion to colonel of the 13th Infantry

Regiment into chaos.[36] "Had a clap of thunder come out of a clear sky, it could not have shocked me more than did this despatch," he wrote his wife.[37] Rosecrans was furious, as the attack was in reality a veiled assault on him. Rosecrans immediately prepared a statement for newspapers denouncing the attack. He wrote to Halleck in protest of the report and sent an aide, Major Frank S. Bond, to carry the letter and report verbally to him.[38] Rosecrans also ordered Bond to press the matter of getting troops from outside Missouri posted to the state.[39] Rosecrans voiced to Congressman James A. Garfield his indignation about the Sanderson "slander." The colonel was "just beginning to bring order out of chaos and with impartial intelligence and sagacity to change the system from a machine for political and pecuniary profit to something rational." Suddenly, his usefulness was "paralysed." He immediately suspected that Charles Dana was the source for the attack. After Chickamauga, he wrote, he had heard Dana ask around if he did not see Sanderson. "I inquired and no one had heard or seen aught to his discredit." Dana was a spy and calumniator, he concluded. Furthermore, he had asked for Sanderson to take up the Saint Louis job precisely "because he was an able impartial sagacious & unprejudiced officer of the regular army, without a stain on his reputation."[40] Sanderson also denounced Dana as a "dirty dog," "scoundrel," and "infamous libeller," and assured his wife that the truth would emerge and all would be well.[41] However, Secretary Stanton ordered Major Bond arrested on his arrival at Washington for violating an edict prohibiting officers to travel to the capital without specific War Department permission. Stanton ordered Bond back to Saint Louis and ordered Rosecrans to convene a court martial to try him for the violation. The tribunal quickly acquitted him of any offense.[42] Though the arrest of Bond was itself an insignificant matter, it would have significance months later in the tense relations between Rosecrans and Washington leaders. In the meantime, Sanderson received messages of support from influential politicians in Washington and Missouri expressing their outrage at the scandalous affair. In time, the Senate confirmed his promotion to colonel.[43]

Sanderson's Detectives

Work went on, however, and in the latter part of March, Sanderson opened up the throttle of his bureaucratic machine and roared ahead with investigations of the secret organization. He assigned paroled rebel officers "to ferret out the operations of the secret order in this department."[44] Many operated under assumed names, and it is today difficult to identify the actual names of some of these spies. However, one of these former rebel officers was Dr. Willis Bledsoe, who went by the alias William Jones. Bledsoe became one of the star detectives for Sanderson and other commanders from New York and Washington to Indianapolis and Chicago. Another was Dr. C. F. Mercer, a resident of Johnson County, Missouri, who had served in Sterling Price's Confederate forces as an assistant regimental surgeon in 1861 and who worked for Sanderson and others under the name William Taylor. Another detective, working under the assumed name Edward F. Hoffman, was Lawrence A. Hudson, a well-educated easterner who had earlier served in the Missouri State Militia. In early 1863, Hudson wrote to then Missouri governor Hamilton R. Gamble that he had been clerking in a district provost marshal's office, as his health was too poor for active service, but that he had been offered a teaching position at the University of Missouri and wished to be discharged from the militia.[45] Sanderson described "Hoffman" as a "New England man by birth, education, and habits—in a word, a shrewd, cool, cautious, wide-awake Yankee—of undoubted fidelity and integrity, and of unquestioned loyalty."[46] However, Sanderson and his successors found him eccentric and intractable and later fired him from the detective staff, but still later rehired him. Sanderson also employed a newspaper correspondent of the *Cincinnati Daily Gazette* and *Cincinnati Daily Times*, Edward Betty, as a detective.[47] Betty had followed Rosecrans from the time the general commanded in northern Mississippi, and, except for a stint writing about Grant's Vicksburg campaign, had attached himself to Rosecrans's headquarters. Surviving personal letters from Betty to the general are replete with fawning toadyisms.[48] His pieces for the *Gazette* and *Times* were no less full of praise of Rosecrans.[49] Betty wrote letters for the newspapers while on his missions for Sanderson that sometimes revealed in veiled terms his government work.[50] His occupation as a newspaperman provided cover to travel widely and ask questions. Sanderson detailed these and other detectives to gather information on the secret organizations in Missouri and elsewhere. They ranged widely throughout the Northwestern states and Kentucky.

Starting in early March, after learning of the existence of the OAK in parts of Missouri, "William Jones" (Willis Bledsoe) worked himself into OAK lodges and provided information to Sanderson. He reported that the organization claimed to stretch across the whole North, from Rhode Island to Missouri, and boasted one million members. He joined the "grand temple" at Saint Louis, which was presided over by a wealthy and prominent Democrat, Charles L. Hunt. Hunt also served as the Belgian consul in the city. Hunt's deputy as state commander of the order was Charles E. Dunn, a city official. In April, Hunt told Bledsoe that he was going to travel to Detroit and thence to Canada for a special conference with Vallandigham; the meeting was to "determine the precise time for action throughout Northern States." En route, Hunt was to meet with the organization's leader in Indiana, named Dodd, with whom he would travel to Canada for the conference. Hunt told "Jones" that "all kinds of munitions of war are in process of manufacture in Indianapolis," and a person there was "preparing infernal machines for the use of this order."[51]

Based on Bledsoe's information, on April 13 Sanderson gave orders to Edward Betty to follow Hunt to Detroit. Betty boarded a train and arrived at Detroit; he found Hunt registered in the city's principal hotel. He watched Hunt make his way on two consecutive days across the Detroit River to Windsor to Hirons House, the hotel where Vallandigham resided, and overheard parts of conversations he had with other persons, most of whom Betty could not identify. Watching in Windsor on the second day, April 15, he reported that "perhaps as many as thirty gentlemen arrived during the day," and they all were passed upstairs. Hunt remained in the hotel all the day and into the evening, with Betty keeping watch; later, Betty observed him back in Detroit "in earnest conversation with a tall, large-built, remarkable-looking gentleman, who wore glasses and had the air of a man usually seen at capitals and other places where the great of a country assemble." The remarkable-looking gentleman registered in his Detroit hotel as "A. James, New York." (Sanderson identified him as James A. McMaster, the influential editor of the *Freeman's Journal,* published in New York, a leading antiwar newspaper.[52]) All the men in Detroit showed great solicitousness toward "James," including Hunt, who "showed him a respect and consideration amounting to sycophancy." Nearly twenty men (including Hunt) met in "James's" Detroit hotel room for several hours. Betty confessed that he could glean nothing about the meeting but revealed that he conferred with Lieutenant Colonel Bennett H. Hill, the acting assistant provost marshal general in Detroit, and the attorney general of Michigan, William Rogers, who informed him of the "character of Mr. Hunt's companions, excepting Mr. James, whom no one knew." Betty also reported information "from a reliable source" that Vallandigham "receives his mail from the United States under cover, directed to S. Dow Elwood and John H. Harmon, both of Detroit." (This information was later used to intercept Vallandigham's communications.) He concluded his report with the information that Hunt left Detroit on April 16 for Chicago.[53]

Back in Missouri, Bledsoe also gathered information in the guerrilla-infested hinterlands. Brigadier General E. B. Brown, stationed at Warrensburg, reported to departmental headquarters that Bledsoe had "seen letters from (Arkansas) [rebel General Sterling] Price's army, which say that Price has two brigades of mounted troops and is mounting two brigades of infantry, the whole to make a raid into Missouri." Bledsoe thought that the information was "worthy of consideration," adding that he had other sources that corroborated that Price intended to return to Missouri during the summer.[54]

Another agent, "Edward F. Hoffman" (Lawrence A. Hudson), gradually ingratiated himself into Saint Louis's secret circles, posing as a rebel sympathizer who wished to go south to enlist in the Confederate service. He reported that city businessmen, among them Green B. Smith, an arms merchant, were members of the organization. One businessman informed him of the best ways to travel to the South and avoid arrest by federal authorities; he also learned that when traveling in the South one was at risk of arrest by the rebel authorities unless possessed of the proper signals "by a secret order."[55] In April, "William Taylor" (Dr. C. F. Mercer) also became a member of the organization in Saint Louis and attended meetings in different lodges in the city. At meetings in mid-April "all seemed to await Hunt," who had gone to Canada to confer with Vallandigham. "They spoke of receiving news from the grand council when Hunt returned," Mercer reported. He noted in passing "They hear from Vallandigham regularly." At subsequent meetings he spoke with leaders of the organization who volunteered extensive information on its strength, activities, and plans. "I have had several interviews with Chief Commander Hunt," wrote Mercer. Among other things, Hunt expressed his wish for the members to "kill every one of the detectives" who were then dogging them. The spy added his thought that "you will soon hear of a good many detectives being killed. It will be done slyly and privately. I most fervently believe what I say." He described an organization that seemed well informed of the activities in Rosecrans's headquarters and that planned to infiltrate headquarters staff, as well as Sanderson's staff, but "from the tenor of the conversation I don't think they have yet accomplished it."[56]

Besides infiltrating secret organizations in Missouri, Rosecrans used his intelligence resources for other pressing concerns. Security of the prisoner-of-war camps under his jurisdiction was a constant worry. In April he telegraphed to warn the commander at the camp at Alton, Illinois, that he had information that the camp was "undermined" and to "look out immediately for escape from your prison."[57] He also suggested to the commanding naval officer on the Mississippi River, Admiral David D. Porter, that a "thoroughly reliable Detective officer" at Memphis would be of great value to the service. "With such an officer there, having a clear and full understanding with the

Provost Marshal General of this Dept, I am persuaded the contraband trade and travel on the river, between here and Memphis, could be broken up, and a great public good accomplished," he wrote. He recommended that J. B. Devoe, a U.S. Navy officer then employed at Saint Louis as a detective, be assigned to Memphis for the task.[58]

Rosecrans Shares His Findings

Soon after his arrival, Rosecrans's intelligence sources alerted him to a planned Confederate raid into Missouri and that a large and active secret organization collaborated with the rebels throughout the state, as well as in Northern states. As well, an active rebel mail and contraband trade flourished in the department. To help counteract these interrelated problems, Rosecrans needed secret-service funds. He had transferred his own supply of "contingent funds" to Major General Thomas when superseded in the command of the Army of the Cumberland. When Lafayette C. Baker's detectives working for the Treasury Department were hot on the trail of counterfeiters in Saint Louis and requested $3,500 from the general, Rosecrans scrambled to borrow funds with which to assist them. He applied to Secretary of the Treasury Salmon P. Chase for funds, stating that the exigencies of the provost marshal service "demand that I should have some contingent fund at my disposal," and explaining that he had just loaned funds to detectives working for Chase.[59] When replacement funds were not forthcoming, he notified Stanton that he had loaned funds to officers working for the Treasury Department, resulting in a "large haul" of counterfeiters.[60] When no reply and no funds came, he repeated his request: "the wants of the Department are pressing," he wrote.[61] However, the War Department was not forthcoming. "No funds available," was the eventual reply.[62]

In late April, on the eve of Grant's multifront offensives to press the rebels at all points simultaneously, the supreme army commander wired to Rosecrans to send troops from the Department of the Missouri to Major General William T. Sherman's army then massing in northern Georgia. All troops were needed at the front, wrote Grant. In an exchange of telegrams, Rosecrans adamantly resisted the orders. He cited the great importance of securing the Saint Louis riverfront wharves, depots, and huge accumulations of army supplies then protected by an already small infantry force. He had too few troops as it was, he telegraphed (via cipher). Serious dangers in the department, including the "existence of secret rebel organizations diffused through the state," the general fear of "bushwhackers and rebel raids," and the exposed city supply depots compelled him to oppose Grant's order.[63] Days later, he reiterated his protest to sending away troops, noting that "secret dangers which I know to exist and hope soon to circumvent," as well as affairs in Arkansas and Louisiana, rendered it too dangerous to strip the state bare. "Rest assured that what I say about secret dangers is well considered and based on facts."[64] When Sherman sent a sharp message, saying that the plots were merely to hold back troops from the front, Rosecrans replied, "You mistake me. I do not speak of stories, threats and ruses to keep back troops but of what I know."[65] Grant waved off the concern, replying that Rosecrans could use militia and one-hundred-day troops against the secret plotters. But Rosecrans considered the Missouri militia to be unreliable and replied that rebel raids had begun in the south of his department and that the emergency in Missouri was a "present one."[66] Grant lost his patience and sent a rebuke asking why Rosecrans had defied his orders, forcing the Saint Louis general to bow to orders and send away his troops:

> I telegraphed to say that if these guards are sent away and not re-placed the 8000 secret society men whose intended rising has been postponed for which rebel cavalry from the south were already be-ginning—would seize that opportunity, burn our depots and do us irreparable damage. This matter of the secret society must be kept perfectly silent until I can secure names and evidence which will en-able me to seize and convict the ring leaders and crush the organiza-tion which is wide spread. If you think it safe after my statement of these facts to risk sending off these troops without bringing some disciplined infantry to take their place your orders will be obeyed.[67]

Thus, weakened by the lack of secret-service funds and the loss of troops, Rosecrans reached out to share information about secret conspirators with commanders and political leaders in the Northwestern states where his detec-tives had prowled about. By cooperating with his neighbors in the Northern Department, Rosecrans would be able to counteract the growing threat of insurrection and mitigate his shortage of available, trustworthy troops. He began to make plans to travel eastward to confer with officials.[68] Writing to his wife at home in Yellow Springs, Ohio, he warned her not to be surprised if he dropped in on her unexpectedly one of these days. "I want to know your proposed movements a few days in advance," he wrote.[69] A week later he wrote her to be ready if he had business in Columbus.[70]

Sanderson's detectives continued to file reports on the machinations of the conspirators in Saint Louis and elsewhere. Bledsoe (a.k.a. William Jones) went to Illinois, where he had heard the OAK existed. There he reported contacts with members in Springfield, including prominent local and state officials.[71] Hudson (a.k.a. Edward F. Hoffman) and another detective known as James M. Forrester traveled to Louisville, where they mingled with rebel sympathizers and found members of the secret groups conspiring with rebels.[72] Sanderson himself wrote to a Gettysburg, Pennsylvania, acquaintance to share what he had learned and to warn of possible Confederate raids. Sources informed him that Missouri rebel sympathizers anticipated that "considerable support" would be given to rebel general Robert E. Lee by a "large force of laborers represented to be employed on some public works in the neighborhood of your town" when the rebels would again invade the state.[73]

Meanwhile, Rosecrans's staff made arrangements for the general to travel to Cincinnati and Columbus. On May 10 he traveled east and met with General Heintzelman and Governor John Brough of Ohio at the Cincinnati home of former governor William Dennison. There they had a long discussion about the secret organizations in the North.[74] The following day Rosecrans telegraphed to his staff in Saint Louis, "Arrived safely. I want those names by telegraph, Dayton, Columbus, Cincinnati. Have you reports from L J.B.[?] Here today. Columbus tomorrow care of Genl Heintzelman."[75] In answer, Sanderson sent the names of the persons who channeled mail secretly to Vallandigham that Edward Betty had supplied. "The names are John H. Harmon and S. Dow Elwood at Detroit. Going on smoothly. Reports from Kentucky favorable," he wired.[76] The next day, in Columbus, Rosecrans, Heintzelman, Brough, and Dennison again conferred. Heintzelman recorded in his journal that "Rosecrantz"

> Came here to consult Govs Dennison, Brough and myself about these secret societies and what had better be done on Sat. (tomorrow) when some of the leaders will be at the opening of the Sanitary fair at St. Louis. It is decided not to disturb them for fear of an outbreak and we are not prepared in Ind. and Ill. to meet it. They left in the afternoon and he [Rosecrans] will go to Indianapolis and Springfield.[77]

After the meeting, Major Bond, who accompanied Rosecrans, telegraphed to Sanderson to postpone action for the time being: "The Genl thinks you had better not make arrests at present, but keep careful watch on the parties. He will return Saturday night."[78]

The exchange of messages by telegraph, and Heintzelman's journal entries, afford a fleeting glimpse into the thinking of Rosecrans and the others. First, this was Rosecrans's initial effort to share information on the secret organizations with his neighbors in the Northern Department. No evidence exists to suggest that Rosecrans and Heintzelman had communicated with each other to compare notes on the subject before these meetings. Heintzelman had met with the governors of Illinois, Indiana, and Ohio in the previous month at Indianapolis concerning the threat of the secret organizations in his Northern Department, but Rosecrans had not been privy to that discussion. Rosecrans took the initiative to travel to his neighbor's department to share intelligence he had collected. Second, Rosecrans and Sanderson had planned to arrest leaders of the organizations in the Department of the Missouri and perhaps other states. The great sanitary fair sponsored by the Western Sanitary Commission at Saint Louis attracted thousands of visitors from far and wide and furnished the opportunity to collar the leaders while they were in the city. Organizers had named Rosecrans honorary president of the fair.[79] He and Sanderson must have believed that they had already accumulated adequate evidence to arrest, hold, and perhaps try in federal civil or military courts the leaders of the conspiracy. However, as reported by Heintzelman, the officers assembled at Columbus did not believe they could effectively resist an "outbreak" in the event of arrests of the secret organization's leadership. Heintzelman cited the parlous situation in Illinois and Indiana: "we are not prepared in Ind. and Ill. to meet it." His assessment reflected the information he had received to date from General Carrington both on the strength of the secret organization as well as the army's weakness in the two states. Heintzelman probably shared with Rosecrans the information that Carrington, his spymaster, had collected and analyzed. Ohio and Michigan, apparently, were viewed to be in less danger of outbreak.

Finally, Rosecrans shared his information on the communications network between Vallandigham, in exile in Windsor, and his followers in the United States. The general probably enlisted the assistance of the assembled officials to try to understand the secret mail system used by the conspirators. Evidence suggests that the meeting may have borne fruit in this regard. Days afterward, Cincinnati's postmaster reported to Sanderson that he had received a letter to a designated person in Toledo and asked what he was to do with it. Sanderson replied that he should send it to Saint Louis and that it would be returned if requested—that it concerned the secret Detroit mail system.[80] Later in the month Rosecrans requested a "special agent" of the postmaster general's office at Sandusky, Ohio, to forward him letters that had been intercepted.[81] Rosecrans exhibited few qualms about seizing and opening private mails.

After meeting with the Ohio leaders, Rosecrans tried to meet with Morton. However, the governor was away in New York City at the time. Rosecrans made no effort to meet with Carrington. Returning to Saint Louis on May 18, he wired Governor Yates at Springfield, Illinois, "I will try and visit you at Springfield tomorrow."[82] He and a staff officer arrived in the Illinois capital the next day, met at the depot by the governor. Yates hosted the general at the governor's residence and treated him to a "grand impromptu serenade" by a crowd of well-wishers. No record of the substance of the meeting with Yates survives except Rosecrans's cryptic statement in a letter to his wife, Ann: "Remaining there two days and accomplishing my mission I returned to St Louis."[83] The next day the general returned to Cincinnati in another attempt to meet with Morton. However, the meeting failed to occur.[84] Rosecrans's exertions to meet with the political leaders of the Northwestern states reflected the urgency he felt to act in concert with army and state authorities against the dangerous secret organizations. Two weeks later he tried again to arrange a meeting with Morton, telegraphing to Indianapolis, "Will you please appoint a time and place where I can meet you on business? Official."[85]

In the meantime, Rosecrans's subordinates continued the work of collecting information on the secret conspirators and their activities. Sanderson's corps of detectives continued to gather information. Among the detectives was the U.S. Navy officer James B. Devoe, who by May had been seconded to the army and was working for Rosecrans and Sanderson in New York City. A native New Yorker, born in 1820, Devoe was a newspaperman who had lit out for California in the 1849 gold rush. By 1850 he was publisher of the *California State Journal* at San Jose (and later of the *San Francisco Times and Transcript*), served as California state printer, and was involved in other business ventures and California politics.[86] By 1858 he had returned to New York and was a partner in a sporting and humor newspaper called *Porter's Spirit of the Times*.[87] In early 1864, Devoe obtained an acting ensign commission in the U.S. Navy (later promoted to acting master in September 1864) and was promptly assigned by Admiral David D. Porter to espionage work on the Mississippi River.[88] Rosecrans and Sanderson sent Devoe to New York City without explicit instructions or information. On May 19, Sanderson wrote him that Rosecrans "has been absent in Ohio, Indiana and Illinois, which will account to you for not hearing from him. On his return yesterday he handed me yours of the 9th." Together, they decided that Devoe should remain in New York. "Though things are not yet ripe for development, and cannot be too cautiously and carefully kept a profound secret," wrote Sanderson, he outlined to Devoe what his spies had uncovered to date and what he believed was accurate information. The secret organization was called the Order of American Knights, created at the Confederate capitol at Richmond, Virginia, "at the time Vallandigham was there."

The exiled Ohioan was currently the "supreme head" of the order. Its object was the "separation of the Western States from New England, and the creation of a Northwestern Confederacy." It was spread across all the Northern states and was "very strong" in Missouri, Kentucky, and the Northwestern states, and "growing rapidly" in Pennsylvania, New Jersey, and New York. Members planned to have Vallandigham appear at the Democratic national convention, then scheduled for July 4 at Chicago, where he would make a speech bidding "defiance to the national authorities." If the government attempted to arrest him, the order would "commence a revolution in the Free States, which is to result in the breaking up of the Union, and the establishment of a Northern Confederacy." Sanderson noted that he had complete information on rituals, oaths, grips, and signs used by members of the organization, but it wasn't necessary to impart that information for the moment. "I have already given you enough to show that it is a most dangerous, as well as formidable, organization," he wrote. "Now go to work and see what what [*sic*] you can find out in your own city and State." McMaster was the state grand commander and representative in the OAK's supreme council, "which has had several meetings at Vallandigham's headquarters in Canada. . . . If you could get hold of his correspondence I have no doubt you would obtain a clue. Would it not be well for you to see your City Postmaster and have his letters inspected?"[89] Devoe would subsequently provide much information to aid Rosecrans and Sanderson in their investigations. He collaborated with the military chief in New York City, Major General John A. Dix, commander of the Department of the East and a prominent Democrat before the war, to discover information about the secret organization in the city.[90]

By May 25 affairs had advanced, information had accumulated, and Rosecrans was prepared for decisive measures. He reported to Heintzelman the status of his investigations. "Since seeing you in Columbus," he wrote, he had conferred with Governor Yates "as to the matter which we discussed." He added that "evidence is coming in daily of a most important character, tending to confirm all that I explained to you as to the organization and its objects." Heintzelman had not been given access to the army's telegraphic cipher code, and Rosecrans noted that he had contacted the head of the military telegraph, Colonel Anson Stager, to have the general in Columbus provided with "No. 1 Cipher" to allow them to communicate securely and rapidly.[91] Also that day, Rosecrans asked Congressman Garfield, in Washington, to arrange a meeting with Lincoln: "It is important that I should have a personal interview, or send an officer to communicate directly with the President of the United States, on matters of grave public interest, that I do not think it prudent or proper under the circumstances to put in writing and trust to the mails." Garfield should "ask him [Lincoln] to telegraph me either to come in person or send an officer to communicate with him any time during the next twenty days." Since the "exhibition of petty malice on the part of the War Department in the case of Maj Bond," he added, he wished to "avoid the inconvenience and trouble of any conflict at a time when more important matters are in hand."[92]

In the following days, Rosecrans gave orders to arrest many of the leaders of the secret organization all over Missouri. Sanderson sent orders to his district provost marshal officers to arrest men in Fulton, Mexico, Macon, Liberty, Saint Joseph, and Hannibal and in Callaway County. He issued arrest orders for the state leaders of the OAK in Saint Louis: Charles L. Hunt, Charles E. Dunn, Dr. James A. Barret, and Green B. Smith. Sanderson named over thirty men to be arrested. The orders came based on no prompting from the War Department or other Washington officials.[93]

Rosecrans and his assistant Sanderson, through prompt, energetic action and commitment of significant staff resources, had quickly gathered information on the existence of secret organizations in Missouri and neighboring states. They believed the threat they posed was real, significant, and imminent. By the end of May, Rosecrans had communicated with political and military leaders in the Old Northwest and had taken steps to call the danger to the attention of President Lincoln. He also took the bold step of arresting the leaders of the organization in Missouri without waiting for orders from Washington or closer coordination with his colleagues in the Northern Department. Rosecrans, who had placed great reliance on intelligence operations in his previous commands, continued to trust in his far-ranging spies and detectives to seek out and discover threats. In doing so, he received little or no support from the War Department, where he was a pariah. His continued efforts to "ferret out" the secret organization would place him in conflict with War Department functionaries, who were slow to see the danger it posed.

EIGHT

"When Government Determines to Act"

How Carrington's Detectives Infiltrated the Secret Organizations in 1864

IN THE late spring and early summer of 1864, General Carrington and Governor Morton spearheaded efforts to gather intelligence on the conspiracy they knew to be developing in Indiana and the Old Northwest. Spies provided new information that pointed to collaboration between conspirators and Confederate General John Hunt Morgan to raid Kentucky. As well, army detectives learned that exiled Clement L. Vallandigham planned to return to Ohio simultaneous to the Morgan raid. The growing strength of military-espionage efforts fortified government's response to the raid and gave Union leaders the initiative over the conspirators for the first time during the war.

Carrington Appeals for Support

Brigadier General Henry Carrington, his health gradually improving, labored on quietly at his Indianapolis desk. Seconded to Governor Morton's staff, he worked to organize the Indiana Legion, drill new volunteer units raised in the state, and superintend the camps around the city where new recruits gathered to organize and drill. More important, out of the public eye he gathered information on the looming threat posed by the existence of the secret organizations in Indiana and neighboring states. His skill and ability impressed Major General Samuel Heintzelman, commander of the Northern Department, who assigned him to gather intelligence in Illinois as well. In his anomalous position, working for both Morton and Heintzelman, Carrington lacked staff. He had only the services of a lieutenant from a regiment guarding the Camp Morton prisoner-of-war grounds. Burdened with paperwork and responsibilities, he pleaded with the War Department for staff assistance. He requested an experienced staff officer from his 18th U.S. Infantry regular-army regiment be sent to him. "The protection of the border entrusted to me by the Governor, under orders of the Secretary of War, and the examination of disloyal societies, confided to me by Maj Gen Heintzelman, involve more labor than any field duty whatever." He and his aide were "overtasked day and night," he wrote. His pleas met only with contempt from War Department staff officers in Washington, who passed Carrington's letter around and recorded their caustic comments on it. One wrote, "If Genl C finds himself overtasked it would be a good idea for him to apply for a Brigade. He has never been in the field." Major General Henry W. Halleck, who harbored particular animus against Carrington, summarily denied the request.[1] Later, functionaries insulted him over the matter of some missing paperwork. An assistant secretary of war wrote to him for an explanation, sneering, "Please state if you have been wounded in battle, and if so, when."[2]

Besides staff help, Carrington requested secret-service funds to support his investigations. On April 18 he requested $5,000 from Washington but was refused.[3] Writing three days later, he asked for even more, revealing, "I have information that shows the [previous] sum to be inadequate." He stated, "I now have the evidence, of a purpose to make an armed resistance to the Government & to revolutionize the North western states." To combat that purpose, he requested authority "to organize a special police of not to exceed twelve persons, with which to operate for the detection of disloyal organizations, at reasonable compensation." He added that "spies from Kentucky abound. My private office was broken open at night, papers overhauled with [aims?] to find private papers; and I must so multiply agents as to keep control of the organization." He reported, "Only last night a detective, (a Kentuckian) in my employ, returned, having obtained the full confidence of one of the leaders, under the plea that he aimed to establish lodges in Kentucky. Correspondence with Kentucky may show that my detective is a union man and I deem it of sufficient moment to urge immediate authority, such as asked for."[4] Carrington upped his request to $10,000, "for use in employing agents to investigate disloyal societies in Northern Department."[5] The request fell on deaf ears. Other military officers in Indiana wrote to army leadership in his support. Colonel Conrad Baker told his superior in Washington that the general was "embarrassed in his operations from want of funds."[6] Lacking support from the War Department, Carrington resorted to makeshifts. Instead of civilian detectives, he employed soldiers to do his espionage work and cooperated with officers in the Provost Marshal General's Bureau.[7]

Sargent Parker Coffin, Spy

On the same day that he wrote to the War Department to ask for funds, Carrington wrote to Northern Department headquarters to report the latest information gathered by one of his detectives, the "Kentuckian" who had gained the confidence of a leading conspirator. He submitted parts of the second- and third-degree oaths of the "American Knights" order (OAK), which showed that the organization was "very complete," revolutionary, and hostile to the United States. "The evidence accumulates of their intentions," he wrote. "I shall increase the detective force so that discovery of one or more, will not embarrass operations."[8] Carrington also voiced his concerns about having enough detectives to keep an eye on the conspirators. "If I have adequate force I hope to keep posted in movements here." He asked Heintzelman to endorse his request for secret-service funds. The extracts of the third-degree OAK oath, his most recent discovery, "are more significant than the one you read here," referring to Heintzelman's visit to Indianapolis on April 15.[9]

The "Kentuckian" detective whom Carrington mentioned was a remarkable man named Sargent Parker Coffin. A North Carolina–born member of the Quaker (Society of Friends) Christian sect, then in his mid-forties, he had resided in Wayne County for many years, in the heart of the "burned-over district" of eastern Indiana where Quakers were numerous. In 1846, Coffin had scandalized the Quaker community in North Carolina by abandoning his wife and children and "eloping" with another married woman. Though he soon returned to his family, a newspaper explained that "Coffin is a man of fine person—of shrewd mind—and, though his associations have not been of the best, his manners [are] agreeable and insinuating. Being what is termed a 'trading character,' he has travelled much over the country, and has an acute knowledge of human nature, which he knows how to turn to his own advantage."[10] Coffin's acuity explains his subsequent success as a spy. In Indiana he was a neighbor and "good friend" of Governor Morton, who hailed from Centreville, in Wayne County.[11] At the beginning of the rebellion, Coffin resided in Warsaw, Gallatin County, Kentucky. Evidence shows that he was one of the persons who kept Morton apprised of Kentucky affairs when Governor Beriah Magoffin attempted publicly to maintain the commonwealth as a neutral party while covertly supporting the Confederacy.[12] In 1862, Morton employed him in various odd jobs along the Ohio River border, including arresting persons who were deemed disloyal.[13] Later in the year Morton loaned him to army headquarters in Henderson, Kentucky, on secret service. The governor's private secretary explained to the local commander, "Coffin has been much in our employ as a detective and is a good hand at the business."[14] He reported to the army commander at Louisville that Morton was sending a "spy" to Henderson to assist the local commander on a job. There, Coffin gained the confidence of former Kentucky governor and then current U.S. senator Lazarus W. Powell, who gave him a letter of introduction to prominent rebel sympathizers at Madisonville. Coffin represented to them that he had a loom with which to weave cloth to supply the Confederate army.[15] The Henderson commander subsequently asked for Coffin's services: "I want him on an important but not dangerous business."[16] Back home in Indiana, the detective moonlighted as a deputy federal marshal and assisted in various jobs such as the arrest of the "butternut" rioters at Centreville in May 1863.[17] He also served briefly as a draft enrollment officer in Wayne County.[18]

In March 1863, while Coffin was still working for the commander at Henderson, Kentucky, "respecting treasonable societies in Indiana, the Knights of the Golden Circle, etc.," Carrington (then commander of the District of Indiana) instructed the detective to arrest any deserters whom he encountered, as well as "to bring to light any cases of smuggling" that he might notice.[19] In the latter capacity, Coffin discovered a large contraband smuggling operation undertaken by Evansville, Indiana, merchants to supply rebels in Kentucky. As John Hanna, the U.S. attorney at Indianapolis, explained it to Attorney General Edward Bates, Coffin "made the acquaintance of certain known disloyal persons" in Evansville who were suspected of being in the contraband trade. He posed as a rebel sympathizer and purchased ready-made coats and pants to be shipped down the Ohio River beyond rebel lines. Coffin had "no trouble" in gaining their confidence as a rebel sympathizer. "Coffin you will understand," wrote Hanna, "is really a Union Man but in these transactions pretended to be Secesh."[20] By the spring of 1864, Coffin had been an important spy for three years. But he did not draw a federal salary for his espionage activities. Carrington, who employed him as chief of his "Special Service Department,"[21] endeavored to get the War Department to hire him as a regular salaried detective. In describing his exploits, Carrington noted that Coffin "has made valuable discoveries and is of special value in the present condition of things here," adding, "He is the man who went within the enemy's lines and first gave notice of the movement of Gen Bragg into Ky in advance of the movement [in 1862]."[22]

While Coffin was an effective spy, Carrington and Morton had other sources of information. In early April, Major John W. Tucker of the 80th Indiana Volunteer Infantry Regiment, a resident of Orleans, Orange County, in southern Indiana, visited his home on a brief furlough. He took the pulse of his community. Dr. William A. Bowles, the owner of the nearby French Lick Springs hotel and spa, the commander of the Indiana regiment that fled in the battle of Buena Vista during the Mexican War and prominent antiwar Democrat in the current conflict, was up to no good, he informed state authorities:

> Dr Bowles and others are working it is thought for the purpose of
> being ready to raise an insurrection, in southern Ind. against. thier
> [sic] friends, reaches here. they openly declare that the Rebels will
> be here by May, all Such talk of course would have no impression
> if it was not for some letters and other facts I have in my possession.
> if a Secret police could be Sent here it would be well.[23]

Carrington and his detectives already had been watching Bowles, but the "letters and other facts" in Tucker's possession intrigued them. Tucker soon visited Indianapolis to meet with Governor Morton and handed over Bowles's letters.[24] They included letters Bowles wrote to his wife in the spring of 1861, expressing himself in favor of the Southern rebels. Also among them was a letter of introduction to the Confederate general Gideon Pillow for a young Indiana man who wished to join rebel forces.[25] Later, Morton had some of the letters printed in the *Indianapolis Daily Journal* at opportune times to embarrass Bowles.[26]

Felix Grundy Stidger, Spy

In response to Tucker's request for a "secret police" to visit Orange County, Carrington and Morton sent Coffin. In his ingratiating way he "obtained the full confidence" of Bowles under the veil of organizing lodges of the secret organization in Kentucky. Coffin likely obtained the OAK oaths that Carrington furnished to Heintzelman. However, Carrington perceived a problem. As he noted, Coffin was well known in Kentucky, and his true identity as a "Union man" might be revealed. Carrington needed someone to be in contact with Bowles and work in Kentucky who would not be suspected as a Union man and spy. Without funds of his own to hire civilian detectives, he turned to military authorities in Kentucky. On May 2, Carrington wrote to the acting assistant provost marshal general in Kentucky for the loan of a detective; his letter was hand-delivered by Sergeant James Prentice, the general's confidential messenger. Carrington explained that "an armed disloyal organization exists in Indiana, Illinois & Ohio for treasonable purposes." He suggested that Bowles be watched, as he regularly visited Kentucky to establish new lodges.[27] In reply, the Kentucky officer noted that General Stephen G. Burbridge, the commander of the District of Kentucky, "has matters of the nature communicated more immediately under his control and has also the means of sending out proper agents etc which I have not." He forwarded Carrington's letter to Burbridge's staff for action.[28]

Kentucky—and Louisville, specifically—was a hotbed of intrigue and espionage during the Civil War. A major Ohio River port and the principal city of Kentucky, Louisville was a busy commercial center. The Louisville and Nashville Railroad served as the chief conveyance of supplies to federal forces then in Tennessee and northern Georgia. Consequently, it was frequently a target for raids by Confederate cavalry and guerrillas. While the commonwealth avoided secession and Union sentiment was strong, as a slave state many of its citizens sympathized with and supported the Confederates in rebellion against the United States. A lively rebel mail existed, as did a flourishing trade in contraband goods. Army detectives crisscrossed Kentucky in search of rebel mails, smugglers, and spies who found safe havens among families and friends. The ease with which persons could cross from rebel- to federal-controlled areas greatly vexed local federal commanders, who maintained a large "detective police" force that worked to suppress rebel activities in Louisville and the countryside.

Major General Stephen Gano Burbridge, a Kentucky attorney and politician before the war, rose to command of the District of Kentucky in early 1864, where he worked to combat the growing threat of guerrilla raids.[29] In addition to fighting guerrillas, he endeavored to detect the existence of organized efforts that collaborated with the rebels. In March his officers reported the existence of an oath-bound "association" in Kentucky and the Northern states intent on cooperating with a rebel invasion and the release of Confederate prisoners of war. It planned to burn cities and traffic on the inland rivers that supplied federal armies. The leaders of the association maintained regular communication with rebels in Canada, as well as with Confederate authorities at Richmond, Virginia, officers reported. Military authorities at Louisville shared this information with their counterparts at Cincinnati, who relayed it to departmental headquarters at Columbus.[30] Heintzelman in turn forwarded the report to Halleck at the War Department, noting that the Coles County, Illinois, "outbreak," the raid on Paducah by Forrest, and other signs showed that "these warnings should not be unheeded."[31]

Army commanders at the front, focused on the success of their offensive plans, took notice of the existence of the conspiracies as a threat to their vital but exposed supply lines. In April, Major General William T. Sherman, preparing for his Atlanta campaign, received warning from the War Department of "boatburner" conspiracies and wrote to Burbridge to take sharp action against the threat to supply lines. Anyone detected as engaged in sabotage should be "drowned or killed on the spot. . . . I dont care to have our military prisons or Courts encumbered with such cases."[32]

Accordingly, when Burbridge's Lexington-based staff received Carrington's forwarded request for assistance against conspiracy, they acted promptly. Captain Stephen E. Jones, the provost marshal general for the district, stationed at Louisville, selected a detective and sent him to Orange County, Indiana, with orders to gather as much information as possible. Jones explained to Lexington,

> as this is a very important and delicate subject, requiring above all things that whatever information was secured should be *known* to be reliable and accurate, I took the liberty of going outside the police department, none of the members of which I *knew*, in selecting the person, to send on the mission. The desirability of dispatch justified me in sending off the party employed without waiting to communicate with the Genl Comdg.[33]

The detective Jones sent was Felix Grundy Stidger. Born in 1838 in Spencer County, Kentucky, in October 1862, he enlisted in the 15th Kentucky Volunteer Infantry Regiment (U.S.) with the promise of clerking in division headquarters. He remained in the army until February 1864, when he claimed to be tubercular and obtained a medical discharge in order to return home to care for his dying mother. After she died, he went to Louisville intent on obtaining work as an army detective. While at home, he served as an informer to the provost marshal's office about local movements.[34] He continued to do so after arriving in Louisville, borne out in surviving reports he filed informing on rebel soldiers in the city and the return of women who had been kicked out of the city for disloyalty.[35]

According to his memoir, Stidger visited Jones's office to report his latest information, but Jones called him into his private office and handed him a letter to read. It was Carrington's letter to the Kentucky authorities warning of Bowles's activities in Kentucky in organizing a treasonable organization known as the Sons of Liberty, formerly known as the Knights of the Golden Circle and Order of American Knights. Jones hired Stidger to go to Indiana for one month on a trial basis: "if my services were not satisfactory I would be dropped."[36] Jones preferred him, an outsider, instead of detectives already on the payroll because the Louisville army "secret police" detective force under the post provost marshal was riddled with corruption; commanders had lately fired detectives for shaking down saloonkeepers and other misdeeds. In April, Burbridge ordered the force reorganized under new leadership.[37] Jones called Prentice, Carrington's messenger, into his office to help brief the new detective on the secret organization in Indiana, which Stidger recalled was not very helpful. He departed Louisville on the first northbound train, crossing the river into southern Indiana.[38]

Not knowing Indiana, Stidger mistakenly got off the train at Salem, in Washington County, and had to wait half a day to board a train to take him nearer to French Lick, about thirty miles to the west. His wait was fortuitous, however, as he fell in with local men who soon revealed themselves as members of the secret organization. He met Horace Heffren, a leading local Democrat, who had formerly been lieutenant colonel of the 50th Indiana Volunteer Infantry Regiment but who had resigned his commission in protest of Lincoln's Emancipation Proclamation. He now opposed the war. In his first report to his military spy masters, Stidger reported, "Upon [Heffren] learning that I was from Kentucky, and of Southern sympathy, he supposed me to be a commissioner or Courier, I could not learn which, that he was looking for from [Kentucky]." Stidger encouraged Heffren in the belief that he came with information on the disbanded cavalry regiments of Confederate general Nathan Bedford Forrest. Heffren remarked that he understood that Confederate general Robert E. Lee was to establish a "permanent occupation" in Pennsylvania, and likewise General James Longstreet in Kentucky. Stidger eventually made his way to French Lick and met Bowles. Bowles bluntly asked him "if I knew anything of a democratic organization in our state." Stidger replied that he did, and in reply to questions said he was a member of the first degree. As the organizer of the society in Kentucky, Bowles took umbrage at this, wanting to know from whom he had obtained the first degree and how that person "derived his authority" to administer it. He asked Stidger if he could recite the oath, to which the detective replied that he could. However, Bowles "did not attempt to test me but let that part drop there seemingly satisfied," Stidger reported. Bowles told the visitor that he was leader of the organization. He also said that the organization was a continuation of the "original" Knights of the Golden Circle, of which he had been a member, "and after the death of that order, that he was the one that from its fragments originated this secret democratic organization; *that he was the Chief Military Executive,* and a man by the name of Wright of St Louis was the Chief in the Civil department." Bowles's plan "was to make Ky. the Battle-Ground," to arm as many men as possible and to join rebel forces and hold Kentucky for the Confederacy. He intimated that there would be "plenty of Bloodshed" in Indiana as well. Thousands of armed men from Missouri, Illinois (led by a man named Holloway), and Ohio would join them, he said. He also planned to raid and seize the arms in the arsenals at Indianapolis, Louisville, and Frankfort. Stidger noted that "Bowles' principal trouble seems to be the procuring of arms." Bowles revealed that the organization met regularly at the state level, with two councils located in Indianapolis and Vincennes in Indiana, and at multistate regional level, with meetings held in Columbus, Chicago, New York City, and Indianapolis. "Their first council in Chicago was delayed several days by the closing of the Times office by the Military on the morning in which they were to meet in the building," Stidger reported. The organization corresponded mostly by couriers, and when sent through the post, messages were coded. Stidger concluded his first report:

> Bowles tells me there is quite a division of policy among the leaders.
> The politicians advocating the policy of waiting a move until they
> come to the Ballot Box, while the war leaders wish to show their
> hand at the earliest possible time. Bowles advocates the latter policy,
> is very much opposed to await the opening of the ballot box. Heffren
> says he fears that the party will not await the proper time, but rise
> too soon.[39]

Stidger returned to Louisville and composed his written report of his mission to Indiana. In his memoir, he recorded that Jones "did not seem to receive my presence with an air of any appreciative satisfaction of the services of his newly appointed Secret Service Agent." Jones bluntly told him that he "'did not believe a word of it.'" He could not understand how anyone could "ingratiate himself" and get so much useful information so quickly. After further discussion and explanations, when asked what his orders for the detective were, Jones replied, "Well Mr. Stidger, I do not know what to tell you to do. Do whatever you think is best, and tell me what you have done."[40]

In the meantime, Carrington was in the dark about Stidger's adventures in southern Indiana.[41] He pressed forward, using other detectives he had at hand to gather information. He employed a former officer in the 9th Kentucky

Volunteer Cavalry Regiment (U.S.), Major John F. Faris, to travel through western Kentucky to gather intelligence on Forrest's Confederate command and guerrilla activity, especially the Kentucky Confederate cavalry units that the rebel general disbanded in the commonwealth shortly after the attack on Paducah. Faris left Indianapolis in April and traveled to Henderson, Kentucky, working his way south into the countryside. In Webster County, Confederate guerrillas under a Captain "Benit" (possibly Captain J. C. Bennett of Colonel Adam Johnson's 10th Kentucky Cavalry Regiment [CSA]) captured him, robbed him of his valuables, and questioned him closely as to why he was in the area. The guerrillas held him as a prisoner for two days, during which "they talked freely of their movements and intentions." The guerrilla captain told him that "southern leaders" planned to "put into the border counties of Indiana from 2500 to 3000 men under the pretense of hunting work as refugees." The "refugees" were to cause trouble in the south of Indiana by aiding deserters, preventing enlistments, destroying government property, inducing a "colision [sic] between the civil and Military authority," and generally were to "stir up strife," "Criple the Government," and "control the Election." Faris described the two guerrilla companies he encountered as well-armed and dressed in civilian clothing; some of them had crossed into southwestern Indiana on the day he left them. Faris concluded by noting that the guerrilla captain told him, "It was the intention of the people to have a north western confederacy and that the time was not far off when the men of the north west would withdraw from the new England states & a greater Rebelion than the one on hand would be the result."[42]

Armed with this sort of information, Carrington requested secret-service funds from Washington. "I furnished Mr. Dana, Asst Secretary of War, a synopsis of the Ritual of the treasonable societies," he wrote, "and have found that numerous rebel soldiers, and spies from Forrest are in the State. I do not over-estimate the importance of these examinations." He added that Heintzelman had ordered him to send detectives to Canada, so that consequently he had "increased expense, well expended, to anticipate movements on the border." Furthermore, Carrington reported that Governor Morton was then "willing that my repeated wish to take the field shall be gratified, in the movement of the new Indiana [hundred-day] regiments." He stated it was then necessary to wrap up the "pending investigations and leave the matter well organized." However, his request for funds again met with a denial from Secretary Stanton.[43]

Carrington's wish to see action in the field was to be again deferred. Captain Potter, Heintzelman's aide, informed him that the commanding general wished to restore him to command of the District of Indiana, replacing the doddering and ineffectual Simonson. The commanding general planned to apply to Stanton for approval, and wished that Governor Morton would forward his own endorsement to strengthen the application.[44] Indeed, Morton complied and telegraphed to Stanton, "Please appoint Gen Carrington military commander of this district it is important to have it done today. Answer by telegraph."[45] Stanton agreed, and days later Carrington assumed command of the district from which he had been ignominiously relieved thirteen months before. In that time, Carrington had accumulated a year's worth of information on the secret undercurrents that flowed in Indiana and neighboring states. Better informed, he was better prepared to respond effectively to the threats that he, Morton, Heintzelman, and other leading Unionists genuinely feared. Though his wish to see battle action was deferred, he could take solace in a sense of vindication.

Restored to command, Carrington sprang into action, appointing several junior officers to be his staff officers and securing Heintzelman's approval to appoint S. P. Coffin as a "Special Agent of Police."[46] He quietly ordered reinforcements for the federal and state arsenals in Indianapolis.[47] Also at this time, Heintzelman tried to strengthen the prison camp garrisons, mostly manned by "overworked" sick and wounded VRC troops. He noted in his journal that he wanted extra troops "to keep down copperheads" and assist Governor Brough in the upcoming draft in Ohio.[48] To his relief, the War Department replied that he could employ one-hundred-day troops to guard prisoners if required.[49] On the intelligence front, information flowed into Indianapolis headquarters. A detective reported that he had tailed a "suspicious character" from Windsor, Canada, to Hamilton, Ohio.[50] Also, Sergeant Prentice reported that Stidger had met with Bowles and succeeded in getting significant information from him; however, Carrington did not receive a copy of Stidger's report until Captain Jones sent him one, on May 23.[51]

Meanwhile, Stidger had gained the trust of Bowles and returned to Louisville with an introduction from the Indiana leader. He met with leaders of the growing secret organization in Kentucky such as Dr. Henry F. Kalfus, formerly regimental surgeon of Stidger's 15th Kentucky Volunteer Infantry Regiment (U.S.), who had been dismissed from the army for opposing the Emancipation Proclamation, and Joshua F. Bullitt, chief justice of the Kentucky Court of Appeals. These Kentucky leaders promptly appointed him secretary of the Kentucky branch of the organization. He worked out of Kalfus's medical offices, in Louisville. In his post he initiated new members into the organization and thereby learned all the oaths and rituals for the different degrees, something he had bluffed his way through to date. He also obtained the complete membership rolls for Kentucky. In the last days of May, going back and forth between Louisville and French Lick, Stidger learned significant details of plans then in the works among leaders of the organization, including the development of the so-called Greek Fire, a chemical developed by an Indiana artillery officer, Captain R. C. Bocking, to burn buildings and steamboats.[52] In early June, he returned to Indianapolis carrying a letter of introduction from Bullitt to Harrison H. Dodd, the grand commander of the organization in Indiana, a prominent Democrat in state and city politics, and owner of a large printing firm. Dodd received him warmly and invited him to sit in on a meeting of the Indiana council. Stidger, in his capacity as the new Kentucky secretary, asked Dodd for copies of the rituals, constitution, and other records of the order. Dodd obliged and ordered the secretary for the Indiana branch, William M. Harrison, to assist his Kentucky counterpart with the paperwork. Harrison loaned him a sheaf of printed materials to take back to Louisville, including the rosters of leaders of the organization in several states. The records received from Harrison were a gold mine of information. While still in Indianapolis, on Sunday night, June 5, Stidger found Sergeant Prentice, who guided him to General Carrington's headquarters via a backdoor route. He met Carrington for the first time. Handed the secret records, the general and staff members worked feverishly through the night to copy the records in their entirety. Stidger also quietly visited (again, for the first time) Governor Morton at his house in the city, and in an hour's conversation briefed the governor on the organization. Early the next morning, Prentice returned the copied records to Stidger, who boarded the early train for Louisville.[53]

Obtaining the records provided by Stidger constituted a major coup for the army. On Monday, June 6, Carrington promptly communicated to departmental headquarters that the new "revelations of the last two days give fuller outline of the designs and operations of the treasonable societies." In a long report, he detailed the intentions, several states' leadership, and the structure of the organization. All was under the leadership of Clement Vallandigham, he reported. The leaders intended to raise revolution in the North while federal armies fought in the South. Recent instances of steamboats loaded with government stores burning at Louisville were due to sabotage by the organization. Moreover, the leadership in Kentucky was in communication with John Hunt Morgan, the Confederate cavalry commander, to coordinate a raid into the state. "The foregoing statements are not rumors or gossip, but taken from documents and reliable witnesses who are in the confidence of these men," he wrote, noting that "if numbers, money, and oaths can give them the power and will to strike they are a dangerous body of men, and it will pay to be ferreted out." He renewed his appeal for secret-service funds and asked that Heintzelman come to Indianapolis in the next few days to confer with him and Governor Morton; Rosecrans could probably come, too.[54] Carrington shared with Rosecrans a briefer synopsis of the records. "The sworn objects of this order are revolution in favor of the South," he noted. It also planned to attack supply steamboats on the rivers, recruit for the rebel army, and "plot to throw the North into civil disorder." He asked Rosecrans to come to Indianapolis to confer. "I did hope to visit you personally before this, and if you cannot come, can you not send a confidential member of your staff to meet me here?"[55] Impressed by the new information, Heintzelman forwarded Carrington's report to Halleck, at the War Department, and added, "There can be no longer any doubt as to the object and wide extent of this treasonable association."[56] Carrington shared the records that Stidger obtained with Governor Morton and forwarded copies along with reports of other detectives to Heintzelman.[57] In turn, the department commander met with Governor Brough and "read him some long letters about these secret societies out West" with the intention "to get him to do something, now necessary." The general added generously that Brough, who wielded great influence in Washington's political circles, was "always ready to do all he can."[58]

While highly significant and useful, Carrington did not reply solely on Stidger's records and reports for intelligence on the conspiracy. The general had other detectives at work. In a letter written May 31, predating Dodd's loan of records to Stidger, Colonel Conrad Baker reported that Carrington's detectives had access to the records of the secret organization and were not suspected.[59] This suggests that other detectives besides Stidger and Coffin had worked their way into the organization. Carrington received information from military commanders in other states on the movements of rebel officers traveling in the North. Colonel Sanderson, at Saint Louis, and Captain Mark Flanigan, the district provost marshal at Detroit, both forwarded information on the whereabouts of a Missouri guerrilla commander called Colonel Snyder who had traveled from Windsor and was in hiding in eastern Illinois, near Vincennes, Indiana. Indeed, rebel officers frequently passed through Indiana to and from Canada, and district provost marshals had uncovered rebel mail routes through the state.[60] Carrington received queries from Lieutenant Colonel Joseph Smith, the military commander at Detroit, to confirm information they had received.[61] Rebel deserters in Canada also supplied information, and Carrington planned to send detective Coffin to Canada "as soon as I have funds." A writer at Chicago with the pseudonym Jones furnished information on arms and ammunition, and David Turnbull in Warren County, Illinois, continued on the job.[62] The Enrollment Act of 1863, creating the Provost Marshal General's Bureau, required the bureau to arrest spies, and acting assistant provost marshal for Indiana, Colonel Conrad Baker, tried diligently to do so. His officers arrested and imprisoned rebel soldiers as spies, learned that they were members of the secret organization, and suggested that Carrington's detectives pose as prisoners to elicit information from them.[63] Stidger provided information to Carrington that Indianapolis businessman Richard J. Gatling (inventor of the Gatling Gun, which sprayed bullets from a revolving ring of rifle barrels) was involved in the conspiracy. Carrington wrote in his June 6 report that the inventor was a member of the order. Stidger subsequently noted that the inventor attended the organization's state council meeting in mid-June.[64] Previous to that, however, the general had written to the Ordnance Bureau of the War Department to inquire about the army's relationship with Gatling.[65] Evidence suggests that Carrington obtained his initial information on Gatling from another source besides Stidger. Finally, as he had received no secret-service funds from the War Department, he continued to employ soldiers as detectives. To Smith at Detroit he wrote, "I send a detective, George W. Bewley, soldier under my orders, who will spend a day in Detroit. . . . He is posted in the first degree of the Order." Carrington gave Smith leave to send him across the border to Windsor.[66] In January Carrington had ordered another soldier, Sergeant Edmund Klamroth of the 63rd Indiana Volunteer Infantry Regiment, to join a secret lodge in Indianapolis to learn about their deliberations. As the lodge members knew Klamroth was a soldier, to allay suspicions Carrington had him arrested and tried by a mock court-martial.[67] In sum, Carrington possessed many sources of information. Indeed, Stidger noted in his memoir that Carrington had eighteen detectives working for him at the time he began his stint as a detective.[68] Again and again, Carrington expressed the crippling effect the lack of secret-service funds from the War Department had on his espionage work. He reported that an Indianapolis bank had advanced him as a stopgap $1,500 to aid the work.[69]

Well informed by many sources, Carrington had a plan for how to use the information. He wished to build a legal case against the conspirators. In June he contacted the judge advocate for the Northern Department, Major Henry L. Burnett, to request that the District of Indiana be assigned its own judge advocate to handle the growing case load then accumulating. Someone needed to sort out the mess; as well, he noted, many cases pertaining to disloyal societies required examination and action. If things continued as they were then progressing, "it will require a district judge advocate's time almost wholly." General Heintzelman deferred to Burnett's judgment in the matter, he added.[70] However, Carrington did not intend to try cases involving persons arrested for disloyalty by military tribunals. Rather, he intended that a judge advocate for the district merely prepare the evidence for the conspiracy cases before referral to the federal grand jury in Indianapolis to obtain indictments that would lead to trials before federal civil courts. During the previous week he wrote that he wished to "make a clear case against Col Bowles" before the federal grand jury for "secreting rebel officers and plotting war against the government."[71] In taking the cases to the federal courts, Carrington intended to follow the course he had taken in the spring of 1863, the course that prompted Burnside to oust him from the Indiana command.

John Hunt Morgan's Kentucky Raid of 1864

In late May and early June, the attention of military commanders north of the Ohio River turned to events in Kentucky. In mid-May, General Burbridge obtained intelligence that Confederate general John Hunt Morgan planned a raid into Kentucky from Virginia through the Appalachian mountain pass of Pound Gap. He telegraphed this news to Kentucky governor Thomas E. Bramlette, at Frankfort, and proposed that he call out the state militia.[72] Halleck forwarded intelligence that confirmed the reports of Morgan's plans; information also arrived that Forrest was gathering forces in northern Mississippi, preparatory to raiding Tennessee and Kentucky.[73] Burbridge determined to go to eastern Kentucky with what cavalry force he could scrape together to meet Morgan and prevent his passage. He telegraphed Morton to ask that he prepare and send troops to the border to defend Louisville, which was bereft of troops.[74] Morton promptly sent three regiments of hundred-days troops to Louisville, which were then distributed about Kentucky to guard railroad lines.[75] Despite Burbridge's efforts, Morgan's force slipped into Kentucky on June 1, and the federal general pursued the rebels northwestward through the state. Morgan's forces attacked and destroyed railroad tracks and bridges, cut telegraph lines, and attacked a federal garrison at Mount Sterling, capturing hundreds and seizing the town. Morgan took part of his command and pressed northward toward Lexington, while Burbridge caught up to the rebel force left behind at Mount Sterling and routed them, inflicting heavy casualties.[76]

On May 31, the day before Morgan entered Kentucky, Colonel Conrad Baker, in Indianapolis, reported to the War Department his personal conviction that the secret conspirators intended to make an attempt "in favor of the enemy at the first favorable opportunity." He was privy to Carrington's espionage operations and conferred with the general on the latest developments. Leaders of the secret organization (which he still termed the Knights of the Golden Circle) had recently met in Indianapolis, with representatives present from Missouri and Kentucky. The leaders expected John Hunt Morgan to enter Kentucky via Pound Gap, he wrote; Kentucky members of the organization were collaborating with the Confederate raider.[77]

That same day, Morton telegraphed Stanton to ask a sensitive question: "Can the fidelity of Gov Bramlette of Kentucky be relied on? It is important for me to understand this immediately. Answer in cipher."[78] Bramlette, a War Democrat, had been a regimental commander and brigadier general before his election as governor in 1863. However, he clashed frequently with the Lincoln administration over the protection of slavery in Kentucky. As Kentucky had not seceded from the Union and remained under federal control, slavery remained intact in the commonwealth under the Emancipation Proclamation. But the increasingly radicalized army stationed in Kentucky had become an agent of social change that undermined slavery in the commonwealth. He vehemently opposed the enlistment of African American men as soldiers in the federal armies and threatened violence to stop it. This vocal opposition to Lincoln's policies and war measures, all in an effort to preserve slavery in Kentucky, prompted questions about Bramlette's loyalty. Morton shared the distrust felt by many Republicans and War Democrats about the Kentucky governor's motives. He also may have distrusted Bramlette owing to David Turnbull's report that the Kentucky governor was in communication with conspirators. In reply, Stanton furnished Morton a qualified endorsement of the Kentucky governor, noting that he thought Bramlette could be relied on, "especially as present appearances are not very encouraging to disloyalty. I believe the Governor is a firm Union man."[79] Reassured, Morton wired Bramlette that he had "satisfactory evidence that a formidable conspiracy is being put on foot in Kentucky." He asked that Bramlette send an aide to confer with him on the subject.[80] Bramlette quickly replied that his adjutant general, Major General D. W. Lindsay, would embark for Indianapolis the next day to confer.[81] Morton met with Lindsay and no doubt shared information on the secret organization in Kentucky and its collaboration with John Hunt Morgan.

In the meantime, Morgan's rebel forces advanced northward from Lexington in the direction of Covington, but were also in striking distance of a nearly undefended Louisville. Detective Coffin, telegraphing from Jeffersonville, Indiana, opposite the Kentucky city, warned Morton that "300 men can take Louisville."[82] Rallying to the city's defense, Carrington traveled to Louisville with additional Indiana troops to coordinate the defense in the border area and sent a regiment to the defense of Frankfort, which also was threatened. Morgan's main force appeared to be driving toward Covington and Cincinnati. Heintzelman left Columbus and went down to Cincinnati to superintend the organization of city defenses, throwing Ohio units across the river as a forward defense. There he met Brigadier General E. H. Hobson, whom Burbridge had sent to organize a force to push south to meet Morgan's advancing troops. He also met Governor Brough, who was on his way to Indianapolis to meet with Morton.[83] Hobson and a small force of Ohio troops crossed the river and rode the rails to Cynthiana, Kentucky, where they clashed with Morgan's forces. The rebel forces overwhelmed the Ohioans, but Hobson delayed Morgan for several hours in negotiations over surrender terms. The delay allowed Burbridge to catch up and, in a night attack, the federal cavalry smashed and scattered Morgan's forces, the remnants of which fled to Virginia.[84] The result delighted Heintzelman, who wrote in his journal that had not Hobson held up Morgan, the rebels could have advanced on Covington. "A few shots fired into Cincinnati would have been heard all over the United States and been repeated in Surprise, Morgan is Shelling Cincinnati!!" The previous day Heintzelman had ordered the seizure of that day's issue of the *Cincinnati Daily Enquirer,* the city's main Democratic newspaper, for what he termed a "treasonable article calling on the Kentuckians to rise."[85]

Federal military commanders and political leaders believed that Morgan's raid into Kentucky was intended to coincide with a rising among the members of the secret organization. Their earnest preparations betrayed their anxiety. Along with messages about troop movements, worried telegrams about captured spies and the arrest of a Michigan man in Louisville with the 1863 KGC oath in his pocket exhibited their fears.[86] Stidger's reports from this period indicated that conspirators from several states were actively recruiting and organizing in Kentucky. He reported that a Springfield, Illinois man, B. B. Piper, a member of the national council of the organization, was going to Frankfort to organize the eastern portion of the state.[87] Curiously, Piper was in the state capital during the "siege" of the town and was noticed by a newspaper correspondent of the *Cincinnati Daily Commercial* as "indulging largely in fierce rebel talk." The writer suggested that he "deserves to be ventilated" with bullet holes.[88]

From the reports of Stidger and other army detectives, military commanders and Morton knew that the leaders of the secret organization in Indiana planned a meeting in Indianapolis on June 14. Stidger, as secretary of the Kentucky branch, was in attendance. The meeting was attended by about fifty Indiana delegates, he reported, and he was the only non-Indiana person in attendance.[89] Delegates from about twenty-six counties attended; they reported that fifty-one of Indiana's ninety-two counties were organized under the new Sons of Liberty reorganization, seven were in a "partial state of organization," and thirty-five were still organized under the "Old Order," which Stidger supposed was the KGC, with hundreds of members in each of those counties. The council discussed a variety matters, including political educational objectives once they controlled the state (e.g., that the organization proscribe all teachers who did not hew to Democratic principles and that only orthodox Democratic ideology be taught in the schools). They discussed the immediate formation of a military organization and setting a time for action. They also reported a breach in their internal security: S. P. Coffin had been fingered as a spy for General Carrington! The Kentucky council determined that Coffin should be killed. They ordered Stidger and Bowles to make arrangements to assassinate him. H. H. Dodd, the state commander of the organization, volunteered to find and kill the spy.[90]

Vallandigham's Return

Stidger also learned at the meeting that the exiled Clement L. Vallandigham would appear the next day at Hamilton, Ohio, to speak at a Democratic rally. Indeed, two weeks previous, Stidger had reported that leaders of the organization knew that Vallandigham planned to return from exile sometime between June 20 and the end of the month.[91] The Ohioan had now moved up the date of his return. Dodd, Stidger, and other Indiana members planned to travel to Hamilton to hear him speak. That night, after the council meeting adjourned, Stidger found Sergeant Prentice and told him to alert Carrington both that the Ohioan was to appear in Hamilton and that Coffin had been discovered; he was to find and warn the exposed spy. But Prentice took the wrong train and failed to contact Coffin. In the early morning of June 15, however, as Stidger was making his way to the Indianapolis train station to travel to Ohio, he saw Coffin walking from the station. He was safe, but no longer useful.[92]

At this time, Carrington was in Louisville superintending the city's defenses; thus, Prentice could not alert him to Vallandigham's imminent appearance at Hamilton. The sergeant instead told Governor Morton. Morton immediately wired Heintzelman and asked him to come to Indianapolis the next day. He did not inform the general why he urgently requested his presence, noting only that "it is important" and that Carrington was requested as well.[93] This was coded language that the matter had to do with intelligence. Morton possessed access to War Department ciphers, but he knew that Heintzelman inexplicably did not. Consequently, the governor dared not send such explosive news to Heintzelman by the open and nonsecure telegraph network. The general replied that he would come the next day. Morton also telegraphed Carrington that Heintzelman would be in Indianapolis the next day. "You must be here," he added.[94]

Morton's urgent request for Heintzelman to travel to Indianapolis almost produced disaster. The general decided to travel to Indianapolis on the train alone; "I won't take any of my staff along," he recorded in his journal. Nor did he take the first train west, but only arrived in Indianapolis at nine o'clock the next evening. Carrington was waiting for him at the train station and immediately informed him that Vallandigham had appeared at Hamilton. "I passed through there last [night;] all appeared quiet," Heintzelman noted. Telegrams sent to him from his Columbus staff officers and awaiting his arrival in Indianapolis also told him of Vallandigham's appearance. The general went to a hotel to get some supper, but Morton and Carrington importunately called on him. Writing in his journal, Heintzelman thought the only course to pursue was to arrest Vallandigham. "I could have decided what to do tonight," he wrote, "but I saw the Governor wants to have a meeting tomorrow." He stayed the night in Indianapolis. That night his Columbus staff telegraphed that the acting assistant provost marshal general for Ohio had ordered the arrest of Vallandigham and was sending several companies of troops from Johnson's Island and Cincinnati to be on hand.[95] He replied that he would be back in Ohio the next evening and that there was no need for "so much haste." Besides, being privy to the machinations of the extensive secret organization, he knew that more troops would be required to make the arrest. The next day, the sixteenth, he again conferred with Morton and Carrington. "A detective came in who was at Hamilton and at Dayton, saw Valandigham [sic] and heard him speak," he recorded. Taking the 2:00 p.m. train for Columbus, he rode through Dayton, which still appeared quiet as far as he could tell. At Springfield, Ohio, between Dayton and Columbus, he learned he had boarded the wrong train and had to stay overnight at a local hotel, backtrack to Xenia, and go on to Columbus. He arrived at his headquarters from his errant journey only on the seventeenth.[96]

While the departmental commander was either incommunicado on trains or lost in Ohio, other political and military leaders were busy trying to gather the facts regarding Vallandigham's return and decide what to do. On June 15, Morton telegraphed Governor Brough at Columbus and Secretary Stanton at Washington to alert them to Vallandigham's presence at Hamilton and

Dayton. To Stanton he added that Vallandigham's presence "was known to his friends for a month. The intention is to try the strength of the government."[97] That same day he also requested artillery equipment with which to prepare two batteries then in organization and asked the secretary to send a confidential officer to Indianapolis immediately. Stanton replied that no officer was available to send at the moment but that there "could be none in whom I have more confidence than in you, and any confidential communication from you will be treated as such."[98]

At Saint Louis, Rosecrans and Sanderson learned of the appearance of Vallandigham in Ohio almost immediately, thanks to the presence at Hamilton of one of their detectives. Alerted to the congressional district convention at Hamilton and the possibility that the former congressman might return to appear at the convention, Sanderson had sent one of his staff, a newspaperman named William Thorpe, to Ohio. Thorpe, who had formerly worked for the *Detroit Advertiser and Tribune,* arrived at Hamilton on the morning of June 15, the day of the convention, in the guise of a "volunteer correspondent" (freelance reporter) for the *Chicago Times,* the Northwest's leading antiwar journal.[99] His guise gave him near celebrity status among many of the Democrats present, and he promptly heard broad hints and outright assertions from knowing persons that Vallandigham was there and would speak that afternoon. At lunchtime he left the convention hall and went to the telegraph office nearby, where he took a chance, confided in the telegraph operator, and wired to Sanderson that Vallandigham was there. He added that he thought Vallandigham would return to Canada and that he would follow him and with help from other detectives would arrest him. He also confided in a local deputy federal marshal, who refused to believe that Vallandigham was there.

After lunch and the reassembly of the convention, printed handbills circulated in the crowd that Vallandigham would address the convention. "Immense applause, shouts, and yells" arose from those present. Convention business continued but was soon halted by noise outside the hall of a great crowd approaching. Pandemonium erupted in the hall and people rushed to the doors and windows to look outside. "Vallandigham! Vallandigham!" they cried as they "climbed on benches, chairs, and tables, waving their hats and yelling like lunatics." Vallandigham came into view and forced his way through the throng to the platform, shaking outstretched hands on all sides. Finally, after several minutes, order was restored, when the throng called on the returning hero for a speech. Moving outside to accommodate the crowds, Vallandigham mounted a platform and spoke from a prepared text. Thorpe recorded his speech verbatim, along with the many exclamations of the enthusiastic audience. In his speech, Vallandigham bid defiance to arbitrary power (military authority) and offered to be tried by civil authorities. He said the existence of "Loyal Union Leagues" that supported the Lincoln administration and the war effort justified the existence of secret organizations of patriots dedicated to the preservation of the Constitution. He warned that a "vast multitude" bound themselves together by holy ties "to defend by whatever means the exigencies of the times shall demand, their natural and constitutional rights as freemen at all hazards, and to the last extremity." When the meeting broke up, Thorpe rushed to the telegraph office and wired Sanderson and Governor Brough what had happened; thoughtfully, he also alerted the *Chicago Times*. A local attorney and supporter of Vallandigham told him that Vallandigham's "friends" intimated that if military authorities attempted to arrest him Dayton would be razed and converted to a cornfield. En route to Cincinnati, Thorpe rode with a Vallandigham supporter who carried the original speech to the major daily newspapers of the city to be set in type for publication. Acting on Sanderson's instructions, Thorpe rode to Columbus and met with Brough on the sixteenth. Also present were the adjutant general of Ohio, B. R. Cowen, and Colonel J. H. Potter, the new acting assistant provost marshal general for Ohio. All were well posted on the "secret order," he reported. Brough, he wrote, understood that Vallandigham and his followers intended to organize the "supreme circle" for Ohio while at Hamilton and asked Thorpe if it had been done. The detective replied that he had not joined the organization to learn its secrets, so he could not say, but expressed his surprise that the leadership of the organization in Ohio was not already established. "Governor Brough said that such was the case—that the order was thoroughly organized up to the fifth degree, but no higher."[100] Brough said that he had considered arresting Vallandigham but would await instructions from Washington. Besides, the governor noted that the "military condition of the State" could not "justify an attempt" to arrest him, meaning that there were then too few effective federal troops in the state to make the attempt. He also awaited the return of Heintzelman.[101]

The news of Vallandigham's appearance filled military commanders at Saint Louis with consternation. Rosecrans, alerted by Thorpe, telegraphed Brough to warn the governor. He urged a tough response to the provocation. "Please have him arrested. Gen H—— can find force I presume to make sure against a rescue."[102] Sanderson wired Governor Yates at Springfield, Illinois, that his "worst anticipations are being realized."[103] In response to requests from Indianapolis for artillery to meet the crisis, Rosecrans offered to send some but changed his mind in order to keep them handy for his own defense.[104] To

Heintzelman he wired the question "What will be done? The question affects us!"[105] When informed that Heintzelman and Brough had contacted Washington and awaited instructions, Rosecrans wired back, "Glad to know you and Brough have put the responsibility where it belongs[.] let me know everything of [Vallandigham's] movements which threatens mischief."[106]

The political and military leaders in the Northwest and Missouri awaited word from Lincoln, but they waited in vain. Wisely, the president did not rise to the bait. Vallandigham's return was an effort to provoke an arrest by military authorities, an action that would have produced mass protest and the uprising that leaders of the secret organization desired. Certainly, some commanders and politicians were eager to put him in prison again and vindicate the authority of the federal government. Ohio congressman James A. Garfield hoped that Lincoln would rearrest the former exile. He wrote, "There will be a great indignation here if the Pres. don't at once arrest Val. I fear he will not. How can we live under such imbecility?"[107] In this instance, however, passivity and inactivity—a stance that governed much of Lincoln's approach to affairs in the Northwest—paid off. Lincoln received the appeals from Brough and Heintzelman, waited several days, and then drafted and signed a letter to the two leaders:

> Both of you have official responsibility as to the U.S. Military in Ohio, and generally—one, in organizing and furnishing, the other in directing, commanding, and forwarding. Consult together freely, watch Vallandigham and others closely, and, upon discovering any palpable injury, or imminent danger to the Military, proceeding from him, them, or any of them, arrest all implicated. Otherwise, do not arrest without further order; meanwhile report the signs to me from time to time.

But the letter sports the endorsement in the handwriting of one of the president's secretaries: "not sent."[108] On reflection, Lincoln probably realized that the letter was general and unhelpful. He rightly did not send it. Significantly, in it he grouped Vallandigham with "others" and enjoined the leaders to watch "him, them, or any of them," suggesting that he associated Vallandigham with the secret organization about which he had so often heard from the governors. The Northwestern governors who called on him after the April 15 conference at Indianapolis to discuss the hundred-days-regiments proposal undoubtedly shared the preeminent problem on their minds: the existence of the Northwest Confederacy conspiracy. He would have heard what Carrington's and the governors' detectives reported to them of Vallandigham's leadership of the organization and its intentions. We lack documentation of the president's response to the visitors, but the evidence points to the conclusion that Lincoln did not have a good idea of how to deal with the problem of Vallandigham and the conspirators except not to provoke them.

Heintzelman, Morton, and Carrington, all well advised by their detectives inside the secret organization, knew that the conspirators wished to provoke a rising. Morton warned Stanton of their intention. No evidence exists to suggest that any of them advised rearresting Vallandigham. As well, Brough of Ohio took a wait-and-see approach and passed the responsibility to Washington. From the conversation reported by detective Thorpe, the governor and his circle were well posted on the organization in their state and believed that there weren't enough troops in Ohio to put down an outbreak. It was Rosecrans who advised arrest. But he deferred to the commanders in Ohio, the War Department, and Lincoln.

In the minds of Morton and Carrington, the Morgan raid into Kentucky and the appearance of Vallandigham at Hamilton, Ohio, were not coincidental occurrences. They knew the conspirators were in communication with the Confederates and that the two groups collaborated in common cause. Morton was able to convince Governor Bramlette of that fact when, in early June, he telegraphed and asked him to send a reliable officer to confer. After Burbridge's troopers defeated and scattered Morgan's force and the immediate threat dissipated, Bramlette wrote a private letter to Morton to express his "grateful thanks for your prompt assistance during Morgan's recent raid." The Indiana troops sent to defend the commonwealth had relieved them of danger. Furthermore, he wrote,

> The appearance of Vallandigham in Ohio simultaneously with
> Morgan's raid into Kentucky fully confirms the matters made
> known to me, through General Lindsay by you.
>   The defeat of Morgan has frustrated their movement for the
> present, but vigilence [sic] in the future must still guard us against
> those machinations of evil doers.[109]

On receipt of Bramlette's letter, Morton telegraphed to request his permission to publish it.[110] It was granted, and the letter appeared in the *Indianapolis Daily Journal* and was reprinted in Union and Republican newspapers throughout the Northwest.[111]

In the aftermath of the latest Morgan raid, Heintzelman was convinced that the rebel raider had aimed for Cincinnati. In his journal he wrote that the interrogation of captured rebel officers "confirms . . . that Morgans intention was to decend [sic] the valley of the Licking [River], plunder Covington, and shell

Cincinnati. I suspected as much," he congratulated himself, and noted that the "stubborn resistance" made by Union troops he had helped organize and send into Kentucky "was all that prevented it." The material damage of the shelling would have been negligible, but the "report of the shelling of Cin. by Morgan would have created a most disastrous effect, both here and in Europe."[112]

An Internal Debate

With the successful infiltration of spies into the secret organization, a subtle but significant change occurred in the counsels of Union leaders in the region. They had achieved an advantage over their foes. Good intelligence of the intentions of the conspirators allowed military commanders and the governors to contemplate taking the initiative. As a result, a debate arose between Morton, Carrington, and Heintzelman about how best they should use the information. In short, the governor wanted to employ the information the detectives had collected for political purposes, but the generals opposed such action and wished to defer revealing their hand in order to learn more about the enemy in their midst.

On Friday, June 17, Carrington wrote to Secretary Stanton to ask advice about a newly arisen policy dispute with the governor: "Governor Morton requests me to give publicity on Monday to the documents of the secret treasonable order." The governor wished to use them "as a warning to the people of its nature." Carrington explained that his own wish was to keep the records under wraps, "the better to undermine their operations and to enable the Government to have proof ample, if they should conclude to make simultaneous arrests of the leaders in the various Western States." The records he referred to were the constitution, rituals, oaths, and other documents that Stidger and other detectives had obtained, including the OAK degrees obtained by Coffin, as well as the new Sons of Liberty "secret forms" that superseded the OAK's. He added that the organization's printing office was in Indianapolis, and were it to be seized other records would be obtained. He disclosed that he had a spy who was an official in the organization who was to attend the organization's national council meeting to coincide with the Democratic national convention at Chicago on July 4. Carrington suggested that the question of public disclosure of the records of the organization was "worthy [of] the grave consideration of the President, his Cabinet, and the General-in-Chief." Separate from the question of immediate disclosure of the records, he assured the secretary that Brough and Morton, Heintzelman and Rosecrans all "concurred in the policy of secrecy, with a view to contemporaneous arrests."[113]

This last statement suggests that the leaders had been in agreement up to that time, but now Morton had changed his mind and wanted immediate publication. Indeed, Rosecrans had already made sweeping arrests of leaders of the organization in Missouri. That put the generals in a fix, and they sought instructions. Heintzelman, finally back in Columbus from his wayward wanderings, communicated his views on the matter to Halleck in his cover letter to Carrington's June 6 report. He stated that there could no longer be any doubt about the existence of the organization, its extent, and its leadership. He repeated Carrington's information that the secret organization's records could be seized. "I have been urged to seize them and to make some arrests," he wrote, "but I do not think it advisable now." He shared Carrington's view that seizure and arrests "would prevent our obtaining any further information; would create alarm and enable many of the leaders to escape or precipitate an outbreak." He put the matter in Washington's hands. "When Government determines to act, troops should be collected at suitable points and the arrests should be made simultaneously in the different States where the leaders are known."[114]

Back in Indianapolis, Carrington issued orders to increase the guard at the federal and state arsenals in the city.[115] He reported to headquarters Stidger's findings on the proceedings of the secret organization's state meeting, held shortly before. He also noted that he was "preparing the copy of the whole work of the order. Gov Morton wishes it published, and has asked of the Secy of War authority." His own opinion was that if Washington authorities intended to arrest Vallandigham and the others, there then should be no publication in advance of the arrests. But, he thought, "if there are to be no arrests it may be well to put the people on their guard" about the conspiracy.[116] Morton, Heintzelman, and Carrington waited for instructions from Washington. But no word came from federal leadership. Days later, with no orders from the War Department or the president, Carrington wrote to Heintzelman to complain of the lack of instructions and the pressure he was under from Morton. The governor "daily urges me to permit the publication" of the records of the secret society. The governor had telegraphed Washington but received no answer. Carrington also complained that Morton had leaked the new name of the organization, the Sons of Liberty, to the *Indianapolis Daily Journal*, which published it on June 18 with the information that Vallandigham was its top leader. Carrington regretted the disclosure. The governor also "wishes to publish the address of the Grand Commander [Dodd] of this State, thinking it will be of value, and develop a re-action against them." He asked "whether I shall be governed" by Morton's wishes regarding publication. Noting growing tensions within the Democratic Party, he added that the "timid portion" of the party had succeeded in postponing the Chicago national convention, "against the wishes of the Western members: but the Supreme Council of the Order will meet at Chicago on the first."[117] In the meantime, Carrington drafted versions of a report outlining the organization, leadership, and intentions of the organization, with the full text of its records incorporated, and forwarded them to Columbus. In turn, Heintzelman sent them on to the War Department, reiterating that it was "inexpedient to make the matter public before receiving orders from [the] War Dept."[118]

There matters rested, awaiting instructions from a seemingly uninterested or paralyzed Washington leadership. The information obtained by Coffin, Stidger, Tucker, Faris, and others gave military and political leadership in the Old Northwest knowledge of the plans of the conspirators that allowed them to steal a march on the plotters and take the initiative. This wealth of intelligence created the temptation in a consummate politician like Morton to use it for immediate political effect. The upcoming elections were paramount in his mind. On the other hand, the generals saw the benefits of gathering more information and awaiting the best moment to strike. Morton pressured Carrington and Washington authorities to divulge the information, but the generals resisted and looked for orders from their superiors. As we shall see, convincing a preoccupied president to see the threat that existed in his home state and region proved to be an unforeseen hurdle.

NINE

"I Feel Provoked beyond Measure at the Indifference of the President"

Convincing Lincoln of the Danger of Insurrection, Summer 1864

IN JUNE, having amassed strong evidence of a significant threat to internal security in the North, General Rosecrans took steps to report his findings to President Lincoln. However, the president was intent not to receive his courier and instead sent his own assistant to Saint Louis to gather the facts. Still, the president rejected the premise of Rosecrans's report, and the general scrambled to find alternative means to convey his information to Washington. Congressional leaders forced a hearing of Rosecrans's report at the White House, but the president failed to act on it. Leaders in the Old Northwest voiced exasperation at Lincoln's "indifference" to the dire situation in the region. Meanwhile, continued efforts to gather information on the conspiracy produced detailed information on planned uprisings. Lacking guidance from Washington, politicians and commanders in the region formulated their own plans to combat the threat. They continued to pressure Lincoln's administration to act. Under such pressure, federal leaders sent trusted official Joseph Holt west to gather information on conditions. Holt's reports finally convinced leaders that the threat of revolution in the Northwest was serious.

John Hay's Mission to Missouri

After his efforts to share intelligence findings with the governors and military commanders of the Old Northwest, General Rosecrans asked Congressman James A. Garfield, his former chief of staff, to go to the White House and persuade President Lincoln to allow him to travel to Washington to speak with him. On May 30, Garfield wrote back that the president told him to have Rosecrans write to him "freely and fully on the whole matter." Garfield's opinion was that Lincoln seemed "afraid of a collision between you and someone else—probably Gl Grant, and he would rather have the matter written about at a little distance." Garfield believed the unpleasantness surrounding the arrest of Major Bond continued to embarrass Lincoln. "There were several gentlemen by—and I think he felt it a little."[1]

Rosecrans was disappointed by the president's dodge, but he dutifully sat down to compose a letter as Lincoln requested. He warned that "detailed information of high national importance of a plot to overthrow the government which you should know about cannot be entrusted to the mails." He requested an order to send an officer who would convey the documents he wished him to see. He did not wish to repeat the "outrage" committed on Major Bond by sending an officer without orders.[2] He also shared the secret with a curious Garfield. "I have followed the conspiracy through Mo, Ill, Ind Ohio and into Mich, New York, & Kentucky," he explained. "The evidence considering the nature of the case is voluminous, and has important bearing not merely upon the possibilities of the future but the actualities of the present. Could I see [you] I would like to take counsel with you. We have 30 or 40 in prison."[3] While he waited for Lincoln's reply, Rosecrans asked the War Department for reinforcements. "The strong probability of the advance of a heavy rebel force upon the southern border of this State impels me to make the request," he wrote.[4] He continued his efforts to meet with Governor Morton, with whom he had yet to confer. Also in the meantime, Sanderson began to draft a report outlining the development of Rosecrans's and his own understanding of the conspiratorial organization in Missouri and neighboring states. He incorporated the numerous reports of the several spies as evidence. The result was a document several inches thick, numbering nearly one thousand pages, with hundreds of letters, reports, and memoranda outlining the work of the provost marshal general's detective force.[5]

A game of telegraphic ping-pong between Saint Louis and Washington ensued. Lincoln wired in reply to Rosecrans to send the information he had by express service. "There will be no danger of its miscarriage."[6] On receipt,

Rosecrans protested that "the nature of the information is too grave involving the interests of the country & the safety of individuals to admit of transacting the business through the express. A sense of duty obliges me to refrain from so transmitting it."[7] Lincoln, exasperated, replied that he was "unable to conceive how a message can be less safe by express than by a staff officer. If you send a verbal messenger the messenger is one additional person let into the secret."[8] The general enlisted Illinois governor Yates, who telegraphed to Lincoln that the general's information was of "most vital importance to the Govt" and could not be "conveyed to you in its full import by mail or by express." He suggested that either Rosecrans or Sanderson be ordered to Washington immediately to report.[9] Insistent that neither Rosecrans nor one of his staff come to Washington, Lincoln ordered one of his private secretaries and close confidants, John Hay, to go to Saint Louis to meet with the general.[10]

Hay, a recent Brown University graduate, young, cultured, witty, an occasional writer for various newspapers, recorded in his diary Lincoln's explanation for sending him: "'If it is a matter of such overwhelming importance,' said the President 'I dont think Sanderson is the proper person to whom to entrust it. I am inclined to think that the object of the General is to force me into a conflict with the Secretary of War and to make me overrule him in this matter. This at present I am not inclined to do.'" Hay set out on the long rail journey to Missouri on June 10.[11] The cars were uncomfortable, crowded, and "malodorous." He endured a delay at Cincinnati on the twelfth while the city was convulsed by the Morgan raid in Kentucky. Arriving in Saint Louis at eleven o'clock on the morning of June 13, he reported immediately to Rosecrans's headquarters. The general was tied up at the moment but proposed supping together and meeting early in the evening to "talk business." After their meal the two men retired to Rosecrans's hotel room. The general "began to talk, in a loud easy tone at first, which he soon lowered, casting a glance over his shoulder and moving his chair nearer." Rosecrans told him in detail of the "secret conspiracy" of a society called the Order of American Knights, which was led by Clement Vallandigham in the North and General Sterling Price in the South. The organization was strong in Missouri, Illinois, Indiana, Ohio, and Kentucky. Rosecrans told him that Vallandigham was soon to leave Canada and appear at a Democratic convention in Ohio, "and if the Government should see fit to rearrest him, then his followers are to unite to resist the officers and protect him at all hazards." Rosecrans's "secret service men" had infiltrated the organization and obtained this information.[12] Rosecrans poured out the details of the conspiracy for about two hours, when Sanderson entered and provided additional details. "I went over to Sanderson's room &

read papers with him for another hour."[13] "He read to me his voluminous report to Rosecrans in regard to the workings of the order and showed me some few documents," wrote Hay, "among them a letter from Vallandigham to the Abbé McMaster dated June 1 in which he at first complains that the 'orders issued' are not properly executed—hints at a scarcity of funds—expresses himself a little dubious as to his own action in relation to the Chicago convention—and concludes by referring to the 'Household of Faith.'"[14]

After thumbing through Sanderson's report, the two men returned to Rosecrans's room. Hay told them that he would return to Washington and "lay the matter before the President as it had been presented to me and I thought he would look upon it as I did, as a matter of importance." Hay noted that he made no suggestions nor asked to convey Sanderson's report to Washington. This was because he "saw in both R. & S. a disposition to insist on Sanderson's coming to Washington in person to discuss the matter without the intervention of the Secretary of War." Hay speculated as to Rosecrans's motives: his hostility to Stanton; Sanderson was proud of his effort in "ferreting out this business" and wanted to "impress" the president; Rosecrans wanted to determine a plan, and "finally they want money for the secret service fund." While Hay was in Saint Louis, the general composed a letter to Lincoln that the secretary carried back to Washington. In it, Rosecrans candidly explained his motives, outlined what he had told Hay, and added that what Hay learned was merely the tip of the iceberg but should suffice to show that one of his officers should go to Washington to lay the whole matter before him. A policy could then be adopted to "give adequate security to public interests." He reiterated that the "organization not only threatens great danger in case our military operations are unsuccessful or indecisive," but was "spreading discontent" and doing "mischief" among the people. He also wrote that the conspirators assisted guerrillas and threatened supply depots in Missouri. "The present raid in Kentucky was invited and as you will observe unquestionably received aid from the organization[,] bridges having been destroyed and other mischiefs done at distances of thirty to forty miles from the rebel raiders. I knew this raid was contemplated and my men warned the military authorities some weeks ago." He could not in good conscience send the records collected into Sanderson's report by mail or express. "My duty to you to the country and the persons whose lives would be endangered by want of prompt and proper action all forced such a course." He asked for "contingent fund" to cover his expenses in this investigation, noting that the War Department's refusal had been "most injurious to the public interest and unwarranted." He also wanted the obstacles to communicating with Lincoln eliminated. He concluded by noting that July 4—the date of the Democratic national convention at Chicago—was the chosen date for the conspirators to act, so that prompt action was needed.[15]

Hay's return trip from Saint Louis was even more arduous than his westward ride, with extra delays and missed connections adding to the toil. Reaching Washington on June 17, he met with President Lincoln immediately and told him all he had learned from Rosecrans. Since leaving Saint Louis, the "Avatar of Vallandigham in Ohio" had occurred, he wrote in his diary. "The President," he recorded,

> seemed not overwell pleased that Rosecrans had not sent all the necessary papers by me, reiterating his want of confidence in Sanderson, declining to be made a party to a quarrel between Stanton and Rosecrans, and stating in reply to Rosecrans' suggestion of the importance of the greatest secrecy, that a secret which had already been confided to Yates Morton Brough Bramlette & their respective circles of officers could scarcely be worth the keeping now. He treats the Northern section of the conspiracy as not especially worth regarding, holding it a mere political organization, with about as much of malice and as much of puerility as the Knights of the Golden Circle.

As to Vallandigham's appearance in Ohio, the president said that the "question for the Government to decide is whether it can afford to disregard the contempt of authority & breach of discipline displayed in Vallandigham's unauthorized return." But, he added, it "cannot but result in benefit to the Union cause" for the "violent and indiscreet . . . firebrand" Vallandigham to go to the Chicago convention. Lincoln noted that he had considered annulling the Ohioan's exile order, "but had been too much occupied to do it." Allowing Vallandigham back into the United States would give the Democratic Party two presidential candidates and thereby divide the party. Lincoln placed his trust in "the people," and said that the political opposition could not control the convention and guide "the honest though misguided masses" into the course of violence. Hay recorded in his diary that he disagreed with the president and told him he thought the Democratic convention managers from New York would be overwhelmed by the western "barefooted Democracy." "The President said he would take the matter into consideration and would write tomorrow the 18th to Brough & Heintzelman about Val. and to Rosecrans at an early day."[16] Hay also described Lincoln's reaction and his own disagreement with the president to fellow secretary John G. Nicolay: "The Tycoon thinks small beer of Rosey's mare's nest. *Too* small, I rather think."[17] As noted, Lincoln drafted but did not send a letter to leaders in Ohio, and no letter to Rosecrans on the subject survives. Indeed, Lincoln failed to communicate any directions to the military and political leaders in the Northwest on the issue. His trust in the people to oppose violent opposition was his guiding principle, and it served as the substitute for formulating a policy, as Rosecrans requested. It is possible that the president did not trust his political allies—both the governors and subordinate military commanders—sufficiently to communicate with them. Lincoln's nonaction and failure to communicate, even that he planned to do nothing, vexed his military and political friends. Contrary to the president's mistaken view, to date they had successfully kept their thorough knowledge of the conspiracy a secret, leaking only small nuggets to the press. Perhaps Lincoln's saving grace was that his inaction came unexpectedly to Vallandigham and the other leaders of the secret organization, who had banked on a military response to the Ohioan's return. Presidential passivity may have prevented a violent outbreak.

Rosecrans was not alone in attempting to convey the imminence of revolution in the Northwest to the president. Governor Yates was gravely concerned by the reports of masses of armed men who openly bid defiance to the federal government and resisted the draft enrollment and the arrests of deserters. As well, guerrilla bands from Missouri found refuge in Illinois and posed a dangerous internal threat.[18] He saw clearly the growing danger in Illinois and the Northwest. He had pressed Secretary Stanton to allow him either to recruit troops to serve solely in Illinois or to send him thousands of guns with which to arm local chapters of the Union League. However, Stanton chose to do neither. Apprised of both Heintzelman's and Rosecrans's espionage efforts, Yates added his voice to Rosecrans's request to send an officer to Washington.[19] When that failed, he sent his own messenger. The governor dispatched Brigadier General Julius White, a Chicagoan who had recently served as commander of the draft rendezvous at Springfield, to call on the president. Accompanied by Illinois Republican congressman Isaac N. Arnold and the president's close friend, Leonard Swett, White saw Lincoln at the White House and "represented [Yates's] views . . . regarding affairs in our State." The president again dismissed their concerns. "The President," wrote White,

> does not appear to apprehend any serious disturbances north of the
> Ohio, but admits that situated as you are, with no efficient militia
> law, and with no troops stationed within the State, except as are
> guarding prisoners, the State authorities would be in an embarrass-
> ing position if any considerable uprising of Copperheads should

occur, and directed me to say to your Excellency, that any measure you should think proper to submit in a definite form, should receive consideration. As I was not authorized to do so, I did not attempt to propose anything, but said that there were two things requisite to secure the State against such outbreaks. One was troops, and the other a military commander having jurisdiction co extensive with the State.[20]

Lincoln's response to Yates's request for help was twofold: to deny the problem existed and to deflect the question back on Yates and ask him for real policy suggestions to meet the problem should it exist. Yates's call to station troops in Illinois was a nonstarter. Troops simply were not available. Lincoln was consistent in his responses to Brough and Heintzelman, Rosecrans, and now Yates: he would do nothing aggressive but would trust in the wisdom of the people to reject appeals for revolutionary violence by a radical and militant fringe.

Back in Saint Louis, Rosecrans believed he had made a persuasive case to Lincoln and was "an[x]iously looking for a decisive position" from him. He made preparations accordingly.[21] For his own part, Sanderson asked Yates if he had received any reply to his telegram to Lincoln of June 9.[22] He also prepared to go east, wiring detective Devoe in New York City to "hold yourself in readiness to meet me at Harrisburg [Pennsylvania] in the coming week: Will give you a timely notice."[23] Before going east, Sanderson set out for Springfield to update Yates. He carried with him a letter from Rosecrans with new information on the conspiracy. "The southern branch of the O.A.K.," reported Rosecrans, was talking about a "general movement and rising" planned for July 4. Reports from all over Missouri pointed to Confederate cavalry commander General Joseph Shelby commencing a raid into the state with several thousand troops. Rosecrans asked the governor for state militia reinforcements should they be needed.[24] Yates lamented that Illinois "is in worse condition to render you assistance, or to suppress uprising at home, than at any period during the rebellion—We have not a company to give you in case of trouble in Missouri." Sanderson had shown him the proofs of a "most formidable and dangerous" conspiracy. "I feel provoked beyond measure at the indifference of the President," he continued. "I am amazed," he wrote, that Rosecrans had not heard from Lincoln since Hay's visit. "The return of Vallandigham and his appointment as Delegate" were "proof" that Sanderson was correct, and "further proof that he (Val.) thinks he is strong enough to resist the Govt." He confessed his unease at the prospect of Vallandigham coming to the Chicago convention "with impunity."

If he had "proper backing" he would have him arrested and sent to Washington. "But how do I d̶o̶ know but that the President has told his friends that if he came back and behaved himself *tolerably,* he would not be disturbed—So upon the whole there is no telling what should be done *even* with the power to do it."[25]

Rosecrans continued to run the intelligence machine under his command. Problems arose that required his intervention. He wrote a stinging telegram to the officer in charge of the detectives in Cincinnati not to interfere with "an important detective plan" of his own. "You have done a public injury. Please don't do so again."[26] He asked Carrington if he had a cipher key and asked if Morton was home.[27] When Heintzelman sent him copies of some of Carrington's intelligence reports, he thanked him and noted that "they confirm and consolidate the evidence we previously had." He sent the information he had shared with Yates and repeated that they were pressing the president to take some sort of policy stand, one way or other. Showing his impatience with Lincoln's inactivity, indecisiveness, and uncommunicativeness, he added that he was glad that Heintzelman and Governor Brough had "taken the course of requiring the Government to adopt and announce its measures based on some policy in reference to the matter." They must be prepared and keep "full watch of all movements" or they would be hit hard at "inopportune moments."[28] Rosecrans also informed Lincoln that Vallandigham's cohorts circulated information that two army corps were being sent from Sherman's army to reinforce Grant in Virginia, warning the president of a possible leak in War Department communications and demonstrating that his intelligence operations had intercepted Vallandigham's mail.[29]

Rosecrans determined to use every means at his disposal to press the president to make a decision. He recruited every person who might have influence at the White House. A week after Hay's departure, he penned a follow-up report to the president with updated information based on information gathered by his detectives. In the last week "we have added much information" on the conspiracy's "Southern Connections" and operations, he wrote. His operatives in New York City (Devoe's New York detective force) had uncovered a "new element" called the McClellan Minute Men. He urged the president to follow his policy recommendations. He was sending Sanderson east, along with his report, "covering a thousand pages of foolscap," to show you the extent of the conspiracy. He outlined the colonel's report, stressing the conspiracy's "formidable power" in collaboration with Confederate rebels to achieve "the overthrow of the existing national Government & the dismemberment of this nation."[30]

Sanderson's Mission to the East

Rosecrans and Sanderson left Saint Louis together and traveled eastward.[31] The general collected his wife at Yellow Springs, Ohio, and arrived at Columbus on the morning of June 24. The two officers called on Heintzelman; Brough was unfortunately absent. That evening at nine o'clock Sanderson went to Heintzelman's headquarters office and laid out the report. Over the next three hours they pored over the papers. Heintzelman recorded,

> They had near a ream of Reports and statements in relation to these secret societies. They are connected North and South and [have] a most complete Military organization. It is surprising how well the information is corroborative. The information Gen. Carrington has, corresponds with what Gen. Rosecrantz and Col. Sanderson collected at Saint Louis. This also agrees with what they got of a woman who was a Lieutenant in Forrest's cavalry.
>
> Col. Sanderson goes to Gov. Curtain [Curtin] with his documents and a letter from Gen. Rosecrantz. Unfortunately the President and authorities in Wash. cannot, or do not realize the gravity of these matters. If these people with their perfect organization should act promptly and energetically, it would defeat our Armies and it might force us to a disgraceful peace.[32]

Rosecrans's letter to Governor Andrew Curtin of Pennsylvania explained that he had ordered Sanderson to Harrisburg to show him the report he was conveying to President Lincoln. The report exposed the "machinations of a powerful and widely extended politico revolutionary organization working nominally within the Democratic party for the overthrow of our Government and [to] dismember the nation." He suggested that "any advice or view you may feel bound to express to the Government as to what ought to be done in the premises will I think be timely at this crisis."[33] In the morning Sanderson and Rosecrans parted; the colonel went to Pennsylvania, and the general escorted his wife back to Yellow Springs and returned to Saint Louis.[34]

Sanderson rode the rails and arrived at Harrisburg at six o'clock in the morning on the twenty-sixth. He called on Major General Darius N. Couch, commander of the Department of the Susquehanna, and spent the whole day with him uninterrupted ("he having no visiters [*sic*]"). They went through the report carefully. Couch briefed him on affairs in Pennsylvania that augmented Sanderson's knowledge.[35] The colonel wrote that when he returned to Saint Louis he would "be able to throw light on many subjects which here at times

[have] been dark & mysterious to us." The following morning, detective Devoe arrived from New York City with "important additional information in regard to the McClellan secret organization proving its identification with the—OAK—." Devoe spent the morning sifting carefully through the pages of the massive report, and in the afternoon he and Sanderson called on Governor Curtin, with whom they had a "long & very satisfactory conference." "Our information startled him," Sanderson wrote. "He had seen and felt the thing, but did not know what it was. He knew at times that he had been hurt but knew not from whence, by whom, or how. Now all was clear as day-light to him, & he entered fully & earnestly upon the subject of pressing prompt action upon the President." Devoe would leave for Washington that night armed with "letters from here that will effect if any thing can, a favorable reception & audience" from Lincoln and other leaders. "All here agree that I should be ordered to Washington, & have directed their energy & influence to that point. We shall soon see with what effect. If it fails to accomplish the object, no other movement, I am sure, can effect it." Sanderson remained at Harrisburg and awaited developments.[36]

Along with Sanderson's massive report, Devoe carried with him letters of introduction from Governor Curtin and Sanderson to several U.S. senators and representatives. He was himself well connected with California and New York politicians. After arriving in Washington after his nine-hour train ride, he went directly to the capitol to meet with congressmen. The end of the legislative session loomed, and members he wished to buttonhole were preoccupied. Representative James K. Moorhead of Pennsylvania, to whom Curtin had directed the detective, was busy with legislation on the floor but introduced Devoe to Representatives Henry T. Blow and Samuel Knox of Missouri, Robert C. Schenck (who defeated Vallandigham in 1862) and Garfield of Ohio, Godlove Orth of Indiana, and Henry Winter Davis of Maryland. Moorhead also introduced him to Lincoln's "Assistant Private Secretary," William O. Stoddard, who was in the capitol monitoring legislative action. Stoddard took Devoe to the White House and introduced him to John Hay, who informed him that Lincoln was temporarily out of the office. Devoe reported, "I waited till about 5 P.M. I then left, leaving all the testimony with Maj. Hay, who promised to lay it before the President as soon as he returned, & I was to call and have an interview to-morrow morning." He invited Garfield and Schenck, and Senators John Conness of California and Ira Harris of New York to accompany him to meet the president before Congress reconvened the next day. "I intend," wrote Devoe, "to bring such a pressure of Congressional influence upon President Lincoln as will force him to take prompt & efficient action in this matter." From Hay he inferred that "some influence is at work to hood-wink the President & deceive him as to the real designs of the organizations. . . . It is only another proof of the potency and vigilance of the members of that organization." He hoped that Lincoln would not "perversely shut his eyes to the evidence now before him" and that Sanderson could himself report to Lincoln.[37] He telegraphed Sanderson, waiting at Harrisburg, that he had seen several representatives and senators, "all of whom were taking an active interest."[38]

Sanderson's report remained at the White House overnight, where President Lincoln presumably had an opportunity to examine it. The next morning Devoe, accompanied by Garfield and Conness, met with the president at the White House. During the meeting, Secretary of State Seward wandered in and joined the discussion. That evening, the detective dashed off a triumphant note to Rosecrans signaling success. He could not send details of the meeting at that moment but would when he met with Sanderson at Harrisburg. "Suffice it to say," he hurriedly wrote, "you need not release [conspiracy leader and Belgian consul in St. Louis Charles L.] Hunt. The President nor the Department of State, did not [sic] understand the case thoroughly till it was presented by myself. As to other matters I will communicate personally to Col. S. . . . ."[39]

Devoe believed he had persuaded Lincoln of the serious threat posed by the secret organization. But there is no evidence to show that Lincoln and other Washington leaders produced a plan at this time to deal with the problem in the Northwest. No documentation signals a change in how the White House or the War Department addressed the issue. The records suggest that matters simply returned to normal, as if Lincoln had never seen Sanderson's report.

Sanderson returned to Saint Louis on July 6 after being away for nearly two weeks.[40] Meanwhile, Rosecrans told his wife that a "clandestine application for my removal" had been sent to Washington by a group of Missouri politicians, among them Governor Willard P. Hall.[41] He also mused on the invasion of Pennsylvania and the occupation and burning of Chambersburg by forces under Confederate General Jubal Early. "What a lively effect this raid into Pennsylvania will have on the mind of Gov Curtin who from Col S. learned that we had information of the desire and intention of the rebels to make it if they could."[42] The War Department continued to plague the general with orders to send what few troops he had out of the department. Rosecrans protested an order to send two hundred-days regiments to Chicago, to replace regiments that Halleck ordered Heintzelman to send south.[43] He asked Heintzelman if he could get by without the two regiments, and complained to Stanton that the order left Missouri vulnerable to guerrilla raiders who were working with the "home conspiration." He expected a raid by Shelby's rebel forces as well. He asked that Illinois militia be used at Camp Douglas at Chicago instead of the regiments.[44] Moreover, the War Department renewed pressure to release the conspirators Hunt and James A. Barret, arrested in the sweep. Rosecrans sent messages to Lincoln in protest, arguing that the thousand-page report that the president had recently seen showed them to be dangerous men whose release would "endanger the public peace and security."[45] On his return to Saint Louis, Sanderson informed Devoe that he was still "embarrassed" for lack of secret-service funds.[46] In mid-July, Sanderson lamented to him that Washington had still not sent policy direction.[47] Bowing to pressure and the lack of response from Lincoln, Rosecrans released Barret and Hunt on $5,000 and $10,000 bonds, respectively, with provisos that neither man leave the department and to report to headquarters by letter weekly.[48]

Part of Rosecrans's problem in getting Washington authorities to pay heed was due to his failure to win the support of the political factions in Missouri. Notwithstanding his efforts to place impartial officers in posts, he suffered the same fate as his predecessors in provoking both factions' ire in managing the state's military affairs. John G. Nicolay, Lincoln's other private secretary, visited Missouri in late June to take the pulse of the problematic state. While there, he composed for the president an unflattering report on Missouri politics and the administration of state affairs under Sanderson. The report was strongly influenced by information from Governor Hall and one of Rosecrans's subordinate generals, Clinton B. Fisk, who did not like Sanderson and blamed him for several problems. Nicolay doubted that the colonel was the "proper man for inquisitor-general for this State. This affair greatly shakes my faith in the truth of his Val. conspiracy."[49]

Events soon provided a measure of vindication for Rosecrans and Sanderson. Between three and four o'clock in the morning of July 15, arsonists set six steamboats loaded with army supplies ablaze at the Mississippi River levee at Saint Louis. The main Republican newspaper carried headlines of "Guerrilla Incendiarism" and printed the report of the post provost marshal, Minnesota colonel James H. Baker, noting that military authorities had received advance warning of an attack and had increased the night watch posted on the levee from four to thirteen guards.[50] Several nights before, an attempt to burn a steamboat by a man using some combustible material from his pocket had been foiled when a watchman saw and caught the man.[51] Rosecrans promptly promulgated an order, General Orders 119, warning that an organized body of boatburners was abroad and directing that all affairs at the levee were to be under the command of a military harbor master.[52] With the city's businessmen, insurance companies, and residents up in arms, the War Department reacted by promising to send Rosecrans $10,000 from the secret-service fund as soon as possible.[53] However, two months passed and the money failed to arrive. The general reminded the War Department that he had paid out money to help treasury detectives arrest counterfeiters but had not been repaid, and "although you advised me some time since that funds had been sent me none has yet been received."[54] Washington explained that heavy demands on the treasury had compelled them to withdraw the request for funds for him.[55] It took prompting from Rosecrans that he had information giving him an important opportunity to catch the leaders of the boatburner operation after an "infernal machine" hidden in a valise and operated by a timer planted in the army's main quartermaster storage warehouse exploded, endangering $1.5 million worth of supplies. Watchmen on the scene put out the fire, but he needed money to catch the perpetrators.[56] Finally, Washington loosened their grip on secret-service funds.[57]

Another significant event in Missouri was the so-called Paw Paw rising. In July, around the same time as the spectacular attack on the steamboats packed with army supplies, Rosecrans reported to Washington the occurrence of a "very serious rising" in northwestern Missouri among the "Paw Paw" militia units. These units consisted largely of former Confederate soldiers recruited into the militia; Missouri Unionists and military commanders deemed them to be highly unreliable. Over a thousand militia soldiers changed their allegiance, went back to the Confederate side, and rallied under the standard of a rebel colonel operating in the region. Rosecrans's depleted forces scrambled to put down the rising, which the general considered a premature attempt by the conspirators. Rosecrans used the uprising to put off Governor Yates's request for troops for Illinois by replying that he was in pursuit of an armed foe and could not help him.[58]

More Reports from Stidger

Meanwhile, in the Northwest, military commanders continued to investigate the secret organization and gather mounting evidence of conspiracy. Among the scores of detectives and spies employed by the U.S. Army in this effort, perhaps the most effective spy was Felix Stidger. The Kentuckian continued his insider efforts in his capacity as the secretary of the commonwealth's branch. He participated in leadership meetings during which plans were made for concerted action with Confederate guerrilla forces. He served also as a courier between Kentucky and Indiana conspirators.

In the aftermath of the Morgan raid into Kentucky in June of 1864, Stidger filed reports on the secret organization's plans with both Captain Jones, the provost marshal general of Kentucky, and General Carrington, military commander at Indianapolis. Some members suspected him, he reported, but Bullitt, the grand commander of Kentucky, defended him. Stidger managed to deflect blame for recent exposures of the organization in the Indiana press onto detective S. P. Coffin, who had been recognized as a Union man and fingered as a spy. He also employed an article deliberately planted in the *Indianapolis Daily Journal* on June 20 by Carrington and Morton that put the spotlight on Bowles. The article featured the 1861 letters, noted that Bowles was frequently in Indianapolis in conference with leading Democrats, and suggested that he had indiscreetly exposed the organization through loose talk.[59] By this piece of deception, Carrington and Morton succeeded in taking suspicion off their valuable spy. Still, wary of exposure, Stidger asked that the *Journal* be given no more information that he had supplied on the organization or Vallandigham, "but let it go ahead with what it has and comment all it can."[60] He suggested to Carrington that military authorities delay any plan to raid headquarters and seize records of the organization until the quarterly reports from the local and county lodges were collected and filed. Authorities would then have a fuller grasp of the scope of the order. He would try to attend the upcoming national meeting, to be held in Chicago at the time of the (now delayed) Democratic national convention in August, but he did not believe he would be allowed to attend. He provided additional information that the conspirators were in regular communication with rebel commanders.[61] Stidger added that Captain R. C. Bocking, the commander of an Indiana artillery battery and inventor, was in Louisville working with Kentucky conspirators to use his Greek Fire formula in arson attacks. He later witnessed a demonstration of the chemical, a hand grenade containing the chemical, as well as a timing device by which a fire could be started and which could be hidden in a box or trunk. Stidger suggested to Captain Jones that Bocking and other Kentucky leaders be arrested. He reported that large quantities of arms and ammunition were being purchased, hidden, and distributed to members.[62] Days after Stidger wrote about Bocking's Greek Fire chemical, a major Louisville warehouse full of army hospital stores caught fire at three o'clock in the morning and burned down. Arson was the cause.[63]

Stidger informed commanders that conspiracy leaders in Kentucky feared the recruiting and arming of African American men; armed blacks would subjugate the state's white people. Leaders in the grand council in Louisville advanced plans to sabotage and attack a troop train traveling south on the

Louisville and Nashville Railroad carrying U.S. Colored Troops. "There will be an effort made to get up a force, and throw the train from the track and murder as many of the negroes as possible," he reported. In Indiana, Bowles and others wished to attack Camp Morton, at Indianapolis, and other prisoner-of-war camps to release Confederate soldiers. "I think a general arrest of the leaders will put down the whole thing at once. They are very apprehensive of arrest," he opined.[64] In his report of July 1 written to Carrington, he disclosed that B. B. Piper, who acted as Vallandigham's courier to leaders in the different states, told Bullitt that "action" was to occur on either August 3 or August 15; the "Supreme Commander" (Vallandigham) was to decide the date, pending developments. Their plan was to release prisoners from camps in the Northwestern states and tear up railroad tracks in Kentucky. Captain Thomas Henry Hines, one of John Hunt Morgan's officers, was to lead an attack on Johnson's Island, in Lake Erie. To prevent it, the army should make a sweep of the leadership after the next state council meeting, on the fifteenth. "The leaders are so anxious that I would not be surprised at hostilities commencing in this state even before 3rd August," Stidger wrote.[65]

General Burbridge's Plan

While military and political leaders in the Northwestern states, Missouri, and Kentucky had developed intelligence networks that supplied them with vital information, they lacked direction and support from national leadership in Washington. Commanders and politicians were left to their own devices to counteract the threat from the conspirators. Each leader developed his own plan for dealing with the problem. In some cases, leaders cooperated among themselves to strike at the organization.

General Burbridge, encouraged by his recent victory over John Hunt Morgan, concluded that a hardhanded military policy would crush the guerrilla insurgency in Kentucky. Likewise, he consumed the reports he received from Stidger and other sources that apprised him of the secret organization's activities and decided to strike at and destroy the subversive movement before it could act. He was strongly influenced by orders received from General Sherman, then campaigning in Georgia, who continued to be concerned about the threat to tenuous supply and communications lines. Sherman told Burbridge that the recent Morgan raid and guerrilla activities in Kentucky "call for determined action" by the army to suppress "anarchy."[66] In response, Burbridge's plan, influenced by Stidger's reports, proposed a coordinated effort by Union leaders in the Northwest to arrest the leaders of the secret organization in those states. He appointed Lieutenant Colonel Thomas B. Fairleigh, 26th Kentucky Volunteer Infantry Regiment and commandant of the post of Louisville, to take direction of detective Stidger's investigations and ordered him to convince the governors and generals north of the Ohio River to act in concert. Fairleigh traveled to Indianapolis, Springfield, and Columbus "to make personal visits and have a personal consultation, in order that some plan in common may be adopted by all concerned and particularly *the time* agreed on" to arrest both the "large as well as the small fry."[67]

In the coming days, Fairleigh communicated with commanders north of the Ohio River to coordinate action. Though he wished to avoid using the mail, thankfully for historians he did commit some words to paper. He asked Carrington to press Indiana authorities to act. Echoing Stidger's report that the leaders of the conspiracy planned an uprising in early August, he insisted that "indications are sure that a much longer delay on our part will be exceedingly hazardous. I think I am certain in saying that a delay beyond the 1st proximo [August 1] will be disastrous. . . . Please write me at once on the subject."[68]

In the meantime, Burbridge received information of an impending rebel raid into Kentucky and scrambled to gather reinforcements to combat it.[69] He alerted Major General John M. Schofield, commanding the Army of the Ohio, then outside Atlanta, Georgia, that he had "positive information" of a new rebel invasion of Kentucky, which he believed was to be "more formidable" than the last. Worse, the day was fixed for a "general insurrection" among the rebel sympathizers to assist the raiders. He requested troops to combat it.[70] Rather disappointingly, Schofield replied that he could not spare any troops at that time but could possibly send dismounted cavalry back north after Atlanta was taken, which, he thought, would not be later than August 1. He supposed that an insurrection could not be planned quickly and asked when it was set to occur. In the end, he advised Burbridge to call on the Northern states for reinforcements.[71] Burbridge replied that he had already contacted Morton and Heintzelman who had responded promptly, but he noted that the "conspiracy referred to is much more formidable" north of the Ohio River than in Kentucky.[72]

At this time, affairs in Ohio were surprisingly quiet, given Vallandigham's return to the state. This may have been due to the stunted development of the secret organization in Ohio. The wave of excitement of Vallandigham's return subsided as the former exile returned to his Dayton home and led a seemingly quiet life. Nonetheless, Governor Brough received word from one of his spies on the inside of the conspiracy regarding preparations for armed insurrection in Ohio. The governor's adjutant general, B. R. Cowen, reported that their spy, "Newcomer," had visited while the governor was away and had provided "detailed statements of his operations for some time past." Newcomer's report about the "organization and purposes of the K.G.C. is merely corroborative of former statements and have resulted in confirmation of his former views." The spy advised that "nothing should be done now to stop their operations in the way of arrests or exposures, as any arrest will be almost sure to hasten the uprising while if let alone nothing will be done until after the Chicago convension [sic], at which time a general up rising is intended." Conspirators aimed "merely to draw off troops from the front . . . , thus weakening the force in front of Lee." Newcomer advised a "close watch" on their movements, "that we may be fully apprised of any change of their plans and time of development." He also said that the conspirators "acquiesce quietly in the posponment [sic] of the convention." Newcomer, the adjutant general continued,

> has ascertained to a certainty that shipments of arms are made from Cincinnati to the western counties of the State in nail kegs and marked as nails. He names the party making the shipment and also parties in Logan, Allen, Auglaize and Ashland [Counties] who have received them. He leaves tonight for Cincinnati to further investigate this buisness [sic] and also if possible to get upon some traces of the class of incendiarys who are infesting western boats and seeking every opportunity to fire depots of government supplies and provisions. He says these men are most dispatched from Canada under the directions of leading rebels there. . . . His idea is they should be spotted in Canada by sharp detectives and followed down to their points of opperations [sic] this is becoming a serious evil and merits the immediate attention of the war Department.

Cowen reported that he had ordered Newcomer to communicate to Brough as soon as the governor returned or if the spy obtained any important information at Cincinnati.[73] Unfortunately, we hear no more of the governor's spy. Military dispositions in Ohio were reassuring. The return of the USS *Michigan* to Sandusky Bay to guard Johnson's Island after a cruise around the lakes brought relief to officials, as did an adequate supply of arms and ammunition for the Ohio National Guard troops (state militia) stationed there to guard rebel prisoners.[74] In the following month, Brough reported to Stanton that he had "no present fears of outbreak," but that he would "try & be prepared for it if it comes."[75] At the same time, the deputy to the acting assistant provost marshal general for Ohio supervising the draft conveyed advice to one of the state's district provost marshals. Yes, he replied, his office knew of the existence of a secret organization in the state and had solicited legal advice from the U.S. attorney on how to deal with it. Flamen Ball, the attorney for the southern district of Ohio, advised:

> until some overt act is committed, so long as they confine themselves to secret, *or open* meetings, and simply '*Resolve*,' without doing anything, they are not amenable. There must be an overt act to constitute treason. They must do something to oppose the draft, or counsel some other person to do something, to make [them] amenable to section 25 of the Enrollment Act. . . . All we can do, then, is to watch them, and get hold of something tangible, something overt.

The attorney advised the district officer, "If you can manage to get a shrewd, observing man into the association, it would be well."[76]

At Detroit, in late spring and early summer, military authorities continued to watch affairs in Windsor and send their detectives across the Detroit River to shadow rebel officers, escaped prisoners, refugees, and the masses of deserters. Since the arrest of Phineas C. Wright, keeping an eye on Vallandigham's movements and visitors remained an important task. In late May, Lieutenant Colonel Bennett H. Hill replaced Lieutenant Colonel Smith as the military commander at Detroit, retaining his position as acting assistant provost marshal general. Hill took over Smith's detective operations and worked to intercept couriers to the Ohioan sent through federal lines from the South.[77] After Vallandigham's stealthy move to his home state, detectives working out of Detroit focused their attention on watching rebel movements in Canada. In July, Hill reported to Columbus headquarters that he had recently been approached by persons from Canada who said that they had information to sell. "They promised to put me in possession of papers, etc" for the price of $5,000. Hill replied to them that the government might already have the information being offered for sale, "but if they were really in possession of information valuable they could communicate it and rely upon the Gov't to pay what it was worth. This was declined in both cases." The last person to make the proposition, with whom Hill continued contact, was an Englishman employed in a Windsor bank who had "joined the scheme or plot and can give me full information" but only if paid for it.[78] The next day Hill reported that he had received information from other sources that rebel refugees in Canada planned to destroy cities on the U.S. side of the Great Lakes. "This coincides more with the suspicion I formed in the interviews referred to with the persons who were desirous of selling information. There is more frequent communication between the refugees in Windsor and Messers Saunders

[Sanders] & Co. at Niagara Falls, and a telegraphic dispatch was yesterday received at Windsor from Saunders, summoning three of the most prominent of the refugees to Niagara." He also reported that there were "floating rumors" that the rebels had "some machines to be mounted on vessels etc."[79]

In Illinois, Governor Yates was almost frantic with worry about both internal threats and guerrilla raids from Missouri and Kentucky. For nearly a year he and Stanton had angrily sparred about supplying arms to loyalists and providing a state force for home defense. But by mid-June, Yates's tone changed from truculence to abject servility. "I am in trouble—the State is in trouble, and the country will be in trouble resulting there from." Enlistments of the hundred-days troops would soon be up, while "we have a bold and defiant enemy in our midst—ready at the first pretext to rise in arms and put down the Government. . . . Will you not send me arms, as have been sent to other States?" He also asked that an officer be appointed to command in the state in case of emergency.[80] He implored Lincoln to send arms to his home state to arm loyal men against invasion and "political troubles" fomented by disloyal persons. Disaffection was more widespread than ever before, and the secret organization was better organized and armed, and more determined, than ever. He asked that three or four regiments be raised solely for state service, to be under Heintzelman's command. "You have sent arms to other States, given other States Dist. Commanders & the result is a strong positive force constantly at hand to meet emergencies," he observed. "I cannot possibly imagine why you should not do the same for Illinois."[81] Stanton at last relented and issued orders to the ordnance department to supply fifteen thousand stands of arms for Yates to use.[82] Relieved, Yates made provision with Colonel Oakes to beef up protection for the state arsenal.[83] He also requested Oakes and Heintzelman to keep the company of VRC invalids stationed at Paris as peacekeepers. He would not be surprised if there was an outbreak in Edgar County or nearby, he wrote.[84] The knowledge of Confederate soldiers in the state training and guiding the armed groups was disquieting. Yates asked Heintzelman to do something about tracking those "rebel emissaries."[85]

In late June in Indiana, Carrington continued to try to use William A. Bowles as a way to divert suspicion from his spy Felix Stidger. At a public reception for troops mustering out, he branded Bowles a "traitor colonel" and declared that he had proof that Bowles had recruited for the rebels.[86] Other exposures planted in the Republican newspapers continued the pressure on the conspirators.[87] At the end of June, Governor Morton left for the East on state business in New York City and Washington and was gone for three weeks. He lobbied federal leaders for his plan to publicize the records

Stidger had obtained from Dodd, Harrison, and other leaders of the secret organization.[88] Carrington awaited Washington's decision. No word came. In the meantime, Carrington employed his spies to keep abreast of the conspirator's plans and activities. Lacking troops, he resorted to temporary security makeshifts. He asked for permission to detain a veteran Ohio regiment then passing through the state after escorting nine hundred Confederate prisoners of war to Camp Morton. He obtained an agreement from Colonel Baker for an Indiana veteran regiment due to return to the front to be allowed to stay for a couple more weeks. His immediate concern was the state Democratic convention set to meet at Indianapolis on July 12. A petition was circulating around the state to invite Vallandigham to address the meeting, "which will beget much excitement." He assured headquarters that he was taking quiet steps to preserve order, "but the disloyal element is very bold."[89] Carrington's detectives alerted him to secret activities in the city. One detective, Frank C. Overturf, warned that "from what I can learn there will be an attempt made to release the prisoners at Camp Morton" during the week of the convention. Armed men would "make a dash on the camp," release the prisoners, arm and mount them as best as possible, and march to the Ohio River.[90] Stidger, then on a tour through Kentucky in his capacity as state secretary of the organization, was not available to provide inside information about Indiana activities.[91] Tensions rose in the days leading up to the convention. "Prominent Democrats" in the city "formally advised" Carrington that if the military interfered with the meeting in any way, or a soldier injured a Democrat, "they will kill Gov. Morton, or in his absence the highest government officials." Party leaders and the *Indianapolis Daily State Sentinel* called on Democratic faithful to attend the convention armed. Carrington planned to keep troops in their camps far away from the meeting but wanted as many on hand as possible to be called out if needed. He also made special arrangements to guard government arms in the city.[92]

The state convention passed off without violence, thanks in part to careful efforts to keep soldiers out of the way and avoid conflicts with Democrats. Leaders in the party establishment frustrated the radical faction and took control of the meeting to steer its course.[93] Carrington, who was present, observed that the gathering was sparsely attended and held in a hall with guards at the door to admit only those who had obtained tickets at the *Sentinel* office. This was unlike previous party conventions, which were well attended and open to all. "By a shrewd policy," Carrington noted, "the Bowles faction kept quiet when they found that [Joseph] McDonald would be selected for Governor" over their own candidate, northern Indiana attorney and conspirator Lambdin P. Milligan. The majority of the Democrats desired to await the Chicago national convention, which had been postponed to the end of August, where there would be a "*mass popular* convention for the north." Carrington also reported that Fairleigh had visited "to agree upon concert of action in the border states. He is waiting for Gov Mortons return from the east." Fairleigh expected an "open outbreak" in the first week of August. Indiana Legion commanders on the river border reported that over two thousand rebel guerrillas, led by cadres of the rebel Kentucky regiments disbanded by Forrest, were recruiting in Kentucky near the Ohio River and raiding and looting. Carrington also noted that Confederate agent Captain Hines had again visited Harrison County, where there was "nearly a regiment of disloyal men prepared to cooperate with Kentucky." Unfortunately, he wrote, Hines had eluded arrest. Informers "authenticated" that Bocking's Greek Fire formula had started the Louisville warehouse fire, which arsonists had started by dropping the chemical through a skylight.[94]

Stidger returned to Louisville from his trip around Kentucky to report that mutual distrust had arisen in the organization's leadership. At the Kentucky grand council meeting, Bullitt had reported on his recent visit to Indianapolis to confer with Indiana leaders Dodd, Indiana Secretary of State Dr. James Athon, State Auditor of Indiana Joseph Ristine, and Michael Bright, brother of the expelled U.S. Senator Jesse D. Bright, all members of the conspiracy. The Indiana men disappointed Bullitt by telling him that Indiana would not rise to rescue the Kentucky leaders should they be arrested and taken north in custody through Indiana, though they assured him that twenty thousand men would come to Kentucky's assistance in a general rising. Dodd was willing to attempt to free the prisoners at Camp Morton, but if he failed he would escape as best he could. Given this lukewarm support, Bullitt stated that he had no faith in any assistance for Kentucky except from Confederate leader Jefferson Davis. Illinois might help Missouri if the latter state rose, he said. He was going to Chicago for a secret conference on July 20 and proposed meeting with the rebel guerrilla commander George M. Jessee on his return to set a day for Kentucky to act alone. He had had a long meeting with Kentucky lieutenant governor Richard T. Jacob but did not secure his full support. Bullitt reported that Vallandigham was showing signs of fear and would not attend the Chicago meeting on the twentieth.[95]

Carrington apprised Heintzelman of the latest reports. He awaited Morton's return from Washington. On July 20 he sent word that Judge Bullitt of Kentucky had been in Indianapolis the previous day to confer with Indiana counterparts for aid for Kentucky and had departed for the meeting in

Chicago. The Illinois organization was to have its state council at Springfield on August 3. The leading conspirators were desperate men who would not be stopped even if federal forces were successful in the field, he warned. He also forwarded information from William Phelps, a detective working for Governor Yates, who reported on plots to free rebel prisoners. Disclosure of intelligence his detectives collected in carefully crafted articles in the newspapers had already had a significant impact on the political landscape in Indiana, he wrote, and it had "nearly broken in two the Peace party in this State." He reminded headquarters that he still had no secret-service funds. If he had funds, "the whole [conspiracy] can be broken up and not only demoralized, but made to work to the benefit of the National cause."[96]

Throughout the region, edgy commanders and political leaders received reports of preparations by the conspirators to rise en masse. They felt vulnerable to attack and craved help from national leaders, who appeared uninterested in their plight. Soon, however, Washington's indifference would change.

Exposés and Holt's Mission to the West

On July 23, Morton finally returned to Indianapolis armed with Secretary Stanton's permission to publish Carrington's report based on the documents obtained by Stidger in early June. He also made arrangements to meet with General Burbridge in the Indiana capital.[97] Heintzelman, also invited, turned down the request but told Carrington, "You will know what to do."[98] Burbridge and Fairleigh arrived in Indianapolis on July 29 and conferred with Morton and Carrington. The next day Carrington apprised Heintzelman of the meeting's outcome. Burbridge, he wrote, believed the crisis was at hand, and action could no longer be put off. His information confirmed what Carrington and Morton knew about affairs along the Ohio River in both states. Burbridge "has ordered the arrest of all the leaders, at Louisville and will send them through to Genl Sherman. He has made requisition for the arrest of Judge Bullit now in this city as supposed in conference with other leaders." Many of the conspirators would be in Indianapolis the following week "to decide whether to make an outbreak." Carrington believed that "the thorough work to be made in Kentucky will smother the fire in Indiana. Otherwise some decided action will be required." Governor Yates had written Burbridge to say that "no arrests of any kind" could be made in Illinois owing to the lack of both troops and a military commander in the state to coordinate action. Most of Illinois was beyond Carrington's effective reach to undertake the arrests himself; besides, "I have not three hundred troops to send anywhere."

Moreover, the hundred-days troops sent south would not be back in Indiana for three more weeks. "If any movement is made" by the conspirators, "it will be as Genl Burbridge says *early,* or not until the issues of the election are known." Carrington voiced misgivings about "premature action" by Burbridge and others, but assured headquarters that he would act promptly in case of trouble.[99] That day Burbridge telegraphed Heintzelman for authority to arrest Judge Bullitt at Indianapolis. "[I] Agreed to it, and to another arrest, if Gen. Rosecrantz desires it, but no others," Heintzelman wrote in his journal.[100] The other provisional arrest order, if Rosecrans desired it, was for John Richard "Dick" Barret, a former Democratic congressman and prominent pro-rebel leader from Saint Louis. Heintzelman ordered Carrington to arrest Bullitt and Barret but not to arrest any others "as their cases are in the hands of the Gov't."[101] Accordingly, military authorities arrested Bullitt en route to Louisville and held him under close confinement at Louisville headquarters.[102] Using Stidger's information, Burbridge rounded up other members of the secret organization in Kentucky.

Heintzelman's message that "cases are in the hands of the Gov't" indicates that the War Department had been contacted about Burbridge's plan for coordinated arrests of leading conspirators. In response, on August 1 and August 5, Assistant Secretary of War Charles A. Dana sent Burbridge, Heintzelman, and other commanders lists of "disloyal persons" with orders to "cause them to be kept under surveillance" and to arrest them "upon their detection in any act of hostility to the United States." The names of the persons on the watch lists are not known.[103] Significantly, the War Department had issued orders to watch and arrest suspected persons. This may be the first instance in U.S. history of a comprehensive, centralized internal-security watch list of persons deemed to be threats to the state. Prompted by appeals from commanders like Heintzelman and Burbridge and issued at a time when Lincoln feared that he would lose the election, the evidence shows that Washington officials had decided on desperate measures.

Morton's return from Washington set in motion another significant action. With Stanton's approval, on July 30 Morton splashed Carrington's report based on records obtained by Stidger across the pages of the *Indianapolis Daily Journal.*[104] The report filled column after column in small type. The full text of the various oaths and rituals appeared, along with other heretofore secret records of the order. The exposé electrified Indiana and was soon reprinted in newspapers around the state and region. Its publication did not please Carrington, who preferred to pursue his investigations in secrecy. Writing to departmental headquarters on the day of its appearance, he noted that "Gov.

Morton, as you see, has published my report made to him. He says that Mr. Stanton has no objection to its publication. I have felt that the time was not ripe for it: but the Governor thought otherwise."[105] It had required weeks of lobbying by Morton to obtain Washington's approval to publish it, but he had finally succeeded.

Two days before the publication of Carrington's report, Sanderson's report to Rosecrans appeared in the *Saint Louis Daily Missouri Democrat,* which, despite its name, was the leading Republican newspaper in the state. The report exposed in detail the rituals and oaths of the organization, laid out its intentions to overthrow the Lincoln administration and named the leaders in the various Northern states, with Vallandigham its leader in the North, and rebel General Sterling Price its leader in the South. It divulged much of the evidence gathered by Sanderson's corps of detectives and spies.[106]

Thus, in short order, three important developments occurred at the end of July 1864: Morton obtained permission from Stanton to publish Carrington's report; the War Department issued a watch list and ordered arrests of suspected person, also giving Heintzelman and Burbridge permission to make arrests of leading conspirators in Kentucky, and Rosecrans published Sanderson's report. Evidence shows that Morton went to Washington expressly to obtain approval from federal leaders to publish Carrington's report, and that Heintzelman had laid the matter of arrests of the conspiracy's leadership in the hands of the War Department. On the other hand, no documentation shows that Rosecrans obtained prior approval from Washington officials to publish Sanderson's exposé.

What had happened in Washington to change the minds of the Lincoln administration in approving the exposés and ordering surveillance of leading conspirators? Evidence shows that during July federal officials opened their minds to the possibility of insurrection in the Northwest. In mid-July, Stanton dispatched trusted hand Joseph Holt, judge advocate general in the War Department, to Louisville and Saint Louis on a fact-finding mission. His orders were to confer with the governors and generals regarding "secret and open organizations against the Government" that "intended to afford aid and comfort to the enemy."[107] He arrived in Louisville during Burbridge's efforts to convince the generals and governors to make sweeping arrests. Three written reports of Holt's mission survive showing that he fully grasped the reality of the threat, its imminence, and wide scope. The evidence, he wrote on July 29 from Louisville, "indicates clearly the existence of a conspiracy" in Kentucky and the states to the north "looking to an armed rising against the government."[108] Two days later, he wrote from Saint Louis that "careful investigation" showed that the threat encompassed Missouri as well. The organization was most "numerous and formidable" in Illinois and Indiana. "It is not to be endured that these conspirators should be permitted" freedom to act. He endorsed Burbridge's get-tough plan of arrests in Kentucky. Unfortunately, he wrote, there were not enough troops in the states north of the river to safely arrest leading conspirators there.[109] Finally, having returned to Washington, on August 5, Holt summarized his findings. The investigations of Carrington ("this vigilant and faithful officer") "have laid bare in a manner too distinct for future question the intensely disloyal nature and revolutionary aims of this association," he wrote. The confessions of Hunt, Smith, and others arrested at Saint Louis, as well as the reports of Rosecrans's spies, were "entirely reliable" in showing its operations and intentions. "It is for the Government to determine," he concluded, "whether, consistently with its own safety or with its duty to the country, it can longer endure this knife of the domestic traitor at its throat."[110]

If Washington officials, including Lincoln, had questioned the cries of the governors and officers in the Northwest, Holt's conclusive pronouncement ended their doubts. Still, recognition of the problem and tangible assistance for Northwestern officials were different matters. The region had yet to endure anxiety and uncertainty as threats continued and disorder hung in the balance.

TEN

A "Narrow Escape from a Civil War"

The Triumph of Military Intelligence in August 1864

IN AUGUST 1864 commanders, acting with little assistance from Washington, made their own plans to meet the threat of insurrection in the Northwest. Coordination among generals and governors produced consensus that action had to be taken to head off feared uprisings known to be in the offing. However, commanders lacked troops with which to confront the large numbers of revolutionaries they faced. They deemed the few reinforcements sent by the War Department to be insufficient. Quite by chance, fragments of veteran regiments sent north from the front to muster out arrived in Indianapolis and helped reinforce the garrison precisely at the moment when conspirators planned their attack on Camp Morton. Similarly, two weeks later, false rumors that five thousand troops had arrived to reinforce the garrison guarding Camp Douglas, outside Chicago, helped intimidate plotters who planned a rising during the Democratic National Convention. As well, Governor Morton received notice from an anonymous source that large shipments of arms and ammunition for use by the conspirators were en route to Indianapolis. Troops seized the shipments in Indianapolis and New York City and also intercepted other arms shipments.

To date, military and political leaders had successfully employed detectives and spies to gather information on the intentions of the plotters. During

August, a series of lucky breaks allowed them to forestall two planned uprisings in Indiana and Illinois. Commanders seized the moment to contain and control the revolutionary movement in the Old Northwest.

Bracing for Revolution

General Burbridge of Kentucky, the initiator of the plan for leaders in the Northwestern states and Kentucky to act together to arrest prominent conspirators, wanted his plan carried out in full. He had arrested leaders of the Sons of Liberty secret organization throughout Kentucky and held them in military prisons.[1] Now he wanted to see similar action taken north of the Ohio River. Telegraphing Secretary Stanton, he suggested that General Heintzelman of the Northern Department "be ordered to arrest" conspirators in Illinois and Indiana. Otherwise, he added, "my action will be of little effect." He also advised that the Confederate prisoners held at Rock Island and Indianapolis should be moved farther north, as there was "great danger of their being released and armed by traitors at those points."[2] Stanton, convinced by Joseph Holt's reports of the imminent danger of insurrection in the Northwest, replied, "Your proceedings against disloyal persons in your command are approved" and that he was forwarding his message to Heintzelman at Columbus, Ohio.[3] Encouraged, Burbridge made preparations to meet with Heintzelman and press action. He ordered his spymaster at Louisville, Colonel Fairleigh, to gather records and travel with him to Cincinnati, where Heintzelman agreed to meet them.[4] They arrived in the river city on a blazing-hot summer afternoon and that evening proceeded to departmental judge advocate Major Henry L. Burnett's offices. Burbridge, Fairleigh, and two staff officers arrived in full uniform; Heintzelman and Burnett greeted them in shirtsleeves. After a moment of embarrassment resulting from the indecorous reception, the visitors removed their woolen coats and sat down to business. Heintzelman recorded, "We exchanged opinions and soon found that we agreed in our views of the situation and as to what should be done." Heintzelman fell in with Burbridge's plan to arrest the leaders of the conspiracy. After returning to Columbus, Heintzelman wrote to Governor Yates and asked General Carrington to consult with Governor Morton to "learn their opinions as to the propriety of arresting the leaders of this conspiracy." Days before, shortly before his journey to Cincinnati, he had met and spoken with Governor Brough of Ohio and sounded him out on the subject of arrests in Indiana. The governor "feels a delicacy in giving his opinion," he recorded, "but says if the state of affairs there was such as here, he would wish them arrested." Heintzelman knew that "Gov. Morton wishes it done and I am of the decided opinion that it should be; but not before a force is collected to prevent an outbreak."[5]

Heintzelman prudently believed he needed more troops before trying to arrest leading conspirators in the Northern Department. Aside from prison camp garrisons, he had only a few VRC companies of invalids acting as provost guards protecting district provost marshal offices and helping arrest deserters and draft dodgers, plus some hundred-days troops whose short enlistments were soon to expire. He wrote to the War Department that the recent publication in the newspapers of the exposés had "created considerable excitement" among the Democrats, who had organized mass meetings "without any previous public notice." He believed that these crowds could constitute enough force "to release prisoners and create revolution." The good news was that the revolutionary undercurrents in Democratic affairs had spooked many established members of party hierarchy, he wrote. Prominent Ohio Democrats had "come forward and repudiated any connection with such a treasonable association" and he thought that the leading conspirators would "scarcely dare make the attempt" at revolution. However, the danger was real and required more troops.[6]

The situation was similar in the Department of the Missouri in the aftermath of the publication of Sanderson's report. Intelligence gathered by Rosecrans's spies pointed to an invasion of Missouri by Sterling Price's rebel army sometime in the fall, simultaneous with a rising by the secret organization. Shortly before publication, military authorities rearrested a number of the leaders of the organization, including Charles L. Hunt. In late July and early August, these leaders, grand commander Hunt, deputy commander Charles E. Dunn, and secretary Green B. Smith, a Saint Louis gun dealer, recanted their previous denials of the existence of the organization and gave full confessions. They acknowledged that the organization was created by Phineas C. Wright, maintained communications with the Southern rebels through secret mails and couriers, and acted to aid them in various ways, including supplying arms to members in northern Missouri.[7] Authorities released Smith's long and detailed statement to the press and on August 5 the *Saint Louis Daily Missouri Democrat* published it verbatim, filling several columns.[8] Newspapers throughout the North reprinted Smith's confession, adding significantly to the exposure of the secret organization and its activities.

Sometime in August, Sanderson fell seriously ill, perhaps suffering a heart attack or stroke. The colonel lay prostrate on his bed, unable to do much business. His health deteriorated slowly and soon he could do no more work. A new assistant provost marshal general, Lieutenant Colonel Joseph Darr, Jr., experienced in intelligence work, arrived from West Virginia at Rosecrans's request to pick up the slack while Sanderson lay ill. Sanderson died in Saint Louis on October 14, the victim, as newspaperman-detective Edward Betty wrote, of the "constant strain of mind and body" that the work of the office wrought on a man of "unflinching devotion" to duty.[9]

In Ohio, apprehensive military and state authorities made preparations against both insurrection and invasion from Canada. The governor's staff had been alerted to domestic threats and the risk of invasion from Canada from both their own sources as well as from Heintzelman. In preparation, Adjutant General Cowen undertook a tour of Sandusky and Johnson's Island, inspecting the facilities of the garrison and the placement of the USS *Michigan* in the bay. He recommended an additional artillery battery be placed there to repel attack from the lake.[10] Governor Brough informed Heintzelman of a plot to attack the arsenals in Columbus and release the prisoners in Camp Chase. The general asked for specifics, but, according to Heintzelman's account, the governor

> would give me no definite information, but wished me to order
> the Light battery to Camp Chase from Sandusky. I would not do
> it, without further information and he took great offense. I went
> and saw him in his office and he found it advisable to give me full
> information. I did not ask him who gave him the information, only
> what it was. I ordered the Battery and also an extra guard of 25 men
> to the U.S. Arsenal.[11]

At this time, after Holt's return from his fact-finding mission in the West, Stanton became more helpful to the governors of the Northwestern states. He agreed to station two state militia batteries at Cleveland and Camp Chase and to supply them fully.[12] He promised to assume full costs for the state militia should Brough call on it to repel invasion or quell uprisings.[13] Responding to Yates's repeated pleas, he reauthorized the creation of a military district in Illinois. The secretary also requested a report on the advisability of the arrests of the leaders of the conspiracy in the Northwestern states. Wanting the information quickly, General Halleck ordered that Heintzelman telegraph his thoughts in cipher.[14] This irked Heintzelman, who, despite requests from himself and Rosecrans, had been denied the use of the army's secret codes by the officious and spiteful army general-in-chief. "I telegraphed to Gen. Halleck that I have no cipher and he replie[d] use the Telegraph operators," recorded Heintzelman in his journal. "He is determined not to let me have the Cipher, although I could not use it, for any purpose but to communicate with the Government."[15] While Stanton became more helpful, Halleck remained a stumbling block.

Heintzelman dutifully wrote *a letter* to Halleck explaining that he and Brough agreed that the conspirators should be arrested. Brough and others had given him "undoubted information" that resistance to the draft would occur in Ohio. He also knew of "combinations, the leaders of which are in this city," who plotted to seize the arsenals and release the prisoners in Camp Chase. To counteract the scheme, the commandant of the camp had been alerted, the prison guard had been quietly increased, and a light battery had been shifted from Sandusky to guard the Columbus prison. His opinion was that draft resistance would be "more extensive" in Indiana and Illinois and, indeed, he feared disturbances would occur in those states before the draft would occur. He reiterated that he had "no available force in either of those States in case of a disturbance." Moreover, his garrisons at the prison camps were insufficient to make an "effectual resistance, should the prisoners be aided, as is threatened, from the outside." The combination of the "large disloyal element" in Indiana and Illinois with released Confederate prisoners would be "truly formidable." He recommended that the prisoners held in camps in the two states be immediately shipped "to some loyal State in the East." He added that he believed Governor Morton shared his decided belief that the leaders of the conspiracy should be arrested, but he had not met with Governor Yates and did not yet know his views. He advised that before any action was taken he should confer with both governors to learn their views; the new military commander of Illinois should also be installed before action was taken. It would be "impolitic" to attempt the arrests without a sufficiently strong force in place with which to "overawe any attempt at resistance." He suggested that a minimum of five thousand troops would be required in Ohio, and ten thousand each in Indiana and Illinois! As an afterthought and reminder, he added in conclusion that he had no secret-service funds to employ detectives and asked for $5,000.[16]

Affairs on the northern frontier of Heintzelman's command continued to be lively. Lieutenant Colonel Hill, commander at Detroit, kept a watchful eye on rebel activities across the river in Windsor. In early August he reported that rebels continued to contact him seeking amnesty. One such rebel refugee, George W. Young, had first applied for amnesty in July and offered information on secret rebel activities as a proof of his renewed loyalty. Hill told him that the government would consider whatever information he offered as part of his amnesty appeal. Young recounted "that a plot is now matured for the release of the rebel prisoners at Camp Douglas" in Chicago and "that he (Young) had joined it with the intention of disclosing it." Two hundred men were involved whose headquarters were at Toronto, where they received money, arms, and orders. They were then to make their way "in small parties" to Chicago, where the rebel prisoners in the camp awaited them. Young added that the "release of these prisoners would be a signal for an outbreak in the States of Indiana and Illinois and that there was an armed organization in Chicago of 5000 men who are hostile to the Government." Young assured him that he would write from Toronto with any more information he could gather. He would also contact the commandant of Camp Douglas directly. Hill offered his opinion that he had no doubt "that there is something afoot among the rebel refugees" and that Young was forthright in his desire to gain amnesty through good works.[17] He shared the information with Colonel B. J. Sweet, commander at Chicago, adding that Young would try to contact him once he was in Chicago by calling at the Tremont House hotel under the alias George Wallace.[18] Hill also provided the same information to the commander at Johnson's Island prison camp, adding that "some of our detectives however in Windsor have observed a great interest expressed among the refugees there about Port Stanley and the 23rd Inst. was mentioned as when something will occur." Such movements, he believed, targeted Johnson's Island.[19]

Hill also reported to headquarters that there were signs of unrest in Michigan and expressed unease about the safety of the Dearborn Arsenal. He sent a small detachment—all that he had available—to augment the guard at Dearborn, but he knew that the soldiers were under orders to be sent away. He requested two companies of troops permanently to guard the arsenal and its large quantities of arms.[20] However, headquarters replied that there were no troops to be had in the department.[21] At this time, new reports of the existence of a secret organization in communities in Michigan reached commanders. Its members attempted to procure arms with the aim of resisting the draft; arms were on order and being shipped from Philadelphia. Commanders took steps to intercept the shipments and ordered the seizure at railroad depots of boxes that they believed contained arms.[22] One officer noted that the "copperheads are evidently cleaning up their arms and buying new ones."[23]

Army commanders in Detroit scored a minor coup when they learned of a collection of papers in the private safe of S. Dow Elwood, a Detroit bookseller, president of the city common council and former member of the state central committee of the Democratic Party. On August 27 the provost marshal seized the papers, which turned out to be records of the OAK placed in Elwood's safe by Phineas C. Wright, who had been arrested in Michigan in April. (Elwood, it will be recalled, was one of the secret conduits for mail sent to and from Clement Vallandigham while at Windsor; Rosecrans's detectives intercepted letters to and from Vallandigham addressed to Elwood as the secret intermediary.) Officers turned over the records to city Republicans who made certified transcriptions, which the Republican newspaper in Detroit published.[24] The records included an address and oaths for members of the supreme council of the organization to swear, and a resolution of thanks to Wright signed by state commanders of the organization: Charles L. Hunt of Missouri, Thomas E. Massey of Ohio, Robert Holloway and Amos Green of Illinois, James A. McMaster of New York, E. W. Goble of New Jersey, and H. H. Dodd of Indiana. The document was also signed by Emile Longuemare as clerk of the supreme council.[25] Also included in the papers were records pertaining to building the organization in Michigan, in which task Wright was engaged when he was arrested in late April.[26] Military investigations in Detroit had successfully uncovered the plans of conspirators but had not eliminated their dangers.

Illinois Developments

Nowhere was the situation worse than in Illinois. Governor Yates had repeatedly requested that his state again be a military district and a district commander be appointed. It was needed, he believed, as guerrillas operating in the state continually disturbed the peace and armed groups massed together to resist the arrest of draft dodgers and deserters.[27] At last, his repeated requests, hitherto rebuffed or ignored, received favorable responses. In early August, Stanton issued orders to appoint a state military commander. As well, he ordered the quartermaster at Springfield to allow the governor to distribute arms to loyal groups around the state. He also ordered that the guard at the arsenal be increased, as the governor requested.[28] Days later, the War Department authorized the raising of one regiment of infantry to serve solely in Illinois and to be under Heintzelman's orders.[29]

At this time, conditions in Illinois were precarious and reports arrived at Springfield from numerous sources that danger was imminent.[30] Brigadier General Eleazer A. Paine, an Illinoisan then in command of the District of Western Kentucky at Paducah, wrote to Yates that his detectives reported a "deep-laid scheme" in Illinois and adjoining states to resist the draft and carry the upcoming election by "foul means." Illinois people worked in concert with the Southern rebels, he added, and had supplied themselves well with arms and ammunition. Paine suggested that the state be placed under martial law to deal with the emergency and a "strict surveillance" be enacted throughout the state to root out the secret associations.[31] From Galena, in northwestern Illinois, authorities learned of an armed group that drilled regularly in secret.

The district provost marshal watched the group closely, assisted by local persons (probably members of the Union League secret society), and learned that it had recently received a shipment of arms and ammunition. Similar groups existed in neighboring communities in the district. "It is understood that the object of these organizations is, forcible resistance to the Draft," the officer reported.[32] Days later he reported the existence of another armed company in a nearby town where men known to be too poor to afford firearms now had guns provided. These armed groups "freely declared" their intention to resist the draft in the district. They also planned to attend the upcoming Democratic National Convention at Chicago, then just two weeks away.[33] Further information arrived that the armed group in Galena had sported their recently obtained arms in a public drill by which it was clear that they possessed "quite a number." But most of their drills occurred in their hall, away from prying eyes. A former sheriff of Jo Daviess County investigated and spoke to some of the men who were members of the armed group: "They say it is for the purpose of protection this fall Election, but when some one of them gets tight and that is often, they say it is to resist the draft. They are getting quite bold. A number of men in good standing tells me that they heard them cheering for Jeff. Davis last night."

The Galena group was drilled by a man who claimed to have been a captain in the Confederate army and was led by local Democratic Party leaders Madison Y. Johnson, Louis Shisler, and others.[34] Johnson had been arrested in August 1862 by Stanton's order for seditious speech and suspicion that he was a member of the KGC. He spent a long spell in Fort Lafayette and Fort Delaware military prisons.[35] Yates alerted Heintzelman to the Galena group and suggested the importance of watching Johnson, an especially dangerous person.[36] In reply, Heintzelman asked the governor what his views were on the propriety of arresting the "leaders of the secret organization and the leader M. Y. Johnson at Galena. Should you deem it advisable I will be glad if you will furnish me a list of names with any suggestions as to the best mode of proceeding against them."[37]

Having revived the military District of Illinois, the War Department chose Brigadier General Halbert E. Paine, then in Washington, to assume command and repair to Springfield. Paine, a Milwaukee attorney born and educated in Ohio and formerly commander of the 4th Wisconsin Volunteer Infantry Regiment, had lost a leg in battle at Port Hudson, Louisiana, in June 1863.[38] En route west he stopped at Columbus, Ohio, to confer with Heintzelman. The departmental commander recorded in his journal that he had a "long talk" with Paine "about the situation of affairs. A gentleman from Quincy Ill.

was here and gave him and me a great deal of information about the situation."[39] Heintzelman gave Paine written instructions in which he stressed the dangers of internal unrest: "Recent disclosures have shown a secret organization whose object is no less than the overthrow of the Government. You will keep yourself advised of their movements and take such measures as you may deem necessary and proper to thwart their intentions. The District is not however under martial law."[40]

Traveling westward, Paine followed orders and stopped in Indianapolis to consult with Carrington and be briefed by the de facto chief of intelligence for the department.[41] He arrived at Springfield on August 18 and promptly wrote Rosecrans for information on the danger of insurrection in the state. Rosecrans loaned a copy of Sanderson's voluminous report with the proviso that it be returned.[42] Paine conferred with Yates and reported to Heintzelman that the governor vetoed the idea of arresting leading Illinois conspirators:

> It is the opinion of Gov. Yates that the arrests to which the Major-
> General Commanding called my attention should not be made
> until the military force within the State is increased. Gen. Carrington
> entertained a similar view but was less decided in his expression of
> it. I am not now prepared to express a different opinion. As soon as
> the investigations which I am making into the condition of affairs
> in the district will enable me to do so I will forward to the Major-
> General Commanding my own recommendation on the subject.
> They were both convinced that in the first clear case requiring the
> use of military force very severe measures will be politic as likely to
> prevent subsequent disorder or bloodshed.

Paine added that he asked Colonel Oakes to obtain information from his district provost marshals about "projects and movements of the disloyal." He characterized the Union League in Illinois as "well organized loyal citizens" and noted that the governor had shared his files on disloyal activities. He hoped to soon have a definite understanding of affairs in the state and a clear plan for addressing its "domestic enemies." He asked authority to hire "two excellent detectives" to assist him.[43]

Oakes's subordinates produced several reports responding to Paine's request, most pointing to serious dangers ahead.[44] The district provost marshal for the 7th District, in eastern Illinois, reported "emphatic indications" that violence was planned by armed oath-bound groups in military or semi-military organizations. He did not know when the revolutionary movement would happen but believed it would be no earlier than August 29 (the start of the Democratic convention at Chicago) and no later than the upcoming draft.[45] From the 9th District, in western Illinois, came the report that organized bands existed in all counties to resist the draft and the arrest of deserters. The "organization is uniform, widespread throughout the District," and had as a "common object" a "symultanious [sic] resistance." The district officer furnished the names of the county leaders and the strengths of their organizations and asked for authority to hire spies to watch them.[46] The officer in the 12th District, in southwestern Illinois, reported, "There are certainly secret organizations throughout the District & I should say all over the State" who threaten to resist the draft. Many bushwhacker bands from Missouri roamed the district as well.[47] The 5th District man, in west-central Illinois, replied that he knew of no plans for violence and did not rate the current threat as great as that of the summer of 1863. He supposed that "disloyal men" were arming for self-defense but thought that much depended on the action of the Chicago convention. If the convention nominated a peace candidate, he concluded, "it will take several regiments of good soldiers to keep the peace in this State."[48]

The commandant of Camp Douglas, outside Chicago, also shared his thoughts concerning secret movements. Colonel Benjamin J. Sweet had formerly commanded the 21st Wisconsin Volunteer Infantry Regiment until badly wounded in battle at Perryville. He joined the VRC and assumed command of the 8th VRC Regiment at Camp Douglas in early 1864; he assumed command of the post of Chicago in early May.[49] The security of Camp Douglas had been a significant concern since the summer of 1863, when the influx of John Hunt Morgan's raiders increased the number of successful escapes. Evidence materialized that rebel prisoners communicated with and received assistance from persons outside the camp. In early May 1864, Captain Stephen E. Jones, at Louisville, warned Sweet that Chicago citizens aided prisoners to escape. Jones's information came from a rebel prisoner who had escaped from the camp that spring but had been recently recaptured in Kentucky. During interrogation, the prisoner revealed that a man living near the camp thought to be named Walsh or Welch "was the principal instrument in assisting prisoners to escape. This he manages through his little daughter who plays around in the vicinity unsuspected & manages to slip in to the prisoners letters containing money & other articles." The recaptured prisoner also provided information that the "copperheads of northern Ill. lend active aid to [the prisoners] and have a large fund subscribed to assist them with this[,] Walsh being the party entrusted with the distribution of the money." The prisoner said citizens furnished him a horse kept near the camp on which to escape.[50] Accordingly, Sweet informed Paine that Colonel Hill, at Detroit, had informed him that rebels in Canada were planning an attack on Camp Douglas; he had hired "competent detectives" to find the rebels from Canada supposed to be in the city. But the detectives failed to find them, and "if there is an organization in this city meaning mischief, I have not yet been able to detect it."[51]

Indeed, Sweet had acted promptly on Hill's information about the rebel plan to attack Camp Douglas and hired two detectives to watch all trains coming from the east. He had also investigated whether an armed organization existed in Chicago. In his reports he downplayed the threat of uprising and attack on the camp. While he had "little, if any, doubt" that a numerous secret organization existed in the city that was hostile to the government, "I do not believe it to be armed" and its leaders did not intend to initiate "open armed hostility" to the government. Unless some public crisis should push both the leadership and membership into open disloyalty, "I do not apprehend danger, here, as the result of my investigations."[52] On August 16, Hill sent Sweet additional information on Young, confirming his belief that the rebel's "statements are entitled to respect." One hundred and fifty men had already left for Chicago, Young had reported, and Young and his fifty men awaited orders from Captain Thomas Henry Hines, the commander of the "expedition." Hines had left Toronto for Chicago last Thursday, August 11, Young said, "and at this time is doubtless at Niagara Falls, making the final arrangements with the chief rebel agents." The plan was to release Camp Douglas prisoners with the aid of armed citizens. Young told Hill that once released, the prisoners would be armed and mounted and would march to Camp Morton in Indianapolis to release the prisoners held there, and that "for months, rebel emissaries have been traveling through the North-west, and that all their arrangements are fully matured, that they expect to receive large accessions of force from Ohio, Indiana, and Illinois, and will cross into Kentucky, which state they expect to be in sufficient strong force to be able to hold for the rebel government." Young was to stay at the City Hotel, at the corner of Lake and State Streets in Chicago, under the name George Wallace and would contact Sweet.[53]

Indiana Developments

Meanwhile, Felix G. Stidger, the spy working for military commanders in both Kentucky and Indiana, remained at work on the inside of the conspiracy. But his personal plans butted up against his work. He planned to marry in September and his fiancée, who knew of his secret labors, suffered from anxiety. At the end of July, to aid in maintaining his secret identity, he suggested to Burbridge that if the general was to make his planned sweep of the leadership of the organization in Kentucky, he should be among those arrested. But because of his wedding plans, he wrote, "I cannot be arrested and remain in prison any length of time." He added that should Indiana's organizational headquarters be raided to seize its records and other papers, the records would mostly be found in rooms on the fourth floor of H. H. Dodd's building in Indianapolis.[54] Later, after Bullitt's arrest, Stidger reported to Fairleigh that Dodd thought it was "unfortunate for the operations of the order." Stidger would have to take Bullitt's place as courier to communicate plans to the Kentuckians. Any forcible attempt to release the Kentucky conspirators should be coordinated with Bowles, Dodd told him. He also informed him that the organization's leadership had discarded secret meetings in favor of conferring during mass Democratic Party gatherings, a series of which was to commence at Peoria, Illinois. The rank-and-file members were also to rise simultaneously and attack Chicago, Springfield, Indianapolis, Camp Douglas, Camp Chase, and Rock Island, release prisoners, seize arms, and concentrate at Louisville, which would be captured by Bowles's command. "They hope for five States to act simultaneously," reported Stidger. "The one preliminary that was to have been settled yesterday was whether they should await for a rebel force to be shown into Kentucky and Missouri, or whether they should act on the 15th or 16th of this month (August) anyway. They have unanimously decided to act on one of those days." The plan for Indianapolis was to call a mass meeting in the city with no advance publicity in the newspapers. "Dodd says he will have three times the number of men . . . there necessary to take the place and Camp Morton." Stidger added, "This may look wild but Dodd talks continually and earnestly." Dodd cursed Bullitt for carrying papers on him that were probably seized during his arrest, and he thought that the Kentuckian's travels to Canada (under the pseudonym Charles Smith) had been the reason he had attracted the attention of the authorities. Turning to other matters, Stidger made clear to his Kentucky handler that Governor Morton wanted the Indiana leaders arrested and tried; the governor "is quite anxious I should testify in person against Dodd. He says without my testimony they cant make out a case against him." However, Stidger had his doubts and told the governor so. "I am willing to do anything for the interests of our Government, at the same time taking all precaution against assassination: Or if I am provided with a sufficiency to live hereafter in protection."[55]

Stidger's reports reveal the divergence of views of the two military commanders to whom he reported. Burbridge favored an aggressive policy of military arrests, while Carrington, at odds with Morton, opted for a wary wait-and-see approach. Stidger sided with Burbridge's view and hoped that "the work of arrest go bravely on." He commented to Fairleigh that they should try to induce Bowles to travel to Louisville where he could be arrested by Kentucky authorities, which would "give them more confidence in Indiana," as Carrington "is afraid to do anything." He complained,

> I fear the result in Indiana, I fear they will not arrest anyone, and
> I know the programme that Genl C. will pursue, it is good, only
> I fear he will not have sufficient strength. The Gov. seems to place
> but little reliance in Dodd's audacity in attempting to carry out
> what he says he will, but I believe that without the arrest of all the
> leaders anyway, that the work will be attempted notwithstanding
> the arrests in this state [Kentucky].[56]

Stidger next called on Bowles at French Lick Springs, where they discussed the decision to act regardless of cooperation with rebel forces. Bowles indignantly remarked that "Dodd had no right to change the programme as laid down by them at Chicago." There they had agreed to await support from a Confederate force. Bowles had sent his messenger (a man named Dickerson, of Baltimore) through federal lines to the Confederate capital of Richmond to arrange it. Dodd had already told Bowles of the new decision by a message carried by his son, Harvey Dodd, but the old Mexican War veteran had answered that "he would not act until he got ready—which would be when he could have the [assistance] of rebel troops on Louisville." They also discussed the purchase of arms through merchants in Cincinnati and New Albany, Indiana, and the possibility of proceeding with just the assistance of rebel guerrillas operating in Kentucky. Stidger opined to Fairleigh that the Kentucky arrests did not deter Bowles from the plan of an armed rising. "They have made up their minds that they are bound to act—leave the country or go to prison." He hoped that Carrington would arrest Bowles.[57] In a report to Carrington of the same date, he repeated the information given to Fairleigh but suggested only that a shipment of ammunition to a merchant at New Albany should be seized.[58]

While Carrington relied heavily on the information he received from Stidger, he supplemented his knowledge with information from other sources. A Washington County, Indiana, man warned that Horace Heffren and others publicly intimated that a "Volcano" was shortly set to explode in a series of simultaneous strikes. The letter writer, "a reliable and well known citizen," advised that Heffren should be arrested, "as he is the leading spirit among them & without him they would be lost for a leader for this county."[59] On receipt, state authorities immediately put the letter in print in the *Indianapolis Daily Journal,* omitting only the recommendation to arrest Heffren.[60] A man from Noblesville, north of Indianapolis, reported that men were repairing their old muskets, rifles, and pistols, while others tried to buy guns in town. Men "openly say they are arming themselves to resist the *draft* and carry the elections throughout the state."[61] In the meantime, LaPorte County Unionists, in northern Indiana, reported that they had discovered the means by which the conspirators distributed arms to the disaffected.[62] Carrington advised legion officers around the state to watch for efforts to disarm their commands and to keep an eye on refugees streaming into the state from Kentucky.[63]

Carrington cataloged these and other disquieting facts in a report to headquarters. The *Indianapolis Daily State Sentinel,* organ of the state Democratic Party, that day called on the party faithful to arm themselves, he wrote; indeed, one city retailer sold ninety revolvers the day before to "men of disloyal antecedents." Democratic leaders "openly avowed in the streets that [at the] first disturbance, the rebel prisoners will be released." Rebel guerrillas were numerous and active in Kentucky and the low level of the Ohio River afforded them numerous places to ford it. Carrington asked for another regiment with which to control the rampant Democrats, guard the arsenals, as well as deter irate Republicans from attacking the *Sentinel* office.[64]

He soon obtained information with explosive political importance. A Terre Haute draft official telegraphed to report the discovery of "pamphlets of secret disloyal organization" in the local law office formerly occupied by Democratic congressman Daniel W. Voorhees and his law partner, prominent Democrat John E. Risley.[65] The pamphlets turned out to be printed materials of the OAK. Also found was some of Voorhees's correspondence, which included letters from U.S. Senator James W. Wall of New Jersey (who had been arrested and imprisoned by military authority in 1861) regarding the offer of twenty thousand "Garibaldi Rifles" for sale by a Philadelphia dealer.[66] The *Indianapolis Daily Journal* promptly trumpeted the find even before officials sent Carrington the materials.[67] Voorhees vigorously denied that he had anything to do with the records and claimed that they had been planted. In the meantime, Carrington made inquiries with War Department officials about the rifles, noting that if the dealer "is of disloyal tendencies it will explain much regarding the smuggling of arms for disloyal purposes."[68] Carrington and Morton held on to the Voorhees pamphlets and correspondence until an opportune moment arose, which soon came.[69]

Other events at Terre Haute demonstrated the delicate balance in the Northwest. In early August bands of hundreds of armed horsemen entered

Vigo County from Greene and Sullivan Counties in search of two soldiers named Brown of the 43rd Indiana Volunteer Infantry Regiment. The soldiers had attended a community picnic at Fairbanks, in Sullivan County, on July 12. At the picnic a political quarrel commenced, a brawl broke out, and "bullets flew pretty thick around," during which a young Democrat was killed.[70] The soldiers fled and hid with the aid of others. The armed horsemen broke into squads of twenty or more and scoured the countryside south of Terre Haute, stopping persons on the roads and entering farmhouses "under pretense of searching for the escaped soldiers." Andy Humphreys of Greene County, a local Democratic firebrand, was among their leaders. Rumors reached Terre Haute that the armed men intended to raid the town at night to seize district provost marshal Richard W. Thompson and hold him as hostage for the Browns. Thompson credited the reports and with other townspeople barricaded the town and provost marshal's office. However, the armed bands halted four miles from town and part of them instead crossed the Wabash River into Illinois, purportedly to continue their search for the soldiers. Thompson asked Morton for prompt reinforcement, offering his belief that an attack on Terre Haute would be the beginning of "open revolt": "If they come to this town and disturb any thing or any body we shall whip them or they must whip us—but this will be the beginning of a revolution."[71]

At this time, Democrats still fumed about the exposé published in the *Journal* and newspapers throughout the state and Northwest. Democratic newspapers targeted Carrington for abuse, with stories of his supposed drunkenness during the Morgan Raid reappearing in the *Sentinel.* Indiana Democrats took steps to put political pressure on Washington to remove him from his post. But Governor Morton stood up for his ally. He wired to Stanton that "as matters stand here now it would be very unfortunate to remove Gen Carrington from the command and I hope it will not be done. Mr. [Senator Thomas A.] Hendricks is reported to have gone to Washington on a mission to the Government." Morton informed the secretary that he was sending his own "deputation" to report on Carrington's good work and the "condition of affairs in a proper light."[72]

Amid the swirl of events, on August 9, Carrington distilled information gathered by spy Stidger and his other sources and reported to departmental headquarters. Much had happened in the last three days, he announced. He had investigated the threats to Terre Haute personally, holding the 46th Indiana Volunteer Infantry Regiment (a depleted veteran regiment then numbering only 220 men) in Indianapolis in reserve. The armed band that marched on the town acted under the control of Greene County Democratic leader

Andy Humphreys, "(Maj Gen of secret order) . . . who daily appeals to the people to arm and be prepared to resist the draft at all hazards." Armed groups all around the state "*drill openly,* cheer for Jeff Davis, and pledge themselves to resist the draft[,] arrests, etc." His informants told him that two thousand rebel guerrillas under Adam Johnson, George M. Jessee, and other guerrilla commanders were poised to strike from Kentucky. Stidger said that Dodd had ordered a "demonstration" to occur on August 16, but that other leaders protested that no rising should happen without support from rebel troops. "Having due notice of their plans," he warned, "I expect to anticipate them, but it will not do to ignore them. The leaders of the order are desperate men[.] They have little to lose:—all to gain by disorder." He believed that the "conspiracy is a substantial reality of serious concern, or it will fall by its own weight upon exposure." He wished to be on guard in either event. "I have ample evidence of all I furnish you and . . . I do not exaggerate any facts." Governor Morton was sending a messenger to Washington to urge, among other things, that the general be given secret-service funds to assist his detective work. In conclusion, Carrington advised that the government should arrest the leaders of the conspiracy for levying war against the United States.[73] He also wrote to Governor Brough and military commanders in other states to warn them in similar tones, stressing that the conspirators planned an uprising on August 15 and 16, but adding, "I do not believe they will have the nerve to attempt it." Still, he asked for reinforcements from his neighboring commanders.[74]

Heintzelman took special notice of the growing guerrilla threat emerging in Kentucky. He clamored for more troops for his department and rejoiced when the War Department ordered four regiments of hundred-days troops from the East to reinforce prison camp garrisons at Chicago, Indianapolis, Johnson's Island, and Rock Island. He informed Carrington that the units would soon arrive and asserted his own confident assessment that "there is a division in the ranks of the disloyal, and they are not able to make up their minds to fix the day to strike." Reinforcements would give government authorities more time to prepare, he concluded. "It must not for a moment succeed at any point. Before that time it may become necessary to make some arrests." He advised caution and secrecy.[75]

As the blazing-hot and dry days of mid-August passed and the day for the planned uprising approached, military commanders made preparations. Luck was with them. On August 14 veteran troops arrived unexpectedly from the South, sent home to muster out. One regiment, the 32nd Indiana Volunteer Infantry Regiment ("1st German"), consisting of 270 "nonveterans" (men who chose to muster out at the end of their three-year enlistment and not reenlist), had been expected. But two small, badly depleted regiments, the 24th and 18th Indiana, numbering 176 and 140, respectively, arrived at Indianapolis's Union Station without notice. As with each Indiana volunteer unit that returned from the front, Governor Morton received them at the capitol and praised their service. But on this occasion, he expressed additional words of thanks for their presence.[76] The 60th Massachusetts, the hundred-days regiment ordered from the East, one thousand strong but raw and untrained, arrived the next day as promised, strongly reinforcing the Indianapolis garrison.[77] The reinforcements dropped on Morton and Carrington like manna from heaven.

Their forces strengthened, authorities made preparations to resist an uprising. Carrington gave orders to the chief of telegraph operators in the state to send instructions to "reliable" operators to keep their eyes open for "unusual collections of passengers" with train tickets for Indianapolis.[78] The operators, who worked mostly in telegraph offices in train depots around the state, would be able to observe who was boarding trains for the city. Carrington also posted picket guards around the city to warn of the advance of mounted groups into the city. He wired headquarters that "every train brings a large number of strangers many of them armed, but they can do nothing should they wish to. Their whole plot will fail unless they tamper with railroads."[79]

At this moment, startling news arrived at Indianapolis that troops under rebel guerrilla general Adam Johnson had crossed the Ohio River near Shawneetown, in southeastern Illinois, seized three steamboats and was ferrying stolen cattle back across the river to Kentucky. The movement across the river appeared to confirm that the conspirators were acting in concert with rebel guerrillas. Carrington immediately sent the 32nd and 46th Indiana Regiments by train to Mount Vernon, in Posey County, where they joined legion troops under the command of Brevet Major General Alvin P. Hovey, then visiting at home. In the next few days the Indiana troops pursued Johnson's guerrillas deep into Kentucky until forces under Brigadier General E. A. Paine attacked Johnson and broke up his command.[80]

Still, the focus rested on Indianapolis. On August 16, the day of anticipated action, the weather turned from blazing hot to cloudy, rainy, and cool. Carrington reported that during the night nineteen train cars had arrived from Anderson and other towns, full of "rough men." "I am advised of every movement," the general said. His observers watched the men congregating in the city's saloons and milling around the streets. Other information came from unexpected quarters. During the afternoon several prominent Democrats called on Carrington and state officials to warn that the Sons of Liberty planned to make an attempt that night, or in the next few days. These Democrats, whom Carrington described as "property holders," took alarm at the growing revolutionary movement in their party and called for military action to quell unrest. Carrington wrote, "The leading Democrat who called today, long a prominent member of Congress Mr. Wm English, though [he] requested that his name be unknown in the matter, informs me that the arrest of a few of the leaders would soon quiet the whole matter." The leaders in the organization "urging resistance to the government" were Dodd, Heffren, Joseph J. Bingham, the editor of the *Sentinel* and chairman of the state Democratic Party's central committee, Lambdin P. Milligan, and Bowles, he added. The general would consult with Morton when he returned to the city the next day.[81] In the end, to the relief of both military and civil leaders, including establishment Democrats, no rising occurred. The timely arrival of the veteran troops and the 60th Massachusetts and divided party counsels had disrupted the plans of the revolutionaries. Writing to Rosecrans to warn him of the mass meeting quickly planned for Springfield on the seventeenth, Carrington wrote that "the threatened movement here is overawed by arrival of reinforcements."[82]

Seizure of Arms

While the intended Indiana rising failed to happen, thanks in part to good intelligence but mainly thanks to the lucky arrival of troops, military commanders continued to be vigilant. Officers worked to intercept arms shipments, attempted to track down and arrest rebel "emissaries" traveling through Indiana, and pursued persons considered to be suspicious.[83] State authorities requested assistance from the War Department to stem the flow of Confederate deserters, rebel refugees, and other Southern sympathizers who were streaming into the state from south of the Ohio River.[84]

Amid these events, Carrington's sickly seven-month-old son, Morton, died at home in Indianapolis. Carrington obtained permission to carry his son's body to Columbus, Ohio, for burial in his wife's family's cemetery plot.[85] To cover his absence, the general appointed Colonel James G. Jones, then deputy acting assistant provost marshal general in Indiana, to assume temporary command of the district. Carrington buried his son in Columbus on a stormy afternoon, reported to be the heaviest rainfall of the year. Heintzelman, who relied on Carrington's intelligence efforts, meant to attend the funeral but was deterred by the downpour.[86]

On Saturday, August 20, while Carrington was in Ohio, Governor Morton received an anonymous letter, postmarked at Buffalo, New York, and dated August 17:

The facts hereby stated have come to my knowledge in a manner & from a source, such as to leave in my mind no doubt of their validity. The Copperheads of Indiana have ordered and paid for 30000 revolvers with 42 boxes fixed ammunition to be distributed amongst the antagonists of our Govt for the purpose of controlling the approaching Presidential election[.] Aug 5th Steamer Granite State landed in N York 42 boxes of revolvers and ammunition, Aug 5th Steamer City of Hartford landed 22 boxes ammunition destined for Indianapolis. 32 boxes of the above have been forwarded to J.J. Parsons, Indianapolis via Merch. Dispatch and marked Stationary [sic]. The balance is stored 42. Walker St N. York awaiting the convenience of the Copperheads to pay for same before shipping.

The writer identified him- or herself as "C.C.L., Box 239, Buffalo, N.Y." Morton gave the information to Colonel Jones, who quickly investigated the matter. He reported that "32 neat boxes, weighing near two hundred pounds each," addressed to J. J. Parsons, a business partner of H. H. Dodd, had arrived at the city train depot. Ten of the boxes bore no mark of their contents, the others were marked "hardware." The ten boxes had already been removed from the depot before Morton received the anonymous letter. Jones ordered that the boxes be seized and Dodd's place of business be searched. "This I did upon consultation with Gov Morton and with his approval," he reported.[87] Troops that day found 26 of the boxes in the Old Sentinel Building warehouse. Jones notified the War Department immediately on learning of the discovery and received a response from Secretary Stanton approving his "prompt attention" to the matter; he also authorized the seizure of the boxes remaining in New York City.[88]

Morton lost no time in trumpeting the discovery for political effect. On the evening of the twentieth, Republicans held a rally on the Circle, in the center of the city, during which a speaker brandished one of the seized revolvers before the audience and described it as "one of the Sons of Liberty's arguments for peace!"[89] Also that night, in the early morning hours, soldiers entered Dodd's printing shop, where they found and seized six more boxes of arms and searched for and seized papers and pamphlets related to the secret organization. The existence and location of the papers had been supplied by Stidger. Soldiers arrested Parsons, Charles P. Hutchinson, and William M. Harrison, all business partners of Dodd (Harrison was also the secretary of the Indiana branch of the secret organization), and a man named Calvin A. Elliott, who had paid the freight charges for the boxes at the station. Dodd himself was out of town and could not be found. All told, the thirty-two boxes contained nearly four hundred Savage patent revolvers and 135,000 rounds of ammunition.[90]

Morton promptly telegraphed Major General John A. Dix, commander of the Department of the East, in New York City, with the information he had received from the anonymous source. He asked Dix to seize the arms at the Walker Street location, saying that the guns were destined for the use of the Sons of Liberty.[91] Morton also ordered the Marion County sheriff, W. J. H. Robinson, formerly colonel of the 11th Indiana Volunteer Infantry Regiment, to board a train for Buffalo and find the person identified as "C.C.L." Robinson arrived at Buffalo and somehow found the informer, who knew nothing more than what the note contained. Robinson pushed on to New York City.[92]

On Sunday, Indianapolis was "in a ferment" over the news of the seizures and arrests. Army officers showed Morton the records found in Dodd's offices.[93] The following day, Republican newspapers in Indianapolis published details of the seizures and printed the text of the anonymous letter. The *Journal* also published some of the correspondence found earlier in the month in Voorhees's Terre Haute office. The correspondence was revealing as well as highly embarrassing. Printed were letters of Senator Wall to Voorhees about the "Garibaldi rifles" for sale, as well as letters from *Sentinel* editor Bingham and Auditor of State Joseph Ristine expressing their hopes that the South would successfully resist the United States. One particularly embarrassing letter from Joseph E. McDonald, the Democratic Party's candidate for governor, ridiculed Indiana chief justice Samuel Perkins, a fellow Democrat, as insane and suffering from hallucinations. The *Journal* also printed a letter from Carrington to Voorhees, dated August 16, responding to the congressman's denial that the records and papers came from his Terre Haute office. In it, the general noted that 112 copies of the pamphlet ritual of the OAK, issued in the fall of 1863, were found in the office with papers covering his congressional speeches up to March 1864, among Voorhees's law library and office furniture. Also found were letters from Clement Vallandigham when the Ohioan was still in Windsor, as well as other leading Democratic figures.[94]

Grasping the political advantage the discoveries had handed him, that night Governor Morton addressed another Union rally on the Circle. Relying on the figure of thirty thousand revolvers mentioned in the note, he claimed that the seized weapons were merely a "small fraction of an immense shipment" being sent to Indiana to arm the ranks of the secret organization. He reminded the audience that he had warned them of the rise of the conspiracy for the past eighteen months. "This has been well known to me during that time," he thundered.[95] Morton also telegraphed Colonel Oakes at Springfield to investigate Illinois persons whose names appeared in the seized records. One was a sutler at the Camp Douglas prison camp at Chicago. He requested that Oakes immediately remove him. "Safety and the public interest demand it."[96]

The next day, August 23, the *Journal* published some of the papers found in Dodd's office. Dozens of letters and other records to and from Dodd and other leaders of the secret organization appeared in six long columns of the newspaper. Included were letters from Lambdin P. Milligan, John C. Walker, Judge Bullitt, expelled U.S. Senator Jesse D. Bright, Richard T. Merrick, Clement Vallandigham, John G. Davis, and others. A letter from Voorhees's law partner, John E. Risley, in New York City, dated August 8, 1864, lamented that "[Charles L.] Hunt and Company have played the devil, according to reports," referring to the published confession of Green B. Smith. "Does he attempt to implicate any of our friends, and does it affect our people in any way?" The newspaper observed that some of the papers were written in code. Reports also noted that among the seized records was a membership list.[97]

In the meantime, military officers in New York City tracked down the Walker Street location based on the information that Governor Morton supplied. Commanders employed U.S. Marshal Robert Murray, who ran a large detective force (paid for by the surplus of funds generated by the seizure of shipping and goods that entered the port of New York) and hired out their services to the army on a contract basis. Detectives first kept watch on the Walker Street building, then entered it and seized thirty-two boxes and arrested the businessman who worked there.[98] In the boxes were 2,192 large, six-barreled "Navy Revolvers" manufactured by the Savage Arms Company of Middletown, Connecticut (the same type of weapon as seized in Indianapolis). Commanders investigated the sale of the arms and learned that the man at the business house, Andrew Kirkpatrick, an arms broker, had been contacted by a shadowy figure who wished to buy a large supply of revolvers.[99] Kirkpatrick knew that the arms were for a "disloyal purpose" but could not resist the temptation of making several thousand dollars on commission, investigators reported. The boxes seized in New York City had stenciled on them "Stationary" [*sic*].[100] In total, the sixty-four boxes seized in Indianapolis and New York contained nearly twenty-six hundred revolvers and 135,000 rounds of ammunition.

During these events, Henry Carrington was in Columbus, Ohio, to bury his son. While there he visited departmental headquarters and had a long meeting with Heintzelman, who was impressed by the "narrow escape from a civil war" that had occurred in Indiana during the previous week. "Nothing but the arrangement of troops prevented it," recorded Heintzelman, as well as "the determination of some leading Democrats not to aid" the conspirators.[101] Carrington returned to Indianapolis in the evening of August 22.[102] He had been away during the seizure of the arms, ammunition, and records from Dodd's offices, as well as during the initial examination of the papers. He had had no say in the decision to publish the letters found in Voorhees's and Dodd's offices. Morton undoubtedly made that decision, guided solely by political considerations. Carrington had argued against publication of his report on the secret organization and had lamented its appearance in print at the end of July. Now he was presented with a fait accompli and could do nothing about it. The seizure of the arms and papers in Dodd's offices was a testament to the value of his spycraft, but their immediate exposure for political effect was contrary to his plan to continue to gather information on the conspirators.

Carrington returned to his duties as commander of the District of Indiana and intelligence chief for the department. The problem of arms and ammunition in the hands of the conspirators was the pressing issue of the moment. Citizens and officers forwarded reports of surreptitious sales of arms occurring throughout the state and requested that authorities seize them.[103] Reports from Terre Haute arrived at district headquarters that a large supply of gunpowder—110 kegs containing over three thousand pounds of powder—had been unloaded at the train depot consigned to unknown persons in Illinois. Carrington ordered the shipment's seizure.[104] He reported that large shipments of arms were invoiced and being shipped to various points and he was watching them. He also worked to locate Dodd, who had disappeared. "Intercepted letters" suggested that he had gone to Saint Paul, Minnesota.[105] Rebel prisoners in Camp Morton acting as informants supplied reports of new tunnels being dug by the prisoners and of new plans to make a mass breakout and seize arms in the arsenal.[106] Finally, Carrington reported that Bowles, who continued to be defiant, was in contact with rebel agent Captain Hines and publicly vowed to lead three thousand Indiana men to go south to join the Confederate army.[107] Carrington's work as spymaster produced important information on the widespread conspiracy and the secret organization's collaboration with rebel agents.

Carrington Out, Hovey In

Despite Carrington's effectiveness collecting intelligence, his second stint in command of the District of Indiana soon came to an end. On August 22, General Halleck telegraphed Heintzelman that Stanton wanted General

Hovey to replace Carrington. Halleck ordered the departmental commander to find Hovey and tell him.[108] Morton asked Stanton that Carrington be retained in Indianapolis and assigned to the command of the draft rendezvous as cover for his intelligence work. "Carrington has an intimate knowledge of the affairs of the state," he explained; his knowledge was "very important to us just now." He added that "Carrington's business is private. Affairs will require some time to arrange and I ask that he may be put on [draft rendezvous] duty for at least sixty days."[109] Carrington acknowledged the new orders, noting that Morton "desires me to continue my investigations." He explained that he would soon be able to "disclose the whole design of the Order. Members are daily furnishing me with affidavits."[110]

The cause prompting Stanton's order to replace Carrington with Hovey is not precisely known. It is unlikely that the Democratic petitioners led by Senator Hendricks would have swayed the War Department to oust Carrington. Surviving records make clear that Governor Morton wished to retain Carrington in Indianapolis because of his invaluable knowledge of the secret organization and its doings. But two policy differences had arisen between the general and the governor. Since being posted to Indianapolis, Carrington had consistently advocated using military power to contain the secret organizations by arresting conspirators. However, he just as consistently advocated turning over arrested persons to the federal civil courts for trial. He was proud of the large numbers of convictions he obtained in the federal courts in 1863. But now that the political and military authorities in the Northwestern states and Kentucky had agreed to arrest the leading members of the secret organization in the various states, the question arose regarding trial venue: in which type of court would they be tried? For many months Morton had agreed on using the civil courts. The governor changed his mind, however, and now wanted to try them by military commissions. Why? The answer probably lies in what had occurred in federal courts to date. The protracted and so-far-inconclusive proceedings in the U.S. court at Cincinnati involving the Camp Chase conspirators (Cathcart, Medary, Samuel Thomas, et al.) arrested in 1863 were undoubtedly an object lesson in the difficulties of using the federal courts. Ten months had passed since the Camp Chase arrests, but the cases were stalled. Compared to military tribunals, the federal civil courts were glacially slow. Moreover, the difficulties of getting a conviction for treason made such cases rare. The federal attorney at Cincinnati had dropped treason charges against the defendants and instead was pursuing lesser conspiracy charges. As well, by this time the Coles County, Illinois, rioters had been bundled off to languish in Fort Delaware military prison, south of Philadelphia. Colonel Oakes had recommended that they be tried by military commission, and the War Department and Lincoln agreed.[111] The fall elections were fast approaching, and Morton wanted to use the arrests for political effect. Carrington, his erstwhile aide, who consistently advocated civil trials, was now a hindrance and had to be removed from command.

The second policy difference between Carrington and Morton centered on the general's disinclination to see information his networks had collected show up in the newspapers. Though he occasionally divulged tidbits in public (most notably, when he exposed Bowles to shield Stidger), he argued that publication would have a deleterious effect on his ability to learn more about the conspiracy. He had opposed the publication of his June 28 report but had been overridden by Morton, who had lobbied Secretary Stanton for approval. In late September, Carrington wrote to Joseph Holt and referred to this variance of opinion:

> the only difference between Gov. Morton, and myself, during two
> years, has been that of my declining to expose this secret order,
> at his request, when Genl Heintzelman forbade it, and I believed
> it would defeat my plans for learning, not only their complete
> work, but anticipating and defeating their ulterior designs. I am
> convinced that he has since concurred in the wisdom of my course.
> We are now working in perfect accord, and though in another
> sphere of duty, it is [animative?] to me, if I can serve the cause
> common to us all.[112]

Carrington made no mention of the difference about civil versus military trials. If exposing the secret organization was, indeed, the only issue that divided Carrington and Morton, then Carrington had changed his mind and joined with Morton and the others in advocating the use of military commissions to try arrested leaders.

Whatever the reason, Carrington was out and Hovey was in as commander of the District of Indiana. Carrington remained in Indianapolis and took up the reins of the draft rendezvous. More important, he continued his intelligence work. Resigned to his new position, he thanked Heintzelman for the "invariable kindness and confidence" shown him while he had command of Indiana. He would have been grateful had the War Department "permitted me to handle my work through." While he felt mortified by the change, at least he would be "spared the daily and hourly care" that had weighed on him in keeping tabs on the conspirators. "Not an hour for weeks, either day or night could I have been surprised," he wrote, "and Genl Rosecrans has thanked me for it."[113]

While Carrington was the department's chief spymaster, Heintzelman received reports from other sources. Civilians alerted military commanders to the arrival of boxes of arms at local train depots and urged that troops seize them.[114] Officers investigated the arms trade and recommended measures to intercept the traffic. Brigadier General August Willich, appointed to the command of the post of Cincinnati, Covington, and Newport in August, looked into the large traffic in arms and ammunition at Cincinnati.[115] He obtained sales data from Kittredge and Company, the firm that commanders had investigated in 1863 for arms sales to people deemed disloyal. A company official informed him that their sales to civilians of carbine rifles and "cavalry pistols" in the last sixty days had been greater than at any time during the war, selling 750 carbines and 500 revolvers in that period, mostly in small batches and mostly in Ohio, Indiana, and Illinois. However, Willich learned that New York dealers controlled most of the arms business and sold directly to buyers throughout the North, dwarfing Kittredge's sales. Indeed, demand was so great that manufacturers had sold out their production months in advance.[116] Heintzelman forwarded Willich's report to the secretary of war with the comment that arms shipped from the East flooded the Northwest. He asked the administration to "prevent any more being sent here at present."[117] Richard W. Thompson, the district provost marshal at Terre Haute, also reported that "extraordinary efforts are now making by the Sons of Liberty to fill this country with arms & ammunition." Large and heavy boxes passed through town on railroad cars to hot spots such as Greene County, Indiana, and Clark and Coles Counties, Illinois. "These things ought to be stopped & in my opinion the military authorities should put a man on every railroad train *secretly* to examine all the freight—or should have one stationed at every freight Depot."[118] Other officers reported that their sources told them that arms for Ohio copperheads were expected to come from Canada for distribution before the draft.[119] Still others noted that many local militia armories were unguarded and liable to attack.[120]

Heintzelman took these and other warnings to heart and issued orders to local railroads and a dealer in Columbus "not to transport or deliver arms without a permit from me." "The copperheads are arming," he explained in his journal. "The War Dept. won't take the responsibility, so I have to. Gov. Brough will sustain me to the extent of his power. A great many revolvers and Henry rifles are coming every day."[121] The general may have been influenced by an editorial in that day's *Cincinnati Daily Commercial* that complained of "immense purchases of arms" by the opponents of the government. The editorial, which appeared after the discovery of the arms in Dodd's offices in Indianapolis, opined that such "extraordinary purchases of arms" indicated a "concert of action" by the copperheads.[122] Days later, on August 27, Heintzelman extended the ban on the sale, transport, or delivery of arms and ammunition over his multistate command in General Orders 53. Exceptions would be allowed only by permits from military authorities. The ban would last for sixty days, a period covering the upcoming draft and state elections in the Northwest.[123] The order prompted seizures of arms and gunpowder throughout the department as commanders intercepted shipments intended for persons they deemed disloyal.[124]

The Chicago Convention

Amid these remarkable events, the presidential election and the rescheduled Democratic National Convention at Chicago loomed large. Intelligence from sources such as Stidger and Rosecrans's detectives pointed to the likelihood of an armed outbreak occurring during the event. Hill's rebel turncoat and informant, Major George W. Young, indicated that rebel authorities in Canada planned an attempt on Camp Douglas to release prisoners. Additional information pointed to danger in the city. Burbridge told Heintzelman that he had "reliable" information that Confederate officers had gone to Chicago to assist in a plot to release rebel prisoners.[125] Captain William James, the district provost marshal for Chicago, reported that trouble was brewing for the convention. His sources told of a plot to liberate the prisoners and that some of the troops guarding the camp were implicated. "They also propose to set fire to the city in not less than 5 places."[126] Days later he wrote that "vague and unreliable rumors" coming from Chicago's Irish Catholic population caused concern and that a local gunsmith had recently received an order for five hundred gun belts and holsters which he (the gunsmith) thought were meant for use in the city. The local businessmen who ordered the belts and holsters were "Kentuckians and copperhead to an extreme," wrote James. Military authorities later seized the equipment.[127] Headquarters staff at Columbus wrote to Colonel Sweet to "keep an eye on movements of suspicious persons."[128] They also warned him that rebel captain Hines had recently been reported at Niagara Falls but might now be in Chicago. "As this Hines appears to be the leader, the Maj Gen Comd'g deems it advisable to arrest him and send him under proper guard to this place (Camp Chase)." However, Sweet should defer arrest if it would "interfere with any arrangement you have made to break up this organization" and instead, "put a detective to watch him for a time." The general thought that Hines's arrest and confinement far away from Chicago "would do much towards breaking up the organization."[129]

At Detroit, Colonel Hill spoke with Young on August 24. Young related that Hines had returned to Canada from Chicago, where he had finalized arrangements. The rebel soldiers going to Chicago were to hold themselves in readiness to depart on short notice. Hines was to have "entire control of the Chicago matter, and if successful, will receive the commission of Brig Genl in the rebel service."[130] Sweet sent Young's information to Springfield and asked if a physical description of Hines could be sent to him, explaining that if Young failed to show up he would have some means to identify the rebel agent. "A man changes his name easy not his spots," he observed.[131] Hill sent him a vague but accurate description of the rebel expedition's leader: "Hines is said to be a young, slight built man, about 28 years of age, with moustache and light hair." Hill had not been able to meet with Young since his return to Windsor from Toronto. Young "has made discreet appointments to see me," he explained, but "he has been so closely watched by those associated with him, that it has been impossible to keep them." Young told him that the Chicago "business has been postponed for a few days, in order to [illegible] a nomination to be made by the Chicago convention." He expected to leave for that city in the next day or two. Hill added that he would "take the precaution" of sending "a reliable detective unknown as such to Wallace [i.e., Young]" so that he would be sure to establish communication with him.[132]

In the meantime, General Paine at Springfield made preparations for danger in Chicago by requesting one thousand veteran troops and a battery be sent to the city. Heintzelman had no infantry to send, but by shifting around his meager forces he managed to send a battery from Camp Chase to Chicago; he also moved an Ohio state militia battery from Cleveland to Sandusky to help guard Johnson's Island.[133] Lacking forces with which to "overawe" the many thousands of Democrats assembling in Chicago and the Confederate troops known to be in the city, Paine issued orders to Sweet. Officers from the camp garrison were to not go to Chicago during the convention unless on duty, in order to avoid provocation or pretext for disorder. Further, "in the event that rebel emissaries, congregating at Chicago during the convention, shall attempt to rescue the prisoners he will, without using blank cartridges, make haste to inflict upon them punishment so exemplary as to prevent the repetition of such crimes. . . . He will not declare martial law, unless in case of necessity of which he will be the judge."[134]

On the day before the start of the convention, Heintzelman received a telegram (in cipher—he had finally obtained the codes!) from Halleck. As

Secretary Stanton believed that an attempt to free the prisoners at Camp Douglas might be attempted during the convention, he ordered him to go to Chicago to ascertain conditions personally. "It would not be good policy to send troops there now if it can be avoided," Halleck added. "It is probable that if an attempt at rescue is made it will be during the excitement and confusion resulting from the adjournment of the convention."[135] In obedience to orders, at daybreak the next morning Heintzelman and one staff officer boarded a train and rode the rails to Chicago, arriving at eleven o'clock that night. It was a "dirty and unpleasant ride."[136] From the train station they obtained rooms at the Sherman House, described by one of the Chicago newspapers as the head-quarters of the "Vallandighamers" (the Tremont House served as base for the "McClellanites").[137] There the general met Dean Richmond, a Buffalo, New York potentate in that state's Democratic leadership, with whom former Ohio governor Dennison wished him to speak about the threat of disturbance during the convention. Richmond dismissed the possibility and said he had "not even thought of it." Significantly, Heintzelman recorded, "There's a rumor that we have 5,000 troops here. We may as well let them believe so."[138]

Chicago was overflowing with visitors for the convention. Extra horse-drawn street cars ran their routes, restaurants and saloons offered special rates for meals and liquor to the hungry and thirsty, and residents turned their homes into boarding houses and filled them with paying guests. Correspondents for major newspapers reported that the city was full of strangers; every train brought three to five extra cars loaded with conventiongoers.[139] Thousands arrived each day in advance of the convention, far more than the number of official delegates. The streets were jammed with people, elbow to elbow. Excitement bubbled. One of Chicago's Republican newspapers gave credit to the Democrats for the lack of ruffianism in the streets.[140] But pickpockets had easy pickings.[141]

Heintzelman did not attend the convention, held in a huge temporary amphitheater built near the Lake Michigan shore. Instead, the morning after his arrival he went out to Camp Douglas and made a careful inspection of facilities. Sweet "has about 8,000 prisoners and about 1,600 men for duty," he recorded. "In case of emergency he can turn out about 2000 men. No difficulty however is anticipated." The day before, on the first day of the convention, reports of his General Orders 53 prohibiting the sale and distribution of arms and ammunition in the states of the Northern Department became generally known. Speakers railed against the order from the high podium in the convention hall, drawing "great enthusiasm" from Westerners affected by the order.[142] Heintzelman was amused by the uproar he had caused and during the day met many Democrats he had known in Washington. He spoke with Horatio Seymour, the governor of New York, president of the convention and an aspirant for the nomination. He also conversed with August Belmont, New York banker and leading financier of the Democratic Party. "In conversation I soon saw that they believed I got my instructions about arms from Washington. I told the Governor that I alone am responsible for the order," he noted proudly, reminding himself that none in Washington would take responsibility for decisive action in the Northwest. Later, the general had a "pleasant talk" with Clement Vallandigham, the leader of both the secret organization and the antiwar wing of the party.[143]

Heintzelman spent part of the following day completing paperwork for gunpowder permits for blasting and hunting purposes, an onerous new chore that fell on him and other military commanders following his order.[144] The next day, September 1, after meeting with Sweet and Colonel William Hoffman, the War Department's head of military prisons, the general met with members of the Indiana delegation. Speaking with U.S. Senator Thomas A. Hendricks; the party's nominee for governor, Joseph E. McDonald; Indiana secretary of state (and leading member of the secret organization) James Athon; and Judge William E. Niblack, he received assurances "that there would be no organized resistance to the draft" in Indiana.[145] That night, the convention ended and Heintzelman and his aide took a train back to Columbus, Ohio. His presence (as well as Rosecrans's, who had passed through the city intent on meeting Governor Yates and had been called on to speak at the Chicago Board of Trade) had been noted in the press, and he had had a "very pleasant" time in Chicago. He had "learned many things [that] will aid me in my duties," he recorded.[146]

Most important, no uprising or unrest occurred during the convention. Two days after the close of the convention, news of Sherman's army's victorious entrance into Atlanta reached the North, a signal triumph for the federal war effort to crush the rebellion. Back in Columbus, the general remarked in his journal, "What a pity [the news's arrival] did not occur while the democratic convention was in session. It would have been a bombshell in their camp. What a commentary such a remark is on their loyalty."[147]

What became of the plot to release the rebel prisoners of war? It is important to note that Confederate troops were in Chicago throughout the Democratic National Convention. Surviving memoirs of rebels involved in the secret plan furnish a picture of events.[148] Captain Thomas Henry Hines and about seventy soldiers (including Young) dressed as civilians and packing two revolvers each arrived in the city on August 27 and 28, traveling in pairs on different routes and different trains, amid the huge influx of visitors. Most of them stayed in one hotel, the Richmond House, staying ten men to a room packed with six beds, where they anxiously awaited word from local leaders of the secret organization for the beginning of the attack. They were inconspicuous among the mass of people who arrived in the city, many of whose train fares had been paid by Confederate government funds supplied to conspirators and the Democratic candidate for governor of Illinois. Charles Walsh, a local Chicago conspirator who lived near Camp Douglas (where his young daughter played seemingly innocently near the camp walls), had earlier visited Confederate officials in Canada and promised that his two regiments of armed men would assist in the assault on the camp. Hines conferred with Walsh and others at the Richmond House on the nights of August 28 and 29 and learned that their promises of action had evaporated. The principal cause for the waning of their revolutionary ardor were rumors coursing through the streets that federal authorities had significantly reinforced the Camp Douglas garrison. Newspapers circulated rumors that Heintzelman had received orders to send troops to Chicago to suppress the convention, and the press paid close attention to troop trains passing through the city in the days before the event.[149] As one of the Confederate soldiers recalled, "It was soon rumored about that the Camp Douglas Garrison had been reinforced by 5,000 men."[150] Another one of the Confederate soldiers later lamented that the rumor of reinforcements "had its effect upon the leaders of the Sons of Liberty."[151] As well, Hines learned that many of the visitors who had come armed and prepared to assist the attack, along with local conspirators, were scattered throughout the city and could not be marshaled quickly.[152] Hines and his chief deputy, rebel Major John Breckinridge Castleman, realized that they were dealing with timid civilians and politicians ("theorists," as Castleman derisively termed them[153]) and not men of action. The plan was postponed. Hines sent some of his Confederate soldiers back to Canada and joined the rest in downstate Illinois, where they scattered and organized local groups to prepare for another attempt to liberate the prisoners.

In August military authorities had successfully foiled two major plots to rise in arms against the federal government and release Confederate prisoners of war: at Indianapolis on August 16 and at Chicago two weeks later. Their success was due to intelligence efforts targeting the activities of the secret organization that existed in the Northwestern states, as well as surveillance of the rebel officers and officials in Canada who directed the plots. Their success was also largely due to chance: the timely arrival of unexpected reinforcements in Indianapolis the day before the planned rising and the inaccurate rumor of significant reinforcements at Camp Douglas. Generals Carrington and Heintzelman both knew that much of their success in avoiding revolution owed much to luck.

ELEVEN

"I Make No Assertions without Proof"

Preserving the Northwest in the Fall of 1864

THE INTELLIGENCE successes of August did not eliminate the threat of insurrection and upheaval. The secret organizations, assisted by Confederate agents, remained intact and poised to strike. In September army intelligence defeated the *Philo Parsons* attempt on Johnson's Island and another plot to attack Camp Douglas in Chicago in November. Commanders pursued their plan to arrest the leaders of the conspiratorial groups. Washington leaders issued orders to employ military commissions to try them. Starting with the arrest of Harrison H. Dodd, the grand commander of the Sons of Liberty in Indiana, the army set the military trial machinery in motion. After Lincoln's election victory in November 1864 and the subsequent surrender of Confederate armies beginning in April 1865, commanders broke up their espionage bureaus and fired their detectives and spies.

Hovey Takes Command

On August 24, 1864, Brevet Major General Alvin P. Hovey arrived at Indianapolis and took command of the District of Indiana.[1] The former attorney, War Democrat, and Mexican War veteran, having before the war been an associate justice of the Indiana Supreme Court and U.S. attorney for Indiana, informed General Heintzelman that he lacked orders either from him or from the War Department about what to do.[2] His appointment to the command came at the high point of the threat of insurrection in the state. No doubt he met with Governor Morton to confer about the immediate crisis. He was in full accord with Morton regarding the plan to arrest conspirators and try them by military tribunals. He wrote to his daughter that Indiana "is now in great danger—Secret societies armed are threatening to defy the laws and may probably do great mischief before they are suppressed."[3] Tellingly, he asked her to find in his law library and send him a specific legal reference work— William C. DeHart on courts-martial.[4] More to the point, he told a prominent Indianapolis lawyer that he feared civil war in the state and wanted to impose martial law, make arrests, and try prisoners by military commission.[5]

Hovey telegraphed Secretary Stanton to request instructions. He laid out his own draconian ideas for meeting the emergency. "The horizon is dark in this State," he wrote, "but a strong arm can dispel the darkness if supported by your Dept."

> Military arrests, and trials should at once be resorted to; but to do this effectively Martial Law should be first proclaimed. The jurisdiction of Military Courts then could not be denied and offenders could be punished. The press too should be compelled to keep within bounds. Such would be my policy but I await your commands.[6]

The general also requested authority to use the hundred-days troops, soon to be mustered out, to protect against "the progress of treason."[7] General Carrington, now limited to running the spy network, briefed him on the leadership of the Sons of Liberty, the latest name of the secret organization.[8] Now more fully aware of Carrington's espionage program, Hovey requested that $20,000 in secret-service funds be immediately sent to Indianapolis.[9] His request doubled Carrington's unsuccessful request, suggesting both the increased scope of information gathering and the anxiety felt by authorities at the time. Two weeks later Washington sent $5,000 in secret-service funds to Hovey, explaining that that was all they could afford.[10] It was the first secret-service funds sent by the War Department to Indiana commanders. Indeed, the quartermaster officer at Indianapolis was so surprised by their receipt that he requested instructions about handling them.[11]

In mid-September the War Department finally sent instructions to Hovey. Assistant Secretary of War E. D. Townsend reminded him that it was "highly desirable" to foster the "cordial relations which are understood to exist between you and his excellency, Governor Morton," in maintaining "harmony of action between the Federal and State authorities." War Department bureaucrats had learned through hard experience that Morton would tolerate neither fools nor interference in the management of political affairs in his state. As a consequence, a declaration of martial law was out of the question. However, Hovey was "authorized to exercise, within your district, the powers of the commander of a Department, in making military arrests, in the organization of courts-martial, and in carrying their sentences into effect."[12] Thus, the War Department extended Hovey the same latitude and independent powers possessed by General Burbridge of the District of Kentucky and gave him the green light to make arrests and employ military commissions. In bland bureaucratic language, the War Department blessed the plan to try leading conspirators by military tribunals, thus signaling its assent to and complicity in the events that were soon to occur in Indiana and elsewhere.

Continued Apprehensions

Notwithstanding the army's success in forestalling two planned uprisings in the previous month, one in Indianapolis and one in Chicago, officers knew that the conspirators still had the power to raise rebellion in the Old Northwest. Information arrived daily at army headquarters pointing to continuing problems around the region. Detectives and informers reported on the further machinations of the secret organizations, and commanders knew that conspirators were organized, armed, and poised for action. Officers all around the Northern Department maintained strict vigilance.

Lieutenant Colonel Hill, commanding at Detroit, quoted the informant wife of a rebel refugee in Windsor that "rebel fortunes were never so desperate as now." Confederate leaders, she said, still plotted cross-border attacks on Northern cities.[13] In Illinois and other states in the department, troops seized gunpowder shipments in accordance with Heintzelman's general orders banning the sale of arms and ammunition. Informers reported Democratic rumbling that when the Democratic National Convention at Chicago concluded, "they will have everything their way."[14] In early September the commander of the District of Illinois, Brigadier General Halbert E. Paine, estimated that five thousand armed men from slave states, former rebel soldiers or guerrillas, were to be found scattered throughout Illinois. Their intention was both to vote in the upcoming elections and "by terrorism" to deter thousands of Union voters from appearing at the polls. Some of the rebels "congregated in camps" in forests and swamps of the state, but most obtained assistance, "singly or in small squads, by their copperhead friends." Paine suggested that troops be stationed around the state to "hunt down and arrest" these rebel irregulars. The government needed to "turn the tables" on them with "an exemplary chastisement" if they should attempt an armed outbreak.[15]

In Indiana, Carrington collected statements of persons who had joined secret organizations and had heard plans for violent action. Elliott Robertson, who lived north of Richmond in Randolph County, near the Ohio border, had first joined the secret organization in April 1863; his brother-in-law was the lodge captain who told members that they were not to know organizational plans but merely to obey orders. Lodge leaders ordered members to be in readiness for after the Chicago convention. Local members were well armed, having received arms from Samuel Beck's firearms firm in Indianapolis; they paid for arms if able, but those who could not afford them had guns freely provided. "There are not more than half a dozen Democrats in my township who are not members of this Order," stated Robertson.[16] Richard W. Thompson, the district provost marshal at Terre Haute, on the west side of the state, supplied information of another planned attack on the town from Sullivan County: "Those men mean an outbreak." He requested troops be sent to his aid.[17] Hovey voiced his uneasiness about imminent uprisings around Indiana. "I have reason to believe," he wrote to the Indiana Legion commander, "that there are outbreaks contemplated in several localities on the day of the draft." He urged that authorities avoid offering "traitors" a "plausible excuse" for a rising.[18] The new acting assistant provost marshal general for Indiana, Colonel James G. Jones, informed federal leaders that Hovey could furnish no guards for the draft; he estimated that four thousand troops would be required to keep the peace.[19] The return of hundred-days regiments offered commanders a brief respite, but authorities remained anxious in the face of feared unrest.[20]

As well, in late August, Republican political leaders voiced nervousness about their political fates in the upcoming elections. Speaker of the U.S. House Schuyler Colfax, facing a strong Democratic challenger in David Turpie, wrote that "the odds are heavy against us in Indiana." A combination of circumstances would adversely affect their electoral prospects: the imminent draft, "armed traitors at home giving us our hands-ful to manage & control," high prices, a lack of recent military successes, and the outlook of a prolonged war. General William T. Sherman had informed him that he would not send Indiana troops home to vote, ensuring that thousands of Union votes would not be cast. Colfax made two suggestions to President Lincoln: first, offer the rebels an armistice, even if they rejected it; and second, he wrote, "our friends think if the Grand Commander of the Sons of Liberty in our State is not arrested either by civil or military process after the shipment of arms to his [warehouse], there is not much use in having a government." "Arbitrary arrests" of traitors played well with his audiences "out on the stump," he reported. "It is the most popular of all."[21]

Governor Morton and several Republican officeholders (including Colfax) and candidates offered their opinion that Republican election prospects looked poor and that they needed help from the administration. Otherwise, victorious Democrats would end military aid from the state to the federal government. They suggested that the draft be delayed until after the October elections and fifteen thousand Indiana troops be sent home to vote. A delayed draft would allow volunteering—at the moment going well—to continue. However, "if the draft is enforced before the election, there may be required half as many men to enforce it as we ask to secure the election. Difficulty may reasonably be anticipated in from 20 to 26 counties." If Secretary Stanton could see and hear what had occurred in Indiana in the last month, "no word from us would be needed. You would need no argument in proof that a crisis, full of danger to the entire North West, is at hand."[22]

Some assistance from federal authorities had already begun to arrive. Records show that during August, Washington changed its tune and began to take seriously the conspiracy in the Northwestern states, as well as Kentucky and Missouri. But major reinforcements were not forthcoming. Halleck had alerted Lieutenant General U. S. Grant to the "pretty strong evidence" of an organized "combination" to resist the draft in several Northern states and Kentucky and the need for troops to be withdrawn from the front and sent north. "I have not been a believer in most of the plots, secret societies, etc., of which we have so many pretended discoveries," he wrote, but people in the Old Northwest spoke openly of draft resistance, and "it is believed that the leaders of the peace branch of the Democratic party are doing all in their power to bring about this result. The evidence of this has increased very much with the last few days." In a separate letter, Halleck wrote, "Seriously, I think much importance should be attached to the representations of Genl H—— [Heintzelman] in regard to the condition of affairs in the west." Grant, engrossed in directing the Army of the Potomac, replied that sending troops to the North would ensure the defeat of federal efforts in both Virginia and Georgia. "General Heintzelman," he wrote, "can get from the Governors of Ohio, Indiana, and Illinois a militia organization that will deter the discontented from committing any overt act. I hope the President will call on Governors of States to organize thoroughly to preserve the peace until after the election."

President Lincoln, consistent with his belief to trust in the people to defeat antiwar sentiment and the threat of disorder in North, supported Grant's determination not to withdraw troops. "Hold on with a bulldog grip, and chew and choke as much as possible," he wrote the general.[23] Halleck continued to echo Heintzelman's assessment that "the plots of the copperheads to release the rebel prisoners were frustrated only by sending additional guards, and that such attempts will be made at the earliest favorable opportunity." But Grant again dismissed the threat out of hand and wrote, "I cannot believe that Gn. Heintzel[man's] fears are well founded. The class of people who would threaten what he apprehends make a great noise but it is hard to believe that states so largely represented in the Union Army have not friends to the soldiers enough left at home to prevent violence."[24] Top military counsels were divided. Grant, encouraged by the president, dismissed Heintzelman's petitions in order to preserve troop levels in Virginia and Georgia. Consequently, Washington supplied little tangible assistance to the beleaguered Westerners. Instead, the administration gave the go-ahead for military-commission trials of leading conspirators to commence as a political tool to weaken Democratic prospects at the polls.

At this time, Hovey held several civilians in prison and had plans to add to their number. The army had arrested a man named John Campbell for attempting to recruit men to go to Kentucky and enlist in rebel forces.[25] He also held in custody William M. Harrison, the grand secretary of the Sons of Liberty for Indiana, arrested as an accessory to the shipment of arms seized at H. H. Dodd's warehouse.[26] Before his authority to call military tribunals arrived from the War Department, in early September Hovey asked Heintzelman to form a military commission to try Harrison, Campbell, and Charles W. Holland, also implicated in the Dodd arms scheme, and "such other persons as may be brought before it." It was, he wrote, "important to do [it] at once," and suggested the names of Indiana field officers who were then available to serve on a commission.[27] The following day, information arrived at city headquarters that H. H. Dodd, the state leader of the Sons of Liberty, had returned to Indianapolis. Dodd had gone to Chicago for the Democratic National Convention and the concurrent secret convocation of conspirators. Hovey immediately ordered the post commander to arrest Dodd and hold him on a charge of "treasonable conduct."[28] Troops promptly arrested Dodd and placed him in a military prison in the city. Hovey telegraphed Heintzelman that Dodd was under military arrest "for treasonable practices and designs" and noted that there were "several other prominent traitors that ought to be arrested and tried." He added that he would be "pleased to have the Comd'g

General's instructions in regard to the same."[29] Hovey also wired Governor Morton, who was then at Washington, to report that Dodd was under arrest. He pressed Morton to get orders from the War Department as to the course he should pursue: "I hope that instructions will be sent me." He asked the governor to "see the Pres and Secy of War and say that we are in danger and must have the usual means of procuring a knowledge of the movements and designs of traitors. I have not one dollar to employ persons in the secret service."[30] When the orders arrived, a few days later, no doubt thanks in part to Morton's pressure on Lincoln and Washington, Hovey started proceedings to try Dodd before a military commission independent of Heintzelman's authority.

The Holt Report

In August federal leaders showed evidence of finally accepting the reality and imminence of widespread insurrection in the Northwest, taking a number of small steps to aid the generals and governors in policing the region. But to date they had done little to aid Republican political prospects. On the last day of the month, Secretary of War Stanton dumped Colonel Sanderson's massive report on Joseph Holt's desk and directed him "to make a detailed report" based on it and the evidence gathered during his recent fact-finding mission in the West. He was to make "such recommendation as in your opinion the nature of the case may require."[31]

Holt immediately notified military commanders in the West to forward information regarding the secret organizations and their conspiracies. General Rosecrans promptly sent copies of the Charles L. Hunt, Charles E. Dunn, and Green B. Smith confessions, which contained extensive confirmation of the plots planned by the OAK in Missouri, and a week later he sent additional materials.[32] In his cover letter to the supplemental records (addressed to Stanton), Rosecrans provided a brief history of his efforts to uncover the secret organization. "Soon after I assumed command of this Department," he explained, "circumstances came to my knowledge, inducing the belief, that we had in our midst a secret rebel oath bound organization." The group "conducted rebel correspondence, smuggled contraband of war and patronized boat and military store-house burners," all of which was "organized under rebel auspices." Colonel Sanderson's "well-organized and systematic operations by confidential agents . . . gradually developed the facts" of the existence of the organization over much of the North. Rosecrans reminded Stanton that he had "alluded to" the existence of the secret organization "in various dispatches . . . as early as the 10th of March." He outlined the findings of Sanderson's detectives and noted that Governors Brough and Morton and General Carrington had developed information that was "fully confirmatory" of what Sanderson had found. The organization intended to cause "mischief to the National Government," he concluded, "and while many of its members mean only to be anti-Lincoln, or anti-abolition, many others go further and require a wholesome application of retribution and preventive justice."[33]

Carrington, in Indianapolis, received Holt's instructions and set to work. He gleefully communicated to Richard W. Thompson, "I am now preparing for the President a whole history of the secret societies for the public. I am going to go back to the last *legislature* and make something that will *tell*."[34] Carrington forwarded a twenty-three page report outlining his investigations since late 1862, along with copies of reports from the invaluable spy Felix G. Stidger and copies of reports he himself had forwarded to the War Department over the previous two years. Stidger's reports "show consistently and fairly the character & operations of Col. W.A. Bowles, a man who should be the first tried before the military commission, if these cases are to be dealt with by that court." Bowles's arrest "would assure conviction, and he would have no sympathy," he advised. The "peace party," as he termed the antiwar wing of the Democratic Party, was "crumbling" and the secret organization had been demoralized due to the exposures to date; however, it was still alive and strong enough to create disturbances in the West. Indeed, it was "issuing new signs & signals." He added that he had still not received any financial assistance from the War Department for his investigations, which had employed "numerous persons." The $5,000 in secret-service funds that General Hovey had just received was paying for Hovey's current investigations and would not pay off Carrington's outstanding expenses.[35]

Carrington's latest report was a review of nearly two years of investigations and provided new details. He named the "principle agents" for securing habeas corpus hearings in state courts for soldiers to escape military service, as well as spreading the secret organization among soldiers, in late 1862. In reviewing the Morgan County incident of late January 1863, he noted that local people blew horns as warning signals to alert others to the presence of cavalry sent to arrest deserters. In April 1863, Carrington assembled a bipartisan group of Indiana's federal and state officials and influential private citizens, including Governor Morton and both U.S. senators, and informed the "loyal" Democrats present that if they did not wish to be controlled by the KGC, they would need to cooperate with federal authorities "to put [it] down . . . as disloyal and dangerous." Otherwise, the army would crush any outbreak. He obtained the agreement of the Democrats in attendance, he reported. Most intriguingly, Carrington put forward an explanation for the failure of an uprising during the Morgan raid of July 1863, quoting Bowles as saying:

> "the exposure of the Ritual [of the KGC, published in Indianapolis newspapers in April 1863] had demoralized the order, so that they knew not whom to trust, and that his [Bowles's] messenger to Morgan was rudely treated; that, otherwise, they would have drawn arms as minute men, *but would have joined Morgan.*" He also claimed that "Capt Hines, of Morgan's staff, was at his house, a week before they crossed the river, to consult as to his cooperation, and that of the K.G.C.s."

This information from Bowles's lips probably derived from discussions the conspirator had with either or both of Carrington's spies, Coffin and Stidger. Carrington outlined the revival of the KGC in Indiana under the new name, OAK, in the fall of 1863; its renaming as the Sons of Liberty, in May 1864; and Vallandigham's overall leadership of the body. He reported that meetings of Sons of Liberty leadership occurred simultaneous with the Democratic National Convention and had been discussed by convention delegates, some of whom "looked to the contingency of their presenting a communication to that convention." He quoted a speech made by H. H. Dodd to Indiana's grand council of his plans for a national organization to contest the authority of the Lincoln administration by force and to take control of the Democratic Party or break from it. Carrington provided details on the failed August 16 uprising at Indianapolis, downplaying the threat by stating that the day "passed with very feeble efforts at disorder, the number assembling at Indianapolis not exceeding 1,100." The plot had collapsed when "property holders and conservative men" of the Democratic Party "themselves warned the authorities" of the planned uprising. Nevertheless, the order was still active in pushing "for an armistice, and recognition of the South, or the re-establishment of the Union with slavery."[36]

Holt waited impatiently for receipt of materials from Kentucky headquarters regarding the secret organization uncovered there. He pressed Burbridge to finish a report and send it on to him.[37] More days passed, but nothing arrived from Kentucky. Showing the urgency of the matter, Stanton himself ordered Burbridge to send the "testimony asked for by the Judge Advocate General . . . at once."[38] The holdup was with Lieutenant Colonel Fairleigh at Louisville. Duly prodded, Fairleigh dashed off a brief report to district headquarters that was then forwarded to the War Department, which Holt received only on October 3. Accompanying it were copies of records of the organization seized during leaders' arrests, as well as copies of reports filed by Stidger. Conspirators had planned an uprising, but it was foiled by timely arrests, Fairleigh wrote. "Our own employees—detectives" could testify that it had a military organization and that "strenuous exertions and large donations [were] made to procure arms and other munitions of war." However, he hinted that getting members of the organization to testify to these facts would be difficult. They would be loath to turn "state's evidence," he wrote.[39]

Joseph Holt quickly scoured the reports, drawing bits and pieces from here and there and reassembling them into a composite portrait of the national threat posed by the conspiracy. He drew most heavily from materials provided by Sanderson and Rosecrans but paraphrased Carrington's report extensively. Fairleigh's report, arriving late, did not significantly influence Holt's final product.

Holt addressed his report, a distillation of the work of intelligence officers, to Stanton and dated it October 8. He first noted, drawing directly from Carrington's report, that military authorities had known about the existence of secret treasonable organizations for "more than a year." They were affiliated with the Southern rebels and were chiefly military in their character. Breaking down his report into eight chapters, he first addressed the origins of the secret organizations. Echoing Carrington's (mistaken) understanding, Holt asserted that the first appearances of the organization in the Northwest occurred in 1862 and under a variety of names. However, the main organizational name was the KGC. Due to "partial exposure" in the summer and fall of 1863, the organization reemerged as the OAK under the leadership of Phineas C. Wright and later Clement L. Vallandigham. Drawing from the evidence gathered by Sanderson and Rosecrans, he noted that rebel General Sterling Price and Charles L. Hunt were the leaders of the organization in Missouri. He also reported (based on Sanderson's understanding) that Vallandigham had formed the OAK with connivance with rebel officials while the Ohioan was in exile in the South. It changed its signs and rituals in the spring of 1864 when military authorities in Indiana learned of them. It took on the new name the Sons of Liberty. Drawing on the reports, Holt emphasized the continuity from the KGC to the OAK through to the Sons of Liberty. He described the structure of the organization, from top governance by the supreme council through state grand councils to county and township temples. He named Wright as the first supreme commander of the OAK, succeeded by Vallandigham, and assisted by various state grand commanders such as Robert Holloway of Illinois, Hunt of Missouri, H. H. Dodd of Indiana, and others. Holt made no mention of earlier KGC leadership and George Bickley, as neither Carrington nor Rosecrans provided details about him. He described in detail the rituals and oaths of the organizations, voicing astonishment that their view of society's hierarchy—an "ascending scale of humanity"—justified the "whole theory of human bondage": that the strong should enslave the weak. The rituals explicitly espoused state sovereignty ideology, and leaders such as Dodd and Lambdin P. Milligan enunciated such views in public and private speeches in Indiana. Holt borrowed from the Carrington and Rosecrans reports to draw estimates of the size of the secret organization. He credited as probably accurate Vallandigham's estimate of five hundred thousand members made in his Dayton, Ohio, speech on his return to the United States in June. The organization worked hard to arm members during the "revolutionary movement" in the summer of 1863. He noted, echoing Carrington, that had Vallandigham been arrested by military authority on his return to Ohio, arms hidden near Windsor, Canada, would have been put into the hands of the membership to "place the order upon a war footing and prepare it for aggressive movements." Holt listed eleven specific purposes of the organization, ranging from cooperation with the rebels-in-arms to aiding soldiers to desert and resisting the draft and circulating disloyal and treasonable publications throughout the North. Assassination and murder were among their "fiendish" goals. He highlighted plans to kill African American soldiers in Kentucky, assassinate detectives who had infiltrated the secret organization, and stealthily murder U.S. Army officers and soldiers whenever possible. The Charleston, Illinois, riot of March 1864 had been a premeditated "murderous assault" on soldiers. The establishment of a Northwestern confederacy was also noted. "Hating New England, and jealous of her influence and resources," members pressed measures to break up the Union and separate from the Northeast. Holt listed nine categories of "witnesses" who supplied information on the conspiracy, ranging from "shrewd detectives" working for military commanders, rebel soldiers and prisoners of war who had disclosed information, U.S. Army deserters, members and officers of the organization (e.g., Hunt, Dunn, and Smith) who confessed, anonymous informants, to grand jury witnesses. In conclusion, Holt warned that the organization was still busy plotting against the government in order to aid the rebellion.[40]

On receipt, Stanton promptly put Holt's report in publication for wide dissemination. The Republican Party printed large numbers of the report in pamphlet form and newspapers published it in its entirety. The report helped Lincoln in his November reelection effort. It is not clear whether Holt intended his report to be a campaign document, but it was put to that use. It disclosed facts and names that probably were not meant to be disseminated publicly. He named two of the spies who provided important information on the secret organization, the rebel soldier Mary M. (or Ann) Pitman and Felix Stidger. Holt called Pitman a "reliable witness" and praised Stidger for his "rare fidelity."[41] Again, as when Morton secured Stanton's permission to publish Carrington's report in July, politics trumped good practices. By the time of its publication, however, Stidger had already appeared as a witness in the military-commission trial of Dodd in Indianapolis, and his identity as a spy had been splashed across the pages of newspapers from coast to coast.[42]

The *Philo Parsons* Plot and Price's Invasion of Missouri

As Holt assembled his compilation for Stanton and Hovey made preparations to begin the military trial of Dodd in Indianapolis, dramatic events occurred on the northern frontier. In the evening of September 17, Lieutenant Colonel Hill, received a visit from a rebel soldier from across the river in Windsor. The soldier, Maurice Langhorn, reported that "some of the officers of the U.S. Steamer Michigan had been tampered with." Jacob Thompson, commissioner and chief agent of the Confederate government sent to Canada to coordinate efforts with conspirators in the Northern states, planned an attempt by rebel forces, with the assistance of some of the *Michigan's* men, to seize the warship, then anchored near Johnson's Island. The rebels believed that, with the sole warship on the Great Lakes in their hands, they would have "control of the lakes for a couple of months, and would levy contributions on all the lake cities," Langhorn said. Seizure of the *Michigan* would also facilitate the release of rebel officers imprisoned in the Johnson's Island prison camp, the target of numerous rebel plots. That night, Hill sent a telegram to the commander of the naval ship, Captain John C. Carter, alerting him to the plot, noting that officers and crew may have been bribed. Carter acknowledged receipt and replied, "All ready. Cannot be true in relation to the officers or men." Langhorn returned to Detroit the following evening, the eighteenth, to tell Hill that he was to join the rebel force in the plot but would beg off at the last moment. He gave additional details that the force would embark on a small steamboat, the *Philo Parsons*, which regularly carried passengers across the lake between Detroit and Sandusky, when the boat made its regular stop en route at Malden, on the Canadian side. Hill shared the update with Carter and stepped out of his office to walk down to the Detroit docks to examine the *Philo Parsons*. He decided to let the plot proceed, reasoning that the vessel was too small to constitute a threat to shipping on the lakes or to cities and towns on shore. He further concluded, "These plots are being constantly made here. We had the information about this one, and the question was whether it would not be better to let it proceed, and make an example in this case, if the information really amounted to anything." The rebels carried on with their plan and on September 20 a group of them boarded at Malden and shortly afterward seized the vessel, steamed toward Sandusky, encountered another small steamer, and, after seizing it and dropping its passengers and crew on an island, proceeded to within sight of the USS *Michigan,* their objective. However, the rebel crew mutinied at the last minute and the *Philo Parsons* turned back; the rebels scuttled the other small steamer in Canadian waters and half sunk it. Hill expressed disappointment that Carter, having the fastest ship on the lakes, had failed to overtake and capture the *Philo Parsons* and the rebels. But, he surmised, the multiplicity of plots and rumors of plots on the lakes made it "hard to discriminate between those having some reality and those purely fabrications."[43]

Langhorn had provided Hill with information on the rebel agent in Sandusky attempting to bribe the officers and crew of the USS *Michigan.* Plans to seize the warship had commenced months before. Major C. H. Cole of the Confederate army had taken up residence at Sandusky to work on land to assist the lake-borne party in the attack. Alerted by Hill, Captain Carter arrested Cole and others and held them at Johnson's Island. The commandant of the prison camp notified departmental headquarters at Columbus, who in turn alerted the War Department about the attempted attack. Newspapers instantly reported the news of the hijacking of the vessels and the attempt on Johnson's Island. Alarmed and fearing a general attack, Secretary Stanton ordered Heintzelman to go to Johnson's Island to prepare its defenses and call on Governor Brough to mobilize state militia.[44] Stanton also dispatched General Dix from New York City and Major General Ethan Allen Hitchcock, the commissioner for the exchange of prisoners, to assist.[45] But no grand assault took place.

Shortly afterward, Langhorn again visited Hill in Detroit to inform him that an immediate attempt to seize the warship would not be made, as Jacob Thompson and the rest of the rebel plotters involved had left Windsor. Hill provided Washington with information about his informant. Langhorn, he wrote, had served faithfully in the rebel service since the beginning of the war, had been wounded three times, "but that owing to injustice done him by Mr. [Judah] Benjamin, Acting Secy. of War, in not advancing him, he has left the South, and now entertains the most bitter enmity to the Southern cause." Hill suggested that Langhorn should be paid for his services, adding that "he has offered himself as a detective in Canada." He asked that Stanton approve the appointment.[46] Hill ordered Langhorn to travel to Washington to meet with War Department officials. Langhorn asked for no money, but Hill knew that he was broke and could use cash. Stanton met with him and paid him $500 for his information in the *Philo Parsons* affair. Hill continued to employ him in spying on the rebels in Windsor and elsewhere in Canada.[47] Langhorn's valuable information had compromised a serious rebel plot, and the newly recruited double agent would later play a role in other investigations.

Elsewhere, hundreds of miles to the west, a mounted rebel army under General Sterling Price rode northward through Arkansas and invaded Missouri in mid-September with the goal of seizing the state in advance of federal elections. Rosecrans, having long been warned by his spies to expect an invasion, was nonetheless short of troops. His meager forces were scattered over thousands of square miles. Price's army rolled over small federal garrisons in southeastern Missouri and advanced to within forty miles of a weakly defended Saint Louis. Rosecrans reported that he expected Price's forces to "arm the O.A.K in the state wherever he can."[48] Rosecrans informed Governor Yates that "Price's soldiers boast of having large supplies of arms, and that he is to be strongly reinforced from Illinois. I feel confident that he can't get any decent white man from that state who is a real citizen."[49] In actuality, however, the invasion force was poorly armed, had few arms to supply to rebel sympathizers who rallied to the invaders, and Price failed to realize how close he was to seizing both Saint Louis and later the state capital, Jefferson City. The invasion petered out in late October after federal troops attacked and drove the rebels southward out of the state.[50]

Still other events kept military authorities on their toes and concerned for the safety of the region. At the end of September, military authorities in Indiana accidentally captured one of the leaders of the Confederate effort to release the prisoners of war at Camp Douglas, in Chicago, and foment an uprising during the Democratic convention. Major John Breckinridge Castleman had joined Captain Hines in the Chicago expedition. When the local leaders of the secret organization got cold feet at the last minute and backed out of their plans to rise, Hines, Castleman, and a handful of Confederate soldiers slipped out of the city and holed up in southern Illinois to recruit a new force. The rebel soldiers scattered to different towns, with Castleman and ten rebels stationed at Marshall, in Clark County, Illinois. Sent by Hines to meet at nearby Sullivan, Indiana, with men "who were trusted by Hines and me" led by Andy Humphreys, Castleman and two fellow soldiers encountered local vigilantes on the road who mistook them for horse thieves. Though they made an effort to destroy or hide their papers and belongings and gave false names, their captors found on them a map of Camp Douglas, a memorandum book with William Bowles's and Horace Heffren's names in it, and vials of a fluid later identified as the incendiary chemical Greek Fire. Sent to Indianapolis and held in a military prison, the captives could not at first be identified by officers there but were suspected to be "rebel emissaries."[51] Days passed before military authorities learned Castleman's real identity from his mother and sister, who came up from Kentucky and visited him in prison. However, authorities still did not know what exactly he was up to; they vaguely suspected him of being a spy or part of another plot to attack Johnson's Island.[52]

Heintzelman Out, Hooker In

During this time the War Department made changes in the command of the Northern Department. The general's relations with Governor Brough at Columbus had become severely strained. The War Department ordered key officers on Heintzelman's staff be reassigned or mustered out of the service for reportedly "speaking disrespectfully of the President and not supporting the measures of the Govt." The general recorded in his diary that he "could scarcely believe it." Speaking to Brough, who boarded at the same hotel, the governor

> acknowledged that he had been acting the spy and informer. In Aug.
> he was in Washington and saw the Sec. and told him, that [Major]
> Johnson was not in favor of negro soldiers and other matters,
> but told the Sec. not to act on his information but to enquire for
> himself. . . . The Governor also acknowledged that he listens to our
> conversation at the dinner table. As long as he sits there we can't
> speak on public affairs.[53]

Relations between Heintzelman and Brough deteriorated. The general wrote "a long letter" to Secretary Stanton to defend his staff officers but worried that his language in the letter was intemperate. He conferred with U.S. Senator John Sherman, then in Columbus, about the matter. "Gov Brough," he summarized, "has made a mistake this time. Several persons have written to Sec Stanton about it. A speaker the last night mentioned openly to the assemblage [Brough's] mistress being turned out, in the night from one of the principal hotels in their town. This of a man who only a few days since spoke to me of the immoralities of my staff."[54] The next day he wrote, "I am the only person at the dinner table [who] speaks to Gov. Brough and I do only on account of my position. His whole manner shows he feels it."[55] However much Heintzelman believed himself in the right in the matter, Brough was the governor of a politically important state, had won election by a huge majority, and was not a person to cross. In such a situation, Washington authorities sided with the political leader, who could rally voters to the president.[56] A few days later Heintzelman noticed a short article in a Cincinnati Republican newspaper that Major General Joseph Hooker was to command the Northern Department. "Am I relieved?" he wondered. The next day, burning with anger, he recorded his emotions in his journal: "I have not been radical enough— won't arrest people without orders—will not take the responsibility of doing what Mr. Stanton would not do without Mr. Lincoln's orders. They can't make me a radical[.] I will do what I think best for the country and not for a party. I have served my country too long to now commence to serve a party."[57]

The newspaper reports were true. The next morning a staff officer reported to Heintzelman that Hooker was in the hotel. The War Department had not extended the courtesy of advanced notice to expect a replacement. The two comrades-in-arms from their days in the Army of the Potomac met cordially over breakfast, where Hooker presented his orders assuming command of the department. "It is about as nice a piece of petty spite as I have seen for a long time. Can a great man be guilty of such a bitterness?" Heintzelman fumed.[58]

That day he arranged his papers and closed up his office. "I feel quite relieved having got rid of the Dept," he wrote. Everyone he encountered voiced surprise at the news. "I believe my administration gave satisfaction to all the gentlem[e]n. The Governor and his special friends I do not count amongst them." Among his last acts in command was to write to Halleck "informing him what General Carrington did to expose these secret organizations. I wished him to have the credit he deserves, particularly as he was relieved so unceremoniously."[59] Indeed, Heintzelman's letter spoke glowingly of Carrington's services. "Soon after my arrival here to take command," he wrote, "I was informed from the War Dept of recent organizations then forming in some of the States of my command and instructing [me] to try and ferret them out."

> I placed the papers in the hands of BG H.B. Carrington . . . ,
> through whom I have been enabled to keep the War Dept fully
> informed of the measures being taken by the disloyal. Through
> his energy perserverance [sic] and good judgement I am indebted
> for all the information I have been able to transmit. Through this
> information they obtained and the measures taken in consequence
> thereof we are indebted mainly to being saved from the horrors of
> civil war in these state[s]. I cannot be relieved from the duties of

this Dept without putting on record my testimony in Genl Carrington's favor.[60]

After departing Columbus, the general continued to mull over the circumstances of his dismissal. "Gov Brough is no doubt at the bottom of the whole
and moving cause . . . he no doubt reported me as being intimate with copperheads." However, he believed himself blameless on that score. "The inter-
course I had with copperheads and Democrats gave a great deal of information
as to [their] views and feelings and the conservative course." He congratulated
himself that "I preserved I have no doubt . . . the country from civil war."[61]

"Fighting Joe" Hooker, another battle-wizened veteran commander, arro-
gant, ambitious, prone to intrigues and making enemies, former commander
of the Army of the Potomac, now had no army to command but had to con-
tend with the embers of a dangerously restive region. Stanton's instructions
ordered him first to secure the prisoners of war in the department. "You are
aware," he wrote, "that repeated efforts have been made by rebels in Canada
to liberate these prisoners, and, although unsuccessful hitherto, they will no
doubt be repeated." He was to guard against surprise attacks from both the
north and the Ohio River to the south, which "will also require attention."
The secretary ordered him to visit the cities and state capitals in the departments to gather information:

> Apprehensions have been entertained by the Governors of some
> of the States in your Department that organized bodies have been
> formed for the purpose of resisting the draft or preventing its
> enforcement by force of arms. You will employ your diligence in
> ascertaining whether these apprehensions are well founded or not,
> and will adopt such precautionary measures as may be necessary to
> meet the emergency.[62]

Key to Hooker's success would be his employment of the intelligence resources
of his new command. The War Department ordered that his headquarters
be shifted to Cincinnati, no doubt in reaction to the political squabble that
ended Heintzelman and Brough's working relationship.[63]

Instantly on his arrival in the Old Northwest, Hooker faced reports of
insurrection in Crawford and Orange Counties, in southern Indiana. Initial
reports from authorities characterized the actions of the five hundred armed
men involved as an uprising, and Indiana Legion militia units quickly mobi-
lized to subdue it. Troops captured about thirty of the "rioters" and extracted
confessions and information from them. Hooker traveled to Indianapolis to

meet with state officials and military commanders.[64] Reports also spoke of thousands of arms being smuggled into the state to equip the ranks of the secret organization in northeastern Indiana. The deputy provost marshal of Huntington County reported "positive information" that disloyalists had purchased eighteen thousand rifles in Canada, which were being shipped secretly to Fort Wayne and Huntington for distribution.[65] Indiana commanders alerted counterparts in Ohio to watch shipping through Toledo. Hooker ordered all vessels along the Lake Erie coast searched, the USS *Michigan* assisting in the sweep. On shore, army soldiers searched canal shipping, warehouses, and railroad depots and cars but failed to find the contraband arms.[66] Hovey and others briefed him on the then ongoing Dodd trial, the evidentiary backbone of which came from army intelligence efforts, and the extent and threat posed by the secret organization active in the state and region. Hooker received reports from army spies sent into the Seventh Congressional District of western Indiana by the Provost Marshal General's Bureau to ascertain the threat of insurrection there.[67] Hooker agreed to Carrington's request to allow drafted men to go home to vote in state elections to bolster Union turnout.[68] Carrington continued his energetic efforts to ferret out the secret organization, which had gone to ground during the treason trials but had not disappeared. In early November he prepared a long report showing that the Sons of Liberty, thanks to the ongoing military-commission trials now thoroughly exposed, had been succeeded by what was called the Star Organization. "All Sons of Liberty are to be accredited as members," he reported, but the previous organization was to be denounced to provide "cover" for the new iteration. The new organization, headquartered in New York City, sported emblems, rituals, ranks, and signals. "Women as well as men may wear this star," he noted, and the group empowered them to warn of attempts to arrest their husbands. Bowles, Humphreys, Milligan, and John C. Walker were the four generals of Indiana, though three of them were in military custody and under trial. "If Lincoln is elected by soldier's votes, the whole will be treated as illegal and void, and the Democracy will appeal to force."[69] He alerted Joseph Holt to his latest discovery, adding, "I make no assertions without proof."[70] General Hovey spent $25,000 seized from bounty jumpers and brokers and employed it to run a "strong detective force in different parts of the state" as well as to pay off Carrington's intelligence expenses from previous months.[71] The War Department forwarded information that rebels planned more attacks from Canada, and political leaders in neighboring states continued to voice fears of violence.[72] During the fall elections of 1864, military authorities throughout the Old Northwest continued their efforts to collect information on suspected activities.[73] The focus of attention again turned to Chicago's sprawling prisoner-of-war facility, Camp Douglas.

Uncovering the Second Plot to Attack Camp Douglas

In September, after the Democratic National Convention at Chicago, Lieutenant Colonel Hill at Detroit continued to share information from Major George Young with Colonel Sweet. Hill was upset. The rebel double agent Young, now back in Windsor, had made meeting appointments but had "failed to keep them." Nevertheless, other sources informed him that "between twenty and eighty of the rebel officers who went to Chicago have returned to Canada."[74] The rebels were again planning mischief. By this time Sweet had experienced a conversion. Before the convention he had dismissed reports of unrest and threats of uprising and played down the possibility of attack on the prison camp. However, the arrival of General Heintzelman in Chicago to oversee defenses, along with the reliable information shared with him by Hill, appear to have made him more alert to the threat. Consequently, Sweet now stepped up his detective operations to watch suspected Chicago persons. He had the "names[,] descriptions of persons, localities, and data enough, in regard to the Sons of Liberty in this city and state," he reported, so that it would not be "difficult, to shadow officers and prominent men, in their movements for the next sixty days should the government deem it advisable." He estimated that a force of four or five detectives could do the job but that they should not be hired from the Chicago city police department, which was then controlled by a Democratic administration. His detective expenses to date had not been heavy, as he had been using funds dedicated to running the prison camp. But he could not continue to pay their expenses in this way beyond the end of the month and suggested that, "if the government desires to follow this affair up," he should have $2,000 to "pay board bills, hotel bills, transportation," and other expenses. Or, he suggested, "if the govt has experienced and trusted men now in its employ the whole affair [could] be turned over to them."[75] Moreover, the recent *Philo Parsons* attack in Lake Erie to free the rebel officers on Johnson's Island had Camp Douglas connections. Sweet reported both to Colonel Hoffman, who oversaw federal prison camps, and to General Paine that on September 19, "simultaneous with the seizure of the steamboats Parsons and Island Queen," his detectives discovered a "plot . . . on the part of prisoners of war here to make a concerted, and combined attempt to overcome the guards and escape at sundown." At a signal, four to five hundred prisoners working in the garrison square were to seize the camp ordnance office, where "considerable ammunition, and about 2000 muskets" were stored, while the rest of the approximately eight thousand prisoners were to rise up against the guard.[76] Sweet explained that the draft was scheduled for that day and that the prisoners, who were "restive and inventive to an uncommon degree of late," "presumed largely on an outbreak, which they believed had or would occur in opposition to its enforcement." He added, "I determined to let them make the effort and punish them in the act, and made dispositions accordingly—[the prisoners] suspected as much, and failed to carry out their designs."[77]

Despite quelling a mass-breakout attempt, Sweet's action in using his Prison Fund to hire detectives ran into censure from a penny-pinching Hoffman. The bureaucrat ordered Sweet not to pay detectives' accounts from the Prison Fund: "until it is submitted to this office for approval, the account must be accompanied by a report stating the service rendered." He later wrote, "Detectives will not be employed at Camp Douglas without the approbation of this Office." In reply, Sweet explained that after a similar breakout attempt, his predecessor, Brigadier General Orme, had obtained authority to hire detectives in January. Only a month before, when Hoffman had visited Chicago, Sweet had informed him that he paid detectives from the Prison Fund and Hoffman had allowed it. Sweet noted that he had first hired detectives in July and had continuously employed them until September 29, when Hoffman's telegrams arrived. He had no other funds with which to pay detectives and should Hoffman insist on prohibiting such use of the Prison Fund he would have no detectives. Sweet added that "the employment of these detectives has not been without important results." The detectives had disclosed the plot on September 19 by "restless[,] uneasy and inventive" prisoners to break out, which was foiled by the guard. The breakout would probably have been successful had not the detectives learned of it. The detectives had also furnished

> the existence[,] names of officers and influential men[,] workings,
> and ultimate designs of the order of "Sons of Liberty" in this city and
> state; a treasonable organization having for its main object, the suc-
> cess of the rebellion, and overthrow of the Government of the United
> States and incident to its main object, engaged in furnishing facilities
> to prisoners of war to escape, and plotting schemes for them to rise
> at a future day, overpower the guard, be armed and give aid to an
> intended insurrection among the inhabitants of this and other states.

The sympathizers in Chicago who wished to aid the prisoners to break out "number thousands," he added, and "the imployment [sic] of competent detectives, especially during the next sixty or ninety days, is not only desirable, but a failure to employ them would be to disregard the suggestions of ordinary prudence." He asked for funds and permission to hire two detectives for the next three months.[78] The two men fired on September 29 had detected, he explained, "the channels and nature of communications between persons in this city, and prisoners of war in the camp with a view to the escape of such prisoners, in being themselves placed in communication with prisoners of war, as rebel agents, by which information was received of an organization on the part of the prisoners to escape."[79]

Sweet's detectives also worked in Chicago and learned of other plots. He forwarded to Paine's headquarters a statement made on September 26 by a seaman who shipped on the Great Lakes that the rebels intended to use two steamers under construction in a shipyard at St. Catharines, in Canada, in further attempts on prison camps and raids on lake cities. Apprised of the report, General Hooker ordered further investigation. The report circulated widely in various military headquarters around the Great Lakes.[80] During October several rumors of rebel raids across the Great Lakes kept military commanders poised for action.[81] As well, worrisome draft violence occurred in downstate Illinois. Sweet expressed his fears to Washington about the weakness of his garrison against the size of the prison camp population. He had only eight hundred troops to guard eight thousand prisoners, he explained, and he expected another two to four thousand prisoners shortly. His concern arose from the likelihood of a "disturbance in this city growing out of the organizations known to be hostile to the Government."[82]

In reply to Sweet's explanations for the need for detectives, Hoffman offered a bureaucratic gloss. General Orme, he wrote, had requested permission to employ detectives at Camp Douglas, "and not [for] their employment in the city of Chicago for political purposes, or purposes remotely connected with the security of prisoners at Camp Douglas." Both Orme and he doubted that detectives would be effective, "but I left it to his discretion whether to employ them or not, 'for the present,' and at "reasonable rates." Orme ultimately decided that he did not need them and did not hire detectives. "And there the authority terminated," noted Hoffman. General Paine's authority extended only to the post of Chicago and not over Camp Douglas, he officiously explained, and if Paine had ordered the hiring of detectives, it "should be paid for by the Quartermaster Dept not from the Prison Fund." He offered a concession, however: if Sweet could show that detectives had prevented escapes at Camp Douglas, or helped to suppress a prisoner revolt, he would recommend payment from the Prison Fund. However, from his vantage point in Washington, Hoffman asserted that the recent attempt to break out had been stopped by sentinels. "It is clear that no intimation of the contemplated movement was given by the detectives, which shows that they knew little of what was transpiring at Camp Douglas." He concluded, "If the services of detectives are necessary in Chicago to expose the acts of disloyal persons, or to discover the haunts and designs of secret organizations inimical to the government, application for authority to employ them should be made to the General Commanding the Department, as such service is a matter beyond the province of this office."[83] However, two weeks later he wired Sweet a terse message informing him that the War Department approved the accounts of the detectives through September and would pay them.[84] He sent another message that Sweet could pay prisoners to obtain information about escape attempts.[85] It is probable that other officials in the War Department more alive to the threats of riot and revolution than saving money overrode Hoffman's bureaucratic objections. On October 21, Sweet had written to Hoffman to ask instructions about private persons who attempted to aid or encouraged prisoners to escape. On November 7, Hoffman's assistant belatedly replied that Secretary Stanton ordered that anyone found aiding or encouraging prisoners to escape was to be arrested and tried by military commission.[86] By then, events had already overtaken Hoffman's bureaucratic money concerns.

Though Hoffman refused to allow the use of the Prison Fund to pay for detectives, evidence shows that detectives continued to report to Sweet after September 29. One was a Chicago resident named Thomas H. Keefe, who held minor government positions in the city. Army pay records indicate that Keefe worked as a detective in September, October, and November at Camp Douglas and in Chicago. Sweet at this time had no secret-service funds at his disposal.[87] Another person who supplied information was a Chicago homeopathic physician named I. Winslow Ayer. During the summer, Ayer had visited Governor Yates to warn him of a conspiracy then brewing in the city. Yates encouraged him to continue to gather information and passed him to Paine for instructions. Ayer provided information to Colonel Sweet regularly.[88] Maurice Langhorn, the rebel officer who had turned against the Confederacy, also visited Chicago in late October, apparently sent by Secretary Stanton.[89] Another detective, "William Jones" (Willis Bledsoe), who worked for army headquarters at St. Louis, also tailed a Missourian through Illinois to the city.[90]

In the first days of November, Sweet's headquarters received intimations of covert activities in the city. Detectives informed him that large numbers of men from southern Illinois were arriving at the train stations and circulating in the streets. He also learned—probably from Langhorn—that rebel officers had been recognized lodging in city hotels. On November 3, the day that Hoffman wired him to permit the use of prisoners at Camp Douglas to detect escape attempts, garrison commanders and detective Keefe spoke to a prisoner in the camp named John T. Shanks, a Texan who had fought with John Hunt Morgan's cavalry raiders and who had been captured in Ohio during the great raid. He had worked odd jobs in Camp Douglas for camp officers. Colonel Lewis C. Skinner, commander of the 15th Veterans Reserve Corps Regiment, part of the camp garrison, asked Shanks to learn about the assembly of rebel officers in the city hotels. He agreed and that same night left the camp and went to the house of a prominent Chicago attorney and judge, Buckner S. Morris, where he spoke with the judge's wife, Mary. Army authorities knew that the Morrises aided rebel prisoners to escape from the camp; Judge Morris was also a leader in the secret organization in the city. Shanks told Mrs. Morris that he was an escaped prisoner from the camp and sought their help. In conversation, Judge Morris mentioned that there probably would be an uprising in the city. Shanks reported this information to commanders and later in the evening of November 6 went to the Richmond House hotel in the city. There he saw and spoke to George St. Leger Grenfell, a British army officer who had served with Confederate forces since 1862, most prominently as adjutant to General John Hunt Morgan during Morgan's raids in Kentucky, Indiana, and Ohio. Shanks saw other rebel officers in the hotel, some of whom divulged the plot to him: there was to be an uprising at Camp Douglas and in the city on election day, November 8. Rebel soldiers and local members of the secret organization planned to attack the camp. The freed prisoners, armed with weapons furnished by the local organization and seized from the camp armory, were then to rampage through the city.[91]

That evening, alerted to the plot, Sweet dispatched a messenger by rail to Brigadier General John Cook, the new commander of the District of Illinois, at Springfield, who had recently replaced Paine. He did not send his message by wire because, he explained, "I am not entirely sure of the telegraph." He reported, "the city is filling up with suspicious characters, some of whom are known to be escaped prisoners, and others who were here from Canada during the Chicago Convention," in August. He supplied Shanks's and Langhorn's information that Grenfell and other rebel officers were in the city. Most notably, Captain Thomas Henry Hines, the leader of the failed attempt in August, was known to be in the city. He reminded Cook that he had only eight hundred troops to guard more than ten times that number of prisoners. He meant to act on the information before the rebel officers and local conspirators initiated their plans. "I am certainly not justified in waiting to take risks," he added, "and mean to arrest these officers, if possible, before morning. The head gone we can manage the body." He also planned to arrest "two or three prominent citizens who are connected with these officers, of which the proof is ample." He asked for reinforcements, as the arrests "may cause much excitement" in the city. He was going to act without awaiting orders from district or departmental commanders. "I regret that I am not able to consult with you on my proposed action before acting without letting an opportunity pass which may never again occur, and which, so passing, would leave us open to much danger."[92]

Sweet acted promptly. During the early morning hours of Monday, November 7—the day before the state and presidential elections in Chicago and Illinois—VRC troops from the camp garrison made arrests of several rebel officers staying at the Richmond House hotel, as well as Vincent Marmaduke, a pro-Confederate Missouri politician and brother of Confederate General John S. Marmaduke, Judge Morris, Charles Walsh, and others. Sweet identified Walsh as a brigadier general in the Sons of Liberty organization, and Morris as its treasurer.[93] Efforts to capture Hines, the leader of the plot, failed, as that resourceful officer managed to escape and hide in the Cincinnati house of his conspirator friends, Samuel and Mary Thomas. Once the arrests had been made and the prisoners safely housed inside Camp Douglas, Sweet felt secure enough to telegraph Cook the results. In turn, Cook telegraphed departmental headquarters at Cincinnati that Sweet had arrested "noted conspirators" but was "apprehensive" that Camp Douglas would be attacked on election night. Cook had no troops to send to Sweet's aid and asked Hooker to send troops "to his instant relief and support." He added that "large quantities of arms and important papers have been seized."[94] At the time, Hooker was at Sandusky, Ohio, inspecting defenses of Johnson's Island.[95]

As the city awoke on the morning of November 7 to learn of the arrests of rebel soldiers and prominent citizens, a wave of excitement rushed through the population. Crowds met in the streets to learn what was happening. People gathered outside newspaper offices to read the latest reports posted in the windows. Along with the arrests, troops seized quantities of arms and ammunition at Charles Walsh's home near Camp Douglas. Troops also found arms at Walsh's city livery stables. An Indiana soldier serving in one of the VRC units guarding Camp Douglas wrote to his hometown newspaper about the excitement in Chicago on the discovery of the astonishing plot:

> That the plot was real I know, for I formed one of the party that
> seized 450 splendid, serviceable revolvers, and 250 double barreled
> shot guns, all loaded with heavy charges, the latter with "buck and

ball [cartridges preloaded with a musket ball and buckshot]," at the house of Charley Walsh. I knew nothing of the business upon which our party was bound, and was greatly astonished when I saw revealed to me the evidences of a conspiracy, the like of which is seldom met in these modern times. And he, who for months had been collecting this arsenal of arms and ammunition for the fell purpose of murdering my comrades and myself, and of subjecting the people of this State to the tender mercies of the desperadoes we guard. What of him? I never saw a man more confounded. It is always thus with men engaged in enterprises of vast sin and peril. His house is scarcely eighty rods from this camp, and was selected on account of its proximity to Lake Michigan, whence a force could easily reach Chicago from Canada, and also on account of its contiguity to the Camp. . . . He was evidently a man in opulent circumstances, and was surrounded by a young, blooming and affectionate family.[96]

With the captured arms, military commanders equipped an ad hoc militia cavalry force of about 250 men to patrol the streets of the city in the following days. Commanders seized additional records of the secret organization in the city, "some of them valuable," at the home of the secretary of the local "temple." The records, wrote Sweet, showed "the intents and purposes of the organization."[97] Amid the excitement, Chicago voters went to the polls and cast their ballots.

Evidence shows that officers from other army posts supplied important assistance and information to Sweet that assisted his investigations before and immediately after he made the arrests. On November 7, Colonel Adoniram J. Warner at Indianapolis forwarded information to him on Grenfell collected by a detective named C. J. Brown, suggesting that Sweet solicited the information when Grenfell's presence in Chicago became known.[98] Significantly, Colonel Joseph J. Darr, Jr., Sanderson's successor at St. Louis, sent a statement by detective "Jones" (Bledsoe), who had reported the presence of Vincent Marmaduke in Chicago. Sweet thanked Darr for "Jones's" statement, adding that it was "true." "If Marmaduke told him of the plot, even in general terms," wrote Sweet, "he will be an important witness in the trial. There is evidence enough against all the others except Marmaduke."[99] "Jones" had been loaned to General Cook at Springfield to help to expose plots to release prisoners in Illinois camps. Cook had sent him to Chicago, where he identified some of the plotters who otherwise might have escaped.[100] In response to Sweet's request for reinforcements, Indianapolis commanders quickly sent four companies of VRC troops to Chicago "to assist in preventing the anticipated outbreak."[101] Captain William James, the district provost marshal for Chicago in the Provost Marshal General's Bureau, provided important assistance in the crisis. James and his officers arrested ninety-six persons in the city on November 7, 8, 9, and 10. He interrogated many of them and reported that their intent was to liberate the prisoners as well as to vote illegally in the election.[102] Military officers also arrested southern Illinois men who had managed to escape the Chicago dragnets. The deputy provost marshal at Joliet, south of Chicago, arrested thirteen men from Fayette County who gave statements of their participation in the plot. The men admitted to have been paid railroad fare by local leaders of the secret organization from Vandalia.[103]

Throughout the crisis at Chicago, Sweet had received no money to pay for detectives. After the excitement died down, he explained to Cincinnati headquarters that during the frantic two-week period starting November 1 he had had to acquire clothing for disguises, hire hacks, express wagons, and messengers, rent hotel rooms, and purchase other services "in order to detect the presence . . . of rebel officers and leaders, [and] arrest and procure evidence against them." He could not take vouchers and receipts without revealing his operations. He had paid $492 out of his own pocket, as he lacked secret-service funds.[104]

The breakup of the second plot to attack Camp Douglas and release the prisoners was the product of intelligence sharing by Sweet and other commanders in the region. Using that information, Sweet struck first to head off the attempt. The result was a signal victory for army intelligence efforts in the Old Northwest. The Chicago arrests resulted in another military-commission trial of conspirators, which commenced in Cincinnati shortly after the end of the Indianapolis trials, in January 1865.

The Breakup of Military-Intelligence Operations

Army intelligence operations continued into 1865, during the Cincinnati treason trial. General Carrington continued to track the remnants of secret organizations, reporting that a successor organization had been formed from the wreckage of the Sons of Liberty. Detroit officers continued to send detectives into Canada to spy on the rebels who congregated over the border amid numerous reports of plots to attack the northern frontier. In November 1864 the significant plot hatched by Confederate agents to burn New York City failed, primarily because the incendiary chemical they employed failed to react properly.[105] Heightened fears of attacks on urban centers prompted continued espionage activities.

Intelligence operations in the Department of the Missouri continued apace. Sanderson had died in October 1864, and Stanton and Grant removed Rosecrans from command in December,[106] but the intelligence machine continued to hum along. After the failed rebel invasion of Missouri by Sterling Price and the collapse of the major threat of an OAK uprising, the department focused much of its attention on the boatburner scourge and the smuggling operations on the western rivers. Headquarters devoted several detectives to finding out their schemes.[107] Minnesota Colonel James H. Baker, formerly post commander at St. Louis and closely involved in intelligence operations in the department, succeeded Colonel Darr as the departmental provost and vigorously pursued the incendiaries.[108] Baker assigned the department's most effective detective and spy, Lawrence A. Hudson, also known as "Edward F. Hoffman," to an elaborate operation to infiltrate the genteel circles of Louisville, Kentucky, high society to learn of rebel operations.[109] Baker also sent him into Arkansas to try to infiltrate the remnants of Sterling Price's rebel army.[110] Commanders also loaned their detectives to neighboring commands that needed intelligence services; detectives went to Wisconsin, Iowa, and Illinois at the request of commanders in those states. In this way detectives assisted in the infiltration of the Chicago conspiracy in November 1864.[111] Like Carrington, Baker reported that a successor organization to the OAK/Sons of Liberty had emerged.[112]

Significantly, based partly on information received from detectives, department commanders had decided to try the Missouri conspirators (Hunt et al.) by military commission and had begun the process of bringing them to trial in late 1864 through early 1865.[113] However, in February 1865, Joseph Holt wrote to the judge advocate for the department that he had conferred with Secretary Stanton on the subject of continued military trials. Stanton ordered that the trials be postponed until after the final disposition of the Indianapolis cases, "now held under advisement here," was completed.[114] In the end, no military trials of the Missouri conspirators occurred. Authorities took a different tack and in June 1865, federal law enforcement officials brought the Ohio civilians implicated in the *Philo Parsons* plot to trial in the U.S. district court in Cleveland. The court acquitted the defendants, insignificant players caught up in the larger plot, of conspiracy.[115]

With the surrender of the various Confederate armies, in April and May 1865, began the precipitous dissolution of the largely volunteer U.S. Army. Soldiers clamored to return home. Likewise, intelligence bureaus developed by the various military commands in the Old Northwest states broke up. Most commanders quickly dismissed their detectives. With the draft no longer needed, and no longer intent on hunting down deserters and draft dodgers or piercing the networks that harbored and protected them, the Provost Marshal General's Bureau dismissed its bureaucracies and summarily fired their special agents. Federal authorities wanted to quickly minimize the expensive war apparatus and begin to pay off massive war debts. Colonel Baker of the Department of the Missouri, with the largest staff of detectives in the West, got a jump on the rest and began to shed his expensive detective force early in January 1865. "Detectives must earn their money," he warned. "They must show some results to this office, or they will be summarily dropped."[116] He pared his staff in half and later whittled away still more detectives. Eventually he ordered his district commanders to fire all civilian detectives and to use enlisted men in their place.[117] Soon, the detective networks that had aided in breaking up the secret conspiracies in the North disappeared. J. B. Devoe, the naval officer seconded to the army at Rosecrans's request, returned to the Navy and worked under orders of the commander of the Mississippi squadron to intercept rebel communications and secret supply lines, as well as to stop rebel efforts to destroy shipping on the river. He reported that the rebels employed "females of beauty" to entice information out of federal officers; "*They generally hesitate at no sacrifice* to accomplish their designs," he reported, using Victorian innuendo to describe the use of sex to gather information.[118]

Detectives and spies once employed by the federal government reverted to their peacetime occupations. Soldiers who doubled as detectives mustered out of their units and returned to farms and shops. Henry S. Zumro continued in his medical practice and later moved to Nebraska amid harassment from Lambdin P. Milligan and others on whom he had spied. George Goodale focused on his theatrical criticism. Sargent Parker Coffin moved to Peru, Indiana, and operated a hotel. Later, his widow applied for a federal veteran's pension based on her husband's important service as a spy. Her application failed because the War Department had no record of his regular enlistment.[119] Other civilian detectives failed to receive pensions for dangerous service in the war. The federal government and postwar Americans swept the memory of espionage and deception under the carpet. Henry B. Carrington, the Indiana spymaster, returned to the command of the 18th U.S. Infantry and shortly after the war led part of the regiment to Wyoming Territory. In late 1866, Sioux Indians ambushed and killed the entire command of subordinate Captain William J. Fetterman. The army blamed Carrington and relieved him of command. Carrington's military career ended, and in later years he became an historian of George Washington's battles of the American Revolution, undertaking the then pioneering step of consulting original archives of the British and French governments in his research. He died in 1912.

Felix G. Stidger, however, returned briefly to federal employ as a detective. In December 1864 he wrote to Joseph Holt that he had been promised "ample remuneration" by military commanders for testifying in the Indianapolis trial. He was "liable to assassination" and wanted sufficient funds to set up in business in a city "large enough to be in some safety to myself."[120] Holt was greatly impressed by Stidger's testimony in the Indianapolis trial and lobbied Stanton on his behalf. At "extraordinary personal risk and with a rare fidelity," he wrote, Stidger had infiltrated the secret conspiracy and testified in the trials of Dodd, Bowles, and Milligan; his testimony was instrumental in their convictions. Holt recommended that Stidger receive additional pay for his "exceptional" services.[121] In April the War Department forwarded Holt's letter to Carrington, still in Indianapolis, for his input. The general warmly praised the spy's services, highlighted the dangers he undertook, and affirmed that "his labors mainly furnished the basis for, and ensured the success of the Union cause in Indiana; and the government could well compensate him liberally." Noting the prejudices of the day, Carrington wrote that Stidger deserved extraordinary solicitude now that his "special capacity" as a spy had become widely known, as even "Union men decline to loan him money to engage in business, because he had been a '*Detective*.'"[122] Convinced, the War Department sent Stidger a check for $10,000. He wrote in acknowledgment: "I am glad to know that my Government thus far appreciates my services, and the great risks incurred by me. I am at its command for any future service I can render."[123] Based on the recommendations of Colonels Darr and Baker, the War Department also rewarded Mary M. Pitman with $5,000 "in view of the manifest importance and value of her disclosures and services."[124]

The Lincoln assassination and subsequent investigations prompted officials in Washington to call Stidger back into secret service. Serving under Colonel Lafayette C. Baker in the War Department's in-house detective branch, he traveled widely and reported on the existence of secret organizations in Baltimore and Cincinnati and horse contract frauds in Ohio. Ambitious for promotion, he informed Holt of Baker's extravagant personal spending, hinted at corruption, and suggested that should his boss be removed from the command of the bureau, he himself would like the position.[125] Though Baker soon lost his job amid extortion charges, Stidger did not gain it. His second stint as detective did not last long. The Kentuckian was shortly in private business in Indianapolis.[126]

As the years passed, life was not kind to Felix G. Stidger. Divorce, unemployment, and poverty plagued him in later years. Living in Chicago, he resorted to selling illicit birth control information by mail using the alias "Madame A. M. Josephine." Arrested and indicted by federal authorities in 1902 for violating federal laws prohibiting distribution of such information in the mails, he pled guilty and was fined one hundred dollars in federal court.[127] Newspapers reported that Stidger showed the prosecuting U.S. attorney a copy of Joseph Holt's October 8, 1864, report, which named Stidger as a government detective. "This man rendered good service to the cause of the Union at a critical time," the attorney told the judge, and asked the judge to suspend the fine. Federal Judge Christian C. Kohlsaat agreed. Stidger's important service to the country had been remembered. His story as a spy in the service of the Union soon spread across the land. Interviewed by reporters, he told of being employed to infiltrate the secret organization in Kentucky and Indiana.[128] The *New York Times* reported that "while his story might seem exaggerated, he could prove it by persons yet living or by authentic documentary evidence."[129] The following year, as if to prove his point, Stidger wrote and privately published his memoir, *Treason History of the Order of Sons of Liberty*, an extraordinarily detailed and surprisingly accurate account of his service as a spy. Newspapers later noted that Stidger resided in Chicago in poverty and "fear of assassination."[130] He died May 11, 1908, in Chicago, "scarcely known by his neighbors," and was buried in a small ceremony supervised by a local post of the Grand Army of the Republic.[131]

The Scope of Army Intelligence Efforts

In the first months of the war, residents in the Old Northwest observed unsettling developments in their communities. Many reported to authorities their fears of a growing undercurrent of opposition to government and the war effort. Local efforts by both state and federal law enforcement officials detected the growth of secret groups intent on obstructing the mobilization of the federal war effort, but failed to effectively curb the groups' activities. Gradually, in an unsystematic, ad hoc fashion, the U.S. Army intervened. Owing to their need to suppress desertion, draft dodging, and disaffection within the ranks of the army itself, beginning in 1863 commanders in the region created small detective bureaus to counteract mounting resistance. In a few months these intelligence operations succeeded in detecting combinations intent on obstructing the draft and attacking prisoner-of-war camps. In 1864 army spies succeeded in infiltrating the leadership of the secret organizations and learning their plans, which included collaboration with Confederate troops and continued attacks on prison camps to free Confederate soldiers and foment insurrection in the North. Effective intelligence aided commanders in the North when they had few troops available to quell uprisings. Arrests of the leaders of the conspiracies led to military-commission trials and convictions for treason. As the war ended and the army demobilized, commanders disbanded their military-intelligence operations.

To date, these intelligence operations have been hidden from the view of historians of the Civil War. Nevertheless, all told, the army's network of spies, detectives, and informers was substantial. In 1871, when Lambdin P. Milligan's civil suit for illegal arrest came to trial in a U.S. federal court in Indianapolis, Henry Carrington testified as a defense witness. "I had," he stated, "probably two or three thousand men, employed in the Western States, that were in communication with me, for the purpose of furnishing information, and every railroad train that came to [Indianapolis] I knew exactly how many men were on it, and their character."[132] While sounding bombastic, could the numbers of hired civilian and soldier detectives, special agents of the Provost Marshal General's Bureau, Union League informers, store clerks who reported on gun sales, railroad agents who supplied information on travelers or told of heavy shipments of arms and ammunition, local postmasters who allowed military officers to intercept and open U.S. mails, and telegraph operators scattered in the cities and small towns of the multistate region who wired information to headquarters be added together, the number of eyes and ears that contributed to U.S. Army surveillance in the Northwest would be substantial. This hidden army played a significant part in defending the United States from widespread conspiracy in the North during the American Civil War.

The Evidence of Conspiracy

THE FOCUS of this study has been the rise of army intelligence operations in the Midwest during the Civil War. We have seen how the U.S. Army reacted to widespread desertion, draft resistance, and obstruction of the war effort by conducting military surveillance and information-gathering efforts. This study has delved deeply into the archives to uncover records showing commanders' grave fears of organized resistance to the government and the threat of insurrection in the region. The records demonstrate clearly that army officers, along with the regional political leaders with whom they cooperated, credited the existence of secret organizations whose members conspired against the federal government. While officers at headquarters occasionally scoffed at some of the reports they received, commanders believed the information their detectives, informers, and spies supplied regarding the plans of the conspirators and the wide scope of the threat. They came to believe that the conspiracies posed a threat to order in the Northwest, the integrity of the army as an efficient fighting force, and, indeed, the survival of the national Union. Most notably, Major General William Rosecrans, neither a shrinking violet nor an alarmist, expressed his concern that the secret groups posed an existential threat to the United States. On June 22, 1864, he warned President

Lincoln that the conspiracies aimed at the "overthrow of the existing national Government & the dismemberment of this nation."[1] Two days later, he used similar language to Governor Andrew Curtin of Pennsylvania to warn of a "powerful and widely extended politico revolutionary organization working nominally within the Democratic party for the overthrow of our Government and [to] dismember the nation."[2] It is for these reasons that commanders took steps to counter the perceived threat by developing their capacity to spy on the conspiracy's leaders, infiltrate their circles, and gather information about their plans.

The extensive surviving documentation in the National Archives and other records and manuscript repositories of intelligence operations in the North shows the earnestness of military commanders' beliefs in the imminent threat of disorder and insurrection. Contrary to long-standing assertions by some historians (most notably Frank L. Klement), no documentation exists to show that these officers and the political leaders with whom they communicated conspired to fabricate or concoct evidence or magnified the threat of revolution or insurrection in the Northwest beyond what their intelligence reports showed. Given the vast quantities of surviving army records, the fact that there is no documentation of collusion among Republican politicians and "politically-minded" army commanders to "smear" their Democratic rivals with cooked-up evidence of treasonous plots must warn historians to be wary of such assertions. The fact that political leaders in Washington, DC, and the Northwest, together with the commanding generals in the region, resorted to military arrests of the leading conspirators and military commission trials just before the fall elections of 1864 in a clear-cut effort to make political capital of the conspirators' machinations does not alter the fact that the army had collected copious evidence of conspiracy and treason. That political leaders chose not to try the conspirators in civilian courts speaks to their lack of faith in the judicial process at a time of national emergency rather than the lack of evidence of conspiracy.

Notwithstanding the vast quantities of army records documenting military operations in the Old Northwest, there are significant gaps in archival holdings. For example, records of the District of Indiana in 1863 and much of 1864 covering Colonel Henry Carrington's first tenure as commander, followed by those of Generals Hascall and Willcox and Colonel Simonson, do not survive in the National Archives. Nor do records survive of General Nathan C. McLean, commander of the Provost Marshal General's Department in the Department of the Ohio under General Burnside. McLean oversaw the department's intelligence operations in 1863 and the employment of military commissions to try violators of General Orders 38. These are gaping holes in the archival record that hinder the historian's efforts to piece together the army's intelligence efforts. But those records that do survive paint a clear picture of a military bureaucracy that carefully observed conditions in the regions around them and forthrightly documented their thoughts in letters, reports, and telegrams. They neither deluded themselves about the reality of widespread opposition nor crafted "cock-and-bull" fictions about nonexistent plots. They knew what was happening in their geographical commands, and the documentary record they created is a reliable gauge of their observations.

While the surviving archival records of the army are our best sources for documenting the existence of conspiracy and secret organizations in the North during the Civil War, they are not the only records available. Some scattered records of the secret groups and individuals active in them survive. Like most criminal conspiracies, the secret organizations kept records but covered their tracks when threatened. Spy Felix Stidger reported to his handlers that organizational records of the group in Indiana could be found in Harrison H. Dodd's warehouse in Indianapolis and suggested that the army delay any raid on the building until regular reports on membership numbers arrived from around the state.[3] During the conspiracy trials in Indianapolis and Cincinnati in late 1864 and 1865, witnesses who had been members testified that members wrote each other in code, or employed couriers to convey verbal instructions. Members destroyed organizational records in times of peril. For example, William M. Harrison, secretary of the grand council in Indiana, first of the OAK and then the Sons of Liberty, testified, "I destroyed all the papers belonging to the organization after the exposition in the Indianapolis *Journal*," referring to Carrington's exposé published on July 30, 1864.[4]

Despite Harrison's efforts to destroy records, the army found and seized a number of records at Dodd's warehouse in August after discovery of a large shipment of revolvers and ammunition from New York. Governor Morton had many of the records published in the *Indianapolis Daily Journal*, filling the paper's columns with compromising letters of Democratic leaders. Other records seized during raids or arrests included KGC records found when military authorities arrested George Bickley in New Albany, Indiana, in July 1863; records seized during the arrests of persons involved in the Camp Chase plot, in November 1863; those belonging to OAK organizer Phineas C. Wright found in the private safe in Detroit and published in Detroit newspapers in September 1864; and correspondence of Clement L. Vallandigham intercepted by postal and military authorities. In addition, army detectives and spies managed to carry records out of the secret groups, some of which survive. See, for example, the records that Stidger spirited into Carrington's hands in early June 1864, which formed the newspaper exposé that spooked Harrison into torching organizational papers. Likewise, organizational records smuggled out by Rosecrans's and Sanderson's detectives appeared in the Saint Louis newspaper exposé. Other records dropped into the hands of military investigators quite by accident, as in the case of the incriminating records found in Indiana congressman Daniel W. Voorhees's vacant Terre Haute office by his landlord, who notified local military authorities. Many of these records survive in the files at the National Archives, most notably in military-commission trial case files; however, many originals have disappeared or were destroyed through careless handling.

Very few records pertaining to the secret organizations survive in private manuscript collections. Again, it is likely that the persons who were implicated in criminal conspiracy destroyed documentary evidence of their wartime misdeeds. Nonetheless, some unsanitized tidbits can be found. For example, an OAK fundraising letter from Secretary William M. Harrison from February 1864 survives in the papers of Indiana legislator Charles B. Lasselle at the Indiana State Library.[5] As noted in this study, army detectives reported that Lasselle attended OAK and Sons of Liberty meetings in that year. Also, the James A. McMaster Papers at the University of Notre Dame Archives show that influential New York journalist to have been active in the OAK and the Sons of Liberty in 1863 and 1864. Indeed, the papers show that he became a close friend of the Confederate agent Emile Longuemare, who served as an intermediary between the Confederate government and the conspirators in the North as secretary of the OAK and Sons of Liberty supreme councils. Later, while based in New York City, Longuemare participated in the failed plot to torch the city in November 1864. He escaped to Mexico and communed with other Confederate exiles. McMaster also corresponded with Confederate commissioners in Canada who ran secret agents into Northern states and coordinated plans with the secret groups. He obtained instructions from them about how to respond to George McClellan's repudiation of the Democratic peace plank, in September 1864.[6] He also warned James W. Singleton, the Democratic candidate for governor of Illinois in that year (whose campaign was bankrolled by Confederate secret-service funds) that the "more scheming and politic of the leading officers of the 'Sons,'" meaning fellow Sons of Liberty members, might jump ship and join forces with McClellan.[7] The paucity of manuscripts pertaining to the internal functions of the secret societies is paralleled by the relative scarcity of papers of both leading and rank-and-file antiwar Democrats from the Civil War–era North. In 1864, nearly half of

Northern voters—Democrats—voted against Lincoln's reelection. Yet surviving papers of Northern antiwar Democrats in manuscript repositories are few. It would seem that while the descendants of northern pro-war Democrats and Republicans cherished and preserved the letters of soldiers and noncombatants who supported the great patriotic struggle to suppress the rebellion, those whose ancestors opposed the Union war effort and the Lincoln administration have not preserved their families' papers.

While few records pertaining to the secret organizations survive in private manuscript collections, numerous confessions of membership in them reside in government records. We have seen that men confessed to membership in secret societies in Ohio in the fall of 1861, both in so-called mutual protection groups and the KGC. Men also confessed to KGC membership in Ohio and Indiana in 1862 and 1863. These confessions occurred on the witness stand in judicial hearings, before grand juries, and while under military arrest. Soldiers admitted to joining secret groups in affidavits and courts martial. As well, military commission trials produced a long string of admissions of membership in the KGC, OAK, and Sons of Liberty. These confessions provide important details about how these societies functioned, their numerical strength, and how their members understood their goals and plans. Military authorities placed great store in these statements and built their prosecutorial efforts on them.

A good example of a confession of membership in a secret society is that of James Ingraham Adams, a self-described forty-seven-year-old "poor man" from Bond County, Illinois, a rural area about twenty-five miles northeast of Saint Louis. Military authorities from the Department of the Missouri arrested him on July 4, 1864, and held him for months in the Gratiot Street Prison in Saint Louis. In late September he made a statement that was transcribed and survives in the National Archives. In it, he described being "duped" into joining the Sons of Liberty, which previously was known in his locale as the Knights of Light. Adams named both the men who recruited him into the organization and the state leadership, and described their rituals of initiation, meetings, and occasional drills. Leaders spoke, he said, of a planned "outbreak" in the North by the organization's many thousands of members who would "take up arms & create a revolution, against the Government of the United States, or as they said—the Administration." They also spoke of carving out a "Northwestern Hemisphere." The organization communicated with Confederate rebels and guerrillas, he said, and he himself corresponded with the notorious guerrilla Clingman. He also revealed that a rebel officer had resided at the home of the local Bond County leader and assisted in coordinating plans. Apprised of Adams's confession in early October, the commander of the District of Illinois requested departmental commanders to arrest and try the local leaders whom Adams named, but Major Henry L. Burnett, who was then busy prosecuting the Indiana conspirators, demurred.[8] Confessions such as these convinced military commanders around the Northwest of the seriousness of the threat of insurrection from secret conspiratorial organizations.

Finally, another category of sources that provides important evidence of conspiracy in the North during the Civil War is the body of postwar memoirs of ex-Confederate soldiers who had served the rebel cause in secret operations in the North and Canada. As secret agents, these soldiers crisscrossed the Northern states to communicate between rebel officials stationed in Canada and the South. They also conferred with Midwestern sympathizers who planned efforts to assist the rebellion. These veterans were proud of fighting for what had become for many ex-Confederates the glorious Lost Cause memory and wrote candidly of their collaboration with Northern conspirators to raise insurrections to aid the rebellion. Captain Thomas Henry Hines, a leader of rebel secret operations, described in broad terms the Northwestern Conspiracy. Writing in the 1880s, he carefully avoided naming important collaborators who were then active in Northern state and federal politics. However, his deputy, Major John Breckinridge Castleman, writing decades later, identified the Cincinnati couple who sheltered Hines during his escape after the second collapsed effort to release prisoners at Camp Douglas, in Chicago. He also recounted the help that Indiana politician Bayless W. Hanna offered when he himself was captured in Indiana after being mistaken for a horse thief. Confederate soldiers John W. Headley and Emile Longuemare wrote of their participation with Northerners in the plots to set New York City ablaze, while Adam R. Johnson described his operations as a Confederate guerrilla in collaboration with Northern sympathizers on the Ohio River border. Finally, George "Lightning" Ellsworth wrote of his participation under Hines in the two Camp Douglas plots, as well as the assassination of army spy Robert L. Jeffries, who had infiltrated Hines's network in Kentucky. All these writers forthrightly described the participation of Northern collaborators, and their memoirs add significant detail to historians' understanding of conspiratorial movements in the North. These writings should not be dismissed.[9]

In conclusion, while most of the evidence of conspiracy and collaboration with the Confederate rebels in the North resides in the archives of the U.S. Army, a small number of private papers and memoirs exist to augment our understanding of events during the Civil War. It was a period the memory of which many in the North tried to sweep under the carpet. Many had been caught on the wrong side of history, which goes far to explain the paucity of surviving private sources to document embarrassing thoughts, wishes, and actions. The surviving government records in the National Archives that tell of military efforts to investigate and quell rampant unrest must guide historians' understanding of events in the Northwest during the war.

NOTES

Abbreviations in Notes

ALPL	Abraham Lincoln Presidential Library, Springfield, Illinois
E	Series or Entry number in record groups in National Archives
IHS	Indiana Historical Society
ISA	Indiana State Archives
ISL	Indiana State Library
LC	Library of Congress, Washington, DC
NARA	U.S. National Archives and Records Administration, Washington, DC
NARA-CP	NARA, College Park, Maryland
NARA-GLR	NARA, Provost Marshal General's Bureau Records
n.d.	no date
OHS	Ohio Historical Society
OPMTB	Gov. Oliver P. Morton Telegraph Books
OR	United States, War Department, *The War of the Rebellion: A Compilation of the Official Records of the Union and Confederate Armies*
ORN	United States, Naval War Records Office, *Official Records of the Union and Confederate Navies in the War of the Rebellion*
RG	record group
RIHS	Rhode Island Historical Society
SC	Small Collection
ser.	series

Introduction

1. See Edwin C. Fishel, "Military Intelligence, 1861–1863," *Studies in Intelligence* 10, nos. 3 and 4 (Summer–Fall 1966): 81–96, 69–93; Fishel, "The Mythology of Civil War Intelligence," *Civil War History* 10, no. 4 (December 1964): 344–67; Fishel, "Pinkerton and McClellan: Who Deceived Whom?" *Civil War History* 34, no. 2 (June 1988): 115–42; Fishel, *The Secret War for the Union: The Untold Story of Military Intelligence*

in the Civil War (Boston: Houghton Mifflin, 1996). Despite its title, the latter volume treats only intelligence operations in the Army of the Potomac. See also William B. Feis, *Grant's Secret Service: The Intelligence War from Belmont to Appomattox* (Lincoln: University of Nebraska Press, 2002); Feis, "'There Is a Bad Enemy in This City': Colonel William Truesdail's Army Police and the Occupation of Nashville, 1862–1863," *North and South* 8, no. 2 (March 2005): 35–45.

2. For a scholarly treatment of a woman spy in the Civil War, see Elizabeth R. Varon, *Southern Lady, Yankee Spy: The True Story of Elizabeth Van Lew, a Union Agent in the Heart of the Confederacy* (New York: Oxford University Press, 2003). The popular appetite for accounts of women as spies in the Civil War began long before the rebellion ended, with sensational newspaper stories feeding demand. During the war, actress Pauline Cushman toured and lectured on her experiences. Publishers quickly cranked out potboilers to satisfy demand, which has yet to be satisfied by a long line of books about women spies. See, for example, S. Emma E. Edmonds, *Nurse and Spy in the Union Army: The Adventures and Experiences of a Woman in Hospitals, Camps, and Battle-fields* (Hartford: W. S. Williams, 1865); Ann Blackman, *Wild Rose: Rose O'Neal Greenhow, Civil War Spy* (New York: Random House, 2005): William J. Christen, *Pauline Cushman: Spy of the Cumberland* (Roseville, MN: Edinborough, 2006).

3. General accounts of Civil War espionage include Nathan Miller, *Spying for America: The Hidden History of U.S. Intelligence* (New York: Marlow, 1989); Rhodri Jeffreys-Jones, *American Espionage: From Secret Service to CIA* (New York: Free Press, 1977); Jeffreys-Jones, *Cloak and Dollar: The History of American Secret Intelligence,* 2nd ed. (New Haven: Yale University Press, 2003); Christopher Andrew, *For the President's Eyes Only: Secret Intelligence and the American Presidency from Washington to Bush* (New York: Harper Collins, 1995). Potboilers and unreliable self-promoting memoirs include William Gilmore Beymer, *On Hazardous Service: Scouts and Spies of the Civil War* (New York: Harper, 1912; repr., Lincoln: University of Nebraska Press, 2003); Lafayette C. Baker, *History of the United States Secret Service* (Philadelphia: King and Baird, 1867); Allan Pinkerton, *The Spy of the Rebellion: Being a True Story of the Spy System of the United States Army during the Late Rebellion* (New York: G. W. Carlton, 1883).

4. Joan M. Jensen, *Army Surveillance in America, 1775–1980* (New Haven: Yale University Press, 1991), 21–28.

5. Kenneth M. Stampp, *Indiana Politics during the Civil War* (Indianapolis: Indiana Historical Bureau, 1949; repr., Indiana University Press, 1978), 241. Stampp incorporates text on Morton written by William Dudley Foulke, *Life of Oliver P. Morton, Including His Important Speeches,* 2 vols. (Indianapolis: Bowen-Merrill, 1899), 1:374.

6. Historian Robert H. Churchill writes of "Republican paranoia" and states, "Though members of the Sons of Liberty were conspiring against the Union in 1864, one must distinguish between the real details of the plot and representation thereof within the Republican imagination." See Churchill, *To Shake Their Guns in the Tyrant's Face: Libertarian Political Violence and the Origins of the Militia Movement* (Ann Arbor: University of Michigan Press, 2009), 315n18. See also Churchill, "Liberty, Conscription, and a Party Divided: The Sons of Liberty Conspiracy," *Prologue* 30, no. 4 (Winter 1998): 295–303.

7. See Frank L. Klement, *The Copperheads in the Middle West* (Chicago: University of Chicago Press, 1960); Klement, *Dark Lanterns: Secret Political Societies, Conspiracies, and Treason Trials in the Civil War* (Baton Rouge: Louisiana State University Press, 1984); Klement, *The Limits of Dissent: Clement L. Vallandigham and the Civil War* (Lexington: University Press of Kentucky, 1970; repr., Fordham University Press, 1998). A comprehensive bibliography of Klement's works can be found in Klement, *Lincoln's Critics: The Copperheads of the North,* ed. Steven K. Rogstad (Shippensburg, PA: White Mane, 1999), 239–51.

8. For examples of works that follow Klement's lead, see Hubert H. Wubben, *Civil War Iowa and the Copperhead Movement* (Ames: Iowa State University Press, 1980); Arnold M. Shankman, *The Pennsylvania Antiwar Movement, 1861–1865* (Rutherford, NJ: Fairleigh Dickinson University Press, 1980); Grace Palladino, *Another Civil War: Labor, Capital, and the State in the Anthracite Regions of Pennsylvania, 1840–1868* (Urbana: University of Illinois Press, 1990); Robert M. Sandow, *Deserter Country: Civil War Opposition in the Pennsylvania Appalachians* (New York: Fordham University Press, 2009); Jean H. Baker, *Affairs of Party: The Political Culture of Northern Democrats in the Mid-Nineteenth Century* (Ithaca: Cornell University Press, 1983; repr., Fordham University Press, 1998); Mark E. Neely, Jr., *The Fate of Liberty: Abraham Lincoln and Civil Liberties* (New York: Oxford University Press, 1991); Melinda Lawson, *Patriot Fires: Forging a New American Nationalism in the Civil War North* (Lawrence: University Press of Kansas, 2002); Adam I. P. Smith, *No Party Now: Politics in the Civil War North* (New York: Oxford University Press, 2006). Historian Jennifer L. Weber has partially challenged the Klement thesis by noting that significant evidence of conspiracy exists in archival records, but hedges her bets by suggesting that the argument is not "airtight." See Weber, *Copperheads: The Rise and Fall of Lincoln's Opponents in the North* (New York: Oxford University Press, 2006), 148. For a cogent assessment of Weber's differences and similarities to Klement's work, see Thomas E. Rodgers, "Copperheads or a Respectable Minority: Current Approaches to the Study of Civil War-Era Democrats," *Indiana Magazine of History* 109, no. 2 (June 2013): 114–46.

9. In a study of the 1864 presidential election, David E. Long correctly notes that Klement "is often errant" and his scholarship is "the product of a selective and biased reading of the evidence." Long highlights a significant error repeated over and over throughout Klement's corpus as symptomatic of the historian's sloppiness and tendentiousness. However, he buries his comment deep in an endnote, where few scholars have bothered to look. See David E. Long, *The Jewel of Liberty: Abraham Lincoln's Re-election and the End of Slavery* (Mechanicsburg, PA: Stackpole, 1994; repr., New York: Da Capo Press, 1997), 314–15n71.

10. Recent studies on the KGC have joined a body of scholarship that has focused on its filibustering activities in the South. See Mark A. Lause, *A Secret Society History of the Civil War* (Urbana: University of Illinois Press, 2011); David C. Keehn, *Knights of the Golden Circle: Secret Empire, Southern Secession, Civil War* (Baton Rouge: Louisiana State University Press, 2013). For older works, see C. A. Bridges, "The Knights of the Golden Circle: A Filibuster Fantasy," *Southwestern Historical Quarterly* 44, no. 1 (January 1941): 287–302; Ollinger Crenshaw, "The Knights of the Golden Circle: The Career of George Bickley," *American Historical Review* 47, no. 1 (October 1941): 23–50;

William H. Bell, "Knights of the Golden Circle: Its Organization and Activities in Texas Prior to the Civil War" (MA thesis, Texas College of Arts and Industries, 1965); Ray Sylvan Dunn, "The KGC in Texas, 1860–1861," *Southwestern Historical Quarterly* 70, no. 4 (April 1967): 543–73; Linda S. Hudson, "The Knights of the Golden Circle in Texas, 1858–1861: An Analysis of the First (Military) Degree Knights," in *The Seventh Star of the Confederacy: Texas during the Civil War*, ed. Kenneth W. Howell (Denton: University of North Texas Press, 2009): Keehn, "Strong Arm of Secession: The Knights of the Golden Circle in the Crisis of 1861," *North and South* 10, no. 6 (June 2008): 42–57. Research on the KGC should be seen as part of the growing scholarly interest in secret societies and male fraternal culture in nineteenth-century America. Examples of works in the field include Lynn Dumenil, *Freemasonry and American Culture, 1880–1930* (Princeton: Princeton University Press, 1984); Dorothy Ann Lipson, *Freemasonry in Federalist Connecticut, 1789–1835* (Princeton: Princeton University Press, 1977); Mark C. Carnes, *Secret Ritual and Manhood in Victorian America* (New Haven: Yale University Press, 1989); Mary Ann Clawson, *Constructing Brotherhood: Class, Gender, and Fraternalism* (Princeton: Princeton University Press, 1989); Jason A. Kaufman, *For the Common Good? American Civil Life and the Golden Age of Fraternity* (New York: Oxford University Press, 2002); Ami Pflugrad-Jackisch, "We Are All Brothers: Secret Fraternal Organizations and the Transformation of the White Male Political Culture in Antebellum Virginia" (PhD diss., State University of New York at Buffalo, 2005); Michael A. Halleran, *The Better Angels of Our Nature: Freemasonry in the American Civil War* (Tuscaloosa: University of Alabama Press, 2010).

Chapter 1

1. Billy Davis, *The Civil War Journal of Billy Davis: From Hopewell, Indiana, to Port Republic, Virginia,* ed. Richard S. Skidmore (Greencastle, IN: Nugget, 1989), 1.

2. The Amish; Mennonites; German Baptist Brethren, or "Dunkards"; and the Society of Friends, or "Quakers" were Christian groups known as peace churches who espoused nonresistance to violence. Their numbers were small and, except for the Quakers in eastern Indiana, did not have significant political influence among the mainstream political parties. See James O. Lehman and Steven M. Nolt, *Mennonites, Amish, and the American Civil War* (Baltimore: Johns Hopkins University Press, 2007); Jacquelyn S. Nelson, *Indiana Quakers Confront the Civil War* (Indianapolis: IHS, 1991).

3. I am guided by the analysis of federalist ideologies outlined in Michael Les Benedict, "Abraham Lincoln and Federalism," *Journal of the Abraham Lincoln Association* 10, no. 1 (1988): 1–45. Lincoln received over 1.8 million votes in the 1860 election, while Stephen Douglas received nearly 1.4 million and John Breckinridge received almost 850,000. Combined, the two Democratic candidates would have polled over 2.2 million votes. A fourth national candidate, John Bell of the Constitutional Union Party, received close to 600,000 votes, drawn heavily from pro-slavery, moderate ex-Whigs in the border states. See Michael F. Holt, *The Political Crisis of the 1850s* (New York: Wiley, 1978; repr., New York: Norton, 1983), 215–16; Sean Wilentz, *The Rise of American Democracy: Jefferson to Lincoln* (New York: Norton, 2005), 762–67.

4. *Huntington Indiana Herald,* January 9, 1861, quoting the *Huntington Democrat,* December 27, 1860.

5. For studies of crowd violence in the United States in the nineteenth century, see Paul A. Gilje, *Rioting in America* (Bloomington: Indiana University Press, 1996); David Grimsted, *American Mobbing, 1828–1861: Toward Civil War* (New York: Oxford University Press, 1998). For a study of violence against newspapers with special attention paid the Civil War era, see John Nerone, *Violence against the Press: Policing the Public Sphere in U.S. History* (New York: Oxford University Press, 1994). For a comprehensive study of newspaper violence in Indiana during the Civil War, see Stephen E. Towne, "Works of Indiscretion: Violence against the Democratic Press in Indiana during the Civil War," *Journalism History* 31, no. 3 (Fall 2005): 138–49.

6. Parker Earle and Charles Colby to Yates, April 21, 1861, and T. M. Seawell to Yates, April 23, 1861, both in box 2, folder 4, Yates Family Papers; Thomas A. Burgess to Oziah M. Hatch, April 27, 1861, box 2, folder 4, Oziah M. Hatch Papers, all in Abraham Lincoln Presidential Library, Springfield, Illinois (hereafter cited as Yates Family Papers, Hatch Papers, and ALPL respectively).

7. John Gilbert to Yates, July 29, 1861, box 3, folder 3, Yates Family Papers, ALPL.

8. William R. William, letters of June 6, June 7, and June 8, 1861, all in box 2, folder 7, Yates Family Papers, ALPL.

9. Thomas A. Burgess to Oziah M. Hatch, April 27, 1861, box 2, folder 4, Hatch Papers, ALPL.

10. John B. Perry to Yates, May 18, 1861, box 2, folder 6, Yates Family Papers, ALPL.

11. A. Clybourn to Yates, May 3, 1861, and David Davis to Yates, May 9, 1861, both in box 2, folder 5, Yates Family Papers, ALPL.

12. Orville Hickman Browning, *The Diary of Orville Hickman Browning,* vol. 1, *1850–1864,* ed. Theodore C. Pease and James G. Randall (Springfield: Illinois State Historical Library, 1925), 465, entry for April 22, 1861.

13. James M. West to Yates, August 2, 1861, box 3, folder 4, Yates Family Papers, ALPL.

14. J. M. Galbraith to Yates, August 4, 1861, box 3, folder 7, Yates Family Papers, ALPL.

15. Milo Jones to Yates, September 10, 1861, box 3, folder 9, Yates Family Papers, ALPL.

16. Lewis Hammach to Yates, August 20, 1861, box 3, folder 6, Yates Family Papers, ALPL. Previously, a Perry County correspondent reported on the secret movements of Dr. William E. Smith to Kentucky and that he was conferring with like-minded men and making treasonous speeches in the county, where he had influence among the illiterate. The writer suggested that the governor assign a detective to watch him. John B. Perry to Yates, May 18, 1861, box 2, folder 6, Yates Family Papers, ALPL.

17. J. A. Britterman to Yates, August 22, 1861, box 3, folder 6, Yates Family Papers, ALPL. For a study of Hancock County, see Susan Sessions Rugh, *Our Common Country: Family Farming, Culture, and Community in the Nineteenth-Century Midwest* (Bloomington: Indiana University Press, 2001), 110–13.

18. J. M. Kelly to Yates, October 6, 1861, box 1, folder 8, Richard Yates Papers, Mss. 232, Southern Illinois University-Carbondale Special Collections Research Center, Morris Library (hereafter cited as Yates Papers–SIUC).

19. See Parker Earle and Charles Colby to Yates, April 21, 1861, David Davis to Yates, May 9, 1861, John B. Perry to Yates, May 18, 1861, R. J. Wheatley to Yates, July 26, 1861, J. M. Galbraith to Yates, August 4, 1861, and Lewis Hammach to Yates, August 20, 186, all in Yates Family Papers, ALPL.

20. Richard Yates to J. I. McCawley, August 10, 1861, box 1, folder 9, Richard Yates Papers (Wabash College), Abraham Lincoln Presidential Library, Springfield, Illinois (hereafter cited as Wabash Yates Papers, ALPL).

21. Yates to John C. Frémont, August 6, 1861, box 3, folder 4, Yates Family Papers, ALPL.

22. See Ulysses S. Grant, *The Papers of Ulysses S. Grant*, ed. John Y. Simon, 32 vols. (Carbondale: Southern Illinois University Press, 1970), 3:117–20.

23. Ibid., 3:117–19. The original letter is found in the Ulysses S. Grant Collection, Chicago Historical Society. See also T. K. Kionka, *Key Command: Ulysses S. Grant's District of Cairo* (Columbia: University of Missouri Press, 2006), 149–50.

24. Charles G. Back to Lazarus Noble, May 29, 1861, Lawrence County Correspondence, box 16, Indiana Legion Records, Indiana State Archives, Commission on Public Records, Indianapolis (hereafter cited as ISA).

25. W. B. Squire to Governor Oliver P. Morton, June 25, 1861, Sullivan County Correspondence, box 27, Indiana Legion Records, ISA.

26. Union Bethell to Morton, July 8, 1861, Warrick County Correspondence, box 31, Indiana Legion Records, ISA.

27. David W. Voyles to Morton, July 20, 1861, Washington County Correspondence, box 32; William L. Carter to Morton, July 21, 1861, Harrison County Correspondence, box 10, both in Indiana Legion Records, ISA.

28. J. F. Duckwall to Lazarus Noble, August 3, 1861, Adjutant General of Indiana Records, A4017 024596, folder 11, ISA. The full text of the letter appears in Richard F. Nation and Stephen E. Towne, eds., *Indiana's War: The Civil War in Documents* (Athens: Ohio University Press, 2009), 127–28.

29. William C. Kise to Morton, August 6, 1861, 10th Indiana Volunteer Infantry Regiment Correspondence, ISA.

30. Samuel Lawson to [?], August 7, 1861, Harrison County Correspondence, box 10, Indiana Legion Records, ISA.

31. A. J. Axtell to [John H. Vajen], Quartermaster General of Indiana, August 13, 1861, Greene County Requisitions, box 9, Indiana Legion Records, ISA.

32. Charles G. Back to Lazarus Noble, September 25, 1861, Lawrence County Correspondence, box 16, Indiana Legion Records, ISA.

33. William C. Kise to Morton, August 6, 1861, 10th Indiana Volunteer Infantry Regiment Correspondence, ISA.

34. William Muir to Morton, August 17, 1861, Lawrence County Correspondence, box 16, Indiana Legion Records, ISA.

35. J. Mortimer Smith to Lazarus Noble, August 19, 1861, Vermillion County Correspondence, box 31, Indiana Legion Records, ISA.

36. E[phraim] Young to Morton, August 27, 1861, Oliver P. Morton Correspondence, ISA.

37. *La Porte Herald,* August 31, 1861, quoted in *Logansport Journal,* September 7, 1861. At this time, soldiers in La Porte arrested and forced persons suspected of rebel sympathy to take oaths of allegiance to the United States. On one expedition soldiers arrested a man for having a small flag featuring a palmetto tree, a serpent, and the words "Jeff. Davis." *La Porte Union,* n.d., reprinted in *Plymouth Marshall County Republican,* September 5, 1861. A La Porte man observed, "Secessionists are being hunted here like sheepkilling dogs. They tried one last week [Brain] and bound him over under $6000 bond,—nobody dared offer to bail him. Several wer[e] taken yesterday and let off by taking the oath of allegiance." D. Tyrrell to L. J. Brooks, September 2, 1861, Daniel Tyrrell Letters, Small Collection (hereafter cited as SC) 2702, William Henry Smith Library, Indiana Historical Society, Indianapolis (hereafter cited as IHS). Historians who have noted Brain's Indiana arrest have dismissed the episode as the workings of a mere charlatan and swindler. Historian Frank L. Klement writes, "excited LaPorte citizens [were] unable to distinguish between a fool and a traitor," and federal investigators found Brain to be merely an "'unmitigated scoundrel' and an idle babbler—a man of moronic nature and mischievous bent." Klement asserts that Brain's arrest "was offered for years as proof that agents of the Golden Circle were active in the Midwest." Klement, *Copperheads in the Middle West,* 138. See also G. R. Tredway, *Democratic Opposition to the Lincoln Administration in Indiana,* vol. 48, Indiana Historical Collections (Indianapolis: Indiana Historical Bureau, 1973), 113. Neither historian notes that after federal authorities released Brain, after six months' imprisonment, in 1862, on oath not to commit acts against the United States, he resumed an active career in the Confederate States Navy and secret operations in Canada. Brain (whose name often was incorrectly spelled Braine) commanded the operation that seized the steamer *Chesapeake* off the coast of Maine in 1863, killed an officer of the ship, and took the vessel into Canadian waters, where a U.S. Navy vessel captured the ship, thus precipitating a tense international dispute between the U.S. government and the government of Great Britain. Brain escaped. See Robin Winks, *Canada and the United States: The Civil War Years* (Baltimore: Johns Hopkins University Press, 1960), 244–63; Greg Marquis, *In Armageddon's Shadow: The Civil War and Canada's Maritime Provinces* (Halifax: Saint Mary's University; Montreal: McGill-Queen's University Press, 1998), 139ff. In 1864 military commanders in New York City received information that the crew who seized the *Chesapeake* were members of the KGC. See A. P. Howard to Gen. N. P. Banks, October 20, 1864, record group 393, pt. 1, Department of the East Records, E 1403, Letters Received, box 3, U.S. National Archives and Records Administration, Washington, DC (hereafter cited as NARA). Later he commanded vessels that captured ships in the Atlantic. In 1866 federal authorities located and arrested him in Brooklyn, New York, and held him for the murder of the officer of the *Chesapeake.* Seized also were records of a shadowy filibustering organization in which Brain was involved called the Knights of Arabia, which had designs on Haiti. However, after former Confederate naval authorities confirmed that Brain held a commission from the rebel government, authorities released him in 1869. Brain was reputed to have been the last rebel prisoner released. He returned to the South,

lectured on the history of the Confederate Navy and his own exploits, and swindled funds from Confederate veterans. He died in Florida in 1906. Contrary to Klement and Tredway, nothing in his subsequent career of piracy, fraud, and deception is inconsistent with Brain having been a conspirator and recruiter of rebel sympathizers in Indiana in 1861.

38. See John C. Brain records printed in United States, War Department, *The War of the Rebellion: A Compilation of the Official Records of the Union and Confederate Armies* (Washington, DC: Government Printing Office, 1897), ser. 2, vol. 2, 711–21 (hereafter cited as *OR*).

39. Sidney Keith to Morton, November 12, 1861, 46th Indiana Volunteer Infantry Regiment Correspondence, ISA. Another protested that Dr. White had been a "rabid sesessionist [*sic*] of our county and we have some pretty hard ones." John Crum to Morton, November 13, 1861, Medical Appointments Correspondence, Adjutant General of Indiana Records, ISA.

40. Morton to Assistant Secretary of War Thomas A. Scott, August 29, 1861. *OR*, ser. 1, vol. 4, 255.

41. Morton to Scott, August 31, 1861, in Gov. Oliver P. Morton Telegraph Books, vol. 1, 182–83, ISA (hereafter cited as OPMTB), reprinted in *OR*, ser. 3, vol. 1, 473–74; Wood Gray, *The Hidden Civil War: The Story of the Copperheads* (New York: Viking Press, 1942), 71. Fears of railroad sabotage were widespread during the war, and several reports of sabotage and attempts to burn bridges, obstruct trains, or run them off the rails appeared in the Indiana press. See *Logansport Journal*, April 27, 1861; *Richmond Broad Axe of Freedom*, October 5, 1861; *Indianapolis Daily Evening Gazette*, March 4, 1863; *Delphi Journal*, July 15, 1863; *Greencastle Putnam Republican Banner*, July 16, 1863; *Indianapolis Daily Evening Gazette*, September 3, 1863; *Columbia City Whitley County Republican*, n.d., reprinted in *Richmond Quaker City Telegram*, September 5, 1863.

42. *Rockville Parke County Republican*, August 7, 14, 1861.

43. Endorsed "Memorandum handed me by J. P. Usher on the 26th Nov 1861 (Opposition to the War and Lincoln's Administration)," in Lane-Elston Papers, M 180, IHS. The full text of the report is printed in Nation and Towne, *Indiana's War*, 173–77. In his book on Democratic opposition in Indiana, historian G. R. Tredway characterizes the mutual protection societies, or "MPs," as a distinctly different organization and unrelated to the Knights of the Golden Circle; the MPs "existed only in the imaginations of excited patriots." Tredway, *Democratic Opposition*, 113–14.

44. *Indianapolis Daily Journal*, December 30, 1861, January 1, 16, 29, 1862; *Indianapolis Daily State Sentinel*, December 31, 1861, January 3, 15, 17, 1862; *Terre Haute Daily Wabash Express*, January 3, 1862; *Sullivan Democrat*, January 9, 1862; *Rockville Parke County Republican*, February 5, 1862; *Marshall (IL) Flag of Our Nation*, February 7, 1862. For the original newspaper report by journalist Joseph K. C. Forrest that created the dispute about "strange stories" circulating during the Illinois State Constitutional Convention in 1862, see *Chicago Daily Tribune*, February 11, 1862. Forrest was a close political ally of Governor Yates. Klement erroneously asserts that U.S. Marshal David L. Phillips and Yates "apologized" to the members of the convention for the assertions. Both Phillips and Yates admitted that they possessed no tangible proof of

disloyalty, but that did not constitute an apology. See Klement, *Dark Lanterns*, 19. See also his accounts of the convention in Klement, *Copperheads in the Middle West*, 142–45; Klement, "Copperhead Secret Societies in Illinois during the Civil War," *Journal of the Illinois State Historical Society* 48, no. 2 (Summer 1955): 154–56. For an Ohio instance of Republican editors being duped, see *Cincinnati Daily Enquirer*, March 10, 11, and 13, 1862. For newspaper "hoaxes" in Michigan, see See Klement, *The Copperheads in the Middle West*, 140–41; Klement, *Dark Lanterns*, 17–18, Klement, "Franklin Pierce and the Treason Charges of 1861–1862," *Historian* 23, no. 4 (August 1961): 436–48; Klement, "The Hopkins Hoax and Golden Circle Rumors in Michigan, 1861–1862, *Michigan History* 47, no. 1 (March 1963): 1–14.

45. Laz Noble to Edward B. Allen, May 10, 1862, in Edward B. Allen Papers, SC 10, IHS. The Terre Haute Democrat was Bayless W. Hanna, who in the next year was arrested for disloyal speech. See *Indianapolis Daily Journal*, March 27, 1863. In 1864 he aided Confederate secret agent John Breckinridge Castleman when the latter was captured while on a mission to meet with Indiana conspirators. See Castleman, *Active Service* (Louisville: Courier-Journal Job Printing, 1917), 174–75, 207–8.

46. *Indianapolis Daily Journal*, June 19, 25, 1862; *Indianapolis Daily State Sentinel*, June 24, 1862. The *Sentinel* printed a reply from Brown County legislator James S. Hester that all men in the county were loyal and supported the suppression of the rebellion. Ten months later, however, Hester alluded privately to the existence of secret political organizations in Brown County, and wrote, "The first collision between the military and the citizens of any magnitude, will be the signal for a general uprising not only in this State but throughout the Northern States." Hester to Morton, April 23, 1863, RG 94, Records of the Adjutant General of the United States, E 159, Generals' Papers: General Ambrose E. Burnside Papers, NARA), reprinted in Nation and Towne, *Indiana's War*, 168.

47. Morton to Stanton, June 25, 1862, Oliver P. Morton Records, Letter Press Book vol. 1, 9–17, ISA, also in *OR*, ser. 3, vol. 2, 176–77, also in Nation and Towne, *Indiana's War*, 177–79.

48. James H. Lutgen to William Dennison, August 23, 1861, vol. 5, p. 105, ser. 147, Adjutant General of Ohio Records, Ohio State Archives, Ohio Historical Society, Columbus (hereafter cited as OHS). *Columbus Daily Ohio State Journal*, May 15, 20, 1861.

49. Wiley R. Johnston to Dennison, July 16, 1861, vol. 2, ser. 147, OHS.

50. Thomas P. Belt to Dennison, July 25, 1861, vol. 2, ser. 147, OHS; O. Bennett to Catharinius P. Buckingham, July 25, 1861, vol. 2, ser. 147, OHS.

51. C. D. Brooks to Buckingham, July 31, 1861, vol. 3, p. 120, ser. 147, OHS.

52. R. G. Andrews to Dennison, August 17, 1861, vol. 5, p. 149, ser. 147, OHS.

53. William H. Trimble to Buckingham, July 28, 1861, vol. 3, p. 99; James H. Lutgen to Dennison, August 23, 1861, vol. 5, p. 105; Lutgen to Buckingham, September 11, 1861, vol. 7, p. 206; Nathan A. Reed to [?], August 22, 1861, vol. 5, p. 137; L. M. Conklin to Buckingham, September 2, 1861, vol. 6, p. 159, all in ser. 147, OHS.

54. A. J. Wright to Buckingham, September 14, 1861, vol. 8, p. 67; L. H. Hamilton to Buckingham, September 15, 1861, vol. 8, p. 63; W. B. Starr to Buckingham, September 19, 1861, vol. 8, p. 167, all in ser. 147, OHS.

55. C. A. Croniger to Buckingham, August 31, 1861, vol. 6, p. 89, ser. 147, OHS.

56. Samuel Rothgeb to Buckingham, September 2, 1861, vol. 6, p. 207, ser. 147, OHS.

57. Edward Hall to Buckingham, September 3, 1861, vol. 6, p. 129, ser. 147, OHS.

58. John Rose to Buckingham, September 23, 1861, vol. 9, p. 102; Sylvester D. Leamon to [?], September 25, 1861, vol. 9, p. 189, both in ser. 147, OHS.

59. Diary of William T. Coggeshall, entries for July 28, 31, 1861, SC 2208, ALPL.

60. Samuel Galloway to David Davis, August 14, 1861, box 2, David Davis Papers, ALPL.

61. See Rita W. Cooley, "The Office of United States Marshal," *Western Political Quarterly* 12, no. 1 (March 1959): 123–40; Frederick S. Calhoun, *The Lawmen: United States Marshals and Their Deputies, 1789–1989* (Washington, DC: Smithsonian Institution Press, 1989).

62. Kenneth W. Munden and Henry Putney Beers, *The Union: A Guide to Federal Archives Relating to the Civil War* (Washington, DC: National Archives and Records Administration, 1986), 418.

63. The historical literature on the role of federal law enforcement officers in the Civil War is negligible. Historians have been deterred from study of their actions during the war by the almost complete lack of surviving records of U.S. marshals in the National Archives. Holdings for federal district attorneys are better, but far from complete.

64. See Marvin R. Cain, *Lincoln's Attorney General: Edward Bates of Missouri* (Columbia: University of Missouri Press, 1965), 226–315.

65. E. Delafield Smith to Edward Bates, April 15, 1861, box 3, New York, folder "Southern District of New York (US Attorney January 15, 1858–December 9, 1861)"; Edwin C. Larned to Bates, April 20, 1861, box 2, Illinois, folder "Northern District of Illinois US Attorney"; W. H. F. Gurley to Bates, April 22, 1861, box Iowa, folder "Iowa (US Attorney) June 18, 1842–December 9, 1870"; Flamen Ball to Bates, May 1, 1861, box Ohio, folder "Southern District of Ohio (US Attorney)," all in RG 60, General Records of the Department of Justice, E 9 Letters Received, National Archives and Records Administration, College Park, Maryland (hereafter cited as NARA-CP).

66. Earl Bill to Bates, April 29, 1861, box Ohio, folder "Northern District of Ohio (US Marshal)," RG 60, E 9, NARA-CP. Earl Bill assumed his office on April 25, 1861. *Daily Cleveland Herald,* April 26, 1861.

67. *Daily Cleveland Herald,* July 2, 1861, copied from *Cincinnati Daily Gazette,* n.d.

68. Edward Bates to William M. Addison [and seven other U.S. attorneys], May 6, 1861, in M-699, Letters Sent by the Department of Justice: General and Miscellaneous, 1818–1904, vol. B2, roll 5, RG 60, General Records of the Department of Justice, National Archives; see entries of Caleb B. Smith to Bates, September 17, 1861; Bates to William M. Addison, May 5, 1861; E. G. Bradford to Bates, May 20, 1861; R. H. Dana to Bates, May 25, 1861; Wingate Hayes to Bates, May 20, 1861; Hiram Willey to Bates, May 20, 1861, all in E 6, Registers of Letters Received [Office of the Attorney General of the United States], RG 60, NARA-CP; David H. Carr to Bates, July 16, 1861, E 9, box Connecticut, folder "Connecticut (US Marshal)," RG 60, NARA-CP; *Daily Cleveland Herald,* June 1, 1861.

69. James Harlan to Bates, September 17, 1861, E 9, box Kentucky, folder "Kentucky (US Attorney)," NARA-CP.

70. David H. Carr to Bates, May 26, 1861; Carr to Bates, May 30, 1861; Carr to Bates July 1, 1861, all in E 9, box Connecticut, folder "Connecticut (US Marshal)," RG 60, NARA-CP. See Bates to Carr, July 23, 1861, in vol. B4, on microfilm roll 6, M-699, NARA.

71. George A. Coffey to Bates, May 14, 1861, E 9, Pennsylvania box 2, folder "Eastern District of Pennsylvania (US Attorney)," RG 60, NARA-CP.

72. David L. Phillips to Caleb B. Smith, May 12, 1861, box 231 Southern Illinois 1860–1863, E 58, Letters Received re Judiciary Accounts, RG 60, NARA-CP; Phillips to Bates, May 13, 1861, E 9, Illinois box 2, folder "Southern District of Illinois (US Marshal)," RG 60, NARA-CP.

73. David L. Phillips to Richard Yates, September 21, 1861, box 1, folder 8, Yates-SIUC.

74. Phillips to Yates, October 16, 1861, box 4, folder 5, Yates Family Papers, ALPL.

75. W. H. L. Gurley to Bates, August 24, 1861, E 9, box Iowa, folder "Iowa (US Attorney) June 18, 1842–December 9, 1870," RG 60, NARA-CP. Bates endorsed the letter, "some ill-defined scheme of treason." The letters written in cipher do not survive.

76. H. M. Hoxie to Bates, August 30, 1861, E 9, box Iowa, folder "Iowa (US Marshal)," RG 60, NARA-CP.

77. Edward J. Chase to Bates, September 2, 1861, E 9, New York, box 3, folder "Northern District of New York (US Marshal)," RG 60, NARA-CP.

78. Edwin D. Morgan to Bates, August 30, 1861, E 9, New York, box 3, folder "Southern District of New York (State Officials)," RG 60, NARA-CP.

79. Richard Bates to Flamen Ball, May 4, 1861; Titian J. Coffey to Montgomery Blair, May 8, 1861; Edward Bates to Asa S. Jones, May 21, 1861; Edward Bates to Robert F. Paine, May 24, 1861, all in vol. B2, roll 5; Titian J. Coffey to Robert F. Paine, September 19, 1861, vol. B4, roll 6, M-699, NARA.

80. Bates to Jones, May 21, July 1, 1861, vol. B2, roll 5, M-699, NARA; Bates to George A. Coffey, June 4, 1861, vol. B4, roll 6, M-699, NARA.

81. Flamen Ball to Bates, August 30, 1861, entry 9, box Ohio, folder "Southern District of Ohio (US Attorney)," RG 60, NARA-CP; Titian J. Coffey to Ball, September 2, 1861, vol. B4, roll 6, M-699, NARA.

82. Titian J. Coffey to marshals at Cleveland and Cincinnati, Ohio, and La Porte, Indiana, September 5, 1861; Richard Bates to James Harlan, September 11, 1861; Edward Bates to Earl Bill, November 8, 1861, all in vol. B4, roll 6, M-699, NARA.

83. The text of the Withers letter was entered into evidence in the preliminary hearing before the U.S. commissioner at Cleveland on October 15, 1861. See *Cleveland Daily Plain Dealer*, October 16, 1861; *Daily Cleveland Herald*, October 16, 1861. Bill described how he obtained the letter in his testimony. *Cleveland Daily Plain Dealer*, October 17, 1861.

84. *Cleveland Daily Plain Dealer*, October 17, 1861.

85. Mansfield Hedges Gilkison (1811–85) had served as a town constable and deputy sheriff in Mansfield and Richland County over the years and was described as "fearless." In the summer months he worked as a brick mason. *Mansfield Herald*, February 26, 1885.

86. Withers was probably William Temple Withers (1825–89), born in Kentucky and educated at Bacon College in that state. He served as a lieutenant in a Kentucky infantry regiment in the Mexican War and was severely wounded in the battle of Buena Vista. He survived and managed to return to Kentucky, married, practiced law, and moved to Mississippi to run large cotton plantations. The letter includes the sentence: "We must not forget to go to the K.G.C. at Cynthiana in July, by that time we can tell what is to be done." Withers resided in Cynthiana, Kentucky, before removing to Mississippi; his brother, James S. Withers, continued to reside at Cynthiana. Biographical sources do not establish where Withers was in June 1861, but in July, "at the solicitation of Jefferson Davis," Withers went to Kentucky and established a recruiting camp, Camp Boone, just over the Tennessee state line and worked to raise the First Kentucky Brigade, nicknamed the Orphans Brigade. He later commanded the Mississippi Light Artillery regiment through the rest of the Civil War. After the war he returned to Kentucky and became a prominent horse breeder. He died when one of his Mexican War wounds reopened. See E. Polk Johnson, *A History of Kentucky and Kentuckians: The Leaders and Representative Men in Commerce, Industry and Modern Activities,* 3 vols. (Chicago: Lewis Publishing, 1912), 3:1571–72; Ida Withers Harrison, *Memoirs of William Temple Withers* (Boston: Christopher Publishing House, 1924).

87. Earl Bill to Caleb B. Smith, box Ohio, August 28, 1861, folder "Northern District of Ohio (US Marshal)," E 9, RG 60, NARA-CP.

88. Robert F. Paine to Bates, September 11, 1861, box Ohio, folder "Northern District of Ohio (US Attorney)," E 9, RG 60, NARA-CP.

89. Titian J. Coffey to Paine, September 16, 1861, vol. B4, roll 6, M-699, NARA. Congress passed a law on August 2, 1861, for the attorney general to permit district attorneys to hire counsel to assist them. The law also authorized the attorney general to supervise the activities of marshals and attorneys, and authorized the hiring of two additional clerks to augment the attorney general's staff. See Appendix to the Cong. Globe, 37th Cong., 1st Sess., Laws of the United States, 32; Paine to Bates, September 26, 1861, box Ohio, folder "Northern District of Ohio (US Attorney)," E 9, RG 60, NARA-CP.

90. *Cleveland Daily Plain Dealer; Columbus Daily Ohio State Journal,* both October 8, 1861.

91. One Republican newspaper observed that "had the developments of the past few days occurred a month sooner," Union voters would have turned out in even larger numbers. *Daily Cleveland Herald,* October 11, 1861. Days before the arrests the chairman of the county military committee wrote to state officials that though one Democrat planned to apply to recruit a volunteer company, his real goal was to distract and embarrass local recruiting efforts, and that he was an open secessionist, KGC member, and county leader of war opponents. See Jonathan J. Williams to "Dear Sir," October 5, 1861, vol. 12, p. 18, ser. 147, OHS.

92. *Daily Cleveland Herald,* October 16, 17, 18, 19, 1861; *Cleveland Daily Plain Dealer,* October 16, 17, 18, 19, 1861.

93. *Daily Cleveland Herald,* October 19, 1861.

94. *Daily Cleveland Herald,* November 6, 8, 1861; *Chillicothe Scioto Gazette,* November 12, 1861.

95. *Cleveland Daily Plain Dealer,* October 19, November 5, 1861; *Daily Cleveland Herald,* November 5, 13, 1861; Thomas H. Smith, "Crawford County 'Ez Trooly Dimecratic': A Study of Midwestern Copperheadism," *Ohio History,* vol. 76, nos. 1–2 (January 1967): 1–2, 40.

96. Gilkison went on to serve as a deputy U.S. marshal. See *Columbus Ohio Daily State Journal,* July 1, 1862. He also continued as the town marshal of Mansfield, where rioters nearly beat him to death. See *Daily Cleveland Herald,* December 1, 4, 1863.

97. *Cincinnati Daily Enquirer,* October 19, 24, 31, November 1, 17, 1861. Historian Frank L. Klement refers frequently to the 1861 northern Ohio episode as an example of Republican concoctions, fabrications, and forgeries in creating partisan smears. He quotes at length the Democratic press's denials and accepts them at face value. He also erroneously refers to the pretrial hearing as a "trial" and asserts that the arrested persons were "acquitted" and vindicated by the outcome. See Klement, *Copperheads in the Middle West,* 138–40; Klement, *Dark Lanterns,* 15–17; Klement, "Ohio and the Knights of the Golden Circle: The Evolution of a Civil War Myth," *Cincinnati Historical Society Bulletin* 32, no. 1 (Spring–Summer 1974): 11–12; Klement, "Civil War Politics, Nationalism, and Postwar Myths," *Historian* 38, no. 3 (May 1976): 423; "President Lincoln, the Civil War, and the Bill of Rights," *Lincoln Herald* 94, no.1 (Spring 1992): 10–23.

98. *Daily Cleveland Herald,* July 18, 1863.

99. Richard J. Thomas, "Caleb Blood Smith: Whig Orator and Politician—Lincoln's Secretary of Interior" (PhD diss., Indiana University-Bloomington, 1969); Doris Kearns Goodwin, *Team of Rivals: The Political Genius of Abraham Lincoln* (New York: Simon and Schuster, 2005), 245, 316, 338.

100. Smith's biographer argues that Smith had "little liking or aptitude for administrative detail; when he was engaged in these repetitive and dull tasks he appeared to some observers as 'indolent and dreadfully unhappy.' Therefore, he left the control of the major bureaus of his department in the hands of his subordinates." Thomas, "Caleb Blood Smith," 187.

101. Caleb B. Smith to Abraham Lincoln, May 10, 1861, E 190, Letters Sent Concerning the "Judiciary," 1854–69, box 4, book 20, 89–102, in RG 48, Records of the Department of the Interior, NARA-CP. Historian James G. Randall refers to Smith's letter to Lincoln arguing against payment of the posse comitatus in Kansas, and notes Smith's conclusion that the apprehension of guerrillas was an executive function, not a judicial one. However, Randall overlooks the issue of the payment from the Judiciary Fund and the concomitant issue of fees for services versus salaries. Randall, *Constitutional Problems under Lincoln,* rev. ed. (Urbana: University of Illinois Press, 1964), 159–61.

102. Caleb Smith to Lincoln, June 14, 1861, RG 48, E 190, book 20, 177–83.

103. Caleb Smith to E. Delafield Smith, April 16, 1861; Smith to George A. Coffey, May 22, 1861, both ibid., 34–35, 127–29.

104. Ibid. I found no evidence that either officer forwarded a detailed statement to Smith as suggested, or that Smith authorized payment as requested. However, it is possible that Smith forwarded funds to Earl Bill to fund his investigation of the Knights of the Golden Circle in northern Ohio in the summer of 1861. On August 28, 1861, Bill

wrote Smith a detailed report of his investigations, and internal evidence in the report shows that Bill had written to Smith at least once, on July 9, 1861, and perhaps before that date, about his uncovering the Withers letter. He also noted in the August report that he had hired a "secret agent" (Gilkison) to watch and gather information on the conspirators. Though I have not found record to show that Smith sent funds to Bill, we may presume that the funds were sent by the fact of Gilkison's employment by Bill.

105. Smith to Bates, September 16, 1861, ibid., 387–88.

106. Smith to Simon Cameron, October 15, 1861, RG 48, E 190, box 4, book 21, 71, NARA-CP.

107. Smith to William H. Seward, November 7, 1861; Smith to Simon Cameron, November 7, 1861, ibid., 119–20, 123–24.

108. Smith to "First Auditor" [D. W. Mahon], November 7, 1861, ibid., 121–22. At this time in 1861, Smith was caught up in a feud with Secretary of War Simon Cameron, who had suggested the propriety of arming former African American slaves to fight against the rebels. Smith, who held conservative views on slavery, attacked Cameron's argument in a cabinet meeting. R. Thomas, "Caleb Blood Smith," 204–7.

109. Smith to W. H. F. Gurley, January 16, 1862, RG 48, E 190, book 21, 248–49.

110. United States, Department of Justice, *Digest of the Official Opinions of the Attorneys-General of the United States,* vol. 1 (1789–1881), comp. A. J. Bentley (Washington, DC: Government Printing Office, 1885), 252.

111. Smith to Salmon P. Chase, March 15, 1862; Smith to Bates, March 20, 1862, both RG 48, E 190 , box 4, book 21, 353–57, 366–69; Smith to Elisha Whittlesey, June 21, 1862, RG 48, E 190, box 4, book 22, 107–8, NARA-CP (emphasis added).

112. Attorney General Bates responded to a question from Ohio senator John Sherman about the fee schedule and offered the advice that reducing the rates paid for court services would be problematic. Furthermore, reducing the number of court officers would be harmful to the government. See Bates to John Sherman, January 17, 1862, vol. B4, roll 6, M-699, NARA.

113. See Baker, *Secret Service,* 378–83. Baker devotes surprisingly little of his memoir to efforts to arrest counterfeiters.

114. See David R. Johnson, *Illegal Tender: Counterfeiting and the Secret Service* (Washington, DC: Smithsonian Institution, 1995). See also Munden and Beers, *Union,* 202–4.

115. Morton to Edward B. Allen, July 14, 1862, Edward B. Allen Papers, SC 10, IHS.

116. *Indianapolis Daily Journal,* August 4, 1862. The Democratic newspaper cast aspersion on the presentment and claimed it was a partisan product. *Indianapolis Daily State Sentinel,* August 5, 1862. The *Journal* replied that the jury included Democrats and that Illinois federal judge Samuel H. Treat, a Democrat substituting for the ill Indiana judge, had ordered the report published. *Indianapolis Daily Journal,* August 6, 1862.

117. Mark E. Neely, Jr., *The Fate of Liberty: Abraham Lincoln and Civil Liberties* (New York: Oxford University Press, 1991), 52–53.

118. Affidavit of Thomas Simpson, August 12, 1862; affidavit of Calvin B. Hess, August 14, 1862; A. C. Sands to L. C. Turner, August 18, 1862; Turner to Sands, August 21, 1862; Turner to Sands, November 5, 1862, all in RG 94, file 154, Turner-Baker Papers, M-797, Case Files of Investigations by Levi C. Turner and Lafayette C. Baker,

1861–1866, roll 6, NARA. See also *Cincinnati Daily Enquirer,* August 17, 1862, which printed the full texts of the three affidavits.

119. See H. M. Hoxie to Edwin M. Stanton, September 18, 1862; Hoxie to L. C. Turner, October 31, 1862, both in RG 94, file 743, Turner-Baker Papers, M-797, roll 22, NARA.

Chapter 2

1. Kate Andrews to Yates, May 3, 1862, box 6, folder 1, Yates Family Papers, ALPL. An endorsement on the letter, probably written by Yates's secretary, reads, "Send this letter to Hon. D. L. Phillips and suggest this lady as a valuable correspondent."

2. See R. W. Waterman to Yates, July 21, 1862; J. M. Kelly to Yates, July 22, 1862, both in box 6, folder 8; Joshua H. Bates to Yates, August 7, 1862, box 7, folder 4, all in Yates Family Papers, ALPL.

3. *Chicago Daily Tribune,* June 14, 1862.

4. Phillips to Jesse K. Dubois, June 28, 1862, box 1, folder 12, Wabash Yates Papers, ALPL.

5. "Gen. Strong has for a long time been aware of their [KGC's] proclivities, and through the instrumentality of Capt. Merrill has at last succeeded in obtaining such proofs of their complicity with the rebellion as warranted him in ordering" the arrest of four men. *Chicago Daily Tribune,* June 14, 1862.

6. *Chicago Daily Tribune,* August 26, 1862. Unfortunately, few records of Gen. Strong's tenure as commander of the District of Cairo in the Department of the Mississippi appear to have survived at the National Archives. The exceptions are two lists of prisoners arrested at Cairo by Captain (later Major) J. W. Merrill, post provost marshal, covering March 1862 to March 1863. The lists provide the reasons for the arrests, including "drunkenness," "abuse of family," and other incidental causes, but also many arrests for "disloyal[ty]," "aiding rebels," "wearing Secesh badges," "treason," and "treasonable sentiments." See vol. 249, in E 1105, Miscellaneous Records, in RG 393, pt. 2, Cairo, no. 28, NARA.

7. Scott Owen Reed, "Military Arrests of Lawyers in Illinois during the Civil War," *Western Illinois Regional Studies* 6, no. 2 (1983): 5–22. Reed errs in stating that the arrests were ordered by U.S. Marshal Phillips. Other historians have ignored the role of Major Merrill in ordering the arrests. See Gary Ecelbarger, *Black Jack Logan: An Extraordinary Life in Peace and War* (Guilford, CT: Lyons Press, 2005), 117. Both Reed, Ecelbarger, and others have been misled by Frank Klement's erroneous depictions of the August 26, 1862, article from the *Chicago Daily Tribune.* Klement asserts that Joseph K. C. Forrest was the author of the report but presents no evidence to support the assertion. Forrest, he wrote, "was responsible . . . for this effusion" and "was the central figure in every 'exposé' in Illinois during the entire Civil War." Klement, "Copperhead Secret Societies," 159. The August 26 article was signed by "B." Forrest sometimes signed his pieces for the *Tribune* with either his own name or with no name or identifier. He also used "Zeta." His pieces for the *St Louis Missouri Democrat* he signed with "Junius." During the time that Forrest posted reports from Springfield for publication in the *Tribune,* another unnamed correspondent sent numerous

letters from Cairo for publication in the newspaper. The letters contained detailed information of events in Cairo that Forrest could not have written from Springfield. Moreover, in an egregious case of misreading evidence, Klement suggests that a letter written after August 26 was incorporated in the *Tribune* article. See footnote 20, ibid. See also Klement, *Copperheads in the Middle West,* 150–51. In discussing the *Tribune* article, Klement also dismisses the evidence of eyewitnesses based on the faulty spelling of their letters, suggesting that "atrocious grammar and misspellings often revealed the credulity and ignorance of the authors." Klement, "Copperhead Secret Societies," 159. Klement is so intent on attacking Forrest and Phillips as authors of numerous perceived fabrications and lies that he mistakenly overlooks the fact that Merrill undertook the investigation and was praised for it by the *Tribune* correspondent. On the basis of his investigatory work, General Strong later recommended Merrill to be appointed provost marshal for the entire state of Illinois. See Strong to Yates, October 8, 1862, box 9, folder 6, Yates Family Papers, ALPL.

8. *Chicago Daily Tribune,* August 26, 1862; Neely, *Fate of Liberty,* 54–55; Ecelbarger, *Black Jack Logan,* 118–20. A local judge, arrested in the sweep, also argued that it was impossible for him to have been present at the secret meeting in question. See A. D. Duff, *Arbitrary Arrests in Illinois. Letter of Judge A.D. Duff, of Franklin County, to the Public of South Illinois, Relative to His Arrest and Imprisonment by the Abolition Despotism* (Springfield: State Register Steam Print, 1863), 15–16.

9. Benjamin P. Thomas and Harold M. Hyman, *Stanton: The Life and Times of Lincoln's Secretary of War* (New York: Knopf, 1962), 201–2.

10. In his official postwar account of Indiana's recruiting efforts, the adjutant general of Indiana noted that Stanton's order "was a most unfortunate step, but all efforts to have the order recalled were unavailing." W. H. H. Terrell, *Indiana in the War of the Rebellion. Reports of the Adjutant General of the State of Indiana,* 8 vols. (Indianapolis: Douglass and Conner, 1869) 1:17–18.

11. Morton to Stanton, August 11, 1862, OPMTB, vol. 15, 76, ISA.

12. *Indianapolis Daily State Sentinel,* August 19, 1862; *Indianapolis Daily Journal,* August 19, 1862.

13. Morton to Stanton, August 21, 1862, OPMTB, vol. 15, 166, ISA. Frank L. Klement erroneously claims that Morton "had [Carrington] appointed" to the position, and that Carrington "became the creator of all Indiana KGC exposés." Klement, *Copperheads in the Middle West,* 153. Also, by being vague about the date that Carrington arrived in Indianapolis, Klement erroneously insinuates that Carrington was behind the "Judge Hughes Letter" of June 1862 and the grand jury report of early August 1862. Klement, "Carrington and the Golden Circle Legend in Indiana during the Civil War," *Indiana Magazine of History* 61, no. 1 (1965): 36. Klement later corrects his insinuation but vaguely states that Carrington arrived in Indianapolis in "mid-year of 1862." See Klement, *Dark Lanterns,* 21. Carrington serves as one of Klement's special targets of criticism; however, most of Klement's assertions regarding Carrington are erroneous.

14. Catherine McKeen, "Henry Beebee Carrington: A Soldier's Tale," (PhD diss., State University of New York at Stony Brook, 1998), 34, 47–48.

15. Ibid., 56, 59–61; *Cleveland Herald,* January 8, 1853. Margaret Irvin Carrington later authored the remarkable narrative of life on the western frontier *Ab-sa-ra-ka,*

Home of the Crows: Being the Experience of an Officer's Wife on the Plains (Philadelphia: J. B. Lippincott and Co., 1868). After her death, Carrington married the widow of another army officer and encouraged her to record her frontier experiences. See Frances C. Carrington, *My Army Life and the Fort Phil. Kearney Massacre, with an Account of the Celebration of "Wyoming Opened."* (Philadelphia: J. B. Lippincott Co., 1910).

16. *Daily Cleveland Herald*, March 17, 1855.

17. Carrington wrote a history of the formation of the Republican Party in Ohio. See H. Carrington, "Early History of the Republican Party in Ohio, 1854–5," *Ohio Archaeological and Historical Quarterly* 2, no. 2 (September 1888): 327–31.

18. See Mathew Oyos, "The Mobilization of the Ohio Militia in the Civil War," *Ohio History* 98, no. 2 (Summer–Autumn 1989): 147–74; Noel Fisher, "Groping toward Victory: Ohio's Administration of the Civil War," *Ohio History* 105, no. 2 (Winter–Spring 1996): 25–41.

19. See entries for May 31, June 15, 1861, in William T. Coggeshall Diary, SC 2208, ALPL; Samuel Galloway to David Davis, August 14, 1861, box 2, David Davis Papers, ALPL. A Dennison biographer has written that Carrington was "too excitable and disorganized to be a chief of staff" for the governor. Thomas C. Mulligan, "Lest the Rebels Come to Power: The Life of William Dennison, 1815–1882, Early Ohio Republican" (PhD diss., Ohio State University, 1994), 168.

20. Eugene H. Roseboom and Francis P. Weisenburger, *A History of Ohio*, 2nd ed. (Columbus: Ohio Historical Society, 1967): 186–87; Richard G. Curry, "McClellan's Western Virginia Campaign of 1861," *Ohio History* 71, no. 2 (1962): 83–96. See also H. Carrington, *Ohio Militia and the West Virginia Campaign, 1861*, rev. ed. (Boston, 1904).

21. *Columbus Daily Ohio State Journal*, June 8, 1861.

22. *Columbus Daily Ohio State Journal*, June 22, 1861. Years later, Carrington wrote an account of a visit of General Winfield Scott to Columbus, who told him, "you ought to be in the army," and remembered him when war came. See H. Carrington, "Winfield Scott's Visit to Columbus," *Ohio Archaeological and Historical Quarterly* 19, no. 3 (1910): 286–87; McKeen, "Carrington," 77.

23. *Columbus Daily Ohio State Journal*, August 25, 1861.

24. *Columbus Daily Ohio State Journal*, September 7, 1861 and October 12, 1861.

25. *Columbus Daily Ohio State Journal*, December 10, 1861.

26. *Rockville Parke County Republican*, March 1, 1865. In later years, Carrington admitted to an addiction to smoking cigars. "Perhaps you know that . . . I have seldom been seen without a cigar in my mouth; and that the use of tobacco, larger [lager] beer, and other stimulants are generally presumed to belong to the army, as a kind of legitimate usage. Having for two months left off cigars, which I had used to excess, as intimated, for nearly twenty five years, and having given up *all alcoholic prescriptions for constitutional lung difficulties*, I find mind body, and spirit more healthy than ever. If I could have one minute with all my friends . . . who have seen me smoke, it would be occupied in saying one single sentence: *Do not smoke or drink!* Popular opinion would sneer at me. It is, nevertheless, a sound philosophy. For example: At this post there is but one man of my regiment in the guard house, and he is in for intemperance. Not a captain of my regiment at this post either drinks or smokes.

They have abandoned it. It is, for my self, a source of deep humiliation that I did not earlier abandon tobacco. I believe that an after dinner cigar may be enjoyed with comparative impunity. . . . A half hour's walk is better, however, as an aid to digestion. The [smoking] habit is expensive, needless, and incompatible with the evenness of temper and living which gives weight to example, and prepares the Christian for the life beyond the present." *Cincinnati Christian Herald,* n.d., quoted in *Daily Cleveland Herald,* April 7, 1869 (emphasis added). In Indianapolis, Carrington rebuked an officer for swearing and instructed new recruits that, along with fighting rebels, soldiers should fight four other enemies: swearing, gaming, drinking, and uncleanliness. *Indianapolis Daily Journal,* September 3, 1862.

27. See the law of Congress passed July 29, 1861, Appendix to Cong. Globe, 37th Cong., 1st Sess., chap. 24, 30–31.

28. *Indianapolis Daily Journal,* August 19, 1862.

29. See Kenneth W. Noe, *Perryville: This Grand Havoc of Battle* (Lexington: University Press of Kentucky, 2001); Stephen D. Engle, *Don Carlos Buell: Most Promising of All* (Chapel Hill: University of North Carolina Press, 1999).

30. A regular-army staff officer in Indianapolis characterized Simonson as the "most fearful of responsibility of any man I ever met—[he] avoids every possible case." Capt. John Farquhar to Fanny M. Farquhar, March 2, 1863, in Correspondence of John Farquhar, box 50, Eugene Gano Hay Papers, Library of Congress (hereafter cited as Farquhar Correspondence, LC). Governor Morton's staff continued to try to get rid of Simonson at this time, noting that he was too old to perform arduous duties and recommending Farquhar take his place as permanent post commander. See William R. Holloway to Maj. Gen. Horatio G. Wright, February 13, 1863, in RG 393, U.S. Army Continental Commands, pt. 1, E 3489, Department of the Ohio, Register of Letters Received, vol. 2, 237, NARA.

31. *Indianapolis Daily Journal,* October 17, 1862.

32. *Indianapolis Daily Journal,* October 21, 1862.

33. *Indianapolis Daily State Sentinel,* November 19, 1862.

34. Carrington to William Cullen Bryant, November 14, 1862, in Henry B. Carrington Collection, S229, Manuscripts Section, Indiana State Library, Indianapolis (hereafter cited as ISL).

35. Carrington to Richard W. Thompson, November 11, 1862, Richard W. Thompson Papers, ISL.

36. Proclamation of October 4, 1862, in RG 110, Provost Marshal General's Bureau Records, E 5083, Letters and Telegrams Sent, 330 (hereafter cited as NARA-GLR); *Indianapolis Daily Journal,* October 6, 1862.

37. J. P. Siddall to Thomas M. Browne, October 11, 1862; Capt. James A. Stretch to [headquarters], October 13, 1862, both in OPMTB, vol. 9, 81, 88, ISA.

38. Carrington to Brig. Gen. Lorenzo Thomas, October 4, 1862, RG 110, E 5083, 342, NARA-GLR. Carrington received instructions to arrest Reynolds. See L. C. Turner to Carrington, October 7, 1862, RG 110, E 5084, Register of Letters, Telegrams, and Reports Received, 29, NARA-GLR.

39. Stampp, *Indiana Politics,* 147–48.

40. Ibid., 155.

41. *Indianapolis Daily Journal,* October 17, 1862. See Thomas E. Rodgers, "Republicans and Drifters: Political Affiliation and Union Army Volunteers in West-Central Indiana," *Indiana Magazine of History* 92, no. 4 (December 1996): 321–45.

42. Holloway to Nicolay, October 24, 1862, Letter Press Book, vol. 1 (June 1862–January 1863), Morton Records, ISA; full text of the letter is found in Nation and Towne, *Indiana's War,* 132–33. Hendricks's speech is quoted in full in *Indianapolis Daily State Sentinel,* January 9, 1862. See Stampp, *Indiana Politics,* 131–33.

43. Morton to Lincoln, October 27, 1862, in vol. 9, Edwin McMasters Stanton Papers, Library of Congress (hereafter cited as Stanton Papers, LC), full text printed in W. H. H. Terrell, *Report of the Adjutant General of Indiana,* vol. 1, *Containing Indiana in the War of the Rebellion and Statistics and Documents* (Indianapolis: Alexander H. Conner, 1869), 21–22. The *Sentinel* editors reported that Governor Morton told Indiana Legion officers that a secret organization existed in the state with the plan to separate the Northwestern states from the Union and that they (the officers) should work to resist it in their communities. *Indianapolis Daily State Sentinel,* October 31, 1862.

44. James G. Randall, *Constitutional Problems under Lincoln,* rev. ed. (Urbana: University of Illinois Press, 1964), 428–30.

45. Carrington to Perkins, October 21, 1862, letter book of Henry B. Carrington (1862; 020176), 10–11, in Henry B. Carrington Papers, ISA.

46. Perkins to Carrington, October 23, 1862, in RG 110, E 5084, 201, NARA-GLR. See also Emma Lou Thornbrough, "Judge Perkins, the Indiana Supreme Court, and the Civil War," *Indiana Magazine of History* 60, no. 1 (March 1964): 79–96.

47. Carrington to Stanton, December 31, 1862, ser. 1, box 1, folder 4, in Carrington Family Papers, Manuscripts and Archives, Yale University Library, New Haven (hereafter cited as Carrington Family Papers); Carrington to Lorenzo Thomas, January 24, 1863, RG 153, Judge Advocate General Records, Court-Martial Case Files, Military Commission Trial of Harrison H. Dodd, NN-2716, box 1808, NARA. One prominent observer to the incident noted that Perkins issued the writ to arrest the captain, "but he could not enforce it, as he had no troops. He threatened to call upon the Governor to call out the State Militia, but did not do so." See Holloway to Nicolay, January 2, 1863, in Abraham Lincoln Papers, Library of Congress (hereafter cited as Lincoln Papers, LC). The letter is reprinted in Nation and Towne, *Indiana's War,* 134–35. See an account in the *Indianapolis Daily State Sentinel,* January 15, 1863. Perkins continued to be rankled by Lincoln's abuses of civil liberties and expansion of the war powers of the president and expressed his views on executive power in a case that came before the Indiana Supreme Court, Griffin v. Wilcox. See Neely, *Fate of Liberty,* 87–90. See also Thornbrough, "Judge Perkins," 88–91. In March 1863, Perkins spoke from the Supreme Court bench to refute rumors that he was a member of the Knights of the Golden Circle: "I was engaged in a sort of conspiracy to aid in getting soldiers out of the service by encouraging writs of habeas corpus, and granting decisions thereon. . . . The object of these charges is manifest, and I deem them of importance enough to justify me in noticing them as I do in this public manner and placing that notice in the record of my judicial proceedings. The charges are false in every particular." When first he heard it, "my first impulse was to refuse to hear any more writs, but reflection leads me to a better judgement; I shall continue to discharge my duty in

the premises as I have done to all without distinction of party." See Indiana Supreme Court Records, L1195 021132, ISA.

48. Carrington to Lt. Col. J. P. Garesche, December 18, 1862, in Carrington Letter Press Book 020177, Henry B. Carrington Papers, ISA.

49. Henry W. Halleck to Stanton, February 18, 1863, vol. 11, Stanton Papers, LC. In her study of desertion during the Civil War, Ella Lonn notes that "though no attempt was made to estimate the exact proportion of those who were sick or on furlough, it is certain that a large portion were deserters and stragglers." See Ella Lonn, *Desertion during the Civil War* (Gloucester, MA: American Historical Association, 1928; repr., Lincoln: University of Nebraska Press, 1998), 151.

50. Maj. Gen. William S. Rosecrans to Brig. Gen. Horatio G. Wright, February 21, 1863, in RG 393, pt. 1, Department of the Ohio Records, E 3491, Telegrams Received, vol. 3, 115, NARA. Rosecrans also wrote to the governors of the Northern states to ask for their cooperation. See Rosecrans to Morton, February 16, 1863, in Adjutant General of Indiana Records, A4017 024596, folder 18, ISA.

51. Rosecrans to Wright, February 21, 1863, in RG 393, pt. 1, Department of the Ohio Records, E 3489, vol. 2, 91, NARA.

52. Wright to Rosecrans, February 21, 1863, in RG 393, pt. 1, Department of the Ohio Records, E 3487, Telegrams Sent, vol. 2, 6, NARA. For records documenting Hascall's efforts, see Brig. Gen. Milo S. Hascall to Lt. Col. C. Goddard, February 12, 1863; Hascall to Rosecrans, February 25, 27, 1863, both in RG 94, E 159, subser. 2, Generals' Papers, box 15, folder 2, NARA. See also Hascall to Wright, February 25, 27, 1863, in RG 393, pt. 1, E 3489, vol. 2, 201–2, NARA. Hascall also assisted military commanders from Grant's army besieging Vicksburg to arrest deserters in the three-state region. See Maj. E. S. Jones to Hascall, April 3, 1863, in Jacob Ammen Papers, ALPL.

53. Affidavit of Washington F. Andrews [also spelled Andrus], Company L, 3rd Indiana Cavalry regiment, December 18, 1862, ser. 1, box 1, folder 4, Carrington Family Papers. Troops arrested an Amos Conway (Conaway), resident of Fayette County, on February 20, 1863, for discouraging enlistments and enlisting soldiers into the KGC. Taken to Indianapolis, he gave bond and was released. *Rushville Jacksonian*, February 26, 1863; *Indianapolis Daily Evening Gazette*, February 26, 1863.

54. Carrington to Stanton, December 22, 1862, in *OR*, ser. 2, vol. 5, 108.

55. The phrase was commonly employed in Indiana and neighboring states by Democrats and Democratic newspapers to describe their political goals. The editors of the *Huntington Democrat*, a partisan Democratic newspaper in northern Indiana, published as a motto on its front banner: "The Union as it was, the Constitution as it is, and the Negroes where they are." *Huntington Democrat*, April 30, 1863.

56. Carrington to Stanton, December 22, 1862, in RG 153, Court-Martial Case Files, Military Commission trial of William A. Bowles, Stephen Horsey, Lambdin P. Milligan, Andrew Humphries, NN-3409, box 1879, NARA.

57. Morton to Stanton, January 2, 1863, in RG 107, Records of the Office of the Secretary of War, E 17, Letters Received by the Secretary of War (Main Series), 1861–70, M-221, roll 229, NARA.

58. Morton to Stanton, January 2, 1863, OPMTB, vol. 16, 70–71.

59. Edward D. Townsend to Morton, January 3, 1863, ibid.

60. At the same time, Morton endorsed a petition made by officers of eight Indiana volunteer units to have Carrington placed in command over them in the field. He praised Carrington's energy in preparing the Indiana regiments. Morton to Maj. Gen. Henry W. Halleck, January 2, 1863, in Lincoln Miscellaneous Manuscripts, Special Collections Research Center, University of Chicago Library, Chicago.

61. An artillery soldier stationed in Indianapolis wrote, "we was ordered out one night to town to blow up the state house[.] the representative[s] could not agree and some truble when we got their they agreed and we fired A few rounds of blank catrages and returned to camp." See William H. Ringwalt to Eli Ringwalt, January 23, 1863, reprinted in Nation and Towne, *Indiana's War*, 136–37. A Democratic newspaper complained, "Gov. Morton trains the Arsenal guns upon the State House, during the session of the Legislature, needlessly keeps a large number of troops in Indianapolis and arms the Abolition secret societies . . . with government arms." *Plymouth Weekly Democrat*, January 29, 1863.

62. Morton to Carrington, January 30, 1863, Morton Papers, L113, Indiana State Library. The document transferring control of the arms states, "Sir, All arms & equipments belonging to the United States in the arsenal in this city are hereby turned over to your possession and control." Carrington noted: "executed by Governor Morton at 11:30pm Jan 30, 1863 at my room in the Bates House, on his request for advice how to avoid trouble on anticipated demand of 'House Committee on the Arsenal,' to turn over arms etc to legislative control." See also Morton and Laz Noble to Stanton, January 31, 1863, OPMTB, vol. 16, 106, ISA.

63. Evidence suggests that military commanders employed Stober as a spy to infiltrate the secret organizations while his company was stationed at Rockport, Spencer County, in southern Indiana. A letter writer from the 5th Indiana Cavalry regiment wrote to his hometown newspaper that "one of the corporals of Co. B is on secret service, catching up Knights of the Golden Circle. His name is ___ of Hagerstown. He comes as near being a fox as 'any other man.'" *Centreville Indiana True Republican*, January 22, 1863.

64. Case file of John O. Brown, in RG 153, Court-Martial Case Files, NN-3980, NARA. Testimony identified Thomas A. Hendricks, only days before selected to be U.S. senator, as one of the attorneys who would help soldiers get out of the army.

65. Carrington to Lincoln, January 14, 1863, Lincoln Papers, LC.

66. Affidavit of Eli Wells, January 12, 1863, RG 153, Court-Martial Case Files, NN-3409, box 1879, NARA.

67. Carrington to Wright, January 15, 1863, RG 393, pt. 1, E 3489, vol. 2, 82, NARA.

68. Wright to Carrington, January 17, 1863, RG 393, pt. 1, E 3482, Letters Sent, vol. 2, 22, NARA.

69. Carrington to Lorenzo Thomas, January 26, 1863, RG 94, Records of the Adjutant General of the United States, M-619, Letters Received by the Office of the Adjutant General, Main Series, roll 164, NARA. Carrington also wrote to Joseph Holt, the judge advocate general in the War Department, to suggest a legislative remedy to strengthen the government's hand against the conspirators. Holt wrote back to Carrington that he had forwarded his letter to the House Judiciary Committee for their action. See Holt to Carrington, February 28, 1863, ser. 1, box 1, folder 6, Carrington Family Papers.

70. *Indianapolis Daily Journal,* February 3, 26, 1863.

71. Carrington to Wright, February 2, 1863, in RG 393, pt. 1, E 3491, vol. 3, 94, NARA.

72. Carrington to Lorenzo Thomas, February 2, 1863, in RG 153, Court-Martial Case Files, NN-3409, box 1879, NARA. Carrington reported he had suppressed telegraphic messages from Democratic newspapers, that dispatches sent by them stated, "'it was ordered by Col Carrington & Gov Morton to arrest all democrats—that ten thousand soldiers could not hold these men arrested, under arrest this night—that civil war and blood shed was inevitable.' The dispatch was designed for certain papers of worst kind, was long, inflammatory and false," intended to provoke a "collision." Carrington also wrote to the president to urge Congress to confer "more ample authority" to cover such incidents. Carrington to Lincoln, February 2, 1863, Lincoln Papers, LC.

73. *Indianapolis Daily Journal,* March 2, 1863.

74. *Indianapolis Daily Journal,* February 16, 25, 16, 28, March 2, 4, 5, 1863; *Indianapolis Daily State Sentinel,* February 17, 19, 28, 29, 1863.

75. Carrington to Lincoln, March 2, 1863, Lincoln Papers, LC.

76. Carrington to Joseph Holt, March 5, 1863, RG 94, M-619, roll 165, NARA. Among those indicted were Shelby County men involved in the secret organization with which John O. Brown associated. He reported that Lincoln had suspended the death sentence of Brown, "as I need him for a witness." Carrington appears also to have complained about Judge Smith's actions, as Holt replied, "The decision of the Judge excusing the witnesses from answering would seem to render the prosecution of these offenses and conspirators difficult, if not absolutely impracticable." Holt to Carrington, February 28, 1863, ser. 1, box 1, folder 6, Carrington Family Papers.

77. General Orders 13, March 3, 1863, in *Indianapolis Daily Journal,* March 4, 1863.

78. Transcripts of Grand Jury Presentments of Jesse McHenry and George Hughes, dated February 16, 17, 1863, respectively, file 358, RG 153, E 6, Letters Received, box 3, NARA. See *Indianapolis Daily Journal,* February 18, 19, 21, 1863.

79. Morton to Stanton, February 9, 1863, in vol. 10, Stanton Papers, LC. Owen had worked as an agent for Governor Morton in purchasing arms in New York and other arms markets and had done important work for both the Indiana governor and the War Department. Stanton appointed Owen to important commissions to audit war contracts and inquire into the social condition of freed ex-slaves. Richard William Leopold, *Robert Dale Owen: A Biography* (Cambridge, MA: Harvard University Press, 1940; repr., New York: Octagon, 1969), 349–60.

80. Robert Dale Owen to Morton, February 13, 1863, in Morton Records, ISA.

81. G. M. Mitchell to Oziah M. Hatch, April 14, 1863, in box 3, Hatch Papers, ALPL.

82. *Marshall (IL) Flag of Our Union,* April 10, 1863.

83. William A. French to Yates, March 16, 1863, box 2, folder 2, Wabash Yates Papers, ALPL.

84. C. S. Beach to Isaac Funk, February 19, 1863, Isaac Funk Papers, SC 537, ALPL.

85. Capt. Stephen E. Jones to Morton, March 17, 1863, Morton Records, ISA.

86. Walter Q. Gresham to Laz Noble, March 25, 1863, 53rd Indiana Volunteer Infantry Regiment Correspondence, Adjutant General of Indiana Records, ISA.

87. J. K. Morrow to Charles J. Ball, May 23, 1863, in 100th Indiana Volunteer Infantry Regiment Correspondence, Adjutant General of Indiana Records, ISA.

88. Thomas W. Bennett to Laz Noble, February 7, 1863, 69th Indiana Volunteer Infantry Regiment Correspondence, Adjutant General of Indiana Records, ISA. In another letter Bennett reported that he had been appointed president of a board of examiners by Major General U. S. Grant to cull disloyal officers from the army besieging Vicksburg. "We are having a good time. We will give the army a good *purge* and a healthy *puke* of all 'Copperheads.' Resignations are played out with such fellows, they are to be *kicked out*." Bennett took great pleasure in *"weeding* out the infernal scoundrels. The army shall be purified if the people at home all prove traitors." He boasted that no soldier in his regiment was disloyal, and that they were eager to "clean out" the traitors at home. Bennett to Noble, February 23, 1863, ibid. Bennett also wrote to the governor that there had been a few "croakers" in the regiment, but meetings and "a little plain talk" silenced them. Democratic newspapers and speech texts "poured in by every mail," but he had "'ironplated' and 'copper-bottomed'" the regiment. Bennett to Morton, February 17, 1863, ibid.

89. Campbell Young to Jacob Ammen, June 4, 1863, in Ammen Papers, ALPL.

90. Historian Mark E. Neely, Jr., has characterized the petitions and resolutions sent from regiments in the field as immoderately "chilling" in their denunciation of Democratic Party actions. See Neely, *The Union Divided: Party Conflicts in the Civil War North* (Cambridge, MA: Harvard University Press, 2002), 42–46, 57. However, he and other historians have overlooked the immediate and dangerous effects that the letter-writing campaign, along with the more overt criticisms of the war effort and the calls for a peace settlement with the rebel South, had on the welfare of the troops.

91. *Portland Jay Torch-Light,* April 30, 1863. Examples of letters sent to soldiers to induce them to desert, which soldiers in turn sent to Indiana newspapers for publication, can be found in *Plymouth Marshall County Republican,* April 2, 1863; *Greencastle Putnam Republican Banner,* April 23, 1863; *Liberty Weekly Herald,* April 29, 1863; *Mishawaka Enterprise,* April 4, 1863; *New Castle Courier,* April 16, 1863; *Seymour Times,* May 14, 1863; *Indianapolis Daily Journal,* March 14, 25, 27, 1863. For an example in an Illinois newspaper, see *Mattoon Independent Gazette,* April 4, 1863. An Ohio example is found in the *Daily Cleveland Herald,* May 2, 1863.

92. Uri Manly to Yates, February 14, 1863, box 1, folder 17, Wabash Yates Papers, ALPL.

93. *Indianapolis Daily Journal,* February 20, 1863; Holloway to Hanna, February 24, 1863, in Letter Press Book, vol. 2, 295, Morton Records, ISA; *Centreville Indiana True Republican,* February 26, 1863. Later in the spring military authorities in Illinois arrested a Jonesboro newspaperman, Commodore Harris, for writing letters to soldiers inducing them to desert. See Joseph H. Newbold to Napoleon B. Buford, April 22, 1863; R. M. Harrison to Buford, April 24, 1863, both in RG 393, pt. 2, no. 28, Records of Post of Cairo, Illinois, E 1090, Register of Letters Received, 8–9; Buford to Newbold, May 16, 1863, RG 393, pt. 2, Records of Post of Cairo, Illinois, E 1088, Telegrams Sent, 9, all in NARA.

94. Carrington to Holt, March 5, 1863, in RG 94, M-619, roll 165, NARA.

95. Albert Fletcher Bridges, "The Execution of Private Robert Gay," *Indiana Magazine of History* 20, no. 2 (June 1924): 174–86.

96. For an analysis of the Constable arrest, see Stephen E. Towne, "'Such Conduct Must be Put Down': The Military Arrest of Judge Charles H. Constable during the Civil War," *Journal of Illinois History* 9, no. 1 (Spring 2006): 43–62. See also Carrington to Col. C. W. Foster, March 12, 1863, in RG 94, M-619, roll 165, NARA; Uri Manly to Yates, March 16, 1863, box 2, folder 2, Wabash Yates Papers, ALPL. Frank L. Klement uses the Constable arrest in several of his works to paint a portrait of Carrington as an incompetent blunderer who exceeded orders in a political drive to fabricate the existence of secret organizations. However, the Constable arrest serves as a case study for how Klement misinterprets and ignores evidence, makes erroneous assertions based on no evidence, and paints a misleading portrait based on selective evidence. Klement makes a number of errors in his depiction, most notably by asserting that Carrington acted without orders from his military superiors, that troops in Indiana were barred from entering Illinois, that Morton attempted to cover up Carrington's "blunders," and that the arrest was a part of Carrington's and Morton's "smear campaign" against Democratic opponents of the war. See Klement, "Copperhead Secret Societies," 165; *Copperheads of the Middle West*, 68–70; "Carrington and the Golden Circle," 41–42; *Dark Lanterns*, 26, 141.

97. Carrington to Wright, March 20, 1863, in RG 393, pt. 1, E 3491, vol. 3, 152, NARA. See accounts of the incident in *Indianapolis Daily Journal*, March 21, 1863; *Indianapolis Daily State Sentinel*, March 21, 25, 1863; *Rushville Jacksonian*, March 25, 1863; *Connersville Weekly Times*, April 2, 1863.

Chapter 3

1. Daniel Aaron, *Cincinnati: Queen City of the West* (Columbus: Ohio State University Press, 1992).

2. See Mark R. Wilson, *The Business of Civil War: Military Mobilization and the State, 1861–1865* (Baltimore: Johns Hopkins University Press, 2006); Clinton W. Terry, "The Most Commercial of People: Cincinnati, the Civil War, and the Rise of Industrial Capitalism, 1861–1865" (PhD diss., University of Cincinnati, 2002).

3. Tertullus W. Brown to J. Wesley McFerren, January 25, 1863, in RG 21, Records of U.S. Federal Courts, U.S. District Court of the Southern District of Ohio [Cincinnati], Criminal Case Files, box 2, file 102, NARA-GLR. The quoted letter found its way into federal court in a roundabout fashion. A lieutenant of Company G, 78th Ohio, wrote to the editor of the *Noble County Republican* and enclosed the letter written by Brown to McFerren. The editor in turn sent the letter to Ohio governor David Tod, who sent it to U.S. Attorney Flamen Ball at Cincinnati. Ball put the matter in the hands of a deputy U.S. marshal and later called on the U.S. Army post commander at Cincinnati, who sent troops to Noble County to assist the marshal. See ibid., files 88–97. See also Wayne Jordan, "The Hoskinsville Rebellion," *Ohio History* 47, no. 4 (October 1938): 319–54.

4. J. T. Davidson to Capt. Harrington R. Hill, March 13, 1863; Capt. Hill to Capt. Andrew C. Kemper, March 14, 1863, both in RG 393, pt. 4, Post of Cincinnati, Ohio, Records, E 217, Letters Received, box 1, NARA.

5. Carrington to [Lorenzo Thomas], March 7, 1863, RG 393, pt. 1, E 3489, vol. 2, 99, NARA.

6. Capt. R. D. Mussey to [Wright], March 13, 1863, ibid., 334.

7. Wright to Simeon Draper, March 13, 1863, RG 393, pt, 1, E 3487, vol. 2, 39, NARA.

8. Lorenzo Thomas to Wright, March 14, 1863, RG 393, pt. 1, E 3491, vol. 3, 138, NARA.

9. George Conkle to Governor Oliver P. Morton, March 10, 1863, OPMTB, vol. 10, 139, ISA; *Richmond Quaker City Telegram,* March 14, 1863; *Indianapolis Daily State Sentinel,* March 16, 1863.

10. Maj. N. H. McLean to Carrington, March 17, 1863, RG 393, pt. 1, E 3487, vol. 1, 50, NARA.

11. *Indianapolis Daily State Sentinel,* March 18, 1863. According to a federal officer in Indianapolis, the arms sale order prompted "considerable excitement" in the city, "but no difficulty" ensued. John H. Farquhar to Fannie M. Farquhar, March 18, 1863, Farquhar Correspondence, LC.

12. Andrew C. Kemper to Maj. N. H. McLean, March 17, 1863, RG 393, pt. 4, Post of Cincinnati, Ohio, Records, E 212, Letters Sent, vol. 1, 118, NARA.

13. See "Report of Persons and Articles Employed and Hired at Cincinnati, Ohio" for May, 1863, RG 92, Quartermaster General Records, E 238, Persons and Articles Hired, file 1863–315, NARA. An endorsement dated June 15, 1863, by department headquarters ordered that the "Quartermaster Department will pay the detectives employed by Lt Col Eastman in excess of the numbers authorized in the endorsement of Mar 19th 1863." Ibid.

14. For studies of military intelligence of federal armies in the field, see Edwin C. Fishel, *The Secret War for the Union: The Untold Story of Military Intelligence in the Civil War* (Boston: Houghton Mifflin, 1996); William B. Feis, *Grant's Secret Service: The Intelligence War from Belmont to Appomattox* (Lincoln: University of Nebraska Press, 2002). Fishel focuses on the Army of the Potomac, while Feis follows U. S. Grant from the Western armies to the Army of the Potomac.

15. For a study of Truesdail's operations, see Feis, "'There Is a Bad Enemy'"; Feis, *Grant's Secret Service,* 178. See also Stanley F. Horn, "Dr. John Rolfe Hudson and the Confederate Underground in Nashville," *Tennessee Historical Quarterly* 22, no. 1 (1963): 38–52; Walter T. Durham's two volumes on the Tennessee capital during the war, *Nashville: The Occupied City* (Nashville: Tennessee Historical Society, 1985); *Reluctant Partners: Nashville and the Union, 1863–1865* (Nashville: Tennessee Historical Society, 1987).

16. See Account Book, vol. 250, RG 393, pt. 2, Post of Cairo, Illinois, Records, E 1105, Miscellaneous Records, NARA.

17. Fishel, *Secret War,* 595–96.

18. See Frank Morn, *"The Eye That Never Sleeps": A History of the Pinkerton National Detective Agency* (Bloomington: Indiana University Press, 1982), 44–45.

19. For a biography of Baker, see Jacob Mogelever, *Death to Traitors: The Story of General Lafayette C. Baker, Lincoln's Forgotten Secret Service Chief* (Garden City, NY: Doubleday, 1960).

20. Laz Noble to Henry W. Halleck, April 4, 1862, in Letter and Order Book no. 1 [November 23, 1861–January 28, 1863], 189, ISA.

21. John Newbury to John Potts, April 7, 1863, RG 110, Provost Marshal General's Bureau Records, E 95, Accounts of Secret Service Agents, box 2, NARA.

22. Potts to Commissary General of Subsistence, July 14, 1863, ibid., box 3.

23. John Newbury and John B. Pollard to [?], March 23, 1863, RG 393, pt. 1, E 3489, vol. 2, 379, NARA.

24. Carrington to Ambrose E. Burnside, April 17, 1863, ibid., 637.

25. Pollard and Newbury to Carrington, April 22, 1863, RG 153, NN-3409, box 1879, NARA; *Indianapolis Daily Gazette,* June 11, 1863.

26. Capt. R. H. Hall to "whom it may concern," October 14, 1863, pension file of widow Eliza A. Pollard, file 285,780, NARA.

27. See endorsement of Maj. C. W. Foster, April 21, 1863, on Newbury and Pollard to Burnside, April 20, 1863, RG 393, pt. 4, E 217, NARA.

28. For the history of the development of policing in the United States, see Roger Lane, *Policing the City: Boston, 1822–1885* (Cambridge, MA: Harvard University Press, 1967); James F. Richardson, *Urban Police in the United States* (Port Washington, NY: Kennikat Press, 1974); David R. Johnson, *American Law Enforcement: A History* (St. Louis: Forum Press, 1981); Eric H. Monkkonen, *Police in Urban America, 1860–1920* (Cambridge: Cambridge University Press, 1981); Monkkonen, "The Organized Response to Crime in the Nineteenth and Early Twentieth Centuries," *Journal of Interdisciplinary History* 14, no. 1 (1983): 113–28; Samuel Walker, *Popular Justice: A History of American Criminal Justice* (New York: Oxford University Press, 1980); Wilbur R. Miller, *Cops and Bobbies: Police Authority in New York and London* (Chicago: University of Chicago Press, 1977); Phillip J. Ethington, "Vigilantes and the Police: The Creation of a Professional Police Bureaucracy, 1847–1900," *Journal of Social History* 21, no. 2 (1987): 197–227. Unfortunately, little has been written about detective forces in nineteenth-century American police forces.

29. See *Cincinnati Daily Times,* April 17, 22, May 6, June 9, 10, 1863. See also K. Luci Petlack, "A Dilemma of Civil Liberties: Cincinnati's Black Community, 1862–1863," *Ohio History* 120 (2013): 47–69.

30. See Reports of Persons and Articles Employed and Hired for 1863 and 1864, RG 92, NARA.

31. See "Receipts for money received by various individuals employed as scouts," September 10–December 31, 1861, William S. Rosecrans Papers, box 80, Department of Special Collections, Charles E. Young Research Library, University of California-Los Angeles (hereafter cited as Rosecrans Papers, UCLA). See also Ruffin to Rosecrans, October 23, 1861; and secret-service accounts of William Reany, December 20, 1861, both in RG 110, E 31, Correspondence, Reports, Accounts, and Related Records of Two or More Scouts, Guides, Spies, and Detectives, box 1, NARA.

32. Wright to Eastman, March 15, 1863, RG 393, pt. 1, E 3482, vol. 2, 130, NARA.

33. Kemper to Ruffin, March 15, 1863, RG 393, pt. 4, E 212, vol. 1, 116, NARA.

34. Kemper to Ruffin, March 22, 1863; Kemper to Samuel Davis, March 22, 1863; Kemper to B. Kittredge and Co., March 22, 1863; Kemper to nine businesses, March 22, 1863; Kemper to [?], March 21, 1863; Kemper to McLean, March 28, 1863, all in RG 393, pt. 4, E 212, vol. 1, 119–25, NARA.

35. Wright to Carrington, March 14, 1863, RG 393, pt. 1, E 3487, vol. 2, 42, NARA. An Indianapolis newspaper reported Carrington returned to Indianapolis from Cincinnati on March 17. See *Indianapolis Daily Journal*, March 18, 1863.

36. Carrington met with Democratic and Republican Party leaders on several occasions to bring calm to the situation. After one meeting he wired Wright, "I had a conference with officers of state and leading men of both parties as to condition of affairs here. They propose an address to the people connected with my taking command [of] this district. They meet again on Weds. If I receive the order [to command district] by that time it will be of great immediate good." Carrington to Wright, March 23, 1863, RG 393, pt. 1, E 3491, vol. 3, 159, NARA.

37. Less than a week later Carrington reiterated the idea of a popular reaction to the rise of opposition to the government. In a letter to Morton written when the governor was away in the East, Carrington reported the end of the state Democratic Party convention in Indianapolis and that the people were "alarmed" by the party's rhetoric. "I think a favorable re-action will come." Carrington to Morton, March 25, 1863, Morton Records, ISA.

38. Carrington to Lincoln, March 19, 1863, Lincoln Papers, LC, also in *OR*, ser. 2, vol. 5, 363–67.

39. J. W. King to Wright, March 26, 1863, RG 393, pt. 1, E 3489, vol. 2, 285, NARA.

40. James J. Langdon to Wright, March 26, 1863, ibid., vol. 2, 309. One of Wright's staff officers forwarded the letter to General Ammen with instructions to inform Langdon of the general orders. See Langdon to Wright, March 26, 1863, Ammen Papers, ALPL.

41. J. A. Potter to Wright, March 27, 1863, RG 393, pt. 1, E 3489, vol. 2, 425, NARA.

42. R. S. Bennett to Eastman, April 8, 1863, RG 393, pt. 4, Post of Cincinnati, Ohio, Records, E 216, Register of Letters Received, vol. 1, 26, NARA.

43. Kittredge and Co. to Eastman, April 6, 1863, ibid., vol. 1, 198, NARA.

44. Kemper to Mason, April 14, 1863, RG 393, pt. 2, District of Ohio Records, E 961, Letters Received, NARA.

45. S. N. Pike to Wright, March 25, 1863, RG 393, pt. 1, E 3489, vol. 2, 425, NARA.

46. Lt. Alonzo Eaton to [Burnside], March 31, April 13, 1863, both in RG 393, pt. 1, E 3489, vol. 2, 129, 130; Eaton and W. S. Mason to Ammen, March 31, 1863; Ammen to Eaton, April 14, 1863; Eaton to Ammen, April 17, 1863, all in Ammen Papers, ALPL.

47. Wright's Senate confirmation was held up by reports that he had ordered the recapture of escaped slaves while serving in North Carolina. Wright considered the reports a lie. Wright to Brig. Gen. George W. Cullom, March 16, 1863, RG 393, pt. 1, E 3487, vol. 2, NARA.

48. William Marvel, *Burnside* (Chapel Hill: University of North Carolina Press, 1991), 151–217.

49. Burnside to Halleck, March 24, 1863, RG 393, pt. 1, E 3487, vol. 2, 67, NARA.

50. Lincoln's proclamation of March 10 is to be found in *OR*, ser. 3, vol. 3, 60–61. The proclamation stated that "evil-disposed and disloyal persons . . . have enticed and procured soldiers to desert and absent themselves from their regiments, thereby weakening the strength of the armies and prolonging the war, giving aid and comfort to the enemy." See also Lonn, *Desertion*, 169.

51. Carrington to Burnside, March 26, 1863, RG 94, E 159, Ambrose E. Burnside Papers, box 6, NARA.

52. Carrington to Burnside, March 26, 1863, RG 94, E 159, Burnside Papers, box 6, NARA.

53. Richard Yates to Salmon P. Chase, February 2, 1863, vol. 10, Stanton Papers, LC. Included with Yates's letter was one from Edward Lusk to Yates, January 30, 1863, describing the mutinous sentiments in the 101st Illinois Volunteer Infantry regiment. As was the custom with Yates's letters to Lincoln, the other Republican state officers (who also knew the president) endorsed the letter with their comments. Secretary of State Oziah M. Hatch added that "great danger of a rebellion" existed and that the government would be defied. President Lincoln read the letter and wrote on it on February 10, "I suppose these papers are superseded, by what the Secy did yesterday." On February 9, Stanton approved the request for four regiments but later rescinded the order.

54. John M. Palmer, *Personal Recollections of John M. Palmer: The Story of an Earnest Life* (Cincinnati: Robert Clarke Co., 1901), 152–53.

55. William H. Pierce to Newton Bateman, March 11, 1863, box 2, Newton Bateman Papers, ALPL.

56. William L. Harper to Yates, March 27, 1863, RG 393, pt. 1, E 3489, vol. 2, 212, NARA.

57. Memorandum of March 21, 1863, Ammen Papers, ALPL.

58. Yates to Burnside, April 3, 1863, RG 94, E 159, box 6, Burnside Papers, NARA.

59. Burnside to Samuel Curtis, April 4, 1863, RG 393, pt. 1, E 3487, vol. 2, 125, NARA.

60. Brig. Gen. Thomas J. McKean to Curtis, April 8, 1863, Ammen Papers, ALPL.

61. Flamen Ball to [Wright], March 24, 1863, RG 393, pt. 1, E3489, vol. 2, 43, NARA.

62. *Cincinnati Daily Commercial,* April 9, 1863.

63. *Cincinnati Daily Commercial,* April 20, 1863.

64. Carrington to Burnside, April 13, 1863, RG 393, pt. 1, E 3489, vol. 2, 616, NARA.

65. Buford to Ammen, April 19, 1863, Ammen Papers, ALPL.

66. Buford to Burnside, April 22, 23, 1863, both in RG 393, pt. 1, E 3489, vol. 2, 53–54, NARA.

67. Burnside to Ammen, April 17, 1863, Ambrose E. Burnside Collection, letter book no. 1, 112, Rhode Island Historical Society, Providence, Rhode Island (hereafter cited as Burnside Collection, RIHS).

68. Affidavit of J. B. Allen, April 17, 1863, RG 94, E 159 A, box 1, Alexander Asboth Papers, NARA.

69. Asboth wrote, "The citizen giving [the statement] is here in person—yet I consider the report exaggerated." Asboth to Burnside, April 17, 1863, RG 393, pt. 1, District of Kentucky Records, E 2175, Telegrams Received and Sent, District of Western Kentucky, box 1, NARA; Asboth to Burnside, April 22, 1863, RG 393, pt. 2, Post of Cairo, Illinois, Records, no. 24, E 986, Letters Sent, vol. 1, 205, NARA.

70. Capt. Thomas J. Larison to Asboth, April 21, 1863, RG 94, E 159 A, Asboth Papers, box 1, NARA.

71. Brig. Gen. Alexander Asboth to Burnside, April 17, 1863, RG 393, pt. 1, E 2175, box 1, NARA.

72. Burnside to Ammen, April 20, 1863, letter book no. 1, 135, Burnside Collection, RIHS; Burnside to Ammen, April 21, 1863, Ammen Papers, ALPL. The officer sent to arrest White botched the effort but reported that that he had found ample evidence of the existence of the KGC in the community. Members met and drilled regularly and posted pickets on the roads to turn back persons who came too close to meeting places, he reported. Lt. James E. Moss to Ammen, April 24, 1863, Ammen Papers, ALPL.

73. H. Binmore to Asboth, April 18, 1863, RG 393, pt. 1, E 2175, box 1; Asboth to Buford, April 23, 1863, RG 393, pt. 2, E 986, vol. 1, 206–7, both NARA.

74. *Indianapolis Daily Journal,* April 20, 22, May 5, 1863. See other accounts in *Indianapolis Daily State Sentinel,* April 20, 21, 1863, and *Indianapolis Daily Gazette,* April 20, 21, 1863.

75. The newspaper accounts, including eyewitness reports, are contradictory. See *Indianapolis Daily Journal,* April 20, 22, 23, 25, 28, 1863; *Indianapolis Daily State Sentinel,* April 21, 23, 27, 29, 1863; *Indianapolis Daily Gazette,* April 20, May 2, 1863; *Cincinnati Daily Enquirer,* May 5, 1863; *Cincinnati Daily Commercial,* April 29, 1863; *Greencastle Putnam Republican Banner,* April 30, 1863; *Shelby Volunteer,* April 30, 1863; *Delphi Weekly Times,* May 2, 1863; *Worthington White River Gazette,* April 30, 1863; *Seymour Times,* May 14, 1863.

76. J. J. Johnson to Laz Noble, April 28, 1863, Adjutant General of Indiana Records, A 4017 024596, folder 13, ISA, printed in Nation and Towne, *Indiana's War,* 167.

77. Carrington to Burnside, April 19, 1863, RG 94, E 159, Burnside Papers, box 6, NARA.

78. Carrington to Burnside, April 20, 1863, ibid.

79. Carrington wrote in 1908 that Halleck's "statement 'I do not know General Carrington personally' is a subterfuge, if not a deliberate falsehood. He *did* have a brief personal interview with [me] in June, 1862 at the City of Washington, which gave him offense." Carrington explains the episode in "Major General H. W. Halleck's Statements Confronted by Actual Facts," Carrington Papers, ISA, 11–14.

80. Halleck to Burnside, March 21, 1863, RG 94, E 159, Burnside Papers, box 7, NARA.

81. Burnside to Halleck, March 24, 1863, RG 393, pt. 1, E 3487, vol. 2, 67, NARA.

82. Halleck to Burnside, March 30, 1863, RG 94, E 159, Burnside Papers, box 6, NARA, also in *OR,* ser. 1, vol. 23, pt. 2, 193–94.

83. Burnside to Stanton, April 6, 1863, letter book no. 1, 43, Burnside Collection, RIHS.

84. Stanton to Burnside, April 6, 1863, RG 94, E 159, Burnside Papers, box 6, NARA.

85. Burnside to Carrington, April 20, 1863, RG 393, pt. 1, E 3487, vol. 2, 224, NARA.

86. Carrington to Burnside, April 21, 1863, RG 94, E 159, Burnside Papers, box 6, NARA.

87. Hascall instituted a policy of suppression of Democratic newspapers that enraged Morton, prompting the governor to try to remove both Hascall and Burnside.

See Stephen E. Towne, "Killing the Serpent Speedily: Governor Morton, General Hascall, and the Suppression of the Democratic Press in Indiana, 1863," *Civil War History* 52, no. 1 (March 2006): 41–65.

88. *Indianapolis Daily Journal,* April 2, 6, 1863.

89. See proclamation of March 24 in *Indianapolis Daily Journal,* March 27, 1863, reiterated in General Orders 6 of April 19, 1863, *Indianapolis Daily Journal,* April 20, 1863.

90. See General Orders 5, April 11, 1863, *Indianapolis Daily Journal,* April 13, 1863.

91. *Indianapolis Daily Gazette,* April 9, 1863; *Indianapolis Daily Journal,* April 13, 1863.

92. See Smith's charge to the grand jury in *Indianapolis Daily Journal,* April 3, 1863.

93. James S. Hester to Morton, April 23, 1863, RG 94, E 159, Burnside Papers, box 7, NARA, printed in Nation and Towne, *Indiana's War,* 167–68.

94. See John Farquhar to Fannie Farquhar, April 27 and May 1, 1863, Farquhar Correspondence, LC.

95. Morton to Jesse J. Brown, April 29, 1863, OPMTB, vol. 10, 234, ISA.

96. Carrington to Chase, May 26, 1863, Salmon P. Chase, *The Salmon P. Chase Papers,* vol. 4, *Correspondence, Apr., 1863–1864,* ed. John Niven (Kent, Ohio: Kent State University Press, 1997), 42–46.

97. Uzziah Kendall, Jr., to [Kemper], April 14, 1863: George N. C. Fraser and Will. Smith to [Kemper], April 25, 1863, both in RG 393, pt. 4, Post of Cincinnati, Ohio, Records, E 216, Register of Letters Received, vol. 1, 199–200, 67, NARA.

98. H. T. Anderson to Kemper, [May 23, 1863?], RG 393, pt. 4, E 217, box 1, NARA.

99. Lt. Col. Thomas C. Boone to Kemper, May 26, 1863, ibid.

100. See reports of Daniel Lesh to Kemper, May 12, 14, 28, June 1, 1863, all ibid.

101. Kemper to J. C. Baum, April 23, 25, 1863; Kemper to Provost Marshal of Nashville, April 25, May 22, 1863; Kemper to Daniel R. Larned, May 20, 1863, all in RG 393, pt. 4, E 212, 143–44, 145, 159, 164, NARA.

102. Brig. Gen. Jeremiah T. Boyle to Brig. Gen. E. H. Hobson, April 29, 1863, RG 393, pt. 1, E 2175, box 1, NARA.

103. W. F. Comly to [?], May 19, 1863, RG 393, pt. 1, E 3489, vol. 2, 625, NARA.

104. Capt. W. P. Anderson to [?], April 24, 1863, RG 393, pt. 2, District of Ohio Records, E 960, Register of Letters Received, vol. 2, 385, NARA.

105. See special orders of April 26, 1863, RG 393, pt. 2, District of Ohio Records, E 967, Special Orders, NARA.

106. *Indianapolis Sentinel,* August 3, 1857, reprinted in *Washington (DC) Daily National Intelligencer,* August 11, 1857; *Cleveland Herald,* September 11, 1852; *Ripley Bee,* August 1, 1857, July 30, 1859; *Philadelphia Press,* February 3, 1859; *Altoona (PA) Tribune,* September 15, 1859.

107. See various special orders detailing Reany and his men, RG 393, pt. 2, E 967, NARA.

108. General Orders 15, July 15, 1863, ibid.

109. Cox to Tod, July 10, 1863, RG 393, pt. 2, District of Ohio Records, E 957, Press Copies of Letters and Telegrams Sent, vol. 6, NARA. The detective whom Tod offered to General Cox was a Corporal James Pike, an Ohio soldier in Tennessee who had

served as a "scout" in the field and who contacted the governor to volunteer his spy services to "ferret out certain secret Political Societies in Ohio. . . . I am confident that there is an understanding between the Knights of the Golden Circle South and the Copperhead organization North. My own father (Samuel Pike the newspaperman) is one of the Copperhead party. I know that the leaders of that party are as base conspirators as Jeff Davis." The War Department issued a Special Field Order, no. 114, to send Pike to meet with Tod. See Pike to Tod, April 28, 1863, Adjutant General of Ohio Records, ser. 147, vol. 85, box 50, 332, folder 5, OHS. Pike later wrote a fanciful memoir of his adventures. See James Pike, *The Scout and Ranger: Being the Personal Adventures of Corporal Pike of the Fourth Ohio Cavalry* (Cincinnati: J. R. Hawley, 1865).

110. Mason wrote, "I have just learned that there is a consultation of Butternuts from different parts of the State to resist any interference with the *Crisis*. They must get their information from [Samuel] Medary, as I have acted discretely in that matter." See Mason to Cox, May 19, 1863, RG 393, pt. 4, Post of Columbus, Ohio, Records, E 270, Letters Sent, vol. 1, NARA.

111. *Daily Cleveland Herald*, April 16, 20, 22, 1863.

112. Mason to Cox, May 8, 1863, RG 393, pt. 4, E 270, vol. 1, NARA, also in RG 393, pt. 2, E 960, vol. 2, 252, NARA.

113. Maj. C. M. Bascom to Mason, May 18, 1863, RG 393, pt. 2, E 957, vol. 5, 444, NARA.

114. Cox to Mason, May 26, 1863, ibid., 483, also in RG 393, pt. 4, Post of Columbus, Ohio, Records, E 273, Register of Letters Received, vol. 1, 49, NARA.

115. Capt. J. M. Hiatt to Col. F. A. Dick, March 20, 1863; Horace Everett to J. M. Hiatt, March 13, 1863; Capt. J. H. Summers to Hiatt, March 9, 1863; Hiatt to Dick, March 15, 1863, all in RG 393, pt. 1, Department of the Missouri Records, E 2786, Letters Received, Provost Marshal General, box 1, NARA. Dan Elbert Clark, *Samuel Jordan Kirkwood* (Iowa City: State Historical Society of Iowa, 1917), 276.

116. Stanton to Burnside, Maj. Gen. John Pope, Maj. Gen. Samuel R. Curtis, May 8, 1863, RG 107, Office of the Secretary of War Records, E 5, Letters Sent by the Secretary of War Relating to Military Affairs, 1800–1889, vol. 52, 313–14, M6, NARA.

117. Receipt of J. M. Hiatt, May 8, 1863, RG 110, E 95, box 2, NARA. In the same box is an abstract compiled by the chief clerk of the War Department, John Potts, who had charge over the secret-service funds, which noted that Hiatt and the two Quartermaster Department detectives Newbury and Pollard were the only recipients of secret-service funds from the West for the period April through June, 1863! All other recipients of War Department secret-service funds worked in the East. Lafayette Baker and Allan Pinkerton received the vast majority of the funds.

118. Brig. Gen. Nathaniel C. McLean to Col. Richmond, May 13, 1863, Charles F. Gunther Collection, Chicago Historical Society.

119. G. Edmonds and Jackson Grimshaw to [Burnside], June 4, 1863, RG 393, pt. 1, E 3489, vol. 2, 131; Capt. Robert B. Rutledge to J. D. Templin, June 11, 1863; Rutledge to Maj. Thomas Duncan, June 24, 1863, both in RG 110, Provost Marshal General's Bureau Records, E 6393, Letters Sent 1st District of Iowa, vol. 1, 28, 59–60, all in NARA.

120. J. L. Langdon to Ammen, April 27, 1863; Col. John W. Foster to Ammen, May 5, 1863, both in Ammen Papers, ALPL.

121. Ammen to Burnside, May 8, 1863, RG 393, pt. 1, E 3489, vol. 2, 19, NARA.

122. Kemper to Captains Hill and Means, April 30, 1863, RG 393, pt. 4, E 212, vol. 1, 147, NARA.

123. Journal of Daniel Read Larned, entry for May 14, 1863, Daniel Read Larned Papers, Library of Congress (hereafter cited as Larned Papers, LC).

124. Burnside to Stanton, March 30, 1863, RG 393, pt. 1, E 3487, vol. 2, 105, NARA.

125. Larned to Amelia Larned, April 24, 1863, Larned Papers, LC.

126. Journal entry for May 16, 1863, Larned Papers, LC.

127. Truesdail to Rosecrans, April 22, 1863, RG 393, pt. 1, Department of the Cumberland Records, E 1095, Register of Letters Received, vol. 1, NARA.

128. Truesdail to [Kemper], May 6, 1863, RG 393, pt. 4, E 216, vol. 1, 400, NARA. Letters to Kemper recorded in the same volume from a "Captain J. M. Palmer" from Louisville and Saint Louis refer to a "Mrs. Johnson" of Cincinnati, suggesting that Palmer followed her to Louisville and Saint Louis. See Palmer to Kemper, May 12, 16, 17, June 21, 1863, all ibid., 312, 313, 316; Kemper to Palmer, May 13, 20, 1863, RG 393, pt. 4, E 212, vol. 1, 154, 161, NARA. Palmer may have been Capt. John M. Palmer of Findlay, Hancock County, Ohio, an attorney who had helped to recruit the 57th Ohio Volunteer Infantry regiment and who obtained a brigade commissary appointment in the Army of the Cumberland before being discharged, in March 1863.

129. See affidavits and correspondence, RG 393, pt. 2, E 961, box 2, NARA. Secretary of the Treasury Salmon P. Chase also played a part in the business.

130. Kemper to Lt. William M. McClure, June 2, 3, 1863, RG 393, pt. 4, E 212, 175, 177, NARA.

131. Willcox to Burnside, June 9, 16, 17, 19, 22, 1863, RG 94, E 159, Burnside Papers, box 7, NARA; Burnside to Willcox, June 11, 16, 1863, letter book no. 2, Burnside Collection, RIHS.

132. Willcox to Burnside, June 11, 1863, RG 94, E 159, Burnside Papers, box 7, NARA.

133. Willcox to Burnside, June 27, 1863, ibid.

134. Willcox to Burnside, June 25, 1863, ibid. See also Willcox to Burnside, July 2, 7, 29, 1863, all ibid.; Willcox to Burnside, July 30, 1863, RG 393, pt. 1, E 3489, vol. 3, 558, NARA.

135. Willcox to Burnside, June 22, July 1, 1863, RG 94, E 159, Burnside Papers, box 7, NARA; Burnside to Willcox, June 23, 1863, letter book no. 2, Burnside Collection, RIHS. Troops arrested Lafayette gunsmiths Bixler and Iddings on July 1, 1863, in connection with the court-martial trial and conviction of Reuben Stout for desertion and murder. *Delphi Journal,* July 8, 1863.

136. Wilson Morrow to Laz Noble, August 24, 1863, Franklin County Correspondence, Indiana Legion Records, ISA. See also Orlando B. Willcox, *Forgotten Valor: The Memoirs, Journals, and Civil War Letters of Orlando B. Willcox,* ed. Robert Garth Scott (Kent, Ohio: Kent State University Press, 1999).

137. Burnside to Halleck, June 22, 1863, letter book no. 2, Burnside Collection, RIHS; printed in *OR,* ser. 1, vol. 23, pt. 1, 397.

138. See statements of Capt. J. S. Hobart, *Indianapolis Daily Gazette,* July 18 and 20, 1863. Colonel L. S. Shuler, who commanded the vanguard of the pursuit force

for part of the time, wrote in his official report, "I am sorry to state that there were few points along the line of our march w[h]ere we did not find men who had been rendering assistance to John Morgan and who were then willing to do every thing in their power to help him on his expedition of robbery and plunder. Their sympathies were all for Vallandigham, and there was no one among them who could not render valuable information in regard to the 'Order of the K.G.Cs.' I would most respectfully suggest the propriety of sending scouts [detectives] throughout the southern part of our State, whose duty it should be to arrest parties who are declaring themselves friends of *Vallandigham* and of the *Southern Confederacy.* Had it not been for the aid and encouragement which these sympathizers gave Morgan could never have made a successful raid through our own state." L.S. Shuler to Laz Noble, July 20, 1863, 103rd Indiana Volunteer Infantry Regimental Correspondence, ISA.

139. Col. Conrad Baker to Col. James B. Fry, August 11, 1863, RG 393, pt. 1, E 3489, vol. 3, 46, NARA.

Chapter 4

1. William Fiscus to Maj. Gen. Alvin P. Hovey, September 29, 1864, RG 110, E 5381, Letters Received, box 1, NARA-GLR.

2. Works on the Civil War conscription system include Eugene C. Murdock, *Patriotism Limited, 1862–1865: The Civil War Draft and the Bounty System* (Kent, Ohio: Kent State University Press 1967); Murdock, *One Million Men: The Civil War Draft in the North* (Madison: State Historical Society of Wisconsin, 1971); James W. Geary, *We Need Men: The Union Draft in the Civil War* (DeKalb: Northern Illinois University Press, 1991).

3. Printed in *OR,* ser. 3, vol. 3, 88–93. See also Robert E. Sterling, "Civil War Draft Resistance in the Middle West" (PhD diss., Northern Illinois University, 1974).

4. *Congressional Globe,* 37th Congress, Third Session (Washington, DC, 1863), 1215, 1218, 1226, 1250, 1291, 1478. James W. Geary devotes a chapter of his book to the debate over the introduction of Wilson's enrollment bill but makes no mention of the "inquire into" language that alarmed Democrats. Further, his book fails to touch on the system of espionage that the Enrollment Act created. See Geary, *We Need Men,* 49–64. Robert E. Sterling makes only passing reference to congressional debate about the implications of the bill for intrusions into the privacy of citizens. Sterling, "Draft Resistance," 148.

5. *OR,* ser. 3, vol. 3, 125–46.

6. See ibid., 322–23.

7. Capt. Benjamin F. Westlake to James Oakes, November 11, December 19, 1863, RG 110, Provost Marshal General's Bureau Records, E 5729, 9th District Illinois, Letters Sent, vol. 1, 298, 407–8, NARA-GLR; Sterling, "Draft Resistance," 527–29.

8. Oakes to Capt. Abel Longworth, August 1, 1863, RG 110, E 5679, 6th District Illinois, Letters Received, NARA-GLR.

9. Oakes to Longworth, September 15, 1863, ibid.

10. Circular 99, November 5, 1863, *OR,* ser. 3, vol. 3, 995.

11. Oakes to Capt. John V. Eustace, November 16, 1863, RG 110, E 5614, 3rd District Illinois, Letters Received, box 16, NARA-GLR.

12. Capt. James M. Allan to Oakes, May 12, 1864, RG 110, E 5651, 5th District Illinois, Letters Sent, vol. 2, 428–34, NARA-GLR.

13. Col. B. H. Hill to James B. Fry, July 31, 1863, RG 110, E 5904, Endorsements Sent by the Acting Assistant Provost Marshal General, vol. 1, 22, NARA-GLR.

14. Capt. P. E. Hall to J. P. Eaton, June 28, 1863, RG 110, E 6403, 2nd District Iowa, Letters Sent, vol. 1, 83–84, NARA-GLR.

15. Capt. William James to Oakes, June 6, 10, 1863, RG 110, E 5382, Letters Received from District Provost Marshals, 1st District Illinois, box 3, NARA-GLR.

16. Capt. James Mathews to George May, June 5, 1863, RG 110, E 6445, 4th District Iowa, Letters Sent, vol. 1, 17–18, NARA-GLR.

17. Capt. James Mathews to Maj. Thomas Duncan, October 2, 1864, RG 110, E 6445, vol. 3, 492–95, NARA-GLR.

18. Sterling, "Draft Resistance," 183. Klement asserts that draft enrollments in the spring and summer of 1863 produced "negligible violence" and passed off more peacefully than fear-mongering Republican authorities expected. Klement, *Copperheads in the Middle West,* 80.

19. Capt. Isaac Keys, to James B. Fry, November 26, 1863, RG 110, E 5714, 8th District Illinois, Letters Sent, vol. 1, 356, NARA-GLR.

20. Mathews to Thomas Craig, July 13, 1863, RG 110, E 6445, vol. 1, 125, NARA-GLR.

21. Oliver White to Allan, August 24, 1863, RG 110, E 5653, Letters Received 5th District Illinois, NARA-GLR.

22. Allan to James B. Fry, April 28, 1864, RG 110, E 5651, Letters Sent 5th District Illinois, vol. 2, 338–39, NARA-GLR.

23. Geary, *We Need Men,* 108.

24. Westlake to Oakes, August 7, 1863, RG 110, E 5382, box 3, NARA-GLR.

25. Westlake to Oakes, June 25, 1863, ibid.

26. Capt. Henry Asbury to James B. Fry, May 31, 1864, RG 110, E 5382, box 3, NARA-GLR.

27. Brig. Gen. William Orme to James, April 18, 1864, RG 110, E 5557, Letters Received 1st District Illinois, box 15, NARA-GLR.

28. Oakes to James B. Fry, June 5, July 3, 1863, both in RG 110, E 5359, Letters and Circulars Sent, vol. 1, 9–10, 352, NARA-GLR.

29. Westlake to Oakes, July 15, 1863, RG 110, E 5382, box 3, also in E 5729, both in NARA-GLR.

30. *Chicago Daily Tribune,* May 19, 1863. Some of the letters Forrest quoted or paraphrased in the article survive in the collections of Governor Richard Yates's papers. See Yates Family Papers and Wabash Yates Papers, ALPL.

31. Another source reported that a guerrilla captain from Missouri drilled Clark County rebel sympathizers. See Joshua Ricketts to Allan C. Fuller, May 18, 1863, Ammen Papers, ALPL.

32. Oakes to James B. Fry, June 8, 1863, RG 110, E 5359, vol. 1, 26–41, NARA-GLR.

33. Buford to [Burnside], June 3, 1863, RG 393, pt. 1, E 3489, vol. 2, 62, NARA.

34. Buford to Ammen, June 4, 1863, Ammen Papers, ALPL.

35. Jack J. Nortrup, "Yates, the Prorogued Legislature, and the Constitutional Convention," *Journal of the Illinois State Historical Society* 62, no. 1 (Spring 1969): 29–34.

36. Ammen to [Burnside], May [?], 1863 [recd. June 2, 1863], RG 393, pt. 1, E 3489, vol. 2, 21, NARA.

37. W. P. Ammen to Buford, June 16, 1863, RG 393, pt. 2, Post of Cairo, Illinois, Records, no. 28, E 1106 Miscellaneous Records, NARA.

38. Jesse Rosson to Yates, June 14, 1863, box 1, folder 14, Wabash Yates Papers, ALPL.

39. James H. Hale to Yates, June 15, 1863, box 2, folder 5, Wabash Yates Papers, ALPL.

40. B. Pilkington to Yates, June 13, 1863, box 12, folder 5, Yates Family Papers, ALPL. Pilkington also wrote to General Buford for protection, stating that the local secessionists were armed, drilled in numbers from fifty to five hundred, and threatened that after the Springfield convention they would drive the loyal citizens out of town. He asked for arms for protection. B. Pilkington to Buford, June 16, 1863, RG 393, pt. 2, E 1090, 27, NARA. Buford replied that his letter "presents a sad state of affairs" and that he would forward it to Burnside. He wrote that he had "information of what I consider treasonable proceedings in other counties near you, which ought to be treated judiciously." However, he asked, would not arming loyal men "bring on a collision and inaugurate in Illinois the unhappy condition of Missouri?" Buford to Pilkington, June 17, 1863, RG 393, pt. 2, Post of Cairo, Illinois, Records, no. 28, E 1085, Letters Sent, 54–55, NARA.

41. See Craig D. Tenney, "To Suppress or Not to Suppress: Abraham Lincoln and the *Chicago Times*," *Civil War History* 27, no. 3 (1981): 248–59.

42. Yates to Stanton, June 15, 1863, box 12, folder 5, Yates Family Papers, ALPL. Testimony given at the Indianapolis and Cincinnati military commission trials in 1864 and 1865 revealed that the June 17, 1863, Democratic convention at Springfield served as the pretext for the reorganization of the secret organization in Illinois into the Order of American Knights.

43. Oakes to James B. Fry, July 3, 1863; Lt. James M. Davidson to Oakes, July 8, 1863, both in RG 110, E 5359, vol. 1, 352, 409–17, NARA-GLR.

44. Lt. Thomas G. Barnes to Oakes, July 4, 1863, RG 110, E 5381, box 1, NARA-GLR.

45. G. W. Rives and Thomas C. W. Scott to Oakes, July 21, 1863, ibid.

46. Eben Noyes to Oakes, July 22, 1863, ibid.

47. Capt. Wells Sponable to Oakes, July 28, 1863, ibid.

48. Lt. Lorenzo Eaton to Buford, August 1, 1863, RG 393, pt. 2, Post of Cairo, Illinois, Records, no. 28, E 1091, Telegrams Received, 40, NARA; Eaton to Ammen, August 2, 1863, Ammen Papers, ALPL.

49. W. B. Archer to Oakes, July 27, 31, 1863; Capt. Mortimer O'Kean to Oakes, July 27, 31, 1863, all in RG 110, E 5382, box 3, NARA-GLR.

50. Buford to Asboth, July 6, 1863, RG 393, pt. 2, Post of Cairo, Illinois, Records, no. 24, E 991, Letters Received, box 3, NARA.

51. Maj. Charles H. Beres to Ammen, July 14, 1863, Ammen Papers, ALPL.

52. Oakes to Capt. Isaac N. Phillips, August 4 and 19, 1863, RG 110, E 5823, Letters Received 13th District Illinois, box 26, NARA-GLR.

53. O'Kean to Oakes, July 14, 1863, RG 110, E 5381, box 1, NARA-GLR.

54. Westlake to Oakes, August 7, 1863, RG 110, E 5382, box 3, NARA-GLR.

55. Westlake to Oakes, August 27, 1863, ibid.

56. O'Kean to Oakes, August 29, 1863, ibid.

57. *Lafayette Daily Courier,* August 25, 1863; *Danville Globe,* August 27, 1863, reprinted in *Logansport Democratic-Pharos,* September 9, 1863; Maj. George R. Clarke to Ammen, August 29, September 2, 1863, Ammen Papers, ALPL.

58. See Ammen to Burnside, July 8, 13, 21, 22, 30, 1863, all in RG 393, pt. 1, E 3489, vol. 3, 2–4, NARA.

59. Yates to Stanton, July 14, 1863, *OR,* ser. 3, vol. 3, 487–88.

60. Ammen to Yates, August 12, 1863, box 13, folder 1, Yates Family Papers, ALPL.

61. Stanton to Yates, August 22, 1863, vol. 40, Stanton Papers, LC.

62. Yates to Stanton, August 5, 17, 1863, both in *OR,* ser. 3, vol. 3, 626–27, 685; Yates to Stanton, October 6, 1863, letter book C, 983–84, box 16, folder 2, Wabash Yates Papers, ALPL.

63. Capt. William M. Fry to Oakes, November 11, 1863, RG 110, E 5382, box 3, NARA-GLR.

64. Lt. Col. George R. Clarke to Capt. W. P. Ammen, November 28, 1863, Ammen Papers, ALPL.

65. Affidavit of Peter Thompson, December 17, 1863, RG 110, E 5382, box 5, NARA-GLR.

66. William P. Ammen to Jacob Ammen, November 30, 1863, Ammen Papers, ALPL.

67. Buford to Maj. Gen. John M. Schofield, June 17, 1863, RG 393, pt. 2, E 1085, 55, NARA.

68. Col. William T. Shaw to Asboth, July 31, 1863, RG 393, pt. 2, E 991, box 2, NARA.

69. Col. Conrad Baker to [?], June 4, 1863, RG 110, E 5055, Letters Sent, vol. 1, NARA-GLR; Brig. Gen. Orlando B. Willcox to Burnside, June 17, 1863, RG 94, E 159, Burnside Papers, NARA; Capt. Richard W. Thompson to Lt. J. C. Conner, June 5, 1863; Thompson to Baker, June 6, 1863, both in RG 110, E 5236, Letters Received 7th District Indiana, box 7, NARA-GLR.

70. Baker to James B. Fry, June 11, 1863, RG 110, E 5055, vol. 1, NARA-GLR.

71. Baker to Fry, June 17, 1863, ibid., 124–25; printed in *OR,* ser. 3, vol. 3, 375.

72. Admission Book no. 1, 519, Indiana Hospital for the Insane, Central State Hospital Records, ISA. See Nation and Towne, *Indiana's War,* 99.

73. Baker to Fry, June 20, 1863, RG 110, E 5055, vol. 1, 146–47, NARA-GLR, printed in *OR,* ser. 3, vol. 3, 392–93.

74. Willcox to Burnside, June 17, 1863, RG 94, E 159, Burnside Papers, NARA, printed in Nation and Towne, *Indiana's War,* 143–44.

75. Baker to Fry, June 11, 1863, RG 110, E 5055, vol. 1, 67–69, NARA-GLR.

76. Brig. Gen. John L. Mansfield to Morton, May 25, 1863, Switzerland County Reports, Indiana Legion Records, ISA.

77. Mansfield to Morton, June 5, 1863, Warren County Reports, Indiana Legion Records, ISA; Joseph H. Brown and Alvin High to Morton, n.d., 33rd Indiana Volunteer Infantry Regiment Correspondence, ISA.

78. William R. Holloway to Brig. Gen. Jeremiah T. Boyle, June 19, 1863, RG 393, pt. 1, E 2175, box 2, NARA; Baker to Capt. A. J. Welch, June 15, 1863, RG 110, E 5055, vol. 1, 103–4, NARA-GLR.

79. Thomas Gullenger to Laz Noble, RG 110, E 5149, Letters Received 1st District Indiana, box 4, NARA-GLR.

80. Capt. John B. Meriwether to Fry, July 5, 1863, RG 110, E 5166, Letters Sent 2nd District Indiana, vol. 1, 158, NARA-GLR.

81. C. R. Van Trees to Blythe Hynes, June 18, 20, 30, 1863, all in RG 110, E 5149, box 4, NARA-GLR.

82. Blythe Hynes to James W. Waterman, June 26, 1863, RG 110 E 5148, Letters Sent 1st District Indiana, vol. 1, NARA-GLR.

83. Blythe Hynes to Fry, August 20, 1863, ibid., 141–42.

84. Hynes to Ezra Atwood, June 26, 1863, ibid.

85. J. S. Power to Hynes, June 18, 1863, RG 110, E 5149, box 4, NARA-GLR.

86. Meriwether to Baker, June 17, 1863, RG 110, E 5166, vol. 1, 47, NARA-GLR.

87. Capt. Simeon Stansifer to Baker, July 28, 1863, RG 110, E 5176, Letters Sent 3rd District Indiana, vol. 1, 140, NARA-GLR.

88. Capt. Calvin Cowgill to James M. Bratton, July 7, 1863, RG 110, E 5290, Letters Sent 11th District Indiana, vol. 1, 102–3, NARA-GLR.

89. Cowgill to Bratton, July 10, 1863, ibid., 110.

90. Cowgill to Morton, July 25, 1863, ibid., 165.

91. Cowgill to Baker, August 2, 4, 1863; [?] to [?], n.d., all ibid., 181, 187, 188–89, 191.

92. Cowgill to Fry, August 20, 1863, ibid., 254.

93. Cowgill to Fry, August 10, 1863, ibid., 216.

94. Baker to Fry, June 12, 1863, RG 110, E 38, Correspondence and Reports Relating to Disloyal and Suspect Persons in Connection with the Lincoln Assassination Plot, folder "Disloyal-1863," NARA.

95. Baker to Capt. John C. McQuiston, June 15, 1863, RG 110, E 5055, vol. 1, 108–9, NARA-GLR.

96. Baker to Fry, July 2, 1863, ibid., 234–35.

97. Baker to Capt. Isaac Kinley, June 29, 1863, ibid., 191; Kinley to Baker, July 11, 1863, RG 110, E 5204, Letters Sent 5th District Indiana, vol. 1, NARA-GLR.

98. Affidavit of James Oard, July 27, 1863, RG 110, E 5205, Letters Received 5th District Indiana, NARA-GLR.

99. Merriwether to Gen. J. T. Boyle, July 16, 1863, RG 393, pt. 1, E 2175, box 2, NARA.

100. Capt. William Wiles to Lt. Kessler, July 9, 1863, RG 393, pt. 1, Department of the Cumberland Records, E 1091, Letters and Telegrams Sent, 126, NARA.

101. Wiles to Burnside, July 9, 1863, ibid., 127.

102. Burnside to Boyle, July 17, 20, 1863, letter book no. 3, Burnside Collection, RIHS. Klement erroneously suggests that Morton and Carrington used the Bickley arrest to announce the existence of the KGC. However, the Republican state organ reprinted articles from the Louisville press and stated merely that Bickley would be tried and executed as a spy. *Indianapolis Daily Journal*, July 21, 23, 29, 1863.

103. Maj. J. M. Wright to Brig. Gen. N. C. McLean, August 8, 16, 1863, RG 393, pt. 1, District of Kentucky Records, E 2218, Press Copies of Letters Sent, Judge Advocate of the District of Kentucky, vol. 1, 17–18, 26–27, NARA.

104. [?] to Burnside, August 6, 1863, RG 109, M-345, Union Provost Marshals' File of Papers Relating to Individual Citizens, roll 26, NARA; Capt. Stephen E. Jones to Boyle, October 23, 1863, RG 393, pt. 1, District of Kentucky Records, E 2239, Press Copies of Letters Sent, Capt. S. E. Jones, vol. 1, 310, NARA. In an attempt to gain release, Bickley wrote a letter to Governor Tod fraudulently claiming that authorities had confused him with his nephew, but authorities did not believe it. Bickley to David Tod, September 3, 1863, RG 109, M-345, roll 26, NARA.

105. Augustus W. Drury, *History of the City of Dayton and Montgomery County, Ohio*, 2 vols. (Chicago: S. J. Clarke, 1909), 2:713–15.

106. Charles P. McIlvaine to Tod, April 1, 1863, Governor David Tod Papers, MS 306, MIC-999, roll 22, OHS (hereafter cited as Tod Papers, OHS).

107. Jacob Low to Tod, April 7, 1863, roll 22, Tod Papers, OHS.

108. W. S. Latham to Tod, April 7, 1863, roll 22, Tod Papers, OHS.

109. Capt. Daniel S. Brown to Parrott, May 25, 1863, RG 110, E 4455, Letters Received, box 1, NARA-GLR.

110. Capt. B. F. Cory to Parrott, June 9, 1863, RG 110, E 4452, Register of Letters Received, vol. 1, NARA-GLR.

111. Capt. William Shunk to Parrott, June 10, 1863, RG 110, E 4685, Letters Sent 8th District Ohio, 11, NARA-GLR.

112. Parrott to Fry, May 11, 1863, RG 110, E 4447, Register of Letters Sent, vol. 1, 144, NARA-GLR.

113. Fry to Parrott, May 12, 1863; Henry Stone to Parrott, May 21, 1863, both in E 4455, box 1, NARA-GLR.

114. Parrott to Capt. F. A. Nash, June 6, 1863, RG 110, E 4447, vol. 1, 132, NARA-GLR.

115. Brown to Parrott, June 10, 1863, RG 110, E 4619, Letters Sent 5th District Ohio, 20, NARA-GLR.

116. Parrott to Capt. James L. Drake, June 2, 1863, RG 110, E 4447, vol. 1, 70, NARA-GLR.

117. Parrott to B. F. Cory, June 8, 1863, RG 110, E 4447, vol. 1, 64, NARA-GLR.

118. Drake to Parrott, June 11, 1863, RG 110, E 4833, Letters Sent 14th District Ohio, vol. 1, 5, NARA-GLR.

119. Parrott to Fry, June 12, 1863, *OR*, ser. 3, vol. 3, 349–50.

120. The Holmes County draft resistance incident has received attention from historians, most notably Kenneth H. Wheeler, "Local Autonomy and Civil War Draft Resistance: Holmes County, Ohio," *Civil War History* 45, no. 2 (June 1999): 147–59. Unfortunately, the author relied on published secondary sources and the *War of the Rebellion* edition, and ignored the original records found in Record Groups 110 and 393 in the National Archives. Moreover, he echoes the erroneous Klement interpretation by discounting the existence of secret organizations that opposed federal government war measures and suggesting that "Republican politicians used the specter of the [KGC] to win votes and smear their opponents." Ibid., 151–52. See also James O. Lehman and Steven M. Nolt, *Mennonites, Amish, and the American Civil War* (Baltimore: Johns Hopkins University Press, 2007), 172–74.

121. Drake to Parrott, June 11, 13, 1863, both in RG 110, E 4833, vol. 1, 5, 6, NARA-GLR.

122. Drake to Parrott, June 15, 1863, ibid., 7.

123. Mason to Wallace, June 16, 1863, RG 393, pt. 4, E 270, vol. 1, NARA.

124. See Wallace's report, Cox's orders, and Parrott's request for troops, *OR,* ser. 1, vol. 23, part 1, 395–97.

125. Parrott to Drake and Shunk, both June 19, 1863, both in RG 110, E 4447, vol. 1, 71, 164, NARA-GLR.

126. Two reports of "J. P." to John Doane, June 18, 20, 1863, RG 110, E 4649, Letters Received 6th District Ohio, box 20, NARA-GLR.

127. See James A. Ramage, *Rebel Raider: The Life of John Hunt Morgan* (Lexington: University Press of Kentucky, 1986), 173–82.

128. See criminal case files for Edward Hughes and Peter Hartinger, RG 21, Records of U.S. Federal Courts, U.S. District Court for the Southern District of Ohio (Cincinnati), box 2, NARA-GLR.

129. Parrott to Capt. A. E. Jones, Capt. T. R. Roberts, and Capt. John Mills, RG 110, E 4447, vol. 1, 109, 129, 157, NARA-GLR.

130. Parrott to Drake, July 22, 1863, ibid., 72.

131. Drake to Parrott, July 23, 1863, RG 110, E 4833, vol. 1, 16, NARA-GLR.

132. John Krug to Capt. A. C. Deuel, July 24, 1863, RG 110, E 4609, Letters Received 4th District Ohio, box 10, NARA-GLR.

133. Brown to Parrott, July 24, 1863, RG 110, E 4619, 64, NARA-GLR.

134. Parrott to Fry, July 24, 1863, RG 110, E 4447, vol. 1, 196, NARA-GLR; printed in *OR,* ser. 3, vol. 3, 567.

135. Parrott to Capt. James A. Wilcox, July 28, 1863, RG 110, E 4447, vol. 1, 175, NARA-GLR; Parrott to Cox, September 5, 1863, RG 393, pt. 2, E 960, vol. 2, 312, NARA.

136. Parrott to Capt. John A. Sinnet, July 28, 1863, RG 110, E 4447, vol. 1, 167, NARA-GLR.

137. Parrott to Maj. C. W. Bascom, August 3, 1863, ibid., 52, also in RG 393, pt. 2, E 960, vol. 2, 310, NARA.

138. W. P. Anderson to Shunk, August 8, 1863, RG 110, E 4664, Letters Received 8th District, box 11, NARA-GLR.

139. Cox to Mason, September 14, 1863, RG 393, pt. 2, District of Ohio Records, E 957, Press Copies of Letters and Telegrams Sent, vol. 6, 386, NARA.

140. The deputy provost marshal of Coshocton County reported a bloody gunfight between armed Union citizens and draft dodgers who tried to escape arrest. Two deserters and one civilian were shot dead in the exchange. The deputy wrote that the people in the area were "considerably scared, and not at all disposed to fight." He believed that the deserters and their supporters now understood that "arresting parties carry guns and are not afraid to use them." William A. Johnston to Capt. John A. Sinnet, August 26, 1863, *OR,* ser. 3, vol. 3, 724–25.

141. Klement, *Limits of Dissent,* 210–28.

142. Brown to Franklin Collins, August 12, 1863, RG 110, E 4619, 80, NARA-GLR.

143. Brown to Parrott, August 10, 1863, RG 110, E 4619, 80, also in E 4452, vol. 2, both in NARA-GLR.

144. Brown to Parrott, August 10, 1863, RG 393, pt. 1, E 3489, vol. 3, 41, NARA. The man overheard in conversation with Pugh was Dr. J. N. Hetzler, a physician of Celina, Mercer County, Ohio, who served as the Democratic mayor of the town during the Civil War. Lester J. DeFord, "Mercer County, Ohio, during the Civil War" (MA thesis, Ohio State University, 1948), 45.

Chapter 5

1. Lt. Col. Joseph R. Smith to Burnside, August 27, 1863, RG 393, pt. 1, E 3491, vol. 4, 66, NARA, also in RG 393, pt. 4, Post of Detroit, Michigan, Records, E 384, Telegrams Sent and Received, NARA; printed in *OR*, ser. 2, vol. 6, 231.

2. *Detroit Free Press*, August 18, 1863.

3. *Detroit Free Press*, August 25 and 26, 1863. For an account of Vallandigham's arrival at Windsor, see Paul Taylor, *"Old Slow Town": Detroit during the Civil War* (Detroit: Wayne State University Press, 2013), 109–10.

4. W. P. Anderson to Smith, August 27, 1863, RG 109, M-345, roll 273, NARA.

5. Willcox to Smith, August 27, 1863, ibid.; printed in *OR*, ser. 2, vol. 6, 231–32.

6. Smith to Willcox, August 27, 1863, RG 393, pt. 4, E 384, NARA.

7. Capt. Robert J. Barry to Capt. John S. Newberry, June 16, 1863, RG 110, E 5949, Letters Received 1st District Michigan; Barry to Lt. Col. B. H. Hill, June 16, 1863, RG 110, E 5903, Letters Received by the Military Commander at Detroit, box 1, Capt. John A. Gordon to Hill, June 24, 1863, RG 110, E 5897, Letters Sent by the Acting Assistant Provost Marshal General, Michigan, vol. 1, 200, all in NARA-GLR.

8. Endorsement of Capt. James McMillan, July 16, 1863, on letter of Alfred Russell to [?], July 14, 1863, RG 393, pt. 4, Post of Detroit, Michigan, Records, E 382, Endorsements Sent and Received, 170, NARA.

9. See Iver Bernstein, *The New York City Draft Riots: Their Significance for American Society and Politics in the Age of the Civil War* (New York: Oxford University Press, 1990).

10. Endorsement of Hill to James B. Fry, July 15, 1863, RG 110, E 5904, vol. 1, 18, NARA-GLR.

11. Hill to Fry, August 18, 1863, RG 110, E 5897, vol. 2, 124–25, NARA-GLR.

12. See several letters and reports regarding their behavior in Detroit in 116th Indiana Volunteer Infantry Regimental Correspondence, ISA.

13. Smith to Willcox, August 28, 1863; Smith to Col. William C. Kise, August 29, 1863, both in RG 393, pt. 4, E 384, NARA.

14. Smith to Cdr. J. C. Carter, August 29, 1863, ibid.

15. Smith to Willcox, August 29, 1863, ibid.

16. Report of John Macafee, September 26, 1863, RG 110, E 5949, NARA-GLR.

17. *Detroit Advertiser and Tribune*, January 21, 1864.

18. Accounts of Lt. Col. J. R. Smith, RG 110, E 95, box 4, NARA.

19. George S. Goodale to [?], September 17, 1863, RG 393, pt. 1, E 3489, vol. 3, 194; Capt. Stephen E. Jones to Goodale, September 30, 1863, RG 393, pt. 1, E 2239, vol. 1, both in NARA.

20. Smith to [provost marshal], September 16, 1863, RG 110, E 5895, Letters Sent by the Military Commander at Detroit, vol. 2, 1, NARA-GLR.

21. Smith to Capt. Frederick A. Nash, September 8, 1863, RG 393, pt. 4, E 384, NARA.

22. Goodale to Stanton, November 3, 1863, RG 94, Turner-Baker Papers, M-797, roll 39, NARA.

23. D.C. Gile to [?], October 21, 1863, RG 393, pt. 4, Post of Louisville, Kentucky Records, E 1635, Register of Letters Received, vol. 1, NARA.

24. Smith to [?], November 10, 1863 and Goodale to [?], November 7, 1863, both in RG 393, pt. 1, E 3489, vol. 3, 502, 200, NARA.

25. Smith to Willcox, September 9, 1863, ibid.

26. Willcox to Anderson, September 9, 1863, RG 393, pt. 1, E 3491, vol. 4, 84, NARA.

27. Willcox to Cox, n.d. [September 14, 1863], ibid., 72.

28. Cox to Mason, September 10, 1863, RG 393, pt. 2, E 957, vol. 6, 301, NARA.

29. Smith to Anderson, September 14, 1863, ibid., 87.

30. Smith to [?], September 25, 1863, RG 393, pt. 1, E 3489, vol. 3, 490, NARA.

31. Smith to Cox, October 12, 1863, RG 393, pt. 4, E 384, NARA.

32. Klement, *Limits of Dissent,* 252.

33. Cox to Burnside, September 10, 1863, RG 393, pt. 2, E 957, vol. 6, 364, NARA.

34. Cox to Lt. John Eadie, September 12, 1863; Cox to Lorenzo Thomas, September 12, 1863, both ibid., 378–80, 383.

35. Brig. Gen. Mason Brayman to Cox, October 14, 1863, RG 393, pt. 2, E 960, vol. 2, 39, NARA.

36. Cox to George Sage, September 18, 1863, RG 393, pt. 2, E 957, vol. 6, 418, NARA.

37. Cox to Brig. Gen. E. P. Scammon, September 26, 1863, ibid., 448–50.

38. Capt. John Mills to Parrott, September 23, 1863, RG 110, E 4583, Letters Received 3rd District Ohio, NARA-GLR.

39. Capt. Isaac Kinley to James B. Fry, October 10, 1863, RG 110, E 5204, vol. 1, NARA-GLR.

40. Mason to Hoffman, October 27, 1863, *OR,* ser. 2, vol. 6, 427. For a study focusing on Camp Chase, see Roger Pickenpaugh, *Camp Chase and the Evolution of Union Prison Policy* (Tuscaloosa: University of Alabama Press, 2007).

41. Mason to Col. William Hoffman, November 6, 1863, RG 393, pt. 4, E 270, vol. 2, 260–61, NARA.

42. Capt. Green to Lt. Col. Edwin L. Webber, October 12, 1863, RG 393, pt. 4, E 270, vol. 2, 236, NARA. General Cox wrote later that troops were ordered to be "carefully out of sight" but under arms in their barracks, with no leaves allowed, during the election. See Jacob D. Cox, *Military Reminiscences of the Civil War,* 2 vols. (New York: C. Scribner's Sons, 1900), 2:53.

43. Mason to Hoffman, November 6, 1863, RG 393, pt. 4, E 270, vol. 2, 260–61, NARA. Soldiers temporarily stationed at Camp Chase months before had sacked the office of the *Crisis.* Reed W. Smith, *Samuel Medary and the* Crisis: *Testing the Limits of Press Freedom* (Columbus: Ohio State University Press, 1995), 106–8.

44. Amid the preparations to attack Camp Chase, on October 19 Cathcart tendered his resignation as state school commissioner to Governor Tod. Tod accepted

the resignation and promptly replaced him with a man to fill out his elected term. Charles W. H. Cathcart to Tod, October 19, 1863, roll 22, Tod Papers, OHS. Authorities arrested Cathcart at the home of antiwar Democrat Sabin Hough, who shortly before had returned from a visit to Vallandigham at Windsor. *Cincinnati Daily Times*, November 2, 1863.

45. *Daily Cleveland Herald*, November 3, 1863, reprinting articles of *Cincinnati Daily Gazette* and *Cincinnati Daily Commercial*, both November 2, 1863. See also *Cincinnati Daily Times*, November 2, 1863.

46. *Daily Cleveland Herald*, November 3, 1863. For an account of the escape and recapture of Colonel Patton and one Sterling King that probably triggered army investigations that broke up the plot, see *Cincinnati Daily Enquirer*, October 22, 1863.

47. *Daily Cleveland Herald*, November 3, 1863.

48. *Cincinnati Daily Enquirer*, November 14, 1863.

49. *Cincinnati Daily Times*, November 24, 1863.

50. *Cincinnati Daily Times*, November 11, 1863.

51. Criminal Case File no. 109, RG 21, U.S. Circuit Court for the Southern District of Ohio (Cincinnati), Criminal Case Files, box 2, NARA-GLR.

52. Ibid.; *Cincinnati Daily Enquirer*, November 17, 1863.

53. Flamen Ball to Edward Bates, April 26, 1864, RG 60, E 9, Letters Received, folder Ohio "Southern District of Ohio (U.S. Attorney), NARA-CP. President James Buchanan appointed Medary to be territorial governor of Minnesota, where he served from 1857 to 1858. Buchanan reappointed him territorial governor of Kansas, where he served from 1858 to 1860. See R. Smith, *Samuel Medary*, 56–60. Ball's description of Medary as a defendant was premature in April 1864; authorities arrested and indicted Medary only in May 1864. Given his knowledge of Medary's complicity in the Camp Chase plot, Ball perhaps anticipated that Medary would be arrested and tried for treason.

54. Samuel Medary's biographer overlooks the evidence that Medary was implicated in the Camp Chase conspiracy and writes, "The charge astounded Medary, who denied any involvement with Cathcart." R. Smith, *Samuel Medary*, 137–39.

55. *Daily Cleveland Herald*, November 5, reprinting article from *Cincinnati Daily Commercial*, n.d.

56. Mason to Hoffman, November 6, 1863, RG 393, pt. 4, E 270, vol. 2, 260–61, NARA. Historian Frank L. Klement dismisses the "Cathcart Conspiracy," stating merely that it "proved to be a figment of Republican imagination," and offers no analysis of the facts. Klement errs by giving Cathcart the wrong first name, "Samuel." See Klement, "Ohio and the Knights," 21, 26n73.

57. See Thomas Henry Hines wedding record, box 1, folder "July–December, 1864," in Thomas Henry Hines Papers, collection 46M97, Special Collections, University of Kentucky, Lexington.

58. John Breckinridge Castleman, *Active Service* (Louisville: Courier-Journal Job Printing, 1917), 193–94.

59. *Daily Cleveland Herald*, November 3, 1863, reprinting report in *Cincinnati Daily Gazette*, November 2, 1863.

60. Affidavit of R. L. Jeffries, November 2, 1863, RG 110, E 5149, box 4, NARA-GLR. An official copy, also signed by Conrad Baker, is also found in RG 110, E 5177, Letters Received 3rd District Indiana, NARA-GLR.

61. Lt. Col. T. E. Boone to [?], April 22, 1863, RG 393, pt. 4, E 216, vol. 1, 33, NARA.

62. Robert L. Jeffries to [?], April 29, May 3, 1863; Maj. J. L. Van Buren to [?], May 26, 1863, all ibid., 186, 187, 302.

63. See RG 92, Quartermaster General Records, E 238, file 1864–84, NARA.

64. For details on how Confederate agents identified and assassinated detective Jeffries, see George A. Ellsworth, "'Everything Is Fair in War': The Civil War Memoir of George A. "Lightning" Ellsworth, John Hunt Morgan's Telegraph Operator," ed. Stephen E. Towne and Jay G. Heiser, *Register of the Kentucky Historical Society* 108, nos. 1, 2 (Winter–Spring 2010): 3–110.

65. Frank L. Klement asserts that the OAK was the "daydream" creation of Phineas C. Wright, a disgruntled "romancer" who tried to generate a membership for it but was unsuccessful; the OAK "was alive but neither active nor effective" during its brief existence. See Klement, "Phineas C. Wright, the Order of American Knights, and the Sanderson Exposé, *Civil War History* 18, no. 1 (March 1972): 12. Klement's erroneous assertions about the OAK are based on perjured testimony given in treason trials by men eager to deflect personal culpability. For example, he asserts erroneously that Wright "revived" the order in December 1863, after it had received no takers in Illinois and Indiana during the summer and fall. See Klement, *Copperheads in the Middle West,* 168. Jeffries's affidavit alone shows that the OAK was active in eastern Illinois and western Indiana in September 1863. Other records showing OAK activity predate Klement's false December 1863 claim. Gilbert R. Tredway provides a more cogent and useful analysis of the OAK but also errs in asserting that it was the first ambitious and effective secret organization to arise, discounting the Knights of the Golden Circle, which preceded it. See Tredway, *Democratic Opposition,* 128–29.

66. David Turnbull to Capt. James Woodruff, November 6, 1863, RG 109, M-416, Union Provost Marshal's File of Papers Relating to Two or More Civilians, roll 73, NARA.

67. "M" to Maj. Gen. John M. Schofield, December 8 [1863], RG 110, E 5381, box 1, NARA-GLR. An endorsement on the copied letter notes that Schofield's headquarters forwarded it to Lt. Col. James Oakes in early February, 1864.

68. See *Richmond Palladium,* October 16, 1863. The district provost marshal at Richmond telegraphed Governor Tod to alert him to armed men entering Ohio: "I have just arrested twelve men on Cincinnati RR all well armed with revolvers and knives two of them have confessed that they were going to assist in the election of Vallandigham." Isaac Kinley to Tod, October 9, 1863, roll 24, Tod Papers, OHS.

69. "The Eastern portion of the State is still quiet and the case of Powderhorn is still under investigation." William P. Ammen to Jacob Ammen, November 30, 1863, Ammen Papers, ALPL. "John Powderhorn" attained nearly the status of living legend in Clark County, Illinois, where he appeared at the head of armed Democrats in drills and armed parades. See J. L. Wallar to "Dear Sir," May 31, 1863, RG 110, E 5381, box 1, NARA-GLR. See also *Marshall (IL) Flag of Our Union,* July 24, August 7, October 9, 1863, February 26, March 18, 1864.

70. John H. S. Jones to Levi Croniger, October 10, 1863, RG 110, E 5149, box 4, NARA-GLR.

71. Reany to Capt. O. D. Green, November 4, 1863, RG 393, pt. 1, Department of the Missouri Records, E 2593, Letters Received, box 10, NARA. In the corner of the letter from Reany is written "By Slade Clerk," suggesting that detective Private Slade did double duty at headquarters.

72. Baker to Hynes, November 9, 1863, RG 110, E 5149, box 4, NARA-GLR.

73. Kinley to Capt. J. R. Martin, November 12, 1863, RG 110, E 5204, vol. 1, NARA-GLR.

74. Martin to Kinley, November 16, 1863, ibid.

75. Confederate naval commanders developed plans to attack Johnson's Island in February 1863. See the report of Confederate naval officer Lt. William H. Murdaugh of February 7, 1863, United States, Naval War Records Office, *Official Records of the Union and Confederate Navies in the War of the Rebellion* (Washington, DC: Government Printing Office, 1895), ser. 1, vol. 2, 828–29, hereafter cited as *ORN*.

76. Smith to Lorenzo Thomas, November 13, 1863, RG 110, E 5895, vol. 2, 17, NARA-GLR.

77. Goodale to Capt. W. P. Anderson, November 7, 1863, RG 110, E 31, box 5, NARA.

78. Smith to Cox, November 7, 1863, RG 393, pt. 4, E 384, NARA.

79. Cox to Lt. Col. W. S. Pierson, November 8, 1863, RG 393, pt. 2, E 957, vol. 6, 608, NARA.

80. Pierson to Cox, November 9, 1863, RG 393, pt. 2, District of Ohio Records, E 962, Telegrams Received, NARA; Pierson to Cox, November 10, 1863, ibid.

81. Cox to Pierson, November 9, 1863, RG 393, pt. 2, District of Ohio Records, E 957, Press Copies of Letters and Telegrams Sent, vol. 6, 616, NARA.

82. Cox to Joshua R. Giddings, November 9, 1863, ibid., 616.

83. Smith to Cox, November 10, 1863, RG 393, pt. 2, E 962, NARA.

84. Cox to Hoffman and Cox to Mason, both November 10, 1863, RG 393, pt. 2, E 957, vol. 6, 618, 619, NARA; Cox to Hoffman is reprinted in *OR*, ser. 3, vol. 3, 1012–13.

85. Cox to Pierson, November 10, 1863, RG 393, pt. 2, E 957, vol. 6, 620, 624, NARA.

86. Hill to Giddings, November 9, 1863, RG 110, E 5897, vol. 2, 409–10, NARA-GLR.

87. Hill to James B. Fry, November 9, 1863, ibid., 414–15, printed in *OR*, ser. 3, vol. 3, 1008.

88. Smith to Lorenzo Thomas, November 13, 1863, RG 110, E 5895, vol. 2, 17, NARA-GLR.

89. Smith to Pierson, November 11, 1863, RG 393, pt. 4, E 384, NARA.

90. Smith to Capt. G. A. Scroggs, November 11, 1863; Scroggs to Smith, November 11, 1863, both ibid.

91. Smith to Pierson, November 12, 1863, ibid.; Smith to Capt. John C. Carter, November 11, 1863; Smith to Capt. Charles Wilkins, November 12, 1863; Smith to B. B. Vincent, November 12, 1863, all ibid.

92. Smith to Cox, November 13, 1863, ibid.

93. In his official report on the expedition, Confederate naval officer Lt. R. D. Minor surmised that a Canadian named McCuaig who sympathized with the rebel

cause had become "alarmed at the last moment" and had betrayed the plan to the Canadian government. See Minor to Confederate Adm. Franklin Buchanan, February 2, 1864, *ORN*, ser. 1, vol. 2, 822–28. For an alternate view of the source who divulged the plot to Monck, see Winks, *Canada and the United States,* 149–50.

94. Winks, *Canada and the United States,* 146–50.

95. Stanton to Andrew G. Curtin et al., November 11, 1863, *OR,* ser. 3, vol. 3, 1013–14.

96. Minor to Buchanan, February 2, 1864, *ORN,* ser. 1, vol. 2, 822–28.

97. Cox to Tod, November 13, 1863, RG 393, pt. 2, E 957, vol. 6, 631, NARA.

98. Smith to Cox, November 14, 1863, RG 393, pt. 4, E 384, NARA.

99. Cox to Anderson, November 15, 1863, RG 393, pt. 1, E 3491, vol. 5, 39, NARA.

100. Smith to Cox, November 17, 1863, RG 393, pt. 4, E 384, NARA.

101. Smith to [Anderson?], November 10, 1863, RG 393, pt. 1, E 3489, vol. 3, 502; Burnside to Anderson, November 12, 1863, RG 393, pt. 1, E 3511, Telegrams Sent by Ambrose E. Burnside, 25, both in NARA. See also Smith to [Cox?], November 15, 1863, RG 393, pt. 2, E 960, vol. 3, 319, NARA.

102. Hill to James B. Fry, December 9, 1863, RG 110, E 5897, vol. 2, 563–65, NARA-GLR.

103. Hoffman to Smith, December 16, 1863, RG 393, pt. 4, E 384, NARA.

104. Carter to Gideon Welles and Cox to Carter, both November 20, 1863; Welles to Carter, December 1, 1863, all in *ORN,* ser. 1, vol. 2, 499, 508.

105. Stanton to Brig. Gen. J. G. Totten, November 21, 1863; Stanton to Tod, December 3, 1863, letter book vol. 41, 58, 65; Stanton to William H. Seward, December 3, 1863, letter book vol. 42, 156, all in Stanton Papers, LC.

Chapter 6

1. Journal entries for January 9, 12, 1864, microfilm roll 7, Samuel Peter Heintzelman Journal, Samuel P. Heintzelman Papers, Library of Congress (hereafter cited as Heintzelman Papers, LC). Heintzelman kept two journals during the Civil War: a pocket diary written on small, commercially printed diary books with short, daily entries to act as an aide-mémoire, and a journal with longer, sometimes expansive daily entries written with the aid of the pocket diary. References to the first journal will be to the "pocket diary," and to the second, more expansive journal, to the "journal."

2. Jerry Thompson, *Civil War to the Bloody End: The Life and Times of Major General Samuel P. Heintzelman* (College Station: Texas A&M University Press, 2006), 130, 132.

3. Ibid., 45.

4. Journal entry for January 13, 1864, Heintzelman Papers, LC.

5. Journal entry for January 14, 1864, Heintzelman Papers, LC.

6. Journal entry for January 15, 1864, Heintzelman Papers, LC; Heintzelman to Maj. Granville E. Johnson, January 15, 1864, RG 393, pt. 1, Northern Department Records, E 3338, Letters Sent, vol. 1, 1–2, NARA; Heintzelman to E. D. Townsend, January 18, 1864, RG 94, M-619, roll 283, NARA.

7. Marvel, *Burnside,* 334.

8. Journal entry for January 22, 1864, Heintzelman Papers, LC.

9. Heintzelman to Townsend, February 14, 1864, RG 94, M-619, roll 283, NARA.

10. Heintzelman to Townsend, February 18, 1864, RG 94, M-619, roll 283, NARA.

11. Journal entry for January 23, 1864, Heintzelman Papers, LC.

12. Heintzelman to Townsend, February 14, March 25, 1864, both in RG 94, M-619, roll 283, NARA.

13. Journal entry for January 14, 1864, Heintzelman Papers, LC.

14. "Dr. Blackburn" was Luke P. Blackburn, a Kentucky physician and future governor of Kentucky. See Nancy D. Baird, *Luke Pryor Blackburn: Physician, Governor, Reformer* (Lexington: University Press of Kentucky, 1979), 20–24.

15. Johnson to Heintzelman, January 26, 1864, RG 393, pt. 1, Northern Department Records, E 3349, Letters Received, box 2, NARA.

16. Parrott to Hill, January 7, 1864, RG 110, E 4447, vol. 2, 311, also in RG 110, E 5903, box 1, and E 5900, Register of Letters Received by the Acting Assistant Provost Marshal General, 223, all in NARA-GLR.

17. Lt. Col. A. H. Poten to Col. William Wallace, January 17, 1864, RG 393, pt. 4, E 270, vol. 2, 319–20, NARA.

18. Brig. William W. Orme to Col. William Hoffman, January 29, 1864, RG 94, M-619, roll 287, NARA; court-martial case file for Dr. William D. Lee, NN-1327, RG 153, NARA. Orme wrote to a friend, "I have had much to do here in straightening out affairs at Camp Douglas. Money flows freely towards the prisoners, and I have strong suspicions of much bribery to effect their escape. There are very many open sympathizers in this city. I permit no person to visit the camp, but with my most stringent efforts unauthorized persons occasionally slip in and out. But I think I am getting some order out of what was chaos." Orme to David Davis, January 15, 1864, box 2, David Davis Papers, ALPL.

19. Capt. Richard W. Thompson to Baker, January 26, 1864, RG 393, pt. 1, Northern Department Records, E 3362, Two or More Name File, box 1, NARA.

20. Capt. B. F. Cory to Parrott, February 4, 1864, RG 110, E 4755 Letters Sent 11th District Ohio, vol. 2, 365–66, NARA-GLR.

21. Carrington to Heintzelman, February 2, 1864, roll 10, Heintzelman Papers, LC.

22. No record of Secretary Stanton or other War Department official acceding to the transfer of Carrington to Morton's staff has been found in records in the National Archives or the ISA.

23. *Indianapolis Daily Gazette,* July 7, 1863. The *Indianapolis Daily Journal* of July 8, 1863, stated that Carrington's duty would also comprehend the organization of the six-months regiments then ordered to be raised. Capt. John H. Farquhar, who had served as chief mustering and disbursing officer at Indianapolis, was also ordered back to Indianapolis from Springfield, Illinois, suggesting that Morton insisted with the War Department that he have army officers in command in Indianapolis whom he trusted. Farquhar's return also suggests that Morton did not request Carrington's return as a personal favor, but as a military and administrative necessity. In reporting Carrington's summons to Indianapolis during the Morgan raid, the Republican newspaper in Cleveland noted, "We know that Gen. Carrington has been advised that this raid would be made, and has used every effort to arouse attention to it." See *Daily Cleveland Herald,* July 9, 1863.

24. *Indianapolis Daily Journal,* July 11, 1863.

25. See Carrington, "The Morgan Raid through Indiana July 1863—Military Status of Indiana, " 17–18, Carrington Papers, ISA.

26. *Centreville Indiana True Republican,* July 24, 1863. The report in the paper was anonymous but was probably written by Congressman George W. Julian, who had volunteered to fight the invaders and was on the troop train that was delayed at the station. He was owner of the newspaper, which was edited by his brother Isaac. Julian also later wrote about the incident in his memoirs. See Julian, *Political Recollections 1840 to 1872* (Chicago: Jansen, McClurg and Co., 1884; repr., New York: Negro University Press, 1970), 232–33. Other officers' reports also ascribed Carrington's collapse to drunkenness. See reports of Morgan raid regimental commanders in the ISA. Frank L. Klement notes that Hascall's published report of the train platform incident was "doctored" to excise language implicating Carrington for being "very drunk and utterly unfit to trust with that or any other duty," and that Morton and his staff "covered up" Carrington's drunkenness. See Klement, "Carrington and the Golden Circle Legend in Indiana during the Civil War," *Indiana Magazine of History* 61, no. 1 (March 1965): 46–47. In her dissertation on Carrington, Catherine McKeen correctly observes that the image of Carrington as drunkard is "strangely at odds with Carrington's entire background and self-perceptions. Carrington thought of his public self as temperate, reliable, self-possessed. At fourteen, he had taken a temperance pledge; at Columbus he joined and led a local temperance group; he enjoined temperance on soldiers. Adjutant General W. H. H. Terrell, to whom [Hascall's] report was submitted, sanitized Hascall's remarks, leaving out the ruinous comment, when he published his official report in 1869. That discrepancy discovered, the image of Carrington as irresponsible drunkard became a fixture of Indiana Civil War history." McKeen, "Carrington," 111. Another contemporary newspaper account took the middle ground in the matter, stating that Carrington refrained from alcohol, suffered from tuberculosis, had labored without sleep for days, and while awaiting the clearance of the tracks was persuaded by his physician "to take a little stimulus, which he accordingly did at a drug store. Being taken on an empty stomach, and the General not having taken anything of the kind for years, was, of course, a little affected by it." *Lafayette Daily Courier,* August 13, 1863.

27. *Delphi Weekly Times,* December 5, 1863; *Indianapolis Daily State Sentinel,* November 9, 1863; *Plymouth Weekly Democrat,* September 24, 1863.

28. *Weekly Vincennes Western Sun,* May 7, 1864.

29. *Indianapolis Daily State Sentinel,* April 1, 1864. Frank L. Klement misinterprets a letter that Carrington sent to the assembled legion companies in Johnson County, Indiana, in lieu of attending and speaking in person. Carrington wrote of the duties of soldiers, and especially to avoid "mere party issues" as the soldier took orders and "owes constant allegiance to the ruling powers, which change from time to time." But, he added, it was "absurdity to assume that a soldier should close his lips as to the cause he fights for. The *nation* is at peril! The cause of humanity is being tried through the ordeal which Providence has brought upon us," and no stone should be left unturned "to thwart every form of treason to the government, wherever it may be developed." He went on to say, "I am not in favor of secret societies and have never joined even

the Union League, but your companies of the Legion are essentially the development of Washington's own plans, and may become the safeguard to liberty." Carrington to "State Militia and citizens of Johnson County," October 3, 1863, letter book of Henry B. Carrington [1863–64] ("Willard Book"), 60–62, Henry B. Carrington Papers, ISA. Klement erroneously equates the legion with the Union League secret organization of Republicans, and interprets "Washington's own plans" to mean plans devised by the Lincoln administration at Washington: "Governor Morton even provided arms from the state armory for Union Leagues that organized military 'legions.'" See Klement, *Dark Lanterns*, 56. Carrington was later to write important histories of the military campaigns of the American Revolution and General George Washington. Rather, it is more plausible to understand Carrington to mean that the legion (state militia) was essentially the embodiment of George Washington's ideal of the citizen-soldiery.

30. Carrington to Heintzelman, January 21, 1864, letter book of Henry B. Carrington [1863–64] ("Willard Book"), 92, Henry B. Carrington Papers, ISA; Carrington to Heintzelman, February 7, 1864, RG 393, pt. 1, Northern Department Records, E 3350, Telegrams Received, 1864–865, NARA.

31. Pocket diary entry for February 16, 1864, Heintzelman Papers, LC.

32. Journal entry for March 2, 1864, Heintzelman Papers, LC.

33. D. J. Van Doren to Yates, February 1, 1864; Eli Wiley to Yates, February 4, 1864; John Monroe to Yates, February 6, 1864, all in box 15, folder 1, Yates Family Papers, ALPL.

34. See reports in *Paris Prairie Beacon*, n.d., reprinted in *Rockville (IN) Parke County Republican*, February 10, 1864; *Sullivan Democrat*, February 11, 1864; *Logansport Journal*, February 6, 1864; *Indianapolis Daily Journal*, February 5, 1864.

35. Maj. A. K. Campbell and Capt. N. Van Sellar to Brig. Gen. Julius White, n.d.; Julius White to Yates, February 7, 1863 [1864], box 1, folder 17, Wabash Yates Papers, ALPL. The property purportedly threatened by the soldiers was the office of the *Paris (IL) Times and Democratic Standard*, a Democratic newspaper. For more on Amos Green, see Peter J. Barry, "Amos Green, Paris Illinois: Civil War Lawyer, Editorialist, and Copperhead," *Journal of Illinois History* 11, no. 1 (Spring 2008): 39–60. Michael E. O'Hair was the sheriff of Edgar County.

36. Yates to Stanton, March 2, 1864, Lincoln Papers, LC.

37. *Terre Haute Daily Wabash Express*, March 1, 1864.

38. Halleck to Oakes, March 2, 1864, box 15, folder 6, Yates Family Papers, ALPL.

39. *Indianapolis Daily Journal*, March 4, 1864.

40. George W. Rives to Yates, March 7, 1864, box 3, folder 1, Wabash Yates Papers, ALPL.

41. Journal entry for March 8, 1864; see also pocket diary entries for March 2, 3, 4, 5, 6, 1864, all in Heintzelman Papers, LC.

42. Heintzelman to Halleck, March 8, 1864, RG 393, pt. 1, E 3338, vol. 1, 67–68, also in RG 94, E 159, subser. 2, Samuel P. Heintzelman Papers, box 15, folder 15, both in NARA.

43. Baker to James B. Fry, March 5, 1864, RG 393, pt. 1, E 3349, box 3, NARA.

44. Ibid.

45. Ibid., also in RG 107, E 5, vol. 54A, 454, M-6, roll 53, NARA.

46. Capt. Carroll H. Potter to Carrington, March 10, 1864, ser. 1, box 12, folder 19, Carrington Family Papers.

47. Heintzelman to Carrington, March 12, 1864, RG 393, pt. 1, E 3338, vol. 1, 71, also in RG 393, pt. 3, District of Indiana Records, E 222, Letters Received, box 2, both in NARA.

48. Carrington to Heintzelman, March 15, 1864, RG 393, pt. 1, E 3349, box 1, NARA.

49. Heintzelman to Oakes, March 14, 1864, RG 393, pt. 1, E 3338, vol. 1, 72–73, NARA. See also Carrington to Heintzelman, March 26, 1864, RG 393, pt. 1, E 3349, box 1, NARA.

50. David Turnbull to Capt. James Woodruff, November 6, 1863, RG 109, M-416, roll 73, NARA.

51. A. C. Harding to Heintzelman, March 1, 1864, RG 153, NN-3409, "exhibit 'Q,'" box 1879, NARA. The document appears to be three separate undated reports by Turnbull, all collected on March 25, 1864, with notes in Carrington's handwriting.

52. Report of Henry Henly, February 26, 1864, RG 153, NN-2716, box 1808, NARA.

53. Affidavit of Thomas Elliott, March 4, 1864, RG 153, NN-3409, box 1879, NARA.

54. Affidavit of John Jackson, March 4, 1864, RG 153, Records of the Judge Advocate General, Court-Martial Case Files, NN-2716, box 1808, NARA.

55. Henry S. Zumro to Morton, March 19, 1864, 101st Indiana Volunteer Infantry Regimental Correspondence, ISA. This remarkable document probably survives because it was misfiled with regimental correspondence, as it was endorsed by Morton's secretary as a remonstrance against an appointment in the regiment and was collected with other correspondence for the regiment. Colonel L. S. Shuler of Hendricks County, Indiana, had commanded cavalry in the vanguard of the pursuit of John Hunt Morgan during his raid in July 1863 and had reported that he saw evidence of collaboration by Indiana citizens with the rebels. It is possible that he assisted Governor Morton in uncovering secret activities in the state.

56. Carrington to Capt. James M. Bratton, March 25, 1864, letter book of Henry B. Carrington [1863–64] ("Willard Book"), 212, Henry B. Carrington Papers, ISA; Carrington to Baker, April 4, 1864, box 1, folder 1, Conrad Baker Papers, M 8, IHS.

57. See Stephen E. Towne, "The Persistent Nullifier: The Life of Civil War Conspirator Lambdin P. Milligan," *Indiana Magazine of History* 108, no. 4 (December 2013): 303–54.

58. Smith to Johnson, March 10, 1864, ser. 1, box 2, folder 19, Carrington Family Papers, also in RG 110, E 5895, vol. 2, 61–62, NARA-GLR.

59. Smith to Johnson, March 19, 1864, RG 110, E 5895, vol. 2, 71–72, NARA-GLR.

60. Potter to Smith, March 23, 1864, RG 393, pt. 3, District of Michigan Records, E 329, Letters Received from Northern Department Headquarters, NARA.

61. Smith to Potter, March 25, 1864, RG 393, pt. 1, E 3349, box 2, NARA, also in RG 110, E 5895, vol. 2, 80–82, NARA-GLR.

62. Heintzelman to Halleck, March 24, 1864, RG 393, pt. 1, E 3338, vol. 1, 94, NARA.

63. Journal entry for February 19, 1864, Heintzelman Papers, LC.

64. Journal entries for February 20, 25, 1864, Heintzelman Papers, LC.

65. Brig. Gen. E. R. S. Canby to Heintzelman, March 14, 1864, RG 107, E 5, vol. 55A, 10, M-6, roll 54, NARA.

66. Journal entry for March 19, 1864, Heintzelman Papers, LC.

67. Heintzelman to Halleck, March 15, 1864, RG 393, pt. 1, E 3338, vol. 1, 76, NARA.

68. Baker to Potter (two letters), March 4, 1864, RG 110, E 5055, vol. 3, 563–64, 565, NARA-GLR.

69. For works on the Charleston riot, see Robert Sampson, "'Pretty Damned Warm Times': The 1864 Charleston Riot and 'the Inalienable Right of Revolution,'" *Illinois Historical Journal* 89, no. 2 (Summer 1996): 99–116; John Scott Parkinson, "Bloody Spring: The Charleston, Illinois Riot and Copperhead Violence during the American Civil War" (PhD diss., Miami University, 1998); Peter J. Barry, *The Charleston, Illinois Riot, March 28, 1864* (privately printed, 2007).

70. Oakes to Heintzelman (two telegrams), March 30, 1864, RG 393, pt. 1, E 3350, NARA

71. Carrington to Heintzelman, March 30, 1864; Carrington to Brig. Gen. Julius White, March 30, 1864, both in letter book of Henry B. Carrington [1863–64] ("Willard Book"), 245, Henry B. Carrington Papers, ISA. See also Col. James R. Slack to Ann Slack, April 1, 1864, James R. Slack Papers, L145, Manuscript Section, Indiana State Library.

72. Carrington to Maj. Gen. Stephen G. Burbridge, March 30, 1864, letter book of Henry B. Carrington [1863–64] ("Willard Book"), 239, Henry B. Carrington Papers, ISA.

73. Carrington to Col. W. E. Hollingsworth, March 30, 1864, ibid.

74. Carrington to Morton, March 30, 1864, ibid., 240.

75. Thomas W. Fry to Carrington, April 11, 1864, RG 393, pt. 1, Northern Department Records, E 3351, Confidential Correspondence re O.A.K., 8–9, NARA.

76. Carrington to Potter, March 30, 1864, RG 393, pt. 1, E 3349, box 1, NARA, also in letter book of Henry B. Carrington [1863–1864] ("Willard Book"), 248–49, Henry B. Carrington Papers, ISA.

77. Oakes to Potter, April 18, 1864, RG 94, M-619, roll 285, NARA; Oakes to Fry, April 16, 1864, *OR*, ser. 1, vol. 32, part 1, 630–33. For the eventual disposition of the prisoners, see Peter J. Barry, "The Charleston Riot and Its Aftermath: Civil, Military, and Presidential Responses," *Journal of Illinois History* 7, no. 2 (Summer 2004): 82–106; Barry, "'I'll Keep Them in Prison Awhile . . .': Abraham Lincoln and David Davis on Civil Liberties in Wartime," *Journal of the Abraham Lincoln Association* 28, no. 1 (2007): 20–29.

78. Carrington to Potter, April 7, 1864, RG 393, pt. 1, E 3351, 1–7, NARA.

79. Smith to Potter, April 1, 1864, RG 110, E 5895, vol. 2, 87–88, NARA-GLR.

80. Smith to Moses A. Share, April 1, 1864, ibid., 88; George Irvine to J. M. Howard, April 12, 1864, RG 393, pt. 1, E 3349, box 3, NARA.

81. Hill to Heintzelman, April 5, 1864, RG 393, pt. 1, E 3349, box 1, NARA.

82. Matthew Hale Smith to Seward, April 4, 1864, RG 107, E 17, M-221, roll 255, NARA.

83. Col. James A. Hardie to Heintzelman, April 20, 1864, vol. 41, 116, Stanton Papers, LC, also in Heintzelman Papers, LC. Klement misuses the general's journal entry for April 23, 1864, to claim that federal officials "knew that they had no damaging evidence concerning" Phineas C. Wright when they arrested him. See Klement, *Copperheads in the Middle West,* 181.

84. Journal entry for April 23, 1864, Heintzelman Papers, LC; Potter to Lt. Col. Paul von Radowitz, n.d., RG 393, pt. 1, E 3338, vol. 1, 155, NARA.

85. Smith to Potter, April 28, 1864, RG 110, E 5895, vol. 1, 112–13, NARA-GLR; Heintzelman to [Hardie], April 29, 1864, RG 107, Records of the Office of the Secretary of War, M-22, Registers of Letters Received by the Office of the Secretary of War, Main Series, 1800–1870, roll 112, vol. 128, NARA.

86. Frank L. Klement erroneously claims that Wright was "arrested upon the orders of Major General Samuel P. Heintzelman." See Klement, *Dark Lanterns,* 74. See also Klement, *Copperheads in the Middle West,* 181; Klement, "Phineas C. Wright," 15.

87. Journal entry for April 4, 1864, Heintzelman Papers, LC.

88. Journal entry for April 5, 1864, Heintzelman Papers, LC.

89. Journal entries for April 5, 12, 1864, Heintzelman Papers, LC.

90. Journal entries for April 16, 17, 1864, Heintzelman Papers, LC. Frank L. Klement erroneously suggests that Major General William S. Rosecrans and Colonel John P. Sanderson of the Department of the Missouri were "interested" in the Indianapolis conference between Heintzelman and the governors. Klement cites no evidence in making the claim, nor does any documentation exist that Rosecrans and Sanderson knew of the meeting. See Klement, *Copperheads in the Middle West,* 181–82. For an account of the governors' tender of short-term enlistment troops to Lincoln, see Jim Leeke, ed., *A Hundred Days to Richmond: Ohio's "Hundred Days" Men in the Civil War* (Bloomington: Indiana University Press, 1999), xi–xiii.

Chapter 7

1. The term *Missouri imbroglio* was employed by Ohio congressman James A. Garfield, who had served as Rosecrans's chief of staff in 1863 and who wrote to congratulate his former general on the new appointment. Garfield to Rosecrans, February 2, 1864, box 9, Rosecrans Papers, UCLA. Rosecrans also used the term in reply to Garfield in describing his agenda. Rosecrans to Garfield, March 12, 1864, ser. 4, vol. 6, roll 12, James A. Garfield Papers, Library of Congress (hereafter cited as Garfield Papers, LC).

2. William M. Lamers, *The Edge of Glory: A Biography of General William S. Rosecrans, U.S.A.* (New York: Harcourt, Brace and World, 1960, repr., Louisiana State University Press, 1999), 8–19.

3. For an assessment of Rosecrans's performance in western Virginia, see Albert Castel and Brooks D. Simpson, *Victors in Blue: How Union Generals Fought the Confederates, Battled Each Other, and Won the Civil War* (Lawrence: University Press of Kansas, 2011), 11–28.

4. See Peter Cozzens, *The Darkest Days of the War: The Battles of Iuka and Corinth* (Chapel Hill: University of North Carolina Press, 1997).

5. Ibid., 301–2, 311–15.

6. Peter Cozzens, *No Better Place to Die: The Battle of Stones River* (Urbana: University of Illinois Press, 1990).

7. Peter Cozzens, *This Terrible Sound: The Battle of Chickamauga* (Urbana: University of Illinois Press, 1992).

8. Peter Cozzens, *The Shipwreck of Their Hopes: The Battles for Chattanooga* (Urbana: University of Illinois Press, 1994).

9. Rosecrans to Lorenzo Thomas, October 1863, *OR*, ser. 1, vol. 30, part 1, 64.

10. Journal entry for January 28, 1864, in War Journal of John Philip Sanderson, box 1, John P. Sanderson Papers, Ohio Historical Society, Columbus (hereafter cited as Sanderson Papers, OHS).

11. Journal entry for February 6, 1864, Sanderson Papers, OHS.

12. Journal entries for September 8, November 1, 1863, Sanderson Papers, OHS.

13. Journal entries for February 10, 11, 23, 1864, Sanderson Papers, OHS. See also George Bergner to Lincoln, February 5, 1864, Lincoln Papers, LC.

14. Erwin S. Bradley, *Simon Cameron, Lincoln's Secretary of War: A Political Biography* (Philadelphia: University of Pennsylvania Press, 1966), 143, 154, 180; Tyler Anbinder, *Nativism and Slavery: The Northern Know-Nothings and the Politics of the 1850s* (New York: Oxford University Press, 1992), 242.

15. Sanderson is one of the principal targets for abuse by Frank L. Klement, who, in his attempts to cast aspersions on the army officers who played significant roles in uncovering the conspiracies in the Northwestern states, characterized him as a "second-rate politician who became a third-rate army officer." In the course of attacking Sanderson, Klement errs on numerous occasions, many of which will be pointed out below. For example, Klement errs when he writes that Sanderson "moved from one unimportant assignment to another, for West Pointers who held commands would not trust him with a field assignment." See Klement, ""Phineas C. Wright," 5. Unfortunately, historians have accepted Klement's erroneous assertions without question. For example, see Louis S. Gerteis, *Civil War St. Louis* (Lawrence: University Press of Kansas, 2001), 196–99.

16. Lamers, *Edge of Glory*, 417–18. Rosecrans wrote to Lincoln to request that "two able Brigadiers, not politicians, nor interested in local politics," be sent to replace the existing district commanders. The incumbents were "good fighting men" but were mixed up in local politics. Rosecrans to Lincoln, March 12, 1864, RG 393, pt. 1, Department of the Missouri, E 2587, Telegrams Sent, vol. 4, 67, NARA.

17. See RG 393, pt. 4, Post of St. Louis, Missouri, Records, E 1747, Special Orders Received from the Provost Marshal General by the Chief of U.S. Police at St. Louis, Missouri, vol. 1, 184ff., NARA.

18. R.S. Thom to Garfield, February 13, 1864, ser. 4, vol. 6, roll 12, Garfield Papers, LC. In the same letter, Thom wrote, "We have asked for Old Sanderson for Provost Marshal which is a secret but I hope he wont come for I don't particularly like him."

19. Rosecrans to Lincoln, February 11, 1864, RG 393, pt. 1, E 2587, vol. 4, 42, NARA. See also Rosecrans to Lincoln, February 12, 20, 1864, Abraham Lincoln Papers, LC. The February 12 telegram is the same as the February 11 message, but arrived in Washington overnight and was consequently dated later. After writing to Lincoln,

Rosecrans received the suggestion from the former provost marshal general to appoint a neutral person, unconnected to Missouri politics, from the former provost marshal general under Schofield. James O. Broadhead, a Missouri attorney closely allied to Edward Bates, advised the incoming general, "Your administration here will have fully as much to do with civil as with military affairs at least so long as martial law is in force." Broadhead to Rosecrans, February 14, 1864, box 2, James O. Broadhead Papers, Missouri Historical Society, Saint Louis. See also Rosecrans to Garfield, February 14, 1864, ser. 4, vol. 6, roll 12, Garfield Papers, LC.

20. Lincoln to Rosecrans, February 22, 1864, in Abraham Lincoln, *The Collected Works of Abraham Lincoln*, ed. Roy P. Basler (New Brunswick, NJ: Rutgers University Press, 1953), vol. 7, 198; Maj. Frank S. Bond to Sanderson, February 23, 1864, RG 393, pt. 1, E 2587, vol. 4, 53, NARA.

21. Journal entries for March 3, 8, 1864, Sanderson Papers, OHS.

22. For a study of the Missouri guerrilla conflict, see Michael Fellman, *Inside War: The Guerrilla Conflict in Missouri during the American Civil War* (New York: Oxford University Press, 1989).

23. Journal entry for March 5, 1864, Sanderson Papers, OHS.

24. Journal entry for March 12, Sanderson Papers, OHS.

25. Diary entry for March 9, 1864, box 79, Rosecrans Papers, UCLA.

26. Journal entry for March 7, 1864, Sanderson Papers, OHS; Lt. Col. C. W. Marsh to provost marshal at Nashville, Tennessee, February 2, 1864, RG 393, pt. 1, E 2587, vol. 4, NARA.

27. Journal entry for April 10, 1864, Sanderson Papers, OHS.

28. Journal entry for March 9, 1864, Sanderson Papers, OHS.

29. Journal entry for March 10, 1864, Sanderson Papers, OHS.

30. Sanderson to Rosecrans, May 31, 1864; Sanderson to Rosecrans, June 12, 1864, G. Byron Jones statement, March 10, 1864, all in box 2, folder 3, Sanderson Papers, OHS, printed in *OR*, ser. 2, vol. 7, 228–40.

31. Reid also wrote, "There seems to be no doubt but that there is a regular line from St Louis to Price[']s Army carrying Rebel mail and contraband goods—I sent a man to St Louis with the Dr to be initiated who confirms most of what he says but did not succeed in being initiated on account of their getting alarmed from some cause." Brig. Gen. Hugh T. Reid to Rosecrans, March 8, 1864, box 2, folder 3, Sanderson Papers, OHS.

32. See account book entries for March 3, 8, 1864, RG 393, pt. 2, no. 28, E 1105, vol. 250, 105, NARA. Sanderson echoed Reid's statement about "Dr. Everett," who was not trustworthy and who disappeared shortly after making his statement at Saint Louis. Sanderson to Rosecrans, June 12, 1864, *OR*, ser. 2, vol. 7, 229.

33. Reports of Capt. Isaac M. Talmadge, February 8, March 8, 1864, enclosed with Reid to Rosecrans, March 8, 1864, box 2, folder 3, Sanderson Papers, OHS. The date of February 8, 1864, is probably a copying error, as the report mentions the February 22 meeting in New York City. The information on the February 22 meeting at New York City matches that from Carrington's detective David Turnbull. No evidence exists that information was shared by military commanders at Indianapolis and Cairo on the New York City meeting, suggesting that detectives obtained information on the meeting independently.

34. Lt. Robert Maes to Capt. George E. Leighton, July 25, 1862; William C. Street to Leighton, August 12, 1862, RG 109, M-345, rolls 258, 133, respectively, NARA; Capt. James F. Dwight to Maj. Gen. Samuel R. Curtis, April 11, 1863; Maj. J. M. Barrett to James O. Broadhead, June 15, 1863; affidavit of Aaron Smith, July 27, 1863; affidavit of Andrew J. Bryant, August 1, 1863, all in RG 109, M-416, rolls 16, 19, 21, 22, respectively, NARA; J. M. Barrett to Col. F. A. Dick, April 13, 1863, RG 393, pt. 1, Department of the Missouri Records, E 2786, Letters Received, box 1, NARA.

35. Daniel Bates et al., to Rosecrans, February 25, 1864, RG 393, pt. 1, Department of the Missouri Records, E 2593, Letters Received, box 12, NARA.

36. Rosecrans's biographer erred in writing that Sanderson had been nominated for brigadier general. Lamers, *Edge of Glory,* 419.

37. Journal entry, March 18, 1864, Sanderson Papers, OHS.

38. Rosecrans to Halleck, March 22, 1864, box 46, Rosecrans Papers, UCLA.

39. Diary entry, March 22, 1864, box 79, Rosecrans Papers, UCLA.

40. Rosecrans to Garfield, March 22, 1864, ser. 4, vol. 6, roll 12, Garfield Papers, LC.

41. Journal entry for March 25, 1864, Sanderson Papers, OHS.

42. General Orders 55, April 11, 1864, General Orders 1864–65, Department of the Missouri, box 84, Rosecrans Papers, UCLA. See Sanderson to Lincoln, March 31, 1864; Rosecrans to Sanderson, April 2, 1864; Maj. Frank S. Bond to Sanderson, April 4, 1864, all in Lincoln Papers, LC.

43. *St. Louis Daily Missouri Democrat,* July 7, 1864.

44. Sanderson to Rosecrans, June 12, 1864, *OR,* ser. 2, vol. 7, 229.

45. Lawrence A. Hudson to Hamilton R. Gamble, January 1, 1863, Hamilton R. Gamble Papers, box 10, Missouri Historical Society, St. Louis.

46. Sanderson to Rosecrans, June 12, 1864, *OR,* ser. 2, vol. 7, 230.

47. Sanderson to Edward Betty, March 26, 1864, RG 393, pt. 1, Department of the Missouri Records, E 2777, Letters and Instructions Sent to Members of the U.S. Police, 1, NARA. Several other letters with orders for Betty are to be found in the same volume.

48. Rosecrans to Ann Rosecrans, October 15, 1862, box 59; Edward Betty to Rosecrans, February 7, March 9, 1864, January 8, 1865, boxes 8, 9, 10, respectively, all in Rosecrans Papers, UCLA.

49. *Cincinnati Daily Gazette,* March 26, April 4, 28, 1864.

50. *Cincinnati Daily Gazette,* May 13, 16, 18, June 6, 9, 25, 30, 1864; *Cincinnati Daily Times,* April 12, 25, 1864. For more on Betty, see J. Cutler Andrews, *The North Reports the Civil War* (Pittsburgh: University of Pittsburgh Press, 1953), 376, 404, 751.

51. Report of William Jones, n.d., *OR,* ser. 2, vol. 7, 244–45. "Dodd" is undoubtedly H. H. Dodd of Indianapolis. The person making "infernal machines" was probably Capt. R. C. Bocking.

52. Sanderson to Rosecrans, June 12, 1864, *OR,* ser. 2, vol. 7, 238–39.

53. Betty to Sanderson, April 18, 1864, ibid., 286–89.

54. Brig. Gen. E. B. Brown to Maj. O. D. Greene, April 20, 1864, *OR,* ser. 1, vol. 34, part 3, 238.

55. Lawrence A. Hudson to [Sanderson], April 26, 28, 1864, RG 393, pt. 1, E 2786, box 2, NARA, printed in *OR,* ser. 2, vol. 7, 254–55.

56. William Taylor to [Sanderson], April 29, 1864, RG 393, pt. 1, E 2786, box 2, NARA, printed in *OR*, ser. 2, vol. 7, 251–54.

57. Rosecrans to Col. William Wier, April 13, 1864, RG 393, pt. 1, E 2587, vol. 4, 94, NARA.

58. Rosecrans to Adm. David D. Porter, April 13, 1864, RG 393, pt. 1, Department of the Missouri Records, E 2571, Letters Sent, vol. 6, 220, NARA.

59. Rosecrans to Salmon P. Chase, April 19, 1864, RG 393, pt. 1, E 2587, vol. 4, 101, NARA.

60. Rosecrans to Stanton, May 10, 1864, RG 393, pt. 1, E 2571, vol. 6, 273–74, NARA.

61. Rosecrans to Stanton, May 30, 1864, RG 393, pt. 1, E 2571, vol. 6, 307, NARA.

62. Hardie to Rosecrans, June 13, 1864, RG 107, vol. 56B, 127, E 5, M-6, roll 55, also in RG 107, E 17, M-221, roll 254, both in NARA.

63. Rosecrans to Grant, April 26, 1864, RG 393, pt. 1, E 2571, vol. 6, 205–6, NARA.

64. Rosecrans to Grant, April 29, 1864, RG 393, pt. 1, E 2587, vol. 4, 113, NARA.

65. Rosecrans to Sherman, April 29, 1864, RG 393, pt. 1, E 2587, vol. 4, 114, printed in *OR*, ser. 1, vol. 34, part 3, 345.

66. Rosecrans to Grant, April 30, 1864, RG 393, pt. 1, E 2587, vol. 4, 114, printed in *OR*, ser. 1, vol. 34, part 3, 363.

67. Rosecrans to Grant, May 1, 1864, RG 393, pt. 1, E 2587, vol. 4, 116, NARA, printed in *OR*, ser. 1, vol. 34, part 3, 381.

68. In late April, Rosecrans had written to William Dennison, former governor of Ohio, but then Ohio's Republican Party chairman and influential voice in Washington, evidently wishing to arrange a meeting. "The matter is one of national importance and must be confidential. Some days hence will probably do but time is important," Rosecrans telegraphed. Rosecrans to William Dennison, April 22, 1864, RG 393, pt. 1, E 2587, vol. 4, 105, NARA.

69. Rosecrans to Ann Rosecrans, May 1, 1864, box 59, Rosecrans Papers, UCLA.

70. Rosecrans to Ann Rosecrans, May 8, 1864, ibid.

71. William Jones to Sanderson, May 7, 8, 1864, RG 393, pt. 1, E 2786, box 2, NARA, printed in *OR*, ser. 2, vol. 7, 241.

72. James M. Forrester to Sanderson, May 7, 1864; statement of Edward F. Hoffman, May 28, 1864, both in *OR*, ser. 2, vol. 7, 258, 262–66.

73. Sanderson to David Willis, RG 393, pt. 1, Department of the Missouri Records, E 2776, Letters Sent Provost Marshal General Department, vol. 1, 74, NARA.

74. Pocket diary entry for May 10, 1864, Heintzelman Papers, LC.

75. Rosecrans to Sanderson, May 11, 1864, RG 393, pt. 1, Department of the Missouri Records, E 2788, Telegrams Received, vol. 3, 55, NARA.

76. Sanderson to Rosecrans, May 11, 1864, RG 393, pt. 1, Department of the Missouri Records, E 2787, Telegrams Sent, vol. 4, 175, NARA.

77. Journal entry for May 13, 1864, Heintzelman Papers, LC.

78. Bond to Sanderson, May 13, 1864, RG 393, pt. 1, E 2788, vol. 3, 55, NARA.

79. Gerteis, *Civil War St. Louis*, 230–33.

80. J. C. Baum to Sanderson, May 17, 1864, RG 393, pt. 1, Department of the Missouri Records, E 2778, Letters Sent Relating to the Secret Service, 4, NARA.

81. Rosecrans to Rush R. Sloan, May 30, 1864, RG 393, pt. 1, E 2587, vol. 4, 149, NARA.

82. Rosecrans to Yates, May 18, 1864, RG 393, pt. 1, E 2587, vol. 4, 132, NARA.

83. Rosecrans to Ann Rosecrans, May 24, June 30, 1864, both in box 59, Rosecrans Papers, UCLA.

84. "To my extreme disgust I was obliged to wait all Saturday [May 21] in Cincinnati to hear from Gov. Morton. Sunday came without a telegram from him. I resolved to leave C. on the O. & M. RR by the Sunday evening train. The [hour?] had been changed and the Burnett House people by not informing me missed the to miss the train [*sic*]. Reached here Tuesday morning 2. oc was sick on the way Went without breakfast." Rosecrans to Ann Rosecrans, May 24, 1864, box 59, Rosecrans Papers, UCLA.

85. Rosecrans to Morton, June 3, 1864, RG 393, pt. 1, E 2587, vol. 4, 156, NARA, also in OPMTB, vol. 5, 242, ISA.

86. Edward Cleveland Kemble and Helen Harding Bretnor, *A History of California Newspapers, 1846–1858* (New York: Plandome Press, 1927; repr., Los Gatos, CA: Talisman Press, 1962), 218.

87. Norris W. Yates, *William T. Porter and the Spirit of the Times: A Study of the Big Bear School of Humor* (Baton Rouge: Louisiana State University Press, 1957).

88. Rear Adm. David Dixon Porter to Ensign J. B. Devoe, February 20, 1864, box 62, folder Correspondence with J. B. Devoe, "Special Secret Service Duty," February, 1864–June, 1865, Samuel Phillips Lee Papers, Library of Congress (hereafter cited as Lee Papers, LC). Devoe is noted by historians of espionage for having successfully broken a Confederate cipher system in 1865. See David Kahn, *The Codebreakers: The Story of Secret Writing*, rev. ed. (New York: Scribners, 1996), 218.

89. Sanderson to Devoe, May 19, 1864, RG 393, pt. 1, E 2778, 1–3, NARA.

90. Devoe to Sanderson, June 17, 1864, box 2, folder 5, Sanderson Papers, OHS, printed in *OR*, ser. 2, vol. 7, 355–56.

91. Rosecrans to Heintzelman, May 25, 1864, Heintzelman Papers, LC. Rosecrans telegraphed to Stager that Heintzelman "has no key to the cipher in use. Please send him a key to number one cipher." Rosecrans to Stager, May 24, 1864, RG 393, pt. 1, E 2587, vol. 4, 136, NARA. Heintzelman would subsequently write that Stager said War Department consent was required to have access to cipher codes, but that Stager had requested it for Heintzelman and it would be sent. Heintzelman to Rosecrans, June 14, 1864, box 10, Rosecrans Papers, UCLA.

92. Rosecrans to Garfield, May 25, 1864, box 46, Rosecrans Papers, UCLA.

93. See arrest orders from Sanderson to district provost marshal officers, May 26–30, 1864, RG 393, pt. 1, E 2776, vol. 1, 122–38, NARA. See also files of Charles L. Hunt et al., RG 109, M-345, roll 137, NARA.

Chapter 8

1. Carrington to Thomas, April 1, 7, 1864, both in RG 94, M-619, roll 245, NARA.

2. E. D. Townsend to Carrington, June 11, 1864, RG 94, Letters Sent by the Office of the Adjutant General, Main Series, 1800–1890, M-565, roll 24, NARA.

3. Carrington to [Thomas], April 18, 1864, RG 107, Office of the Secretary of War Records, M-493, Registers of Letters Received by the Secretary of War from the President, Executive Departments, and War Department Bureaus, 1862–70, vol. 7, roll 4, NARA.

4. Carrington to Thomas, April 21, 1864, RG 94, M-619, roll 245, NARA, also in letter book of Henry B. Carrington [1863–64] ("Willard Book"), 272–73, Carrington Papers, ISA.

5. Carrington to Thomas, n.d., RG 94, M-619, roll 245, NARA.

6. Col. Conrad Baker to James B. Fry, May 31, 1864, RG 110, E 5055, vol. 4, 128–30, NARA-GLR.

7. Carrington to Capt. James M. Bratton, April 25, 1864; Special Order dated April 25, 1864, both in letter book of Henry B. Carrington [1863–64] ("Willard Book"), 278–79, Carrington Papers, ISA; Carrington to Sargent P. Coffin, May 30, 1864, pension application file of Frances E. Coffin, widow of Sargent P. Coffin, NARA.

8. Carrington to Capt. Carroll H. Potter, April 21, 1864, RG 393, pt. 1, E 3351, 12–14, NARA.

9. Carrington to Heintzelman, April 20, 1864, letter book of Henry B. Carrington [1863–64] ("Willard Book"), 274, Carrington Papers, ISA.

10. *Greensboro (NC) Patriot*, October 31, 1846. My thanks to Prof. Thomas Hamm for this reference. Frank L. Klement erroneously names Coffin "Samuel P. Coffin." Klement, *Dark Lanterns*, 157.

11. *Centreville Indiana True Republican*, July 30, 1863. The newspaper reported that Coffin, noted to be a "good friend" of both Morton and Brigadier General Solomon Meredith, a Morton ally, had publicly criticized Morton for omitting mention of Meredith in a July 4 speech at Cambridge City.

12. See Morton to Brig. Gen. Robert Anderson, October 3, 1861, pension application file of Frances E. Coffin, NARA.

13. Laz Noble to S. P. Coffin, April 12, 1862, Letter and Order Book no. 1 [November 23, 1861–January, 1863], Adjutant General of Indiana Records, ISA; *Lawrenceburg Democratic Register*, July 11, 1862; *Indianapolis Daily Journal*, August 8, 1862.

14. William R. Holloway to Col. J. M. Shackelford, October 8, 1862, OPMTB, vol. 9, 61, ISA.

15. Holloway to Brig. Gen. Jeremiah T. Boyle, November 14, 1862, RG 393, pt. 1, District of Kentucky Records, E 2173, Letters Sent, box 1, NARA.

16. Col. John W. Foster to Morton, February 23, 1863, OPMTB, vol. 10, 123, ISA.

17. *Richmond Palladium*, May 8, 1863.

18. *Richmond Palladium*, June 5, 1863.

19. Carrington to Coffin, March 24, 1863, pension application file of Frances E. Coffin, NARA.

20. John Hanna to Edward Bates, April 14, 1863, RG 60, E 9, box "Indiana," folder "Indiana (US Attorney)," NARA-CP.

21. Carrington to Coffin, May 30, 1864, pension application file of Frances E. Coffin, NARA.

22. Carrington to Lorenzo Thomas, May 30, 1864, RG 393, pt. 3, District of Indiana Records, E 218, Letters Sent, vol. 1, 5, NARA.

23. Maj. John W. Tucker to Laz Noble, April 10, 1864, 80th Indiana Volunteer Infantry Regimental Correspondence, Adjutant General of Indiana Records, ISA.

24. Tucker to Morton, May 7, 1864, 80th Indiana Volunteer Infantry Regimental Correspondence, Adjutant General of Indiana Records, ISA.

25. The letters are found in RG 109, M-345, roll 31, NARA. A letter of Bowles to his wife, Eliza, of April 25, 1861, and one to General Gideon Pillow of August 18, 1861, are printed in Nation and Towne, *Indiana's War*, 56–57.

26. *Indianapolis Daily Journal*, June 20, July 7, 1864. The *Journal* noted that the letters were in the possession of General Carrington.

27. Carrington to Maj. William H. Sidell, May 2, 1864, RG 393, pt. 1, District of Kentucky Records, E 2241, Registers of Letters Received and Endorsements Sent by Capt. S. E. Jones, vol. 2, 32, NARA.

28. Maj. William H. Sidell to Carrington, May 3, 1864, box 2, folder 23, Carrington Family Papers.

29. Louis De Falaise, "General Stephen Gano Burbridge's Command in Kentucky," *Register of the Kentucky Historical Society* 69, no. 2 (1971): 101–27; Daniel E. Sutherland, *A Savage Conflict: The Decisive Role of Guerrillas in the American Civil War* (Chapel Hill: University of North Carolina Press, 2009), 222–23.

30. Capt. H. B. Grant to Capt. Stephen E. Jones, March 25, 1864; Lt. Col. Robert Vaughn to Provost Marshal at Cincinnati, Ohio, March 29, 1864, both in RG 393, pt. 4, E 217, box 2, NARA.

31. Heintzelman to Halleck, April 5, 1864, RG 393, pt. 1, E 3338, vol. 1, NARA.

32. Maj. Gen. William T. Sherman to Maj. Gen. Stephen G. Burbridge, April 23, 1864, RG 393, pt. 4, Post of Louisville, Kentucky, Provost Marshal Records, E 1636, Letters Received, NARA.

33. Carrington to Sidell, May 2, 1864, RG 393, pt. 1, E 2241, vol. 2, 32, NARA.

34. Felix G. Stidger, *Treason History of the Order of Sons of Liberty, formerly Circle of Honor, succeeded by Knights of the Golden Circle, afterward Order of American Knights* (Chicago, 1903), 15–31. Frank L. Klement asserts that Stidger's memoir was "replete with errors of contradiction and omission" and that he told "tales" and "legends" in describing his activities. He claims that Stidger fabricated evidence of collaboration between citizens in Kentucky and Indiana and Confederate soldiers: "Stidger could find no tangible evidence of treason, nor any secrets of the subversive society he sought to expose." Klement, *Copperheads in the Middle West*, 250, 192. In his subsequent publications, Klement repeats the same assertions that Stidger fabricated evidence and told lies about secret activities. See especially *Dark Lanterns*, 156–59. Klement errs in castigating Stidger as liar and fabricator, and completely misstates the facts in regard to army investigations of secret organizations and Stidger's role in those investigations. In reality, Stidger's memoir is remarkably accurate for a document written forty years after the fact.

35. Reports of F. G. Stidger, May 4, 1864, RG 393, pt. 1, E 2241, vol. 2, 227, NARA, also in E 1637, Registers of Letters Received Relating to Prisoners, vol. 1, NARA.

36. Stidger, *Treason History*, 32.

37. Vaughn to Burbridge, April 7, 1864; Vaughn to Jones, April 30, 1864; Lt. Col. J. H. Ward to B. F. Livingston, May 9, 1864, all in RG 393, pt. 4, Post of Louisville, Kentucky, Records, E 1633, Press Copies of Letters Sent, 88, 110–12, 117–18, NARA.

38. Stidger, *Treason History,* 32–33. Stidger's memoir follows closely the narrative of events that he reported to his commanders, first Captain Jones, and later Colonel Fairleigh in Louisville and General Carrington in Indianapolis. This strongly suggests that Stidger had access to copies of the reports he wrote to his commanders when he compiled his memoir.

39. Stidger to Capt. S. E. Jones, May 13, 1864, RG 153, Office of the Judge Advocate General Records, E 33, Reports on the Order of American Knights, Sanderson Reports (1864), box 5, NARA. Klement errs in writing that Stidger used the pseudonym, "J. J. Eustiss [Eustis]," for his first report of May 13, 1864. Stidger employed that name for the first time on his June 29, 1864 report. Klement, *Dark Lanterns,* 157n12.

40. Stidger, *Treason History,* 41–42. Jones hit on the essence of the conspirators' worst weakness: they were seemingly constitutionally unable to limit the membership of their organization and the sharing of information of its plans and activities. The leaders viewed it as a hybrid of a political organization and a fraternal organization, for which "the more the merrier" and "strength in numbers" were seen as advantageous attributes, and they welcomed new members with an evangelical fervor akin to the rejoicing for newly saved souls. The fraternal character of the organization allowed detectives and other outsiders to infiltrate it with comparative ease. Since the earliest months of the war, civilians, army detectives, and soldiers posing as deserters had joined the organizations found in their communities and subsequently revealed them to be acting against the federal government and federal laws. Stidger's and Coffin's ability to ingratiate themselves with Bowles the conspirator was far from singular.

41. Carrington to Provost Marshal General of District of Kentucky, May 10, 1864, RG 393, pt. 1, District of Kentucky Records, E 2166, Register of Letters Received, NARA. Curiously, Jones forwarded Carrington's letter to the new chief of police for the District, Major B. F. Livingston. The fact that Sergeant Prentice, Carrington's confidential messenger, was in Louisville and present at Stidger's hiring suggests that Prentice reported back to Indianapolis and informed the general in person.

42. J. F. Faris to Carrington, May 7, 1864, RG 153, E 33, box 5, NARA. Frank L. Klement erroneously asserts that Faris (Farris) was a pseudonym of F. G. Stidger. See Klement, *Dark Lanterns,* 156–57n11.

43. Carrington to Lorenzo Thomas, May 9, 1864, RG 94, M-619, roll 245, NARA. Carrington on the same day wrote to Governor Morton to express his wish to lead the Indiana hundred-days regiments and return to Indianapolis in the fall, when the danger from "disloyal parties" was expected to be greatest. Carrington to Morton, May 9, 1864, ebay auction accessed October 13, 2005.

44. Potter to Carrington, May 18, 1864, RG 393, pt. 1, E 3338, vol. 1, 204–5, NARA.

45. Morton to Stanton, May 23, 1864, RG 94, Adjutant General's Office Records, E 159, subser. 2, Generals Papers, Papers of H. B. Carrington, box 6, folder 6, NARA.

46. Special Order dated May 27, 1864, pension application file of Frances E. Coffin, NARA.

47. Col. Adironam J. Warner to Capt. J. N. Cross, May 14, 1864, RG 110, Provost Marshal General's Bureau Records for Indiana, E 5314, Letters Received, Draft Rendezvous, box 7, NARA-GLR; Carrington to Warner, May 25, 1864, RG 393, pt. 4, Post of Indianapolis Records, E 591, Register of Letters Received, 3, NARA.

48. Journal entry for May 23, 1864, Heintzelman Papers, LC.

49. Heintzelman to E. D. Townsend, May 28, 1864, RG 94, M-619, roll 284, NARA.

50. T. H. Huntington to Laz Noble, May 24, 1864, ser. 1, box 2, folder 24, Carrington Family Papers.

51. Stidger, *Treason History,* 55, 47. Capt. S. E. Jones to Carrington, May 23, 1864, RG 393, pt. 1, District of Kentucky Records, E 2239, Press Copies of Letters Sent of Capt. S. E. Jones, vol. 2, 456, NARA.

52. Stidger, *Treason History,* 42–51. In the previous year, Bocking had attempted to sell artillery shells loaded with a "Greek Fire" formula of his own devising to Cincinnati and Indianapolis army commanders. He gave public demonstrations, but the shells failed. See *Cincinnati Daily Times,* April 10, May 30, June 29, August 4, 1863; *Indianapolis Daily Journal,* June 26, 1863.

53. Stidger, *Treason History,* 59–66. On May 21, 2004, a fragment of a diary written by a private soldier named Dewitt C. Markle of the 57th Indiana Volunteer Infantry regiment was sold in an auction by Cowan's Historic Americana of Cincinnati, Ohio. The online catalog description of the diary fragment noted that it covered the period March 14–September 19, 1864, and was the continuation of another diary fragment in the possession of the [Anderson Public Library] and published in Dewitt C. Markle, "'. . . The True Definition of War': The Civil War Diary of Dewitt C. Markle," ed. Erich L. Ewald, *Indiana Magazine of History* 89, no. 2 (June 1993): 125–35. Markle at the time was recovering from disability and was seconded to the district headquarters and serving as a clerk. The text of the June 5, 1864, entry in Markle's diary appeared in the online description: "Gen. H. B. Carrington came in and Whiting and Nichols were in bed but the Gen. told us that he wanted us to come up to his house and write all night for him, for he had a lot of copying to do, which had to be done immediately and it must be kept a perfect secret. On entering his dwelling he conducted us quietly to a rather small back room I should think a sitting room) in which was seated one of his aids-de-camp and on which was spread writing material for us. He then spoke and said he supposed it was unnecessary to caution us, but were it known what we were doing our lives would not be safe twenty minutes. And if the object in view can only be carried out fully, or reached in time, it may be of incalculable value to the Government. . . . The room was kept closed that no one might see us, and much of our conversation was in a whisper. He also had a large Revolver lying on the table." http://www.liveauctioneers.com /auctions/ebay/302546.html, accessed May 12, 2004.

Before the sale date I contacted the auction house for more information, and, when the auction came, attempted to purchase the Markle diary fragment. However, the bidding was quickly beyond my means and the diary sold for several thousand dollars. After the sale I contacted the auction house and asked them to contact the successful bidder and ask the buyer to contact me, to which was kindly agreed. However, I received no word from the buyer. I renewed my request to the auction house more recently, but have heard nothing from the buyer. I have also inquired around Indiana about the whereabouts of the diary to no avail. It is unfortunate that an historically valuable record is inaccessible for use by historians and other scholars.

54. Carrington to Potter, June 6, 1864, RG 393, pt. 1, E3351, 21–26, NARA, also in box 2, folder 5, Sanderson Papers, OHS, printed in *OR*, ser. 2, vol. 7, 341–42. After Rosecrans's trip to Ohio to meet with Heintzelman and Brough, evidence suggests that some cooperative efforts arose between the intelligence operations of the two departments.

55. Carrington to Rosecrans, June 6, 1864, box 2, folder 5, Sanderson Papers, OHS, printed in *OR*, ser. 2, vol. 7, 340–41.

56. Heintzelman to Halleck, June 18, 1864, RG 393, pt. 1, E3351, 20–21, 26–27, NARA.

57. Carrington to Potter, June 7, 1864, RG 393, pt. 3, E 218, vol. 1, 16, NARA.

58. Journal entry for June 8, 1864, Heintzelman Papers, LC.

59. Baker to Fry, May 31, 1864, RG 110, E 5055, vol. 4, 128–30, NARA-GLR.

60. Carrington to Potter, May 31, 1864, RG 393, pt. 1, E 3349, box 1, NARA.

61. Carrington to Lt. Col. J. R. Smith, June 3, 1864, RG 393, pt. 3, E 218, vol. 1, 12, NARA.

62. Carrington to Potter, June 1, 1864; E. R. Jones to Schuyler Colfax, April 29, 1864, both in RG 393, pt. 1, E3351, 20–21, 17–18, NARA, also in box 2, folder 5, Sanderson Papers, OHS, printed in *OR*, ser. 2, vol. 7, 339–40. The date of Carrington's letter in the *OR* is erroneously given as June 5.

63. Col. Conrad Baker to Carrington, June 1, 1864, RG 110, E 5055, vol. 4, 132–33, NARA-GLR.

64. Stidger to Jones, June 17, 1864, RG 153, NN-2716, box 1808, NARA. A biography of Richard Gatling ignores Gatling's associations with the secret organization's conspirators in Indianapolis. See Julia Keller, *Mr. Gatling's Terrible Marvel: The Gun That Changed Everything and the Misunderstood Genius Who Invented It* (New York: Viking, 2008), 124–45.

65. Carrington to [?], June 2, 1864, RG 107, M-493, vol. 7, roll 4, NARA.

66. Carrington to Smith, June 3, 1864, RG 393, pt. 3, E 218, vol. 1, 12, NARA; Carrington to Coffin, May 30, 1864, pension application file of Frances E. Coffin, NARA.

67. Klamroth's activities as a spy arose in the postwar civil suit that Lambdin P. Milligan filed against those who participated in his arrest and military commission trial. Klamroth and Carrington testified in 1871 that the soldier joined an Indianapolis lodge of the OAK in January 1864. See *Indianapolis Journal*, May 25, 26, 1871; *Indianapolis Daily Sentinel*, May 26, 1871.

68. Stidger, *Treason History*, 55. Stidger provided the figure of eighteen detectives working for Carrington as a way to magnify the importance of his own services and discoveries. The detective was quick to praise his own feats and eager to tarnish the accomplishments of others. He seems to have had an especial rivalry with S. P. Coffin and is at pains to note that he saved the other spy's life. See *Treason History*, 32–33.

69. Carrington to Potter, June 7, 1864, RG 393, pt. 3, E 218, vol. 1, 16, NARA.

70. Carrington to Maj. Henry L. Burnett, June 8, 1864, RG 393, pt. 3, E 218, vol. 1, 18, NARA.

71. Carrington to Potter, June 1, 1864, RG 393, pt. 1, E3351, 20–21, NARA.

72. Burbridge to Bramlette, May 19, 20, 1864, RG 393, pt. 1, District of Kentucky Records, E 2164, Letters Sent, vol. 119, 12, NARA.

73. Capt. J. Bates Dickson to Burbridge, May 26, 1864, RG 393, pt. 1, E 2164, vol. 119, 22, NARA.

74. Ramage, *Rebel Raider*, 212–13; Burbridge to Morton, May 23, 1864, RG 393, pt. 1, E 2164, vol. 119, 18, NARA.

75. Morton to Burbridge, May 23, 1864, OPMTB, vol. 13, 154, ISA.

76. Ramage, *Rebel Raider*, 219.

77. Baker to James B. Fry, May 31, 1864, RG 110, E 5055, vol. 4, 128–30, NARA-GLR.

78. Morton to Stanton, May 31, 1864, OPMTB, vol. 5, 240, ISA.

79. Stanton to Morton, June 1, 1864, OPMTB, vol. 5, 241, ISA.

80. Morton to Bramlette, June 2, 1864, OPMTB, vol. 13, 162, ISA.

81. Bramlette to Morton, June 3, 1864, OPMTB, vol. 13, 163, ISA.

82. Coffin to Morton, June 8, 1864, OPMTB, vol. 13, 165, ISA.

83. Journal entries for June 9, 10, 11, 1864, Heintzelman Papers, LC.

84. Ramage, *Rebel Raider*, 221–22.

85. Journal entries for June 12, 13, 1864, Heintzelman Papers, LC.

86. Capt. T. E. Hall to Dickson, June 10, 1864, RG 393, pt. 1, District of Kentucky Records, E 2174, Telegrams Received, 49, NARA; Carrington to Morton, June 12, 1864, OPMTB, vol. 13, 187, ISA.

87. Stidger to Jones, June 2, 1864, RG 153, E 33, box 5, NARA. Curiously, Stidger later reported that on June 13 Bowles told him that he (Bowles) had received a letter from a man who had shortly before been in Richmond, Virginia, who informed him that Morgan remained in Virginia and was not then in the current Kentucky raid. This confusion suggests disorganization and confusion among the leadership of the secret organization. It also came at the time of reports of Morgan's defeat by Burbridge and may reflect wishful thinking. Stidger to Jones, June 17, 1864, RG 153, NN-2716, box 1808, NARA. Klement writes erroneously that "no members [of the Sons of Liberty] were enrolled" in Kentucky. Klement, *Copperheads in the Middle West*, 175. Stidger's reports are evidence of the widespread recruiting of the organization in Kentucky.

88. *Cincinnati Daily Commercial*, June 18, 1864.

89. Among Carrington's papers is a list of names of persons who attended a "traiter [*sic*] convention" at Indianapolis on June 14 and 15, 1864, in the "old Sentinell [*sic*] Building." The list contains 141 names of men identified as being from Indiana, twenty-three Ohioans, and four from Michigan. The author of the report, whose name is not given, states that he and "Mess. Gordon, Ullendorff, and McClure" worked hard to gather these names. See [?] to Carrington, June 16, 1864, ser. 1, box 1, folder 12, Carrington Family Papers. Stidger wrote in his memoir, "It was reported to General Carrington by some of his detectives that there were delegates from Illinois, Ohio, and Michigan, present at this meeting, while I know that there was not a man in that room besides myself" except Indiana officers and members. Stidger, *Treason History*, 71. Why there is this discrepancy in the accounts is not known. A possible explanation is that the larger meeting may have been a parallel one of members of a lower degree in the organization. Only one name appears in common on the two lists: Indiana Democratic state legislator Charles B. Lasselle of Logansport, Cass County.

90. Stidger to Jones, June 17, 1864, RG 153, NN-2716, box 1808, NARA; Stidger to Jones, June 2, 1864, RG 153, E 33, box 5, NARA; Stidger, *Treason History*, 57–59.

91. Stidger to Jones, June 2, 1864, RG 153, E 33, box 5, NARA.

92. Stidger, *Treason History*, 75–76.

93. Morton to Heintzelman, June 14, 1864, RG 94, Adjutant General Records, E 159, subser. 2, Heintzelman Papers, box 15, folder 15, NARA.

94. Morton to Carrington, June 14, 1864, OPMTB, vol. 13, 200, ISA. Carrington wired Burbridge his departure from Louisville to meet with Heintzelman. Carrington to Burbridge, June 15, 1864, RG 393, pt. 1, E 2174, 69, NARA.

95. Frank L. Klement misrepresents Heintzelman and erroneously states that "Gov. Brough, excited at the news of Vallandigham's return, promptly asked military authorities to arrest him," citing the journal entries for June 17 and 18, 1864. Klement, *Limits of Dissent*, 275. Actually, Heintzelman's journal entry for June 16 specifically states, "I had gone to bed last evening when I got a telegram from Capt Potter that Col. Potter P.M.G. of Ohio had ordered the arrest of Valandigham [*sic*], and that he had ordered two companies at Johnson's Isld and 2 at Cincinnati to be ready to assist." Nothing is said of Governor Brough in the journal entries for June 16, 17, 18, 1864. As we shall see, Brough awaited instructions about arresting Vallandigham from Washington.

96. Journal entries for June 14, 15, 16, 17, 1864, Heintzelman Papers, LC; Heintzelman to Potter, June 16, 1864, RG 393, pt. 1, E 3350, NARA. Frank L. Klement misrepresents the meeting at Indianapolis between Heintzelman, Morton, and Carrington. He writes that Morton "urged Heintzelman to rearrest Vallandigham, but the general procrastinated." Klement cites the Heintzelman journal entries for June 15 and 16, 1864. Klement, *Limits of Dissent*, 276. In fact, neither journal entry states that Morton urged the arrest of Vallandigham. Indeed, it was Heintzelman himself who mused to himself in his journal that the "only thing I can see that should be done is to arrest Valandigham and his attendants. I could have decided what to do tonight, but I saw the Governor wants to have a meeting tomorrow." See journal entry for June 15, 1864.

97. Morton to Brough, June 15, 1864, OPMTB, vol. 5, 242; Morton to Stanton, June 15, 1864, OPMTB, vol. 5, 244, both in ISA.

98. Morton to Stanton, June 15, 1864; Stanton to Morton, June 15, 1864, both in OPMTB, vol. 5, 242, 244–45, ISA.

99. A month before, Thorpe had been in Detroit and was feted by his former newspaper: "William Thorpe, of this city, formerly a[n] attaché of this paper, has been commissioned First Lieutenant of enrolled Missouri militia, now in active service, and has also been selected as member of the Board of Examiners of the Provost Marshal General office for the Dept of the Missouri." *Detroit Advertiser and Tribune*, May 10, 1864. Because of Thorpe's stenographic skills, Sanderson employed him extensively at his headquarters in examining and recording the statements of prisoners, detectives, and others. It is probable that Thorpe was in Detroit to watch activities in Windsor.

100. Brough's statement that the organization was not fully organized in Ohio is confirmed by Carrington, who reported that the Hamilton, Ohio, gathering was outwardly a Democratic congressional district convention but secretly was to organize the grand council for the state. Carrington to Potter, June 18, 1864, RG 393, pt. 3, E 218, vol. 1, 19–20, NARA.

101. Report of William Thorpe, June 18, 1864, box 2, folder 5, Sanderson Papers, OHS, printed in *OR*, ser. 2, vol. 7, 321–34. Frank L. Klement erroneously

identifies Thorpe as William Taylor, the pseudonym of another of Sanderson's detectives, Dr. C. F. Mercer. According to Klement, the detective "happened" to be in the crowd and was not sent by Sanderson, and "neither Vallandigham nor his immediate friends trusted the garrulous fellow; they surmised that he was a spy and evaded answering his questions." Klement, *Limits of Dissent,* 274–75. Klement misrepresents and reverses the meaning of Thorpe's report, which clearly suggests that Vallandigham's friends were aware of Vallandigham's presence in advance of his appearance, were eager to talk to the man representing himself as working for the *Chicago Times,* and volunteered significant information. Indeed, Thorpe noted in his report that one of Vallandigham's lieutenants told him, "Mr. Vallandigham was anxious to see me, but as he was unable to do so, requested him (McGinnis) to furnish me with a copy of the speech and with such other information as he could." For Thorpe's orders to call on Brough, see Sanderson to Thorpe, June 15, 1864, RG 393, pt. 1, E 2587, vol. 4, 171, NARA.

102. Rosecrans to Brough, June 15, 1864, RG 393, pt. 1, E 2587, vol. 4, 171, NARA.

103. Sanderson to Yates, June 15, 1864, RG 393, pt. 1, E 2587, vol. 4, 172, NARA.

104. Rosecrans to Carrington, June 17, 18, 1864, RG 393, pt. 1, E 2587, vol. 4, 173, 175, NARA.

105. Rosecrans to Heintzelman, June 17, 1864, RG 393, pt. 1, E 2587, vol. 4, 173, NARA.

106. Heintzelman to Rosecrans, June 18, 1864, RG 393, pt. 1, E 2593, box 14, NARA; Rosecrans to Heintzelman, June 18, 1864, RG 393, pt. 1, E 2587, vol. 4, 175, NARA, also RG 393, pt. 1, E 3350, NARA.

107. Garfield to Rosecrans, June 15, 1864, box 10, Rosecrans Papers, UCLA.

108. Lincoln to Brough and Heintzelman, June 20, 1864, Abraham Lincoln Papers, LC. Historians have overlooked the fact that Lincoln did not send the letter to Brough and Heintzelman. See Larry T. Balsamo, "'We Cannot Have Free Government without Elections': Abraham Lincoln and the Election of 1864," *Journal of the Illinois State Historical Society* 94, no. 2 (Summer 2001): 193.

109. Bramlette to Morton, June 22, 1864, Morton Records, ISA.

110. William H. H. Terrell to Bramlette, June 26, 1864, OPMTB, vol. 5, 250, ISA.

111. *Indianapolis Daily Journal,* June 28, 1864. The letter appeared in the *Cincinnati Daily Commercial* on June 29 and in other newspapers.

112. Journal entry for June 19, 1864, Heintzelman Papers, LC.

113. Carrington to Stanton, June 17, 1864, box 2, Carrington Family Papers, printed in *OR,* ser. 2, vol. 7, 376.

114. Heintzelman to Halleck, June 18, 1864, RG 393, pt. 1, E 3351, 26–27, NARA.

115. Capt. James M. Whittimore to Carrington, June 16, 1864, RG 110, E 5314, box 7, NARA-GLR; Col A. J. Warner to Col. J. S. Simonson, June 17, 1864, RG 393, pt. 3, District of Indiana Records, E 222, Letters Received, box 2, NARA.

116. Carrington to Potter, June 18, 1864, RG 393, pt. 3, E 218, vol. 1, 20–21, NARA.

117. Carrington to Potter, June 25, 1864, RG 393, pt. 3, E 218, vol. 1, 31–32, NARA. An explanation for the postponement of the Chicago convention appears in Irving Katz, *August Belmont: A Political Biography* (New York: Columbia University Press, 1968), 126–27.

118. Heintzelman to Carrington, June 23, 1864, RG 393, pt. 3, District of Indiana Records, E 221, Letters Received, vol. 1, 292, NARA; also Heintzelman to Carrington, June 27, 1864, RG 393, pt. 1, E 3351, 28, NARA.

Chapter 9

1. Garfield to Rosecrans, May 30, 1864, box 9, Rosecrans Papers, UCLA.

2. Rosecrans to Lincoln, June 2, 1864, RG 393, pt. 1, E 2587, vol. 4, 155, NARA, also in box 46, Rosecrans Papers, UCLA and in Abraham Lincoln Papers, LC.

3. Rosecrans to Garfield, June 4, 1864, ser. 4, vol. 6, roll 12, Garfield Papers, LC. Also, he composed a message for public consumption renouncing interest in a vice presidential nomination at the Union convention at Baltimore. See Rosecrans to Garfield, June 7, 1864, ser. 4, vol. 6, roll 12, Garfield Papers, LC

4. Rosecrans to Brig. Gen. Lorenzo Thomas, June 5, 1864, box 46, Rosecrans Papers, UCLA.

5. Sanderson's first draft report to Rosecrans is dated May 31, 1864; he supplemented that report with additional reports and prepared a long cover letter summarizing the whole, addressed to Rosecrans, on June 12, 1864. See box 2, Sanderson Papers, OHS.

6. Lincoln to Rosecrans, June 7, 1864, RG 393, pt. 1, E 2593, box 15, NARA, printed in Lincoln, *Collected Works,* vol. 7, 379.

7. Rosecrans to Lincoln, June 8, 1864, box 46, Rosecrans Papers, UCLA, also Abraham Lincoln Papers, LC, and RG 393, pt. 1, E 2587, vol. 4, 163, NARA.

8. Lincoln to Rosecrans, June 8 [received in St. Louis June 9], 1864, RG 393, pt. 1, E 2593, box 15, NARA.

9. Yates to Lincoln, June 9, 1864, Lincoln Papers, LC.

10. Lincoln to Rosecrans, June 10, 1864, box 10, Rosecrans Papers, UCLA, printed in Lincoln, *Collected Works,* vol. 7, 386.

11. Hay wrote two accounts of his journey to St. Louis in his diary, a short version on June 15 and a long version on June 17. See John Hay, *Inside Lincoln's White House: The Complete Civil War Diary of John Hay,* ed. Michael Burlingame and John R. Turner Ettlinger (hereafter cited as Hay diary) (Carbondale: Southern Illinois University Press, 1997), entry for June 17, 1864, 203.

12. Ibid., entry for June 17, 1864, 204–6.

13. Ibid., entry for June 15, 1864, 202.

14. Ibid., entry for June 17, 1864, 206. Rosecrans's detectives had discovered the means by which Vallandigham secretly corresponded with his friends, followers, and his subordinate leaders of the organization. His operatives made transcriptions of intercepted letters to and from Vallandigham, copies of which are to be found in box 80, Rosecrans Papers, UCLA, and vol. 21, Stanton Papers, LC. The letter of Vallandigham to McMaster of June 1, 1864, may be that of June 1 found among the intercepted letters in the Rosecrans Papers. In it, Vallandigham acknowledged receipt of the writer's letter of May 23 through Klotz, and commiserated about subordinates who failed to follow instructions: "Not an order has been obeyed: not a request complied with except that from Indiana, Illinois and Missouri the letters calling on me for a *Peace Letter,* have been received. But we must be patient and wait a little yet, before we give

up. I will determine for myself before the Chicago Convention whether I will retain my present position or not." He discussed the coming Hamilton, Ohio, convention, and says, "I should be *glad* to have you there as a speaker & for consultation, if convenient." He concluded with this sentence: "Just now all is suspense, & there seems to be no disposition to do anything. But let us 'who are of the household of Faith,' stand firm." The letter does not refer to scarcity of funds as does the one to which Hay refers, suggesting the possibility that Hay saw a different letter, dated the same day, in which Vallandigham refers to similar topics and employed similar phrases. See Vallandigham to "My Dear Sir," June 1, [1864], box 80, Rosecrans Papers, LC. In his biography of Vallandigham, Frank L. Klement omits mention of these letters.

15. Rosecrans to Lincoln, June 14, 1864, box 46, Rosecrans Papers, LC.

16. Hay diary, entry for June 17, 1864, 207–8.

17. John Hay to John G. Nicolay, June 20, 1864, in John Hay, *At Lincoln's Side: John Hay's Civil War Correspondence and Selected Writings,* ed. Michael Burlingame (Carbondale: Southern Illinois University Press, 2000), 85. Klement erroneously asserts that Hay was "unimpressed" with Sanderson's and Rosecrans's evidence. See Klement, *Copperheads in the Middle West,* 183.

18. See Donald F. Tingley, "The Clingman Raid," *Journal of the Illinois State Historical Society* 56, no. 2 (June 1963): 350–63.

19. Sanderson to Yates, June 14, 1864, RG 393, pt. 1, E 2587, vol. 4, 169, NARA.

20. Brig. Gen. Julius White to Yates, June 19, 1864, box 3, folder 4, Wabash Yates Papers, ALPL.

21. Rosecrans to Ann Rosecrans, June 21, 1864, box 59, Rosecrans Papers, LC. In his letter, Rosecrans noted that along with Governor Yates, U.S. Supreme Court Justice David Davis had also telegraphed Lincoln on the issue.

22. Sanderson to Yates, June 13, 1864, RG 393, pt. 1, E 2587, vol. 4, 166, NARA.

23. Sanderson to Devoe, June 13, 1864, RG 393, pt. 1, E 2587, vol. 4, 166, NARA.

24. Rosecrans to Yates, June 20, 1864, L. U. Reavis Collection, Chicago Historical Society.

25. Yates to Rosecrans, June 21, 1864, box 10, Rosecrans Papers, LC.

26. Rosecrans to Capt. And. C. Kemper, June 12, 1864, RG 393, pt. 1, E 2587, vol. 4, 166, NARA.

27. John D. Congden to telegraph operator, Indianapolis, June 17, 1864, RG 393, pt. 1, E 2587, vol. 4, 173, NARA.

28. Rosecrans to Heintzelman, June 20, 1864, Heintzelman Papers, LC.

29. Rosecrans to Lincoln, June 21, 1864, RG 393, pt. 1, E 2587, vol. 4, 177, NARA.

30. Rosecrans to Lincoln, June 22, 1864, box 46, Rosecrans Papers, UCLA, and Lincoln Papers, LC.

31. An Indianapolis newspaper reported that Rosecrans passed through the city on the evening of June 22 en route to Washington. There is no indication that he stopped to confer with anyone. *Indianapolis Daily Journal,* June 25, 1864.

32. Journal entry and pocket diary entry for June 24, 1864, Heintzelman Papers, LC. The woman mentioned by Heintzelman was Mary M. Pitman (also called Mary Ann Pitman), who served as a lieutenant in the forces of her uncle, rebel general N. B. Forrest. Pitman was captured in Memphis in the spring of 1864, having been a courier

between Confederate forces and sympathizers in Saint Louis. She provided information first to the provost marshal at Memphis, who forwarded her to Sanderson at Saint Louis. See DeAnne Blanton and Lauren M. Cook, *They Fought Like Demons: Women Soldiers in the American Civil War* (Baton Rouge: Louisiana State University Press, 2002), 10–11, 40, 49, 68–71, 87–90; Elizabeth D. Leonard, *All the Daring of the Soldier: Women of the Civil War Armies* (New York: Norton, 1999), 181–82; Michael Fellman, "Women and Guerrilla Warfare," in *Divided Houses: Gender and the Civil War,* ed. Catherine Clinton and Nina Silber (New York: Oxford University Press, 1992), 162. Klement dismisses the information that Pitman provided Sanderson and other federal officers out of hand, saying merely that she was an "accomplished liar" about her service in the rebel army and her knowledge of secret activities by the OAK. See Klement, "Phineas C. Wright,"16. In making the assertion, Klement took his cue from Vallandigham's testimony during the military commission trial in Cincinnati for the Chicago conspirators. Vallandigham denied that he and Jefferson Davis had collaborated to form an organization: "That was the testimony of Mary Ann Pitman, a lady of whom I have no knowledge, and alluded to in the judge advocate general's report." See *Executive Documents Printed by Order of the House of Representatives during the Second Session of the Thirty-ninth Congress, 1866–67* (Washington, DC: Government Printing Office, 1867), 509.

33. Rosecrans to Andrew G. Curtin, June 24, 1864, box 46, Rosecrans Papers, UCLA.

34. Journal entry for June 25, 1864, Heintzelman Papers, LC. Major Bond, Rosecrans's close aide, appears also to have traveled east to New York City at this time, though for what purpose is not known. F. Bond to William Bond, June 26, 1864, RG 393, pt. 1, E 2587, vol. 4, 185, NARA.

35. For works on opposition to the war in Pennsylvania, see Arnold M. Shankman, *The Pennsylvania Antiwar Movement, 1861–1865* (Rutherford, NJ: Fairleigh Dickinson University Press, 1980); Grace Palladino, *Another Civil War: Labor, Capital, and the State in the Anthracite Regions of Pennsylvania, 1840–1868* (Urbana: University of Illinois Press, 1990); Robert M. Sandow, *Deserter Country: Civil War Opposition in the Pennsylvania Appalachians* (New York: Fordham University Press, 2009). All three works show the influence of the Klement thesis by dismissing the influence of secret organizations in the North during the rebellion.

36. Sanderson to Rosecrans, June 27, 1864, box 10, Rosecrans Papers, LC. In early August the adjutant general of Illinois, Allen C. Fuller, traveled to Washington and while waiting for a connecting train at Harrisburg called on Governor Curtin. He had a two-hour conversation with the governor, who raised the issue of insurrection in Illinois: "In relation to difficulties in Illinois [Curtin] enquired very particularly for he says he had information some time since that the first blow was to be struck there & was to be soon followed up in other states. In fact he talks about that matter substantially as Gen Rosecrans does. He asked me if we were apprized of these things & I told him yes. He then said 'if you have arms in your arsenal look out for them for the leading democrats are bent on breaking up the Government & will seize your arsenal if you don't look out.'" Allen C. Fuller to Yates, August 3, 1864, box 17, folder 4, Yates Family Papers, ALPL.

37. Devoe to Rosecrans, June 28, 1864, box 10, Rosecrans Papers, UCLA. Devoe reported other matters to Rosecrans in this letter, including his need for funds to pay for his New York City detective operations. He also reported that several congressmen told him that "a week or ten days since, a serious effort was made to have you removed from your present command." Garfield, Schenck, and Knox of the Military Affairs Committee remonstrated against the move.

38. Sanderson to Rosecrans, June 28, 1864, box 10, Rosecrans Papers, UCLA.

39. Devoe to Rosecrans, June 29, 1864, box 10, Rosecrans Papers, UCLA.

40. Sanderson to Frank G. Porter, July 6, 1864, RG 393, pt. 1, E 2587, vol. 4, 195, NARA.

41. Rosecrans to Ann Rosecrans, July 6, 1864, box 59, Rosecrans Papers, UCLA.

42. Rosecrans to Ann Rosecrans, July 8, 1864, box 59, Rosecrans Papers, UCLA.

43. Rosecrans to Halleck, July 6, 1864, RG 393, pt. 1, E 2587, vol. 4, 196, NARA; pocket diary entry for July 5, 1864, Heintzelman Papers, LC.

44. Rosecrans to Heintzelman, July 8, 1864, and Rosecrans to Stanton, July 9, 1864, both in RG 393, pt. 1, E 2587, vol. 4, 199, 201, NARA.

45. Rosecrans to Lincoln, July 8, 11, 1864; Rosecrans to Capt. L. H. Pelouze, July 8, 1864, all in RG 393, pt. 1, E 2587, vol. 4, 199, 203, 204, NARA.

46. Sanderson to Devoe, July 6, 1864, RG 393, pt. 1, E 2776, vol. 1, 208, NARA.

47. Sanderson to Devoe, July 15, 1864, RG 393, pt. 1, E 2778, 11–12, NARA.

48. *St. Louis Daily Missouri Democrat,* July 16, 25, 1864.

49. See two letters of John G. Nicolay to Hay, June 29, 1864, Abraham Lincoln Papers, LC. The three-page cover letter requested that Hay show the second, eight-page letter, to President Lincoln. See also Fellman, *Inside War,* 172. A month later, James O. Broadhead, a prominent Missouri political figure and Sanderson's predecessor as provost marshal general, wrote to his friend Edward Bates to complain vigorously of Rosecrans's management of Missouri affairs. See Broadhead to Bates, July 24, 1864, box 2, James O. Broadhead Papers, Missouri Historical Society, Saint Louis.

50. *St. Louis Daily Missouri Democrat,* July 16, 1864. See also Rosecrans to Stanton, July 15, 1864, RG 393, pt. 1, E 2587, vol. 4, 217.

51. *St. Louis Daily Missouri Democrat,* July 14, 1864.

52. *St. Louis Daily Missouri Democrat,* July 16, 1864.

53. Charles A. Dana to Rosecrans, July 20, 1864, RG 393, pt. 1, E 2593, box 16, NARA.

54. Rosecrans to Dana, September 6, 1864, RG 393, pt. 1, E 2587, vol. 5, 15, NARA.

55. Dana to Rosecrans, September 7, 1864, RG 393, pt. 1, E 2593, box 12, NARA.

56. Rosecrans to E. D. Townsend, September 7, 16, 1864, RG 393, pt. 1, E 2587, vol. 5, 23, 51, NARA.

57. Rosecrans to Townsend, September 17, 1864, RG 393, pt. 1, E 2587, vol. 5, 53, NARA.

58. Rosecrans to Yates, July 29, 1864, RG 393, pt. 1, E 2587, vol. 4, 245, NARA. See also Fellman, *Inside War,* 174–75.

59. *Indianapolis Daily Journal,* June 20, 1864.

60. Stidger to Jones, June 17, 1864, RG 153, Court-Martial Case Files, Case of Harrison H. Dodd, NN-2716, box 1808, NARA. Stidger's June 17 report contained an addendum dated June 21, 1864.

61. Stidger to Carrington, June 23, 1864, RG 153, Court-Martial Case Files, Case of Harrison H. Dodd, NN-2716, box 1808, NARA.

62. Stidger to Jones, June 28, 1864; "J. J. Eustis" [Stidger] to Jones, June 29, 1864, both in RG 153, E 33, box 5, NARA.

63. *Cincinnati Daily Commercial,* July 2, 1864. See G. E. Rule, "The Sons of Liberty and the Louisville Warehouse Fire of July 1864," *Lincoln Herald* 107, no. 2 (2005): 68–74.

64. "J. J. Eustis" [Stidger] to Jones, June 29, 1864, RG 153, E 33, box 5, NARA. The June 29 report is the first surviving report in which Stidger used the pseudonym J. J. Eustis.

65. "J. J. Eustis" [Stidger] to Carrington, July 1, 1864, RG 153, Court-Martial Case Files, Case of Harrison H. Dodd, NN-2716, box 1808, NARA.

66. Sherman to Burbridge, June 21, 1864, RG 107, E 17, M-221, roll 255, NARA. Sherman enclosed a copy of his letter to Burbridge with a letter to Stanton giving his recommendations for the disposition of guerrillas and suspected rebels. He suggested that exiling them to Honduras, British or French Guiana, Santo Domingo, Madagascar, or Lower California was fitting. "But one thing is certain," he wrote, "there is a class of people, men women and children who must be killed or banished before you can hope for [?] and order, . . . as far south as Tennessee." Sherman to Stanton, June 21, 1864, ibid. See also Sutherland, *Savage Conflict,* 222–23.

67. Lt. Col. Thomas B. Fairleigh to Dickson, July 4, 1864, RG 393, pt. 1, E 2173, box 4, NARA.

68. Fairleigh to Carrington, July 13, 1864, RG 393, pt. 4, Post of Louisville Records, E 730, Press Copies of Letters Sent, 206, NARA. In mid-July Burbridge was also forced to beat back an effort by Halleck at the War Department to reassign Fairleigh. See Burbridge to Halleck, July 17, 1864, RG 393, pt. 1, District of Kentucky Records, E 2175, Telegrams Received and Sent of the District of Western Kentucky, box 5, NARA.

69. Burbridge to Morton, July 16, 1864; Burbridge to Heintzelman, July 16, 1864, both in RG 393, pt. 1, E 2175, box 5, NARA; Heintzelman to Burbridge, July 16, 1864, RG 393, pt. 1, District of Kentucky Records, E 2174, Telegrams Received, 145, NARA.

70. Burbridge to Maj. Gen. John M. Schofield, July 16, 1864, RG 393, pt. 1, E 2164, vol. 119, 156, NARA.

71. Schofield to Burbridge, July 18, 1864, RG 393, pt. 1, E 2174, 151, NARA.

72. Burbridge to Schofield, July 20, 1864, RG 393, pt. 1, E 2175, box 5, NARA. Amid the reports of another rebel raid, Burbridge issued his infamous General Orders 59, instituting stringent measures against guerrillas, stating that rebel sympathizers living within five miles of any act of violence against a Unionist would be liable to arrest and banishment beyond federal lines, rebel sympathizers' property would be seized, and that four captured guerrillas would be summarily executed for each unarmed Union person killed. *Cincinnati Daily Commercial,* July 21, 1864.

73. B. R. Cowen to Brough, June 30, 1864, RG 107, E 17, M-221, roll 259, NARA. The letter features an endorsement written on it by a clerk in Stanton's office, "do not copy," and dated August 12, 1864, meaning that the letter was received by the War Department in August and intentionally not recorded in the registers of letters received. The identity of "Newcomer" is not absolutely certain, but he was probably Henry

"Harry" Newcomer of the 11th Indiana Light Artillery Battery. He was a former police detective in Pittsburgh who enlisted to fight in the army but was detailed to work for Truesdail's Army Police in the Army of the Cumberland. See Lt. Col. George Spalding to Capt. A. Nevin, January 6, 1864, RG 110, Provost Marshal General's Bureau Records, E 36, Correspondence, Reports, Appointments, and Other Records Relating to Individual Scouts, Guides, Spies, and Detectives, box 36, NARA. For a sensationalized account of his Civil War service, see Linus Pierpont Brockett, *Scouts, Spies, and Heroes of the Great Civil War* (Cincinnati: E. R. Curtis, 1891), 73–100. An Ohio newspaper noted, "Mr. Henry Newcomer, the great scout of the Department of the Cumberland, was at the Spencer House yesterday. He left for Cleveland this morning, his presence being required at the U.S. Court now in session there." *Cincinnati Daily Times,* January 6, 1864. "William Taylor," the alias of spy Dr. C. F. Mercer, mentioned a rebel captain "Newcomer, alias Thompson" as active in the secret organization in Saint Louis, and Green B. Smith, secretary of the OAK in Saint Louis also referred to "Newcomer" as a rebel mail carrier in his statement of August 2, 1864. For both see *OR,* ser. 2, vol. 7, 251–52, 648, 656.

74. Lt. Col. Bolander to Potter, July 14, 1864; Col. C. W. Hill to Potter, July 16, 1864, both in RG 393, pt. 1, E 3350, NARA.

75. Brough to Stanton, July 28, 1864, RG 107, E 17, M-221, roll 259, NARA.

76. Maj. L. V. Bierce to Capt. D. S. Brown, July 28, 1864, RG 110, Provost Marshal General's Bureau Records for Ohio, E 4626, Letters Received 5th District Ohio, box 10, NARA-GLR.

77. Clinton F. Taggart to Lt. Col. B. H. Hill, June 15, 1864, RG 110, E 5949, NARA-GLR.

78. Hill to Potter, July 29, 1864, RG 393, pt. 3, District of Michigan Records, E 327, Press Copies of Letters Sent, 92–93, NARA.

79. Hill to Potter, July 30, 1864, RG 393, pt. 3, E 327, 95–96, NARA. George N. Sanders was one of the Confederate officials then operating out of Canada to superintend secret operations. The other main officials were Jacob Thompson and Clement C. Clay. See William A. Tidwell, *April '65: Confederate Covert Operations in the American Civil War* (Kent, Ohio: Kent State University Press, 1995).

80. Yates to Stanton, June 18, 1864, RG 107, E 17, M-221, roll 252, NARA.

81. Yates to Lincoln, June 24, 1864, letter book F, 451–52, box 15, folder 2, Wabash Yates Papers, ALPL.

82. Stanton to Brig. Gen. G. D. Ramsay, July 1, 1864, letter book vol. 43, 1, Stanton Papers, LC.

83. Yates to Oakes, July 18, 1864, RG 110, E 5381, box 1, NARA.

84. Yates to Oakes, July 14, 1864; Yates to Heintzelman, July 15, 1864, both in RG 393, pt. 1, E 3349, box 2, NARA.

85. Yates to Heintzelman, July 11, 1864, letter book F, 607–8, box 15, folder 2, Wabash Yates Papers, ALPL.

86. *Indianapolis Daily Journal,* June 24, 1864.

87. H. H. Dodd's speech of June 25 was printed in full in the *Indianapolis Daily State Sentinel,* June 28, 1864.

88. *Indianapolis Daily Journal,* July 6, 1864.

89. Carrington to Potter, July 1, 1864, RG 393, pt. 1, E 3349, box 2, NARA, also in RG 393, pt. 3, E 218, 38–39, NARA.

90. Frank C. Overturf to Carrington, July 8, 1864, ser. 1, box 3, folder 34, Carrington Family Papers.

91. "J. J. Eustis" [Stidger] to Fairleigh, July 3 and 10, 1864, RG 153, E 33, box 5, NARA.

92. Carrington to Potter, July 9 and 14, 1864, both in RG 393, pt. 1, E 3349, box 1, NARA.

93. Stampp, *Indiana Politics*, 233–34.

94. Carrington to Potter, July 14, 1864, RG 393, pt. 1, E 3349, box 3, NARA. Indiana Democrat David Turpie served as president of the convention. In his memoir, Turpie writes that Carrington, "with certain members of his staff in full uniform, had seats upon the stage." Turpie, *Sketches of My Own Time* (Indianapolis: Bobbs-Merrill, 1903), 208.

95. "J. J. Eustis" [Stidger] to Fairleigh, July 16, 1864, RG 153, E 33, box 5, NARA.

96. Carrington to Potter, July 20, 1864, RG 393, pt. 3, E 218, vol. 1, 53–54, NARA. For records regarding William Phelps, see Capt. C. P. Horton to Carrington, July 15, 1864, RG 393, pt. 1, E 3338, vol. 1, 329–30, NARA; Carrington to [?], July 27, 1864, RG 107, M-493, vol. 7, roll 4, NARA.

97. *Indianapolis Daily Journal*, July 23, 1864; Morton to Burbridge, July 26, 1864, OPMTB, vol. 5, 256; Burbridge to Morton, July 27, 1864, RG 94, E 159, subser. 2, General's Papers of S. G. Burbridge, box 5, folder 1, NARA.

98. Heintzelman to Carrington, July 28, 1864, RG 393, pt. 1, Northern Department Records, E 3341, Telegrams Sent (Northern Department), vol. 1, 375, NARA.

99. Carrington to Potter, July 30, 1864, RG 393, pt. 1, E 3349, box 1, NARA.

100. Journal entry for July 30, 1864, Heintzelman Papers, LC.

101. Heintzelman to Carrington, July 31, 1864, RG 393, pt. 1, E 3341, 379, NARA.

102. Lt. C. C. Adams to Maj. Alexander Magruder, July 30, 1864, RG 393, pt. 4, E 730, 233, NARA. Stidger describes a meeting with Morton, Carrington, Burbridge, Bramlette, and Fairleigh in Indianapolis on July 29, and the arrest of Bullitt, on July 30, in his *Treason History*. 100–107.

103. Dana to Heintzelman and Burbridge, August 1, 1864, RG 107, E 5, vol. 56A, M-6, roll 55, 378, NARA. Similar orders were sent to Maj. Gen. John A. Dix commanding the Department of the East, Maj. Gen. C. C. Augur commanding the Department of Washington, Maj. Gen. Benjamin F. Butler commanding the Army of the James, Maj. Gen. Henry Slocum at Vicksburg, Maj. Gen. C. C. Washburne at Memphis, and Maj. Gen. George H. Thomas commanding the Department of the Cumberland. Ibid., vol. 56B, 370, 377–78, 383, 394, 395, vol. 56B, 424, 425, 428. Oddly, the War Department did not generate a watch list for Rosecrans and the Department of the Missouri.

104. In his books and articles, Frank L. Klement erroneously states that Carrington's report appeared on June 29 or 30, 1864. See *Copperheads in the Middle West*, 189–90, 308n75–76; *Dark Lanterns*, 131. Historian David E. Long was the first scholar to note Klement's error, correctly adding, "Klement's information regarding the Indiana Sons of Liberty is often errant or the product of a selective and biased reading of

the evidence." Unfortunately, Long buried his important criticism of Klement's accuracy in a footnote, where few people have paid heed. See Long, *The Jewel of Liberty: Abraham Lincoln's Re-election and the End of Slavery* (Mechanicsburg, PA: Stackpole, 1994; repr.,, New York: Da Capo Press, 1997), 315n71.

105. Carrington to Potter, July 30, 1864, RG 393, pt. 1, E 3349, box 1, NARA.

106. *St. Louis Daily Missouri Democrat,* July 28, 1864.

107. E. D. Townsend to Holt, July 12, 1864, *OR,* ser. 3, vol. 4, 488.

108. Joseph Holt to Stanton, July 29, 1864, vol. 22, Stanton Papers, LC. Morton invited Holt to participate in the meeting between Indiana and Kentucky officials regarding plans to arrest leading conspirators. See Morton to Holt, July 26, 1864; Holt to Morton, July 27, 1864, both in OPMTB, vol. 5, 256–57.

109. Holt to Stanton, July 31, 1864, *OR,* ser. 1, vol. 39, part 2, 212–15.

110. Holt to Stanton, August 5, 1864, *OR,* ser. 3, vol. 4, 577–79.

Chapter 10

1. For the names of ten persons arrested at Covington, Kentucky, see *Cincinnati Daily Commercial,* August 1, 1864.

2. Burbridge to Stanton, August 6, 1864, RG 393, pt. 1, E 2164, vol. 119, 154, NARA.

3. Stanton to Burbridge, August 7, 1864, RG 393, pt. 1, E 2174, 179, NARA. Stanton's reply noted that the secretary of war had received a letter from the general carried by Joseph Holt regarding the plan to arrest leading conspirators. Unfortunately, the letter cannot be found. This and the language in Stanton's reply strongly suggest that he had not previously been aware of Burbridge's plan for concerted arrests.

4. Burbridge to Fairleigh; Burbridge to Maj. Henry L. Burnett, both August 9, 1864, RG 393, pt. 1, E 2164, vol. 119, 160, NARA.

5. Journal entries for August 9, 10, 11, 12, 1864, Heintzelman Papers, LC.

6. Heintzelman to E. D. Townsend, August 4, 1864, RG 393, pt. 1, E 3351, 39–40, NARA, also in RG 94, M-619, roll 286, NARA.

7. See statements of Charles L. Hunt, Charles E. Dunn, and Green B. Smith in Sanderson to Rosecrans, August 20, 1864, box 2, folder 6, Sanderson Papers, OHS. printed in *OR,* ser. 2, vol. 7, 626–59. Frank L. Klement asserts that Sanderson ordered the arrest of the three leaders and "promised them their freedom if they would confess their role . . . and implicate 'bigger names.'" However, he cites no source for his claim. See Klement, "Phineas C. Wright," 17.

8. *St. Louis Daily Missouri Democrat,* August 5, 1864.

9. *Cincinnati Daily Gazette,* October 18, 1864.

10. Cowen to Brough, August 5, 1864, vol. 22, Edwin McMasters Stanton Papers, LC.

11. Heintzelman noted that commanders at Camp Chase had intercepted a letter to a prisoner written in "sympathetic [invisible] ink" telling of plans to release rebel prisoners. See journal entries for August 6, 7, 1864, Heintzelman Papers, LC.

12. T. W. Vincent to Heintzelman, August 11, 1864, RG 393, pt. 1, E 3350, NARA.

13. Order of Stanton, August 15, 1864, in letter book vol. 43, 15, Stanton Papers, LC.

14. Halleck to Heintzelman, August 7, 1864, RG 393, pt. 1, E 3350, NARA.

15. Journal entry for August 7, 1864, Heintzelman Papers, LC.

16. Heintzelman to Halleck, August 9, RG 393, pt. 1, E 3351, 42–44, NARA. See also journal entry for August 13, 1864, Heintzelman Papers, LC.

17. Lt. Col. Bennett H. Hill to Potter, August 9, 1864, RG 393, pt. 3, E 327, 111–13, NARA, also in RG 393, pt. 1, E 3349, box 1, NARA.

18. Hill to Col. B. J. Sweet, August 8 [?], 1864, RG 393, pt. 3, E 327, 121–23, NARA.

19. Hill to Col. C.W. Hill, August 9, 1864, RG 393, pt. 3, E 327, 116–17, NARA.

20. Hill to Potter, August 11, 1864, RG 393, pt. 3, E 327, 132–33, NARA.

21. Potter to Hill, August 13, 1864, RG 393, pt. 3, E 329, NARA.

22. J. J. Newell to Lt. Butler, August 28, 1864, RG 110, E 5949, NARA-GLR.

23. See endorsement of Capt. Mark Flanigan to Hill, September 1, 1864, on Newell to Butler, August 28, 1864, RG 110, E 5949, NARA-GLR. See also *Detroit Advertiser and Tribune,* September 1, 1864.

24. See *Detroit Advertiser and Tribune,* August 30, 31, September 3, 1864. See Elwood's protest published in the *Detroit Free Press,* September 1, 1864.

25. Emile Longuemare was a Confederate agent who worked with Northern conspirators. He came from a prominent Saint Louis family and had a brother, Eugene Longuemare, who edited a pro-Breckinridge and pro-secession newspaper in the city, the *Bulletin.* Emile Longuemare obtained a commission in a pro-secession Missouri unit and later was an intermediary between Jefferson Davis and the Northern conspirators. He was closely associated with New York editor James A. McMaster. See John W. Headley, *Confederate Operations in Canada and New York* (New York: Neale, 1906). At the time of publication of Headley's first-person account of operations in the North, Emile Longuemare wrote a letter to a New York newspaper in response. See Longuemare letter, *New York Sun,* September 13, 1906; Longuemare, "New Light on Wartime Plot," *New York Sun,* September 16, 1906.

26. The documents transcribed and certified and published in the newspaper had signatures of P. C. Wright dated May 3, 1864. As Wright was arrested on April 26, 1864, the documents had probably been misdated by the transcribers or prepared in advance.

27. Yates to Stanton, July 29, 1864, RG 107, E 17, M-221, roll 258, NARA; Yates to Heintzelman, July 29, 1864, RG 393, pt. 1, E 3349, box 2, NARA.

28. Yates to Stanton, August 4, 1864, vol. 22, Stanton Papers, LC.

29. Fry to Yates, August 6, 1864, RG 110, Provost Marshal General's Bureau Records for Illinois, E 5633, Letters Received 4th District Illinois, box 17, NARA-GLR.

30. Yates to Oakes, August 9, 1864, RG 110, E 5381, box 1, NARA.

31. Brig. Gen. E. A. Paine to Yates, August 3, 1864, box 17, folder 4, Yates Family Papers, ALPL.

32. Capt. John V. Eustace to Oakes, August 6, 1864, RG 110, E 5382, box 3, NARA-GLR.

33. Eustace to Oakes, August 9, 1864, RG 110, E 5382, box 3, NARA-GLR.

34. Eustace to Oakes, August 10, 1864, ibid.; enclosed with it is S. K. Miner to Eustace, August 9, 1864. Eustace later reported a happy ending to the problem: "I like to write you a pleasant thing once in a while; so must tell you how the Copperhead Military co. in Galena has been considerably interfered with. Some three weeks since, Mr. Huntington, the Post Master there told a man (who he knew would repeat it) *in perfect confidence;* and with promise of secrecy, that the Govt. was aware of the

existence of the company, and did not intend to interfere with it, until it got pretty well perfected in drill, when the intention was, to *press the whole co into service.* The result has been that that company has had but one drill since; and that the members generally have taken the cars, for other places; their leaders being unable to quiet their apprehensions." Eustace to Oakes, September 30, 1864, ibid.

35. For Johnson's diary of his incarceration , see Madison Y. Johnson Papers, Chicago Historical Society. After the war, Johnson was invited to the "Prisoners of State" convention held in New York City in 1868, organized by Phineas C. Wright.

36. John Lorrain to Yates, July 24, 1864, box 17, folder 1, Yates Family Papers, ALPL. An endorsement on the letter noted that a letter was sent to Heintzelman on August 6, 1864.

37. Heintzelman to Yates, August 12, 1864, RG 393, pt. 1, E 3351, 29, NARA. Unfortunately, Yates's response, if he wrote one, does not survive.

38. Halbert Eleazer Paine, *A Wisconsin Yankee in Confederate Bayou Country: The Civil War Reminiscences of a Union General,* ed. Samuel C. Hyde, Jr. (Baton Rouge: Louisiana State University Press, 2009), xi, xvii–xviii; Halbert E. Paine manuscript, Fred Benton Collection, Center for Southeast Louisiana Studies and Archives, Southeastern Louisiana University, Hammond, Louisiana (hereafter cited as Paine MS).

39. Journal entry for August 16, 1864, Heintzelman Papers, LC.

40. Heintzelman to Paine, August 16, 1864, RG 94, Adjutant General Records, E 159, subser. 2, General's Papers of Halbert E. Paine, NARA.

41. Paine MS; *Indianapolis Daily Journal,* August 17, 1864.

42. Brig. Gen. Halbert E. Paine to Rosecrans, August 20, 1864, RG 393, pt. 3, District of Illinois Records, E 196, Letters Received, box 1, NARA. See Rosecrans's endorsement of August 30, 1864.

43. Paine to Potter, August 21, 1864, RG 393, pt. 1, E 3349, box 2, NARA; Paine MS. Paine noted in his report that Morton was away from Indianapolis on the day he conferred with Carrington, and could not sound him on the plan to arrest the leading conspirators.

44. Paine to Oakes, August 21, 1864, Paine MS; Oakes to Paine, August 22, 1864, RG 393, pt. 3, E 196, box 1, NARA.

45. Capt. William Fithian to Oakes, August 23, 1864, RG 110, E 5382, box 4, NARA-GLR.

46. Capt. Benjamin F. Westlake to Oakes, August 30, 1864, RG 110, E 5382, box 3, NARA-GLR.

47. Capt. George Abbott to Oakes, n.d. [September 2, 1864?], RG 110, Provost Marshal General's Bureau Records for Illinois, E 5800, Letters Received 12th District Illinois, box 26, NARA-GLR.

48. Capt. James M. Allan to Oakes, August 25, 1864, RG 110, E 5651, vol. 3, 350–51, NARA-GLR.

49. Sweet is a target of severe censure by Frank L. Klement, who characterizes him as incompetent, devious, cowardly, and a liar. Worst of all, he was "politically minded" and "ambitious." He also asserts that Sweet's battle wounds were "greatly exaggerated by friends" in order to "stifle an investigation of his errors of judgment on the battlefield." In Klement's erroneous account, Sweet fabricated the existence of a

plot to attack Camp Douglas. See Klement, *Dark Lanterns,* 191–92. A more informed and reliable account of Sweet's field service with the 21st Wisconsin is found in Noe, *Perryville,* 250–51, 260.

50. Jones to commanding officer, Camp Douglas, May 6, 1864, RG 393, pt. 1, E 2239, vol. 2, 403, NARA. The man named Walsh was Charles Walsh, a leader of the secret organization in Chicago.

51. Sweet to Paine, August 23, 1864, RG 393, pt. 3, E 196, box 1, NARA.

52. Sweet to Potter, August 12, 1864, RG 393, pt. 3, E 196, box 1, NARA.

53. Hill to Sweet, August 16, 1864, RG 393, pt. 1, E 196, box 1, NARA.

54. "J. J. Eustis" [Stidger] to Burbridge, July 30, 1864, RG 153, case file of Harrison H. Dodd, NN-2716, box 1808, NARA. Carrington wrote in the margin of the report that authorities found records in the places Stidger identified.

55. "J. J. Eustis" [Stidger] to Fairleigh, August 3, 1864, RG 153, E 33, box 5, NARA.

56. "Eustis" [Stidger] to Fairleigh, August 3,1864, RG 153, E 33, box 5, NARA.

57. "J. J. Eustis" [Stidger] to Fairleigh, August 7, 1864, RG 153, E 33, box 5, NARA.

58. "J. J. Eustis" [Stidger] to Carrington, August 7, 1864, RG 153, Case File of Harrison H. Dodd, NN-2716, box 1808, NARA.

59. D. W. Vogle to Laz Noble, August 3, 1864, RG 153, Case File of Harrison H. Dodd, NN-2716, box 1808, NARA. Carrington wrote on the letter that other southern Indiana sources reported similar information about Heffren's speech.

60. *Indianapolis Daily Journal,* August 5, 1864.

61. S. Layton to Carrington, August 3, 1864, RG 393, pt. 3, E 222, box 2, NARA.

62. William Copp to Carrington, August 11, 1864, RG 393, pt. 3, E 222, box 2, NARA.

63. Carrington to Capt. John P. Reynolds, August 5, 1864; Carrington to J. J. Brown, August 8, 1864, both in RG 393, pt. 3, E 218, vol. 1, 65–66, 67–68, NARA.

64. Carrington to Potter, August 3, 1864, RG 393, pt. 3, E 218, vol. 1, 63–64, NARA. Heintzelman noted the receipt of Carrington's letter: "He is in great alarm about a copperhead outbreak and want [*sic*] a Regt."; and "I . . . answered Gen. Carrington's letter and sent it to Washington. I must have more troops for here, both in Ind and Ill." Journal entries for August 5, 6, 1864, Heintzelman Papers, LC.

65. A. G. Preston to Carrington, August 3, 1864, RG 393, pt. 3, E 221, vol. 1, 334, NARA.

66. See open letter of L. F. Muzzy to Voorhees, August 30, 1864, in *Terre Haute Daily Wabash Express,* September 2, 1864.

67. *Indianapolis Daily Journal,* August 6, 8, 1864; Carrington to Potter, August 9, 1864, RG 393, pt. 3, E 218, vol. 1, 68–71, NARA.

68. Carrington to Ramsay, August 11, 1864, RG 393, pt. 3, E 218, vol. 1, 76, NARA.

69. Carrington to Muzzy, August 15, 1864, RG 393, pt. 3, E 218, vol. 1, 79, NARA. Frank L. Klement erroneously asserts that Voorhees's office in which the pamphlets and letters were found was in Indianapolis. Indeed, Klement errs in nearly every detail regarding the matter by stating that Carrington, "desperately in need of evidence," ordered a "raid" on the Indianapolis office, and that "Carrington and others broke down the door to the empty law office on August 4 and carted off some letters, as well as a stack of Sons of Liberty materials." See Klement, *Dark Lanterns,* 140, 162. This episode illustrates the unreliable invention of events and facts frequently found in Klement's works.

70. Testimony in the courts-martial of the Browns reveals the political origins of the quarrel between civilians and soldiers in which ten to fifteen shots were fired. See RG 153, Judge Advocate General Records, Court-Martial Case Files of Sgt. Matthias M. Brown and Pvt. Sergeant J. Brown, NN-2997, NARA.

71. Richard W. Thompson to Morton, August 5, 1864, Carrington Family Papers. See also *Terre Haute Daily Wabash Express,* August 4, 6, 1864.

72. Morton to Stanton, August 6, 1864, OPMTB, vol. 5, 266, ISA.

73. Carrington to Potter, August 9, 1864, RG 393, pt. 3, E 218, vol. 1, 68–71, NARA.

74. Carrington to Brough; Carrington to Rosecrans; Carrington to Col. A. J. Johnson, all August 9, 1864, all in RG 393, pt. 3, E 218, vol. 1, 72–73, 73, 73–74, NARA.

75. Heintzelman to Carrington, August 12, 1864, RG 393, pt. 1, E 3351, 30–31, NARA. See also Potter to Heintzelman, August 10, 1864, RG 393, pt. 1, E 3350, NARA.

76. *Indianapolis Daily Journal,* August 15, 1864.

77. *Indianapolis Daily State Sentinel,* August 16, 1864; Capt. Charles Booth to Carrington, August 12, 1864, RG 393, pt. 1, E 3338, vol. 2, 16, NARA; Carrington to Potter, August 15, 1864, RG 393, pt. 1, E 3350, NARA.

78. Carrington to Mr. Wallach, August 15, 1864, Rg 393, pt. 3, E 218, vol. 1, 79, NARA.

79. Carrington to Potter, August 15, 1864, RG 393, pt. 1, E 3350, NARA.

80. Carrington to Potter, August 15, 1864, RG 393, pt. 1, E 3350, NARA. See report of Bvt. Maj. Gen. A. P. Hovey, September 8, 1864, in *Report of the Adjutant General of the State of Indiana* vol. 1 (Indianapolis: 1869), 281–82. In his postwar memoir, Adam Rankin Johnson detailed how he had been ordered by Confederate authorities in Richmond to operate in western Kentucky in cooperation with the Sons of Liberty with the intent of freeing rebel prisoners of war. See Johnson, *The Partisan Rangers of the Confederate States Army,* ed. William J. Davis (Louisville: George G. Fetter, 1904), 161–74. See also the enclosed memoir of Terah Major Freeman, "The Sons of Liberty," 428–37.

81. Carrington to Potter, August 16, 1864, RG 393, pt. 1, E 218, vol. 1, 82–84, NARA. See also Carrington to Potter, August 16, 1864, ibid., 80–82. William H. English (1822–96) was a Democratic congressman for several terms, and Democratic candidate for vice president in 1880.

82. Carrington to Rosecrans, August 16, 1864, RG 94, Adjutant General Records, E 159, subser. 2, General's Papers of Halbert E. Paine, NARA.

83. Capt. J. P. Reynolds to Carrington, August 15, 186; Eden H. Davis to Carrington, August 17, 1864, both in RG 393, pt. 3, E 222, box 2, NARA; Col. Conrad Baker to Carrington, August 16, 1864, RG 110, E 5055, vol. 4, 401–2, NARA-GLR; Col. A. J. Warner to Carrington, August 18, 1864, RG 109, M-345, roll 136, NARA.

84. Morton to Stanton, August 19, 1864; Stanton to Morton, August 20, 1864, both in OPMTB, vol. 5, 270, 272, ISA.

85. Carrington to Heintzelman, August 18, 1864, RG 94, Adjutant General Records, E 159, Subser. B, General's Papers of Henry B. Carrington, box 6, folder 6, NARA.

86. Journal entry for August 20, 1864, Heintzelman Papers, LC; *Columbus Daily Ohio Statesman,* August 22, 1864.

87. Col. James G. Jones to James B. Fry, August 20, 1864, RG 110, Provost Marshal General's Bureau Records for Indiana, E 5059, Registers of Letters Received, vol. 1, 141–42, NARA-GLR.

88. Stanton to Jones, August 21, 1864, RG 110, E 5059, vol. 1, 295, NARA-GLR.

89. *Indianapolis Daily Journal*, August 22, 1864.

90. Jones to Fry, August 20, 1864, RG 110, E 5059, vol. 1, 142, NARA-GLR; Col. A. J. Warner to Capt. Charles F. Flowers, August 25, 1864, RG 393, pt. 4, Post of Indianapolis, Indiana Records, E 588, Letters Sent, 268–69, NARA.

91. Morton to Maj. Gen. John A. Dix, August 20, 1864, OPMTB, vol. 5, 274, ISA.

92. W. J. H. Robinson to Morton, August 22, 1864, Morton Records, ISA.

93. *Indianapolis Daily Evening Gazette*, August 22, 1864; Jones to Warner, August 21, 1864, RG 393, part 4, E 591, 19, NARA.

94. *Indianapolis Daily Journal*, August 22, 1864.

95. *Indianapolis Daily Journal*, August 23, 1864, *Indianapolis Daily Evening Gazette*, August 23, 1864. Morton subsequently received another letter explaining that the reference to thirty thousand revolvers should have been $32,000 worth of revolvers. Morton did not correct his public statement. See [?] to Morton, August 23, 1864, Morton Records, ISA.

96. Morton to Oakes, August 22, 1864, OPMTB, vol. 9, 230, ISA.

97. *Indianapolis Daily Journal*, August 22, 23, 1864; *Indianapolis Daily Evening Gazette*, August 24, 1864. Some of the original letters survive in the records of the military commission case files for the Indiana conspirators. See RG 153, Case File of Harrison H. Dodd, NN-2716, box 1808; Case File of Humphreys, Horsey, Milligan, and Bowles, NN-3409, box 1879, both in NARA. Morton sent a copy of the *Indianapolis Daily Journal* of August 23 to Stanton for his reference. William H. Schlater to Stanton, August 25, 1864, RG 107, E 17, M-221, roll 258, NARA.

98. Maj. Gen. John J. Peck to Robert Murray, August 21, 1864; Peck to Stanton, August 21, 1864; Peck to Maj. C. O. Joline, August 22, 1864; Joline to Brig. Gen. L. C. Hunt, August 23, 1864, all in RG 393, pt. 1, Department of the East Records, E 1394, Letters Sent, vol. 3, 62–63, 63, 64, 65, 68; Stanton to Dix, August 22, 1864, RG 393, pt. 1, Department of the East Records, E 1402, Registers of Letters Received, vol. 3, 410, all in NARA.

99. A memorandum in the personal papers of Confederate agent Captain Thomas Henry Hines notes that John C. Walker of La Porte, Indiana, purchased the arms and ammunition in New York using funds supplied by Confederate agent Clement Claiborne Clay, Jr. See box 1, Folder July–December, 1864, Thomas Henry Hines Papers, Special Collections, University of Kentucky, Lexington.

100. Peck to Stanton, August 29, 1864, RG 107, E 17, M-221, roll 260, NARA, also in RG 393, pt. 1, E 1394, vol. 3, 83–86, NARA.

101. Journal entry for August 21, 1864, Heintzelman Papers, LC.

102. *Indianapolis Daily Journal*, August 23, 1864; *Indianapolis Daily State Sentinel*, August 23, 1864; *Indianapolis Daily Evening Gazette*, August 23, 1864. Frank L. Klement erroneously credits Carrington for being in Indianapolis on August 20 and ordering the seizures of the arms and ammunition that day. He also erroneously writes, "Carrington next raided and ransacked Dodd's office, carrying off a stack of

material," and says that he arrested and held the business partners of Dodd, lied to the press that the boxes containing the arms were marked "Sunday school books" and "greatly exaggerated the number of revolvers taken." Klement, *Dark Lanterns,* 166–67. The "Sunday School Books" story appeared in the *Indianapolis Daily Evening Gazette* of August 22, 1864, when Carrington was still in Columbus, Ohio. As noted above, the original reports by the military officers who reported the seizures said the boxes were either unmarked or marked "hardware." The boxes of arms seized in New York City were marked "Stationary [*sic*]."

103. John R. Martin to Carrington, August 22, 1864, RG 393, pt. 3, E 221, vol. 2, 187, NARA; Warner to Carrington, August 22, 1864, RG 393, pt. 4, E 591, 19, NARA.

104. *Terre Haute Daily Wabash Express,* August 25, 26, 27, 1864; Carrington to Richard W. Thompson, August 24, 1864, RG 110, Provost Marshal General's Bureau Records for Indiana, E 5237, Telegrams Received 7th Indiana District, NARA-GLR; Thompson to Baker, August 24, 1864, RG 110, E 5314, box 7, NARA-GLR.

105. Carrington to Lt. Col. L. H. Lathrop, August 24, 1864, RG 393, pt. 3, E 218, vol. 1, 88, NARA.

106. Carrington to Lathrop, August 23, 24, 1864, RG 393, pt. 3, E 218, vol. 1, 87, 88–89, NARA.

107. Carrington to Lathrop, August 23, 1864, RG 393, pt. 3, E 218, vol. 1, 86–87, NARA. Carrington spoke publicly at a reception rally for a returning Indiana cavalry regiment on August 26 about Hines: "Colonel Hines, of John Morgan's staff, has been four times in consultation with Colonel Bowles, in reference to an uprising of the Democrats of Indiana, and this morning the General [Carrington] had received over twenty letters from different parts of the State, giving information of the open arming of men to resist the draft." *Indianapolis Daily Journal,* August 27, 1864.

108. Halleck to Heintzelman, August 22, 1864, RG 94, Adjutant General's Records, E 159, subser. 2, General's Papers of Alvin P. Hovey, box 16, folder 9, NARA.

109. Morton to Stanton, August 23, 1864, RG 94, M-619, roll 267, NARA, also in OPMTB, vol. 5, 276, ISA. The War Department agreed to Morton's request. Townsend to Morton, August 29, 1864, OPMTB, vol. 5, 277, ISA.

110. Carrington to Lathrop, August 24, 1864, RG 393, pt. 3, E 218, vol. 1, 89, NARA.

111. See Barry, "Charleston Riot and Its Aftermath," 99; Barry, "'I'll Keep Them in Prison," 20–29.

112. Carrington to Holt, September 22, 1864, RG 107, E 17, M-221, roll 257, NARA.

113. Carrington to Heintzelman, August 27, 1864, Heintzelman Papers, LC. Rosecrans's message of thanks to Carrington does not survive.

114. [Anonymous] to [deputy provost marshal at Urbana, Ohio], August 16, 1864, RG 110, E 4609, box 10, NARA-GLR; Thomas Drake to R. B. Cowen, August 25, 1864, RG 393, pt. 1, E 3350, NARA.

115. *Cincinnati Daily Commercial,* August 15, 1864.

116. Kittredge and Company to Brig. Gen. August Willich, August 20, 1864, RG 94, M-619, roll 286, NARA.

117. Willich to Potter, August 22, 1864, RG 94, M-619, roll 286, NARA. Heintzelman endorsed Willich's report on August 25.

118. Thompson to Baker, August 24, 1864, RG 153, Case File of Humphreys, Horsey, Milligan, and Bowles, NN-3409, box 1879, NARA.

119. Col. James G. Jones to Hovey, August 26, 1864, ibid.

120. O. Aldrich to Brough, August 22, 1864, RG 393, pt. 1, E 3349, box 1, NARA.

121. Journal entry for August 22, 1864, Heintzelman Papers, LC.

122. *Cincinnati Daily Commercial,* August 22, 1864. Other Ohio newspapers reported a large influx of arms. See *Zanesville Courier,* August 22, 1864, reprinted in *Columbus Daily Ohio State Journal,* August 25, 1864.

123. Heintzelman wrote to Carrington, "I have just issued an order to seize arms and ammunition." Heintzelman to Carrington, August 27, 1864, RG 393, pt. 1, E 3338, vol. 2, 55, NARA.

124. Lt. Charles F. Flowers to Warner, August 24, 1864; Warner to Capt. Walker, August 31, 1864, both in RG 393, pt. 4, E 588, 19, 131, NARA; Warner to Hovey, August 30, 1864, RG 393, pt. 3, E 221, vol. 2, 129, NARA.

125. Burbridge to Heintzelman, August 12, 1864, RG 393, pt. 1, E 2164, vol. 119, 163, NARA.

126. Capt. William James to Oakes, August 19, 1864, RG 110, E 5382, box 3, NARA-GLR.

127. James to Oakes, August 24, 1864, RG 110, E 5382, box 3; James to Sweet, August 31, 1864, RG 110, Provost Marshal General's Bureau Records for Illinois, E 5551, Letters and Endorsements Sent 1st District Illinois, vol. 3, 489–90, both in NARA-GLR.

128. Lathrop to Sweet, August 17, 1864, RG 393, pt. 1, E 3338, vol. 2, 18, NARA.

129. Lathrop to Sweet, August 20, 1864, RG 393, pt. 1, E 3351, 36, NARA.

130. Hill to Sweet, August 26, 1864, RG 110, E 5897, vol. 5, 43–44, NARA-GLR, also in RG 393, pt. 3, E 196, box 1, NARA.

131. Sweet to Lt. E. L. Deane, August 27, 1864, RG 393, pt. 3, E 196, box 1, NARA.

132. Hill to Sweet, August 31, 1864, RG 110, E 5897, vol. 5, 73–74, NARA.

133. Paine to Heintzelman, August 27, 1864, RG 393 pt. 1, E 3349, NARA; pocket diary entry for August 27, 1864; journal entries for August 27, 28, 1864, Heintzelman Papers, LC.

134. District of Illinois Special Orders 8, August 27, 1864, RG 393, pt. 1, E 3349, box 2, NARA.

135. Halleck to Heintzelman, August 28, 1864, RG 393, pt. 1, E 3350, NARA; pocket diary entry for August 28, 1864, Heintzelman Papers, LC.

136. Pocket diary entry for August 29, 1864, Heintzelman Papers, LC.

137. *Chicago Evening Journal,* August 26, 1864.

138. Journal entry for August 29, 1864, Heintzelman Papers, LC.

139. *Chicago Daily Times,* August 27, reprinted in *Cincinnati Daily Commercial,* August 28, 1864.

140. *Chicago Evening Journal,* August 29, 1864.

141. Theodore J. Karamanski, *Rally 'Round the Flag: Chicago and the Civil War* (Chicago: Nelson-Hall, 1993; repr., Lanham, MD: Rowman and Littlefield, 2006), 202.

142. *Cincinnati Daily Commercial,* August 29, 1864.

143. Journal entry for August 30, 1864, Heintzelman Papers, LC.

144. Journal entry for August 31, 1864, Heintzelman Papers, LC.

145. Journal entry for September 1, 1864, Heintzelman Papers, LC.

146. Journal entries for September 1, 2, 1864, Heintzelman Papers, LC; *Chicago Evening Journal*, August 27, 30, September 1, 1864. Evidence points to Rosecrans paying a quiet visit to Indianapolis on August 25. One of his spies telegraphed him at Indianapolis that Governor Yates had traveled to St. Louis to see him that day and wished the general to return by way of Springfield to confer. Edward Hudson (alias E. F. Hoffman) to Rosecrans, August 25, 1864, RG 393, pt. 1, E 2587, vol. 4, 282, NARA.

147. Journal entry for September 3, 1864, Heintzelman Papers, LC.

148. Four useful memoirs survive of Confederate soldiers who participated in the plot to attack Camp Douglas during the Democratic national convention at Chicago. They are Thomas Henry Hines [and John B. Castleman and W. W. Cleary as unnamed coauthors], "The Northwestern Conspiracy," *Southern Bivouac* 2, nos. 7–9, 11 (1886–87): 437–45, 500–510, 567–74, 699–704; Castleman, *Active Service;* Terah Major Freeman, "The Sons of Liberty," in Adam Rankin Johnson, *The Partisan Rangers of the Confederate States of America*, ed. By William J. Davis (Louisville: George G. Fetter, 1904), 428–37; Ellsworth, "'Everything Is Fair.'"

149. *Cincinnati Daily Commercial*, September 1, 1864; *Chicago Evening Journal*, August 22, 1864.

150. Ellsworth, "'Everything Is Fair,'" 95.

151. See Freeman, "Sons of Liberty," 428–37.

152. Hines, "Northwestern Conspiracy," 573.

153. Castleman, *Active Service*, 146.

Chapter 11

1. Earl J. Hess, "Alvin P. Hovey and Abraham Lincoln's 'Broken Promises': The Politics of Promotion," *Indiana Magazine of History* 80, no. 1 (March 1984): 35–50.

2. Bvt. Maj. Gen. Alvin P. Hovey to Heintzelman, August 25, 1864, RG 94, Office of the Adjutant General Records, E 159, subser. 2, Generals' Papers, Alvin P. Hovey, box 16, folder 9, NARA.

3. Hovey to Essie Hovey, August 26, 30, 1864, Alvin P. Hovey Papers, Lilly Library, Indiana University, Bloomington (hereafter cited as Hovey Papers).

4. Hovey to Essie Hovey, August 25, 1864, Hovey Papers. William C. DeHart's *Observations on Military Law, and the Constitution and Practice of Courts Martial* (New York: Wiley and Halsted, 1859) became a standard text on military law.

5. David McDonald, "Hoosier Justice: The Journal of David McDonald, 1864–1868," ed. Donald O. Dewey, *Indiana Magazine of History* 62, no. 3 (September 1966): 188.

6. Hovey to Stanton, August 26, 1864, RG 393, pt. 3, E 218, vol. 1, 97, NARA. While Hovey did not receive authority to declare martial law, he instructed the superintendent of the telegraph in Indianapolis that all dispatches alluding to military affairs sent from Indianapolis must be cleared through district headquarters before sending. Hovey to J. F. Wallack, September 3, 1864, ibid., 107.

7. Hovey to Stanton, August 26, 1864, ibid.

8. Carrington to Hovey, August 28, 1864, RG 393, pt. 3, E 221, vol. 2, 43, NARA. While most branches of the Order of American Knights changed their name to the Sons of Liberty, the Missouri branch retained the OAK label.

9. Hovey to Stanton, August 29, 1864, RG 393, pt. 3, E 218, vol. 1, 95, NARA.

10. Charles A. Dana to Hovey, September 12, 1864, RG 393, pt. 3, E 221, vol. 2, 380, also in RG 107, E 5, vol. 57A, 84, M-6, roll 56, both in NARA; E. D. Townsend to Hovey, September 14, 1864, RG 94, Office of the Adjutant General Records, E 159 subser. 2, Generals' Papers, Alvin P. Hovey, box 16, folder 9, NARA.

11. Col. James A. Ekin to Capt. J. L. Trumbull, September 20, 1864, RG 393, pt. 3, E 222, box 2, NARA.

12. Townsend to Hovey, September 14, 1864, RG 94, Office of the Adjutant General Records, E 159 subser. 2, Generals' Papers, Alvin P. Hovey, box 16, folder 9, NARA, also RG 110, E 5314, box 7, NARA-GLR, also letter book vol. 43, 27–28, Stanton Papers, LC.

13. Hill to Potter, August 25, 1864, RG 393, pt. 1, E 3351, 99, 102–3, NARA.

14. D. B. Wood to Capt. Isaac Keys, August 30, 1864, RG 110, Provost Marshal General's Bureau Records for Illinois, E 5716, Letters Received 8th District Illinois, NARA-GLR; A. G. Meacham to Yates, August 24, 1864, box 3, Hatch Papers, ALPL; Capt. James Campbell to Brig. Gen. H. E. Paine, August 25, 1864, RG 393, pt. 3, E 196, box 1, NARA.

15. Paine to Stanton, September 8, 1864, vol. 23, Stanton Papers, LC.

16. Statement of Elliott Robertson, August 23, 1864, RG 153, Case File of Harrison H. Dodd, NN-2716, box 1808, NARA.

17. Thompson to Col. James G. Jones, August 31 and September 1, 1864, RG 393, pt. 3, E 222, box 2, NARA.

18. Hovey to Gen. James Hughes, September 3, 1864, RG 393, pt. 3, E 218, vol. 1, 112, NARA.

19. Jones to Fry, September 13, 1864, RG 110, E 5059, vol. 1, 147, NARA-GLR.

20. Carrington to Heintzelman, August 31, 1864, Heintzelman Papers, LC; Morton to Stanton, August 31, 1864, RG 393, pt. 3, E 218, vol. 1, 100, NARA.

21. Colfax to Stanton, August 29, 1864, vol. 23, Stanton Papers, LC. See Willard H. Smith, *Schuyler Colfax: The Changing Fortunes of a Political Idol,* Indiana Historical Collections, vol. 33 (Indianapolis: Indiana Historical Bureau, 1952), 199–200.

22. Morton et al. to Stanton, September 12, 1864, vol. 23, Stanton Papers, LC.

23. Halleck to Grant, August 11, 1864; Grant to Halleck, August 15, 1864; Lincoln to Grant, August 17, 1864, all in *OR,* ser. 1, vol. 42, pt. 2, 111–12, 193–94, 243; Halleck to Grant, August 12, 1864, in Grant, *Papers,* 11:425.

24. Grant, *Papers,* 12:103–4.

25. Kemper to Col. Adoniram J. Warner, August 30, 1864, RG 393, pt. 3, E 218, vol. 2, 4–5, NARA.

26. Warner to Capt. J. W. Walker, August 31, 1864, RG 393, pt. 4, E 588, 132, NARA.

27. Hovey to Potter, September 2, 1864, RG 393, pt. 3, E 218, vol. 1, 104, NARA.

28. Walker to Warner, September 3, 1864, RG 393, pt. 3, E 218, vol. 1, 106, NARA.

29. Hovey to Potter, September 3, 1864, RG 393, pt. 3, E 218, vol. 1, 107, NARA.

30. Hovey to Morton, September 3, 1864, RG 393, pt. 3, E 218, vol. 1, 108, NARA.

31. Stanton to Holt, August 31, 1864, letter book vol. 43, 24, Stanton Papers, LC.

32. Rosecrans to Holt, September 5, 14, 19, 1864; Rosecrans to Townsend, September 19, 1864, both in RG 393, pt. 1, E 2587, vol. 5, 14, 48, 58, 59, NARA. See Sanderson

to Maj. O. D. Greene, September 3, 1864, called "Third Report of Col. J.P. Sanderson," and accompanying records, in box 2, Sanderson Papers, OHS, and in RG 153, E 33, boxes 2 and 4, NARA.

33. Rosecrans to Stanton, September 11, 1864, RG 393, pt. 1, E 2571, vol. 7, 34–36, NARA.

34. Carrington to Thompson, September 7, 1864, Richard W. Thompson Papers, L 158, Indiana State Library. Carrington also informed Thompson, "I hope to get permission to speak & shall invite Vorhees [sic] to meet me in Clay, Owen & Sullivan How would it do to give one of the papers I sent you. . . . ? How do you like my letter to Vorhees? Mr. [John D.] Defrees says he showed it to the President who liked it?" Carrington referred to his public reply to Voorhees's denial that the records found in his Terre Haute office were his. See *Indianapolis Daily Journal,* August 22, 1864.

35. Carrington to Holt, September 16, 1864, RG 153, Case File of Humphreys, Horsey, Milligan, and Bowles, NN-3409, box 1879, NARA.

36. Report entitled "Outline of Disloyal Organizations 'O.A.K.' and 'O.S.L.' in Indiana, and Adjoining States," n.d. (attached to Carrington's letter to Holt, September 16, 1864), RG 153, Case File of Humphreys, Horsey, Milligan, and Bowles, NN-3409, box 1879, NARA.

37. Holt to Burbridge, September 13, 1864, RG 393, pt. 4, Post of Louisville, Kentucky Records, E 731, Telegrams Sent, vol. 363, 86, NARA.

38. Stanton to Burbridge, September 19, 1864, RG 393, pt. 1, E 2174, 258, NARA.

39. Fairleigh to Dickson, September 20, 1864, RG 393, pt. 4, E 730, 278–82, NARA, also in RG 153, E 33, box 5, NARA.

40. Holt to Stanton, October 8, 1864, *OR,* ser. 2, vol. 7, 930–53. Holt's friend, Professor Francis Lieber of New York City, praised his work for exposing the "hellish conspiracy." He juxtaposed it to Confederate vice president Alexander Stephens's public letter to President-elect Lincoln during the secession crisis in early 1861 on state sovereignty. "And these are the Conservatives!" he wrote, adding that he believed the secret societies dated back to before 1850 in the South with the filibustering schemes. See Lieber to Holt, October 16, 1864, vol. 45, Joseph Holt Papers, Library of Congress (hereafter cited as Holt Papers, LC). Phineas C. Wright, imprisoned at Fort Lafayette, in New York Harbor, wrote to Holt to complain that he had read the report in the *New York Daily Tribune* and that he had "brought me before the public in a character which is not *mine."* Wright to Holt, October 17, 1864, vol. 45, Holt Papers, LC. Holt received hate mail as a consequence of the publication of his report.

41. Holt to Stanton, October 8, 1864, *OR,* ser. 2, vol. 7, 946, 951.

42. Historian Elizabeth D. Leonard notes Joseph Holt's important role in bringing to justice the conspirators who murdered President Lincoln. However, in her discussion of Holt's October 8, 1864, report, Leonard makes no mention of the reports of the military commanders that formed the evidentiary basis of Holt's report. See Leonard, *Lincoln's Avengers: Justice, Revenge, and Reunion after the Civil War* (New York: Norton, 2004), 30–31; Leonard, "Lincoln's Chief Avenger: Judge Advocate General Joseph Holt," in *The Lincoln Assassination: Crime and Punishment, Myth and Memory,* ed. Harold Holzer, Craig L. Symonds, and Frank J. Williams (New York: Fordham University Press, 2010), 115–35; Leonard, *Lincoln's Forgotten Ally: Judge Advocate General*

Joseph Holt of Kentucky (Chapel Hill: University of North Carolina Press, 2011). Frank L. Klement devotes a chapter of one of his books to "this excursion into the world of make-believe." Klement, *Dark Lanterns,* 136–50. See also Klement, *Copperheads in the Middle West,* 202–5.

43. Hill to Potter, September 21, 1864, RG 110, E 5897, vol. 5, 212–17, NARA, reprinted with related records in *OR,* ser. 1, vol. 43, pt. 2, 233–47. An officer of the naval vessel who in the following years gained fame as a detective wrote that he had followed the rebel Cole to Sandusky and was instrumental in breaking up the plot. John Wilson Murray, *Memoirs of a Great Detective: Incidents in the Life of John Wilson Murray,* ed. Victor Speer (New York: Baker and Taylor, 1905), 19–29. However, Murray's account was challenged for inaccuracies and bombast by a Buffalo, New York, researcher who relied on the account of another officer of the *Michigan,* John Hunter, who claimed the credit for arresting Cole. See Frederick J. Shepard, "The Johnson's Island Plot. A Historical Narrative of the Conspiracy of the Confederates, in 1864, to Capture the U.S. Steamship *Michigan* on Lake Erie, and Release the Prisoners of War in Sandusky Bay," *Publications of the Buffalo Historical Society* 9 (1906): 1–51.

44. Col. C. W. Hill to Heintzelman; Stanton to Heintzelman, both September 20, 1864, RG 393, pt. 1, E 3350, NARA.

45. Dix to Stanton, September 24, 1864, vol. 23, Stanton Papers, LC. See also David W. Francis, "The United States Navy and the Johnson's Island Conspiracy: The Case of John C. Carter," *Northwest Ohio Quarterly* 52, no. 3 (June 1980): 229–43.

46. Hill to Fry, September 22, 1864, RG 110, E 5897, vol. 5, 222–24, NARA.

47. Hill to Fry, October 4, 1864, RG 110, E 95, box 4, NARA.

48. Rosecrans to Halleck, September 24, 1864, RG 393, pt. 1, E 2587, vol. 5, 72, NARA.

49. Rosecrans to Yates, September 26, 1864, RG 393, pt. 1, E 2587, vol. 5, 83, NARA.

50. See Albert Castel, *General Sterling Price and the Civil War in the West* (Baton Rouge: Louisiana State University Press, 1968), 208–37; Lamers, *Edge of Glory,* 426–30; Mark A. Lause, *Price's Lost Campaign: The 1864 Invasion of Missouri* (Columbia: University of Missouri Press, 2011).

51. Castleman, *Active Service,* 174–77; Warner to Kemper, October 12, 1864, RG 393, pt. 4, E 588, 181–83, NARA. A Confederate private soldier accompanying Castleman also wrote an account of the arrest. See H. G. Damon, "Perils of Escape from Prison," *Confederate Veteran* 15, no. 5 (May 1907): 223–26.

52. Warner to Kemper, October 15, 17, 1864, RG 393, pt. 4, E 588, 190, 191–92, NARA.

53. Journal entry for September 12, 1864, Heintzelman Papers, LC.

54. Journal entry for September 16, 1864, Heintzelman Papers, LC.

55. Journal entry for September 17, 1864, Heintzelman Papers, LC.

56. Stanton telegraphed to Grant: "It is important to remove Heintzelman from any command, and perhaps Rosecranz," and suggested Hooker as a replacement. Grant wired back giving his approval. Stanton to Grant; Grant to Stanton, both September 25, 1864, in *Papers of Ulysses S. Grant,* vol. 12, 203.

57. Journal entry for September 29, 30, 1864, Heintzelman Papers, LC.

58. Journal entry for October 1, 1864, Heintzelman Papers, LC.

59. Ibid.

60. Heintzelman to Halleck, October 1, 1864, RG 393, pt. 1, E 3338, vol. 2, 131, NARA.

61. Journal entry for October 7, 1864, Heintzelman Papers, LC. For an account of Heintzelman's quarrel with Brough and removal, see J. Thompson, *Civil War to the Bloody End*, 305–8.

62. Stanton to Maj. Gen. Joseph Hooker, September 28, 1864, letter book vol. 43, 31–33, Stanton Papers, LC.

63. See Walter H. Hebert, *Fighting Joe Hooker* (Indianapolis: Bobbs-Merrill, 1944; repr., Lincoln: University of Nebraska Press, 1999).

64. Merriwether to Jones, October 2, 1864; Jones to Fry, October 6, 1864, both in RG 110, E 5059, vol. 1, 163, 331, NARA-GLR; Hovey to Hooker, October 4, 1864, RG 393, pt. 1, E 3350; Hooker to Townsend, October 4, 1864, RG 94, Adjutant General's Records, E 159, subser. 2, Generals' Papers, box 16, folder 8, Joseph Hooker file; Brig. Gen. Henry Jordan to Hovey, October 7, 1864, RG 393, pt. 3, E 221, vol. 2, 141, all in NARA.

65. Capt. James M. Bratton to Jones, September 25, 1864; Jones to Hovey, October 3, 1864, both in RG 393, pt. 3, E 221, vol. 2, NARA.

66. Hovey to Hooker, October 4, 1864, RG 393, pt. 3, E 218, vol. 2, 59; Hooker to Col. C. W. Hill, October 4, 1864, RG 393, pt. 4, Post of Johnson's Island, Ohio Records, E 653, Telegrams Sent and Received, vol. 1, 29; Lt. Col. B. H. Hill to Hooker, October 5, 1864; Col. C.W. Hill to Hooker, October 5, 1864, RG 393, pt. 1, E 3350; Col. C. W. Hill to Potter, October 11, 1864, RG 393, pt. 4, Post of Johnson's Island, Ohio Records, E 649, Press Copies of Letters Sent by the Commanding Officer, 56, all in NARA.

67. W. H. Riley to Fry, September 28, 1864, RG 393, pt. 1, E 3349, box 1, NARA.

68. Carrington to Hooker, October 5, 1864, RG 393, pt. 1, E 3349, box 1, NARA.

69. Carrington to Hovey, November 4, 1864, RG 393, pt. 3, E 222, box 2, NARA.

70. Carrington to Holt, November 4, 1864, *OR*, ser. 2, vol. 7, 1089.

71. Hovey to Lorenzo Thomas, January 16, 1865, RG 393, pt. 3, E 218, vol. 2, 9–10, NARA.

72. Brough to Col. C. W. Hill, October 12, 1864, RG 393, pt. 4, E 653, vol. 1, 30; Brig. Gen. H. E. Paine to Potter, October 8, 1864, RG 94, Adjutant General's Records, E 159, subser. 2, Generals' Papers, NARA.

73. Hovey to Stanton, October 12, 1864, RG 393, pt. 3, E 218, vol. 2, 68, NARA.

74. Lt. Col. B. H. Hill to Sweet, September 7, 1864, RG 110, E 5897, vol. 5, 117, NARA-GLR. Several words in this letter are nearly or fully illegible. Hill later wrote to Gen. Fry describing Young, noting that he was from Missouri but had served with Morgan's force and had twice been captured and had escaped both times, once from Camp Douglas and once from Camp Morton. Young "enjoys the [full?] confidence of the Rebel agents in Canada and is in a condition to furnish [information on everything that is being projected?]." Hill wanted to employ Young to range throughout Canada to keep him posted. Gen. Hooker was agreeable to employing Young. Hill to Fry, November 4, 1864, ibid., 488–90.

75. Sweet to Brig. Gen. Halbert E. Paine, September 20, 1864, RG 393, pt. 3, E 196, box 1, NARA.

76. Sweet to Capt. G. W. Carter, October 7, 1864, RG 393, pt. 4, Post of Chicago, Illinois Records, E 415, Letters Sent, vol. 2, 448–50, NARA.

77. Sweet to Col. William Hoffman, September 22, 1864, RG 393, pt. 4, E 415, vol. 2, 426–27, NARA; Sweet to Carter, September 22, 1864, RG 393, pt. 3, E 196, box 1, NARA.

78. Sweet to Hoffman, October 1, 1864, RG 393, pt. 4, E 415, vol. 2, 438–42, NARA. The two detectives Sweet hired at the end of July and employed through August were S. C. Storer and C. P. Bradley. He hired them at the request of department and district headquarters "to put different persons under surveillance." Sweet to Carter, October 11, 1864, RG 393, pt. 4, E 415, vol. 2, 453–54, NARA.

79. Sweet to Hoffman, October 11, 1864, ibid., 454–55, NARA.

80. Sweet to Carter, October 4, 1864, ibid., 444, and in RG 393, pt. 1, E 3349, box 2, both in NARA; Potter to Capt. William F. Rogers, October 11, 1864, RG 110, Provost Marshal General's Bureau Records for New York, E 2285, Letters Received 30th District , box 42, NARA.

81. Stanton to Hooker, October 24, 1864, RG 393, pt. 1, E 3349, box 3; Stanton to Dix, October 24, 1864, RG 393, pt. 1, Department of the East Records, E 1402, Register of Letters Received, vol. 4, 421; Potter to Col. C. W. Hill, October 30, 1864, RG 393, pt. 4, E 653, 34–35; B. R. Cowen to Hooker, November 1, 1864, RG 393, pt. 1, E 3349, box 1, all in NARA. In late October, Hill dismissed the threat of raids from Canada. Hill to Dix, October 17, 1864, RG 393, pt. 1, E 1402, vol. 4, NARA.

82. Sweet to Fry, October 31, 1864, RG 393, pt. 4, E 415, vol. 2, 474–75, NARA.

83. Hoffman to Sweet, October 17, 1864, RG 393, pt. 4, Post of Chicago, Illinois Records, E 418, Letters, Telegrams, and Orders Received, vol. 2, 6, NARA. For a study of Hoffman's administration of prisoner-of-war camps, see Leslie Gene Hunter, "Warden for the Union: General William Hoffman, 1807–1884" (PhD diss., University of Arizona, 1971).

84. Hoffman to Sweet, November 3, 1864, RG 393, pt. 4, E 418, vol. 2, 16, NARA.

85. Hoffman to Sweet, November 2, 1864, RG 393, pt. 4, E 418, vol. 2, 18, NARA.

86. Maj. G. Bladen to Sweet, November 7, 1864, RG 393, pt. 4, E 418, vol. 2, 17, NARA.

87. Sweet to Brig. Gen. H. W. Wessells, November 28, 1864, RG 393, pt. 4, E 415, vol. 3, 31; vouchers for Thomas H. Keefe, RG 110, E 95, box 5, both in NARA.

88. I. Winslow Ayer to Yates, December 2, 1864, box 19, folder 5, Yates Family Papers, ALPL; affidavit of I. Winslow Ayer, June 1883, RG 153, Judge Advocate General Records, MM-2185, case file of George St. Leger Grenfell, box 1113, NARA. Ayer wrote two accounts of his exploits, neither of which is reliable. See Ayer, *The Great Northwestern Conspiracy in All Its Startling Details* (Chicago: Rounds and James, 1865); Ayer, *The Great Treason Plot in the North during the War* (Chicago: U.S. Publishing, 1895).

89. Thomas H. Keefe, "How the Northwest Was Saved: A Chapter from the Secret Service Records of the Civil War," *Everybody's Magazine* 2, no. 1 (January 1900): 89. Keefe's account is highly self-aggrandizing and cannot be relied on for accurate details. He also published a pamphlet on the episode. See Keefe, *The Great Chicago Conspiracy of 1864* (Chicago: Desplaines Press, 1898).

90. Edmunde Kirke, "The Chicago Conspiracy," *Atlantic Monthly* 16, no. 93 (July 1865): 113. "Kirke," the nom de plume of J. R. Gilmore, had access to and quotes army records.

91. For a Confederate account of the plot to release the rebel prisoners at Camp Douglas in November 1864, see Ellsworth, "'Everything Is Fair,'" 96–103.

92. Sweet to Brig. Gen. John Cook, November 6, 1864, *OR*, ser. 1, vol. 45, pt. 1, 1081.

93. Sweet to Cook, November 7, 1864, ibid., 1082.

94. Cook to Potter, November 7, 1864, RG 393, pt. 1, E 3349, box 1, NARA.

95. Potter to Hooker, November 7, 1864, RG 393, pt. 1, E 3350, NARA.

96. *Evansville Daily Journal*, November 21, 1864. The letter, written by "M," was dated November 14.

97. Sweet to Capt. B. F. Smith, November 23, 1864, RG 393, pt. 4, E 415, vol. 3, 17–29, NARA. See also RG 393, pt. 3, E 196, box 1, NARA. Sweet's report was published in *OR*, ser. 1, vol. 45, pt. 1, 1077–83.

98. Warner to Sweet, November 7, 1864, RG 393, pt. 4, E 588, 233, NARA.

99. Sweet to Darr, November 12, 1864, RG 393, pt. 4, E 415, vol. 3, 3, NARA.

100. Cook to Potter, November 26, 1864, RG 110, E 36, box 9, NARA.

101. Report of 5th Veterans Reserve Corps Regiment, n.d., in Adjutant General of Indiana Records, box 268, folder 7, L523, 022663, ISA. Cincinnati headquarters praised Hovey for his promptness in sending reinforcements. "However well planned and matured may be the schemes and plots of our adversaries, they will be anticipated and defeated, and in the end their authors forever disgraced." Potter to Hovey, November 14, 1864, Hovey Papers.

102. James to Oakes, November 11, 1864, RG 110, E 5551, vol. 4, NARA-GLR. See also *Chicago Daily Journal*, November 8, 11, 1864; *Chicago Daily Tribune*, November 9, 10, 1864.

103. James to Sweet, November 15, 1864, RG 110, E 5551, vol. 4, 522, NARA-GLR; S. [?] Hornback to Sweet, November 15, 1864, letter book G, 812, box 14, folder 2, Wabash Yates Papers, ALPL.

104. Sweet to Potter, November 28, 1864, RG 393, pt. 4, E 415, vol. 3, 30, NARA.

105. Headley, *Confederate Operations;* Nat Brandt, *The Man Who Tried to Burn New York* (Syracuse: Syracuse University Press, 1986).

106. Lamers, *Edge of Glory,* 435–39.

107. William Taylor to Darr, October 8, 13, 30, 1864, RG 393, pt. 1, E 2786, box 4; Rosecrans to Maj. Gen. Cadwallader C. Washburn, September 17, 1864; Darr to Dix, November 28, 1864, both in RG 393, pt. 1, E 2587, vol. 5, 52, 302; Darr to Washburn, September 22, 1864; Darr to Provost Marshal General of Department of the East, November 9, 1864, both in RG 393, pt. 1, E 2778, 18, 44, all in NARA.

108. Baker to Maj. Gen. Grenville M. Dodge, January 31, 1865; Baker to C. A. Dana, February 1, 1865; Baker to Maj. Gen. Joseph J. Reynolds, March 1, 1865, all in RG 393, pt. 1, E 2778, 131–47, 148, 160, NARA. In 1866 the army tried by military commission one of the leaders of the boatburners, employing testimony of detectives and military commanders who had directed intelligence operations to break up the boatburner rings. Witnesses testified that the boatburners acted under orders from

Confederate president Jefferson Davis. See RG 153, case file of William Murphy, MM-3562, NARA.

109. Darr to Hoffman, December 2, 1864; Darr to Lt. Franklin Swap, December 8, 1864; Lt. Col. C. W. Davis to Swap, December 22, 1864, all in RG 393, pt. 1, E 2778, 71, 78, 93; Hoffman to Rosecrans, December 1, 1864; Hoffman to Davis, December 16, 20, 1864; Hoffman to Baker, December 29, 1864, January 3, 15, 18, 21, 22, 27, 1865, all in RG 393, pt. 1, E 2786, boxes 3, 4, NARA.

110. Hoffman to Baker, April 13, 1865, RG 393, pt. 1, E 2786, box 4, NARA.

111. Capt. Theodore Yates to Sanderson, October 7, 1864, RG 393, pt. 1, E 2786, box 5; Darr to Yates, October 10, 1864, RG 393, pt. 1, E 2776, vol. 1, 431; Darr to Maj. Gen. John Pope, November 2, 1864, RG 393, pt. 1, E 2587, vol. 5, 226; Darr to Pope, November 10, 1864; Darr to Cook, November 11, 21, 1864; Darr to Sweet, November 11, 1864; Darr to Brig. Gen. T. C. H. Smith, November 22, 1864, all in RG 393, pt. 1, E 2778, 44, 46, 47, 55, 58, all in NARA.

112. Col. J. H. Baker to C. A. Dana, May 5, 1865, RG 393, pt. 1, E 2778, 219–24, NARA.

113. Col. S. S. Burdett to George W. Cline, June 13, 1864, RG 393, pt. 1, E 2776, vol. 1, 158; Hoffman to Sanderson, August 18, 1864, RG 393, pt. 1, E 2786, box 2, both in NARA.

114. Holt to Lucien Eaton, February 10, 1865, RG 393, pt. 1, E 2786, box 2, NARA.

115. Unfortunately, the case files for the federal trial of J. B. Merrick and Lewis Rosenthal do not survive in the National Archives. The Cleveland newspapers followed the trial and offer the best accounts. Detective John Wilson Murray suggested in his memoir that Generals Heintzelman and Hancock initially considered trying the conspirators by a military commission. "They talked at first of trying [rebel officer] Cole by a military commission." Murray, *Memoirs of a Great Detective*, 28.

116. Baker to Dodge, January 7, 1865, RG 393, pt. 1, E 2778, 106–7, NARA.

117. Baker to Provost Marshal at Kansas City, March 10, 1865, RG 393, pt. 1, E 2778, 170; circular by Baker, March 15, 1865, RG 393, pt. 1, E 2786, box 4, both in NARA.

118. Devoe to Adm. Samuel Phillips Lee, December 1, 1864, box 62, folder "Correspondence with J. B. Devoe, 'Special Secret Service Duty,' February, 1864–June, 1865," Lee Papers, LC.

119. See pension application packet of Frances E. Coffin, widow of Sargent P. Coffin, NARA.

120. Stidger to Holt, December 15, 1864, RG 110, E 95, box 5, NARA.

121. Holt to Stanton, February 16, 1865, RG 110, E 95, box 5, NARA.

122. Carrington to Lorenzo Thomas, April 18, 1865, RG 110, E 95, box 5, NARA.

123. Stidger to John Potts, June 10, 1865, RG 110, E 95, box 5, NARA.

124. Holt to Stanton, April 24, 1865, RG 110, E 95, box 5, NARA.

125. Stidger to Holt, July 15, 1865, vol. 49, Holt Papers, LC. Baker was subsequently tried in a District of Columbia civil court for extortion. A jury found him guilty of false imprisonment but not guilty of extortion. See *Daily National Intelligencer*, January 25, 26, 27, 30, 31, February 2, 1866.

126. Stidger to Holt, September 20, 1865, vol. 50, Holt Papers, LC.

127. See Criminal Case File 3345, U.S. v. Felix G. Stidger, in RG 21, Records of U.S. District Court of Northern District of Illinois, NARA-GLR.

128. *Indianapolis News,* May 26, 1902.

129. *New York Times,* May 25, 1902; *Chicago Daily Tribune,* May 25, 1902.

130. *Hartford (KY) Herald,* August 3, 1904, quoting *Chicago Chronicle,* n.d.

131. *Chicago Daily Tribune,* May 15, 1908.

132. *Indianapolis Journal,* May 25, 1871. The *Sentinel* reported Carrington's testimony slightly differently: "I had reporting to me in the Western States probably two or three thousand. I went myself in disguise among them and learned their plans. Several of my detectives were suspected. I was in the Lodge in Washington Hall [in Indianapolis] one evening myself, so I had a chance to confirm what the detectives said." *Indianapolis Daily Sentinel,* May 25, 1871.

Postscript

1. Rosecrans to Lincoln, June 22, 1864, box 46, Rosecrans Papers, UCLA, and Lincoln Papers, LC.

2. Rosecrans to Curtin, June 24, 1864, box 46, Rosecrans Papers, UCLA.

3. "J. J. Eustis" [Stidger] to Burbridge, July 30, 1864, RG 153, Case File of Harrison H. Dodd, NN-2716, box 1808, NARA.

4. Benn Pitman, comp., *The Trials for Treason at Indianapolis, Disclosing the Plan for Establishing a North-western Confederacy* (Cincinnati: Moore, Wilstach and Baldwin, 1865), 81.

5. Harrison to Lasselle, February 1, 1864, box 17, Lasselle Family Papers, ISL.

6. See resolutions of Supreme Council of the OAK dated December 4, 1863, signed by Emile Longuemare; see also John C. Bennett to McMaster, July 25, 1864; C. C. Clay, Jr., and Jacob Thompson to McMaster, September 22, 1864, all in James A. McMaster Papers, University of Notre Dame Archives, Notre Dame, Indiana.

7. McMaster to James W. Singleton, September 16, 1864, James W. Singleton Papers, Special Collections: Manuscripts, Old Dominion University, Norfolk, Virginia.

8. Confession of James Ingraham Adams, September 27, 1864, in RG 393, pt. 1, E 2786, box 2, NARA.

9. A number of memoirs written by Confederate soldiers who acted in collaboration with Northern conspirators exist. See Hines, "Northwestern Conspiracy"; Castleman, *Active Service;* Headley, *Confederate Operations;* "New Light on Wartime Plot," *New York Sun,* September 16, 1906, page 5 (Emile Longuemare's account prompted by the appearance of Headley's book); see also Longuemare's letter in the *Sun* of September 13, 1906, page 6; A. Johnson, *Partisan Rangers.* Also included in Johnson's volume is a short account by Terah Major Freeman, "The Sons of Liberty," 428–37; Damon, "Perils of Escape; Ellsworth, "'Everything Is Fair." Historian Frank L. Klement preposterously suggests that these Confederates deluded themselves into believing Republican charges of disaffection in the North and "mistook" protest for disloyalty. "In postwar years," he writes, "they brought their claims in line with those of the exposés that Republicans concocted for political ends." Klement, *Copperheads in the Middle West,* 200.

BIBLIOGRAPHY

National Archives and Records Administration Archival Records

Washington, DC (NARA)

RG 92, Records of the Office of the Quartermaster General
RG 94, Records of the Adjutant General of the United States
RG 107, Records of the Office of the Secretary of War
RG 109, M-345, Union Provost Marshals' File of Papers Relating to Individual Citizens
RG 109, M-416 Union Provost Marshals' File of Papers Relating to Two or More Civilians
RG 110, Provost Marshal General's Bureau Records
RG 153, Records of the Office of the Judge Advocate General
RG 393, Records of U.S. Army Continental Commands
Pension application file of Frances E. Coffin

College Park, Maryland (NARA-CP)

RG 48, Records of the Department of the Interior
RG 60, General Records of the Department of Justice

Great Lakes Region, Chicago (NARA-GLR)

RG 21, Records of U.S. Federal Courts
RG 110, Provost Marshal General's Bureau Records

Other Archives and Manuscripts Repositories Cited

Abraham Lincoln Presidential Library, Springfield, Illinois

Jacob Ammen Papers
Newton Bateman Papers
William T. Coggeshall Diary
David Davis Papers
Isaac Funk Papers
Oziah M. Hatch Papers
Yates Family Papers
Wabash Yates Papers

Special Collections Research Center, University of Chicago Library

Lincoln Miscellaneous Manuscripts

Chicago Historical Society

Ulysses S. Grant Collection
Madison Y. Johnson Papers
L. U. Reavis Collection

Special Collections Research Center, Morris Library,
Southern Illinois University-Carbondale

Richard Yates Papers

Indiana State Archives, Commission on Public Records, Indianapolis

Adjutant General of Indiana Records
Henry B. Carrington Papers
Indiana Hospital for the Insane, Central State Hospital Records
Indiana Legion Records
Indiana Volunteer Infantry Regiment Correspondence
Indiana Supreme Court Records
Oliver P. Morton Records
Gov. Oliver P. Morton Telegraph Books

Manuscripts Section, Indiana State Library, Indianapolis

Henry B. Carrington Collection
Oliver P. Morton Papers
James R. Slack Papers
Richard W. Thompson Papers

William Henry Smith Library, Indiana Historical Society, Indianapolis

Edward B. Allen Papers
Conrad Baker Papers
Lane-Elston Family Papers
Daniel Tyrrell Letters

Ohio Historical Society, Columbus

Adjutant General of Ohio Records, Series 147, Ohio State Archives
John P. Sanderson Papers
David Tod Papers

Missouri Historical Society, Saint Louis

James O. Broadhead Papers
Hamilton R. Gamble Papers

Manuscripts and Archives, Yale University Library, New Haven, Connecticut

Carrington Family Papers

Manuscripts Division, Library of Congress, Washington, DC

Correspondence of John Farquhar, Eugene Gano Hay Papers
James A. Garfield Papers

Samuel P. Heintzelman Papers
Joseph Holt Papers
Daniel Read Larned Papers
Samuel Phillips Lee Papers
Abraham Lincoln Papers
Edwin McMasters Stanton Papers

Department of Special Collections, Young Library, University of California-Los Angeles
William S. Rosecrans Papers

Rhode Island Historical Society, Providence
Ambrose E. Burnside Collection

Special Collections, University of Kentucky-Lexington
Thomas Henry Hines Papers

*Center for Southeast Louisiana Studies and Archives,
Southeastern Louisiana University, Hammond*
Halbert E. Paine manuscript, Fred Benton Collection

Lilly Library, Indiana University, Bloomington
Alvin P. Hovey Papers

University of Notre Dame Archives, Notre Dame, Indiana
James A. McMaster Papers

Special Collections: Manuscripts, Old Dominion University, Norfolk, Virginia
James W. Singleton Papers

Published Primary Sources

Ayer, I. Winslow. *The Great Northwestern Conspiracy in All Its Startling Details.* Chicago: Rounds and James, 1865.

———. *The Great Treason Plot in the North during the War.* Chicago: U.S. Publishing, 1895.

Browning, Orville Hickman. *The Diary of Orville Hickman Browning.* 2 vols. Vol. 1, *1850–1864.* Edited by Theodore C. Pease and James G. Randall. Springfield: Illinois State Historical Library, 1925.

Carrington, Frances C. *My Army Life and the Fort Phil. Kearney Massacre, with an Account of the Celebration of "Wyoming Opened."* Philadelphia: J. B. Lippincott Co., 1910.

Carrington, Henry B. "Early History of the Republican Party in Ohio, 1854–5." *Ohio Archaeological and Historical Quarterly* 2, no. 2 (September 1888): 327–31.

———. *Ohio Militia and the West Virginia Campaign, 1861.* Rev. ed. Boston: R. H. Blodgett and Co., 1904.

———. "Winfield Scott's Visit to Columbus." *Ohio Archaeological and Historical Quarterly* 19, no. 3 (July 1910): 278–91.

Carrington, Margaret Irvin. *Ab-sa-ra-ka, Home of the Crows: Being the Experience of an Officer's Wife on the Plains.* Philadelphia: J. B. Lippincott and Co., 1868.

Castleman, John Breckinridge. *Active Service.* Louisville: Courier-Journal Job Printing, 1917.

Chase, Salmon P. *The Salmon P. Chase Papers.* Vol. 4, *Correspondence, April 1863–1864.* Edited by John Niven. Kent, Ohio: Kent State University Press, 1997.

Congressional Globe. 37th Congress, 3rd Sess. Washington, DC, 1863.

———. Appendix. 37th Cong., 1st Sess. Laws of the United States. Washington, DC, 1863.

Cox, Jacob D. *Military Reminiscences of the Civil War.* 2 vols. New York: C. Scribner's Sons, 1900.

Damon, H. G. "Perils of Escape from Prison." *Confederate Veteran* 15, no. 5 (May 1907): 223–26.

Davis, Billy. *The Civil War Journal of Billy Davis: From Hopewell, Indiana to Port Republic, Virginia.* Edited by Richard S. Skidmore. Greencastle, IN: Nugget Publishers, 1989.

Duff, A. D. *Arbitrary Arrests in Illinois: Letter of Judge A. D. Duff, of Franklin County, to the Public of South Illinois, Relative to His Arrest and Imprisonment by the Abolition Despotism.* Springfield: State Register Steam Print, 1863.

Ellsworth, George A. "'Everything Is Fair in War': The Civil War Memoir of George A. "Lightning" Ellsworth, John Hunt Morgan's Telegraph Operator." Edited by Stephen E. Towne and Jay G. Heiser. *Register of the Kentucky Historical Society* 108, nos. 1, 2 (Winter–Spring, 2010): 3–110.

Freeman, Terah Major. "The Sons of Liberty." In *The Partisan Rangers of the Confederate States of America* by Adam Rankin Johnson. Edited by William J. Davis, 428–37. Louisville: George G. Fetter, 1904.

Grant, Ulysses S. *The Papers of Ulysses S. Grant.* Edited by John Y. Simon. 32 vols. Carbondale: Southern Illinois University Press, 1967–2012.

Hay, John. *At Lincoln's Side: John Hay's Civil War Correspondence and Selected Writings.* Edited by Michael Burlingame. Carbondale: Southern Illinois University Press, 2000.

———. *Inside Lincoln's White House: The Complete Civil War Diary of John Hay.* Edited by Michael Burlingame and John R. Turner Ettlinger. Carbondale: Southern Illinois University Press, 1997.

Headley, John W. *Confederate Operations in Canada and New York.* New York: Neale, 1906.

Hines, Thomas Henry [and John B. Castleman and W. W. Cleary]. "The Northwestern Conspiracy." *Southern Bivouac* 2, nos. 7-9, 11 (1886–87): 437–45, 500–510, 567–74, 699–704.

Johnson, Adam Rankin. *The Partisan Rangers of the Confederate States Army.* Edited by William J. Davis. Louisville: George G. Fetter, 1904.

Julian, George Washington. *Political Recollections, 1840 to 1872.* Chicago: Jansen, McClurg and Co., 1884. Reprint, New York: Negro University Press, 1970.

Keefe, Thomas H. *The Great Chicago Conspiracy of 1864.* Chicago: Desplaines Press, 1898.

———. "How the Northwest Was Saved: A Chapter from the Secret Service Records of the Civil War." *Everybody's Magazine* 2, no. 1 (January 1900): 82–91.

Lincoln, Abraham. *The Collected Works of Abraham Lincoln.* 9 vols. Edited by Roy P. Basler. New Brunswick, NJ: Rutgers University Press, 1953.

Markle, Dewitt C. "' . . . The True Definition of War': The Civil War Diary of Dewitt C. Markle." Edited by Erich L. Ewald. *Indiana Magazine of History* 89, no. 2 (June 1993): 125–35.

McDonald, David. "Hoosier Justice: The Journal of David McDonald, 1864–1868." Edited by Donald O. Dewey. *Indiana Magazine of History* 62, no. 3 (September 1966): 175–232.

Murray, John Wilson. *Memoirs of a Great Detective: Incidents in the Life of John Wilson Murray.* Edited by Victor Speer. New York: Baker and Taylor, 1905.

Nation, Richard F., and Stephen E. Towne, eds. *Indiana's War: The Civil War in Documents.* Athens: Ohio University Press, 2009.

Paine, Halbert Eleazer. *A Wisconsin Yankee in Confederate Bayou Country: The Civil War Reminiscences of a Union General.* Edited by Samuel C. Hyde, Jr. Baton Rouge: Louisiana State University Press, 2009.

Palmer, John M. *Personal Recollections of John M. Palmer: The Story of an Earnest Life.* Cincinnati: Robert Clarke Co., 1901.

Pike, James. *The Scout and Ranger: Being the Personal Adventures of Corporal Pike of the Fourth Ohio Cavalry.* Cincinnati: J. R. Hawley, 1865.

Pinkerton, Allan. *The Spy of the Rebellion: Being a True Story of the Spy System of the United States Army during the Late Rebellion.* New York: G. W. Carlton, 1883.

Pitman, Benn, comp. *The Trials for Treason at Indianapolis, Disclosing the Plan for Establishing a North-western Confederacy.* Cincinnati: Moore, Wilstach and Baldwin, 1865.

Stidger, Felix G. *Treason History of the Order of Sons of Liberty, formerly Circle of Honor, Succeeded by Knights of the Golden Circle, afterward Order of American Knights.* Chicago, 1903.

Terrell, W. H. H. *Indiana in the War of the Rebellion: Reports of the Adjutant General of the State of Indiana.* 8 vols. Indianapolis: Douglass and Conner, printers, 1869.

Turpie, David. *Sketches of My Own Time.* Indianapolis: Bobbs-Merrill, 1903.

United States. Congress. *Executive Documents Printed by Order of the House of Representatives during the Second Session of the Thirty-ninth Congress, 1866–67.* Washington: Government Printing Office, 1867.

———. Department of Justice. *Digest of the Official Opinions of the Attorneys-General of the United States.* Vol. 2, *1789–1881,* compiled by A. J. Bentley. Washington, DC: Government Printing Office, 1885.

———. Naval War Records Office. *Official Records of the Union and Confederate Navies in the War of the Rebellion.* Washington, DC: Government Printing Office, 1894–1922.

————. War Department. *The War of the Rebellion: A Compilation of the Official Records of the Union and Confederate Armies.* Washington, DC: Government Printing Office, 1880–1901.

Willcox, Orlando B. *Forgotten Valor: The Memoirs, Journals, and Civil War Letters of Orlando B. Willcox.* Edited by Robert Garth Scott. Kent, Ohio: Kent State University Press, 1999.

Newspapers

District of Columbia

Washington (DC) Daily National Intelligencer

Illinois

Chicago Daily Times
Chicago Daily Tribune
Chicago Evening Journal
Danville Globe
Marshall Flag of Our Nation
Mattoon Independent Gazette
Paris Prairie Beacon
Paris Times and Democratic Standard

Indiana

Centreville Indiana True Republican
Columbia City Whitley County Republican
Connersville Weekly Times
Delphi Journal
Delphi Weekly Times
Greencastle Putnam Republican Banner
Huntington Democrat
Huntington Indiana Herald
Indianapolis Daily Evening Gazette
Indianapolis Daily Journal
Indianapolis Daily State Sentinel
Indianapolis News
Lafayette Daily Courier
La Porte Herald
Lawrenceburg Democratic Register
Liberty Weekly Herald
Logansport Democratic-Pharos
Logansport Journal
Mishawaka Enterprise
New Castle Courier
Plymouth Marshall County Republican
Plymouth Weekly Democrat

Portland Jay Torch-Light
Richmond Broad Axe of Freedom
Richmond Palladium
Richmond Quaker City Telegram
Rockville Parke County Republican
Rushville Jacksonian
Seymour Times
Shelby Volunteer
Sullivan Democrat
Terre Haute Daily Wabash Express
Weekly Vincennes Western Sun
Worthington White River Gazette

Kentucky

Hartford Herald

Michigan

Detroit Advertiser and Tribune
Detroit Free Press

New York

New York Sun
New York Times

North Carolina

Greensboro Patriot

Ohio

Chillicothe Scioto Gazette
Cincinnati Daily Commercial
Cincinnati Daily Enquirer
Cincinnati Daily Gazette
Cincinnati Daily Times
Cleveland Daily Plain Dealer
Columbus Daily Ohio State Journal
Columbus Daily Ohio Statesman
Daily Cleveland Herald
Mansfield Herald
Ripley Bee
Zanesville Courier

Pennsylvania

Altoona Tribune
Philadelphia Press

Secondary Sources

Aaron, Daniel. *Cincinnati: Queen City of the West.* Columbus: Ohio State University Press, 1992.

Anbinder, Tyler. *Nativism and Slavery: The Northern Know-Nothings and the Politics of the 1850s.* New York: Oxford University Press, 1992.

Andrew, Christopher. *For the President's Eyes Only: Secret Intelligence and the American Presidency from Washington to Bush.* New York: HarperCollins, 1995.

Andrews, J. Cutler. *The North Reports the Civil War.* Pittsburgh: University of Pittsburgh Press, 1953.

Baird, Nancy D. *Luke Pryor Blackburn: Physician, Governor, Reformer.* Lexington: University Press of Kentucky, 1979.

Baker, Jean H. *Affairs of Party: The Political Culture of Northern Democrats in the Mid-Nineteenth Century.* Ithaca: Cornell University Press, 1983. Reprint, New York: Fordham University Press, 1998.

Baker, Lafayette C. *History of the United States Secret Service.* Philadelphia: King and Baird, 1867.

Balsamo, Larry T. "'We Cannot Have Free Government without Elections': Abraham Lincoln and the Election of 1864." *Journal of the Illinois State Historical Society* 94, no. 2 (Summer 2001): 181–99.

Barry, Peter J. "Amos Green, Paris Illinois: Civil War Lawyer, Editorialist, and Copperhead." *Journal of Illinois History* 11, no. 1 (Spring 2008): 39–60.

———. *The Charleston, Illinois Riot, March 28, 1864.* Privately printed, 2007.

———. "The Charleston Riot and Its Aftermath: Civil, Military, and Presidential Responses." *Journal of Illinois History* 7, no. 2 (Summer 2004): 82–106.

———. "'I'll Keep Them in Prison Awhile . . .': Abraham Lincoln and David Davis on Civil Liberties in Wartime." *Journal of the Abraham Lincoln Association* 28, no. 1 (2007): 20–29.

Bell, William H. "Knights of the Golden Circle: Its Organization and Activities in Texas Prior to the Civil War." MA thesis, Texas College of Arts and Industries, 1965.

Benedict, Michael Les. "Abraham Lincoln and Federalism." *Journal of the Abraham Lincoln Association* 10, no. 1 (1988): 1–45.

Bernstein, Iver. *The New York City Draft Riots: Their Significance for American Society and Politics in the Age of the Civil War.* New York: Oxford University Press, 1990.

Beymer, William Gilmore. *On Hazardous Service: Scouts and Spies of the Civil War.* New York: Harper, 1912. Reprint, Lincoln: University of Nebraska Press, 2003.

Blanton, DeAnne, and Lauren M. Cook. *They Fought Like Demons: Women Soldiers in the American Civil War.* Baton Rouge: Louisiana State University Press, 2002.

Bradley, Erwin S. *Simon Cameron, Lincoln's Secretary of War: A Political Biography.* Philadelphia: University of Pennsylvania Press, 1966.

Brandt, Nat. *The Man Who Tried to Burn New York.* Syracuse: Syracuse University Press, 1986.

Bridges, Albert Fletcher. "The Execution of Private Robert Gay." *Indiana Magazine of History* 20, no. 2 (June 1924): 174–86.

Bridges, C. A. "The Knights of the Golden Circle: A Filibuster Fantasy." *Southwestern Historical Quarterly* 44, no. 1 (January 1941): 287–302.

Brockett, Linus Pierpont. *Scouts, Spies, and Heroes of the Great Civil War.* Cincinnati: E. R. Curtis, 1891.

Cain, Marvin R. *Lincoln's Attorney General: Edward Bates of Missouri.* Columbia: University of Missouri Press, 1965.

Calhoun, Frederick S. *The Lawmen: United States Marshals and Their Deputies, 1789–1989.* Washington, DC: Smithsonian Institution Press, 1989.

Castel, Albert. *General Sterling Price and the Civil War in the West.* Baton Rouge: Louisiana State University Press, 1968.

Castel, Albert, and Brooks D. Simpson. *Victors in Blue: How Union Generals Fought the Confederates, Battled Each Other, and Won the Civil War.* Lawrence: University Press of Kansas, 2011.

Churchill, Robert H. "Liberty, Conscription, and a Party Divided: The Sons of Liberty Conspiracy." *Prologue* 30, no. 4 (Winter 1998): 295–303.

———.*To Shake Their Guns in the Tyrant's Face: Libertarian Political Violence and the Origins of the Militia Movement.* Ann Arbor: University of Michigan Press, 2009.

Clark, Dan Elbert. *Samuel Jordan Kirkwood.* Iowa City: State Historical Society of Iowa, 1917.

Cooley, Rita W. "The Office of United States Marshal." *Western Political Quarterly* 12, no. 1 (March 1959): 123–40.

Cozzens, Peter. *The Darkest Days of the War: The Battles of Iuka and Corinth.* Chapel Hill: University of North Carolina Press, 1997.

———. *No Better Place to Die: The Battle of Stones River.* Urbana: University of Illinois Press, 1990.

———. *The Shipwreck of Their Hopes: The Battles for Chattanooga.* Urbana: University of Illinois Press, 1994.

———. *This Terrible Sound: The Battle of Chickamauga.* Urbana: University of Illinois Press, 1992.

Crenshaw, Ollinger. "The Knights of the Golden Circle: The Career of George Bickley." *American Historical Review* 47, no. 1 (October 1941): 23–50.

Curry, Richard G. "McClellan's Western Virginia Campaign of 1861." *Ohio History* 71, no. 2 (1962): 83–96.

De Falaise, Louis. "General Stephen Gano Burbridge's Command in Kentucky." *Register of the Kentucky Historical Society* 69, no. 2 (1971): 101–27.

DeFord, Lester J. "Mercer County, Ohio, during the Civil War." MA thesis, Ohio State University, 1948.

Drury, Augustus W. *History of the City of Dayton and Montgomery County, Ohio.* 2 vols. Chicago: S. J. Clarke, 1909.

Dunn, Ray Sylvan. "The KGC in Texas, 1860–1861." *Southwestern Historical Quarterly* 70, no. 4 (April 1967): 543–73.

Durham, Walter T. *Nashville: The Occupied City.* Nashville: Tennessee Historical Society, 1985.

———. *Reluctant Partners: Nashville and the Union, 1863–1865.* Nashville: Tennessee Historical Society, 1987.

Ecelbarger, Gary. *Black Jack Logan: An Extraordinary Life in Peace and War.* Guilford, CT: Lyons Press, 2005.

Engle, Stephen D. *Don Carlos Buell: Most Promising of All.* Chapel Hill: University of North Carolina Press, 1999.

Ethington, Phillip J. "Vigilantes and the Police: The Creation of a Professional Police Bureaucracy, 1847–1900." *Journal of Social History* 21, no. 2 (1987): 197–227.

Feis, William B. *Grant's Secret Service: The Intelligence War from Belmont to Appomattox.* Lincoln: University of Nebraska Press, 2002.

———. "'There Is a Bad Enemy in This City': Colonel William Truesdail's Army Police and the Occupation of Nashville, 1862–1863." *North and South* 8, no. 2 (March 2005): 35–45.

Fellman, Michael. *Inside War: The Guerrilla Conflict in Missouri during the American Civil War.* New York: Oxford University Press, 1989.

———. "Women and Guerrilla Warfare." In *Divided Houses: Gender and the Civil War,* edited by Catherine Clinton and Nina Silber. New York: Oxford University Press, 1992.

Fesler, Mayo. "Secret Political Societies in the North during the Civil War." *Indiana Magazine of History* 14, no. 3 (September 1918): 183–286.

Fishel, Edwin C. "Military Intelligence, 1861–1863." *Studies in Intelligence* 10, nos. 3 and 4 (Summer–Fall 1966): 81–96, 69–93.

———."The Mythology of Civil War Intelligence." *Civil War History* 10, no. 4 (December 1964): 344–67.

———. "Pinkerton and McClellan: Who Deceived Whom?" *Civil War History* 34, no. 2 (June 1988): 115–42.

———. *The Secret War for the Union: The Untold Story of Military Intelligence in the Civil War.* Boston: Houghton Mifflin, 1996.

Fisher, Noel "Groping toward Victory: Ohio's Administration of the Civil War." *Ohio History* 105, no. 2 (Winter–Spring 1996): 25–41.

Foulke, William Dudley. *Life of Oliver P. Morton, Including His Important Speeches.* 2 vols. Indianapolis: Bowen-Merrill, 1899.

Francis, David W. "The United States Navy and the Johnson's Island Conspiracy: The Case of John C. Carter." *Northwest Ohio Quarterly* 52, no. 3 (June 1980): 229–43.

Geary, James W. *We Need Men: The Union Draft in the Civil War.* DeKalb: Northern Illinois University Press, 1991.

Gerteis, Louis S. *Civil War St. Louis.* Lawrence: University Press of Kansas, 2001.

Gilje, Paul A. *Rioting in America.* Bloomington: Indiana University Press, 1996.

Goodwin, Doris Kearns. *Team of Rivals: The Political Genius of Abraham Lincoln.* New York: Simon and Schuster, 2005.

Gray, Wood. *The Hidden Civil War: The Story of the Copperheads.* New York: Viking Press, 1942.

Grimsted, David. *American Mobbing, 1828–1861: Toward Civil War.* New York: Oxford University Press, 1998.

Harrison, Ida Withers. *Memoirs of William Temple Withers.* Boston: Christopher Publishing House, 1924.

Hebert, Walter H. *Fighting Joe Hooker.* Indianapolis: Bobbs-Merrill, 1944. Reprint, Lincoln: University of Nebraska Press, 1999.

Hess, Earl J. "Alvin P. Hovey and Abraham Lincoln's 'Broken Promises': The Politics of Promotion." *Indiana Magazine of History* 80, no. 1 (March 1984): 35–50.

Holt, Michael F. *The Political Crisis of the 1850s.* New York: Wiley, 1978. Reprint, New York: Norton, 1983.

Horn, Stanley F. "Dr. John Rolfe Hudson and the Confederate Underground in Nashville." *Tennessee Historical Quarterly* 22, no. 1 (1963): 38–52.

Hudson, Linda S. "The Knights of the Golden Circle in Texas, 1858–1861: An Analysis of the First (Military) Degree Knights." In *The Seventh Star of the Confederacy: Texas during the Civil War,* edited by Kenneth W. Howell. Denton: University of North Texas Press, 2009.

Hunter, Leslie Gene. "Warden for the Union: General William Hoffman, 1807–1884." PhD dissertation, University of Arizona, 1971.

Jeffreys-Jones, Rhodri. *American Espionage: From Secret Service to CIA.* New York: Free Press, 1977.

———. *Cloak and Dollar: The History of American Secret Intelligence.* 2nd ed. New Haven: Yale University Press, 2003.

Jensen, Joan M. *Army Surveillance in America, 1775–1980.* New Haven: Yale University Press, 1991.

Johnson, David R. *American Law Enforcement: A History.* St. Louis: Forum Press, 1981.

———. *Illegal Tender: Counterfeiting and the Secret Service.* Washington, DC: Smithsonian Institution, 1995.

Johnson, E. Polk. *A History of Kentucky and Kentuckians: The Leaders and Representative Men in Commerce, Industry and Modern Activities.* 3 vols. Chicago: Lewis Publishing, 1912.

Jordan, Wayne. "The Hoskinsville Rebellion." *Ohio History* 47, no. 4 (October 1938): 319–54.

Kahn, David. *The Codebreakers: The Story of Secret Writing.* Rev. ed. New York: Scribners, 1996.

Karamanski, Theodore J. *Rally 'Round the Flag: Chicago and the Civil War.* Chicago: Nelson-Hall, 1993. Reprint, Lanham, MD: Rowman and Littlefield: 2006.

Katz, Irving. *August Belmont: A Political Biography.* New York: Columbia University Press, 1968.

Keehn, David C. *Knights of the Golden Circle: Secret Empire, Southern Secession, Civil War.* Baton Rouge: Louisiana State University Press, 2013.

———. "Strong Arm of Secession: The Knights of the Golden Circle in the Crisis of 1861." *North and South* 10, no. 6 (June 2008): 42–57.

Keller, Julia. *Mr. Gatling's Terrible Marvel: The Gun That Changed Everything and the Misunderstood Genius Who Invented It.* New York: Viking, 2008.

Kemble, Edward Cleveland, and Helen Harding Bretnor. *A History of California Newspapers, 1846–1858.* New York: Plandome Press, 1927. Reprint, Los Gatos, CA: Talisman Press 1962.

Kionka, T. K. *Key Command: Ulysses S. Grant's District of Cairo.* Columbia: University of Missouri Press, 2006.

Kirke, Edmunde [J. R. Gilmore]. "The Chicago Conspiracy." *Atlantic Monthly* 16, no. 93 (July 1865): 108–21.

Klement, Frank L. "Carrington and the Golden Circle Legend in Indiana during the Civil War." *Indiana Magazine of History* 61, no. 1 (March 1965): 31–52.

———. "Civil War Politics, Nationalism, and Postwar Myths." *Historian* 38, no. 3 (May 1976): 4–23.

———. "Copperhead Secret Societies in Illinois during the Civil War." *Journal of the Illinois State Historical Society* 48, no. 2 (Summer 1955): 152–180.

———. *The Copperheads in the Middle West.* Chicago: University of Chicago Press, 1960.

———. *Dark Lanterns: Secret Political Societies, Conspiracies, and Treason Trials in the Civil War.* Baton Rouge: Louisiana State University Press, 1984.

———. "Franklin Pierce and the Treason Charges of 1861–1862." *Historian* 23, no. 4 (August 1961): 436–48.

———. "The Hopkins Hoax and Golden Circle Rumors in Michigan, 1861–1862." *Michigan History* 47, no. 1 (March 1963): 1–14.

———. *The Limits of Dissent: Clement L. Vallandigham and the Civil War.* Lexington: University Press of Kentucky, 1970. Reprint, New York: Fordham University Press, 1998.

———. *Lincoln's Critics: The Copperheads of the North.* Edited by Steven K. Rogstad. Shippensburg, PA: White Mane, 1999.

———. "Ohio and the Knights of the Golden Circle: The Evolution of a Civil War Myth." *Cincinnati Historical Society Bulletin* 32, no. 1 (Spring–Summer, 1974): 7–27.

———. "Phineas C. Wright, the Order of American Knights, and the Sanderson Exposé." *Civil War History* 18, no. 1 (March 1972): 5–23.

———. "President Lincoln, the Civil War, and the Bill of Rights." *Lincoln Herald* 94, no. 1 (Spring, 1992): 10–23.

Lamers, William M. *The Edge of Glory: A Biography of General William S. Rosecrans, U.S.A.* New York: Harcourt, Brace and World, 1960. Reprint, Baton Rouge: Louisiana State University Press, 1999.

Lane, Roger. *Policing the City: Boston, 1822–1885.* Cambridge, MA: Harvard University Press, 1967.

Lause, Mark A. *Price's Lost Campaign: The 1864 Invasion of Missouri.* Columbia: University of Missouri Press, 2011.

———. *A Secret Society History of the Civil War.* Urbana: University of Illinois Press, 2011.

Lawson, Melinda. *Patriot Fires: Forging a New American Nationalism in the Civil War North.* Lawrence: University Press of Kansas, 2002.

Leeke, Jim, ed. *A Hundred Days to Richmond: Ohio's "Hundred Days" Men in the Civil War.* Bloomington: Indiana University Press, 1999.

Lehman, James O. and Steven M. Nolt. *Mennonites, Amish, and the American Civil War.* Baltimore: Johns Hopkins University Press, 2007.

Leonard, Elizabeth D. *All the Daring of the Soldier: Women of the Civil War Armies.* New York: Norton, 1999.

———. *Lincoln's Avengers: Justice, Revenge, and Reunion after the Civil War.* New York: Norton, 2004.

———. "Lincoln's Chief Avenger: Judge Advocate General Joseph Holt." In *The Lincoln Assassination: Crime and Punishment, Myth and Memory,* edited by Harold Holzer, Craig L. Symonds, and Frank J. Williams, 115–35. New York: Fordham University Press, 2010.

———. *Lincoln's Forgotten Ally: Judge Advocate General Joseph Holt of Kentucky.* Chapel Hill: University of North Carolina Press, 2011.

Leopold, Richard William. *Robert Dale Owen: A Biography.* Cambridge, MA: Harvard University Press, 1940. Reprint, New York: Octagon, 1969.

Long, David E. *The Jewel of Liberty: Abraham Lincoln's Re-election and the End of Slavery.* Mechanicsburg, PA: Stackpole, 1994. Reprint, New York: Da Capo, 1997.

Lonn, Ella. *Desertion during the Civil War.* Gloucester, MA: American Historical Association, 1928. Reprint, Lincoln: University of Nebraska Press, 1998.

Marquis, Greg. *In Armageddon's Shadow: The Civil War and Canada's Maritime Provinces.* Halifax: Saint Mary's University, Montreal: McGill-Queen's University Press, 1998.

Marvel, William. *Burnside.* Chapel Hill: University of North Carolina Press, 1991.

McKeen, Catherine. "Henry Beebee Carrington: A Soldier's Tale." PhD dissertation, State University of New York at Stony Brook, 1998.

McPherson, James M. *Battle Cry of Freedom: The Civil War Era.* New York: Oxford University Press, 1988.

Miller, Nathan. *Spying for America: The Hidden History of U.S. Intelligence.* New York: Marlow, 1989.

Miller, Wilbur R. *Cops and Bobbies: Police Authority in New York and London.* Chicago: University of Chicago Press, 1977.

Milton, George Fort. *Abraham Lincoln and the Fifth Column.* New York: Vanguard, 1942.

Mogelever, Jacob. *Death to Traitors: The Story of General Lafayette C. Baker, Lincoln's Forgotten Secret Service Chief.* Garden City, NY: Doubleday, 1960.

Monkkonen, Eric H. "The Organized Response to Crime in the Nineteenth and Early Twentieth Centuries." *Journal of Interdisciplinary History* 14, no. 1 (1983): 113–28.

———. *Police in Urban America, 1860–1920.* Cambridge: Cambridge University Press, 1981.

Morn, Frank. *"The Eye That Never Sleeps": A History of the Pinkerton National Detective Agency.* Bloomington: Indiana University Press, 1982.

Mulligan, Thomas C. "Lest the Rebels Come to Power: The Life of William Dennison, 1815–1882, Early Ohio Republican." PhD dissertation, Ohio State University, 1994.

Munden, Kenneth W., and Henry Putney Beers. *The Union: A Guide to Federal Archives Relating to the Civil War.* Washington, DC: National Archives and Records Administration, 1986.

Murdock, Eugene C. *One Million Men: The Civil War Draft in the North.* Madison: State Historical Society of Wisconsin, 1971.

———. *Patriotism Limited, 1862–1865: The Civil War Draft and the Bounty System.* Kent, Ohio: Kent State University Press 1967.

Neely, Mark E., Jr. *The Fate of Liberty: Abraham Lincoln and Civil Liberties.* New York: Oxford University Press, 1991.

———. *The Union Divided: Party Conflicts in the Civil War North.* Cambridge, MA: Harvard University Press, 2002.

Nelson, Jacquelyn S. *Indiana Quakers Confront the Civil War.* Indianapolis: Indiana Historical Society, 1991.

Nerone, John. *Violence against the Press: Policing the Public Sphere in U.S. History.* New York: Oxford University Press, 1994.

Noe, Kenneth W. *Perryville: This Grand Havoc of Battle.* Lexington: University Press of Kentucky, 2001.

Nortrup, Jack J. "Yates, the Prorogued Legislature, and the Constitutional Convention." *Journal of the Illinois State Historical Society* 62, no. 1 (Spring 1969): 5–34.

Oyos, Mathew. "The Mobilization of the Ohio Militia in the Civil War." *Ohio History* 98 (Summer–Autumn, 1989): 147–74.

Palladino, Grace. *Another Civil War: Labor, Capital, and the State in the Anthracite Regions of Pennsylvania, 1840–1868.* Urbana: University of Illinois Press, 1990.

Parkinson, John Scott. "Bloody Spring: The Charleston, Illinois Riot and Copperhead Violence during the American Civil War." PhD dissertation, Miami University, 1998.

Petlack, K. Luci. "A Dilemma of Civil Liberties: Cincinnati's Black Community, 1862–1863." *Ohio History* 120 (2013): 47–69.

Pickenpaugh, Roger. *Camp Chase and the Evolution of Union Prison Policy.* Tuscaloosa: University of Alabama Press, 2007.

Ramage, James A. *Rebel Raider: The Life of John Hunt Morgan.* Lexington: University Press of Kentucky, 1986.

Randall, James G. *Constitutional Problems under Lincoln.* Rev. ed. Urbana: University of Illinois Press, 1964.

Reed, Scott Owen. "Military Arrests of Lawyers in Illinois during the Civil War." *Western Illinois Regional Studies* 6, no. 2 (1983): 5–22.

Rhodes, James Ford. *The History of the United States from the Compromise of 1850.* 8 vols. New York: Macmillan, 1893–1928.

Richardson, James F. *Urban Police in the United States.* Port Washington, NY: Kennikat Press, 1974.

Rodgers, Thomas E. "Copperheads or a Respectable Minority: Current Approaches to the Study of Civil War–Era Democrats." *Indiana Magazine of History* 109, no. 2 (June 2013): 114–46.

———. "Republicans and Drifters: Political Affiliation and Union Army Volunteers in West-Central Indiana." *Indiana Magazine of History* 92, no. 4 (December 1996): 321–45.

Roseboom Eugene H., and Francis P. Weisenburger. *A History of Ohio.* 2nd ed. Columbus: Ohio Historical Society, 1967.

Rugh, Susan Sessions. *Our Common Country: Family Farming, Culture, and Community in the Nineteenth-century Midwest.* Bloomington: Indiana University Press, 2001.

Rule, G. E. "The Sons of Liberty and the Louisville Warehouse Fire of July 1864." *Lincoln Herald* 107, no. 2 (2005): 68–74.

Sampson, Robert. "'Pretty Damned Warm Times': The 1864 Charleston Riot and 'the Inalienable Right of Revolution.'" *Illinois Historical Journal* 89, no. 2 (Summer 1996): 99–116.

Sandow, Robert M. *Deserter Country: Civil War Opposition in the Pennsylvania Appalachians.* New York: Fordham University Press, 2009.

Shalhope, Robert E. *Sterling Price: Portrait of a Southerner.* Columbia: University of Missouri Press, 1971.

Shankman, Arnold M. *The Pennsylvania Antiwar Movement, 1861–1865.* Rutherford, NJ: Fairleigh Dickinson University Press, 1980.

Shepard, Frederick J. "The Johnson's Island Plot: A Historical Narrative of the Conspiracy of the Confederates, in 1864, to Capture the U.S. Steamship *Michigan* on Lake Erie, and Release the Prisoners of War in Sandusky Bay." *Publications of the Buffalo Historical Society* 9 (1906): 1–51.

Smith, Adam I. P. *No Party Now: Politics in the Civil War North.* New York: Oxford University Press, 2006.

Smith, Reed W. *Samuel Medary and the* Crisis: *Testing the Limits of Press Freedom.* Columbus: Ohio State University Press, 1995.

Smith, Thomas H. "Crawford County 'Ez Trooly Dimecratic': A Study of Midwestern Copperheadism." *Ohio History* 76, nos. 1–2 (1967): 33–53, 92–94.

Smith, Willard H. *Schuyler Colfax: The Changing Fortunes of a Political Idol.* Indiana Historical Collections, vol. 33. Indianapolis: Indiana Historical Bureau, 1952.

Stampp, Kenneth M. *Indiana Politics during the Civil War.* Indianapolis: Indiana Historical Bureau, 1949. Reprint, Indiana University Press, 1978.

Sterling, Robert E. "Civil War Draft Resistance in the Middle West." PhD dissertation, Northern Illinois University, 1974.

Sturckler, James A. "Union Consular Intelligence Collection on Confederate Operations in British North America during the American Civil War." PhD dissertation, State University of New York at Buffalo, 2006.

Sutherland, Daniel E. *A Savage Conflict: The Decisive Role of Guerrillas in the American Civil War.* Chapel Hill: University of North Carolina Press, 2009.

Taylor, Paul. *"Old Slow Town": Detroit during the Civil War.* Detroit: Wayne State University Press, 2013.

Tenney, Craig D. "To Suppress or Not to Suppress: Abraham Lincoln and the *Chicago Times.*" *Civil War History* 27, no. 3 (1981): 248–59.

Terry, Clinton W. "The Most Commercial of People: Cincinnati, the Civil War, and the Rise of Industrial Capitalism, 1861–1865." PhD dissertation, University of Cincinnati, 2002.

Thomas, Benjamin P., and Harold M. Hyman. *Stanton: The Life and Times of Lincoln's Secretary of War.* New York: Knopf, 1962.

Thomas, Richard J. "Caleb Blood Smith: Whig Orator and Politician—Lincoln's Secretary of Interior." PhD dissertation, Indiana University-Bloomington, 1969.

Thompson, Jerry. *Civil War to the Bloody End: The Life and Times of Major General Samuel P. Heintzelman.* College Station: Texas A&M University Press, 2006.

Thornbrough, Emma Lou. "Judge Perkins, the Indiana Supreme Court, and the Civil War." *Indiana Magazine of History* 60, no. 1 (March 1964): 79–96.

Tidwell, William A. *April '65: Confederate Covert Operations in the American Civil War.* Kent, Ohio: Kent State University Press, 1995.

Tingley, Donald F. "The Clingman Raid." *Journal of the Illinois State Historical Society* 56, no. 2 (June 1963): 350–63.

Towne, Stephen E. "Killing the Serpent Speedily: Governor Morton, General Hascall, and the Suppression of the Democratic Press in Indiana, 1863." *Civil War History* 52, no. 1 (March 2006): 41–65.

———. "The Persistent Nullifier: The Life of Civil War Conspirator Lambdin P. Milligan." *Indiana Magazine of History* 109, no. 4 (December 2013): 303–54.

———. "'Such Conduct Must be Put Down': The Military Arrest of Judge Charles H. Constable during the Civil War." *Journal of Illinois History* 9, no. 1 (Spring 2006): 43–62.

———. "Works of Indiscretion: Violence against the Democratic Press in Indiana during the Civil War." *Journalism History* 31, no. 3 (Fall 2005): 138–49.

Tredway, G. R. *Democratic Opposition to the Lincoln Administration in Indiana.* Indiana Historical Collections, vol. 48. Indianapolis: Indiana Historical Bureau, 1973.

Varon, Elizabeth R. *Southern Lady, Yankee Spy: The True Story of Elizabeth Van Lew, a Union Agent in the Heart of the Confederacy.* New York: Oxford University Press, 2003.

Walker, Samuel. *Popular Justice: A History of American Criminal Justice.* New York: Oxford University Press, 1980.

Weber, Jennifer L. *Copperheads: The Rise and Fall of Lincoln's Opponents in the North.* New York: Oxford University Press, 2006.

Wheeler, Kenneth H. "Local Autonomy and Civil War Draft Resistance: Holmes County, Ohio." *Civil War History* 45, no. 2 (June 1999): 147–59.

Wilentz, Sean. *The Rise of American Democracy: Jefferson to Lincoln.* New York: Norton, 2005.

Wilson, Mark R. *The Business of Civil War: Military Mobilization and the State, 1861–1865.* Baltimore: Johns Hopkins University Press, 2006.

Winks, Robin. *Canada and the United States: The Civil War Years.* Baltimore: Johns Hopkins University Press, 1960.

Wubben, Hubert H. *Civil War Iowa and the Copperhead Movement.* Ames: Iowa State University Press, 1980.

Yates, Norris W. *William T. Porter and the Spirit of the Times: A Study of the Big Bear School of Humor.* Baton Rouge: Louisiana State University Press, 1957.

Boyle, Jeremiah T., 80, 108
Bradley, C. P., 399n78
Bragg, Braxton, 42, 44, 176–77
Brain, John C., 18–19, 321n37
Bramlette, Thomas E., 209, 210; thanks Morton for aid during Morgan raid, 217
Breckinridge, John, 318n3
Bright, Jesse D., 241, 266
Bright, Michael, 241
Broadhead, James O., 367n19, 382n49
Brough, John, 165, 172, 190, 205, 270, 288; meets with Heintzelman regarding secret societies, 207; awaits instructions from Lincoln regarding arrest of Vallandigham, 215; receives warning from his spies of armed insurrection, 236–37; recommends arrests of leading conspirators, 247–48; warns Heintzelman of plot to attack Camp Chase, 249; feuds with Heintzelman, 290–92
Brown, C. J., 300
Brown, Daniel S., 112
Brown, E. B., 186
Brown, John O., 49, 51–52
Browning, Orville Hickman, 14
Buell, Don Carlos, 44, 47, 91
Buford, Napoleon Bonaparte, 75–76, 97, 100, 102, 349n100
Bullitt, Joshua F., 205, 235, 242, 266; confers with leading Indiana conspirators, 241; arrested in Indiana, 243, 257
Bull Run, VA, federal defeat at (1861), 14, 17, 21, 150
Burbridge, Stephen G., 9, 167, 200, 278; reorganizes Louisville secret police, 202; obtains intelligence of Morgan's planned raid, 209; defeats Morgan, 211; proposes plan to arrest leading conspirators, 235–36; confers with Morton and Carrington, 242; asks Stanton to order arrest of conspirators, 247; confers with Heintzelman and Burnett, 247–48; informs Heintzelman of plot to release Camp Douglas prisoners, 271; pressed by Holt for report on investigations, 284–85
Burnett, Henry L., 208, 247, 312
Burnside, Ambrose E., 2, 72–81, 117, 308; meets with Wright at Cincinnati, 73; issues General Orders 38, 75–76; removes Carrington from Indiana command, 77; prefers soldiers to civilian detectives, 82–84; removes Hascall from Indiana command, installs Willcox, 86; supplies

secret-service funds to Smith and Cox, 135–36; turns over Army of the Ohio to John G. Foster, 151

Cairo, IL, 14–16, 39–40, 66, 182; martial law declared in, 100
Calhoun, John C., 12
California State Journal, 192
Cameron, Simon, 34
Campbell, John, 281
Camp Chase, OH, 82, 152; plot to free prisoners, 123–27, 130, 249–50, 268, 309
Camp Douglas, IL, 63, 118, 126, 152, 232, 246, 254, 266; plot to free prisoners, 250–51, 255–56, 271–75, 289–90, 294–301, 312
Camp Morton, IN, 20, 127–28, 130, 152, 235, 240, 241, 246; plot to attack, 261–63
Carr, David H., 25–26
Carrington, Henry B., 5–6, 7, 38–60, 63, 68, 149, 172, 195–220, 279, 308; background, 42–44; ordered to Indianapolis, 41–45; ambition of, 45; meets with Indiana chief justice Perkins, 48; uncovers secret organizations among soldiers, 49–51; warns Lincoln of secret societies in Indiana, 52, 70–71; investigates Morgan County incident, 53–54; calls for execution of deserter, 58; reports shipments of arms for disloyal purposes, 73; reports political violence to Burnside, 77–78; sent to Ohio, 79–80; returns to Indiana, 153–56; service during Morgan raid, 154–55; asks for staff, 155–56; diverts regiment to Charleston, IL, 167; sends first major report to Heintzelman, 168–69; asks for secret-service funds from War Department, 195–97; works to get Coffin on federal payroll, 198–99; asks military authorities in Kentucky for a detective, 200; employs Kentucky officer to gather information on Forrest's troops, 203–4; asks Heintzelman to confer with him and Morton, 207; investigates Gatling as member of secret organization, 208; plans to build legal case against conspirators, 208–9, 268–9; goes to Louisville with troops during Morgan's Kentucky raid, 210–11; asks Stanton for direction regarding policy dispute with Morton, 218–19; uses Bowles to deflect suspicion from Stidger, 234, 239; attends Democratic state convention (1864), 240; reports to Heintzelman on conference

420 — Index

with Burbridge and Morton, 242; reports
concerted plans of Kentucky guerrillas
and Indiana conspirators, 261; travels
to Columbus, OH, to bury son, 263,
266; removed from district command,
assigned draft rendezvous command,
269; thanks Heintzelman for kindnesses,
269; briefs Hovey on Sons of Liberty,
277; hopes to challenge Voorhees to
debate, 396n34; provides report to Holt
on secret conspiracies, 283–84; continues
investigations in 1865, 301; postwar career
of, 303–6; testifies at Milligan's civil trial
(1871), 306; tobacco addiction, 331n26;
historian of American Revolution, 362n29
Carter, John C., 287–89
Castleman, John Breckinridge, 275, 289–90,
323n45
Cathcart, Charles W. H., 124, 127, 268
Chandler, Zechariah, 118, 119, 170
Charleston, IL, violence, 166–68, 286
Chase, Salmon P., 34, 36, 43, 80, 188
Chesapeake (steamer), 321n37
Chicago Times, 98, 203, 214, 215
Chicago Tribune, 96–97
Cincinnati Daily Commercial, 211, 270
Cincinnati Daily Enquirer, 125, 211
Cincinnati Daily Gazette, 185
Cincinnati Daily Times, 125, 185
civilian investigations: federal, 23–37; in
Illinois, 13–16; in Indiana, 17–21; in Ohio,
21–23, 28–32
Clark, C. H., 57
Clay, Clement C., 384n79
Cleveland Plain Dealer, 31
Clingman (guerrilla), 311
Coffey, George A., 26
Coffin, Sargent Parker, 197–99, 210,
234, 303, 375n68; obtains OAK oaths,
197; investigates in Kentucky, 197–98;
appointed special agent of police, 205;
identified as spy, 212
Coggeshall, William, 22
Cole, C. H., 288
Colfax, Schuyler, 279–80
Collins, Franklin, 114
Columbus Crisis, 123–24
Confiscation Act (1861), 27
Congress, U.S., 35–36, 90, 230
Conness, John, 230
Constable, Charles H., 59, 156
contraband cotton trade, 85–86
Conway (Conaway), Amos, 334n53

Cook, John, 298, 299, 300
"Copperhead organization." *See* Knights of
the Golden Circle
Corry, William M., 125–26
Cory, B. F., 109
Couch, Darius N., 229
counterfeit treasury notes and coin,
investigation of, 34–36, 188
Cowen, B. R., 215, 236–37, 249
Cowgill, Calvin, 106
Cox, Jacob D., 63, 75, 77, 82, 114; creates
detective force for District of Ohio,
81–82; orders officers to be watchful along
Lake Erie coast, 120; asks Giddings to
investigate report of steamers on lakes,
133; asks Tod to send militia to Sandusky,
135; leaves District of Ohio command,
151, 154
Cox, S. S., 85
Crawford County Forum (Bucyrus, OH), 31
Cresap, J. D., 124
Croniger, Levi, 131
Cunning, A. D., 77
Curtin, Andrew, 229, 230, 231, 308
Curtis, Samuel R., 175
Cushman, Pauline, 3, 316n2

Dana, Charles A., 177, 184, 204; sends
commanders lists of disloyal persons, 243
Darr, Joseph, Jr., 248–49, 300, 302
Davis, David, 14
Davis, Henry Winter, 230
Davis, Jefferson, 99, 161, 241
Davis, John G., 20, 266
Dearborn arsenal, 118, 136
Defrees, John D., 396n34
DeHart, William C., 277
Democratic National Convention (Chicago,
1864), 234, 246, 253, 271–75, 278, 281
Democratic Party, 5, 283, 284; gains strength
from Emancipation Proclamation,
46–47; leaders alarmed at rise of secret
organizations, 71; gunfight at Danville,
IN, rally, 76–77; Illinois state convention
(Springfield, IL, 1863), 97–98; Indiana
state convention (Indianapolis, 1864), 240
"Democratic society." *See* Knights of the
Golden Circle
Dennison, William, Jr., 42–43, 190, 369n68;
receives reports of unrest, 21–23
desertion. *See* Army, U.S.
Detroit Advertiser and Tribune, 119, 214, 252
Detroit Free Press, 117

Hay, John, 223–26, 230–31; reports to Lincoln on his meeting with Rosecrans, 225–26
Headley, John W., 312, 387n25
Heffren, Horace, 202, 258, 263, 290
Heintzelman, Samuel P., 149–53, 157–73, 281; Carrington calls on, 156; confers with Morton and Carrington en route to Illinois, 157; sends intelligence reports to Carrington, 159–61; sends Bickley to Fort Lafayette, 165; receives information about Phineas C. Wright, 170–71; meets with governors in Indianapolis, 172; meets with Rosecrans, Dennison, and Brough, 190–91; forwards Carrington's information to Halleck, 207; goes to Cincinnati during Morgan's Kentucky raid, 211; visits Morton and Carrington in Indianapolis, 213; believes Morgan targeted Cincinnati, 217–18; meets with Sanderson, 229; gathers opinions about arrests of conspirators, 247–48; reports views regarding arrest of conspirators and need for troops, 250; asks Yates for views on arresting leading conspirators, 253; orders bans on arms and ammunition sales, 270–71; in Chicago, 273–74; feuds with Brough, 290–92; is replaced by Hooker, 291–92; praises Carrington for his services, 291–92
Hendricks, Thomas A., 260, 283, 335n64
Henley, Henry, 161
Hertzler, J. N., 354n144
Hester, James, 77, 79, 323n46
Hiatt, J. M., 83
Hill, Bennett H., 118, 133–34, 170, 186; replaces Smith as commander in Detroit, 238; reports plot to attack Camp Douglas, 250–51, 255–56, 271, 294; reports rebel plots to attack northern cities, 278; alerted to *Philo Parsons* plot, 287–89
Hill, Harrington R., 84
Hines, Thomas Henry, 87, 126, 235, 241, 267, 284, 391n99; leader of Camp Douglas expeditions, 256, 271–72, 274–75, 289, 298; escapes arrest in Chicago, 299; postwar writings of, 312; Carrington mentions him in public speech, 392n107
Hines's raid (1863), 87
Hobart, J. S., 87
Hoffman, William, 133, 294–98
Holland, Charles W., 281
Holloway, Robert, 161, 252, 285
Holloway, William R., 47, 58

Holt, Joseph, 54, 247, 269, 335n69; sent west to investigate secret organizations, 244–45; praises Carrington, 245; ordered by Stanton to make recommendations on secret conspiracies, 282–87; emphasizes continuity of KGC to OAK to Sons of Liberty, 285; recommends payments for Stidger and Pitman, 304
Holy Brotherhood. *See* Knights of the Golden Circle
Hooker, Joseph, 299; replaces Heintzelman in command of Northern Department, 291–92; goes to Indianapolis to investigate southern Indiana unrest, 292–93
Hough, Sabin, 356n44
Hovey, Alvin P., 262, 283, 293; replaces Carrington in command of District of Indiana, 267–69; commands District of Indiana, 276–78; asks Stanton for instructions, 277; plans to try civilians by military commission, 281–82
Howard, Jacob M., 170
Hudson, Lawrence A., 185, 187, 190, 302
Hughes, George, 55
Hull, John, 119
Humphreys, Andrew, 260–61, 289, 293
Hunt, Charles L., 185–86, 194, 231, 232, 245, 248, 252, 266, 282, 285
Hunter, John, 397n43
Hutchinson, Charles P., 264
Hynes, Blythe, 105–6

Illinois, 13–16; District of, created, 63; District of, re-created, 252; draft violence in, 98–103; threat of uprisings in, 252–55, 278–79; Union victories at Vicksburg and Gettysburg have little effect on resistance, 101
Illinois army units: 27th Illinois Volunteer Infantry Regiment, 39; 54th Illinois Volunteer Infantry Regiment, 56, 166; 101st Illinois Volunteer Infantry Regiment, 342n53
Illinois Central Railroad, 13, 67, 76
Illinois General Assembly, 96–97
Indiana, 16–21; District of, created, 63; draft violence in, 103–8; and Michigan, District of, 117
Indiana army units: 1st Indiana Cavalry Regiment, 91; 3rd Indiana Cavalry Regiment, 49; 5th Indiana Cavalry Regiment, 51, 335n63; 11th Indiana Light Artillery Battery, 384n73; 14th Indiana Light Artillery Battery, 58; 9th Indiana

Thorpe, William, 214; warns Brough and Sanderson about Vallandigham's return to Ohio, 215

Tod, David, 78, 82, 109, 113, 120, 338n3

Townsend, E. D., 277–78

Tranter, Wesley, 169

Treasury, Department of the, 36

Treat, Samuel, 59, 328n116

Truesdail, William, 66, 384n73; warns of league to overthrow government in North, 85

Tucker, John W., 199

Turnbull, David, 129, 160–61, 208, 210, 367n33

Turpie, David, 279

Union League, 95, 96, 215, 253, 254, 362n29

United States flag, destruction of, 17, 21

Usher, John P., 20

Vallandigham, Clement L., 2, 8, 9, 57, 99; army opens mail of, 81; arrest of, 81; speech in Congress on Enrollment bill, 91; travels through Canada, 113–14; met with representatives of OAK, 161; arrives at Windsor, 116–21; rebels consult with, 163; implicated in plots, 164; communicates with conspirators in Saint Louis, 187; identified as leader of OAK and Sons of Liberty, 193, 206, 223, 235, 244, 285; returns to United States, 212–18; speaks at Hamilton, OH, 214–15; shows signs of fear, 241; correspondence intercepted by Rosecrans, 251–52; correspondence published, 265, 266, 309; denies collaboration with Jefferson Davis, 381n32

Van Lew, Elizabeth, 3

Veteran Reserve Corps (VRC), 95, 152, 157, 205, 239, 248, 299; 8th VRC Regiment, 255; 15th VRC Regiment, 298; reinforcements sent to Chicago, 300. See also Invalid Corps

Voorhees, Daniel W., 20, 91, 114, 266; discovery of OAK records in Terre Haute office, 259, 265, 310

Walker, John C., 266, 293, 391n99

Wall, James W., 259, 265

Wallace, William, 110

Walsh, Charles, 255, 299–300

War Department: order of August 8, 1862, 36; sends division to guard Johnson's Island, 136; sends regiments to reinforce prison camp garrisons, 261

Warner, Adoniram J., 300

Watson, Thomas, 124

Webber, Edwin L., 123

Westlake, Benjamin F., 95

White, Bushnell, 30

White, Charles L., 19

White, Julius, 226–27

White, William, 76

Wiles, William, 66

Willcox, Orlando Bolivar, 86, 104, 117–18, 120, 154, 308; appoints Goodale head of detective unit, 119; leaves District of Indiana and Michigan command, 151

Willich, August, 270

Willson, Hiram V., 31

Wilson, Henry, 90

Windsor, Canada, 116–21, 132–36, 163–65, 170, 250–51, 286; Betty watches Hunt cross to, 186; suspicious character trailed from, 205; Carrington gives leave for detective to cross to, 208; information offered by bank employee in, 238; information supplied by wife of rebel refugee in, 278

Wisconsin army units: 4th Wisconsin Volunteer Infantry Regiment, 253; 21st Wisconsin Volunteer Infantry Regiment, 255

Withers, William T., 29, 326n86

Woodruff, James, 129

Wright, Horatio G., 7; pledges Rosecrans cooperation in stopping desertion, 49; promises Carrington support to break up conspiracies, 53; orders Carrington to arrest judge Constable, 59; reorganizes Department of the Ohio, 62–63; orders ban of arms and ammunition sales, 64, 71–72; creates detective force, 65; orders investigation of arms sales, 69–70

Wright, Phineas C., 160, 161, 203, 248, 251, 285, 309, 357n65; arrest of, 170–72, 238; complains of Holt's report, 396n40; organizes prisoners of state convention, 388n35

Yates, Richard, 95, 215, 233, 247, 250, 252; receives reports of unrest, 13–16, 26, 39; requests regiments be sent to Illinois, 73–74, 226; shares information with Ammen on secret organizations, 84; prorogues General Assembly, 97–98; clashes with Stanton regarding troops in Illinois, 98, 101, 239;

Yates, Richard (*cont.*)
telegraphs Washington regarding violence in Paris, IL, 157; presses Stanton and Lincoln for assistance against internal threat, 226–27; voices anger at Lincoln for indifference to threat, 227; opposes military arrests of conspirators without more troops, 242; advises Heintzelman to arrest conspirators in Galena, 253; advises Halbert Paine regarding arrests of conspirators, 254; visits Saint Louis to see Rosecrans, 394n146

Young, George W., 250–51, 256, 271–72, 294

Zumro, Henry S., 158, 162, 169, 303; investigates secret organization, 162–63